General Business Skills Master Class

Michelle N. Halsey

Silver City Publications & Training, L.L.C.
P.O. Box 1914
Nampa, ID 83653
https://www.silvercitypublications.com/shop/

ISBN-10: 1-64004-044-7
ISBN-13: 978-1-64004-044-1

Contents

12

Chapter 1 – Soft Skills

What are Soft Skills?

What are soft skills, anyway? Simply put, soft skills are the personal attributes that allows us to effectively relate to others. These skills enhance our personal interactions and lead to greater job performance and satisfaction. Unlike hard skills, which are the technical and knowledge skill set we bring to our work, soft skills are interpersonal and can be applied in a broad array of situations. Soft skills encompass both personality traits, such as optimism, and abilities which can be practiced, such as empathy. Like all skills, soft skills can be learned.

Definition of Soft Skills

Soft skills are personal attributes that allow us to effectively relate to others. Applying these skills helps us build stronger work relationships, work more productively, and maximize our career prospects. Often we place the focus of our career development efforts on hard skills – technology skills, knowledge, and other skills that specifically relate to our ability to get work-related tasks done. This means we neglect to develop our soft skills. However, soft skills are directly transferrable to any job, organization, or industry. As a result, they are an investment worth making.

Soft skills include:

- Communication

- Listening

- Showing Empathy

- Networking

- Self-confidence

- Giving and receiving feedback

Empathy and the Emotional Intelligence Quotient

Empathy is perhaps the most important soft skill we can develop for better interpersonal interactions. Empathy is the ability to identify with another person's experience. While we often think of empathy in terms only of identifying with someone's pain or negative experience, we can apply empathy in a variety of situations. Developing empathy allows us to imagine ourselves in another person's shoes, to respond to others, and even to vicariously experience others' feelings of emotions. When we demonstrate empathy, we create connections with others, which can help to build teamwork or otherwise create shared goals. Empathy also helps to forge stronger interpersonal connections between team members and colleagues, which is as important as shared goals or complementary skills when it comes to accomplishing work.

Empathy is one component of what is known as Emotional Intelligence, or EI. Emotional Intelligence is the ability to recognize and manage our feelings so that they are expressed appropriately. Exercising emotional intelligence helps to create harmonious, productive relationships. There are four key components to Emotional Intelligence:

- **Self-awareness**: The ability to recognize our own feelings and motivations

- **Self-management**: The ability to appropriate express (or not express) feelings

- **Social awareness**: Our ability to recognize the feelings and needs of others, and the norms of a given situation

- **Relationship management**: Our ability to relate effectively to others

Taken together, these skills make up our Emotional Intelligence Quotient (EQI). The EQI is a measure of your ability to exercise soft skills such as empathy.

Professionalism

The word "professionalism" often conjures up images of a cold, distant, brusque person in a nondescript navy blue suit. In fact, many people have the sense that to be "professional" is exactly the opposite of demonstrating empathy and emotional intelligence! However, professionalism is a key soft skill, and it doesn't require you to be inauthentic, distant, or detached. Professionalism is simply the ability to conduct yourself with responsibility, integrity, accountability, and excellence. Acting with professionalism also means seeking to communicate effectively with others and finding a way to be productive. Professionalism involves what may seem to be small acts, such:

- Always reporting to work on time and returning promptly from breaks

- Dressing appropriately

- Being clean and neat

- Speaking clearly and politely to colleagues, customers, and clients

- Striving to meet high standards for one's own work

Learned vs. Inborn Traits

Because soft skills are talked about as traits of a person's personality, it may seem as though you have to born with them. While some soft skills come more easily to one person than they might to another, soft skills are not inborn. Like all skills, they can be learned. Because we all have our own preferences and ways of moving through the world, some soft skills may be more difficult to learn than others. But if we think back, there are also aspects of our hard skill set that were difficult at first, though they now seem to come quite naturally to us. We develop soft skills in the same way we develop hard skills – we practice! Spending time with people who seem to be able to effortlessly demonstrate a soft skill that you find challenging is one way to build your soft skill set. Another way is to seek opportunities to practice in which the risk of failure is low, until you feel confident in your ability. You don't have to be born a networker or an empathetic person – you can learn and build these skills throughout your career.

Communication

Communication is the most important soft skill, because all other soft skills are built on the ability to communicate clearly and professionally. Communication is more than just sending a message – it is also the ability to receive messages, listen actively, and "hear" what isn't being said. Many times we focus on learning to speak or write clearly, but this is only one component of communication – and perhaps not even the most important!

Ways We Communicate

Human communication is complex. The first thing that comes to mind when we hear the word "communication" is often words – either spoken or written. But the words we speak and hear are just one way we communicate, and some studies show that most of our communication takes place through other means. Humans communicate in many different ways:

- **Nonverbal communication**: Communication without words, such as eye contact or posture

- **Verbal communication**: Communication with words, both written and spoken

- **Body language**: Communication through gestures, personal space, and touching

- **Artistic communication**: Communication through images and other creative media

- **Musical communication**: Communication through music, whether with lyrics or without

Most of us have a preferred method of communication, but all of use these different forms at one point or another. Learning to communicate effectively in many forms helps not only when you craft your own messages, but when you receive messages as well.

Improving Nonverbal Communication

Studies show that up to 70% of the information we communicate comes through nonverbal communication – gestures, eye contact, posture, personal space, and all the other ways we use our bodies to send messages. Other studies show that if a person's nonverbal communication and verbal communication don't match in terms of message, the listener is more likely to doubt what he or she is saying. Improving your nonverbal communication can help improve your overall ability to both send and receive messages.

Improving your nonverbal communication starts with awareness. Pay attention to how you use your body when you are talking or listening to someone. An open stance, frequent (but not continuous eye contact), nods, and a relaxed posture help to communicate that you are open and approachable, and that you are communicating honestly. A closed stance, folding your arms across your chest, staring at the floor, or refusing to make eye contact all indicate that you are not listening, or that you are not communicating openly. Shifting from foot to foot, pacing, or otherwise moving continuously indicate impatience. We do many things without thinking about them, especially when we are otherwise busy. Take time to notice both your own nonverbal communication and others', and especially your reaction to others.

Listening

The ability to receive messages is as important, if not more important, than the ability to send them. Listening is more than just hearing the words someone speaks. It is a total way of receiving verbal and nonverbal messages, processing them, and communicating that understanding back to the speaker. Many of us listen in order to respond – we are formulating our next message while another is still talking. We should instead listen to understand – to fully take in, process, and comprehend the message that is being sent.

"Active listening" is sometimes thrown around as a buzzword, but it's a valuable soft skill to develop. Active listening is a form of listening where you listen to the speaker and reflect back what you understand the speaker to have said. You may also give the speaker nonverbal feedback through nods of agreement or other techniques which indicate you are listening and understanding. Active listening involves staying focused on the present, both by giving the speaker your full attention and by keeping the discussion to the issue at hand. Reflect back to the speaker what you understand him or her to have said by carefully rephrasing the message, such as, "So, I hear you saying that…." Check for understanding and use "I" statements rather than "you" statements.

Openness and Honesty

Open, honest communication is the key to building workplace relationships and demonstrating professionalism. While you do not need to discuss personal or private topics in the workplace, being transparent and honest about work matters and generally being willing to communicate with others is vital. People can sense when someone is hiding something or withholding information, and tend not to trust him or her. This damages workplace trust and relationships, and may lead to lower productivity and morale. Each of us has a different level of comfort with what we choose to disclose about ourselves, but being willing to share parts of yourself with your colleagues also helps to build rapport.

Teamwork

Even if you work fairly independently most of the time, inevitably you must also work with others. Finding ways to build teams that accomplish what needs to be done in the most efficient and accurate manner is often challenging, especially when bringing together team members with diverse sets of hard and soft skills. There are some basic techniques you can use when building, or working with, a team to help create a cohesive unit that leverages everyone's talents and ensures that each person contributes.

Identifying Capabilities

Einstein said that everyone is a genius, but if you judge a fish by its ability to climb a tree, it will live its life thinking it is stupid. When building a team, it is key to identify the different talents, skills, and capabilities each team member brings. Identifying what each team member does well and can contribute helps ensure that work is allocated in a way that takes full advantage of the talent resources on the team. Assigning a team member work that is completely outside his or her skill set is a recipe for failure! On the other hand, leveraging all the diverse capabilities, skills, and talents on your team helps you achieve the maximum results.

When you build or join a team, take the time at the outset to ask each member what he or she brings to the team. What skills, abilities, and relationships does each team member have that can enhance the project? What does each person feel he or she does well? How can the team use all these talents and capabilities to achieve the best outcome?

Get Into Your Role

When you are given a role on a team, it's important to get into it! Be sure you know what is expected of you, and what you can expect of others. Even if the role is a new one or a stretch for you, it is key to step into it. This also means stepping *out* of others' roles, even if they are roles you have played before. Use your communication skills to create open, honest dialogues with your other team members so that you are all on the same page. Be clear about where your role begins and ends, and be willing to assert those boundaries. Teamwork can be challenging in the best of circumstances, but it is even more so when roles are unclear. A key step in creating a team is clearly outlining what each person's role is (and is not).

Learn the Whole Process

Knowing your role and stepping fully into it is a vital part of effective teamwork. At the same time, it's important not to get isolated in your own piece of the project. Learning the whole process not only ensures that you understand your own role and accountabilities, but helps you know what to expect of and from others. When you take the time to learn the whole process, it puts your work and your relationships with team members into a larger context. Knowing the whole process also means that you can help a colleague troubleshoot if problems arise, and that your colleagues can be of assistance should you need it. In the worst case scenario, having every member of the team know the whole process means that others can step in if there is a crisis or breakdown in the project.

The best way to learn the whole process is to talk to team members who are working parts of a project different from your own. Take the time to ask questions and to listen actively to the answers. This not only demonstrates that you care about the outcome of the project, but that you are interested and invested in each of your teammates' work and success. Learning the whole process helps to build collaborative relationships among team members, which helps to enhance communication and overall productivity.

The Power of Flow

Psychologists define "flow" as a mental state that occurs when we are fully immersed in an activity. When we are a flow state, we are completely absorbed in what we are doing, and this produces a feeling of energized focus and enjoyment. Tapping into flow is a powerful way to increase your own productivity, and the productivity of your team. We are most likely to achieve flow when we are engaged in a task to which our skills are well matched – another reason to identify the capabilities of each person on a team. Flow also comes about more easily when we have clear goals and can focus on the process rather than the end product. Perhaps the most important key to achieving flow is to minimize interruptions when you are working.

When we can find the flow state, time seems to pass quickly without our noticing. We are also more likely to create accurate, high quality work with fewer errors. Because we are focused totally on what we are doing, a flow state may be a key aspect of mastering a new set of skills – stretching your skill set and cultivating flow can be a great tool for professional development.

Problem-Solving

No matter what your industry or your role, problem-solving is part of your job. Whether the problems you encounter are big or small, you solve problems every day. Learning how to apply problem-solving skills helps not only to enhance productivity, but also helps to cultivate relationships by focusing on shared goals and solutions.

Define the Problem

You can't solve a problem if you don't know what it is! The first step in solving any problem should be to define the problem itself. Oftentimes what we think is a problem is only a symptom of a larger issue. Take time to define the problem clearly, whether it's an interpersonal conflict or a hitch in a supply line. Figuring out what the problem is *exactly* and clearly defining it means you can move forward with solutions that will actually solve it, rather than just resolve the symptoms or temporarily stop the chaos. Taking time to define the problem is especially important if emotions are running high or interactions are getting heated – it puts the focus back on shared goals and allows for everyone to be heard.

Generate Alternative Solutions

Once you've defined a problem, you can move on to solutions. It is important not to just choose the first solution that presents itself. Nor should you push your own preferred solution the exclusion of others. Instead, take the time to generate alternative solutions. Ask the others involved what ideas they have for solving the problem. Discuss the ways in which the alternative solutions might play out, problems they might encounter, and how any obstacles can be overcome. Apply active listening and clear communication throughout. When the group has generated many solutions, discuss which one(s) you would all like to move forward with.

Evaluate the Plans

With your list of alternative solutions generated, it is time to make plans and evaluate them. Give all alternative solutions equally fair treatment. Ask the group to brainstorm potential benefits to each alternative solution or plan. Then work with the group to anticipate potential obstacles or problems with each plan. Based on these discussions, evaluate which plan or plans seem to offer the greatest benefit with the fewest drawbacks. Also consider whether the necessary resources – people, time, materials, funding – are available for each proposed plan. As the plans are evaluated, it will quickly become clear which are entirely unworkable. Narrow the list until the most workable plans are found.

Implementation and Re-Evaluation

Once the most workable plan has been chosen, it's time to implement it. It is important to communicate clearly about how the plan will be implemented, what each person's role will be, and what the goals and expected outcomes are. The other soft skills you are developing – communication and teamwork – are vital here. People must feel as though they are part of the solution if you want them to buy in to it. Also provide a timeline for the plan, including the point at which the plan will be re-evaluated.

Re-evaluation of the plan is a step that often gets missed. Sometimes what appears to be the most workable plan on paper does not play out when put into action. It is important to take the time to re-evaluate the plan once it has been implemented so you can gauge how well it's working. Depending on the results, you may need to make some changes to the plan, or implement a new plan altogether. Re-evaluation helps to determine whether the original problem has, in fact, been solved!

Time Management

We all have the same number of hours in the day, so why is it that some people seem to get so much more done? The ability to effectively manage your time is key to productivity. You may not be able to create more time in your day, but applying time management skills can help you make the most of the time you do have!

The Art of Scheduling

We know that if we want to have a meeting, get a haircut, or see our healthcare provider, we need to make an appointment. We schedule our errands and vacations. But when it comes to our own time and work we do independently, too often we take a piecemeal approach and just do whatever comes to hand first. Taking the time to schedule work tasks, even those you do independently, helps you make better use of your time. Instead of doing work as it comes to you, take the time to slot in a block of time on your schedule for each tasks. Don't forget to schedule in breaks, too! Scheduling tasks makes them a priority – after all, you wouldn't just skip a doctor's appointment or other scheduled obligation. Seeing something on your schedule also helps you remember that it needs to get done! Scheduling can take some time to master – you may discover that tasks take much more (or much less) time than you plan for. Spend a week or so keeping track of how you spend you work time so that you can better plan ahead for how much time to schedule a given task or project.

Prioritizing

Managing your priorities is key to managing your time. Taking the time to determine what is most important, whether in terms of value or in terms of completion, is the first step. Take time each day and week to determine what your priorities for the coming days are. Slot these into your schedule first. This allows you to ensure that time is blocked off and resources allocated for the most important tasks and projects. When we don't take time to set priorities, everything becomes equally urgent – which means that we move from task to task in a way that is haphazard and does not make the best use of our time or energy. Setting priorities helps ensure that you take care of the things that are most pressing or which deliver the most value. Prioritizing is especially key when working with others. If people who must work together have differing senses of what the priorities are, this can lead to miscommunication, conflict, and reduced productivity.

Managing Distractions

A major key to productivity, especially if you want to find a flow state, is to manage your distractions. Distractions happen – we can minimize them and manage them, but never eliminate them altogether. Creating a plan for managing distractions is a key time management skill. The first step is to determine what your major distractions are. Is it colleagues popping into your office? Is it your email or voicemail? Do you get bored with routine tasks if you have to focus on them too long? Figuring out what your major distractions are can help you brainstorm solutions and better manage them.

Some common distractions are:

- Colleagues stopping by to chat
- Checking email or voicemail
- Noise in the environment
- Clutter in your workspace
- Boredom after spending too long on one task

You can solve these by:

- Establishing "open door" hours
- Closing your door or otherwise indicating "Please Do Not Disturb"
- Using noise canceling headphones
- Setting a regular time to check voicemail and email
- Letting calls go to voicemail
- De-cluttering your workspace
- Building in breaks

The Multitasking Myth

Multitasking is exactly what it sounds like – trying to do more than one thing at a time. Many of us multitask throughout our day – listening to a colleague while checking email, working on a document while talking on the phone. We have the idea that we get more done when we multitask or that this is the best way to maximize our time. However, studies show that 30-40% more time is spent when you multitask rather than when you mono-task (work on one thing at a time). Multitasking also means your attention is divided, which can lead to miscommunication and errors. Multitasking can also damage relationships, as it may convey that we are not really interested in what another is saying. It can be difficult to break the multitasking habit, but it is key if we are be the best we can be.

Attitude and Work Ethic

Creating a positive attitude is one of the best things you can do for your productivity and your workplace happiness. People who have a consistently positive attitude are seen as approachable and can build more effective workplace relationships. A positive attitude also serves you well when you face challenges or setbacks – it breeds resilience. Coupled with a positive attitude, a strong work ethic helps you build strong relationships with team mates and superiors. A solid work ethic also helps you find reward in the work you do, and shows a dedication not just to goals and outcomes but to your overall professional development.

What Are You Working For?

Being clear about what you're working for is a key part of building a positive attitude and strong work ethic. If you are not sure what you are working for, it can be difficult or even impossible to fully invest in a project or in developing your skills. Take time to clarify what your personal goals are, both in terms of specific projects and in terms of your overall career. Set specific goals and then create plans to achieve them. Tie these goals to your day to day tasks and responsibilities so that you can keep them in sight. When working with a team, it is also vital that you outline clear group goals. Know what each member of the group is working for, and what the group is collectively working for. Find ways to consistently tie individual tasks or steps to the overarching group goals and to individual members' personal goals.

Caring for Others vs Caring for Self

Is there really a difference between caring for others and caring for yourself? Too often, we assume that to show care and concern for others and their needs, we have to put ourselves and our needs at the bottom of the list. We may believe that we can either practice self-care of be a good colleague and team member who demonstrates compassion for others, but that we cannot be both. However, when we come to the realization that we have shared goals with those we work with, we can find a way to both care for ourselves and care for others. We may also realize that caring for ourselves is in itself a way of demonstrating care for others -- that by taking good care of ourselves, we become the best colleague we can be, which demonstrates care for others.

Even more, we may hold the false belief that there can only be one "winner" in any given situation. As a result, we may believe that we can pursue our own goals or help others pursue theirs, but never do both. Seeing the ways in which everyone is interconnected, and the way in which everyone's success benefits the entire group is an important attitude shift. When we can find a way to care for others and ourselves, we develop a more positive, productive workplace.

Building Trust

Nothing undermines productivity and morale in a workplace like lack of trust. If people don't trust you, they find it hard to work with you, invest in you, or pursue shared goals. Take the time to build trust with those you work with, and everyone will thrive. Many of the soft skills help to build trust – effective communication, openness and honesty, a positive attitude and a strong work ethic. Continuously demonstrating that you are trustworthy helps not only to build persona relationships, but also to create buy in for your initiatives and projects. People who are deemed trustworthy by colleagues share some characteristics:

- They are skilled at their jobs

- They are passionate about their work , with a strong work ethic

- They communicate honestly and value transparency

- They have others' best interests at heart

- They care about people and demonstrate this

- They are self-aware

Work Is Its Own Reward

One result of adopting a positive attitude and strong work ethic is that you begin to see work as its own reward. When we operate from this standpoint, we are no longer working with others or completing tasks based on what we will gain financially or professionally from doing so, and this makes us seem more engaged and trustworthy. There is nothing wrong with valuing our salaries and other compensation – they are a vital part of why we work. However, when we take the focus off the material rewards for work and instead focus on the satisfaction we derive from the work itself, we are better able to grow and thrive.

A person who clearly loves what they do and considers it a reward in itself is also more trustworthy, as others do not question his or her motives. If it is difficult for you to consider your work as anything other than the source of a paycheck or path to advancement, it may be time for you to consider why you do the work you do. Learning to practice gratitude around your work is one way to learn to see it as its own reward. What does your work provide you in terms of satisfaction, contentment, excitement, and other nonmaterial benefits? Are you excited to do the work you do? Why or why not? Do you feel content at the end of the day with what you've accomplished? Every day won't be a dream come true – there are always rough days! – but if you can find a way to love the work you do the majority of the time, you are on the path to greater professional and personal happiness.

Adaptability/Flexibility

Two of the most important skills you can have are adaptability and flexibility. Some people mistakenly think that the ability to change according to the needs of a situation or a willingness to compromise show weakness of a lack of conviction. In reality, the ability to compromise, change in response to changing situations and changing needs, and thrive are key to success in the fast-pace workplaces most of us find ourselves in. Change can be scary, but learning to adapt and flex as needed is an investment worth making.

Getting Over the Good Old Days Syndrome

"But that's how we've always done it."

"Things were better back when we….."

Do you find yourself saying these things? Most of us fall prey to the "good old days" syndrome, where we look back at the past and believe that everything was better. This can pose a serious obstacle to our ability to adapt to change. If we are convinced that the good old days were best, we are unlikely to give a new way of doing things a fair try. When you find yourself thinking back to the good old days, give yourself a reality check. Ask yourself if things were really as good as you think you remember. Most of us romanticize the past. Be honest with yourself. Try to recall obstacles, problems, or difficulties you had with the thing you are remembering as so good. (And remember, there were people in the good old days who were wishing for their own good old days!)

Changing to Manage Process

One of the most common situations in which we will need to change, flex, and adapt is when processes change. In order to navigate the new process, and help others to do the same, we need to change not only what we do but how we approach it. New technology, globalizing businesses, and changing needs all lead to changes in our work processes. If we hold on to the old way of doing things, we risk reduced productivity (and revenue), as well as conflict and other challenges. When we adapt to a new process, we are not just learning a new way of doing a specific task – we are demonstrating our ability to adapt to changing circumstances, learn new skills, and work with others.

Changing to Manage People

Managing people is not a one-size-fit-all ability. People need different things from a manager. Some need lots of feedback and guidance. Others prefer to work independently most of the time and to get feedback only at regularly scheduled intervals. Some people needs a great deal of hands-on training with technology or equipment, while others will come into your organization as experts. Taking the time to learn what your people need, and then changing your management style to meet those needs, is hugely important to workplace success. When you adapt your management style to meet the specific needs of the people you manage, this demonstrates that you care for others – that rather than expecting them to conform to your preferred way of doing things, you want to invest in them and help them grow. Take the time to ask the people you manage what they need from you, what their goals are, and how you can be a better manager, supervisor, and colleague. Then take steps to make the changes that you feel will be most helpful.

Showing You're Worth Your Weight in Adaptability

How can you showcase your adaptability at work? Studies show that people who are highly adaptable may be more highly valued at work than those who are highly skilled but less willing to adapt, flex, and change. Take the time to show how adaptable you are, and your workplace is likely to see you as a worthwhile investment. Some ways to demonstrate adaptability on the job are:

- Be open to alternative solutions when your first suggestion does not go over well or succeed

- Be willing to take on new roles, even when they are a stretch for your skills

- Be willing to help others generate alternative solutions or plans

- Be willing to accept the unexpected

- Keep your calm, even when things are moving fast or are stressful

- Demonstrate confidence in your ability to complete the job even when you've had to adapt or flex

Self-Confidence (Owning It)

The single greatest thing you can do for your own success is build and learn to show self-confidence. Self-confidence is not egotistic or acting like you are better than others. Self-confidence is simply the belief that you know what to do and how to do it, that you are good at what you do, and that you can handle whatever comes your way. Demonstrating self-confidence helps to engender trust in you, and demonstrates that you are skilled and adaptable.

Confident Traits

What does it mean to be confident? Studies show that confident people share many of the same traits, even across cultures and industries. Cultivating those traits you already have, and developing those that you do not yet have, will build your overall self-confidence. Remember – self-confidence is about building yourself up, not tearing others down. When you confident, you make others around you feel confident too. Some common traits of confident people include:

- They are not afraid to be wrong

- They are willing to take a stand, even if they end up being wrong

- They value finding out what is right more than they value being right

- They listen more than they speak

- They do not seek the spotlight, and they share the spotlight with others

- They ask for help when they need it

- They think in possibilities, not obstacles – they ask "Why not?"

- They don't put others down

- They aren't afraid to look silly or foolish

- They acknowledge their mistakes

- They seek feedback from only those who matter

- They accept compliments

- They "walk their talk"

Self-Questionnaire

How confident are you? It can be hard to assess our own self-confidence. Taking some time to ask a few questions and answer them honestly can help you gauge the areas where your confidence is high and the areas in which you can develop greater self-confidence. Ask yourself if you agree with these statements:

- I intuitively know what's right for me

- I walk my talk

- I am honest with others

- I am honest with myself

- I feel comfortable being wrong

- I am more interested in finding out what is right than being right

- It is not important to me that I be right all the time

- I feel like I can meet any challenge

- I operate well under pressure

- I do not put others down

- I like to share the spotlight with others

- I have a clear vision for my life

Surefire Self-Confidence Building Tactics

Self-confidence is a trait that can be built. In fact, a few very simple tactics can help you quickly build your self-confidence. And as you become more confident, you will have experiences that will build your confidence even more! Here are ten sure-fire tips for building self-confidence:

- **Dress your best!** Knowing you look good is a key to feeling good about yourself. When you know you look good, you project confidence. Take the time to choose clothes that fit well and which you feel good in. A good haircut that is easy for you to style is also key. If you enjoy make-up, jewelry, or other types of adornment, find pieces you love that make you feel like a million.

- **Stand up straight!** Good posture is a quick, free way to build your confidence. Stand up straight and keep your shoulders back. Don't be afraid to take up space. A bonus of good posture is that you breathe more deeply and get more oxygen, which may mean you have more focus!

- **Practice gratitude!** When you take the time each day to practice gratitude, you see how many blessings you have in your life. This builds your confidence and appreciation for your life.

- **Compliment others!** Confident people take the time to compliment others. When you compliment others, you project that you have concern and appreciation for others.

- **Accept compliments!** When someone compliments you, accept it. Too often we say "Yes, but…" instead of just saying "Thank you."

- **Spend time with people who build you up**. This helps keeping you focused on the positive.

Build Up Others

One key trait of people who have high self-confidence is that they build up others rather than tearing them down. Having self-confidence means that you do not feel competitive with others – their success doesn't take away from your own. Find ways to build up others. Compliment others. Acknowledge their contributions, and express your gratitude. Being a mentor can also help to build others up by helping them develop skills, which will help them develop their own self-confident

Ability to Learn from

No one likes criticism, but the ability to learn from it is key to professional and personal development. Learning to accept and learn from criticism is a valuable investment in yourself. The ability to listen to and accept criticism is a key component of self-confidence. It also demonstrates that you value what others have to say, and helps develop a sense that you are committed to what you do and to your own growth.

Wow, You Mean I'm Not Perfect?

It can come as a shock when we get feedback that we're not as perfect as we might like to think. However, one of the hallmarks of a confident person is the willingness to recognize mistakes and accept that sometimes we are wrong. The key is to keep the focus on improvement, not on defending ourselves or on the reasons why we did the thing we are being criticized for. When you accept that you're not perfect, but that that imperfection doesn't mean you are a bad person, you have gained a valuable skill. Remember that no one expects you to be perfect – they just expect you to be the best you can. And criticism is offered in the spirit of helping you achieve excellence, not to make you feel bad.

Listen with an Open Mind

Your active listening skills come in very hand when you're learning to accept and learn from criticism. It is tempting to defend ourselves when we receive criticism, but it is vital to resist this. When someone offers you feedback or criticism, listen with an open mind. You may not agree with all (or any) of what he or she has to say, but it is important to hear the person out. Reflect back what you understand the person to have said, and check for understanding. Answer any questions non-defensively, and do not interrupt. Listen to understand, not to respond.

Analyze and Learn

After someone has given you feedback or criticism, it is fine to ask for time to consider what he or she has said. Always thank the person for the feedback. Take time to analyze the feedback and decide what items you want to act on. Give yourself time, especially if you feel defensive. Even if you do not agree with everything the person said, see what you can draw out of the feedback that you can learn from. When you have analyzed the feedback, choose some action items that you can use going forward. You should then investigate training, courses, mentoring, or other ways in which you can act on the areas of feedback that you agree with or think are valid. If you have difficulty analyzing the feedback, seek out the help of a mentor, supervisor, or trusted colleague.

Clear the Air and Don't Hold Any Grudges

Even when it's not meant to be, criticism and feedback can feel extremely personal. When someone gives you feedback, it's important to clear the air and not hold onto any bad feelings or grudges. Take the time to thank the person for his or her time, and for caring enough to give you feedback. Affirm the relationship, especially if the criticism has been harsh or difficult to hear. Remember that, when people give you feedback, they are doing so with your best interests at heart. If you find yourself feeling defensive or holding on to negative feelings even after the feedback session, make sure to find a way to clear the air as soon as possible. This demonstrates not only that you are committed to your own growth, but that you value the relationship with the person who gave you the feedback.

Networking

Networking is more than just a buzzword. Taking the time to network and build relationships is a key soft skill. Networking helps you create connections with others, which expands your circle of learning and support. Networking is more than meeting people or connecting with them on the Internet. It involves building mutually beneficial links where you can learn from and benefit from each other and the relationship.

Redefine Need

When many people think of networking, they think of it terms of what they need or what they can get from the networking relationship. Networking can be more beneficial if we instead think of what we can give in our networking relationships. Think about what you have to offer people instead only of what you need from them. When you think in terms of what you can offer as well as what you need from others, it expands your network. You begin to seek out people to whom you can offer yourself, your expertise, and talents rather than just those who have something to offer you. Seeing yourself as someone with much to offer also helps to boost your self-confidence.

Identifying Others' Interests

When you network with others, it's key to identify others' interests. This helps you identify common interests and goals, as well as areas in which you can offer of yourself. When you meet a new person, ask about his or her goals and interests. Ask yourself how they mesh with your own goals and interests. How do they line up with the goals and interests of your organization? How can you integrate your interests with others' to find common ground? What common goals do you have? How can you offer of yourself to help others reach their goals? How can they help you reach your goals? Focusing on ways in which your goals and interests integrate with others' helps create a strong, powerful network that goes beyond simple friendship.

Reach Out

To be able to network, you have to reach out. There are many ways to do this, both online and in person. One of the easiest ways to reach out is to join professional social networking sites such as LinkedIn, and look for people in your industry or who share your interest. Join groups, both online and in person – professional groups and associations, groups which promote skills you want to develop (such as Toastmasters), and groups that work for causes you value are all good choices. No matter what you choose as a method of meeting people, the key part of networking is to talk to people. Approach people and start a conversation, and cultivate a presence that makes you approachable. Be responsive when people contact you via email or phone. Make time in your schedule each week to work on networking – schedule it as you would any other important task. Use your soft skills – listening actively, projecting self-confidence, building others up – as you network.

When to Back Off

As important as knowing how and when to reach out is knowing when to back off. If it becomes clear that the person you are trying to connect with is not responding, it is time to move on. The last thing you want is for someone to feel pursued! Be willing to back off if a person appears to be trying to distance him or herself. Also be aware of being too self-promoting – this can be off putting. Know that you have much to offer to others, and that someone not wanting to build a networking relationship with you is not a reflection of your worth as a person.

Chapter 2 – Communication Strategies

For the better part of every day, we are communicating to and with others. Whether it's the speech you deliver in the boardroom, the level of attention you give your spouse when they are talking to you, or the look that you give to the cat, it all means something. This workshop will help participants understand the different methods of communication and how to make the most of each of them.

By the end of this chapter, you should be able to:

- Understand what communication is

- Identify ways that communication can happen

- Identify barriers to communication and how to overcome them

- Develop their non-verbal and para verbal communication skills

- Use the STAR method to speak on the spot

- Listen actively and effectively

- Ask good questions

- Use appreciative inquiry as a communication tool

- Adeptly converse and network with others

- Identify and mitigate precipitating factors

- Establish common ground with others

- Use "I" messages

Communication Strategy Activity

Think of a situation where you missed an opportunity because of a lack of communication, and what communication skills in particular could have alleviated the problem. Take some time now to share your thoughts.

The Big Picture

When we say the word, "communication," what do you think of? Many people will think of the spoken word. People who are hearing impaired, however, might think of sign language. People who are visually impaired might think of Braille as well as sounds.

In this module, we will explore the different ways in which we communicate.

What is Communication?

The dictionary defines communication as, "the imparting or interchange of thoughts, opinions, or information by speech, writing, or signs."

It is also defined as, "means of sending messages, orders, etc., including telephone, telegraph, radio, and television," and in biology as an, "activity by one organism that changes or has the potential to change the behavior of other organisms."

The effectiveness of your communication can have many different effects on your life, including items such as:

- Level of stress

- Relationships with others

- Level of satisfaction with your life

- Productivity

- Ability to meet your goals and achieve your dreams

- Ability to solve problems

How Do We Communicate?

We communicate in three major ways:

- Spoken: There are two components to spoken communication.

    o Verbal: This is what you are saying.

    o Para verbal: This means how you say it – your tone, speed, pitch, and volume.

- Non-Verbal: These are the gestures and body language that accompany your words. Some examples: arms folded across your chest, tracing circles in the air, tapping your feet, or having a hunched-over posture.

- Written: Communication can also take place via fax, e-mail, or written word.

Other Factors in Communication

Other communication factors that we need to consider.

- Method: The method in which the communicator shares his or her message is important as it has an effect on the message itself. Communication methods include person-to-person, telephone, e-mail, fax, radio, public presentation, television broadcast, and many more!

- Mass: The number of people receiving the message.

- Audience: The person or people receiving the message affect the message, too. Their understanding of the topic and the way in which they receive the message can affect how it is interpreted and understood.

Understanding Communication Barriers

On the surface, communication seems pretty simple. I talk, you listen. You send me an e-mail, I read it. Larry King makes a TV show, we watch it.

Like most things in life, however, communication is far more complicated than it seems. Let's look at some of the most common barriers and how to reduce their impact on communication.

An Overview of Common Barriers

Many things can impede communication. Common things that people list as barriers include:

- I can't explain the message to the other person in words that they understand.

- I can't show the other person what I mean.

- I don't have enough time to communicate effectively.

- The person I am trying to communicate with doesn't have the same background as me, and is missing the bigger picture of my message.

These barriers typically break down into three categories: language, culture, and location.

Language Barriers

Of course, one of the biggest barriers to written and spoken communication is language. This can appear in three main forms:

- The people communicating speak different languages.

- The language being used is not the first language for one or more people involved in the communication.

- The people communicating speak the same language, but are from different regions and therefore have different dialects and or unique subtleties.

There are a few ways to reduce the impact of these barriers.

- As a group, identify that the barrier exists. Identify things that the group can do to minimize it.

- Pictures speak a thousand words, and can communicate across languages.

- If you are going to be communicating with this person on a long-term basis, try to find a common language. You may also consider hiring a translator.

Cultural Barriers

There can also be times when people speak the same language, but are from a different culture, where different words or gestures can mean different things. Or, perhaps the person you are communicating with is from a different class from you, or has a very different lifestyle. All of these things can hinder your ability to get your message across effectively.

If you have the opportunity to prepare, find out as much as you can about the other person's culture and background, and how it differs from yours. Try to identify possible areas of misunderstanding and how to prevent or resolve those problems.

An example: A British restaurant owner needs to talk to a culinary specialist in Australia. Although they speak the same language, their words could mean very different things.

If you don't have time to prepare, and find yourself in an awkward situation, use the cultural differences to your advantage. Ask about the differences that you notice, and encourage questions about your culture. Ensure that your questions are curious, not judgmental, resentful, or otherwise negative.

Differences in Time and Place

The last barrier that we will look at is location, definable by time and by place. These barriers often occur when people are in different time zones, or different places.

Take this scenario as an example. Bill works on the east coast, while his colleague, Joe, works on the west coast. Four hours separate their offices. One day, right after lunch, Bill calls Joe to ask for help with a question. Bill has been at work for over four hours already; he is bright, chipper, and in the groove.

Joe, however, has just gotten to the office and is, in fact, running late. He does not feel awake and chipper, and is therefore perhaps not as responsive and helpful in answering Bill's question as he normally is.

Bill thinks, "Geez, what did I do to make Joe cranky?" In response to the way he perceives Joe's behavior, he, too, stops communicating. Their effort to solve a problem together has failed.

So how can you get over the challenges of time and place? First, identify that there is a difference in time and place. Next, try these tips to reduce its impact.

- Make small talk about the weather in your respective regions. This will help you get a picture of the person's physical environment.

- Try to set up phone calls and meetings at a time that is convenient for you both.

- If appropriate, e-mail can be an "anytime, anywhere" bridge. For example, if Bill had sent Joe an e-mail describing the problem, Joe could have addressed it at a better time for him, such as later on in the day. Clearly, this is not always practical (for example, if the problem is urgent, or if it is a complicated issue that requires extensive explanation), but this option should be considered.

Another thing to watch out for is rushed communication. The pressure of time can cause either party to make assumptions and leaps of faith. Always make sure you communicate as clearly as possible, and ask for playback. The listening and questioning skills that you will learn in this workshop will help you make the most of the communication time that you do have.

Para verbal Communication Skills

Have you ever heard the saying, "It's not what you say, it's how you say it"? It's true!

Try saying these three sentences out loud, placing the emphasis on the underlined word.

- "I didn't say you were wrong." (Implying it wasn't me)

- "I didn't say you were wrong." (Implying I communicated it in another way)

- "I didn't say you were wrong." (Implying I said something else)

Now, let's look at the three parts of para verbal communication; which is the message told through the pitch, tone, and speed of our words when we communicate.

The Power of Pitch

Pitch can be most simply defined as the key of your voice. A high pitch is often interpreted as anxious or upset. A low pitch sounds more serious and authoritative. People will pick up on the pitch of your voice and react to it. As well, variation in the pitch of your voice is important to keep the other party interested.

If you naturally speak in a very high-pitched or low-pitched voice, work on varying your pitch to encompass all ranges of your vocal cords. (One easy way to do this is to relax your throat when speaking.) Make sure to pay attention to your body when doing this – you don't want to damage your vocal cords.

The Truth about Tone

Did your mother ever say to you, "I don't like that tone!" She was referring to the combination of various pitches to create a mood. (Speed, which we will discuss in the next module, can also have an effect on your tone.)

Here are some tips on creating a positive, authoritative tone.

- Try lowering the pitch of your voice a bit.

- Smile! This will warm up anyone's voice.

- Sit up straight and listen.

- Monitor your inner monologue. Negative thinking will seep into the tone of your voice.

The Strength of Speed

The pace at which you speak also has a tremendous effect on your communication ability. From a practical perspective, someone who speaks quickly is harder to understand than someone who speaks at a moderate pace. Conversely, someone who speaks v-e---r----y s---l-----o---w---l---y will probably lose their audience's interest before they get very far!

Speed also has an effect on the tone and emotional quality of your message. A hurried pace can make the listener feel anxious and rushed. A slow pace can make the listener feel as though your message is not important. A moderate pace will seem natural, and will help the listener focus on your message.

One easy way to check your pitch, tone, and speed is to record yourself speaking. Think of how you would feel listening to your own voice. Work on speaking the way you would like to be spoken to.

Non-Verbal Communication

When you are communicating, your body is sending a message that is as powerful as your words.

In our following discussions, remember that our interpretations are just that – common interpretations. (For example, the person sitting with his or her legs crossed may simply be more comfortable that way, and not feeling closed-minded towards the discussion. Body language can also mean different things across different genders and cultures.) However, it is good to understand how various behaviors are often seen, so that we can make sure our body is sending the same message as our mouth.

Think about these scenarios for a moment. What non-verbal messages might you receive in each scenario? How might these non-verbal messages affect the verbal message?

- Your boss asks you to come into his office to discuss a new project. He looks stern and his arms are crossed.

- A team member tells you they have bad news, but they are smiling as they say it.

- You tell a co-worker that you cannot help them with a project. They say that it's OK, but they slam your office door on their way out.

This is the first goal of this module: to help you understand how to use body language to become a more effective communicator. Another goal, one which you will achieve with time and practice, is to be able to interpret body language, add it to the message you are receiving, and understand the message being sent appropriately.

With this in mind, let's look at the components of non-verbal communication.

Understanding the Mehrabian Study

In 1971, psychologist Albert Mehrabian published a famous study called <u>Silent Messages</u>. In it, he made several conclusions about the way the spoken word is received. Although this study has been misquoted often throughout the years, its basic conclusion is that 7% of our message is verbal, 38% is para verbal, and 55% is from body language.

Now, we know this is not true in all situations. If someone is speaking to you in a foreign language, you cannot understand 93% of what they are saying. Or, if you are reading a written letter, you are likely getting more than 7% of the sender's message.

What this study does tell us is that body language is a vital part of our communication with others. With this in mind, let's look at the messages that our body can send.

All About Body Language

Body language is a very broad term that simply means the way in which our body speaks to others. We have included an overview of three major categories below; we will discuss a fourth category, gestures, in a moment.

The way that we are standing or sitting

Think for a moment about different types of posture and the message that they relay.

- Sitting hunched over typically indicates stress or discomfort.

- Leaning back when standing or sitting indicates a casual and relaxed demeanor.

- Standing ramrod straight typically indicates stiffness and anxiety.

The position of our arms, legs, feet, and hands

- Crossed arms and legs often indicate a closed mind.

- Fidgeting is usually a sign of boredom or nervousness.

Facial expressions

- Smiles and frowns speak a million words.

- A raised eyebrow can mean inquisitiveness, curiosity, or disbelief.

Chewing one's lips can indicate thinking, or it can be a sign of boredom, anxiety, or nervousness.

Interpreting Gestures

A gesture is a non-verbal message that is made with a specific part of the body. Gestures differ greatly from region to region, and from culture to culture. Below we have included a brief list of gestures and their common interpretation in North America.

Gesture	Interpretation
Nodding head	Yes
Shaking head	No
Moving head from side to side	Maybe
Shrugging shoulders	Not sure; I don't know
Crossed arms	Defensive
Tapping hands or fingers	Bored, anxious, nervous
Shaking index finger	Angry
Thumbs up	Agreement, OK
Thumbs down	Disagreement, not OK
Pointing index finger at someone/something	Indicating, blaming
Pointing middle finger (vertically)	Vulgar expression
Handshake	Welcome, introduction
Flap of the hand	Doesn't matter, go ahead
Waving hand	Hello
Waving both hands over head	Help, attention
Crossed legs or ankles	Defensive
Tapping toes or feet	Bored, anxious, nervous

What other gestures can you add to the list?

Speaking Like a STAR

Now that we have explored all the quasi-verbal elements of communication, let's look at the actual message you are sending. You can ensure any message is clear, complete, correct, and concise, with the STAR acronym.

This module will explore the STAR acronym in conjunction with the six roots of open questions (Who? What? When? Where? Why? How?), which will be explored in more detail later on in the workshop.

S = Situation

First, state what the situation is. Try to make this no longer than one sentence. If you are having trouble, ask yourself, "Where?", "Who?", and, "When?". This will provide a base for message so it can be clear and concise.

Example: "On Tuesday, I was in a director's meeting at the main plant."

T = Task

Next, briefly state what your task was. Again, this should be no longer than one sentence. Use the question, "What?" to frame your sentence, and add the "Why?" if appropriate.

Example: "I was asked to present last year's sales figures to the group."

A = Action

Now, state what you did to resolve the problem in one sentence. Use the question, "How?" to frame this part of the statement. The Action part will provide a solid description and state the precise actions that will resolve any issues.

Example: "I pulled out my laptop, fired up PowerPoint, and presented my slide show."

R = Result

Last, state what the result was. This will often use a combination of the six roots. Again, a precise short description of the results that come about from your previous steps will finish on a strong definite note.

Example: "Everyone was wowed by my prep work, and by our great figures!"

Let's look at a complete example using STAR. Let's say you're out with friends on the weekend. Someone asks you what the highlight of your week at work was. As it happens, you had a great week, and there is a lot to talk about. You use STAR to focus your answer so you don't bore your friends, and so that you send a clear message.

You respond: "On Tuesday, I was in a director's meeting at the main plant. I was asked to present last year's sales figures to the group. I pulled out my laptop, fired up PowerPoint, and presented my slide show. Everyone was wowed by my prep work, and by our great figures!"

This format can be compressed for quick conversations, or expanded for lengthy presentations. We encourage you to try framing statements with STAR, and see how much more confident you feel when communicating.

Listening Skills

So far, we have discussed all the components of sending a message: non-verbal, para-verbal, and verbal. Now, let's turn the tables and look at how to effectively receive messages.

Seven Ways to Listen Better Today

Hearing is easy! For most of us, our body does the work by interpreting the sounds that we hear into words. Listening, however, is far more difficult. Listening is the process of looking at the words and the other factors around the words (such as our non-verbal communication), and then interpreting the entire message.

Let's start out slowly. Here are seven things that you can do to start becoming a better listener right now. Pick a few of them and write them in your action plan.

1. When you're listening, listen. Don't talk on the phone, text message, clean off your desk, or do anything else.

2. Avoid interruptions. If you think of something that needs to be done, make a mental or written note of it and forget about it until the conversation is over.

3. Aim to spend at least 90% of your time listening and less than 10% of your time talking.

4. When you do talk, make sure it's related to what the other person is saying. Questions to clarify expand, and probe for more information will be key tools. (We'll look at questioning skills later on in the workshop.)

5. Do not offer advice unless the other person asks you for it. If you are not sure what they want, ask!

6. Make sure the physical environment is conducive to listening. Try to reduce noise and distractions. ("Would you mind stepping into my office where I can hear you better?" is a great line to use.) If possible, be seated comfortably. Be close enough to the person so that you can hear them, but not too close to make them uncomfortable.

7. If it is a conversation where you are required to take notes, try not to let the note-taking disturb the flow of the conversation. If you need a moment to catch up, choose an appropriate moment to ask for a break.

Understanding Active Listening

Although hearing is a passive activity, one must listen actively to listen effectively, and to actually hear what is being said.

There are three basic steps to actively listening.

1. Try to identify where the other person is coming from. This concept is also called the frame of reference. For example, your reaction to a bear will be very different if you're viewing it in a zoo, or from your tent at a campsite. Your approach to someone talking about a sick relative will differ depending on their relationship with that person.

2. Listen to what is being said closely and attentively.

3. Respond appropriately, either non-verbally (such as a nod to indicate you are listening), with a question (to ask for clarification), or by paraphrasing. Note that paraphrasing does not mean repeating the speaker's words back to them like a parrot. It does mean repeating what you think the speaker said in your own words. Some examples: "It sounds like that made you angry," or, "It sounds like that cashier wasn't very nice to you." (Using the "It sounds like…" precursor, or something similar, gives the speaker the opportunity to correct you if your interpretation is wrong."

Sending Good Signals to Others

When we are listening to others speak, there are three kinds of cues that we can give the other person. Using the right kind of cue at the right time is crucial for keeping good communication going.

- Non-Verbal: As shown in the Mehrabian study, body language plays an important part in our communications with others. Head nods and an interested facial expression will show the speaker that you are listening.

- Quasi-Verbal: Fillers words like, "uh-huh," and "mm-hmmm," show the speaker that you are awake and interested in the conversation.

- Verbal: Asking open questions using the six roots discussed earlier (who, what, where, when, why, how), paraphrasing, and asking summary questions, are all key tools for active listening. (We will look at questioning skills in a moment.)

These cues should be used as part of active listening. Inserting an occasional, "uh-huh," during a conversation may fool the person that you are communicating with in the short term, but you're fooling yourself if you feel that this is an effective communication approach.

Asking Good Questions

Good questioning skills are another building block of successful communication. We have already encountered several possible scenarios where questions helped us gather information, clarify facts, and communicate with others. In this module, we will look closer at these questioning techniques that you can use throughout the communication process.

Open Questions

We discussed open questions a bit when exploring the STAR model earlier. Open questions get their name because the response is open-ended; the answerer has a wide range of options to choose from when answering it.

Open questions use one of six words as a root:

- Who?

- What?

- Where?

- When?

- Why?

- How?

Open questions are like going fishing with a net – you never know what you're going to get! Open questions are great conversation starters, fact finders, and communication enhancers. Use them whenever possible.

Closed Questions

Closed questions are the opposite of open questions; their very structure limits the answer to yes or no, or a specific piece of information. Some examples include:

- Do you like chocolate?

- Were you born in December?

- Is it five o'clock yet?

Although closed questions tend to shut down communication, they can be useful if you are searching for a particular piece of information, or winding a conversation down.

If you use a closed question and it shuts down the conversation, simply use an open-ended question to get things started again. Here is an example:

- Do you like the Flaming Ducks hockey team?

- Yes.

- Who is your favorite player?

Probing Questions

In addition to the basic open and closed questions, there is also a toolbox of probing questions that we can use. These questions can be open or closed, but each type serves a specific purpose.

Clarification

By probing for clarification, you invite the other person to share more information so that you can fully understand their message. Clarification questions often look like this:

- "Please tell me more about…"

- "What did you mean by…"

- "What does … look like?" (Any of the five senses can be used here)

Completeness and Correctness

These types of questions can help you ensure you have the full, true story. Having all the facts, in turn, can protect you from assuming and jumping to conclusions – two fatal barriers to communication.

Some examples of these questions include:

- "What else happened after that?"

- "Did that end the …"

Determining Relevance

This category will help you determine how or if a particular point is related to the conversation at hand. It can also help you get the speaker back on track from a tangent.

Some good ways to frame relevance questions are:

- "How is that like…"

- "How does that relate to…"

Drilling Down

Use these types of questions to nail down vague statements. Useful helpers include:

- "Describe…"

- "What do you mean by…?"

- "Could you please give an example?"

Summarizing

These questions are framed more like a statement. They pull together all the relevant points. They can be used to confirm to the listener that you heard what was said, and to give them an opportunity to correct any misunderstandings.

Example: "So you picked out a dress, had to get it fitted three times, and missed the wedding in the end?"

Be careful not to avoid repeating the speaker's words back to them like a parrot. Remember, paraphrasing means repeating what you think the speaker said in your own words.

Appreciative Inquiry

Traditional communication often focuses on what is wrong and how we can fix it. Think back to your last performance review, visit to the doctor, or your latest disagreement with a friend or spouse.

Appreciative inquiry does the opposite: it focuses on what is right and how we can make it better. Many organizations have found it to be a refreshing, energizing way of approaching problems and revitalizing their people.

Although we could spend a whole day talking about appreciative inquiry, this module will give you a brief taste of what AI is all about.

The Purpose of AI

To understand the purpose of Appreciative Inquiry, let's look at each of its parts.

- Appreciate is defined by the Random House dictionary as, "to value or regard highly; to be fully conscious of; be aware of; detect; to rise in value."

- In the same dictionary, inquiry is defined as, "the act of inquiring or of seeking information by questioning."

Therefore, appreciative inquiry can be defined as, "the act of seeking information about the things that we value."

The Four Stages

Appreciative Inquiry includes four basic stages. Note that these stages are viewed as a cycle – AI allows people and organizations to grow and evolve through the continuous use of the process.

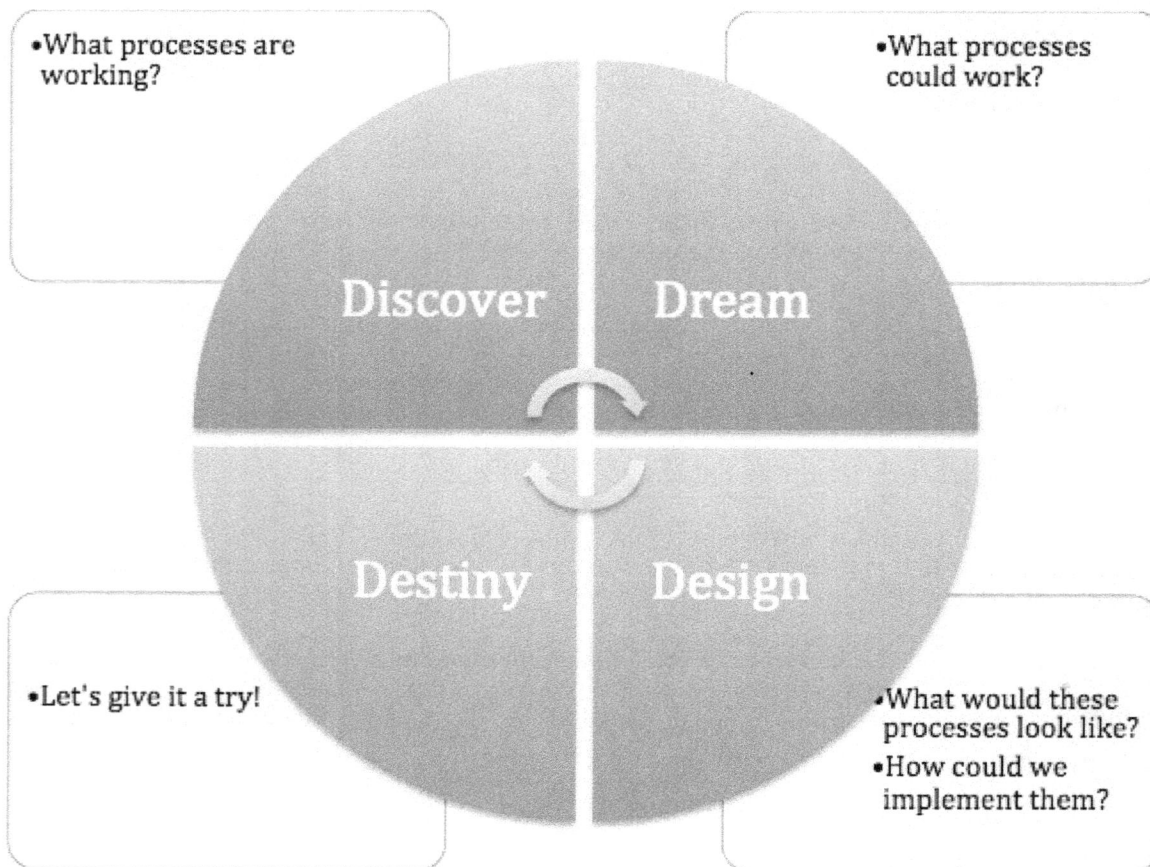

- What processes are working?

- What processes could work?

Discover | Dream

Destiny | Design

- Let's give it a try!

- What would these processes look like?
- How could we implement them?

Examples and Case Studies

Appreciative inquiry has been used in many different ways in many different organizations. Some projects where it has been a key tool include:

- Creation of learning network for organizational psychologists at the California School of Professional Psychology

- Process improvement at John Deere that resulted in millions of dollars in savings

- Relief efforts for children orphaned by AIDS in Zimbabwe.

- Integration of mental health services in England.

Mastering the Art of Conversation

Engaging in interesting, memorable small talk is a daunting task for most people. How do you know what to share and when to share it? How do you know what topics to avoid? How do you become an engaging converser?

Most experts propose a simple three-level framework that you can use to master the art of conversation. Identifying where you are and where you should be is not always easy, but having an objective outline can help you stay out of sticky situations. We will also share some handy networking tips that will help you get conversations started.

Level One: Discussing General Topics

At the most basic level, stick to general topics: the weather, sports, non-controversial world events, movies, and books. This is typically what people refer to when they say, "small talk."

At this stage, you will focus on facts rather than feelings, ideas, and perspectives. Death, religion, and politics are absolute no-no's. (The exception is when you know someone has had an illness or death in the family and wish to express condolences. In this situation, keep your condolences sincere, brief, and to the point.)

If someone shares a fact that you feel is not true, try to refrain from pointing out the discrepancy. If you are asked about the fact, it's OK simply to say, "I wasn't aware of that," or make some other neutral comment.

Right now, you are simply getting to know the other party. Keep an eye out for common ground while you are communicating. Use open-ended questions and listening skills to get as much out of the conversation as possible.

Level Two: Sharing Ideas and Perspectives

If the first level of conversation goes well, the parties should feel comfortable with each other and have identified some common ground. Now it's time to move a bit beyond general facts and share different ideas and perspectives.

It is important to note that not all personal experiences are appropriate to share at this level. For example, it is fine to share that you like cross-country skiing and went to Europe, but you may not want to share the fact that you took out a personal loan to do so.

Although this level of conversation is the one most often used, and is the most conducive to relationship building and opening communication channels, make sure that you don't limit yourself to one person in a large social gathering. We'll offer some ways to mingle successfully in a few moments.

Level Three: Sharing Personal Experiences

This is the most personal level of conversation. This is where everything is on the table and personal details are being shared. This level is typically not appropriate for a social, casual meeting. However, all of the skills that we have learned today are crucial at this stage in particular: when people are talking about matters of the heart, they require our complete attention, excellent listening skills, and skilled probing with appropriate questions.

Our Top Networking Tips

Understanding how to converse and how to make small talk are great skills, but how do you get to that point? The answer is simple, but far from easy: you walk up, shake their hand, and say hello!

If you're in the middle of a social gathering, try these networking tips to maximize your impact and minimize your nerves.

- Before the gathering, imagine the absolute worst that could happen and how likely it is. For example, you may fear that people will laugh at you when you try to join their group or introduce yourself. Is this likely? At most business gatherings, it's very unlikely!

- Remember that everyone is as nervous as you are. Focus on turning that energy into a positive force.

- To increase your confidence, prepare a great introduction. The best format is to say your name, your organization and/or position title (if appropriate), and something interesting about yourself, or something positive about the gathering. Example: "I'm Tim from Accounting. I think I recognize some of you from the IT conference last month."

- Just do it! The longer you think about meeting new people, the harder it will be. Get out there, introduce yourself, and meet new people.

- Act as the host or hostess. By asking others if they need food or drink, you are shifting the attention from you to them.

- Start a competition with a friend: see how many people each of you can meet before the gathering is over. Make sure your meetings are worthwhile!

- Join a group of odd-numbered people.

- Try to mingle as much as possible. When you get comfortable with a group of people, move on to a new group.

- When you hear someone's name, repeat the introduction in your head. Then, when someone new joins the group, introduce them to everyone.

- Mnemonics are a great way to remember names. Just remember to keep them to yourself! Some examples:

    o Mr. Singh likes to sing.

    o Sue sues people for a living.

o   How funny – Amy Pipes is a plumber!

Advanced Communication Skills

During this workshop, we have learned a lot about communication. We would like to wrap things up with a brief discussion on a few advanced communication topics. Adding these skills to your toolbox and using them regularly will make you a more efficient, effective, communicator.

Understanding Precipitating Factors

For many people, life is like a snowball. On a particularly good day, everything may go your way and make you feel like you're on top of the world. But on a bad day, unfortunate events can likewise snowball, increasing their negative effect exponentially.

For example, imagine how each of these events would make you feel if they happened to you first thing in the morning.

- You encounter construction on the way to work.

- Your alarm clock doesn't go off and you wake up late.

- You are out of coffee.

- The cafeteria line is very long.

Each of those things is potentially responsible for creating a crummy morning. Now, imagine this scenario:

You wake up and realize your alarm clock hasn't gone off and you're already late. You get up and go to turn the coffee pot on, but you realize that there is no coffee left in your house. Then, you shower and head out the door – only to encounter construction and massive traffic back-ups on the way to work. Now you're 15 minutes late instead of five. You get to work and head to the cafeteria for some much-needed coffee, but the line stretches out the door.

With the addition of each event, your morning just gets worse and worse. For most people, this is a recipe for disaster – the first person that crosses them is likely to get an earful!

Successful communicators are excellent at identifying precipitating factors and adjusting their approach before the communication starts, or during it. Understanding the power of precipitating factors can also help you de-personalize negative comments. This does not mean that someone having a bad day gets to dump on everyone around them; it does mean, however, that the person being dumped on can take it less personally and help the other person work through their problems.

Establishing Common Ground

Finding common ties can be a powerful communication tool. Think of those times when a stranger turns out not to be a stranger – that the person next to you on the train grew up in the same town that you did, or that the co-worker you never really liked enjoys woodworking as much as you do.

Whenever you are communicating with someone, whether it is a basic conversation, a problem-solving session, or a team meeting, try to find ways in which you are alike. Focusing on positive connections will help you build stronger relationships and better communication.

Using "I" Messages

Framing your message appropriately can greatly increase the power of your communication.

How would you react to these statements?

- Your outfit is too casual for this meeting.

- You mumble all the time.

- You're really disorganized.

Most people would feel insulted and criticized by these statements – and rightly so! They are framed in a way that puts blame on the receiver. These statements can even give the impression that the speaker feels superior to the receiver.

Instead of starting a sentence with "you," try using the "I message" instead for feedback. This format places the responsibility with the speaker, makes a clear statement, and offers constructive feedback.

The format has three basic parts:

- Objective description of the behavior

- Effect that the behavior is causing on the speaker

- The speaker's feelings

Here is an example: "Sometimes, you speak in a very low voice. I often have difficulty hearing you when you speak at that volume. It often makes me feel frustrated."

Be careful not to start the sentence with some form of, "When you…" This tends to create feelings of blame and injustice.

Chapter 3 – Emotional Intelligence

What is Emotional Intelligence?

Emotional Intelligence is a part of you that affects every aspect of your life. Understanding the root causes of your emotions and how to use them can help you to effectively identify who you are and how you interact with others.

With Emotional Intelligence being a fairly new branch of psychology, its definition can be found in various theories and models. We are presenting a definition influenced by a few theories, and mainly popularized by Daniel Goleman's 1995 book Emotional Intelligence.

Self-Management

In order to effectively achieve your overall career objectives or the objectives within a given task, you must use clearly defined methods to carry out those activities. This includes the setting of goals, decision making, planning, and scheduling. Once the tasks are completed, you must evaluate the success of these methods.

The following is a list of five key points to remember to help you master the art of self-management.

- Be consistent. Part of managing oneself is the ability to be stable. The values you hold dear should always be transparent. Always changing can not only cause others to question your beliefs, but it can also cause you to become confused about what you truly believe.

- Stick to the plan. If you are scheduled to complete a particular task, do it. Don't just do it, but make sure it is done in a timely manner. It is easy to feel out of control when you disregard the plan you are to follow.

- Be accountable. There are times when things don't work out as you plan, but you have to be able to admit that and then use your flexibility to get things back on track. The ideal result is that you easily bounce back and complete the task, but even during those times when this is not the case, you are expected to adjust.

- Educate yourself. We live in an ever-changing world and you want to be able to keep up with it. Don't let change pass you by, embrace it. Be an avid reader. Talk and listen to mentors and peers. They may know something that could help you along your journey.

- Stay physically fit. Many people don't think of staying fit when they talk about self-management, but it is a very important part of being able to practice the four preceding points. Exercising your body is just as crucial to self-management as exercising your mind. A body that is not well rested, nutritionally fed, or physically exercised can lead to emotional and physical illnesses.

Self-Awareness

Being 'aware' of one's self is the ability to accurately perceive one's skills and knowledge, value and responsibilities. It is being confident in what you have to offer, whether it is personally or professionally.

Self-awareness is not only important for one's self-esteem, but it is also the first step to the process of full acceptance or change. Without understanding why one thinks the way he thinks or why he acts the way he acts, he may never fully appreciate himself or see the importance of making changes to improve him, if necessary. Self-awareness gives power and a sense of peace or happiness. This newly found strength will more than likely carry over into your work life, how you perform your duties as well as how you interact with others.

The lack of self-awareness can cause you to not realize your worth in the company or even the quality of the work you perform. This can have an even more dramatic effect when you hold a leadership position. Not only will you have doubts about yourself, but the people you lead will also begin to question your competence, which could ultimately lead to a lack of leadership effectiveness.

Self-Regulation is another term for 'self-control', which is defined as the ability to control one's emotions, desires, and behaviors in order to reach a positive outcome. Self-regulation is sometimes difficult because of the phenomenon that it is important to 'express how you feel'. While this may be partially true, the art to finding the balance between expressing one's feelings and avoiding unnecessary tension is self-regulation.

Self-Regulation is a direct reflection of the type of pressure one is experiencing. There are three types of pressure:

- Good Pressure: This type of pressure is the result of an aggressive yet non-critical and non-harmful atmosphere. One aspires to be like the people around them. This motivation leads to the acquisition of self-regulation.

- Bad Pressure: Bad pressure is the when the atmosphere is critical and harmful. One has no motivation and loses self-regulation.

- No Pressure: When one is not experiencing any pressure, they tend to act based on emotion, since there is no one to compare themselves to.

Self-Motivation

Andrew Carnegie said it best with his quote "People who are unable to motivate themselves must be content with mediocrity, no matter how impressive their other talents." Self-motivation is an essential part of excelling at life. You must learn to motivate yourself because you cannot depend on others to do it for you. You have to know how to encourage yourself regardless of how bad the situation. There are several keys to building self-motivation.

- Work towards a cause.

- Don't compare yourself to others.

- Make the conscious effort to not give up.

- Don't live in your past failures or successes.

- Utilize positive thinking.

There are times when you may need motivation to get motivated. Positive thinking may not be doing the trick. What should you do? Consider these suggestions:

- Write down your plan for improvement.

- Briefly think about your past successes.

- Read books that promote self-motivation.

Empathy

Empathy is sharing in the feelings of others, whether joy or sadness is an admirable trait. In order for empathy to work, a person must first be able to recognize, classify, and understand their own feelings.

Empathy has been defined by others as:

- Alvin Goldman: The ability to put oneself into the mental shoes of another person to understand her emotions and feelings.

- Martin Hoffman: An effective response more appropriate to another's situation than one's own

- Carl Rogers: To perceive the internal frame of reference of another with accuracy and with the emotional components and meanings which pertain thereto as if one were the person, but without ever losing the "as if" condition. Thus, it means to sense the hurt or the pleasure of another as he senses it and to perceive the causes thereof as he perceives them, but without ever losing the recognition that it is as if I were hurt or pleased and so forth.

Empathy is most useful when the one empathizing has experienced a variety of feelings. For example, the boss who was once passed over for a promotion generally finds it easier to identify with another person who is passed over for a promotion. Not only is this comforting for the person who is going through the situation, but it's also good for empathizer because it strengthens their ability to positively react to negative situations.

It is not as simple as it sounds. The ideal situation would be for a person to express their issues and you empathize with them, but the fact is, people aren't always as forthcoming with their problems, even though it is obvious that there is something wrong. Since this is the case, you may be forced to ask probing questions or read between the lines of what is said. You can also focus on non-verbal cues such as body language.

Skills in Emotional Intelligence

Developing successful Emotional Intelligence begins by understanding your emotions and their meanings. With this understanding, you must uncover productive ways to manage your emotions, then use them to the benefit yourself and others.

How to Accurately Perceive Emotions

The words that people say are only half of the message they are trying to get across. The tone in which they say it, or the emotion tied to their words, is the other half. For example, if your boss says, "We're going to have to let you go" with the look of concern or in a caring tone of voice, he /she are actually saying, "Unfortunately, we are going to have to let you go." On the other hand, if your boss makes that statement, trying hard to keep from laughing, he / she could be saying, "Fortunately, we are going to have to let you go."

The ability to decide the manner, in which things are being said, lies in your knack of being able to decode the message by looking beyond the words themselves. It is important that you do not allow your emotional state of being to cloud your judgment of what is being said. Focus on the message (verbally and non-verbally) itself in order to accurately perceive the emotions of others.

Use Emotions to Facilitate Thinking

'Use emotions to facilitate thinking' is such a profound statement. How one feels will determine how he/she views situations. If you are in a happy mood, everyday events don't seem so bad. On the contrary, if you are not in a happy mood, even the smallest of situations can seem major to you.

When it comes to the workplace, regardless of your mood, your boss expects you to be a high performer. Make it easy on yourself and 'choose' to be in a good mood.

Understand Emotional Meanings

The underlying reason for why you feel the way you do is very important to understand. If you know why you are unhappy, you can either alter the thing that is making you unhappy or consciously tell yourself that 'thing' is not worth allowing you to be upset, which can ultimately turn your negative mood into a positive one. Having this understanding can not only be used to internally gauge yourself, but can also help with how you interact with co-workers.

Manage Emotions

Knowing what emotion you are exhibiting or understanding the reason for that emotion is not enough to manage your emotions. Managing your emotions is a conscious and active task. This can be done in several ways. The overall goal is to establish strategies that utilize your emotions to help accomplish a goal rather than allowing your emotions to use you to create a futile outcome.

It is important to remember that your emotions are not the 'enemy'. They contain valuable information that if used properly, can help you make sound decisions.

Verbal Communication Skills

Strong verbal communication skills are important in all facets of life. Without these essentials, one may find it hard to get a personal point across, articulate needs and desires or even compete in the business world. There are many factors that contribute to solid communication skills.

Focused Listening

One of the best ways to ensure someone that you are truly listening to what they are saying is to intently listen. To some this may sound like common sense, but it is a skill that is seldom mastered. Usually when engaged in a conversation, the listener is multitasking. They are listening with one part of the brain and preparing a response with the other. It is painfully obvious when a person is not wholeheartedly interested in what someone else has to say. Not only does this make the listener look uncaring, but it may also influence the speaker to go elsewhere when he needs to speak about matters.

Whether you are in a leadership role or an individual contributor, strong listening skills are essential to your success. Hearing something other than what is being said or trying to think of what to say while the speaker is talking, can have dire consequences. Regardless of the industry you work in, focused listening is a great skill to sharpen.

Asking Questions

Asking probing questions is a component that goes hand-in-hand with focused listening. Rarely does someone truly understand everything another is saying without at least asking a couple of probing questions. The key is to not ask questions for the sake of asking questions, or ask questions that do not relate to the conversation. For example, Amy talks to Michelle about a project they are going to work on together. The goal of the project is to create a high school lesson plan for a literature teacher. Michelle has never created a lesson plan and has no idea of what is included in one. The conversation is as follows:

Amy: Hi Michelle. Today we are going to prepare a lesson plan for a high school literature teacher. This lesson is for the book, Teaching to Transgress: Education as the Practice of Freedom. It is not necessary for you to read the book. We have a summary and analysis for each chapter, which is sufficient to develop the plan. There are several sections of the lesson plan that we have to write and it has a non-negotiable deadline.

Michelle: Great, Amy. I look forward to writing the lesson plan with you; however, I have several questions:

- Specifically, what are the sections that we must create?

- Is there a template or certain grammatical rules that we must follow?

- In what format do we complete the lesson plan?

- What is the final due date?

Amy felt like she adequately described the assignment and how it should be done, but because Michelle was listening carefully, she had the opportunity to ask several probing questions to gain a better understanding of what was to be done.

Communicating with Flexibility and Authenticity

When speaking to another, the one rule you want to always observe is that you are being honest about what you are saying. This can be somewhat of a challenge because we are taught to speak with diplomacy; being politically correct, especially in the business-world. While this is true, it is still necessary to make sure you are not sugar-coating or dancing around an issue, as this can cloud the meaning of what is being communicated. Effective communication does not require the speaker to repeat or continuously restate what is being said.

Even though sometimes one is as honest or clear as they could possibly be, it takes a little more work to relay the message. The ability to be flexible in your speech, whether to make your meaning more clear or to 'show off' that diplomacy you have been working so hard at, is significant for verbal communication success.

Non-Verbal Communication Skills

There is more to communication than the words one speaks or message being conveyed. There are also non-verbal cues that all use in everyday conversations. Being mindful of the signals you send others through body language and the manner in which you speak may get your point across a lot faster than your mere words.

Body Language

The saying, 'Actions speak louder than words' is so true in the world of business. It is easy to shower someone with promises, but when it is time to perform, if the actions do not measure up to the words spoken, the words spoken will be forgotten.

The use of body language can have both positive and negative effects. The thing to remember about body language is that if you are not conscious of what your body is doing while you are talking, the wrong message could be conveyed. For example, if you are smiling while giving someone condolences on the loss of their loved one, that could be construed as inappropriate and your words insincere. On the other hand, if you are congratulating someone on a job well done, but do so with a frown on your face, you could appear to be unhappy for the person.

The signals you send to others.

Sending non-verbal signals to someone can be a great way to reinforce that which you've verbally spoken. It can also be used as a tool to further explain what you're trying to say. However, it can be a way of confusing the listener. So, this can be a valuable skill as long as you are conscious of it and have trained it to have a positive effect rather than using it as an uncertain form of communication.

It's Not What You Say, It's How You Say It

The manner in which you say something could be the factor that determines what the listener hears. It is important to be aware of your emotions, body language, tone, speed, and pitch when you speak. It may sound like a lot of work and until it becomes second nature, it may be, but consistently doing so can produce a favorable outcome. It is possible to send the wrong message without intentionally doing it, so be careful. An innocent request such as 'Please shred that document' can sound like a rude command.

Social Management and Responsibility

The terms Social management and responsibility refer to a group or organization's participation in environmental, ethical, and social issues outside of the organization itself. 'Outside of the organization' can refer to issues at the country level, B2B (Business to Business) level or even the individual development of the members within the group or organization.

Benefits of Emotional Intelligence

Emotional intelligence is "*the ability to perceive emotions, to access and generate emotions so as to assist thought, to understand emotions and emotional knowledge, and to reflectively regulate emotions so as to promote emotional and intellectual growth* (Mayer-Salovey, Four Branch Model of Emotional Intelligence).

Focusing on the importance of Emotional Intelligence and developing EI skills serves many benefits. Specifically, it affects one decision-making ability, relationships, and health.

- **Decision-making.** Having an awareness of your emotions, where they come from and what they mean, can allow you to take a more rational, well-planned approach to how you are going to make a specific decision.

- **Relationships.** When one is able to understand why they are the way they are and why they react to things the way they do, they tend to gain more of an appreciation for others and who they are, which can in turn lead to stronger relationships, business and personal.

- **Health.** Many times, internal turmoil expresses itself as physical illnesses. Always harboring negative emotions can lead to higher stress levels in the body, which can temporarily or fatally damage it.

Articulate Your Emotions Using Language

As a child, it may be acceptable to 'act out your emotions' to get your point across, but when you become an adult it is frowned upon and certainly not appropriate in the work place. Emotions will never go away, but that is not an excuse to say, do and behave anyway we want to. It is important to understand your emotions, what they are, and why you feel that way, and then share your feelings via positive and constructive conversation.

When in a leadership role, you may encounter several opportunities to express yourself, whether it is praising a worker for a job well done, or reprimanding an employee for not meeting deadline. But the key to making sure you articulate your emotions in an effective and efficient manner is to channel those emotions so that your message comes across as firm but professional.

Tools to Regulate Your Emotions

The ability to keep your emotions under control requires more than a willing heart. Understanding a situation through the eyes of another and strengthening self-management and self-awareness skills are tools that can be used in your quest to regulate your emotions.

Seeing the Other Side

If you ever want to understand the type of person you are and how you behave, ask other people. It is easy to justify the things you do, so much so that it seems like everything you do is perfect. If you take an honest look at yourself, you would probably say not only is this perfection untrue for you, but it is unattainable for all.

Talk to your boss, co-workers or friends about how they view you. If someone says, 'When everything is good you are a nice person, but if something doesn't go your way, you have an explosive temper', don't get upset and don't automatically say that it is untrue. Gaining this insight is a valuable tool for you to help regulate your emotions. Your emotions and how you express them is your responsibility. If you don't like it, fix it.

Self-Management and Self-Awareness

Self-management can sometimes be a hard quality to tame when self-awareness produces a very arrogant and self-centered result. The strength to self-management and self-awareness lies in the balance between the two. Understanding who you are, the role you play, authority you possess are all very important, but when these things overshadow your ability to be consistent and accountable, this could cause a poor outcome. By the same token, if one lacks understanding of whom they are and their importance, this could also hinder their ability to be consistent and accountable. People who are aware of their methods of dealing with conflict and understand the bearing of their way of doing things aren't as likely to make matters worse than those who are not aware of themselves.

Giving in Without Giving Up

Compromise is an unavoidable part of dealing with others in both the business world and in personal relationships. The ideal situation would be that everyone agrees with everything you say, but that is highly unlikely. Unless you live in a society that does not value diplomacy, this is a skill that will present plenty of opportunities for you to master it.

This can be even more of an issue when you are in a position of less influence. You may be expected to compromise at a greater level or even expected to follow the lead of your superiors, without regard to your own feelings or opinions. In either case, learning how to have your beliefs, while accepting the ideas of others and not causing tension in the relationship is crucial to your success in the work place.

Gaining Control

Just by the very nature of the word, control is a very powerful thing to have. Having control causes companies to become multi-billion dollar entities and nations to crumble. This is no less important when it comes to having control over yourself, your thoughts, and emotions. Having control or the lack thereof could be the difference between building a successful career and no career at all. If you have control over these aspects of your life, pat yourself on the back. If you do not, read the following to obtain the necessary tools to become the master of your fate.

Using Coping Thoughts

The power of the mind is amazing. Every day, you will encounter at least one situation that requires you to use the calming forces of your mind, to overcome the potential anxiety of the issue at hand. In order to use these forces, you must have a reservoir that consists of them. When you find yourself in a situation that requires coping skills, do the following:

- **Take a deep breath.** Deep breathing has an amazingly calming effect on the brain. By taking a deep breath or two, you can easily avoid your first, natural reaction to a stressful situation. This can prevent you from saying something or physically acting out in a manner that is inappropriate and may require you to apologize later on.

- **Step away from the issue.** Mentally take yourself away from the situation and analyze the issue itself. Ask yourself if it is something worth using your emotions on. Does it truly impact you? Will your emotions bring forth a resolution to the problem or just internal conflict for you?

- **Use positive thinking.** Even if the situation requires you to physically act, you do not want to approach it with thoughts of anger, sadness or other negative emotions. Consciously tell your mind to think 'happy thoughts'. Thinking happy thoughts is not a way to avoid the problem, but rather a way to prepare you to tackle it in a productive manner.

Using Relaxation Techniques

Relaxation techniques are not just used to help you 'feel better'; they actually play a major role in reducing the stress on your body and mind that comes from the experiences of everyday life.

According to the Mayo Clinic, relaxation techniques can reduce stress symptoms by:

- Slowing your heart rate

- Lowering blood pressure

- Slowing your breathing rate

- Increasing blood flow to major muscles

- Reducing muscle tension and chronic pain

- Improving concentration

- Reducing anger and frustration

- Boosting confidence to handle problems

There are several common types of relaxation techniques, with three of them being:

- **Autogenic:** This technique uses the senses to promote relaxation. For example one may think about a peaceful place and then use relaxed breathing. Or they might repeat words in their mind to do away with muscle tension.

- **Progressive muscle**: In this technique, individuals purposely tense and then relax each muscle group.

- **Visualization:** With visualization, the individual imagines a calming place and tries to utilize his or her senses to feel like they are really at that place.

Bringing it All Together

Once you have mastered the art of coping with difficult situations, it may not be necessary to engage in relaxation techniques as much. But until you have reached that point and maybe even afterwards, finding effective ways to relax yourself and take control of the situation is highly beneficial. Whether it is dealing with an unruly co-worker or a demanding boss, not allowing negativity to get the best of your emotions can benefit your mind, body and soul, which is the ultimate goal.

Business Practices

There is more to the workplace than the business itself. An employee's makeup, which is emotions and their ability to manage them, level of Emotional Intelligence and communication skills are all a part of whether or not a business is successful.

Understand Emotions and How to Manage Them in the Workplace

As previously stated, having emotions is an inherent part of all human beings. Understanding one's emotions and learning how to use them is the responsibility of each person. Many times, it may feel like the workplace is no place for emotions, whether good or bad. But the truth is, emotions must be utilized!

For example, if you are the manager and your team is about to miss an important deadline, it is up to you to stress how necessary it is for you to meet the deadline. The approach you take is determined by your natural tendencies as well as level of professionalism. One level-headed approach may be to call the team to a meeting and explain the ramifications of not meeting the deadline. This would also be a good time to listen to the team members to find out if there is something out of their control that is preventing them from doing their job.

A less calm and volatile method would be to yell at everyone and tell them to get to work.

Deciding which style is best can be done by weighing the pros and cons of each as well as which would result in the most positive outcome. Do not rely solely on how you feel, but what makes logical sense.

Role of Emotional Intelligence at Work

Emotional Intelligence plays a vital role in the workplace. How one feels about himself, interacts with others, and handles conflict is directly reflected in the quality of work produced. Both social and personal proficiencies are developed as a result of Emotional Intelligence.

Social Proficiencies

- Empathy – Being aware of others' feelings and exhibiting compassion.

- Intuition – An inner sense of the feelings of others'.

- Political Acumen – Ability to communicate, strong influence and leadership skills, and conflict-resolution.

Personal Proficiencies

- Self-Awareness – Understanding one's own emotions. The ability to asses one's self as well as display confidence.

- Self-Regulation – Managing one's emotions. Maintaining trustworthiness and flexibility.

- Motivation - Being optimistic about situations. Having the drive to take initiative and commit until completion.

Disagreeing Constructively

To disagree constructively means to do so in a positive, productive manner. Its purpose is not to disagree for the sake of disagreeing or getting your point across. It is also not used to be negative or destructive of another's thoughts. The workplace is a place where disagreeing is a common occurrence. Companies look for the most effective ways to carry out operations and therefore invest in process improvement strategies, which opens the floor for discussion and compromise.

What does constructively disagreeing look like in practice, you may ask. Well, it is acknowledging and confirming someone else's ideas before presenting your own.

Example:

Ted: Because of the nature of their duties, I feel the customer service phone team should arrive 30 minutes before their shift to bring up their systems and test their equipment to make sure it is properly working so they are ready to take the first call as soon as their shift starts.

Michael: I understand your point, Ted and I agree the phone team should arrive early to prepare themselves for the start of their shift. However, I feel 15 minutes is sufficient time for them to get everything in place.

Optimism and pessimism are two schools of thought adopted by individuals within organizations. Neither extreme is considered better than the other. The proper balance of the two is a fundamental part of best business practices.

Optimism

Possessing the quality of 'optimism' is the ability to find the bright side of every situation. This is an admirable position that not all have. The secret to exhibiting this characteristic is to understand that there are no issues that cannot have a positive spin.

Not only is this beneficial for an individual's personal life, but optimism can be a competitive advantage in the business world. Like every other entity, businesses suffer losses and setbacks, but the trick to maintaining the stability of a company is leadership that knows how to look past the current problem to a nearby resolution. Optimistic employees tend to be more productive in terms of the quality and quantity of their work and therefore make more money for the company.

Who wants to follow a leader that whimpers at the sight of trouble just like the people he is leading? Not many people can honestly say they desire this type of leader.

Optimism is also good for your health. There have been several studies performed that conclude those who live life with a bright outlook, generally live longer than those who do not. Also, optimists are likely to have more long-lasting, successful personal relationships.

Pessimism

Pessimism is the exact opposite of optimism. Instead of viewing the glass as 'half full' or having a positive outlook on situations, pessimists can only see the down side of the issue.

As you would expect, pessimism in the workplace can be very detrimental to the individual's career growth and the well-being of the company as a whole. A pessimist who holds a leadership role can bring down the productivity and morale of the team, just by his or her very nature. An individual contributor with this type of attitude may never get promoted to leadership positions.

What about the health factors associated with this pessimism? Pessimists generally suffer a lot of bodily and mental stress, which can manifest itself in a variety of ways such as heart disease, diabetes, and even cancer. So what's the moral of the story? Don't worry, be happy.

The Balance Between Optimism and Pessimism

Extremism may not be a desirable trait in a person. This is also true when it comes to optimism and pessimism. Being optimistic about every situation could potentially lead a person away from reality and taking the proper steps to resolve a situation. It could also give someone a false hope, which would ultimately lead to disappointment which could in turn cause the person to abandon all optimism.

Making an Impact

There are opportunities we face each day that allow us to make an impact on the lives of others. How we impact others is up to us. It requires a conscious effort on our part to decide if we are going to leave a legacy of good or bad. Whichever you decide, be sure to thoroughly think through who you are and what you want others to remember about you.

Creating a Powerful First Impression

Although some don't like to admit it, many are greatly concerned with the first impression that is made to a new acquaintance. The impact one leaves can be the difference between getting and not getting a job or obtaining and not obtaining a contract for your company. There are several factors to keep in mind when meeting someone for the first time, whether it is through electronic means or face-to-face.

Physical Appearance: It is unfortunate but true that when you are in a face-to-face meeting, you are initially judged on your physical appearance. Always err on the side of caution and present yourself in a conservative light. Avoid flamboyant clothing, jewelry, and make-up. Even though you may be confident in your abilities, these things can send the message that you are unprofessional and not capable of performing the job.

Body Language: Many times, body language speaks so much louder than words. From posture to facial expressions, the message being conveyed can be completely different from the intended message. So, it's important to be aware of how your body is positioned as well as the messages it gives. In addition to posture and facial expressions, be mindful of your eye contact and the tone, pitch and speed of your voice.

Although posture and eye contact may not be as important when you are communicating on the phone, your facial expressions can be very apparent. Smiling while talking is an easy thing to do that says you are professional.

The first handshake should be firm enough to show you are confident, but not so firm that it cuts circulation to the other person's fingers. Be sure to include good eye contact while you are shaking hands.

Spoken Words: This is one of the more obvious but neglected aspects of the first impression. Focusing too much time on your physical appearance or body language can cause you to forget to choose your words carefully. Choosing your words carefully is not about you withholding your true self, but remembering there are some situations that require you to be more politically correct or proper. Stay away from the slang you would use with friends or in other less formal situations. Also avoid using too much jargon or words not typically used in everyday language, as this may cause the listener to tune out what you are saying for the mere fact that they cannot understand you.

Assessing a Situation

Before deciding on the path to take to approach a situation, one must first assess it. Is it worth doing anything about? How will it impact me or others? The overall goal is to be effective when dealing with issues, so make sure you know what you are getting into before embarking on the journey.

The best way to assess a situation is to step away from it. Take yourself out of the equation in order to fully understand what it is about and the effect it will have. This can allow you to make a more reasonable decision rather than one based on emotions.

Being Zealous without Being Offensive

Being a zealous person is a good quality, but being overly zealous can not only send a negative message to others, it may be considered offensive. Every manager would like to hear that their employees are excited about work. This sends the idea that the employees will focus on 'getting the job done'. However, 'getting the job done' is not the most important thing, 'getting the job done' correctly is. The drive to work fast can be a down fall of being overly zealous, as sometimes the individual may lose the focus on quality. The positive side is this individual can bring to the team a renewed excitement that was once lost.

With everything in life, you must strive for balance, not extremism on either end of the spectrum. This balance will not only bring internal stability for you, but it will also allow you to maintain equilibrium within your relationships.

Chapter 4 – Social Intelligence

Social intelligence can seem like a complicated term and can make many of us feel nervous. But social intelligence is something we deal with every day and it can help us navigate better experiences from our social environment. Whether we're at home or at work, knowing how to be more aware of ourselves and our surroundings can help us make the best out of any social situation!

At the end of this chapter, you should be able to:

- Be aware of our own behaviors

- Learn to be empathetic with others

- Know tools for active listening

- Effectively communicate interpersonally

- Recognize various social cues

- Determine appropriate conversation topics

- Know various forms of body language

Before reading this chapter, answer the following questions.

1. In your own words, what is social intelligence? Have you ever heard this term before?

2. Why is social intelligence important at home and work?

3. What areas of social intelligence would you be more interested in learning about?

4. What do you hope to learn or take away from this class?

Increase Your Self Awareness

Many times we wonder why the situations around us change simply because we are relying on the people around us to change. But being aware of our own actions and behaviors is one of the key tools to change not only ourselves, but our surroundings. We must be aware of what communication we are putting out there and how our behaviors can affect others.

Remove or Limit Self-Deception

Self-deception is a tool we commonly use to try and hide something from ourselves or prevent ourselves from accepting something. We can often try to make ourselves believe whatever we want and alter facts in our mind by self-deceiving ourselves. No one is exempt from this habit and we can find ourselves practicing it more often than we think. For instance, we can self-deceive ourselves that our presentation was the best in the group or self-deceive ourselves to believe that people are talking about us when we walk away. It can affect our relationships with others and give people the wrong impression of ourselves. One of the simplest ways we can help prevent this type of deception is to simply be direct with ourselves and others.

Always say what you mean and mean what you say – don't try to deceive with alternative phrases or meanings. When taking in information, review it over before making conclusions. Recognize facts and happenings that could form a final thought. For instance, your presentation may have been very good, but do not assume it was the best out of the group. While it is alright to build confidence and esteem by believing in yourself or believing you know what is best, it is not beneficial to deceive ourselves into thinking over the line since it can cause us to damage our future relationships with others.

Ask For Feedback

We often forget one of the easiest tools to increase our own self-awareness is to simply ask for feedback from those around us. It doesn't have to be a lengthy or complicated process and can be done very professionally or casually. The people around us can see our usual actions and behaviors and can give an honest opinion about them. The thought of asking someone to share their opinions and thoughts about us can seem unnerving and even downright scary, but the advice and thoughts can prove invaluable. If possible, let the person know in advance you will want feedback later so they have time to form an impression and gather any tips or hints. A random request for feedback (such as right after a meeting) can be acceptable too, but keep in mind the person may be caught off guard and will not be able to give a good answer right away.

The most important part about asking for feedback it to prepare yourself for what you may hear. Not all feedback is positive. Take the advice and tips that the person offers as tools to help you improve yourself and style. Don't turn defensive or angry just because the person delivering the feedback may have said something you don't particularly want to hear.

Be Open to Change

Humans are designed to be creatures of habit. We often have the mindset of "we want what we want when we want it", and if something throws a kink in our routine, we can go a little crazy sometimes. But being open to change allows us to adapt to new surroundings and situations and helps us grow as a person. Changing our attitude about ourselves and others can help determine how we build our connections. Sometimes after we receive feedback from our peers, we may need to change how we do things or behave in a group. Perhaps after a meeting we decide we need to change how we plan our presentations. Whatever the reason, it is important to not disregard the importance of your willingness to change and not turn a blind eye to its prospects. Changing how we see ourselves and the people that surround us can have a positive impact on our attitudes and can help build better relationships with our peers.

Tips for accepting change:

- Determine how the change can benefit you

- Don't assume a need for change is negative

- Recognize that change is a chance for improvement

Reflect On Your Actions

While feedback from other people can be a great tool to use, feedback from ourselves can be just as valuable (without being self-deceptive). Being reflective gives us a chance to learn from our past experiences (even our mistakes) and recognize the chance for learning opportunities. By reflecting on our actions, we can see firsthand what actions we took, how they played out, and what kind of effect they had on people. Use all of your senses to recreate an experience in your mind and the actions that you took. What behaviors did you show? What did you feel at the time? What type of reactions did you receive from other people?

Reflect back on any body language cues you may have used and make note of any cues you may have seen in others. What intuitions or gut feelings do you feel from the experience? Do you feel as though you have learned anything new from the experience? These steps and process can help you reflect back on your actions and increase not only your self-awareness, but your awareness of others.

The Keys to Empathy

Empathy is one of our greatest interpersonal skills because it allows us to have better communication with people around us and increases our understanding of others. We know empathy can simply mean to 'put ourselves in the other person's shoes', but it can also mean to take an active role in getting to know the people around you and treating them with the respect they deserve.

Listening and Paying Attention

We all know that there is a difference between hearing and listening, but yet we still seem to confuse the two when we communicate with other people. Listening is considered a skill, so like any other skill it must be implemented and strengthened. Listening allows for you to understand what the person is talking about and register what they are trying to communicate. Building better listening skills starts with learning to pay attention when someone speaks and actively listening to what they are saying. Key tips to help accomplish this are to give your attention to the person by facing them and making eye contact. Turn off any cell phones or pagers or remove any item from the area that can distract you and make you lose focus. You'll find that you will catch more of what the person is saying and be able to retain more. Paying attention and building better listening skills can show support for the other person and build rapport with them.

Tips for better listening skills:

- Remove any distractions

- Make eye contact with the person speaking

- Nod your head periodically

- Ask for follow up details or information

- Ask the person to repeat anything you may have missed

Don't Judge

No matter how many times we hear the old phrase "Don't judge people" or "It's not our place to judge", we more than likely find ourselves doing it anyway – we just don't want to admit it. Whether subconsciously or not, we still find ourselves judging those around us, whether it is based on their clothes, job title, the way the talk or walk, gender, hair color, skin color, and etc. When someone is speaking or completes a task, what do you think in your head? Do you automatically make comments on how their assignment was too easy or that the way they speak is subpar to the group. Of course you would never say this out loud or tell them directly, but in your mind you have already made up your mind about them.

Thoughts like this cause us to judge people more and more, which can create barriers between people and lose connections and chances to network over time. Every person has an "inside person" and an "outside person" – we see the outside person every day and try to form our own opinions without seeing everything first. Don't forget that there is an "inside person" as well that has an entirely different side.

Shift Your View

Empathy is simply defined as putting yourself in another person's shoes and seeing things from their point of view. When communicating with another person, think about how it would feel to be in their shoes and do the things they have to do. How would you feel if you have to complete their assignment in the weekly meeting or if you have to conduct a speech in front of hundreds of people?

Shifting your view does not mean that you have to entirely give up your opinions and what you think. It involves taking a few minutes to stop and reflect on the actions and words of the other person and picturing yourself in their situation. Think about what it would be like to stand in their shoes in the conference room or in front of the new manager. By doing this, we can better understand why they may act or speak a certain way and what can drive them to do what they do. By showing empathy, you are able to connect with this person and create an important relationship to have in the workplace.

Don't Show Fake Emotions

In social situations it is never a good idea to fake our emotions or how we feel toward others. Of course, this does not mean we have full permission to start tearing into people and ripping them to shreds if we didn't like their recent speech. But if you are not entirely happy about something in the group or feel anxious about something else, it is not a good idea to fake a smile or laugh just to appear happy.

This 'fakeness' will more than likely be detected, which can offend others around you or even make them feel insecure. Instead, be honest about how you feel and show honest concern for your peers. Be tactful if delivering negative feedback and offers helpful tips for improvement or changes. Although they may not accept your true feelings at first, and may even seem angry about it, in the end they will appreciate the fact that you were honest with them and didn't show a mask of fake emotions with them.

Active Listening

It is not always enough to simply listen to a person and have the sense of 'waiting to speak'. This type of listening will cause us to lose out on important information and deny us the chance to make any real connection. By using active listening, we are more inept to learn about other people and take an active interest in what they have to say and offer. This concept can not only improve your overall listening skills, but your overall connections with other people as well.

Attunement

Attunement is defined as being aware and responsive to another person. When developing active listening skills, this tool is used to better connect with the person and become more 'in tune' with what they are saying. Since attunement relies heavily on nonverbal communication (such as body language), it is important to pay attention to the signals that the other person gives off, as well as the ones we use. Key gestures such as smiling, hand gesturing, eye contact and body movement can signal a connection or a break in communication. When we use these gestures toward other people, it can make them feel more connected with us and continue to open up with us. These connections can form bonds that can benefit the both of you and build networks for the future.

Don't Jump to Conclusions

It's a common gesture to hear something or witness someone do something and try to jump to a conclusion about it right away. Maybe you didn't like what they said or heard something you didn't think was appropriate, so you reach conclusions that the person has poor speaking skills or doesn't know how to communicate with others. But this quick acting judgment can only harm your business relationships and misses the chance to really listen to someone and make a connection. While you may believe you have all the facts and have reached a final decision, always remember there is another side of the coin and most likely more information to know.

Even if you in fact do have everything you need, you may still not be able to process his thought in way that can be productive or even helpful to anyone since it is based on negativity. If someone says something that makes you jump to a conclusion, ask them to repeat it or clarify what they said. Then take a few minutes to reflect on what was said or done and take enough time to form a logical conclusion about it. Taking a little extra time may seem like a chore at times, but it can save you from jumping to unnecessary conclusions and ruining the chance to build a relationship with another coworker.

Shift Your Focus

Naturally, we often think of ourselves as Number One. We're the first person we try to take care of and try to guard ourselves when necessary. But when it comes to active listening, the role is often reversed in order to focus on the other person. In order to actively listen, we must shift the focus from ourselves to the person speaking at the time and become attune to what they are saying. Steps should include turning to face the person and making eye contact with them. During the conversation, nod your head periodically and give them time to pause or rest before talking yourself.

When they have finished, stay focused on them by asking questions about what they have said. Don't be afraid to ask them to clarify something you didn't catch or something you may have missed. By shifting your focus to them instead of on your thoughts, you should be able to remember and comprehend most of what was said. From here you can be able to offer suggestions or opinions and engage in open conversation with the person. They'll be more likely to openly share with you if they feel as though you can focus on them as well as yourself.

Don't Discount Feelings

One of the biggest faults many of us have is the need to 'fix' things when we something that has gone wrong. When we get some bad news or information about a bad situation, we often try to follow it up with "It's not so bad" or "It could be worse". While this may seem like a helpful gesture, it can actually cause more damage than good because it makes the other person feel as though their feelings about the situation are invalid or void.

It gives the impression that you are not necessarily listening to the problem, but imply trying to brush it over and discount their feelings altogether. When a person is speaking about something they feel strongly about, whether it is about work or personal situations, it is important to recognize that it is the way they feel and that they are entitled to feel that way. Instead of trying to smooth the problem over, listen to what the person is saying and how they are feeling and offer support. Let them know you are there to help and can always lend an ear. They will appreciate the gesture much more than any half-hearted solution or smooth-over phrase.

Insight on Behavior

Behavior can be a complicated concept to try and master, much less understand. Every person is different and can interpret behaviors differently. In social groups, there is a wide range of behaviors occurring, which can seem overwhelming at times. But by having a little insight on not only the behavior others, but our own, we are able to better understand what is going on around us and how to navigate through the situation.

Perception

Perception can be a hard aspect to learn from since most of the time our perception can only be drawn from our own experiences – and we're pretty biased when it come to our own thoughts. Perception is an important tool in controlling behavior because it helps us determine how we can appear to others and how other people's behaviors can influence us. Your belief in yourself can affect your perception and can in turn affect your outward behavior.

We may not always know exactly how people perceive us since many will not say these things out loud, but we can make our own conclusions based on our perception of their behavior. Do they come close when they speak to you or do they try to move away? Do they smile and interact with you or do they seem withdrawn? Do you use these thoughts when you perceive people and their behaviors? It is likely you form some of the same conclusions and determine how to respond to the behaviors they are displaying.

Facts vs. Emotions

The main difference between facts and emotions is that facts are based on definite results while emotions are often involuntary and one-sided. But both facts and emotions can affect our behaviors and change how we act towards others. Facts can drive a conversation and allow people to connect on a logical level. Emotions are involved in everything we do, but sometimes they can affect the impact of our behavior and the information we are talking about.

Any social situation is most likely driven with emotions, and sometimes this can cause facts to become irrelevant and even misconstrue the information given. For example, a male speaker may not be taken seriously at a feminism rally, or a group full of teachers may not listen to a group of school board members. When you recognize that emotion may be driving the situation, it's time to reflect back on the situation and rediscover the facts and figures of the information. You may have to be a leader in the group and remind everyone to focus on the facts and save the emotions for later.

Online Communication

Online communication can be a hard concept to conquer since it can cover a wide range of areas. In our ever-growing world of technology, online communication can include emails, instant chats, video calls, and even text messages. While this form of communication can be a quick and easy way to connect with someone and cut out the need to physically see them or pick up a telephone, it can cause misconceptions in the process.

It is difficult to convey feeling, emotions, or even tone in online communications, so the use of particular words is important to remember. People may not be able to hear the light-heartedness in your words or the stern demeanor in our office warnings. Additionally, online communication can often seem impersonal, since you do not have to take the time to contact someone and speak to them personally, which can cause people to feel insulted or even slighted. When possibly, speak to the person face to face or by phone in order to get your message and feelings across. Save the electronic communications for quick and impersonal messages.

Popular forms of online communication:

- Blogs

- Emails

- Online memo

- Instant messaging

- Video or text chats

Listen and Watch More

One of the best ways to monitor your behavior and the behavior of others is to learn to listen and watch more than you participate. When listening to others talk, focus on their words, not necessarily the person saying them. Don't get caught up in one or two things they say and try to stay focused on the topic at hand. Even though you want to chime in, avoid making your own predictions and assumptions and continue to listen until the end. By watching and listening more, we are able to better to monitor the behaviors of other as well as our own since we are not focused mainly on ourselves. By focusing on the other person and their actions, we can develop better listening skills and catch more information than if we tried to assume it all ourselves.

Tips for better listening:

- Listen for verbal cues

- Watch for nonverbal cues

- Focus on what is being said, not the person

- Be aware of your own behaviors and reactions

Communication

Sadly, talking and listening has often been seen as a tool for simply communicating with other people, but not for building connections and networks. This assumption doesn't recognize the fact that interpersonal communication is a great tool to connect with people on a deeper level and form a connection with them. Speaking interpersonally allows both parties to feel more at ease and open up to one another. Just remember to be an active listener and watch your own body language.

Give Respect and Trust

It is a common courtesy in any conversation to treat the other person respectfully and professionally. By treating their ideas and opinions respectfully and with due consideration, you are showing respect by hearing them out, listening to them, and considering what they have to say with an open mind. When communicating with coworkers, it is important to build rapport and trust by speaking with each other respectfully and giving each other your full attention. After all, they deserved to be treated with dignity and courtesy for their thoughts and opinions. In addition, give your trust to them and let them know that you feel confident enough to speak with them openly. The motions and feelings we put out into the world will come back to us, so don't be afraid to speak openly with your coworkers. They will be impressed that you can give respect and trust so freely and appreciate the effort you are trying to make with them.

Be Consistent

Consistency is a key factor that builds interpersonal relationships. Being consistent in what we say and do shows knowledge and reliability because it helps build a familiar base to start from. People will want to communicate with you because you will become a factor they know they can trust and depend on. In addition, ensure that your actions are consistent with what you say – in other words– do what you say you'll do. If you say you will meet someone after lunch to review a report, ensure that you are there early to greet them. If you volunteered to give a speech at the next work convention, be prepared ahead of time and be ready when the day arrives. Showing you are consistent in turn shows how reliable you are and what an asset you can be for the group.

Take a few minutes to reflect back on your actions and note if they have been consistent over time. Are there behaviors you can change? What can you do differently in the future?

Always Keep Your Cool

Keeping our cool in tight or stressful situations can be tough and takes a lot of skill to make it through gracefully. It is perfectly normal to feel embarrassed or hurt when someone does something you don't like, such as speaking rudely to you or pointing out a mistake you made. Our first instinct is to possibly lash out at them or try to retaliate by hurting them in return. But the key to strong and professional communication is to keep your cool at all times and not let the negative feelings take over. When something happens that may send you over the edge, take a minute to reflect on what was said and what happened. If needed, you should step away for a few moments to compose yourself. Don't deny the other person their opinion, but let them know how you feel and how it affects you. Kinder coworkers will back track their statements and try to address the problem in less negative terms. If the coworker is unwilling to give respect, realize that their opinion may not be worth the fight.

Tips for keeping your cool:

- Try not to take words personally

- Stop and reflect *what* was said, not *how* it was said

- Make a note to learn from this experience

- Ask yourself if the person had reason for what was said – if so, what can you do to change it?

Observing Body Language

Body language can speak volumes between people, even if it does not have words to accompany it. Many times people may say one message, but their body language can say another, meaning they may not be truthful in what they say. By observing and becoming more aware of body language and what it might mean, we can learn to read people more easily and understand some of their body movements. By better understanding their movements, you can be better prepared to communicate with them, while at the same time better understanding the body language you may be conveying to them. Even though there are times that we can send mixed messages, we can try to get our point across using certain behaviors. Our body language affects how we act with others and how we react to them, as well as how they can react to ours.

Social Cues

Social cues are verbal or non-verbal hints that let us know what someone maybe thinking or feeling. When in a social situation, it is important to keep an eye out for these social cues and ensure our behavior isn't contributing to them. While some cues can be obvious, other may be very subtle, so we must train ourselves to be able to recognize them when they do appear.

Recognize Social Situations

Social situations are not a 'one size fits all' situation. Because the people in each situation are different, we must learn to adapt ourselves to this ever-changing group – and know how to handle them. This does not mean we have to change who we are or hide our own personality, but rather we can change how we present ourselves around other people. Some of the best hints we can use are the ones we get from other people around you. How are they behaving? How are they 'working through' the event? Do you know all of them? Are there faces you do not recognize? With this information in mind, determine what type of social situation you may be in. Is this a formal gathering? Is it a business meeting or function with coworkers? Maybe a few friends catching a bite to eat? The key is to recognize your surroundings and the people involved to help determine how to present yourself.

Questions to ask in a social situation:

- "What is the gathering for?"

- "Who is present?"

- "Do we share common interests?"

The Eyes Have It

Not all cues from others can be seen right and may be well hidden, but the eyes will always give them away. Without blatantly staring at a person (of course), try to observe how they are looking at you and others. Do certain words or phrases make them blink more or dart their eyes in another direction? Are they staying focused on a subject for a long period of time? Unfortunately, the eyes cannot lie – often. Many feelings or behaviors we try to hide in ourselves will often be shown through the eyes. Common eye behaviors such as rolling the eyes or looking around frequently can be signs of boredom or discomfort. If a person looks at you while talking or moves their eyebrows while listening to you talk, this can be a sign of interest or curiosity. But since these feelings may not be said out loud, or even gestured, it is a key tool to remember when gauging the people around you.

Common eye behaviors:

- Eye rolling

- Blinking too much or too little

- Wandering eyes; not looking directly at a person

- Long blinks

Non-Verbal Cues

It has been said that non-verbal communication is the most powerful form of communication since it can expand beyond voice, tone, and even words. It accounts for over 90% of our communication methods. Although the differences in non-verbal communication can be different in certain situations (amount of personal space or use of hand gestures), most cues can send the same message across the board. Nonverbal cues can include facial expressions, body movements, eye movement, and various gestures and usually are not associated with supported words or phrases.

Common non-verbal cues include folding the arms, gripping or moving hands while speaking, rolling the eyes and even misusing the tone of voice. Do you notice these gestures when speaking with people around you? When thinking of your behavior, do you find yourself making any of these gestures when you are in a social situation? If so, think of ways you can try to eliminate some of them and replace them with more welcoming or outgoing gestures instead.

Common non-verbal cues:

- Folding the arms

- Looking around frequently

- Tapping the feet or clasping hands

- Fidgeting

- Moving closer/farther away

Verbal Cues

Verbal cues are cues that we are more likely to pick up on and notice right away. They are usually done with some sort of emphasis or tone that causes an effect within us, and is mostly likely to stick with us in the future. Phrases such as "Did you see the new *rules* in the handbook?" or "I *can't* wait to see the projections for this week" add emphasis to certain words to stress a point or effect. Other verbal cues can include appropriate pauses when speaking, pitch, or volume of the voice or even speaking too slowly or quickly. These are cues that we can control and use with our voices (hence the term *verbal*) to get a message across.

When in a social situation, listen to those around you and determine what verbal cues you can pick up on. Do they sound positive or negative? Do they appropriately portray the message being sent? Do you find yourself using these verbal cues on others? Maybe you emphasized the wrong word or spoke in a higher pitch when trying to speak with a group of people. When we can recognize these cues in others and learn to adapt ourselves to them, we can learn to identify them in ourselves and ensure that we are not putting the wrong message out there.

Common verbal cues:

- Voice tone or pitch
- Word emphasis
- Volume
- Uncomfortable pauses or word inserts

Social cues can often enhance, or even downplay, what is being said or portrayed in a situation. But the social cue needs to be interpreted in the right manner for it to better a social situation – not make it worse. People who are better equipped to identify and understand these social cues are more likely to act appropriately to them, and will be better prepared to respond to them and adapt their behavior.

Spectrum of Cues

As in all situations, there is always a possibility for going to one extreme to the other without having any middle ground in between. For social cues, it can be a fairly wide spectrum with plenty of variations. On one side of the spectrum, a person can be very obvious with their cues, such as speaking very loudly or making very large and awkward hand gestures. These types of cues are easy to spot and can often make people feel uncomfortable right away. On the other hand, there are cues that are more subtle and can often be missed if not recognized right away, such as excessive eye blinking or adding a tone to their words.

Unfortunately, these types of cues may go unnoticed and can portray the wrong message when they may not be intended to. They key point is being able to recognize each side of this spectrum and the different ways a social cue can go wrong and right at the same time. When you learn the extremes they can reach, you're better equipped to catch the cues in between and adapt your behavior faster.

Review and Reflect

It's a natural behavior to want to react to a cue we may recognize and want to confront right away. Are you bored? Did I offend you? Did you understand? But these approaches are not the best solution to connect with people and better understand their behavior. When you notice a social cue, such as someone rolling their eyes or speaking in a shrill voice at you, take a moment to stop and review the action. Take notice if it is being directed at you or if others around you are subject to it as well. Does the behavior continue? Maybe the behavior was a onetime occurrence?

Reflect on what you can do to adapt yourself to the situation. Was there something you said to trigger this feeling? Does this person have something they want to share? Or maybe you just need to take a step back from this person. Sometimes they need a moment to review and reflect as well, and may need some personal space to do it. Whatever your results, remember to refrain from jumping to conclusions about the cues we encounter. Always take a minute to two before responding with your own actions.

Being Adaptable and Flexible

Even though there are times we can pick up on these social cues, we may be able to change them or even get away from them as soon as we'd like. These are the times we must learn to be flexible and adapt to the situation. We all know that not all situations will be comfortable for us and we may need to find a way to adapt until it's over. Sometimes the room can have more people than we are comfortable with or maybe the other visitors are sending cues of boredom or annoyance, but don't let these cues sink you. Be flexible to the group and reflect on what you can do to help the situation. Try to start a conversation with people that seem distant or unsure. Lead by example and speak in lower pitches or in casual tones. Many times the people around you will catch onto the cues you are sending out and will become adaptable as well. This great trick doesn't always work in all situations, but it is one way we can help ourselves adapt and manage through a difficult situation.

Personal Space

Edward Hall was one of the first people to define and characterize the space around us – our different level of spaces. The outer most space around us is our public space, such as in a large room. Coming in closer is our social space, such as talking with a group of friends. The next inward space is our personal space, which is usually within arms' reach of us. This space is usually on reserve for 'invitation-only', meaning we do not like for people to be in our personal space unless we initiate it and welcome them over.

In social situations, this can be a hard thing to maintain. The key is to refrain from being rude to someone who may have encroached on your space. If this person is too close, take a few steps to the side instead of backwards, which creates subtle distance and doesn't appear as though you are backing away. If you must leave a group of people, or even just one, that are too close, always excuse yourself politely and move to an open area. If possible, take a few steps around the room every so often, which keeps you mobile and doesn't allow for crowding. Remember, this is the time to be adaptable, so you may need to be flexible with your surroundings to feel more at ease.

Tips for keeping your personal space personal:

- Excuse yourself politely when leaving a group

- Step to the side a step or two to create subtle distance

- Walk often or roam about the area – if possible

- Opt for a handshake when greeting people – it allows for the other person to stay at arm's length

- Be aware of cultural differences in personal space

Conversation Skills

Conversation is like an adhesive that can bring people together. It can make friends, create networks, and even seal a deal. But it can have the opposite effect when used in the wrong way. Some key points about holding a conversation include the topic, the tone, and even presentation. Only you are familiar with how to work on these aspects, conversation in social situations will become second nature.

Current Events

Discussing current events can be a great skill to build conversation and become engaged in the real world around us. Tragic current events, such as war or weather disasters, can bring in many members to a conversation and can share empathy and sorrow among people. Of course more pleasant events, such as economic upswing and the cost of gas going down can be a more uplifting line of topics to discuss and create a lighter atmosphere. Discussing what is going on in the world allows for group members to connect on many levels. After all, we live here and we see what's going on! But be aware of current events that can cross into sensitive topics such as politics or religion, since these can offend some people and cause tension among a group.

Conversation Topics

Sometimes when we speak among other people in social situations, the lines of safe conversation topics can become blurry. We can become too comfortable and begin talking about subjects that can seem fine to some people, but can be offensive or rude to others. It is usually recommended to stick with topics that are considered 'safe' for everyone, such as common work areas or hobbies. Some other safe topics include sporting events, television or movies and even forms of travel. These can help people connections and friendships without crossing into dangerous territories. Some infamous topics to avoid include religion, gossip, risqué jokes, and the government/politics, since these can cause tension and arguments among group members, even if it was not the intention.

If all else fails, you can always talk about the weather!
Topics to avoid in a group:

- Religion

- Politics

- Personal health

- Prejudice topics (racism, sexism, etc.), including jokes

Cues to Watch For

As we've come to learn, we're not psychic and can't always predict what other people are thinking. This is why it is important to learn about verbal and nonverbal cues to look and listen for when in a social situation. Remember the nonverbal cues such as crossing the arms or turning their heads away to signal signs of discomfort or disinterest. These can be signs to change the current subject or recognize that something inappropriate was probably said. However, cues such as full smiles or open hands can be positive in nature and can signal approval and happiness.

Many cues that are given are from the subconscious are not always shared on purpose, especially if some feels offended or angry, in which they may not want to express out loud. So while in the midst of a conversation, look around at the people talking and the people listening. Do you see any of the typical cues, such as eye rolling, loud speaking, turned away bodies or inappropriate laughter? If so, what can you do to change the situation or even adapt yourself to it?

Cues to keep an eye out for:

- Cues signaling boredom or annoyance

- Cues signaling anger or offense

- Cues signaling different types of body language – whether open or closed

- Cues signaling for interest or comfort

Give People Your Attention

Whether you're in a conversation with just one person, a few people, or even a large group, it is important for you to give them your attention. It shows your respect for the person, or people, talking and that you really value what they are saying. When listening to other people, nod your head and make eye contact with them to let them know they have your attention and that you are listening. This can make people feel more at ease with you and make them not only put their trust in you, but feel more confident when speaking with you. If you know a head of time that you will be in a group or be speaking with others, remember to turn off your phone or set it to vibrate, so it will not be a distraction. The emails or notices can usually wait until after your conversation.

Tips to remember:

- Make eye contact

- Nod and show facial movements

- Ask questions or make a follow up comment

- Remove distractions, such as cell phones

Body Language

Body language is a form of language that relies on body movements as gestures. It accounts for over 90% of the language we use in society – the other 10% consisting of actual words or phrases. It can provide cues and hints about how the other person is feeling and thinking. Learning to read body language is an important lesson to know since people may not always simply say what is on their mind, but will definitely show it in their movements.

Be Aware of Your Movements

Unless the room is covered in mirrors, we may not always be aware of the body language we are displaying to people around us. Since the majority of body language is nonverbal, we cannot always control what we show and what we are 'saying', so we must learn to be aware of our own movements and gestures to prevent any miscommunications. Some tips to try out on your own are to look at yourself in a reflective surface, such as a mirror or a piece of glass, and practice saying things from a conversation. Do you show any signs of body language – and what are they? When in the room, listen to what other people are saying when they talk to you. Don't put up defense barriers and block them out. Look at the way they act or behave when they are around you or speak directly to you. Their body language can often let you know how you are coming across and let you know what you may be putting out into the room, even if you are not aware of it.

It's Not What You Say – It's How You Say It

When we rely on our words alone and open our mouths to let them out, we can accidentally let fly all sorts of meanings and phrases that were never meant to come out. Linguistic tools such as tone, emphasis, and even pitch can make even the simplest or nicest phrase come out very wrong. When we speak, the emphasis on certain words comes naturally, which can seem off-putting to others and can lead to a confused message. It can often lead them to question if that is what you meant to say or if you just didn't know what you were trying to say to begin with.

Practice saying the following phrase with tone and emphasis on a different word each time:

- "*I'd* like to help you work on your presentations."

- "I'd like to help you *work on* your presentations."

- "I'd like to help you work on your *presentations*."

Do you hear the different messages that the same phrase can have with different words stressed and tones implied? The words we say only make up half of our message – the rest is in how you say it.

Open vs. Closed Body Language

Our body language can be like a traffic light to the people around us. Open body language can signal a green light for people to approach you and engage in conversations with you. However, closed body language can signal a red light and make people want to keep their distance from you while they can. Open body language includes gestures such as having open hands and palms, making eye contact, and reaching out to greet someone. This can also you seem more persuasive when speaking with other people and gain their trust. Closed body language such as crossing the arms, turning the head away and constantly fidgeting are much less inviting, and will not get other people to come around. This kind of body language can make you seem defensive and withholding from those around you. If you wish to communicate well with others, it is important to realize how to use (and not use) your body to speak out.

Examples of Open Body Language	Examples of Closed Body Language
Feet facing forward	Looking away or around the room
Smiling face	Crossing the arms or legs
Open palms	Turning your body away
Making eye contact	Rolling the eyes or blinking excessively

Communicate with Power

Effective communication is key in any situation. When you communicate with others, you want it to be a powerful message that they will take away with them when you part ways. No one wants their message to come across as week and easily forgotten. Before you even begin to form words, think about what you want to say, and how you want your message to come across. Make notes of any wrongful tones or emphasis might be used and prevent it. When you are done speaking, listen to what the other person has to say and show signs of active listening, such as nodding your head or asking follow up questions. Turn your body to the other person and give them your full attention during the session. As always, remove any distractions that can incur the wrong body language, such as checking a ringing phone or being distracted while checking emails.

Tips for communicating with power:

- Think before you speak

- Be an active listener

- Watch for verbal and nonverbal cues

- Be aware of your body language

Building Rapport

Rapport is used in the business world to build professional relationships and networks. It helps gain confidence and trust in other people and makes them feel more at ease. When in social situations, this can include simple techniques such as mirroring and sharing common interests. Building rapport early on can help you be successful later in business and create less awkward moments in social situations.

Take the High Road

Building rapport is about standing out and standing above others around you to make connections and networks with various people. While this can seem like an aggressive gesture, it is actually just the opposite. Taking the high road is being humble and putting others before yourself. Don't treat the situation like a competition, but rather more of a showcase. Show others that you can be a great listener as well as a contributor to a team or group. While others are scrambling around you to show off their talents and skills to come out as the 'top dog', take the road less taken and have a lower profile to display. Offer your input and take interest in what the other person is saying. By showing you can stand out over the others without trying to crush them shows that you can display great skills without having to put others down in the process, which benefits the entire group. Remember, building rapport is about building connections- not destroying them.

Forget About Yourself

When you want to build rapport with another person, or group, the key element is to actually take yourself out of the equation. Although you have things to say and contribute, spend more time listening to what they have to say and ask follow up questions to expand on their ideas. Yes, you know you have great opinions and ideas and want to share them with the world, but this is not the time. Building rapport requires you to develop an honest interest in another party besides yourself. Become interested in the people around you and what they do and stand for. When people feel that you care about their lives and what they do, they are more inclined to open up and share more, opening the gates to build stronger connections and longer relationships.

Key points to remember:

- Be an active listener

- Show interest in their ideas and thoughts

- Ask for follow up information

- Offer opinions as needed, but focus on them

Remembering People

When we meet new people, sometimes the names or faces can become a blur. Most people are great at remembering one or the other, but rarely both. But rapport depends on being able to recall a person at a later time over many encounters. One of the main reasons we forget a person's name or face is because we are not truly listening or paying attention when we are being introduced. Don't be nervous and put your mind at ease so that you can easily register the person's face and hearing their name with it. When you look at the person, look for any features that stand out, such as hair color, facial features, scars or even the use of makeup. Remembering a key characteristic while fully listening to their name will help keep them associated in your brain to retrieve at a later date when needed.

Tips to remember name and faces:

- Say their name immediately after hearing it

- Don't be afraid to ask them to repeat their name

- Associate a gesture with their greeting, such as a handshake or smile

- Remember distinct features

Ask Good Questions

You cannot expect to get anywhere with people if you do not know more about them and form a connection with them. One of the best ways to start building this connection is to ask good questions that allow them to share their pearls of wisdom and what they have come to know over time. In turn, they will usually ask for your opinions or thoughts after they have shared, pulling you into to create a network of ideas. The key is asking questions about them and their company, which gives them plenty of area to talk about themselves. Ask open-ended questions that pertain to what they do or don't like about their area and what kind of advice they would offer newcomers. Try to avoid simple yes or no questions, or questions that can make you seem as though you are encroaching on their territory. You're trying to build a bridge between people, not burning it behind you.

Sample questions to ask:

- "What do you enjoy most about _____?"

- "What kind of advice would you offer someone like me?"

- "What are some of your accomplishments with the company?"

- "What is one thing you would want everyone to know about your business?"

Chapter 5 – Body Language Basics

The ability to interpret body language is a skill that will enhance anyone's career. Body language is a form of communication, and it needs to be practiced like any other form of communication. Whether in sales or management, it is essential to understand the body language of others and exactly what your own body is communicating.

At the end of this chapter you should be able to:

- Define body language.

- Understand the benefits and purpose of interpreting body language.

- Learn to interpret basic body language movements.

- Recognize common mistakes when interpreting body language.

- Understand your own body language and what you are communicating.

- Practice your body language skills.

Communicating with Body Language

We are constantly communicating, even when we are not speaking. Unspoken communication makes up over half of what we tell others and they tell us. It affects our work and personal relationships. Improves negotiating, management, and interpersonal skills by correctly interpreting body language and important signals.

Learning a New Language

In many ways understanding body language is like learning a foreign language. There are a few tips that make learning any language, even a nonverbal one, easier.

Tips:

- Set Goals: Make sure that your goals are realistic and have specific timelines.

- Devote time to learning: Schedule time to practice. Do not rely on spare time.

- Practice daily: Hone skills by continued practice.

- Enjoy the process: You are not in school. Relax and have fun with your new skill.

The Power of Body Language

Understanding body language does more than improve relationships. You will get insight into the thoughts and feelings of those around you. Because it is not a conscious form of communication, people betray themselves in their body language. Body language is powerful in several ways.

Power of Body Language:

- It is honest: Body language conveys truth, even when words do not.

- Creates self-awareness: Understanding body language helps you identify your own actions that hinder success.

- Understand feelings: Body language shows feelings and motive such as aggression, submission, deception, etc. Use these as cues to your communication.

- Enhance listening and communication skills: Paying attention to body language makes someone a better listener. Hear between the words spoken to what is being said.

More than Words

Much of the way people communicate is nonverbal. Body language specifically focuses on physical, not tone, or pitch. It includes the following characteristics.

Body Language:

- Proximity: The distance between people

- Positioning: Position of a body

- Facial expression: The eyes are particularly noticed.

- Touching: This includes objects, people, and themselves.

- Breathing: The rate of respiration is telling.

Actions Speak Louder than Words

Our impressions of each other are based on more than words. People can have cordial conversations and not like each other. The actions that we take are stronger than our words. For example, a person may dismiss someone using body language and not saying anything negative. Like it or not, our body language makes a lasting impression on the people around us.

What Actions Can Say:

- Deception

- Confidence

- Nerves

- Boredom

- Emotions

- Attraction

- Being open

- Being closed off

Please note that this is not an exhaustive list of what body language can communicate.

Reading Body Language

We are constantly reading the body language of others, even when we are not aware of it. Actively reading body language, however, will provide valuable insight and improve communication. Pay attention to the positions and movements of people around you. Specifically their head positions, physical gestures, and eyes.

Head Position

The head is an obvious indicator of feelings and thoughts. The position of the head speaks volumes, making it the perfect place to start. While it takes practice to accurately interpret head position, the basic positions, and movements that are not extremely difficult to identify.

Movement and Position:

- **Nodding:** Nodding typically indicates agreement. The speed of the nod, however, indicates different things. A slow nod can be a sign of interest or a polite, fake signal. Look to other eyes for confirmation. A fast nod signals impatience with the speaker.

- **Head up:** This position indicates that the person is listening without bias.

- **Head down:** This position indicates disinterest or rejection for what is said. When done during an activity, it signals weakness or tiredness.

- **Tilted to the side:** This means a person is thoughtful or vulnerable. It can signal trust.

- **Head high:** Holding the head high signals confidence or feelings of superiority.

- **Chin up:** The chin up indicates defiance or confidence.

- **Head forward:** Facing someone directly indicates interest. It is a positive signal.

- **Tilted down:** Tilting the head down signals disapproval.

- **Shaking:** A shaking head indicates disagreement. The faster the shaking, the stronger the disagreement.

Translating Gestures into Words

Scientific studies show that the part of the human brain that comprehends words is the same part of the brain that comprehends gestures. Gestures are also called movement clusters because it is more than a body position. We use gestures when we speak, typically hand gestures. They enhance meaning, or can be used by themselves.

Translations:

- **Pointing finger**: This is an aggressive movement. When a wink is added, however, it is a positive confirmation of an individual.

- **Finger moves side to side**: This motion acts as a warning to stop something.

- **Finger moves up and down**: This acts as a reprimand or places emphasis on what is said.

- **Thumbs up**: Thumbs up is a sign of approval.

- **Thumbs down**: This is a sign of disapproval.

- **Touch index finger to thumb**: The sign indicates OK.

Open Vs. Closed Body Language

Body language is often defined as open or closed. Being open or closed has many different causes. Open body language can come from passivity, aggression, acceptance, supplication, or relaxation. Closed body language may be caused by the desire to hide, self-protection, cold, or relaxation.

Closed body language:

- **Arms crossed:** This stance is often defensive or hostile.

- **Legs crossed when seated:** Cross legs can indicate caution. One leg over the other at the knee may indicate stubbornness.

- **Arm or object in front of the body:** This can coincide with nervousness and is a form of self-protection.

- **Legs crossed when standing:** This may mean someone is insecure when combined with crossed arms. By itself, it can signal interest.

Open body language:

- **Legs not crossed:** This is an open, relaxed position.

- **Arms not crossed:** Open arms indicate openness; although the hands may indicate aggression, supplication, or insecurity, depending on their position.

The Eyes Have It

People give a great deal away through their eyes. The eyes are an important factor when reading a person's body language. When combined with body position, the eyes will provide a more accurate translation of body language.

Looks:

- **Looking to the left**: Eyes in this direction can mean someone is remembering something. Combined with a downward look, it indicates the self-communication. When looking up, it means facts are being recalled.

- **Sideways:** Looking sideways means someone is conjuring sounds. Right, is associated with imagination, and may mean a story. Left is accessing memory.

- **Looking to the right**: Looks to the right indicates imagination. It can mean guessing or lying. Combined with looking down, it means there is a self-question. Combined with looking up, it can mean lying.

- **Direct eye contact**: When speaking, this means sincerity and honesty. When listening, it indicates interest.

- **Wide eyes**: Widening eyes signal interest.

- **Rolled eyes**: Rolled eyes mean frustration. They can be considered a sign of hostility.

- **Blinking:** Frequent blinking indicates excitement. Infrequent blinking signals a boredom or concentration, depending focus.

- **Winking:** A wink is a friendly gesture or secret joke.

- **Rubbing eyes:** Rubbing eyes may be caused by tiredness. It can also indicate disbelief or being disturbed.

Body Language Mistakes

There are different factors that will create false body language signals. This is why it is so important to examine the positions and gestures as a whole when attempting to interpret body language. To prevent body language mistakes, become aware of these factors and think carefully when reading body language.

Poor Posture

Posture can lead to unfair judgments and prejudices. Often, poor posture is seen as a closed body language that people assume is caused by a lack of confidence. There are, however, many different reasons why someone can have poor posture. While it is true that most people can improve on their posture, the changes that can be made to a person's musculoskeletal structure are limited. Always pay attention to other cues, and do not make rash judgments based solely on posture.

Some Causes of Poor Posture:

- **Injury**: Both acute injuries and repetitive motion injuries can alter someone's posture.

- **Illness**: Autoimmune diseases, such as arthritis, can damage the skeletal structure.

- **Skeletal structure**: Scoliosis and other problems with the spine will affect posture.

- **Temperature**: People may take a closed posture when they are cold.

Invading Personal Space

Invading personal space is seen as an act of hostility. Western societies typically use five different zones, depending on the social situations.

- **12 feet**: This zone is for the public. The purpose is to avoid physical interaction.

- **4 feet:** This zone is reserved for social interactions such as business settings. Touching requires the individual to move forward.

- **18 inches:** This is a personal zone. It allows contact, and it is reserved for friends and family.

- **6 inches:** This zone is reserved for close relationships. This zone can be invaded in crowds or sports.

- **0 to 6 inches:** This zone is reserved for intimate relationships.

It is essential to remember that these zones are part of most Western cultures. There are reasons why people will invade personal space that have nothing to do with hostility.

Personal Space Differences:

- **Culture:** Each culture has different boundaries and personal space.

- **Background:** Personal history and background will affect an individual's concept of personal space.

- **Activity:** Some activities require people to work closely. This should be considered before assuming someone is invading personal space.

Quick Movements

Quick movements may be interpreted as a sign of nervousness. They may, however, be used to draw attention to specific information when speaking. Consistent jerking movements, however, do not always indicate nerves or negative emotions. Do not make a snap judgment about quick movements. There are reasons why movements may seem quick or jerking.

May alter movement:

- Stress

- Illness

- Exhaustion

- Cold

Fidgeting

Most people fidget from time to time. In interviews and social settings, fidgeting can indicate nervousness, boredom, frustration, stress, or self-consciousness. It is an outlet to release feelings or an attempt at self-comfort. Besides emotions, there are a number of other reasons why people may fidget.

Other Reasons for Fidgeting:

- Attention deficit disorder: ADD and ADHD are often accompanied by fidgeting.

- Hormone imbalances: These may be accompanied by nervous energy.

- Blood sugar imbalances: Fidgeting accompanies sugar highs.

- Imbalanced brain chemistry: These may increase tension.

- Medications: Steroids and other medications can cause imbalances

Gender Differences

Not all body language is universal. There are differences in the way that men and women communicate. Body language is often confused between genders. In order to prevent miscommunications, it is important to understand the signals that are common to most people as well as the different signals that men and women communicate with their body language.

Facial Expressions

Facial expressions will be explored in a separate module. Men and women share the universal facial expressions, but there are some differences in use and perception. For example, women typically tend to smile more often than men. Women frequently smile to be polite or fulfill cultural expectations. The meanings behind smiles are often misinterpreted. Additionally, people judge the same facial expressions on men and women differently. Women, for example, were thought to be angrier and less happy than men, according to a study published by the American Psychological Association, even though they all had the same facial expressions.

Personal Distances

Personal space and personal distance change with each individual. Everyone has his or her own idea of personal distance, which is the comfortable distance that someone wishes to keep from another person. Gender, however, often affects one's sense of personal distance.

Men: Men generally take more space than women, and they employ larger personal distances. Men are less likely to stand close to each other, even when they are all friends. Additionally, they create larger buffer zones using items such as coats, cups, papers, etc. Men usually expect their buffer zones to be respected and do not respond well to someone invading their personal space.

Women: Women generally employ smaller personal distances with each other or with male friends. They tend to increase personal distance with strange men. Women also create buffer zones, but they are typically smaller than male buffer zones. Women are more likely to draw back when their zones are invaded, and female buffer zones are not always respected. People are more likely to move a woman's purse than a man's coat.

Female Body Language

There are some subtle differences to note when interpreting female body language. Culture plays a role in what is considered appropriate body language. Female body language changes over time, and it is not universal to all women. There are, however, some basic actions that many women have in common.

Body Language:

- **Body Position and posture:** Many women use closed body language. This may stem from a cultural convention to appear smaller. Women, however, will straighten their posture to look more attractive.

- **Leaning:** Women will lean forward when they are interested in something or someone. They lean away when displeased or uncomfortable.

- **Smiling:** We have already mentioned that women are more likely to smile. While it is often a friendly gesture, it is a probably a polite gesture when the eyes are not engaged.

- **Eye contact:** Eye contact indicates interest (either in what is said or the individual). Dilated pupils are another sign of interest.

- **Mirroring:** Women often mirror, or copy, the actions of each other. They will occasionally mirror men.

- **Legs and feet:** The legs and feet typically point in the direction of a woman's interest. This includes romantic interest.

- **Touching:** Women are more likely to touch each other than men are.

- **Tapping:** Tapping or fidgeting is a sign that a woman is annoyed or uncomfortable.

Male Body Language

Male body language is not universal to all men. There are, however, certain aspects of body language that are common to many men. Male body language is often seen as more aggressive and dominating. Women are sometimes encouraged to adapt male body language in the workplace.

Body Language:

- **Stance**: Men often choose wide stances to increase their size. Spread legs and a straight back, both sitting and standing, indicates confidence. Closed body language does not.

- **Eye contact:** Men will make eye contact, but eye contact can be seen as a dominating or hostile act when it lasts too long. Occasional eye aversion is normal. Like women, pupils dilate with interest.

- **Mirroring:** Men do not typically mirror each other. They often mirror women to show their interest.

- **Legs and feet:** Like women, the legs and feet typically point in the direction of a man's interest. This includes romantic interest.

- **Smiling**: Men do not smile as often as women in social settings; their facial expressions are often reserved. They do, however, occasionally use forced smiles. Men often smile when happy or to engage someone's interest.

- **Hands**: Men are more likely to fidget than women. This is not necessarily a sign of insecurity or boredom, just a way to use energy.

Nonverbal Communication

We all communicate nonverbally. The image that we project from our nonverbal communication affects the way that our spoken communication is received. While interpreting body language is important, it is equally important to understand what your nonverbal communication is telling others. It takes more than words to persuade others.

Common Gestures

Many gestures that we make are unconscious movements or mannerisms. Being aware of what our gestures mean will make us aware of what we are communicating. The following list is not comprehensive, but it is a good place to start.

Unconscious Gestures:

- **Biting nails**: This may mean insecurity or nerves.

- **Turning away:** Looking away indicates that you do not believe someone.

- **Pulling ears:** Tugging at ears can indicate indecision.

- **Head tilt:** A brief head tilt means interest. Holding a tilt equals boredom.

- **Open palms:** Showing palms is a sign of innocence or sincerity.

- **Rubbing hands together**: Rubbing hands together is a sign of excitement or anticipation.

- **Touching the chin:** This signals that a decision is being made.

- **Hand on the cheek:** Touching the cheek indicates someone is thinking.

- **Drumming fingers:** This is a sign of impatience.

- **Touching the nose:** People often associate touching the nose with lying. It can also signal doubt or rejection.

The Signals You Send to Others

You are always sending signals to other people. These signals come through body language, voice, appearance, and personal distance.

- **Body language**: Body language includes posture, gestures, and facial expressions.

- **Appearance**: A person's hygiene and dress send signals to others. People make negative assumptions based on a disheveled appearance.

- **Personal distance**: Too great a personal distance makes people appear cold. On the other hand, not respecting the personal distance of others will have negative consequences.

- **Voice**: Tone is important to the way we communicate. Emotions are conveyed through tone.

It's Not What You Say, It's How You Say It

Miscommunication is a common problem in personal and business relationships. Paying attention to the way that you communicate will help prevent any miscommunications. You must take note of the tone, pitch, and timbre of your voice.

- **Pitch:** People tend to naturally respect deeper voices. High-pitched voices are viewed as a sign of immaturity. Try a lower, even pitch. Even a neutral tone can make a person appear weak or insecure when there is a higher pitch at the end of a statement, like questions have.

- **Speed:** Keep a moderate pace. Speaking too quickly will cause confusion, and speaking too slowing will make it difficult to keep attention.

- **Loudness**: Speak up; quiet voices can be viewed as submissive. Be careful, however, not accidentally yell.

- **Tone**: Tone conveys emotion, so avoid sarcasm and condescension. Vary your tone to prevent boring listeners with a monotone presentation.

What Your Posture Says

Posture is the basis of body language communication. People respond well to good posture, and having good posture improves physical and emotional health. Slouching is seen as a sign of insecurity or weakness. Confident body language demands good posture.

Posture Communication:

- **Standing or sitting erect**: Standing straight communicates confidence. It will also prevent musculoskeletal pain.

- **Hunching over:** This is closed body language and can signal unhappiness or insecurity.

- **Ducking or shrugging the head**: This is a protective or submissive move to appear smaller. It is not equated with confidence.

Correct Posture:

- **Stand and sit straight:** Straight posture maintains the natural curve of the spine. This is achieved by pulling in the abdominal muscles, pushing the shoulders back, and lifting the chest.

- **Head position:** Hold the head upright and look to the front. This will protect the natural shape of the neck.

- **Relaxation:** Posture should not be forced or stiff. Someone with straight posture should look and feel relaxed.

Facial Expressions

Facial expressions are an important part of body language. We use our faces to express ourselves, and we all interpret the facial expressions we see. While some facial expressions are cultural, some facial expressions are universal. Understanding the basics of facial expressions and decoding them will help you determine what people are feeling and facilitate better communication.

Linked with Emotion

Many scientists agree that facial expressions are linked to emotions. Different feelings create physical responses within the body, and facial expressions are emotional responses to situations. Because of the emotional connection, it is not easy to continually fake facial expressions. A flash of true emotion will typically flicker across the face, even when feelings are kept in check. Not only are emotions shown with facial expressions; the degree of emotion a person feels is visible on the face. For example, you can see the difference between a face that shows sadness and one that shows sorrow.

Micro-Expressions

We all hide negative or unwanted emotions from time to time. We can even mask our facial expressions to fit social situations. Feelings can occasionally slip out in the form of micro-expressions. These brief, involuntary expressions betray emotions, and they typically last 1/25 of a second. For example, someone gives a brief sneer but smiles when running into an acquaintance. Most people do not consciously notice micro-expressions. In fact, roughly ten percent of people will knowingly pick up on the micro-expressions of others.

Most micro-expressions are based on universal facial expressions. Being aware of these facial expressions will make micro expressions easier to catch. Noticing micro-expressions can help determine if someone is lying. It is not foolproof, however. For example, someone can be afraid of being caught in a lie or of not being believed.

Facial Action Coding System (FACS)

The Facial Action Coding System (FACS) is a complex system attributed to Dr. Paul Ekman. This system breaks down the muscle movements of micro-expressions into numbered action units (AUs). The muscles that relax or contract with emotion are identified to show the feeling behind each movement of the face. There are AUs identified in the upper and lower face. The meanings behind these involuntary muscle movements are interpreted by the FACS system. The intensity, duration, and asymmetry of expressions are also noted.

Upper Face:

- Eyebrows

- Forehead

- Eyelids

Lower Face:

- Up/Down

- Horizontal

- Oblique

- Orbital

- Miscellaneous

Example:

- An insincere smile will only trigger the zygomatic major muscle. A sincere smile will also include the lower part of the orbicularis oculi.

Universal Facial Expressions

Many facial expressions are learned from one's family and culture. There are, however, facial expressions that all people are believed to share in common. These are the universal facial expressions. Success with FACS and interpreting micro-expressions requires an understanding of universal facial expressions. There are different lists of universal facial expressions, but most lists include the same six facial expressions.

Facial Expressions:

- **Happiness**: More than a smile is needed to indicate happiness. Genuine happiness should include the eyes. Eyelids crinkle a crow's feet become visible.

- **Anger**: A frown typically accompanies anger. Additionally, the eyes narrow, the chin points forward, and the eyebrows furrow.

- **Fear**: Wide eyes and slightly raised eyebrows signal fear. The lips may be parted or stretched when the mouth is closed.

- **Surprise:** Surprise is similar to fear. The eyebrows fully raise and the eyes are wide with surprise. The mouth, however, is usually open.

- **Sadness:** The mouth turns down when someone is sad. A crease in the forehead and quivering chin accompany this slight frown.

- **Disgust:** The expression of disgust includes the nose. The nose wrinkles, the lips part, and the eyes narrow.

Note: Contempt is not always a universally recognized facial expression. It is useful to recognize, however, and includes a sneer with the side of the mouth elevated.

Body Language in Business

Body language can provide people in business with a key advantage. Learn how to adjust your body language to each situation, as you identify the needs, thoughts, and feelings of those you do business with every day. A basic understanding of body language will strengthen negotiating strategies and other business tactics.

Communicate with Power

Powerful communication breeds confidence and respect. It is important that people sense power without aggression. Communicating with power requires practice, but it is an effective business tool.

Powerful Movements:

- **Stance**: A wide stance with the feet apart indicates power. Hands on the hips with the elbows out take up more space and also indicates power.

- **Positioning**: Avoid open space at your back. It is known to elevate stress. Open spaces can be used to make others more vulnerable.

- **Walk**: Walk quickly and take long strides. Be careful not to run, and keep the back and neck erect.

- **Handshake**: Offer a firm handshake, and keep the hand vertical. Placing the palm up because it is a submissive gesture. The palm down is a dominating gesture.

- **Sitting**: Sit with the legs slightly apart. Another powerful pose is sitting with one leg crossed over the other and hands behind the head. Be careful, however, because this position makes many women uncomfortable.

Cultural Differences

International business means working with different cultural backgrounds. While certain expressions are universally recognized, many gestures are cultural. It is essential to research the etiquette and communication style of any culture you do business with ahead of time.

Examples of Differences:

- **Feet**: Pointing feet at people or showing the soles of the feet is disrespectful in many Middle East and Asian cultures.

- **Eye contact**: Different cultures view prolonged eye contact as disrespectful.

- **Hand gestures**: Avoid Western hand gestures when communicating with people from different cultures. Many of them, such as thumbs up, are rude.

- **Head**: Individuals from certain parts of India may move their heads to the side when they agree.

Building Trust

Monitor body language to build trust with business partners. Personal perception builds trust. There are steps that anyone can take to create a rapport of trust.

Steps:

- **Remove barriers:** Physical barriers create a defensive line and do not increase trust.

- **Smile:** A genuine smile helps build trust. People can typically pick up on fake smiles, and insincerity does not engender trust.

- **Body position:** Remain relaxed to build trust.

- **Listen:** Active listening and repeating information helps connect with people.

Mirroring

Mirroring helps build rapport. Mirroring occurs when we copy the movements and gestures of others to show similarities. The perception that people are similar creates trust. Typically mirroring comes easier to women. Women will mirror each other in social settings. Men usually mirror women in romantic situations. In the business setting, consciously mirroring a client or colleague will have dramatic results.

What to Mirror:

- **Smile**: Smile when the client does.

- **Height:** Some people mirror height by stooping or stretching their bodies.

- **Gestures:** Copy the gestures used.

- **Speech:** Monitor the tone, pitch, and rhythm the individual uses.

- **Breathe:** Matching breathing rates will help create a bond.

Lying and Body Language

Body language can expose deception. Close observation of body language can indicate that someone is hiding something. Be careful about interpreting every action as a lie. A number of factors, including stress and insecurity, will cause suspicious body language. When there are multiple indications of deception in a person's body language, however, further investigation may be warranted.

Watch Their Hands

We all communicate with our hands. We can even communicate deception without knowing what we are doing. Several movements can indicate someone is hiding something.

Hands:

- **Palms down:** Showing your palms is a sign of sincerity. Keeping the palms down signals that someone is hiding something.

- **Self-touching**: Self-touching may be a calming action, but be alert when someone touches this or her face. Hands at the nose and mouth are often seen as an attempt to hide the spoken lie.

- **Hidden hands**: Hand gestures are a natural part of communication. Many people will suddenly hide their hands when telling lies. Lack of hand movement may also indicate lying.

Forced Smiles

We have already mentioned smiling. A forced smile does not reach the eyes. Alone, a forced smile can simply indicate that someone is trying to be polite. Always pay close attention when other deceptive movement clusters accompany a forced smile, as they can add additional proof that a person could be lying.

Smiles:

- **Tight smiles:** A tight, thin-lipped smile can indicate that someone is concealing information.

- **Closed mouth:** Genuine smiles are typically open. A closed smile, however, could be an effort to hide bad teeth.

- **Licking lips:** Lying can cause the mouth to dry out. People who lie are more likely to lick their lips after speaking.

Eye Contact

The eyes are called the "windows to the soul." The eyes continually communicate feelings. A person's eye contact can betray that he or she is being deceptive.

The Eyes:

- **Little to no eye contact:** A complete lack of eye contact may be an indication that someone is nervous and being deceptive, but it is not always an indication of lying. There could be cultural reasons for this behavior, so always be aware of any outside factors.

- **Looking to the left:** Moving the gaze to the left may indicate deception. It signals the imagination is being engaged. Left-handed individuals will shift their eyes to the right.

- **Unmoving eyes:** Some people who lie can look directly ahead without moving their eyes. They will not always shift their gaze or look away.

Changes in Posture

Posture can easily signal when a person is being deceptive. Lying will cause someone to focus more on his or her body language. This can cause people to exercise too much control or shift posture.

- **Being still:** People who try to control their movements may be very still. Slight changes in positioning are normal. Abnormally still individuals may be hiding something.

- **Extreme changes:** Deception causes anxiety in most people. When body language changes from defensive positions to open, friendly postures. The clumsier these transitions increase the likelihood of deception.

- **Voice and movements do not correspond:** Body language typically reflects the voice and message of a speaker. When this is not the case, lying is indicated. For example, someone uses closed, defensive body language with a friendly tone and interaction.

Improve Your Body Language

People make snap judgments about each other based on body language. It is possible to improve your body language and the way that others view you. Give an air of confidence when meeting with colleagues and potential clients. Understanding the subtleties of body language makes it easier to improve your own. Simply pay attention to what you say and do.

Be Aware of Your Movements

It is important to be aware of your movements and what they mean. The best way to do this, however, is to make sure that the movements are genuine. Faked body language typically looks disjointed and unnatural. People can subconsciously pick up on these movements.

Tips:

- **Relax:** Try to relax and implement open body language. This will help prevent any nervous body signals.

- **Watch your hands:** Use comfortable gestures when talking. Do not hide your hands, and try to avoid fidgeting or touching your face.

- **Eye contact:** Maintain eye contact, but do stare at people.

- **Smile:** Avoid fake smiles. Give genuine smiles to instill trust.

- **Watch your head:** Look ahead; tilting is submissive. Nod occasionally to signal your interest.

The Power of Confidence

Improve body language by increasing personal confidence. Everyone has a personal level of confidence that is evident in body language. There are simple ways that can help improve confidence and body language.

Tips:

- **Exercise:** A strong body will boost personal confidence. It can also improve posture.

- **Dress:** Our appearance affects our confidence. Dressing well will help improve our self-esteem.

- **Posture:** An open posture will induce confidence. It will also improve the way others see you.

- **Speech:** Speak in a confident tone to increase your feelings of confidence. Do not mumble.

Position and Posture

Posture and body position are effective forms of communication. Pay attention to your position and posture and think about what they are communicating.

- **Posture:** Straight posture automatically increases confidence and alertness. Avoid slouching, but remain relaxed.

- **Position:** Open body positions communicate a relaxed and confident demeanor. Closed body positions indicate defensiveness.

Practice in a Mirror

Practice is the key to success. Many people have poor body mechanics. They do not realize the mechanics alter their posture or positions. Practicing body language in front of a mirror will give an accurate evaluation of what you are communicating.

What to Practice:

- **Note your posture:** Pay attention to any tendencies to slouch or hunch over. Practice your posture until it is correct.

- **Note your gestures:** Identify any nervous gestures you use, and consciously try to avoid them.

- **Practice talking:** Your tone should match your gestures and body language.

Matching Your Words to Your Movement

The key to instilling trust is matching body language to the words spoken. Movements will confirm or contradict what is said. Gestures will easily match what is said if the words reflect genuine feeling. Emotional awareness is necessary to communicate exactly what you mean. Unresolved emotions can affect body language.

Involuntary Movements

We do not control our involuntary movements. Emotions can affect our breathing, posture, gestures, and micro-expressions. People subconsciously pick up on involuntary movements, particularly when they contradict what is said. For example, increased respiration can indicate stress or anxiety. When practicing body language, be aware of involuntary movements. Reducing stress and finding healthy ways to express emotion will help limit involuntary movements.

Ways to reduce stress:

- Exercise

- Meditation

- Sufficient sleep

- Journaling

- Healthy diet

Say What You Mean

Deception is often part of polite communication. This will affect body language and movement. Communication is much more effective when you say what you mean. You should always practice being respectful and honest in your speech.

Honest Communication:

- **Be specific:** Stick to the facts when communicating. Do not rely on your emotions.

- **Self-edit:** Choose language that is not confrontational.

- **Have a goal:** Know the point of your communication, and do not ramble.

Always Be Consistent

Dependable communication creates trust. The key is to be consistently honest and open when communicating with others. Here are a few tips that will improve your communication style and increase consistency.

- **Speak plainly**: Avoid complex terms, and define any new terms used.

- **Listen:** Invite feedback and clarify information when necessary.

- **Adapt:** Pay attention to the body language and tone of others, and respond appropriately.

- **Be open:** Be open and honest in what is said and in your body language.

Actions Will Trump Words

People pay more attention to actions than words. We typically make decisions about someone within four seconds of a meeting. This is largely based on body language and behavior. If your body language is hostile, it does not matter how kind your words or tone are. Be aware of what your actions and gestures are communicating to those around you. Practice your body language skills and decode the body language of others:

What People Decide?

- Intelligence

- Trustworthiness

- Likability

- Decision to buy

Chapter 6 – Interpersonal Skills

We've all met that dynamic, charismatic person that just has a way with others, and has a way of being remembered. This workshop will help participants work towards being that unforgettable person by providing communication skills, negotiation techniques, tips on making an impact, and advice on networking and starting conversations.

By the end of this tutorial, participants will be able to:

- Understand the difference between hearing and listening

- Know some ways to improve the verbal skills of asking questions and communicating with power.

- Understand what non-verbal communication is and how it can enhance interpersonal relationships.

- Identify the skills needed in starting a conversation, moving a conversation along, and progressing to higher levels of conversation.

- Identify ways of creating a powerful introduction, remembering names, and managing situations when you've forgotten someone's name.

- Understand how seeing the other side, building bridges and giving in without giving up can improve skills in influencing other people.

- Understand how the use of facts and emotions can help bring people to your side.

- Identify ways of sharing one's opinions constructively.

- Learn tips in preparing for a negotiation, opening a negotiation, bargaining, and closing a negotiation.

- Learn tips in making an impact through powerful first impressions, situation assessment, and being zealous without being offensive.

As a pre-assignment, think of a social situation that you consider most stressful. This situation can be within an employment, community, family, or recreational setting. Example: introducing one's self to strangers.

After coming up with the social situation you find most stressful, answer the following questions:

- What aspect of this situation do you find most stressful? Why?

- What do you think are the interpersonal skills needed in order to successfully navigate this situation? List down at least three.

- On a scale of 1 to 5, with 1 being the least effective and 5 being the most, rate your effectiveness in practicing the skills you listed.

- Looking at your responses, which skills do you practice most effectively? What helps you in practicing these skills well?

- Which skills do you practice least effectively? What keeps you from practicing these skills well?

Verbal Communication Skills

Words are powerful tools of communication. Indeed, word choice can easily influence the thoughts, attitudes, and behavior of the people listening to us. Similarly, proper attention to the language of others can give us insight to what it is that they are *really* saying, helping us to respond appropriately and effectively.

In this module, we will discuss important verbal communication skills like the art of listening, asking questions, and communicating with power.

Listening and Hearing: They Aren't the Same Thing

Most people can hear, but few can really listen.

Hearing is simply the process of perceiving sounds within our environment. The best way to illustrate hearing is through the biological processes involved in sensory perception. Specifically: our ears pick up sound waves around us, sends signals to our brain, and our brain in turn tells us what the sound is and where it is coming from.

Listening, on the other hand, goes beyond simply picking up stimuli around us, and identifying what these stimuli are. Listening involves the extra steps of really understanding what we heard, and giving it deliberate attention and thoughtful consideration. It may be said that listening involves a more active participation from a person than simply hearing.

Here is an example to illustrate the difference between hearing and listening:

A secretary entered her boss' office and presented her boss with a copy of the schedule for the next day. The secretary told the boss that she has a packed day for tomorrow, and that she only has an hour of break time for the whole afternoon.

The boss, busy studying a report, merely nodded to the secretary, and motioned for her to place the schedule on her desk. The boss continued to study the report as if there were no interruption. In this case, the boss simply heard what the secretary said; the boss paid just enough attention to make an appropriate but non-committal reaction.

Had the boss been listening, her reaction would have been different.

She would have set aside the report she was reading and paid 100% attention to what the secretary was saying. She could also have processed the implication of the message. For instance, upon learning that she has a packed day ahead, she could have arranged for her lunch to be delivered, or noted to herself that she needs to get a good night's sleep.

Taking the extra step to move from hearing to listening can enhance a person's interpersonal relationships in many ways. Listening promotes a more accurate and deeper understanding of a person's communication, helping a responder to provide the most appropriate response. But more so, when you're listening to a person, you communicate to them that you value not just what they are saying, but their presence as well.

Asking Questions

If communication is the exchange of information between two or more people, then questions are a way to elicit the specific information that you are looking for. But more so, well-crafted questions make for an engaging conversation. It can establish rapport, spark interest, and curiosity in others, break new grounds, and communicate your own sincerity in learning what people around you have to say.

Here are some tips in asking questions effectively:

Ask! First of all, don't be afraid to ask questions! Sometimes shyness, concern over making a faux pas, or fear of being perceived as a busybody, can keep us from asking questions. While some subject matters are not appropriate conversation pieces in the early stages of a conversation (we will discuss this later, in the section on Levels of Conversation), there's nothing wrong in asking questions per se. Start with your inherent curiosity about people, if you're genuinely interested in a person, you won't run out of things to ask.

Ask open questions. There are two kinds of questions based on the scope of the answers they elicit: closed and open questions.

- Closed questions are questions answerable by yes or no. Example: "Are you happy with today's presentation?"

- Open questions, on the other hand, are questions that require a qualified response. Open questions are usually preceded by who, when, where, what, how, and why. Example: "What is it about today's presentation that you find most engaging?"

- Open questions are more effective than closed questions because they evoke thoughtful consideration of the subject and creative thinking.

Ask purposeful questions. There are different reasons why we ask questions, and it is important that we take note of our purpose in asking a question. Doing so can help us frame our questions better, and keep the questions relevant.

For example, we can ask questions with the goal of making the other person feel at ease. Questions like these should be phrased in a pleasant, non-threatening manner, and involves subjects that the other person is likely to be interested in. Example: *"That's a lovely blouse! Where did you get it?"*

Some questions are designed to challenge the other person's thinking, and encourage a lively debate or deliberation. Questions like these should be phrased in a way that is focused and process-oriented. It can also challenge existing assumptions about the subject matter. Example: *"How do you think a leader can better motivate his team?"*

In other times, questions are meant to encourage a person to join an existing discussion. The goal of these questions is to invite participation, as much as gain information. Example: *"I find Matthew's approach very refreshing. What do you think, Frank?"*

For better effectiveness, think of what you and the person you're talking to needs in your stage of relationship, and ask him or her questions that can address that need.

Communicating with Power

Power in communication refers to the ability to influence, persuade, or make an impact. A powerful communication is associated with self-confidence, credibility, and effectiveness.

The following are some ways you can communicate with power verbally:

Stick to the point. Powerful communication is not about saying as many things as you can in a given period of time. Rather, it is about sticking to what is relevant to the discussion, and getting your message across in the shortest --- but most impact-laden --- way possible. Get rid of fillers like *"uhm…"*, *"you know"*, or *"actually"* in your delivery, and avoid off-topic statements. Just provide the bare bones --- the ideas your audience would be most interested in knowing, or the ones that promote your intentions best.

Don't be too casual. Note that phrasing appropriate when talking with friends is not necessarily appropriate for business-related meets. The use of slang, street talk, and poor grammar can detract from your credibility, especially if you're mingling with potential clients, employers, and business partners. Events that require you to come across as impressive may require the use of industry-specific jargon and a formal tone --- so adjust accordingly.

Emphasize key ideas. Stress the highlights of your communication. For example, people who are delivering a sales pitch should emphasize the main features of their product or service. Those who are presenting their opinion on an issue should explain the crux of their arguments, and build from there. Even if you're merely expressing interest or congratulations, make sure the person you're talking to would remember what you have to say. Emphasis in verbal communication comes in many ways, including repetition of key points, giving specific examples, accenting particular adjectives or nouns, or even directly saying that "this is really a point I want to emphasize."

Tailor-fit your communication to your audience. A powerful communication is one that connects with one's audience. In this case, minding the readiness, attention, age, and educational level of your audience is very important, so that you don't overwhelm or underwhelm them. Social skills are primarily about flexibility; the better you can adjust to changes in your audience profile, the better off you'll be.

Connect. Power in communication is sometimes determined by the quality of your rapport with others. You may need to "warm up" your audience, make them comfortable, and show them that you sincerely want to talk with them. The more others see you as "one of them", the better their reception of anything that you have to say will be.

Your non-verbal communication can be a big help in connecting with others.

Non-Verbal Communication Skills

Communication is not just about what comes out of our mouths. In fact, what we don't say --- our body language, voice intonation and use of silence ---- often sends a louder message to other people than the words we say. Unless we actively practice non-verbal communication skills, we can't really be sure if we're actually sending the message that we want to send.

Body Language

Body language refers to the messages we send to other people through our posture, facial expression, gestures, and bodily movements.

It is believed that a listener pays more attention to body language than verbal messages. This implies that if one's body language is inconsistent with the verbal message being sent (e.g. frowning while saying you're happy), the verbal message becomes less credible. In fact, such inconsistency can even nullify the verbal message, and result to the verbal message being perceived as a lie. At the very least, inconsistencies between verbal and non-verbal communication can result in confusion.

The following are some of the components of body language:

Eye Contact: Eye contact is considered one of the most important aspects of non-verbal communication. Steady eye contact often indicates attention to the person one is in conversation with, as well as a willingness and sincerity to connect. The lack of eye connect can be viewed as defensiveness, nervousness and or social withdrawal. Many say that our eyes are the "windows to our soul", and that one can tell if an individual is happy, sad, or angry simply by looking at their eyes.

Facial Expression: It is believed that there are universal facial expressions for different emotions, most of which have an evolutionary basis. For example, anger is often indicated by sharp stares, crunched eyebrows and the baring of teeth. Sadness, on the other hand, can be denoted by teary eyes and drooping lips. Note though that the expression and perception of emotions tend to vary from culture to culture.

Posture: The way we sit down, stand up or even walk can also communicate. For example, slumping in a chair is often considered as a sign of inattention and or disrespect. Walking with one's head and shoulders down can be interpreted as a sign of nervousness or low self-esteem. Withdrawing to a fetal position can also be indicative of fear and or depression. The puffing of one's chest has been traditionally interpreted as pride.

Specific Movements: There are specific movements that have traditionally been associated with certain messages. For example, nodding is generally a sign of assent or agreement. Raising clenched hands are interpreted as a sign of angry challenge. Stomping our feet can be an indication of frustration.

Physical Contact: The way we physically interact with other people is also a part of body language. Shaking of hands, hugging, slapping, punching are forms of communication. The same can be said about our physical closeness and distance with another person. Standing too close to a person can be considered as an invasion of boundaries, while standing too far from a person can be construed as avoidance.

The Signals You Send to Others

Generally, our non-verbal communication is something that we do unconsciously. It can be influenced by many things, including past habits, life experiences, personal models, culture and hidden thoughts and feelings. Because body language is often outside of awareness, most have no idea what it is exactly that they are communicating to other people.

To take control of the signals that we send to others, it's important that we become much more deliberate and purposive in communicating non-verbally.

The following are some tips and techniques you can follow to be able to use body language effectively.

Increase your awareness of your body language. Try to get more information about what you communicate non-verbally, so that you will know what to change and what to retain. Ways you can do this include: watching a videotape of yourself, studying yourself in front of a mirror, and getting feedback from peers and friends.

Know how certain behaviors are typically interpreted. Interpreting body language can be very subjective. There are, however, typical interpretations to specific body language. Increasing awareness of what body language is often associated with what interpretation, can help a person avoid body language incongruent with the message they want to send; as well as deliberately practice the body language congruent with their message.

Practice! Practice! Practice! Body language is a skill. Initially, using body language that is congruent with the message that we want to communicate will feel unnatural. But just keep on working on it. Soon, it'll be second nature to you!

It's Not What You Say, It's How You Say It

Non-verbal communication also includes the way we deliver information. A simple change in tone and inflection can change the meaning of statements. It is important then, to be aware of the way we speak, so that we can communicate more effectively.

The following are aspects of "how we say things" that we should take note of:

Tone of Voice: Voice intonation refers to the use of changing pitch in order to convey a message. The same message, for example, can be delivered using a rising intonation, a dipping intonation, or a falling intonation. Changes in tone can help inject emotions into messages; messages can be upbeat or depressing depending on the speaker's tone. Changes in tone can also help identify what is the purpose of a sentence. There are intonations that better fit a question, and intonations that better fit a declarative sentence.

Stress and Emphasis: Changing which words or syllables you put emphasis on can change its meaning. For example, consider the differences among these three statements below. The italicized word represents where the emphasis is.

- You mean *he* disobeyed his mother?

- You mean he *disobeyed* his mother?

- You mean he disobeyed *his mother*?

Pace and Rhythm: The speed of speech, as well as the appropriate use of pauses can change the meaning of words spoken, and affect the clarity and effectiveness of a communication. For instance, people who speak too fast can be difficult to talk to --- a listener might feel too pressured to catch everything that they have to say! On the other hand, a person who speaks too slowly can bore their listener.

Volume: How softly and how loudly you speak also matters in communication. Ideally, one should generally speak in a moderate volume while in the company of others; a too soft voice can communicate nervousness or lack of assertiveness, while a loud voice can communication anger and aggression. A person should also be flexible, able to whisper or shout when it's appropriate to do so.

Pronunciation and Enunciation. How well a message comes across is influenced by pronunciation and enunciation. Pronunciation refers to speaking a word in a way that's generally accepted or understood, while enunciation is the act of speaking clearly and concisely. Developing one's skills in pronunciation and enunciation ensures that one is accurately understood. Note that accents can cause varieties in what is considered as acceptable pronunciation.

Making Small Talk and Moving Beyond

Small talk is the "ice-breaking" part of a conversation; it is the way strangers can ease into comfortable rapport with one another. Mastering the art of small talk ---- and how to build from this stage--- can open many personal and professional doors. In this module, we will discuss how to start a conversation, as well as how to skillfully ease our conversation starters into deeper levels of talk.

Starting a Conversation

Many people are interested in initiating friendships and productive business networks, but they don't know how to start. Indeed, going up to a stranger and making an introduction can be incredibly anxiety-provoking for some people. The same goes with finding something to talk about with someone you already know, but are not familiar with.

The following are some tips in starting a conversation:

Understand what holds you back. The first step in developing conversation skills is to understand what factors --- attitudes, feelings, and assumptions --- interfere in your ability to skillfully handle a conversation. Is it shyness? Fear of rejection? Difficulty in dealing with people in authority? Awareness of what holds you back can help you manage your anxieties better, and give you more control over how you handle yourself during social situations.

Know what you have to offer. In the same way that you have to make an inventory of your weaknesses during social situations, you also have to take stock of your strengths. Confidence in initiating conversations does not begin with knowing what tried-and-tested lines are out there. It starts with a sincere belief that you have something to contribute to a discussion, and that people would find it a pleasant experience to get to know you. If you have this self-assurance, you can be more at ease and more natural around other people.

Be interested about people. Genuine curiosity and openness makes starting a conversation less threatening; it grants incentive to approach people.

Cultivate the attitude that meeting people is an enriching experience. It shouldn't be that hard; this mantra goes beyond self-talk. Many find that you can actually learn a lot about yourself, about life and about various subject matters, just by simply engaging in constant conversation. And remember: being interested in people doesn't end after you've spent time with them. Even those you've spent years with can still tell you something you don't know!

Create an arsenal of conversation starters. For people not used to skillfully handling conversations, the first few tries can feel awkward. While you're still finding your footing, you can rely on some recommended conversation starters. Among them are:

Introduce yourself. The most straightforward way to start a conversation is to offer your name and your hand. By making the first move in breaking silence, you're sending the other person an invitation into conversation. If you can make the introduction with a smile, better.

Comment on something in your immediate surroundings, maybe the location, or the event you both are attending. Things that you both can relate with are good conversation starters, as it does not alienate anyone. Example: "It's really crowded tonight, isn't it?"

Comment on something the other person or people would find interesting. For example, if you're talking with someone known for his or her art collection, you may call attention to an art piece within your vicinity, or inform him about an exhibit you heard about. Example: "Hey Bob, I just heard that the National Museum is hosting a Renaissance week." And if you have no prior knowledge about the person you want to strike a conversation with, you can take a guess at their interests by subtly checking what they are looking at, or studying their appearance. Example: *"That's a lovely brooch. It looks like an antique."*

Relax. *"Be yourself"* is generally good advice for handling social situations. Conversations are more comfortable and engaging if participants simply relax, and let their personalities do the talking. Don't pressure yourself coming up with something funny, clever, or new. Scripts are okay while you're still developing your social skills, but make sure you also give conversations your personal touch!

The Four Levels of Conversation

The real art of conversation is not only to say the right thing at the right place, but to leave unsaid the wrong thing at tempting moment. It requires sensitivity to the stage of a relationship, the context of the conversation and the comfort level of the person you are talking to.

There are 4 levels of conversation based on the degree and amount of personal disclosure. They are:

Level 1: Small Talk: This is commonly referred to as the 'exchange of pleasantries' stage. In this level, you talk only about generic topics, subjects that almost everyone is comfortable discussing. These subjects include the weather, the location you're both in and current events.

The small talk stage establishes rapport; it makes a person feel at ease with you. It's also a safe and neutral avenue for people to subtly 'size up' one another, and explore if it's a conversation or relationship that they'd want to invest in.

If the small talk goes well, you can proceed into the next level: fact disclosure.

Level 2: Fact Disclosure: In this stage, you tell the other person some facts about you such as your job, your area of residence, and your interests.

This is a 'getting-to-know' stage, and it aims to see if you have something in common with the other person. It's also a signal that you are opening up a little bit to the other person while still staying on neutral topics.

If the fact disclosure stage goes well, you can proceed to sharing viewpoints and opinions.

Level 3: Viewpoints and Opinions: In this stage of the conversation, you can offer what you think about various topics like politics, the new business model ---or even the latest blockbuster. It helps then to read and be curious about many things, from politics to entertainment to current events.

Sharing viewpoints and opinions require the 'buffering effect' of the first two stages for two reasons:

- First, a person needs rapport with another before they can discuss potentially contentious statements, even if they're having a healthy debate.

- Second, sharing viewpoints and opinions opens a person to the scrutiny of another, and this requires that there is some level of safety and trust in a relationship.

The controversial, and therefore potentially offensive, nature of an opinion exists in a range; make sure that you remain within the 'safe' zone in the early stages of your relationship.

Level 4: Personal Feelings: The fourth stage is disclosure and acknowledgment of personal feelings. For instance you can share about your excitement for the new project, or your worry about your son's upcoming piano recital. Depending on the context and the level of the friendship, you can disclose more personal subjects. This stage requires trust, rapport, and even a genuine friendship, because of the intimate nature of the subject.

Different people have different comfort levels when it comes to disclosing feelings, and there are cases when you'd need several conversations before they would trust enough to open themselves. In some cases, you never get to this stage. Just make sure to be sensitive and test the other person's readiness before opening an intimate topic.

Listening is vital in all stages of the conversation but especially so in this fourth stage. Listen with empathy and understanding to acknowledge that you heard the feeling that they have shared.

Moving the Conversation Along

Initiating a conversation is one interpersonal skill, maintaining it is another. An engaging and effective conversation is one that "flows" and "goes forward." To be able to keep a conversation from being stuck, it's best to know techniques in moving a conversation along. In this module we will discuss techniques like asking for examples, using repetition, using summary questions, and asking for clarity and completeness.

Asking for Examples

One way to get a conversation partner to elaborate on what they are sharing with you is to ask for examples. Examples make a specific general statement, and give an insight on the particulars of a disclosure. It can also serve to illustrate principles shared, or personalize an experience.

The following conversation excerpts illustrate how asking for examples can move a conversation along:

Excerpt 1

Person A: C.S. Lewis is one of my all-time favorite writers.

Person B: C.S. Lewis? I am not familiar with his work. *Could you give an example of what he has done?*

Person A: Well, he wrote the Chronicles of Narnia. It's a children's series with seven books. I find it very inspiring.

Excerpt 2

Person A: This is a great company to work for. They really care about their employees.

Person B: *In what ways do they care for the staff?*

Person A: Well, their medical aid program is a good example of how they prioritize health and security. All ABC Company employees are registered with a private insurance firm from their first day of work.

Person B: Wow. That's very generous. *In what other ways are they employee-oriented?*

Person A: The staff members are also scheduled for an annual week-long retreat, all expenses paid for by the company.

Using Repetition

Questions are not the only powerful tools that you can use to keep a conversation going. Repeating certain words, phrases, or even statements that a person discloses to you can also maintain the momentum of your talk, or urge it to a new direction.

In what way can repetition keep a conversation going?

Repetition can be a way of saying *"please go on"* or *"tell me more."* It is a technique of acknowledging that you have heard what the other person said, and or something about their disclosure has picked your attention. It is an encouragement for them to elaborate.

Repetition is also a way of focusing a conversation on an interesting aspect. Your choice of what word, phrase, or statement to repeat will signal to the other person what you'd like to hear more about. One way you can use this technique to your advantage is to repeat a word, phrase or statement that you feel has a lot more story to it. You may also zero in on what you think the other person likes to talk about more, or what you yourself find intriguing.

Lastly, repetition can also be a way of communicating your reaction to what the other person said. Varying the intonation and pitch of your voice can inject your repetition with emotions of surprise, shock, excitement, or confusion.

The following conversation excerpts illustrate how repetition can move a conversation along:

Excerpt 1:

Person A: Mark and I have been married for 40 years now. We'll be renewing our vows in April.

Person B: *Forty years.*

Person A: Yes. Amazing, isn't it? It wasn't always easy but we made it through. Very few people who married the same time as us are still together now. I know I am one of the lucky ones.

Excerpt 2:

Person A: I can't believe it! The guys threw me a surprise party.

Person B: *The guys threw you a birthday party.*

Person A: Yes! It really made my day.

Note that in repetition you don't necessarily have to repeat the same exact phase. You can make changes necessary to make the repetition more effective.

Using Summary Questions

Another way to keep a conversation moving is to summarize what has been discussed, or what you heard from the other person, every now and then.

A summary can communicate that you are really listening, and that you have taken stock of everything the other person has said. More so, it gives a sense of movement to the conversation, because summaries say that one part of the conversation is over, and that it's time to move on to another part.

Note that in repetition you don't necessarily have to repeat the same exact phase. You can make changes necessary to make the repetition more effective.

The following conversation excerpts illustrate how summary questions can move a conversation along:

Excerpt 1:

Person A: I'm really geared up for this coming marathon! I changed my diet, hired a trainer, and I've been practicing 3-4 hours a day. I've never felt more in shape; I feel that I have a real shot at winning this!

Person B: *You're really invested in this marathon; you really think you have a chance to win?*

Person A: Yes. Amazing, isn't it!

Excerpt 2:

Person A: I want this project to be the one of the most successful for this trimester. We've had a run of bad luck the past month, and we need a big break to recoup it all. Judging by the projections the accounting department made, I think we're right on track!

Person B: That's great! How can I help?

Person A: We need a design person. You're good at art, right? Can you make us a logo?

Person B: Sure. Just give me the specs you want and I'm on it.

Person A: And a pamphlet as well? One that has all of the company colors in it. Same with the logo!

Person B: No problem. *Let me see if I understood you right. You need a pamphlet and a logo with the company colors in it. Is this correct?*

Person A: That's it. Thanks!

Asking for Clarity and Completeness

Here's another way of moving a conversation along: asking for clarity and completeness.

It is important to verify your understanding of a communication, and see if you have accurate and or complete information. Often, a speaker presumes that he or she is understood, and therefore tends to miss on certain details. They may think that they have the same frame of reference with the other person, and consequently does not need to expand on the meaning of their statements. At times, intense emotions, like excitement can result in lack of clarity and completeness in communication.

Asking for clarity and completeness can give your conversation depth and richness of idea. It can also communicate your sincere desire to understand what the other person is saying.

The following conversation excerpt illustrates how asking for clarity and completeness can move a conversation along:

Excerpt 1:

Person A: My 7-year old daughter wants to become an actress! She's been begging me to enroll her in this intensive acting community workshop, but I'm afraid it will just spoil her.

Person B: *I don't understand. What do you mean by 'it will just spoil her'?*

Person A: You know…I think it will indulge her too much. I want her to grow up disciplined by school and household chores. I don't want her to be like many young stars nowadays, who don't seem to know what's real and what's not.

Person B: *I think I understand what you mean. Are you saying that she'll miss the normal demands of everyday that keeps people grounded?*

Person A: Exactly!

Remembering Names

Writer and lecturer Dale Carnegie once said that *"a person's name to him or her is the sweetest and most important sound in any language*." When we address people by name, we are telling them that we respect them, consider them as important, recognize their individuality, and warmly relate with them. If you want to be able to cultivate many functional friendships and working partnerships, you need the ability of remembering names.

Creating a Powerful Introduction

Three steps to introducing yourself effectively:

Step 1: Project warmth and confidence. Many people size you up even before you say a word, which is why it's important to mind your body language. When you introduce yourself, stand up straight, relax, and establish eye contact.

Step 2: State your first name and your last name. Depending on the situation, you may also state your affiliation and or your position in the company. Example: *"Hello. I'm Jacqueline Smith. I'm the Quality Control Officer."*

Step 3: When the other person has given their name, repeat it in acknowledgment. *"It's nice to meet you, Mr. Andrews."* or *"It's nice to meet you, Joseph."* Repeating their name is an acknowledgment that you heard their introduction.

Using Mnemonics

One technique that has been known to work in helping improve recall is the use of mnemonic devices. Mnemonic devices are ways of conceptualizing ideas that aim to organize arbitrary things into meaningful data. Things that seem random are harder to remember; mnemonic devices help organize ideas in our minds.

Here are examples of mnemonic devices you can use in name recall:

Clustering by Categories: Grouping the items that you need to remember into categories can help you remember them better. For example, to memorize a list of contacts, group them by company or by profession.

Visualizing Interactive Images: Some people memorize better when they create a scene in their heads where all the items that they have to remember are interacting with each other in some active way. For example, if you have to remember to Mark, Joseph and Martha, imagine a Biblical Joseph being served tea by Martha Stewart while he's playing target shooting (the bulls-eye can remind you of the synonym "mark")

Acronyms: This is a method where you devise a word or expression in which each of its letters stand for a name. An example is SALE for Sally, Andrew, Louise and Ester

Acrostics: This mnemonic device follows the same logic as acronyms except that one forms a sentence rather than a single word to help one remember new words. For example one might remember 'all babies cry loudly' for Allan, Betty, Chris and Lisa.

Uh-Oh…I've Forgotten Your Name

Most of us have been there before: a situation when someone says "hi" to us, but we have absolutely no idea who is talking to us. At best we'd just feel awkward and embarrassed; at worse, we might end up offending the other person. To better manage situations like this, it is recommended that you:

Understand why you forget names. Often, forgetting names is not about memory problems --- it's about attitude problems. Perhaps you don't think remembering names is important. Maybe you don't trust your ability to manage a list of names in your head. Or it's possible that you get easily nervous in social situations, you tend to mentally blank out. Identify what holds you back from remembering people's name. Exert a deliberate effort to improve your rate of name recall. It is only when you have an open attitude that name recall becomes easy.

Ask a third party. One way you can avoid showing your memory lapse is to seek a third person's help subtly. If you see a face in a crowd that looks familiar, but whose name you can't recall, ask a friend: "Hey, do you know the woman at the back?" A little research prior to walking up to a person can help you prevent a potentially embarrassing situation.

Ask for a card. Asking for a calling card can be a way to subtly get the other person's name. For example, you can say: *"Hey, I don't think I have your card yet, here's mine."*

Introduce other people to them. If you have people you know around you, why don't you initiate an introduction? For instance you can say "Hey, have you met my friend Mark? Mark is a PR in this company." Politeness would typically compel the person to introduce himself or herself to Mark, and you can catch their name at that point.

Be honest. And if you really can't recall who the person is, and the other person appears amiable enough, then perhaps you can come clean. You can say: *"I'm sorry; I know that we've met, but I seem to have forgotten your name."* You may also add some details that you do remember, to ease the effect of your memory loss. *"We met at the company dinner, right, last September? You were with your lovely children."* Hopefully, the other person can empathize with your distress and re-introduce themselves.

Influencing Skills

The skill of influencing others is a valuable asset to have; it can help us sell products and ideas, convince people and institutions to assist us, and even get the world to change! After all, while we don't have the power to control other people, we can always do our best to persuade them.

In this module, we will discuss how to improve our influencing skills. Particularly, we will discuss techniques like seeing the other side, building a bridge and giving in without giving up.

Seeing the Other Side

The first step in influencing other people is entering their world. This means setting aside your own point of view, and looking at the situation from another person's perspective. Remember, each person is unique, and consequently sees the world differently. You can't always assume that what's clear to you is clear to the people you are talking to.

In short, you have to be able to answer this question for them: *"what's in it for me?"*

Seeing the other side involves knowing what is important to the other person(s): their values, interests, and preferences. Do they have strong feelings against what you are pitching to them? What would it take to for them to get over their resistance? What are their characteristics, personality traits, social status, or professions that can you use in order to make your point more convincing?

Research, active listening, and keen observation can help you in "seeing the other side."

Consider this example:

How do you convince city-based, working mothers to plant medicinal plants instead of buying factory-made pharmaceuticals?

If you are not practicing the skill of "seeing the other side", you might be tempted to argue that having medicines readily available in the home is more convenient than having to run to the pharmacy every time someone is sick.

But this argument may not be so convincing if you consider the world city-based working mothers live in. As city-dwellers with full time jobs, working mothers would likely find buying from the pharmacy much more convenient than finding space in an urban home for plants. More so, the demand of having to water the plants and expose them to sunlight every day is too much added responsibility.

On the other hand, mothers would always respond to one prime value ---- their child's health and welfare. If you can present a case on how pollution in the city and chemical-based food and drugs lower resistance to diseases among children, and that natural medicines are both a way to improve kids' health and show love, you may be able to build a stronger case for planting medicinal plants at home.

Building a Bridge

A second skill that can help you during situations that need persuasion is bridge building.

Bridge building is the process of increasing rapport and affinity between people. It can involve making the other party feel at ease talking to you, gaining their trust, and identifying common interests.

Bridge building is important in persuasion because people are more likely to agree with someone they like, trust, or see as "one of them." Aside from bridges improving the over-all communication between two parties, bridges can also serve as negotiating grounds. Bridges translate to common interests, which can be the foundation of win-win scenarios.

The following are some of the ways you can build bridges in your interpersonal relationships:

Active Listening. If you want to gain another person's trust, you have to communicate that you value their presence, and that you are exerting the effort to understand what they are saying to you. Listening attentively is a way to do this.

Use Common Language. An indirect way of building bridges is showing by your words, manner of speaking and even by body language, that you are one with the other person. For example, use business language when you're speaking with the company CEO, but use laymen terms when speaking with blue-collared workers. Pay attention to how the other person phrases his statements; if they're formal, be formal, and if they're casual, then follow suit. Similarly, attend to their pace of doing business. Some people like to relax before a deal, others like to go straight to business. Adjust your approach accordingly.

Highlight Similarities. No matter how differently two people appear they will always have at least one thing in common. If you want to persuade a person, find these areas of similarities and emphasize them. An important similarity to emphasize is common interests --- goals that you both share, that the proposal you're pitching can address. The previous skill of "seeing the other side" can assist you in this process.

Sustained Communication. Lastly, consistent and sustained communication about matters of interest can help you in influencing other people. If you feel that there is significant resistance to you or to your proposal, or there are marked differences between you and the other person, just persistently meet with the person and open communication lines. Sometimes, your mere visibility in another person's circle can increase your likeability and credibility.

Giving In Without Giving Up

Issues are rarely black and white. In most cases, there are areas within a contention that you can compromise upon. If you want to improve your chances of influencing other people, be willing to make some concessions ---- even if it's just at the levels of simply agreeing to differ, agreeing that the other person has a right to their opinion, or agreeing that the other person has made a reasonable argument.

The skill of giving in is important because people generally don't want to deal with individuals whose intention is to win at all points, or be declared "right" for the sake of being right. This makes the relationship confrontational rather than collaborative. The discussion becomes an argument, and the atmosphere turns tense. If you want to enhance your chances of winning someone over, be willing to consider ---and even agree upon ---reasonable requests. You may even volunteer to take losses in areas you can afford to give up, as long as you don't lose sight of the main goal.

A person who is willing to "give in" from time to time comes across as sensible and realistic. Moreover, concessions communicate a sincere desire to do what is best for another person. At the very least, it can promote a culture of "quid pro quo"; I will give you something, if you give me something in return.

The trick lies in choosing what you will concede. Understandably, you don't want to "give up" and concede the very thing you are selling. Keep sight of the main goal and judge what you can sacrifice based on this main goal. If you can create a win-win compromise between what you want and what the other person likes, better.

Consider this example:

How can you convince your boss to allow you to take freelance work outside your company --- something that you initially agreed not to do?

What if your boss tells you that you signed a contract that you will work exclusively for them, and that you taking freelance work outside the company will just result in a conflict of interest?

If you start opposing what your boss just said ---- for example you argue that they have never given you a single raise since you started five years ago and the economy has since changed ----- chances are, you'd just make your boss upset and defensive, decreasing your chances of influencing him or her.

However, if you concede that you did sign a contract (which you did!), and that yes, you can see how such a move can create a conflict of interest, then you can "mellow" your boss down.

This doesn't mean you've given up, however. You can follow your concession by presenting an alternative win-win proposal. How about a change in contract that states that you can't take freelance work from the company's main competitors, and that you're obliged to refer to the company any deal worth $5000 and above? The arrangement can give you the extra income you want, without the conflict of interest.

Bringing People to Your Side

In the previous module, we discussed the different ways you can increase your influence over other people, and set the stage for persuasion. We will continue on that thread in this module, and discuss the ways you can bring people to your side. Particularly, we will discuss the persuasive techniques of appealing to a person's emotions and reason.

A Dash of Emotion

Emotions have always been a driving force for people's behavior. Advertisers appeal to emotions all the time; they tell you that so-and-so beauty product can make you feel confident around the opposite sex, while so-and-so theme park can make you forget all your worries. There are those who begin a relationship based solely on how the other person made them feel. More so, advocacies, political campaigns, and even wars are waged, based on a collective sense of anger, contempt, or injustice.

Thus, you can never underestimate emotions as a way of influencing and persuading other people.

Why are emotions powerful? For one, emotions heavily influence a person's sense of comfort and general state of well-being. Positive emotions make us feel good, while negative emotions drive us to do something to make us feel good. But more so, emotions connect all of us to the "human" side of ourselves --- almost all emotions are universal and can cross race, religion, age, and social status.

How can you add a "dash of emotion" to your communication?

Focus on positive emotions as benefits. If you want to bring a person to your side, tell them how good the proposal will make them feel. For example: if you want to convince your spouse to take you on that dream vacation, describe how relaxing a day you'll have. If he can picture it in his mind, then you've succeeded.

Focus on a negative emotion, and then add a call to action. Negative emotions are powerful in influencing behavior because they bring about a sense of dissonance in a person. All people want to feel good, which is why anger, sadness, shock, or indignation doesn't sit well with most. An example of using a negative emotion to bring people to your side is describing the horror of an accident in order to convince people to wear their seat belts.

Show that it's personal. Instead of focusing on the other person's emotions, you can focus on communicating your own. An effective way to persuade others is to show that your conviction is borne of a personal experience, and that you are emotionally attached to an idea. For example, showing your excitement verbally and non-verbally while explaining an ideal can show that you really believe in what you are pitching.

To be able to communicate emotion in your communication, you must use one of the influencing skills discussed earlier: seeing the other side. If you know how the other person looks at the situation, you will know what emotions will appeal to them.

Emotions can be communicated through body language (e.g. raising a fist to show that you are angry), variations in voice pitch, intonation and emphasis, directly saying what you feel or what you want the other person to feel, and painting a picture of situations where an emotional response is expected.

And don't forget: to use emotions effectively, use the appropriate amount. Less can be more, so don't overdo it!

Plenty of Facts

While emotions are a powerful influence to people's behavior, we all know that people are not just a bundle of emotions. Some situations require an appeal to the mind instead of the heart. An effective communication must make sense. More so, it must have basis in facts.

Facts create persuasive arguments because there is no way to dispute facts. If something is true, real, or verified by research, it has to be accepted. More so, presenting facts in communication show the extent that you have studied a subject, which in turn shows that you are serious in what you are saying.

There are two skills that can help in the use of facts during communication.

The first skill is the ability to separate fact from opinion. Facts are objective data, and can be verified by credible procedures such as empirical research or expert opinion. It is considered true on the basis of actual evidence. An opinion, however, is a subjective statement that may be based on personal interpretation.

The second skill is the ability to create logical arguments from facts. Facts can't be disputed, but you also have to use them properly in order to give them impact. Arguments from facts have to follow the rules of deductive or inductive reasoning. For example, from the research finding that watching TV increases attention deficiency among toddlers, "we should reduce TV time for toddlers" is a more valid conclusion than "attention deficiency doesn't exist in adults."

The following is an example of a communication that uses facts *"I believe I deserve this promotion because I was able to increase the department's productivity by 12% since I held office last year."*

Bringing It All Together

For best results, use both emotion and facts to influence people. After all, people use both their heart and mind in their daily lives, and addressing both is a more holistic approach to take.

The key is in being consistent, so that there isn't a dissonance between the emotional and the rational side of your communication. Done correctly, appeals to emotion can balance the coldness of reason, and facts can temper strong emotions.

Here is an example of a communication that has emotions and facts together:

"You should get that wedding dress! It makes you look like a princess --- think of how well it will flow when you walk down the aisle, the lights behind you. Plus, it's on sale --- 30% off. It fits your budget perfectly, leaving you with some extra cash to spend on accessories."

Sharing Your Opinion

In any social situation, you are expected to contribute. Sharing opinions is a way to present your personality to the world, and a way to create the image that you want to project. It is also an invitation for the other person to share their opinion, setting the stage for an engaging discussion or debate. In this module, we will discuss the skills you can use in sharing your opinion. Particularly, we will discuss how to use I-messages, disagree constructively, and build consensus.

Using I-Messages

An I-message is a message that is focused on the speaker. When you use I-messages, you take responsibility for your own feelings instead of accusing the other person of making you feel a certain way. The opposite of an I-message is a You-message.

An I-message is composed of the following:

A description of the problem or issue.

Describe the person's behavior you are reacting to in an objective, non-blameful, and non-judgmental manner.

"When ... "

Describe the concrete or tangible effects of that behavior.

"The effects are ... "

A suggestion for alternative behavior.

"I'd prefer ... "

Here is an example of an I-message:

"When I have to wait outside the office an extra hour because you didn't inform me that you'd be late (problem/issue), I become agitated (effect). I prefer for you to send me a message if you will not be able to make it (alternative behavior)."

The most important feature of I-messages is that they are neutral. There is no effort to threaten, argue, or blame in these statements. You avoid making the other person defensive, as the essence of an I-message is "I have a problem" instead of "You have a problem". The speaker simply makes statements and takes full responsibility for his/her feelings.

Disagreeing Constructively

There is nothing wrong with disagreement. No two people are completely similar therefore it's inevitable that they would disagree on at least one issue. There's also nothing wrong in having a position and defending it.

To make the most of a disagreement, you have to keep it constructive. The following are some of the elements of a constructive disagreement:

- **Solution-focus.** The disagreement aims to find a workable compromise at the end of the discussion.

- **Mutual Respect.** Even if the two parties do not agree with one another, courtesy is always a priority.

- **Win-Win Solution.** Constructive disagreement is not geared towards getting the "one-up" on the other person. The premium is always on finding a solution that has benefits for both parties.

- **Reasonable Concessions.** More often than not, a win-win solution means you won't get your way completely. Some degree of sacrifice is necessary to meet the other person halfway. In constructive disagreement, parties are open to making reasonable concessions for the negotiation to move forward.

- **Learning-Focused.** Parties in constructive disagreement see conflicts as opportunities to get feedback on how well a system works, so that necessary changes can be made. They also see it as a challenge to be flexible and creative in coming up with solutions for everyone's gain.

Building Consensus

Consensus means unanimous agreement on an area of contention. Arriving at a consensus is the ideal resolution of bargaining. If both parties can find a solution that is agreeable to both of them, then anger can be prevented or reduced.

The following are some tips on how to arrive at a consensus:

- **Focus on interests rather than positions.** Surface the underlying value that makes people take the position they do. For example, the interest behind a request for a salary increase may be financial security. If you can communicate to the other party that you acknowledge this need, and will only offer a position that takes financial security into consideration, then a consensus is more likely to happen.

- **Explore options together.** Consensus is more likely if both parties are actively involved in the solution-making process. This ensures that there is increased communication about each party's positions. It also ensures that resistances are addressed.

- **Increase sameness and reduce differentiation.** A consensus is more likely if you can emphasize all the things that you and the other party have in common, and minimize all the things that make you different. An increased empathy can make finding common interests easier. It may also reduce psychological barriers to compromising. An example of increasing sameness and reducing differences is an employer and employee temporarily setting aside their position disparity and looking at the problem as two stakeholders in the same organization.

Negotiation Basics

We can do our best to persuade others to our side --- but what if the other party is as assertive? Then it's time for some bargaining! In this module we will discuss some basic negotiating skills that can help you in both getting the best deal for yourself, and engaging the other person into an amicable discussion. We will discuss negotiation in its four stages: preparation, opening, bargaining, and closing.

Preparation

Half the battle of negotiations is won during the preparation stage. Think of it as similar to strategizing before a war. You have to know ahead of time what the other side's strengths and weaknesses are, as well as your own. This will provide you with the knowledge on which approach to use.

The following are some tips in preparing for a negotiation:

Research what is standard for the area. To make sure that you don't get shortchanged, know the going rate for what you are offering or buying. For example, know what the standard salary is for a person with your background in a particular industry before going to a salary negotiation.

This advice may seem basic, but you'd be surprised at how many people actually forget to look in their backyards before a negotiation. Look for the strengths of your position and capitalize on them. Similarly, identify your weaknesses so that you can anticipate possible attacks.

Know your boundaries. This advice is related to the first one. As you study your interests and position, it is important to reflect ahead of time how much you are willing to concede, and what's non-negotiable for you. Having your boundaries clear in your mind will prevent you from making agreements that you'd regret later.

It will also help you make the right amount of allowances for bargaining. Note though: don't dismiss the possibility that you might change your boundaries in the middle of the negotiation proper.

Step into their shoes. You know what's the best way to prepare a bargaining stance? Pretend to be the other party. Ask yourself: if you were the other side, what do you want to see or hear in order to give in?

If you can do extensive research about the players of the other party, as well as their position, better. Are you going to be dealing with people who are known to be difficult? Well, what makes them difficult? Do they have strong feelings about you? You can use information like these to help you plan your strategy.

Identify areas of bargaining. Now that you have studied your position, as well as the other side's position, it's now time to identify the common ground you can work on. A way to do this is to look for mutual interests. If you can emphasize that a move stands to benefit both parties in a satisfactory way, then you are more likely to get an agreement.

Prepare yourself mentally, emotionally and physically. Negotiations can be a taxing endeavor. You need to be alert; in control and unemotional (but not emotionless) while you negotiate, so make sure you're in the right condition. In some cases, a lot of games and posturing will take place. So before going to the bargaining table, meditate, aim for a clear head, and get a good night's sleep.

Set up the time and venue for the negotiations. A significant element of negotiations is context. You have to make sure that the negotiation will be at a place and time when all parties feel at ease, as uncomfortable people are less likely to make concessions. This means you have to check even the tiny details of room temperature and space before you start a negotiation.

Moreover, you have to ensure that the seating arrangement is conducive to a friendly discussion. Two parties seating themselves from across each other may seem confrontational. Sitting too far away each other can send the message that you're not interested in finding common ground. Using dissimilar chairs can communicate a power play.

Opening

The way that you open a negotiation can set the tone for the whole bargaining session. It is important then that you pay attention to how you or the other party opens the negotiation.

The following are tips and techniques on opening a negotiation:

Express respect for the other party, and openness to the negotiation process. Negotiations have traditionally been perceived as a combative endeavor, but this need not be the case. In fact, simple courtesy can break the ice between two negotiating parties, and promote a reasonable discussion. So invest in pleasantries and small talk. Smile. At the end of the day, you are both just people with interests to pursue, and you can accomplish this without having to put anyone down.

Ask for more or higher than what you really want. Always assume that the other party will want to haggle with you, so ask for something greater than what you would be willing to accept. The excess is your bargaining allowance. Remember too, that the other party might just be willing to give you more than what you think you deserve, so there's nothing wrong with starting immodestly.

Don't accept the first offer. Keep in mind: the other party would expect you to haggle too! Chances are, you'd receive an initial offer lower than what a person or company is willing to give --- so invest in time convincing them you're worthy of more.

Put your strengths on the table. Here's a cardinal rule in negotiation: always negotiate from a position of strength. Don't beg or defend your weak points. Instead, illustrate from the onset the best about what you have to offer, and send the message that you're worth your asking

Bargaining

The heart of a negotiation process is the actual bargaining. There are times when bargaining is easy, especially if the meeting point of two positions does not require much sacrifice from either party. But there are also occasions when bargaining can be quite tedious. Negotiators can hold on to their stances stubbornly, either because they really don't think they can afford a concession, or they want you to be the one to yield.

The following are some tips to bargain more effectively:

Listen. Beginner negotiators are often more focused on what they want to say that they forget an important element of the process: listening. Take time to carefully listen to what the other party is saying to you; they can give you clues as to what is of value to them, and what counter-offer can make them give in. Similarly, note their non-verbal behavior to get clues regarding your pacing and demeanor.

Concede to get concessions. In the previous section, we discussed about the skill of "giving in without giving up." You can use this skill too during negotiations. Your concessions can be a way to sweeten the pot, or communicate to the other party that you also have their best interests at heart. For example: you can concede to lower the price of the goods you're selling, if they agree to buy a higher volume.

Anchor your position on objective data. This tip is related to the skill of using facts to bring people to your side. If you want to strengthen your bargaining position, make references to objective standards. For example, stating that you are offering a lower amount than the standard retail price of a good or service can strengthen your bargaining position.

Present options. Everyone likes to have a choice; it's empowering and keeps a person from feeling trapped. If you can afford it, create packages that the other party can choose from. You can win more if you have a "there's something for everyone approach."

Mind your phrasing. If you want something, make sure that it's phrased in such a way that is positive, and a benefit to the other party. For example, don't say that you want a higher salary because you have a graduate degree. Instead, say that your graduate degree can contribute positively to their bottom line. If you can show how your position furthers the other party's interest, then negotiations can proceed much more smoothly.

Closing

How you close a negotiation is as important as how you open one. You want to make sure that you leave the bargaining table with a satisfactory agreement for both sides. You also want to ensure that you end positively. After all, a settled deal means the possible start of a new relationship.

The following are some tips in closing the deal:

Be sensitive to signals that it's time to close. Always be sensitive to changes in the dynamics of the discussion, so that you will have fair warning that it's time to close. For example, the lessening of objections and counter arguments from the other party can be a sign that they have all the information that they need to make a decision. Similarly, requesting for a contract is an often signal that a decision has been made; all that's needed is to formalize it.

Here is some advice to consider before making a final offer. Haggling back and forth can take a while, but if you took the advice on setting boundaries before a negotiation, you'd know when you've reached your boundaries. If you sense that you are at that point of giving your final offer, and the other party seems to be as well, then issue a gentle but firm warning. For example, you can directly say "this is my final offer" or "I think I've reached a decision." The advice is a signal to the other party to give their final offer as well.

Increase the pressure. If the other party still seems hesitant, and you are ready to close the deal, then perhaps it's time to put pressure on them. Common ways to do this is to give a deadline to the offer ("This offer will expire by 2PM."), or showing that you have other options to consider ("I also have a proposal from XYZ company.")

Summarize. Another way to close a negotiation is to present a summary of what has been achieved so far, highlighting both the issues that have been resolved as well as what actions are expected of the participants so far. For instance you can say "we seem to agree on so-and-so details of the deal; we look forward to signing the contract tomorrow."

> A summary is a positive way of ending a negotiation because it makes everyone feel that the time was well-spent. This is true even if the negotiation did not result in a mutually-agreed upon resolution. By emphasizing the idea that you moved forward despite lingering issues, you set the stage for further discussions.

Seal the commitment. Follow the ceremony that indicates a deal is formalized. Often this means signing the contract. In more informal settings, this can be a handshake. While they may seem like meaningless rituals, they are a sign of commitment to what has been agreed upon, and must be embraced warmly.

Thank. Lastly, end your negotiation with gratitude. Aside from observing the ethics of relationships, it shows your appreciation for the other party's time and consideration.

Making an Impact

Some people stand out, while others fade into the background. But if you want to make the most of interpersonal relationships, you have to be able to leave a lingering positive impression on the people that you meet. People's first impressions of you are what dictate if they want to get to know you any further. You want to make sure, then, that you create an impact on people.

Creating a Powerful First Impression

You've probably heard this saying before: *you don't get a second chance to make a first impression.*

In today's fast-paced world, you have to maximize the time and opportunities you get with the people that you meet. If you managed to secure a conference with a client or potential partner, for example, make sure that you don't leave anything to chance for that meeting. And that goes with the impression that you want to leave behind.

The following are some tips in creating a powerful first impression:

Dress to impress. Beauty is within, but this doesn't mean that people don't make conclusions about you based on your appearance. If you want to create a great first impression make sure that you look your best. Whenever you're presenting yourself to other people, be clean, well-groomed and dressed in clothes that fit and within the prescribed dress code

Be positive. Nobody likes to talk to cranky, irritable, and pessimistic people! Instead, people are drawn to those who smile a lot and radiate a pleasant disposition. If you want to be remembered, make them feel welcomed and appreciated. A positive experience is as easy to remember as a negative one!

Communicate your confidence. Powerful first impressions are those that show you are self-assured, competent, and purposive. Always establish eye contact with the people you are talking to. Shake hands firmly. Speak in a deliberate and purposive way.

Be yourself! Meeting people for the first time can be extremely anxiety-provoking, but do your best to act naturally. People are more responsive to those who don't come across as if they're putting on a front or are very controlled. Let your personality engage the other person.

Go for the extra mile. Do more than the usual that can make you stand out from the rest. For example, if you're going for a job interview, show that you studied the company very well and know their mission and vision. If others can see that you appreciation a social situation, they are more likely to remember you positively.

Assessing a Situation

All interpersonal skills involve sensitivity to what is going on around, especially what is happening with the people you are interacting with. After all, context variables, such as timing and location, can change the meaning of a communication. You want to make sure that you are not just saying the right thing, but you are saying the right thing at the right moment.

If you want to make an impact, you have to factor in the situation.

The following are some tips in assessing the situation:

Listen, not just to what is being said, but also to what is NOT being said. An excellent interpersonal skill to master is a keen observing eye. You have to be able to note the body language of the people around you in order for you to be able to respond appropriately. For example, there is body language that says *"go on, we like what you're saying."* There is also body language that says *"I don't want to hear that right now."*

Identify needs. A second way to assess the situation is to ask yourself: what does this social occasion need right now? A newly formed group, for example, likely has members who still don't know one another. The need then is for someone to help break the ice. A group that is tired from a long working day probably needs an opportunity to relax and unwind. Knowing these needs can help you respond to them more appropriately.

Practice etiquette. Etiquette may seem like a useless bunch of rules to some people but they serve a purpose: they tell you what are generally considered as acceptable and unacceptable for certain situations. It helps then that you know basic etiquette rules so that you don't make a faux pas that can ruin the great first impression that you made.

Being Zealous without Being Offensive

Enthusiasm, diligence, and persistence are all great virtues to have, especially if you're in the business of creating social networks. However, you have to be careful that your persevering doesn't cross the line to pestering --- or worse harassing the person.

The following are some tips in being zealous without being offensive:

Focus on what is important to the other person. Being "other-centered" is the best way to monitor your own eagerness to make contact with other people. Before you do something, make that habit of asking yourself: does this action address the need of the other person, or is it merely addressing my need?

Respect boundaries. Everyone has personal boundaries, and it would do us well to respect them. Not seeing clients without an appointment is an example of a boundary. The same goes for not accepting calls during the weekend or past regular office hours. Work within these boundaries, and you'll be able to communicate your courtesy. And if you don't know what a person's boundaries are, you have nothing to lose in asking!

Make requests, not demands. As mentioned previously, we can always do our best to persuade and influence other people, but we can't force them to do what they don't want to do. So always courteously ask for permission, and verify agreement. And if they say no ---- then accept the no as an answer, unless you have something new to offer.

Note non-verbal behavior. Similar to the tip in the previous section, always be guided by the other person's non-verbal response to you. If you find that they are already showing irritation --- example they speak in a gruff, annoyed tone when talking to you ---- then perhaps it's time to back off. But if they appear open to you --- they look at you with interest while you speak --- then it's advisable to go on.

Chapter 7 – Managing Anger

Anger can be an incredibly damaging force, costing people their jobs, personal relationships, and even their lives when it gets out of hand. However, since everyone experiences anger, it is important to have constructive approaches to manage it effectively.

Anger Management Review

Think of a situation where you experienced anger, preferably one that no longer affects you in the present time. Recall the exact symptoms you experienced, and the way you responded to the symptoms. The following guide questions can help during this process:

During your anger incident,

1. What symptoms did you experience

    A. Physically?

    B. Mentally?

    C. Emotionally?

    D. Behaviorally?

2. What was your response to your anger symptoms?

3. Was your response helpful? If yes, in what way was it helpful? If your response was not helpful, in what way was it unhelpful?

Understanding Anger

Before we discuss specific anger management strategies, it is helpful to first understand the nature of anger. While most are familiar with this emotion, not everyone is aware of its underlying dynamics. In this module, we will discuss the cycle of anger, the fight or flight response, and common myths about anger.

The Cycle of Anger

Anger is a natural emotion that usually stems from perceived threat or loss. It's a pervasive emotion; it affects our body, thoughts, feelings, and behavior. Anger is often described in terms of its intensity, frequency, duration, threshold, and expression.

Anger typically follows a predictable pattern: a cycle. Understanding the cycle of anger can help us understand our own anger reactions, and those of others. It can also help us in considering the most appropriate response.

Illustrated below are the five phases of the anger cycle: **trigger, escalation, crisis, recovery, and depression.**

Phase 1: The Trigger Phase
The trigger phase happens when we perceive a threat or loss, and our body prepares to respond. In this phase, there is a subtle change from an individual's normal/ adaptive state into his stressed state. Anger triggers differ from person to person, and can come from both the environment or from our thought processes.

Phase 2: The Escalation Phase

In the escalation phase, there is the progressive appearance of the anger response. In this phase, our body prepares for a crisis after perceiving the trigger. This preparation is mostly physical, and is manifested through symptoms like rapid breathing, increased heart rate, and raised blood pressure. Once the escalation phase is reached there is less chance of calming down, as this is the phase where the body prepares for fight or flight (to be discussed later).

Phase 3: The Crisis Phase
As previously mentioned, the escalation phase is progressive, and it is in the crisis phase that the anger reaction reaches its peak. In the crisis phase our body is on full alert, prepared to take action in response to the trigger. During this phase, logic and rationality may be limited, if not impaired because the anger instinct takes over. In extreme cases, the crisis phase means that a person may be a serious danger to himself or to other people.

Phase 4: The Recovery Phase
The recovery phase happens when the anger has been spent, or at least controlled, and there is now a steady return to a person's normal/ adaptive state. In this stage, reasoning and awareness of one's self returns. If the right intervention is applied, the return to normalcy progresses smoothly. However, an inappropriate intervention can re-ignite the anger and serve as a new trigger.

Phase 5: The Depression Phase
The depression phase marks a return to a person's normal/ adaptive ways. Physically, this stage marks below normal vital signs, such as heart rate, so that the body can recover equilibrium. A person's full use of his faculties return at this point, and the new awareness helps a person assess what just occurred. Consequently, this stage may be marked by embarrassment, guilt, regret, and or depression.

After the depression phase is a return to a normal or adaptive phase. A new trigger, however, can start the entire cycle all over again.

Below is an example of a person going through the five stages of the anger cycle.

Josephine came home from work to see dirty plates left in the sink (trigger phase). She started to wash them, but as she was doing so she kept thinking about how inconsiderate her children are for not cleaning after themselves. She was already tired from work and does not need the extra chore. She felt the heat in her neck and the tremble in her hands as she's washing the dishes (escalation phase).

Feeling like she can't keep it to herself any longer, she stormed up the room to confront her kids. In a raised voice, she asked them how difficult could it be to wash the dishes. She told them that they are getting punished for their lack of responsibility (crisis phase).

Having gotten the words out, she felt calmer, and her heartbeat slowly returned to normal. She saw that her kids are busy with homework when she had interrupted them. She was also better able to hear their reasoning, as they apologized (recovery phase).

Josephine regretted yelling at her children and told them that she's simply tired and it's not their fault (depression phase).

NOTE: How long each phase lasts differ from person to person. Some people also skip certain phases, or else they go through them privately and/ or unconsciously.

Understanding Fight or Flight

The Fight or Flight theory, formulated by Walter Cannon, describes how people react to perceived threat. Basically, when faced with something that can harm us, we either aggress (fight) or withdraw (flight). It is believed that this reaction is an ingrained instinct geared towards survival.

The fight or flight instinct is manifested in bodily ways. When faced with a threat, our body releases the hormones adrenaline, noradrenaline, and cortisol. These chemicals are designed to take us to a state of alertness and action. They result in increased energy, heart rate, slowed digestion, and above normal strength.

Understanding the fight or flight instinct can help us understand the dynamics of our anger response. The following are some of the implications of the fight and flight theory on anger management:

First, the theory underscores how anger is but a natural response. There is no morality to anger. Anger is a result of perceived harm to self, whether physical or emotional.

Second, this theory reminds us of the need to stay in control. When we are angry, our rational self gets overridden by a basic survival instinct. There's a need to act immediately. This instinct can then result in aggressiveness, over-reactivity, and hyper-vigilance, which are all contrary to rational and deliberate response. Conscious effort towards self-awareness and control is needed so that this instinct does not overpower us.

Common Myths about Anger

Here are five common myths about anger:

Myth 1: Anger is a bad emotion.

There is no such thing as a good or bad emotion; they are instinctual reactions and we don't make conscious decisions for them to come. In fact, some anger reactions are appropriate, such as the anger against discrimination, injustice, and abuse. What can be judged as positive or negative/ healthy or unhealthy is how we react to anger.

Myth 2: Anger needs to be 'unleashed' for it to go away.

It's true that anger needs to be expressed in order for symptoms to be relieved. However, expressing anger in verbally or physically aggressive ways are not the only way to 'unleash' anger. Nor is anger an excuse for a person to be aggressive. The expression of anger can be tempered by rationality and forethought.

Note that venting anger does not necessarily results into the anger disappearing, although venting can relieve the symptoms. At times, processing personal experiences, seeing concrete change and genuine forgiveness are needed for anger to go away.

Myth 3: Ignoring anger will make it go away.

Generally, all kinds of emotions do not disappear when ignored. The anger just gets temporarily shelved, and will likely find other ways of getting expressed. It can get projected to another person, transformed into a physical symptom, or built up for a bigger future blow up. Some of our behaviors may even be unconscious ways of expressing anger.

While there are situations when it's inadvisable to express your anger immediately, the very least you can do is acknowledge that it exists.

Myth 4: You can't control your anger.

This myth is related to the second one. As discussed earlier, the fight and flight instinct can make anger an overwhelming emotion. However, this instinct does not mean that you're but a slave to your impulses. Awareness of anger dynamics and a conscious effort to rise above your anger can help you regain control of your reactions.

Myth 5: If I don't get angry, people will think I am a pushover.

It's true that a person can lose credibility is he makes rules and then ignores violations. However, anger is not the only way a person can show that there are consequences to violations. In fact, the most effective way of instilling discipline in others is to have a calm, non-emotional approach to dealing with rule-breakers. Calm and rationality can communicate strength too.

Do's and Don'ts

Now that we've established that anger is a natural, unavoidable, and instinctual reaction, let's look at how we can respond to anger appropriately. In this module, we will discuss the dos and don'ts in responding to anger.

Unhelpful Ways of Dealing with Anger

The following are unhelpful ways of dealing with anger:

DON'T ignore the anger.
Some people respond to anger by not admitting, even to themselves, that they are angry. Defense mechanisms often used to ignore anger include laughing an issue off, distracting one's self from the problem, and trivializing the trigger's impact.

DON'T keep the anger inside.
There are people who do recognize that they're angry. However, they choose to obsess about their anger in silence rather than express it. They can bear grudges for a long time. People like this, also called 'stuffers', are more likely to develop hypertension compared to others. They are also likely to just 'explode' one day, once the anger has built to the point that they can't keep it inside anymore.

DON'T get aggressive.
The right to vent your anger doesn't extend to doing it in ways that can hurt others, hurt yourself, and damage property. Aggression can be verbal or physical.

DON'T get passive-aggressive.
Passive-aggressiveness refers to indirect and underhanded means to get back at the person who made you angry. Examples of passive-aggressive behaviors are gossiping, tardiness and backbiting.

DON'T use non-constructive communication styles.
Avoid the use of indirect attacks and unproductive statements. These include blaming, labeling, preaching, moralizing, ordering, warning, interrogating, ridiculing and lecturing.

Helpful Ways of Dealing with Anger

The following are helpful ways in dealing with anger:

DO acknowledge that you are angry.

It is important that you know how to recognize that you are angry, and give yourself permission to feel it. This can be as simple as saying to yourself "I am angry." Remember, you can't control something you don't admit exists!

DO calm yourself before you say anything.
In the previous discussions, we saw how there is a biological reason why anger can feel overwhelming --- our body is engaged in a fight or flight response. It helps then to defer any reactions until you have reached the return to normal/ adaptive phase of the anger cycle. Otherwise, you might end up saying or oing something that you'd later regret. Count 1 to 10!

DO speak up, when something is important to you.
This is the opposite to 'keeping it all in.' If a matter is important to you, so much so that keeping silent would just result in physical and mental symptoms, then let it out. If it's not possible to speak to the person concerned, at least look for a trusted friend or a mental health professional.

DO explain how you're feeling in a manner that shows ownership and responsibility for your anger.
Take ownership and responsibility for your feelings. This makes the anger within your control (you can't control other people). One way to take ownership and responsibility for your anger is through the use of I-messages, which would be discussed in a later module.

Gaining Control

Anger is instinctual, yes. It is an emotion that comes unbidden and we often don't have a choice whether we would be angry or not. What we can do however, is take control of our anger when it comes. In this module, we will discuss ways to gain control over our anger. Specifically we will discuss recognizing warning signs, coping thoughts, relaxation techniques and ways to blow off steam.

A Word of Warning

The first step in gaining control of anger is to recognize its warning signs. You have to be aware of symptoms that your anger is about to build up, so that you can catch yourself early and make the necessary intervention. This process involves taking yourself from the 'moment' and observing your own reactions from a third person point of view.

Warning signs of anger exists in a range. Some are very obvious; others very subtle. They differ from person to person.

Signs of anger can be physical, mental, emotional, and behavioral.

Physical signs of anger include:
- rapid heart rate
- difficulty breathing
- headache
- stomachache
- sweating
- feeling hot in the face and neck
- shaking

Mental signs of anger include:
- difficulty concentrating
- obsessing on the situation

- thinking vengeful thoughts
- cynicism

Emotional signs of anger include:
- sadness
- irritability
- guilt
- resentment
- feeling like you need to hurt someone
- needing to be alone
- needing to isolate one's self
- numbness

Behavioral signs of anger include:
- clenching of fist
- pounding of fist on a wall/ table or any surface
- pacing
- raising one's voice
- any act of aggression/ passive-aggression

Using Coping Thoughts

Once you realize that you are angry, or that you're about to get angry, you can start calming yourself mentally. The following are just a few mental scripts you can use to keep your anger under control.

1. Calm down first, and think this through.

2. This may not be as bad as it seems.

3. This is just one incident --- it doesn't define my life.

4. I am capable of managing this situation.

5. It's alright to be upset. / I have the right to be upset in this situation. / I am angry.

6. What needs to be done immediately? (damage control/ solution-focused mode).

7. Bad things/ Mistakes do happen/ Nothings says that things will go right all the time.

8. There is no need to feel threatened here.

9. I have no control over other people and their feelings. But I have control over myself.

10. I have managed anger successfully before and I will again.

Using Relaxation Techniques

Another way to help you control your anger is to intentionally induce yourself to a state of calm. This can help especially in addressing the physical symptoms of anger.

Relaxation techniques that you can do include:

Breathing Exercises

Deliberately controlling your breathing can help a person calm down. Ways to do this include: breathing through one's nose and exhaling through one's mouth, breathing from one's diagram, and breathing rhythmically.

Meditation

Meditation is a way of exercising mental discipline. Most meditation techniques involve increasing self-awareness, monitoring thoughts, and focusing. Meditation techniques include prayer, the repetition of a mantra, and relaxing movement or postures.

Progressive Muscle Relaxation (PMR)

PMR is a technique of stress management that involves mentally inducing your muscles to tense and relax. PMR usually focuses on areas of the body where tension is commonly felt, such as the head, shoulders, and chest area. It's a way to exercise the power of the mind over the body.

Visualization

Visualization is the use of mental imagery to induce relaxation. Some visualization exercise involves picturing a place of serenity and comfort, such as a beach or a garden. Other visualization exercises involve imagining the release of anger in a metaphorical form. An example of this latter kind of visualization is imagining one's anger as a ball to be released to space.

Music

Some people find listening to music as very relaxing. The kind of music that's calming differs from person to person; traditional relaxation music includes classical pieces, acoustic sounds, and even ambient noises.

Art and Crafts

There are people who find working with their hands as a good way to relax. This is especially true for people who feel their tensions in their hands. Drawing pictures, paper construction and sculpting are just some of the ways to de-stress when faced with an anger trigger. Arts and crafts are helpful because it keeps a person from obsessing on the anger while he or she is still in the recovery phase of the anger cycle.

Blowing Off Some Steam

Another way of controlling your anger is by getting the anger energy out--- blowing off steam. These techniques are especially helpful when you are in the crisis phase of the anger cycle.

The following are some constructive ways of blowing off steam:

Screaming

If the place would allow it, screaming can help release the tensions and frustrations that come with anger. Think of the thing that angers you the most, build momentum, and let it out in one big shout. You may also scream out the words you wish you could say if the venue is appropriate; the louder the scream, the better.

Physical Activity

Many people find exercise, sports, dancing and even just pacing about, as effective ways to vent anger. This makes sense; if the fight and flight response gears a person for physical action, then physical action might indeed be the best way to deal with the anger. Physical activity is also believed to release endorphins, our natural mood regulators.

Pillow Punching

The need to fight back may be channeled through punching pillows. Pillows provide a safe way to release tensions; it's safe not just for the object of the anger but also for one's self. Related techniques include wringing out towels and breaking old plates.

Writing

If physical activities are not your thing, you can blow off steam by expressing your thoughts and feelings in writing. You can write in an unstructured way, simply putting on paper the first thing that comes to your mind. You can also be more creative about it, and channel your anger through poetry or song.

Singing

Here's a new one: vent your anger by going to your nearest videoke or karaoke bar. Many people find singing therapeutic, especially if the song lyrics and melody matches one's mood.

Separate the People from the Problem

Anger is not just personal. It can be relational as well. When managing anger that involves other people, it helps to have a problem-oriented disposition, setting personal matters aside. This way the issue becomes an objective and workable issue.

In this module, we will discuss ways to separate people from the problem. Specifically, we will discuss the difference between objective and subjective language, ways to identify the problem, and how to use I-messages.

Objective vs. Subjective Language

One way to make sure that a discussion remains constructive is to use objective rather than subjective language.

Objective language involves stating your position using reference points that are observable, factual, and free from personal prejudices. Objective references do not change from person to person.

This is the opposite of subjective language, which is vague, biased, and or emotional. You are using subjective language when you are stating an opinion, assumption, belief, judgment, or rumor.

The use of objective language keeps the discussion on neutral ground. It's less threatening to a person's self-esteem and therefore keeps people from being in the defensive. More importantly, objective language can be disputed and confirmed, which ensures that the discussion can go towards a solution.

Here are some guidelines in the use of objective vs. subjective language:

1. State behaviors instead of personality traits.

    Subjective: You're an *inconsiderate* supervisor.

    Objective: You approved the rule without consulting with us first.

2. Avoid vague references to frequency. Instead, use the actual numbers.

    Subjective: You are *always* late!

    Objective: You were late for meetings four times in the past month.

3. Clarify terms that can mean differently to different people.

Subjective: You practice *favoritism* when you give promotions.

Objective: The employee ranking system is not being followed during promotions.

4. Don't presume another person's thoughts, feelings, and intentions.

Subjective: You hate me!

Objective: You do not talk to me when we are in a room together.

5. Don't presume an action you did not see or hear.

Subjective: She stole my wallet.

Objective: The wallet was in my desk when I left. It was no longer there when I came back, and she was the only person who entered the room.

Identifying the Problem

You can't separate people from the problem if you don't know what the problem is. A good way to move forward, in a discussion where anger is escalating, is through identifying the problem.

Identifying the problem focuses all energy on the crisis at hand rather than the persons involved in a conflict. The two parties focus their energies on a common enemy that is outside of themselves, a move that puts the two opposing parties back in neutral ground.

There are many processes you can use to identify the problem. Here is one of them:

STEP ONE: Get as much information as you can why the other party is upset.

STEP TWO: Surface the other person's position. Reframe this position into a problem statement. Example: *"I can hear how upset you are. Am I right in perceiving that the problem for you is that you weren't informed of the account being sold?"*

STEP THREE: Review your own position. State your position in a problem statement as well. Example: *"The problem for me is that I don't have the resources to contact you. The phone lines are not working because of the storm."*

STEP FOUR: Having heard both positions, define the problem in a mutually acceptable way. Example: *"I hear that you'd like to be informed of any sales. On my part, I'd like to inform you, but for as long as the phone lines are dead, I can't see how I would do it. I think the issue here is about finding an alternative way to get the information to you on time while the phones are being repaired. Do you agree?"*

If the two parties agree to the problem statement, they can now both work at the surfaced problem and take the focus away from their emotions.

Using "I" Messages

An "I-message" is a message that is focused on the speaker. When you use I-messages, you take responsibility for your own feelings instead of accusing the other person of making you feel a certain way. The opposite of an I-message is a You-message.

An "I-message" is composed of the following:

A description of the problem or issue.

Describe the person's behavior you are reacting to in an objective, non-blameful, and non-judgmental manner.

"When ... "

Its effect on you or the organization.

Describe the concrete or tangible effects of that behavior.

"The effects are ... "

A suggestion for alternative behavior.

"I'd prefer ... "

Here is an example of an I-message:

"When I have to wait outside the office an extra hour because you didn't inform me that you'd be late (problem/issue), I become agitated (effect). I prefer for you to send me a message if you will not be able to make it (alternative behavior)."

The most important feature of I-messages is that they are neutral. There is no effort to threaten, argue, or blame in these statements. You avoid making the other person defensive, as the essence of an I-message is "I have a problem" instead of "You have a problem". The speaker simply makes statements and takes full responsibility for his/her feelings.

Working on the Problem

The escalation of anger in 'hot' situations can be easily prevented, if a system for discussing contentious issues is in place. In this module, we will discuss how to work effectively on the problem. Specifically, we will tackle constructive disagreement, negotiation tips, building a consensus and identifying solutions.

Using Constructive Disagreement

There is nothing wrong with disagreement. No two people are completely similar therefore it's inevitable that they would disagree on at least one issue. There's also nothing wrong in having a position and defending it.

To make the most of a disagreement, you have to keep it constructive. The following are some of the elements of a constructive disagreement:

- **Solution-focus.** The disagreement aims to find a workable compromise at the end of the discussion.

- **Mutual Respect.** Even if the two parties do not agree with one another, courtesy is always a priority.

- **Win-Win Solution.** Constructive disagreement is not geared towards getting the "one-up" on the other person. The premium is always on finding a solution that has benefits for both parties.

- **Reasonable Concessions.** More often than not, a win-win solution means you won't get your way completely. Some degree of sacrifice is necessary to meet the other person halfway. In constructive disagreement, parties are open to making reasonable concessions for the negotiation to move forward.

- **Learning-Focus.** Parties in constructive disagreement see conflicts as opportunities to get feedback on how well a system works, so that necessary changes can be made. They also see it as a challenge to be flexible and creative in coming up with solutions for everyone's gain.

Negotiation Tips

Negotiations are sometimes a necessary part of arriving at a solution. When two parties are in a disagreement, there has to be a process that would surfaces areas of bargaining. When a person is given the opportunity to present his side and argue for his or her interests, anger is less likely to escalate.

The following are some tips on negotiation during a conflict:

Note situational factors that can influence the negotiation process.
Context is an important element in the negotiation process. The location of the meeting, the physical arrangement of room, as well as the time the meeting is held can positively or negatively influence the participants' ability to listen and discern. For example, negotiations held in a noisy auditorium immediately after a stressful day can make participants irritable and less likely to compromise.

Prepare!
Before entering a negotiating table, make your research. Stack up on facts to back up your position, and anticipate the other party's position. Having the right information can make the negotiation process run faster and more efficiently.

Communicate clearly and effectively.
Make sure that you state your needs and interests in a way that is not open to misinterpretation. Speak in a calm and controlled manner. Present arguments without personalization. Remember, your position can only be appreciated if it's perceived accurately.

Focus on the process as well as the content.
It's important that you pay attention not just to the words you and the other party are saying, but also the manner the discussion is running. For example, was everyone able to speak their position adequately, or is there an individual who dominates the conversation? Are there implicit or explicit coercions happening? Does the other person's non-verbal behavior show openness and objectivity? All these things influence result, and you want to make sure that you have the most productive negotiation process that you can.

Keep an open-mind.
Lastly, enter a negotiation situation with an open mind. Be willing to listen and carefully consider what the other person has to say. Anticipate the possibility that you may have to change your beliefs and assumptions. Make concessions.

Building Consensus

Consensus means unanimous agreement on an area of contention. Arriving at a consensus is the ideal resolution of bargaining. If both parties can find a solution that is agreeable to both of them, then anger can be prevented or reduced.

The following are some tips on how to arrive at a consensus:

Focus on interests rather than positions.
Surface the underlying value that makes people take the position they do. For example, the interest behind a request for a salary increase may be financial security. If you can communicate to the other party that you

acknowledge this need, and will only offer a position that takes financial security into consideration, then a consensus is more likely to happen.

Explore options together.
Consensus is more likely if both parties are actively involved in the solution-making process. This ensures that there is increased communication about each party's positions. It also ensures that resistances are addressed.

Increase sameness / reduce differentiation.
A consensus is more likely if you can emphasize all the things that you and the other party have in common, and minimize all the things that make you different. An increased empathy can make finding common interests easier. It may also reduce psychological barriers to compromising. An example of increasing sameness/ reducing differences is an employer and employee temporarily setting aside their position disparity and looking at the problem as two stakeholders in the same organization.

Identifying Solutions

Working on a problem involves the process of coming up with possible solutions. The following are some ways two parties in disagreement can identify solutions to their problem.

- **Brainstorm.** Brainstorming is the process of coming up with as many ideas as you can in the shortest time possible. It makes use of diversity of personalities in a group, so that one can come up with the widest range of fresh ideas. Quantity of ideas is more important than quality of ideas in the initial stage of brainstorming; you can filter out the bad ones later on with an in-depth review of their pros and cons.

- **Hypothesize.** Hypothesizing means coming up with 'what if' scenarios based on intelligent guesses. A solution can be made from imagining alternative set-ups, and studying these alternative set-ups against facts and known data.

- **Adopt a Model.** You may also look for a solution in the past. If a solution has worked before, perhaps it may work again. Find similar problems and study how it was handled. You don't have to follow a model to the letter; you are always free to tweak it to fit the nuances of the current problem.

- **Invent Options.** If there has been no precedence for a problem, it's time to exercise one's creativity and think of new options. A way to go about this is to list down each party's interests and come up proposed solutions that have benefits for each party.

- **Survey**. If the two parties can't come up with a solution between the two of them, maybe it's time to seek other people's point of view. Survey people with interest or background in the issue in contention. Find an expert is possible. Just remember though, at the end of the day the decision is still yours. Identify a solution based on facts, not on someone's opinion.

Solving the Problem

After a constructive discussion of the problem, as well as review of available options, it's now time to go about solving the problem. Solving a problem lessens its 'threat' aspect, making less an anger trigger. In this module, we will discuss elements of solving the problem. Particularly, we would discuss choosing a solution, making a plan, and getting it done.

Choosing a Solution

You've already identified possible solutions to a problem. The next thing to do is how to narrow the list down to the best.

The following are some criteria you can use when choosing solutions.

- **Costs and benefits.** An ideal solution is one that has the least costs and most benefits.

- **Disagreeing parties' interests**. An ideal solution has factored in the impact on all parties concerned and has made adjustments accordingly.

- **Foresight**. An ideal solution doesn't have just short-term gains bit long term ones as well.

Obstacles. An ideal solution has anticipated all possible obstacles in its implementation and has made plans accordingly.

VALUES. An ideal solution is one that is consistent with the mission-vision of the organization and/ or its individual members.

Making a Plan

You've already picked a solution for your problem. Now it's time to create a plan for its implementation.

The following are some guidelines when making a plan.

Keep your goal(s) central to you plan.
Every solution has a goal. The goal is the specific and measurable change that you want to achieve by implementing your solution. When you make a plan, make sure that all the steps and processes you outline are moving towards this goal.

Break down your action plan into concrete steps.
A good plan is concrete instead of abstract, specific instead of generic. Think of the different steps that you need to do in order to get to your ultimate goal and plan along those milestones. Note the deliverable per milestone. Indicate the timeline for each milestone. Identify the people responsible for each task.

Note all the resources you would need.
There are two kinds of resources: human and material. Make a list of all human and material resources that you need to execute the action, and make sure that they are all available. If they are not available, add an extra action plan to procure them. You want to make sure that your plan is realistic given your resources.

Plan how the solution would be evaluated.
A good plan doesn't just include the steps to execute the program. It should also include mechanisms for monitoring progress and evaluating results. An evaluation plan ensures that needs for plan revision can be surfaced.

Getting it Done

An issue in contention will remain a hot issue unless the plan is implemented. It is only when concrete change can be observed that anger can be seriously addressed.

The following are some tips in implementing a solution.

Stick to your plan.

Note the what, where, when and, who of your plan and follow it to the letter. This will keep your end of the bargain explicit and easy to monitor and evaluate. Deviating from the plan can result to additional anger, especially if you deviated in areas important to the other party.

Monitor progress and results.
Keep track of whether or not your solution is accomplishing the goal. Make sure that you put everything on paper for ready reference later. Log down best practices, risks and obstacles encountered.

Reward and revise accordingly.
If the solution is working, note progress and affirm the success. This gives the two parties a sense of accomplishment. More so, the next time they have a conflict, it can serve as testament to their ability to solve a problem.

If the solution is not working, gather feedback. Surface the reason why the solution does not seem to be working. Make the necessary changes so that you can revise the plan as needed.

A Personal Plan

Anger is deeply personal. Effective anger management should take into consideration individual anger dynamics and tailor-fit interventions to them. In this module we will discuss what hot buttons are, how to identify your personal hot buttons, and how you can be benefitted by keeping a personal anger log.

Understanding Hot Buttons

Hot buttons are triggers that make us react with anger. They are not necessarily the real cause of our anger, but they can be the one that 'lights the fuse'. Triggers vary in the intensity of the anger reaction they can evoke; some can evoke uncontrollable rage while others merely mild irritation.

Hot buttons can be things that fall short of your expectations, block your goals, attack your self-esteem, violate your values, and/ or give you a feeling of loss or helplessness. A hot button is usually one that elicits an intense reaction in a person, or the one that frequently sparks anger.

These hot buttons can be:

- Something we **observe** (e.g. injustices happening to other people)

- Something we **think** (e.g. the thinking that we are always the target of a particular person's mockery)

- Something we **feel** (e.g. the feeling of being helpless)

- Something we **do** (e.g. rescuing someone in a jam even if they don't deserve our help)

- Any **combination** of the four

Identifying Your Hot Buttons

Hot buttons differ from person to person. Our personal histories influence what would make us angry. Some triggers are caused by conditioning, modeling, and unresolved issues.

A key to seeing if a hot button is the real cause of the anger, or just a trigger, is to see if your anger reaction is proportionate to what the situation calls for. If you're angrier than you should be, perhaps there is an underlying emotional issue that needs to be surfaced.

Awareness of your hot buttons is already winning half the battle against anger. If you know what can evoke your anger, you can watch out for them.

A Personal Anger Log

More often than not, anger reactions appear in patterns. This means that there is a predictable structure that the anger reactions follow. This pattern is unique to each individual.

Unfortunately, it is difficult to notice this pattern unless you take that third person point of view and study your anger reactions from a distance.

Here is where keeping a personal anger log would help. A personal anger log is a diary of anger reactions including symptoms, triggers and coping styles. It is a way of increasing awareness of anger patterns unique to the individual. With awareness, one can better identify ways to prevent and cope with anger when it comes.

Keeping a personal anger log is also a good way to blow off steam. You may treat is as a diary. Instead of a structured table, as the one that will be presented later, you can make an unstructured one to note your free floating ideas and feelings.

Here is a sample template for a personal anger log:

MY PERSONAL ANGER LOG FOR WEEK 1							
Date/ Time	Symptoms	Before the anger, these are what I was				My Response to the Anger	Effect of my Anger Response
		seeing	thinking	feeling	doing		
1.							
2.							
3.							
4.							
5.							
Insights							

The Triple A Approach

Anger is exacerbated by a feeling of victimization and helplessness. It helps to know then that we always have at least three options when dealing with an anger-provoking situation: you can alter, avoid or accept.

Alter

You are not a victim of your situation; you always have the option of taking a deliberate and well-thought out response to an anger-provoking situation. Your options typically fall into three categories: alter, avoid, or accept.

Alter means that you initiate change. You can change things in your environment that are within your control. You can also initiate changes within yourself.

The following are ways that you can change to deal with anger more effectively.

Change non-productive habits.
If you know that you have a particular way of doing things that often result into an anger situation, perhaps it's time to break the pattern. For example, if you know that mediating a family quarrel while your mind is tired from work often leads to blow-ups, then re-schedule family meetings to times when you're more relaxed.

Respectfully ask others to change their behavior and be willing to do the same.
You can't control other people's thoughts, feelings, and behavior. You can, however, let them know that you'd appreciate a change. Waiting for lightning to strike people with habits that irritate you will never get you anywhere, perhaps proactive communication can.

Change the way you view a situation.
Sometimes, it's our interpretation of a situation that makes us angry, rather than the situation itself. What you can do is change your way of thinking. For example, irrational thoughts like "I have to be perfect at all times" usually result in anger directed at one's self when failures happen. Maybe if you start thinking "It's alright to fail now and then," things would get easier.

Change the way you react to a situation.
You can also deliberately change the way you respond. Anger usually begets anger; we raise our voice when someone raises their voice to us. But if you take a moment and find other ways to respond, then maybe you can manage your anger better.

Avoid

Avoid means steering clear of situations that can make you angry.

The following are 'avoid' ways that you can do to deal with anger more effectively.

Steer clear of people who make you upset.
Anger is often triggered by interactions with difficult people, or people who just 'rub you the wrong way.' If you know that a person is eliciting an intense anger reaction in you, and you feel that you can't control it, then perhaps it's best that you just take action to avoid this individual.

Steer clear of your 'hot buttons.'
One of the advantages of knowing your hot buttons is that it enables you to structure your day in such a way that avoids them. For example, if too many deadlines make you angry and stressed, then learn time management --- or don't take more projects than you can handle. Saying 'no' is a good avoid response.

Remove yourself from a stressful situation immediately.
Another avoid intervention is to immediately remove yourself from a situation that might escalate your anger. For example, if a peer provokes your anger, you don't have to stay around to listen to what he has to stay. You can opt to walk away and address the issue another day.

Accept

Unfortunately, there are some things that we cannot change nor avoid. In this case, we have to accept them. This is true in many things that involve unrecoverable losses, like an accident or financial collapse.

The following are examples of accept responses to dealing with anger:

Find learning.
When you have no choice but to accept a situation, make the most of it by distilling the lessons from the experience. This way you can recover control by making proactive changes to prevent the situation from happening again.

Seek higher purpose.
Finding meaning can help in managing anger. Interpreting a situation based on one's faith life, or personal philosophy, can lessen its threatening impact on the self. For instance, there are people who think that every negative experience is an opportunity, a call for change.

Vent to a friend.
If you can't do anything but accept a situation, at the very least find someone to share your experience with. Venting with a trusted friend or a mental health professional can help you integrate the experience better in your life. This can help you move on faster and more effectively.

Dealing with Angry People

It is not just our own anger that can get overwhelming. Another person's blow up can also trigger intense reactions in us, including shock, fear, and even reactive rage. In this module we will discuss how we can effective deal with angry people. Specifically we will talk about the Energy Curve, de-escalation techniques, and guidelines on when to back away and what to do.

Understanding the Energy Curve

One of the tricky things about handling another person's anger is reacting in a way that will not escalate the anger. This is where an understanding of the Energy Curve can help.

The Energy Curve shows the pattern commonly found in angry reactions. It shows how angry reactions progress in stages, and in each stage there are appropriate responses.

Below is an illustration of the Energy Curve:

Here are some key points to note about the Energy Curve:

RATIONAL BEHAVIOR. The baseline of the curve is rational behavior. This is the stage when a reasonable discussion about the cause of the anger can happen. Before an angry reaction, a person is said to be in that 'rational' frame of mind. However, once the angry reaction takes root, people go into a state of mind not conducive to reasoning. It is important then to get the person *back* to a rational frame of mind.

IMPLICATION: You cannot reason with a person during these times: when their anger is taking off, at the height of their anger/ rage and even at the point when they are cooling down! You'll just waste a perfectly good argument.

TAKE OFF. Angry reaction slowly builds momentum, and the point when the anger is gaining energy is called the 'take off' stage. The way anger builds in intensity differs from person to person. For example, some people start with hostile facial reactions, which progresses to shouting, and which progresses to hitting the table. Other people build up anger in less obvious ways, they start with keeping quiet and then progresses to physically withdrawing themselves from other people. The anger would continue to build energy until it reaches its peak.

IMPLICATION: Anger naturally builds energy during the take off phase. Arguing back at this point in fact, any conversation would just be futile. Don't react! Respond.

SLOW DOWN. In this stage is the most intense of the person's reaction. It is a turning point; the reaction stops gaining momentum and begins a steady decline.

COOL DOWN. Once the angry reaction has reached its height, it will start to subside. You can tell by observing the person's behavior --- often their voices go down to a level tone, they are not moving their hands as much and they seem to breathe easier. Unless provoked further, the person will run out of steam. However, if you start arguing to the person or agitating the person even during this stage, the reaction can take off once again.

IMPLICATION: Only when the angry reaction has slowed down can you introduce supportive behavior. Supportive behavior can be any statement that acknowledges the anger, example: "I can see that this is an upsetting experience for you."

BACK TO RATIONAL BEHAVIOR. Once the individual has returned to this stage, you can begin to start talking about the problem reasonably. You may even start problem solving at this point.

SUMMARY: When a person is angry, just let them vent! It's the fastest way to deal with the situation.

De-escalation Techniques

De-escalation techniques are skilled interventions designed to facilitate a person's cooling down process, reduce the possibility of getting verbally or physically hurt, and gain control of the situation.

The following are examples of de-escalation techniques:

Practice active listening.

MOST OF THE TIME, ALL AN ANGRY PERSON NEEDS IS AN OPPORTUNITY TO TELL SOMEONE HOW THEY FEEL, AND HAVE THEIR ANGER ACKNOWLEDGED. SEEING THAT YOU ARE GENUINELY LISTENING TO THEIR GRIEVANCE CAN HELP LESSEN THE INTENSITY OF THEIR ANGRY REACTION.

THE FOLLOWING ARE SOME HELPFUL COMPONENTS OF ACTIVE LISTENING:

Show non-verbally that you are listening: Make sure that your posture shows openness. Establish eye contact. Speak in a soft, well-modulated, non-threatening tone of voice.

Reflect: Re-state what you hear from the person. Example: "This is what I heard from you: You are mad because the package did not arrive on time." You can also mirror back their body language in a tentative but objective, non-judgmental fashion. Example: "I can see that you're really upset. You are clasping the desk very tightly."

Clarify: Help the person make sense of their garbled, confusing, and or illogical statements. "Could you help me explain to me a bit more about what happened in the cafeteria? What do you mean by 'he bullied you'?

Increase personal space: Anger can escalate if a person feels that he is being stifled. Make sure your body language is non-threatening. Create distance between you and the person.

Help the person recover a sense of control: Angry people may feel victimized by a situation, and may need to recover even a small sense of control. You can help do this by:

Giving them choices.

Example: "Would you like to move to a different area and talk?"

Seeking their permission to speak.

Example: May I tell what I think about what just happened?

Focusing on immediate solutions.

Example: "What do you think we can do today to help solve this issue?"

Orient them to immediacy: People temporarily loses track of their immediate surroundings at the height of getting overwhelmed. Orienting the person to the time, his location, and who he is with can help de-escalate a person. It helps a person feel less threatened if he knows where he is and how he got there. The goal also is to shift him from attending to his overwhelming feelings to recovering rationality.

Invite criticism: Ask the angry person to voice his or her criticism of yourself or the situation more fully. You might say something like, "Go ahead. Tell me everything that has you upset. Don't hold anything back. I want to hear all you have to say."

Agree if possible. If not, agree to disagree: There are cases when anger is triggered by a legitimate grievance. In these cases, it can help a person lose steam by hearing someone validate the presence of injustice. At the very least, agreeing that a person has a right to the opinion they have can help de-escalate anger.

Reiterate your support: Emphasize your willingness to help. Example: "Okay. I don't know how this thing could have happened, but you have my assurance that I'll stay with you until we figure it out."

Set limits: Tell the person that you are willing to listen, but you'd appreciate that the tones down the expression of his anger.

Example is: "I'm listening right now. I'd like to talk, but without the shouting. When you shout it is distracting, and if this issue is important to you, then I want to be able to concentrate without hearing you raise your voice. Can we start again? How did I upset you? "

When to Back Away and What to Do Next

Not all angry reactions can be effectively dealt with. Here are situations when it is more advisable to back away:

When you are too affected by an issue to view it objectively.
De-escalating anger requires that you can take yourself out of an issue, even temporarily, and look at it objectively. However, if the issue has personal meaning for us, or we are too tired to properly intervene, then we don't have the resources to de-escalate the anger.

WHAT TO DO: Withdraw from the situation and talk to someone you trust about your own feelings.

When there are warning signs for verbal and/ or physical violence.
Your priority is always your well-being and safety.

Warning signs for violence include a history of violent behavior, severe rage for seemingly minor reasons, possession of weapons and threats of violence.

WHAT TO DO: Get as far away from the person as you can! Go to a public place.

When there is influence of mood-altering substances.
No de-escalating technique can help you deal with a person who has taken alcohol and mood-altering drugs (both legal e.g. some anti-depressants, and illegal e.g. hallucinogens).

WHAT TO DO: Disengage from the conversation and talk to them when they're sober!

When no amount of rational intervention seems to work.
There are moments when a person is hell-bent on raging, and the anger will escalate regardless of what intervention you use. It is possible that the strength of the anger is significantly more than the person's resources to cope. This is signaled by a tendency for the anger to still take off even after slowing down and cooling down, despite the absence of provocation.

WHAT TO DO: Disengage from the conversation and re-schedule the talk for another time.

When there are signs of serious mental health conditions.
While there are no categories of anger disorders in the Diagnostic Manual of Mental Disorders-IV (the reference of most mental health professionals), some serious mental health conditions are related to anger. In these cases, intensive therapy and/or psychiatric medications may be most appropriate. As a rule, people who suffer impairment of reality testing cannot be expected to be rational or reasonable.

Signs to watch out for: persecutory or paranoid delusions, hallucinations, past history of violence based on delusions.

Chronic and *rigid* patterns of the use of anger as coping mechanism may point to a personality disorder.

WHAT TO DO: Compassionate understanding is key! However, disengage yourself immediately as some psychotic symptoms are correlated with a tendency towards violence. Refer to the appropriate mental health professional.

Pulling It All Together

We've now come to the conclusion of our workshop. So far, we've presented to you different techniques that can help you manage your anger better. In this module, we will show how these different techniques come together. We will also give additional tips to help you in practicing these anger management techniques more effectively.

Process Overview

The following diagram is a summary of all the anger management techniques discussed in this workshop. The techniques can be summarized into four main steps: be informed, be self-aware, take control, and take action.

Putting It into Action

The following are tips in putting anger management techniques into action:

Be Informed	Be Self-Aware	Take Control	Take Action
Know….	Study….	• Use coping thoughts	• Alter, Accept, Avoid
• The anger cycle	• Your warning signs	• Try relaxation techniques	• Identify the problem
• The fight and flight response	• Your hot buttons	• Blow off steam	• Disagree constructively
• Do's and don'ts of anger management	• Your helpful ways of dealing with anger		• Negotiate
	• Your unhelpful ways of dealing with anger		• Find a solution, build a consensus
	• Personal anger dynamics		• Make a plan, get it done
			• De-escalate the other person's anger
			• Back away when needed

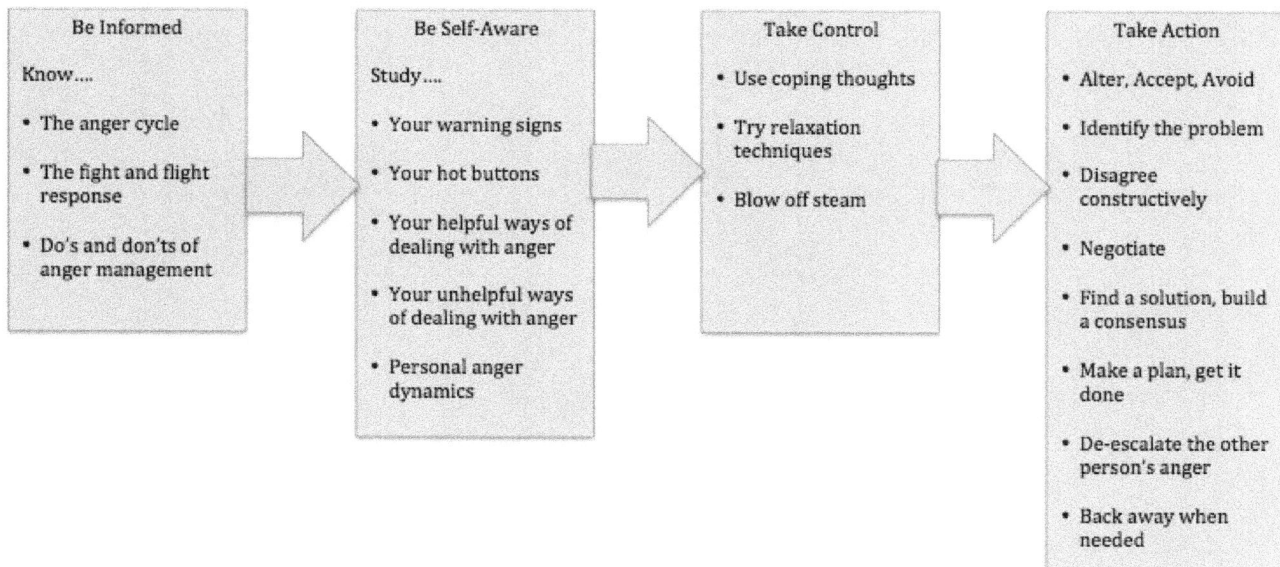

Find your motivation

As with any plan towards behavioral change, it helps to sustain your motivation. Habits are hard to break and unless there is something strong that can inspire you to change, your efforts may not get followed through. So find your motivation! You can remember a negative effect of anger in your life, such as health problems or poor quality of relationships, and use it to encourage. You may also picture how things could be different if you can manage your anger better.

Choose only one change at a time.

Don't expect change to happen overnight. After all, these may be lifetime habits that you are trying to change. Instead, stick to managing one issue at a time. Develop goals that are realistic, otherwise you might just end up frustrating yourself.

Reward yourself for your successes.

If you've successfully managed to change, affirm yourself! Any success, no matter how small, shows that you are capable.

Choose an accountability partner.

It helps to not keep your goals to yourself. Instead, select a trusted friend who knows what you are trying to accomplish. This friend can encourage you when you need additional motivation, can spur you to action when you're lagging, and can check if you are working at the pace you promised you would.

Seek a mental health professional.

If you're really struggling with anger problems, or you just need additional support, remember: you can always seek a mental health professional. Counselors, therapists, and psychiatrist are all trained to address anger and its impact on your life.

Chapter 8 – Assertiveness & Self Control

What Does Self-Confidence Mean To You?

Self-confidence plays an important role in our everyday lives. Being confident allows us to set and reach our goals. It provides stability when we are faced with a challenge; it gives us that push that helps us overcome difficulties. Self-confidence is necessary in our personal and professional lives, as without it one would not be successful in either. It gives us the ability to stand up to face our challenges and to pick ourselves up when we fall.

What is Assertiveness?

An assertive person is confident and direct in dealing with others. Assertive communications promote fairness and equality in human interactions, based on a positive sense of respect for self and others. It is the direct communication of a person's needs, wants, and opinions without punishing, threatening, or putting down another person.

Assertive behavior includes the ability to stand up for a person's legitimate rights – without violating the rights of others or being overly fearful in the process. A skill that can be learned, assertive behavior is situational specific; meaning different types of assertive behavior can be used in different situations.

Assertive behavior involves three categories of skills; self-affirmation, expressing positive feelings, and expressing negative feelings. Each will be explored during this course.

What is Self-Confidence?

Self-confidence is a belief in oneself, one's abilities, or one's judgment. It is freedom from doubt. When you believe you can change things -- or make a difference in a situation, you are much more likely to succeed.

As a self-confident person, you walk with a bounce in your step. You can control your thoughts and emotions and influence others. You are more prepared to tackle everyday challenges and recover from setbacks. This all leads to a greater degree of optimism and life satisfaction.

The Four Styles

There are four styles of communication: passive, aggressive, passive-aggressive, and assertive.

The Passive Person

Passive behavior is the avoidance of the expression of opinions or feelings, protecting one's rights, and identifying and meeting one's needs. Passive individuals exhibit poor eye contact and slumped body posture, and tend to speak softly or apologetically. Passive people express statements implying that:

- "I'm unable to stand up for my rights."

- "I don't know what my rights are."

- "I get stepped on by everyone."

- "I'm weak and unable to take care of myself."

- "People never consider my feelings."

The Aggressive Person

An aggressive individual communicates in a way that violates the rights of others. Thus, aggressive communicators are verbally or physically abusive, or both. Aggressive communication is born of low self-esteem, often caused by past physical or emotional abuse, unhealed emotional wounds, and feelings of powerlessness.

Aggressive individuals display a low tolerance for frustration, use humiliation, interrupt frequently, and use criticism or blame to attack others. They use piercing eye contact, and are not good listeners. Aggressive people express statements implying that:

- The other person is inferior, wrong, and not worth anything

- The problem is the other person's fault

- They are superior and right

- They will get their way regardless of the consequences

- They are entitled, and that the other person "owes" them.

The Passive-Aggressive Person

The passive-aggressive person uses a communication style in which the individual appears passive on the surface, but is really acting out anger in a subtle, indirect, or behind-the-scenes way.

Passive-aggressive people usually feel powerless, stuck, and resentful. Alienated from others, they feel incapable of dealing directly with the object of their resentments. Rather, they express their anger by subtly undermining the real or imagined object of their resentments. Frequently they mutter to themselves instead of confronting another person. They often smile at you, even though they are angry, use subtle sabotage, or speak with sarcasm.

Passive-aggressive individuals use communication that implies:

- "I'm weak and resentful, so I sabotage, frustrate, and disrupt."

- "I'm powerless to deal with you head on so I must use guerilla warfare."

- "I will appear cooperative, but I'm not."

The Assertive Person

An assertive individual communicates in a way that clearly states his or her opinions and feelings, and firmly advocates for his or her rights and needs without violating the rights of others. Assertive communication is born of high self-esteem. Assertive people value themselves, their time, and their emotional, spiritual, and physical needs. They are strong advocates for themselves -- while being very respectful of the rights of others.

Assertive people feel connected to other people. They make statements of needs and feelings clearly, appropriately, and respectfully. Feeling in control of themselves, they speak in calm and clear tones, are good listeners, and maintain good eye contact. They create a respectful environment for others, and do not allow others to abuse or manipulate them.

The assertive person uses statements that imply:

- "I am confident about who I am."

- "I cannot control others, but I control myself."

- "I speak clearly, honestly, and to the point."

- "I know I have choices in my life, and I consider my options. I am fully responsible for my own happiness."

- "We are equally entitled to express ourselves respectfully to one another."

Obstacles to Our Goals

Obstacles are encountered every day of our lives, but what we do and how we react during these events will determine the outcomes of such events. Our reactions to these obstacles will determine if the situation becomes a minor annoyance to a major event. Over reacting to a small annoyance can magnify the issue and make larger than it actually is. These are the types of reactions that should be kept in check, what is an appropriate response to each obstacle that we encounter? Like many things the obstacle will determine the response.

Types of Negative Thinking

Negative thinking is the process of thinking negative rather than positive thoughts. Seemingly, positive thinking requires effort while negative thinking is uninvited and happens easily.

A person who has been brought up in a happy and positive atmosphere, where people value success and self-improvement will have a much easier time thinking positively. One who was brought up in a poor or difficult situation will probably continue to expect difficulties and failure.

Negative thoughts center on the individual, others, and the future. Negative thinking causes problems such as depression, pessimism, and anxiety. Typical types of negative thinking are described below.

Type of Thinking	As the thinker, you:
Overgeneralization	Make a general universal rule from one isolated event
Global labeling	Automatically use disparaging labels to describe yourself
Filtering	Pay attention selectively to the negative, disregarding the positive
Polarized thinking	Group things into absolute, black and white categories, assuming that you must be perfect or you are worthless
Self-blame	Persistently blame yourself for things that may not be your fault
Personalization	Assume that everything has something to do with you, negatively comparing yourself to everyone else
Mind reading	Feel that people don't like you or are angry with you, without any real evidence
Control fallacies	Feel that you have total responsibility for everybody and everything, or that you have no control as a helpless victim
Emotional reasoning	Believe that things are the way you feel about them

Personal Application

We all have situations in our personal lives where the ability to be assertive helps us achieve our goals. Now we'll each practice the opportunity to develop assertive responses. Standing up for yourself will translate into success throughout your personal and professional lives. It will help grow a person's self-confidence, and make the challenges that we encounter every day that much more easily to overcome.

Communication Skills

Strong communication skills are essential for assertive interaction with others. Humans are social animals and communication is a very important part of our daily lives. Every interaction we have with another person including, face to face, over the phone, chatting online or even texting is communication happening, and have strong communication skills will benefit every type of interaction we encounter.

Listening and Hearing; They Aren't the Same Thing

Hearing is the act of perceiving sound by the ear. Assuming an individual is not hearing-impaired, hearing simply happens. Listening, however, is something that one consciously chooses to do. Listening requires concentration so that the brain processes meaning from words and sentences.

Listening leads to learning, but this is not always an easy task. The normal adult rate of speech is 100-150 words per minute, but the brain can think at a rate of 400-500 words per minute, leaving extra time for daydreaming, or anticipating the speaker's or the recipient's next words.

As opposed to hearing, listening skills can be learned and refined. The art of active listening allows you to fully receive a message from another person. Especially in a situation involving anger or a tense interchange, active listening allows you to be sensitive to the multiple dimensions of communication that make up an entire message. These dimensions include:

The occasion for the message: What is the reason why the person is communicating with me now?

The length of the message: What can the length of the message tell me about its importance?

The words chosen: Is the message being made formally? Is it with aloofness or slang?

The volume and pace: What clues do the loudness and speed give me?

The Pauses and Hesitations: How do these enhance or detract from the message?

Non-verbal clues: What does eye contact, posture, or facial expressions tell me about the message?

Empathy is the capability to share and understand another's emotions and feelings. Empathetic listening is the art of seeking a truer understanding of how others are feeling. This requires excellent discrimination and close attention to the nuances of emotional signals. According to Stephen Covey in "The Seven Habits of Highly Effective People", empathetic listening involves five basic tasks:

1. Repeat verbatim the content of the communication; the words, not the feelings

2. Rephrase content; summarize the meaning of the words in your own words

3. Reflect feelings; look more deeply and begin to capture feelings in your own words. Look beyond words for body language and tone to indicate feelings.

4. Rephrase contents and reflect feelings; express both their words and feelings in your own words.

5. Discern when empathy is not necessary – or appropriate.

Asking Questions

Active listeners use specific questioning techniques to elicit more information from speakers. Below are three types of questions to use when practicing active listening.

Open Questions

Open questions stimulate thinking and discussion or responses including opinions or feelings. They pass control of the conversation to the respondent. Leading words in open questions include: *Why, what, or how*, as in the following examples:

- Tell me about the current employee orientation process.

- How do you open the emergency exit door on an A320 aircraft?

Clarifying Questions

A clarifying question helps to remove ambiguity, elicits additional detail, and guides the answer to a question. When you ask a clarifying question, you ask for expansion or detail, while withholding your judgment and own opinions. When asking for clarification, you will have to listen carefully to what the other person says. Frame your question as someone trying to understand in more detail. Often asking for a specific example is useful. This also helps the speaker evaluate his or her own opinions and perspective. Below are some examples:

- I can tell you are really concerned about this. Let me see if I can repeat to you your main concerns so we can start to think about what to do in this situation.

- What sort of savings are you looking to achieve?

Closed Questions

Closed questions usually require a one-word answer, and effectively shut off discussion. Closed questions provide facts, allow the questioner to maintain control of the conversation, and are easy to answer. Typical leading words are: *Is, can, how many, or does*. While closed questions are not the optimum choice for active listening, at times they may be necessary to elicit facts. Below are several examples of closed questions:

- Who will lead the meeting?

- Do you know how to open the emergency exit door on this aircraft?

The following exercise provides practice with questioning techniques to support communications skills.

Body Language

Body language is a form of non-verbal communication involving the use of stylized gestures, postures, and physiologic signs which act as cues to other people. Humans unconsciously send and receive non-verbal signals through body language all the time.

Non-verbal communication is the process of communication through sending and receiving wordless messages. It is the single most powerful form of communication. Nonverbal communication cues others about what is in your mind, even more than your voice or words can do.

According to studies at UCLA, as much as 93 percent of communication effectiveness is determined by nonverbal cues, and the impact of performance was determined 7 percent by the words used, 38 percent by voice quality, and 55 percent by non-verbal communication.

In communication, if a conflict arises between your words and your body language, your body language rules every time.

The Importance of Goal Setting

A strong self-concept depends both upon what you do, and your idea of yourself. Goal setting is the process that allows you to analyze and determine what you do. Goal setting helps you feel strong and in control. Goal setting drives us and gives us a measure for our successes. Setting goals provides an incentive and helps to push us into completing the goals we set.

Why Goal Setting is Important

The process of setting goals helps to provide a clear picture of your wants and needs so you can chart your own life destiny. To get a clear picture of your wants and needs, consider eight types of goals.

To begin building and qualifying your list of goals, answer four key questions that serve as triggers.

Question	Example	Potential Goal
What hurts, or feels bad?	The long commute to work	Explore a telecommuting option
What are you hungry for?	More time in the outdoors	Plan a national park vacation
What are your dreams?	Enhance the yard	Build a rock garden
What are the little comforts?	A new kitten	Adopt or buy a pet

Now classify the goals according to potential timing: long-range, medium-range, and immediate.

Long-Range Goals

Explore a telecommuting option

Medium-Range Goals

Plan a national park vacation

Immediate

Get a kitten

Setting SMART Goals

The SMART method is a straightforward way to qualify and quantify each goal.

Handout Four: Smart Goal Setting describes the SMART criteria and provides examples of how they are used to establish and qualify goals.

SMART is a convenient acronym for the set of criteria that a goal must have in order for it to be realized by the goal achiever.

Specific: Success coach Jack Canfield states in his book <u>The Success Principles</u> that, "Vague goals produce vague results." In order for you to achieve a goal, you must be very clear about what exactly you want. Often creating a list of benefits that the accomplishment of your goal will bring to your life, will you give your mind a compelling reason to pursue that goal.

Measurable: It's crucial for goal achievement that you are able to track your progress towards your goal. That's why all goals need some form of objective measuring system so that you can stay on track and become motivated when you enjoy the sweet taste of quantifiable progress.

Achievable: Setting big goals is great, but setting unrealistic goals will just de-motivate you. A good goal is one that challenges, but is not so unrealistic that you have virtually no chance of accomplishing it.

Relevant: Before you even set goals, it's a good idea to sit down and define your core values and your life purpose because it's these tools which ultimately decide how and what goals you choose for your life. Goals, in and of themselves, do not provide any happiness. Goals that are in harmony with our life purpose do have the power to make us happy.

Timed: Without setting deadlines for your goals, you have no real compelling reason or motivation to start working on them. By setting a deadline, your subconscious mind begins to work on that goal, night and day, to bring you closer to achievement.

Our Challenge to You

Use the SMART goal-setting method to set up an out of class personal goal.

- **Specific**: Be clear on what the goal will be.

- **Measurable**: Make it so you can track your progress.

- **Achievable**: Set a reasonable and achievable goal.

- **Relevant**: Make it relevant to your life at that moment.

- **Timed**: Set a deadline.

Feeling the Part

Being positive and feeling good about one's self is the key, you must feel the part. Positivity is a leading factor in one's self confidence, it will help you keep a feeling of worth. Staying positive will provide you a great asset in regards to self-talk and recognizing and working with your strengths. Everyone has weaknesses and by being positive you can recognize your weaknesses and then work on them to lesson to remove them all together.

Identifying Your Worth

Worth is defined as "sufficiently good, important, or interesting to justify a specified action." People with a sense of self-worth exude confidence in themselves. They feel in change of their own destiny, and are happy. To create a picture of your self-worth, take a self-concept inventory, analyzing multiple attributes in your life.

Attribute	Description
Physical appearance	Height, weight, facial appearance, skin, hair, style of dress, body areas
How you relate to others	Co-workers, friends, family, and strangers in social settings
Personality	Positive and negative personality traits
How other people see you	Positive and negative perceptions, as viewed by others
Performance at work or school	How you handle major tasks
Performance of the daily tasks of life	How you handle health, hygiene, maintenance of your living environment, food preparation, caring for children or parents
Mental functioning	How you reason and solve problems, your capacity for learning and creativity, your knowledge, wisdom, insights

Creating Positive Self-Talk

Positive self-talk allows you to recognize, validate, and apply your full potential with respect to all that you are, and do. Also called affirmations (to make something firm), positive self-talk serves as your own personal accomplishment scale. Below are some tips for positive self-talk:

- Use the present tense; deal with what exists today.

- Be positive – rather than affirming what you don't want.

- Remain personal; self-talk must relate to you and you only.

- Keep sentences short and simple.

- Go with your gut. If it "clicks", then just say it. Self-talk should feel positive, expanding, freeing, and supporting.

- Focus on new things, rather than changing what is.

- Act "as if"; give yourself permission to believe the idea is true right now.

If self-talk is new to you, it is a good idea to first think about the things that are wonderful about you, such as:

- I have someone I love, and we enjoy spending time together

- I am a mother or father, fulfilled in this role

- My career is challenging and fulfilling.

- When I learn something new, I feel proud.

- I am worthwhile because I breathe and feel; I am aware.

- When I feel pain, I love, I try to survive. I am a good person.

Identifying and Addressing Strengths and Weaknesses

After an individual has listed words and phrases for self-attributes, they can be classified as strengths or weaknesses. This exercise also allows participants to re-frame weaknesses into message that don't feed a negative self-worth.

Looking the Part

A person who has a strong sense of personal worth makes a confident, positive appearance. Looking the part is important as it influences the people around us. It will provide a boost to confidence and in turn a boost to your performance. Once higher performance is obtained it will then cycle back and make us more confident. Looking the part is an important part of being more assertive and confident as it is relatively quick and easy to do and pays off great dividends.

The Importance of Appearance

In the dictionary, appearance is defined as an external show, or outward aspect. Your confidence depends significantly on your personal thoughts and perceptions about the way you look. Appearance is as important today as it ever was. The first thing noticed when meeting someone new is their appearance. That is why it is important as you only have one first impression.

The Role of Body Language

Body language is a form of non-verbal communication involving the use of stylized gestures, postures, and physiologic signs which act as cues to other people. Humans unconsciously send and receive non-verbal signals through body language all the time.

One study at UCLA found that up to 93 percent of communication effectiveness is determined by nonverbal cues. Another study indicated that the impact of a performance was determined 7 percent by the words used, 38 percent by voice quality, and 55 percent by non-verbal communication. Your body language must match the words used. If a conflict arises between your words and your body language, your body language governs. The components of body language include:

Eye contact: The impact of your message is affected by the amount of eye contact you maintain with the person with whom you are speaking. One who makes eye contact is normally perceived as more favorable and confident.

Posture: Find comfortable sitting and standing postures that work for you; avoid any rigid or slouching positions.

Excessive or unrelated head, facial, hand and body Movement: Too much movement can divert attention from the verbal message. Your facial expressions should match the type of statement you are making; smile when saying "I like you", and frowning when saying "I am annoyed with you". Occasional gestures that reinforce your verbal message are acceptable.

First Impressions Count

It takes as few as seven seconds – and no more than thirty seconds -- for someone to form a first impression about you. Like it or not, people make judgments about others right away based on a presenting appearance. And you never have a second chance to make a first impression. Below are some tips to help you make that positive first impression when someone.

- **Body language.** Remember that body language makes up to 55% of a communication.

- **Dress and grooming.** It's less about your budget, and more about clean, pressed, and event-appropriate clothing with neat grooming.

- **Handshake.** Use a medium to firm handshake grip, avoiding a weak handshake, or overly firm one that can cause potential discomfort to another.

- **Body Movement.** Use a mirror, or enlist the help of a friend to make sure that your movements are not overly active --and that they support the nature of your message.

Sounding the Part

Feeling and looking the part would not be complete without voice. Given that we know that 38% of communication effectiveness is governed by voice quality, improving your overall voice message delivery is worthwhile.

It's How You Say It

We are all born with a particular tone of voice, which we can learn to improve. The goal is to sound upbeat, warm, under control, and clear. Here are some tips to help you begin the process.

1. Breathe from your diaphragm

2. Drink plenty of water to stay hydrated; avoid caffeine because of its diuretic effects

3. Posture affects breathing, and also tone of voice, so be sure to stand up straight

4. To warm up the tone of your voice, smile

5. If you have a voice that is particularly high or low, exercise it's by practicing speaking on a sliding scale. You can also sing to expand the range of your voice.

6. Record your voice and listen to the playback

7. Deeper voices are more credible than higher pitched voices. Try speaking in a slightly lower octave. It will take some practice, but with a payoff, just as radio personalities have learned

8. Enlist a colleague or family member to get feedback about the tone of your voice.

Sounding Confident

Since 38% of the messages received by a listener are governed by the tone and quality of your voice, its pitch, volume and control all make a difference in how confident you sound when you communicate. Below are some specific tips.

Pitch (Pitch means how high or low your voice is.) Tip: Avoid a high-pitched sound. Speak from your stomach, the location of your diaphragm.

Volume (The loudness of your voice must be governed by your diaphragm.) Tip: Speak through your diaphragm, not your throat

Quality (The color, warmth, and meaning given to your voice contribute to quality.) Tip: Add emotion to your voice. Smile as much as possible when you are speaking.

The need for assertive, confident communication can occur at any time, in virtually any place. So how do you make this all come together? Here are some practice suggestions.

- Start simply and gain some experience in safe environments, such as at the grocery store, or with family or friends

- Set aside time when you can read out loud without being disturbed; listen to yourself

- Challenge yourself to speak with someone new every day

- Set a realistic time frame to make the shift; don't expect to change your speaking style overnight.

Reducing Anxiety

Often, anxiety inhibits your ability to act and sound confident when speaking. Knowing how to perform a quick relaxation exercise can help diffuse anxiety and allow you to speak more confidently.

Using "I" Messages

An "I" message is a statement specifically worded to express your feelings about a particular situation. "I" messages begin with "I", and are an excellent way to share your feelings about particular behaviors -- without accusing the other person. There are four types of "I" messages, each with varying parts.

Powerful Presentations

Presentations made by assertive, self-confident people can achieve the desired outcome. What can be more confident building than giving a powerful presentation? Being prepared is the main tool in giving a powerful presentation. Preparedness provides you with the ability to be ready when the unexpected happens, or when you are called upon to speak up or give a presentation.

What to Do When You're on the Spot

Regardless of the situation, things are guaranteed to happen, and not always according to plan. Irrespective of the presentation venue, four actions can help you convert an interruption into an opportunity.

1. Always expect the unexpected!

2. At the beginning of the program, "work" the audience to pre-frame them, to create a mindset. Through light remarks, humor, or other responses based on your read of the group, leads them to make commitments to be playful, curious, flexible, and energized.

3. Create several positive anchors that you can use later. An anchor is something unique that you do or say that automatically puts the audience in a resourceful or emotional state. Examples include: A unique smile, specific place where you stand, the word "yes" in a strong voice.

4. If something unexpected happens, first smile, and then quickly ask yourself "How can I turn this event into an opportunity to create humor or illustrate a point?"

Using STAR to Make Your Case

STAR is an acronym that stands for **Situation or Task, Thoughts and Feelings, Actions, Results**. The STAR Model helps you deal with recurring problem situations such as repeated mental blocks or anxieties stemming from interpersonal situations. Using the four points of a star as the visual representation, the STAR model prompts questions that allow you to analyze the aspects of a problem situation -- and turn it around.

Coping Techniques

An assertive, self-confident person uses a variety of coping techniques to deal with the challenges of interpersonal communication. Many of these techniques come from the school of neuro-linguistic programming. NLP began in California in the mid-1970s, when graduate Richard Bandler joined a group at the University of Santa Cruz headed by linguistics professor John Grinder. NLP is defined as models and techniques to help understand and improve communication -- and to enhance influencing behavior.

Building Rapport

Rapport is the relation of harmony, conformity, accord, or affinity to support an outcome. The intended outcome is more likely with rapport than if it is not present. There is a sense of a shared understanding with another person.

Mirroring – matching certain behaviors of a person with whom you are interacting -- is the process used to establish rapport. There are four techniques for mirroring to build rapport.

- Voice tone or tempo

- Matching breathing rate

- Matching movement rhythms

- Matching body postures

Levels of rapport range on a continuum from a low of tolerance to a high of seduction. For business, strive for levels of neutral, lukewarm, understanding, identification, or warm, all in the center of the continuum.

Expressing Disagreement

Representations systems determine by the brain give us cues about how individuals process information. People can be classified as predominantly:

- **Visual** (The things we see)

- **Auditory** (The things we hear)

- **Kinesthetic** (The things we feel, touch, taste, or smell)

Both the type of words used, and the speaker's eye movement provide indicators of the system type. In a conversation, once we understand which type our conversation partner is, we can use the same system language to match the person's type, helping to ensure more reception to our message.

Coming to Consensus

Whether there is a disagreement on a particular issue, or you simply need to get a group to agree, neuro-linguistics offers a solution. To plan, make the following decisions:

1. What do you want your outcome to be?

2. How will you know when the outcome is achieved?

3. Who will attend the meeting? (Important: Each person invited to the meeting must have information needed for two out of three agenda items.)

Then, establish rapport as participants come into the meeting.

Now you are ready to use the **PEGASUS** model to achieve your desired outcomes.

Present outcomes
Explain evidence
Gain agreement on outcomes
Activate sensory acuity
Summarize each major decision
Use the relevancy challenge
Summarize the next step.

Dealing with Difficult Behavior

Each of us can probably think of at least one difficult personality with whom we have had to deal with, either at work or in our personal lives. With a strategy, it is possible to learn what the person does to annoy you, and what you might be doing to aggravate the situation.

Dealing with Difficult Situations

A difficult person can be your boss, your co-worker, or anyone else. He or she behaves in a way that is disruptive to business or life outside of work. In a work setting, often the functioning of a team is disturbed leading to a disruption of the work flow, flared tempers, and gossip. The bottom line is that work suffers and difficult situations cost organizations money.

To deal with difficult people, we innately try to apply coping filters, such as:

- Removing virtually all positive attributes about the person. ("He was my worst hiring mistake…")

- Defaming him or her (We build consensus with others against the person)

- Explaining the person in negative terms.

Anger also plays a big part; feeling angry, we instinctively use anger to try to manage the situation.

To break the cycle of negativity, take time to answer the following questions:

- What observable behaviors or statements did the person perform or say?

- What is the most positive interpretation an outside witness would make? The most negative?

- What will you gain by interpreting the difficult person's actions or words in as positive a light as possible?

- What would you do or say when you respond to the difficult person if you viewed his or her actions in a positive light? What is stopping you from responding this way?

Key Tactics

Three strategies will help you gather facts and use targeted strategies to deal with the person or the situation.

Active Listening

The first tactic, and possibly the most important, is to listen empathetically, which is listening while trying to be sensitive to the various components and levels of the message. We've already learned some strategies in module four for active listening. In addition, try to listen for the following information:

- **The Why:** Why is the person communicating with me?

- **The Length:** What can the size of the message tell me about the importance of the message to the person?

- **The Words:** Does the person use formal, aloof language? Impatience?

- The **Volume and Pace**: What emotional pressures can be sensed?

Note taking after a Discussion

A second tactic is to write down your recollection of the discussion that just took place. The notes can be used to support your next communication with the difficult person. Note taking also gives you the opportunity to plan and organize before the next communication takes place.

Writing Your Communication

Putting your thoughts into writing has three important benefits:

- The difficult person cannot interrupt with an objection

- It's easier to provide orderly communication in writing than in a discussion

- Written communication is pure; there is no body language to shape the outcome, reducing the possibility of mixed messages.

Chapter 9 – Attention Management

A distracted workforce is less than effective. Employees who do not pay attention to their work can waste valuable time and make careless mistakes. Attention management is a useful skill that allows managers to connect with their employees on an emotional level and motivate them to focus on their work and how to reach their personal and company goals.

At the end of this tutorial, participants should be able to:

- Define and understand attention management.

- Identify different types of attention.

- Create strategies for goals and SMART goals.

- Be familiar with methods that focus attention.

- Put an end to procrastination.

- Learn how to prioritize time.

Attention Management Assessment

Evaluate the attention management skills you already have along with the skills you need to develop. Understanding what skills you have and being able to communicate these skills clearly will increase your chances of being successful in your career.

Answer the questions quickly and honestly. Do not over think your answers. Use the assessment to gauge which topics demand your immediate attention.

1. I actively listen to both supervisors and employees.	1	2	3	4	5
2. I work efficiently and do not procrastinate.	1	2	3	4	5
3. I keep focused on positive things.	1	2	3	4	5
4. I think strategically about achieving goals.	1	2	3	4	5
5. I easily transition between tasks.	1	2	3	4	5
6. I manage my time well.	1	2	3	4	5
7. I make SMART Goals.	1	2	3	4	5
8. I am able to prioritize well.	1	2	3	4	5
9. I effectively motivate employees.	1	2	3	4	5
10. I understand and apply the 80/20 rule.	1	2	3	4	5

Every company and every manager wants to increase productivity. Constant access to information and the expectations to do more with less is overwhelming the workforce. People are easily distracted at work. Attention management allows managers and employees to increase their productivity as well as their personal job satisfaction.

What Is Attention Management?

Attention management increases the ability to focus attention and can be done at the individual and organizational level. Managers are encouraged to deal with their own attention problems before trying to influence employees in their organization. In order to understand attention management, people must be aware of where they focus most of their attention. Most experts divide attention into four different areas or zones. While the names change, the ideas are all the same.

Four Areas of Attention:

- **Intentional:** When working intentionally, people plan strategically and prioritize their activities.

- **Responsive:** In this area people are responding to the world around them. They spend more time putting out fires than working intentionally.

- **Interrupted:** People spend too much time answering messages and handling situations that interrupt their work.

- **Unproductive:** This occurs when people waste time at work. Unless you are taking a scheduled break, checking Facebook and chatting is unproductive.

Stop Thinking and Pay Attention!

The advice "stop thinking" may seem counterintuitive to attention management. Many people, however, are over thinking everything and focused on the wrong ideas. When we constantly think we do not pay attention to what is really going on around us. Our feelings control how and what we think. If we think that something is boring, bad, or a waste of time, we tend to give it less attention. For example, people are less likely to pay attention during a meeting if they believe it will not be productive. The ability to pay attention allows people to better connect with the world around them, better process their emotions, and organize the way they process cognitively.

What Is Mushin?

Mushin is a Chinese term that loosely translates to "no mind." The concept is used in training for different martial arts. A better way to understand Mushin might be to call it pure mind. Mushin requires people to reach an absence of conscious thought and emotion, which better enables individuals to focus on a task. Meditation is used to reach Mushin and as a result, better intuitive skills.

What is Xin Yi (Heart Minded)?

Xin Yi is a centuries old martial arts used in China. While the fighting techniques may not be helpful when handling situations at the office, the strategies linking the mind and body are useful. Xin Yi involves the ideas of Six Harmonies that also appear in Kung Fu and other martial arts. The three internal harmonies connect the mind with will, energy, and power.

Internal Harmonies

- **XIn** and **Yi**: Connects the mind (Xin) with the heart or will (Yi).

- **Yi** and **Qi**: Connects the will (Yi) with natural energy (Qi).

- **Qi** and **Li**: Connects energy (Qi) with power (Li).

Reaching the internal harmonies is usually done through moving meditation that links the mind and body.

Types of Attention

There are different types of attention that we all use to function in everyday life. Different types of attention are required for different situations. When attempting to manage attention, whether personal or organizational, it is essential to understand the different types of attention and how each type functions.

Focused Attention

Focused attention is what most people would define as paying attention. This is the type of attention that concentrates on a single task and excludes everything else. This can be done while studying or working on a project. Focused attention is difficult to maintain because it is not a natural human state, and it operates on a physiological level. Constant focused attention actually makes people tired.

Sustained Attention

Sustained attention is the type of attention that people use to focus on a particular task that takes time. It is also called the attention span. For example, reading a book requires sustained attention. The brain uses sustained attention to process information and adapt to different situations. Problems with sustained attention occur when there are distractions that keep someone from completing the task at hand. Most people need to refocus and return to the task after 20 minutes. There are three stages of sustained attention.

Three Stages:

- Grab attention

- Keep attention

- End attention

In order to sustain attention, it is important to remove distractions and occasionally refocus.

Selective Attention

Selective attention is what people use when they pay attention to a single stimulus in a complex setting. Having a conversation in a crowded restaurant is an example of selective attention. It is not possible to pay attention to every stimulus that surrounds us. The ability to filter out background noise and focus on one object or message is essential when we are consistently bombarded with information. The drawback to selective attention occurs when people disregard what is happening around them.

Selective attention can be manipulated. Marketing experts, for example, attempt to link their advertising messages to their customers' interests. They do this with the hope of grabbing the selective attention of people.

Alternating Attention

Occasionally people need to perform two tasks that require different cognitive abilities at the same time. These situations require alternating attention. An example of this would be taking notes during a lecture. In order to use alternating attention, the mind needs to be flexible and move between one task and another seamlessly. Alternating attention means that the work on each task is quick and accurate as the brain transitions.

Attention CEO

CEOs guide the direction of their companies. The attention of a CEO will determine the attention management of an organization. CEOs must focus the attention of their employees in ways to drive business and move the company in the right direction. Modern CEOs are faced with the dilemma of attracting and keeping employee attention. Understanding the different types of attention and implementing attention management techniques will allow CEOs to motivate employees towards greater success. In order to accomplish this, CEOs must focus their expectations of internal and external attention.

- **Internal attention**: Paying attention to internal procedures.

- **External attention:** Focusing on objects outside the organization.

Attentional Blink

Attentional blink was first defined in the 1990s. Vision is a key part of attention. Rapid, serial visual presentations show that when people focus on two targets in succession in a visual series, they are likely to miss the second target. This occurs when the second target appears 200 to 500 milliseconds after the first target. Research shows that strong emotions related to the targets make them easier to locate. Meditation is also shown to reduce the errors associated with attentional blink.

Strategies for Goal Setting

Goals are continually linked to attention management. Success, on both a personal and professional level, demands effective goal setting. Goal setting, however, requires careful strategy and execution. Simply writing down a list of things to do is not goal setting. Goals need to be made on an emotional and intellectual level in order to be achieved successfully.

Listening to Your Emotions

People often fail to reach their goals because they ignore the emotional aspect of goal setting. Emotions affect every aspect of a person's life. They influence health and factor into how well people perform at work. Feelings towards goals determine whether or not they are achieved. Feelings of obligation will only motivate someone so far. Goals need to be based on personal vision in order to be effective.

Vision

Vision statements allow people to create goals that relate to their convictions and emotions.

- **Recognize your values**: Reflect on what you truly value and how these values will shape your future.

- **Consider your goals:** What do you want your life to be like in the future?

- **Write it down:** Draft a vision statement, and revisit occasionally to make any necessary adjustments.

Prioritizing

People often fail to achieve goals when the number of things they need to do overwhelms them. Goals must be prioritized. It is not possible to concentrate on every goal at once. They should be ranked in order of importance so that plans can be made accordingly. It is essential to have balanced goals that reflect all areas of life. Personal values and visions should be used to prioritize personal and professional goals.

Examples of Prioritizing

Goals	Priorities
Earn a promotion	B
Buy a house	C
Become a mentor	C
Coach my child's sports team	A
Stay healthy by exercising	A

Re-Gating

Sensory gating is the process that the brain uses to adjust to stimuli. There is a direct connection between the ability to filter out distracting stimuli and performance. Stress, anxiety, and depression can alter the chemistry of the brain and reduce the effectiveness of sensory gating. In order to prevent cognitive issues related to gating, it is important to try re-gating. Gating can be improved by using relaxation techniques that help the mind focus and filter out the distractions. Setting goals require focus and a calm atmosphere. Before setting goals, attempt to use relaxation techniques such as meditation to clear the mind of distractions.

Meditation

The brain travels through different patterns of brainwaves in sleeping and waking states. Meditation affects brain activity and allows users to control these patterns. EEG's show the changes that meditation brings to the brainwave patterns. Each brainwave is connected to specific activities such as sleep, attention, meditation, hypnosis, music, and relaxation. Different meditation techniques will have an impact on the different types of brainwaves. Understanding meditation demands an understanding of the five basic brainwaves.

Beta

Beta brainwaves signal wakefulness. They are associated with concentration and attentiveness. People use Beta brainwaves to solve problems, but they are also connected to feelings of trepidation and anxiety. Anyone who is awake is in Beta. Meditation slows Beta brainwaves and allows practitioners to focus on the other brainwaves.

Alpha

Alpha brainwaves are a sign of relaxed consciousness. Alpha waves are considered to be the brainwave of meditation. They promote creativity and are associated with pleasant feelings and tranquility. In this state, a person is awake but not intently focused. This is the ideal state for intuitive thinking.

Theta

Theta waves appear when someone is in a deep state of meditation, hypnotized, or in a light stage one sleep. At this stage a person is not fully aware of his or her surroundings. Theta waves are linked to dreams and short-term memory. Children naturally have more Theta waves than adults. Theta waves allow people to recall facts easily, which is sometimes why answers to questions seem to come while falling asleep.

Delta

Delta waves accompany deep sleep that is without dreams. This is the slowest brainwave pattern, moving at 1.5 to 4 cycles per second. Few people enter delta when they are meditating. Only experienced practitioners are able to reach delta waves and still remain awake.

Gamma

Gamma waves are the waves associated with the ability to connect and process information. They also improve memory and keep the senses sharp. People with high gamma brainwaves are known to be more compassionate and known to be happier or more content. They are often considered to be more intelligent than those with lower levels of gamma waves. Meditation is known to increase the frequency of gamma brainwaves in individuals.

Training Your Attention

There are different methods that allow people to train their attention. While some of the methods may seem counterintuitive to attention management, there are great benefits to practicing them. Visualization may seem like a waste of time that should be focused on work, but it is not. Each person is different, and it is important to find a method or combination of methods that work best for you.

Mushin

Mushin may be difficult to describe. It is translated as "no thought", "no fear", or "no mind." A martial arts technique, Mushin occurs when the conscious mind does not stand in the way of the body and instinct. Mushin occurs anytime that intuition takes over. There are no logical steps to Mushin, but there are exercises to increase the chances of reaching Mushin.

Exercise:

- Sit comfortably in a quiet room with no distractions.

- Focus on breathing. (There is no need to breathe in tandem; be natural.)

- Try to keep the mind blank, and consciously release each distracting thought as it comes.

Meditation

There are different types of meditation, but most are used to relax the body and calm or focus the mind. Common meditations include Mantra Meditation, Steady Gaze Meditation, Transcendental Meditation, and Chakra Meditation.

- Mantra Meditation repeats sounds or words.

- Steady Gaze Meditation involves visually focusing on an object.

- Transcendental Meditation is done sitting with eyes closed.

- Chakra Meditation uses focused breathing and mantra to explore the chakras.

Each person needs to discover his or her personal meditation style. For example, some people find mantras distracting and prefer steady gaze. Transcendental Meditation is the most popular in a business setting. Beginners, regardless of the style they choose, often benefit from guided meditation with an instructor.

Focus Execute

Attention management requires people to focus and execute. Failure is often caused by a fear of success. When the mind focuses on potential negative outcomes, it is impossible to execute a plan well. Rather than focusing on the potential failures, people need to concentrate on the benefits of a successful plan. Remaining positive will allow people to focus on their goals and execute their actions accordingly.

Visualization

Visualization is a habit of creating a mental picture of a goal and believing that it will happen. Successful people in every field use visualization techniques. The process of visualization may seem odd, but visualizing a goal allows the mind to accept it as a concrete possibility rather than a vague wish.

Steps:

- **Choose a goal**: Visualization needs to be specific. Pick an individual goal to visualize. It is easier to start small.

- **Relax**: Find a time and place to relax and focus on visualization techniques.

- **Visualize:** Picture the goal in detail, visualize it happening in the present. For example, many athletes visualize their performance before a game or competition.

- **Accept:** Believe that the goal will come true. Affirmations are useful tools to bring acceptance.

Attention Zones Model

There are four different attention zones: Reactive, Proactive, Distracted and Wasteful. These zones were introduced in an earlier module. The attention zone determines productivity as well as personal stress levels. Attention management allows people to move out of stressful or unproductive zones and manage their time wisely.

Reactive Zone

Many people, particularly managers, spend most of their time in the reactive zone. Those in the reactive zone spend their time putting out fires and handling urgent needs. The tasks are important, but they demand time that takes away from scheduled projects. An example would be finding someone to fill in for a sick employee. The task is important and demands immediate attention, but it does not help the manager meet any of his or her goals or deadlines. Occasionally, a crisis will need to be handled, but attending to one crisis after another should never be a way of life. In order for people to move out of the reactive zone and stay in the proactive zone, they need to address the time they spend in the distracted and wasteful zones.

Proactive Zone

The proactive zone is where everyone wants to work. People in this zone work strategically. They are able to plan and achieve goals. Spending time in the proactive zone reduces the amount of time that is spent in the reactive zone because contingency plans will be in place. The proactive zone maintains relationships, budgets, systems, and personal well-being. Review your goals and plan accordingly at the beginning of each week to improve performance in the proactive zone.

Distracted Zone

The distracted zone takes up far too much time. Things in this zone seem urgent, but they are not really important. The distracted zone occurs when other people monopolize your attention. Things like emails and phone calls fall under the distracted zone. Important time and energy is given to other people's priorities rather than personal goals.

Leaving the distracted zone:

- **Turn off email alert**: Emails do not always need to be answered immediately. Constant email alerts are distractions that take people out of the proactive zone.

- **Create a time-blocked schedule**: Schedule time to return phone calls and emails and build relationships. Work on projects during the time set aside for them, and do not allow yourself to become distracted by other people.

- **Set boundaries**: Stick to the schedule. Do not allow people to draw you away unless it is a **real** emergency. Be firm, and people will learn to respect your schedule.

Wasteful Zone

The wasteful zone is exactly what it sounds like, the zone where people waste time. Activities that waste time include checking personal email, looking at social media sites, online videos, and other activities that are not productive. It is important to note that people need to occasionally decompress. When time to relax and regroup is not included in a person's schedule, more time will be spent in the wasteful zone.

Leaving the wasteful zone:

Schedule personal time: Take the time to relax, meditate, eat, and socialize. It is not possible to continually focus on a single task, so schedule breaks and take them. It will increase productivity and prevent the need for mind numbing activities.

Limit temptation: Internet junkies should turn off their connection when they do not need the Internet, if possible. Turn off mobile devices when working, and indulge pastimes only when appropriate. Remind yourself that the wasteful zone keeps you out of the proactive zone and away from your goals

SMART Goals

The importance of goal setting has already been addressed. In order to achieve these goals, however, it is essential to create SMART goals. SMART goals guide people as they works towards an end. They eliminate confusion and increase satisfaction. While they are a staple in business settings, SMART goals are able to motivate personal and professional goals.

The Three P's

There are three P's to achieving goals. Approaching goals the wrong way will only end in failure. The three P's can help prevent people from becoming discouraged and motivate them to keep moving forward. When setting goals, make sure that they are positive, personal, and present.

- **Positive:** Goals should be written in a positive light. Rather than writing "stop wasting time", write, "become more productive."

- **Personal**: Goals need to connect on a personal and emotional level.

- **Present**: Similar to visualization, create goals that can be achieved immediately. For example, immediately stop surfing the Internet at work.

The SMART Way

Attention management is used to meet specific goals and objectives. Goals and objectives give participants motivation and a sense of direction. The goals and objectives of any strategy need to be SMART. SMART goals are particularly useful because they break long-term goals into short-term goals. For example, a long-term goal may be "become CEO", but a SMART goal would be "be promoted within a year."

- **Specific:** Goals should have specific directions. An example of a specific goal would be visualizing 10 minutes a day.

- **Measurable:** You should know when you reach your goals. For example, increasing productivity three percent is specific, and becoming more productive is not specific.

- **Attainable:** Goals, especially short-term goals, must be attainable. A goal to double your income in the next month is probably not attainable.

- **Relevant:** Goals need to be relevant to each situation. A goal to increase sales is not relevant to someone in production.

- **Timely:** Goals need specific timeframes. For example, spending less time in the reactive zone within three months is a timely goal.

Prioritizing

SMART goals, like every other goal, need prioritizing. Consider how SMART goals align with your personal vision and values. A goal that does not meet a personal need is less likely to be reached. Use the same criteria to rank SMART goals that you use to rank your general goals. Again, try to balance the goals between different areas of your life.

Goals	Priorities
Earn bonus in two months	B
Learn a new system in a week	C
Finish a project two days early	C
Create a schedule for the week	A
Exercise three times a week	A

Evaluating and Adapting

Once a SMART goal is created, it needs to be evaluated. Is it SMART? Does it follow the three P's? Is it a priority? Consider the steps that are necessary to reach the goal. Even if the goal is achievable, are you willing to do what is necessary to reach it? For example, if saving 100 dollars a month means never eating out, are you willing to give up the luxury? If not, adapt the goal to saving 50 dollars every month.

It is also important to review goals periodically. Circumstances change, and changes will affect goals. Re-evaluate and adapt goals to meet any new requirements or personal visions.

Keeping Yourself Focused

Staying focused is easier said than done. Even with SMART goals and schedules, there is always something trying to distract us. We can become overwhelmed by everything that we have to do. Looking at the big picture can be discouraging and cause us to lose heart. Fortunately, there are useful methods that help people stay focused.

The One Minute Rule

Everyone hates doing the little things. They seem unimportant, but when left to pile up, they can destroy focus and waste time. Did you ever let the sink pile up with dishes? How long did it take to do the pile of dishes? The one minute rule eliminates this type of situation; it reduces stress and creates focus.

The one minute rule advises people to complete any task that only takes a minute. Examples include filing a paper, putting office supplies away, or washing a dish. A minute does not really cut into your schedule, and it saves you the time in the long run. Filing a single paper every day takes a minute. Filing a month of papers will require much more time.

The Five Minute Rule

Schedules help people focus and manage their time better when they are done correctly. A common mistake that people make with schedules is making them too strict. It is not possible to plan the day down to the minute. When creating a schedule, follow the five minute rule. The five minute rule is simple: allow at least five minutes between tasks. A slight buffer will provide time to complete one task before transitioning to another.

What to Do When You Feel Overwhelmed

Everyone becomes overwhelmed. It is important, however, not to let your feelings control your actions. There are steps to take whenever you feel overwhelmed that will make it easier to regain focus.

Steps:

- **Stop**: Slow down before you panic and try to keep perspective. Take a moment to relax and think when you are overwhelmed.

- **Take Breaks**: Plan to take a five-minute break for every hour of work. Use the time to try relaxation techniques.

- **Break down tasks:** Break tasks into smaller steps.

- **Sleep:** Get enough rest to ensure you can think critically.

Procrastination

Everyone is guilty of procrastination from time to time. Procrastination is the enemy of productivity. When we procrastinate, we put off doing what we need to do. We usually procrastinate with leisure activities that gratify us for the moment but hurt our chances of long-term success. There are ways to fight off procrastination.

Why We Procrastinate

We usually do not mean to procrastinate. Sometimes a five minute break can lead to an hour long session of surfing the Internet. Each person procrastinates for different reasons. Identifying the reasons for procrastination will help people overcome it.

Reasons:

- **Stress**: Being stressed and exhausted triggers a fight or flight response. This reduces logical thinking and increases the chance of procrastination.

- **Fear**: Both fear of failure and fear of success result in procrastination.

- **Boredom**: Some people naturally delay gratification better than others. When we are bored, the desire for immediate gratification increases.

Nine Ways to Overcome Procrastination

Your ability to select your most important task at any given moment, and then to start on that task and get it done both quickly and well, will probably have greatest impact on your success than any other quality or skill you can develop! If you nurture the habit of setting clear priorities and getting important tasks quickly finished, the majority of your time management issues will simply fade away.

Here are some ways to get moving on those tough tasks.

- **DELETE IT.** What are the consequences of not doing the task at all? Consider the 80/20 rule; maybe it doesn't need to be done in the first place.

- **DELEGATE.** If the task is important, ask yourself if it's really something that you are responsible for doing in the first place. Know your job description and ask if the task is part of your responsibilities. Can the task be given to someone else?

- **DO IT NOW.** Postponing an important task that needs to be done only creates feelings of anxiety and stress. Do it as early in the day as you can.

- **ASK FOR ADVICE.** Asking for help from a trusted mentor, supervisor, coach, or expert can give you some great insight on where to start and the steps for completing a project.

- **CHOP IT UP.** Break large projects into milestones, and then into actionable steps. As Bob Proctor says, "Break it down into the ridiculous." Huge things don't look as big when you break it down as small as you can.

- **OBEY THE 15 MINUTE RULE.** To reduce the temptation of procrastination, each actionable step on a project should take no more than 15 minutes to complete.

- **HAVE CLEAR DEADLINES.** Assign yourself a deadline for projects and milestones and write it down in your day planner or calendar. Make your deadlines known to other people who will hold you accountable.

- **GIVE YOURSELF A REWARD.** Celebrate the completion of project milestones and reward yourself for getting projects done on time. It will provide positive reinforcement and motivate you toward your goals.

- • **REMOVE DISTRACTIONS.** You need to establish a positive working environment that is conducive to getting your work done. Remove any distractions.

Eat That Frog

There is a saying of Mark Twain's that aptly defines ending procrastination.

If the first thing you do each morning is to eat a live frog, you can go through the day with the satisfaction of knowing that that is probably the worst thing that is going to happen to you all day long!

Your frog is the task that will have the greatest impact on achieving your goals, and the task that you are most likely to procrastinate starting.

Another version of this saying is, "If you have to eat two frogs, eat the ugliest one first!"

This is another way of saying that if you have two important tasks before you, start with the biggest, hardest, and most important task first. Discipline yourself to begin immediately and then to persist until the task is complete before you go on to something else. You must resist the temptation to start with the easier task. You must also continually remind yourself that one of the most important decisions you make each day is your choice of what you will do immediately and what you will do later, or postpone indefinitely.

Finally, "If you have to eat a live frog, it does not pay to sit and look at it for a very long time!"

The key to reaching high levels of performance and productivity is for you to develop the lifelong habit of tackling your major task first thing each morning. Don't spend excessive time planning what you will do. You must develop the routine of "eating your frog" before you do anything else and without taking too much time to think about it.

Successful, effective people are those who launch directly into their major tasks and then discipline themselves to work steadily and single-mindedly until those tasks are complete.

In the business world, you are paid and promoted for achieving specific, measurable results. You are paid for making a valuable contribution that is expected of you. But many employees confuse activity with accomplishment and this causes one of the biggest problems in organizations today, which is failure to execute.

Prioritizing Your Time

Successful attention management demands that you learn to prioritize your time. Establishing priorities shows you where to focus your energy. Priorities should be used to create goals and schedule your time. There are different tools available that will help you prioritize your time.

The 80/20 Rule

The 80 / 20 rule states that 80 percent of our success comes from only 20 percent of our actions. This means that it is necessary to focus on the 20 percent of our actions that are the most effective. Prioritize goals, and focus on the 20 percent of activities that actively move you towards those goals. Give most of your attention to this 20 percent.

The Urgent / Important Matrix

We are often trapped performing urgent tasks that are not important. The distracted zone is an example of tasks that are urgent but not important. They may be important to the people around you, but they do nothing to help you meet your own goals. Important tasks should take priority because they are focused on specific goals. The proactive zone is an example of important activities.

The Urgent/Important Matrix:

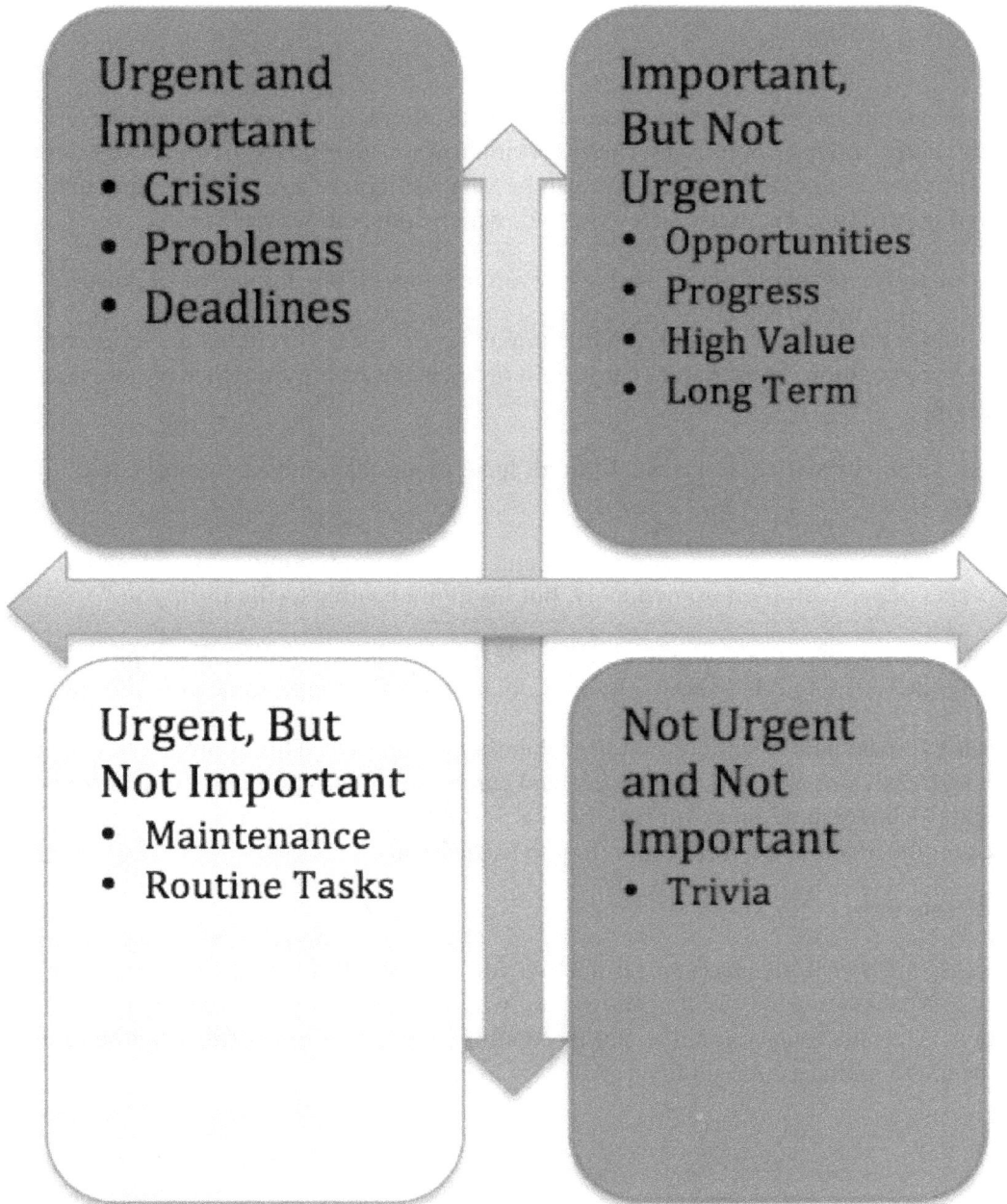

Urgent and Important
- Crisis
- Problems
- Deadlines

Important, But Not Urgent
- Opportunities
- Progress
- High Value
- Long Term

Urgent, But Not Important
- Maintenance
- Routine Tasks

Not Urgent and Not Important
- Trivia

- **URGENT AND IMPORTANT**: Activities in this area relate to dealing with critical issues as they arise and meeting significant commitments. *Perform these duties now.*

- **IMPORTANT, BUT NOT URGENT:** These success-oriented tasks are critical to achieving goals. *Plan to do these tasks next.*

- **URGENT, BUT NOT IMPORTANT:** These chores do not move you forward toward your own goals. Manage by delaying them, cutting them short and rejecting requests from others. *Postpone these chores.*

- **NOT URGENT AND NOT IMPORTANT:** These trivial interruptions are just a distraction, and should be avoided if possible. However, be careful not to mislabel things like time with family and recreational activities as not important. *Avoid these distractions altogether.*

Being Assertive

At times, requests from others may be important and need immediate attention. Often, however, these requests conflict with our values and take time away from working toward your goals. Even if it is something we would like to do but simply don't have the time for, it can be very difficult to say no. One approach in dealing with these types of interruptions is to use a Positive No, which comes in several forms.

- Say no, followed by an honest explanation, such as, "I am uncomfortable doing that because…"

- Say no and then briefly clarify your reasoning without making excuses. This helps the listener to better understand your position. Example: "I can't right now because I have another project that is due by 5 pm today."

- Say no, and then give an alternative. Example: "I don't have time today, but I could schedule it in for tomorrow morning."

- Empathetically repeat the request in your own words, and then say no. Example: "I understand that you need to have this paperwork filed immediately, but I will not be able to file it for you."

- Say yes, give your reasoning for not doing it, and provide an alternative solution. Example: "Yes, I would love to help you by filing this paperwork, but I do not have time until tomorrow morning."

- Provide an assertive refusal and repeat it no matter what the person says. This approach may be most appropriate with aggressive or manipulative people and can be an effective strategy to control your emotions. Example: "I understand how you feel, but I will not [or cannot]…" Remember to stay focused and not become sidetracked into responding to other issues.

Creating a Productivity Journal

Keeping track of how you spend your time and how productive you are will allow you to evaluate your priorities. A productivity journal is a useful tool that shows you where you spend your time and how effectively you are using it. A productivity journal is similar to a time log, and a spreadsheet can be used to create one. The journal needs to include three things:

- Activities

- Time spent on each activity

- Progress or outcome of the activity

The Glass Jar: Rocks, Pebbles, Sand and Water

The "rocks in a glass jar demonstration" is a familiar time management technique that is used to illustrate the importance of establishing priorities. A glass jar is filled with large rocks then pebbles. This is followed by sand and water. The purpose of the exercise is to teach participants that they need to put the large rocks in first or they will not fit later. The large rocks symbolize the priorities in our lives that are aligned with our values and goals.

Chapter 10 – Business and Etiquette

Success in any industry relies on relationships, whether with co-workers, clients, suppliers, or investors. When you're well-mannered and considerate in dealing with others, you create engaging, productive, and long term business relationships. As such, it is important to learn, not just the technical side of a business, but how to conduct one's self in the company of others.

This is where business etiquette comes in. This tutorial will introduce participants to business etiquette, as well as provide guidelines for the practice of business etiquette across different situations.

By the end of this chapter, you will be able to:

- Define etiquette and provide an example of how etiquette can be of value to a company or organization.

- Understand the guidelines on how to make effective introductions.

- Identify the 3 C's of a good impression.

- Identify at least one way to minimize nervousness while in social situations.

- Understand how to use a business card effectively.

- Identify and practice at least one way to remember names.

- Identify the 3 steps in giving a handshake.

- Enumerate the four levels of conversation and provide an example for each.

- Understand place settings, napkin etiquette, and basic table manners.

- Understand the protocol in ordering in a restaurant, handling alcohol in a business meal, paying the bill, and tipping.

- Understand basic guidelines when it comes to the proper form of address, grammar standards, and use of acronyms in e-mails.

- Understand basic guidelines in the use of the telephone, voicemail, and cell phone.

- State the difference between a formal and an informal letter.

- Create an effective 'Thank You' note.

- Understand the meaning of colors in dressing for success.

- Differentiate among the dressy casual, semi-formal, formal and black tie dress code.

- Understand basic guidelines in international etiquette.

Etiquette Principles Assessment

The purpose of the Pre-Assignment is to think about etiquette principles you are already practicing, and situations where you could use greater awareness/ practice of business etiquette.

As a pre-assignment, think of 3 business activities you conducted in the past 7 days. Focus on activities where there's interaction with other people. It doesn't have to be a big activity; it may be routine work like meeting with a client or replying to queries online.

After coming up with 3 activities, write how you had practiced good manners or professional courtesy for each activity; as much as possible, express the response in behavioral terms.

Lastly, what else could you have done in that situation to express good manners and professional courtesy?

The following table could be of help for this activity:

3 Business Activities I Did in the Last Week	How I showed good manners/ professional courtesy in this situation	What else I could have done to have expressed good manners/ professional courtesy.

Take a moment now to look at your responses and reflect on what it says about your current practice of business etiquette. Keep your responses in mind during the day as they provide the context for the etiquette guidelines that will be discussed later on.

Understanding Etiquette

Before we look at etiquette rules across multiple business-related scenarios, it's best to level off everyone on what etiquette means. We would also look at the many ways business etiquette can improve a company or an organization's bottom line.

Etiquette Defined

Josy Roberts, author of *'Business Etiquette Your Questions and Answers'*, defines etiquette as 'conventional rules of polite behavior.' They are guidelines on how to behave befitting good manners while in the company of other people. They show sensitivity to the needs and feelings of the person or people that you are with.

Etiquette covers most aspects of social interactions, including self-presentation, communication, courtesy, and hospitality. Business etiquette, in particular, covers expectations in the interactions between co-workers, the company and their clients, as well as the company and their stakeholders.

Etiquette guidelines are many and can be quite complicated. In this workshop we will focus on basic etiquette guidelines for situations typically found in most business settings.

The Importance of Business Etiquette

Etiquette can help businesses improve the following areas:

- **Branding**: Everything we do will reflect on our company and our products. By acting professionally, we send the message that our business is credible and trustworthy. Personalized care may very well be your edge against the competition.

- **Customer Care**: The best way to show customers that their patronage is valued is to treat them with respect and consideration. This in turn can inspire customer loyalty and positive feedback.

- **Employee Engagement:** Good manners will help improve morale and confidence between employees and team members.

- **Team Synergy**: Good manners will help establish smooth working relationships within a team, which contributes to greater productivity.

After the meeting, George understood where Jordan was going wrong. "You come off as cold", he told Jordan. "You don't shake hands with anyone and you seem very robotic when you talk, as if you're just going through the motions. Next time, try being more warm and open, and treat your clients like potential friends." Following George's advice, Jordan's meetings went much smoother in the future.

Networking for Success

When you're networking, it is important to make the most of the first meeting. In this module, we'll discuss how to create an effective introduction, make a good impression, minimize nervousness, use business cards effectively, and remember names.

Creating an Effective Introduction

Three steps to introducing yourself effectively:

Project warmth and confidence.

Many people size you up even before you say a word, which is why it's important to mind your body language. When you introduce yourself, stand up straight, relax, and establish eye contact.

State your first name and your last name. Depending on the situation, you may also state your affiliation or your position in the company.

Example: *"Hello. I'm Jill Smith. I'm the Quality Control Officer."*

When the other person has given their name, repeat it in acknowledgment.

"It's nice to meet you, Mr. Andrews." or *"It's nice to meet you, Joseph."* Repeating their name is an acknowledgment that you heard their introduction.

When you are networking is not just about presenting yourself. You may also find yourself introducing two strangers to one another. Here are some guidelines to introducing others:

- **Take note of the pecking order**. In business, introductions are made based on a person's seniority in a company. This is regardless of age and gender. When you make an introduction, present a person with the lesser status to the person with the higher status.

- Example: *"Caroline Daniels, I would like you to meet President Andrews. Caroline is the head of the Public Relations Department."*

- **Introduce strangers first**: If you are introducing two persons of equal rank to one another, start with the person that you don't know. This way you can use the introduction to make the newcomer feel welcome.

- **Mind titles**: Unless invited otherwise, stick to using formal address such as "Mr. Gallagher" or "Attorney Louis Harris".

Making a Great First Impression

If you want to make a good impression, know that you need to project 3 C's:

Confidence

- Having a straight but relaxed posture. Hold your head high and steady. Don't slouch or slump.

- Moving in a natural, unaffected manner.

- Maintaining eye contact with the people you are talking to.

Competence

- Exhibiting knowledge of your craft. Know your way around the agenda. Being prepared for the meeting. Bring supportive materials to emphasize your points.

- Answer questions in a clear and professional manner, avoiding the use of slang or technical jargon.

- Asking relevant questions.

Credibility

- Arriving on time.
- Being presentable (well-groomed and mindful of dress codes.

- Keeping true to your word.

Minimizing Nervousness

Meeting people can be anxiety-provoking. The need to impress another person can be a lot of pressure.

Here are some ways to minimize nervousness while in a social situation:

Be informed: If possible, take time to research about the people you're going to meet: their work, values, and preferences. Knowing what is expected from you can prepare you adequately. Nervousness is amplified by going into a situation blind.

Practice! Practice! Practice: Networking is a skill, which means that you can develop it with practice. Practice your introduction in front of a mirror and note what you need to improve. You can also practice with peers. Get feedback from others about the kind of impression you give. Try to meet as many people as you can! The more you do it, the easier it gets!

Learn relaxation techniques: There are many activities that can help relax a nervous person. These activities include:

- Meditation

- Self-talk

- Visualization

- Breathing exercises

- Listening to music.

Identify your triggers: If nervousness is a real problem for you, it is recommended that you identify what triggers your nervousness. Is it lack of confidence? Is it fear of authoritative people? Awareness can help you catch yourself in time and respond accordingly.

Believe in what you have to offer: It's easy to get intimidated by how successful or famous the other person is. But remember, they're people--- just like you! They would be willing to listen to someone who can offer them something that they want or need. Have faith in your business. Have faith in your personal worth. Adopt the mindset that you are doing them a service, and it's your duty to not let them miss the opportunity of meeting you!

Using Business Cards Effectively

Networking is not complete without receiving or giving a business card. The business card is a way for you to follow up on the people you have met. Likewise, it is a way for them to contact you for further meetings.

More than that, your business card is a way to brand yourself. Professional-looking business cards send the message that you're professional. Adding your company motto or tagline in your business advertises you and what you're all about.

5 Tips on Using Business Cards Effectively:

Tip 1: Never be without your business cards! (Make sure there's always a stack in your office desk, and in your wallet. You'll never know; even a trip to the grocery story can present an opportunity to network.

Tip 2: Follow the protocol on hierarchy. Cards should not be given to senior executives that you meet, unless they've asked for one.

Tip 3: Time the presentation of your card.

Don't just hand over your business card at any random moment. Handing a business card in the middle of a discussion can be an interruption, as parties would need to take a moment to give it a look. You also want to make sure that your card is perused at point when the other person can give it his or her full attention.

The best moments to hand a card is when you're asked for one, when you're asked to repeat your name, or when someone offers to send you something.

If the two organizations that you represent are well-known to each other, although you haven't met your host before, offering your card is probably best left to the end of the meeting. If your host is unfamiliar with your company, offering your card at the beginning of the meeting is good practice.

Tip 4: Accompany your business card with an explanation of what you can offer them.

When you hand another person your card, give a brief "action recommendation." This can increase the likelihood of them contacting you again. For instance you may say: "I think I can help with your PR concerns, Mr. Johnston. Here is my card."

You may also ask for referrals. Invite the other person to send your contact details to anyone they know who can use your services or products.

Tip 5: When receiving a business card, show the other person that you value their card.

Look at the business card for a few seconds. Comment about the card. Let them see that you take care in storing their card as well, instead of just jamming it in your pocket.

Remembering Names

Remembering names may be difficult for some people, but it's not impossible. It's a skill: something that you can improve with constant application.

Here are some ways to remember names:

Repeat: When someone is introduced to you, repeat their name. "It's a pleasure to meet you, Mark." This can help reinforce your memory of the name. You may also introduce them to someone else so that you can create an opportunity to use their name.

Use mental imagery: We think in pictures, therefore associating an image with a name can help in assisting recall. For example, after meeting Bill the plumber, imagine the word Bill spelled with pipes. If Jason Smith is marathon runner, imagine Jason running on a treadmill in a gym called Jason's. Or just imagine a person's name written on their forehead. Pick an imagery that works for you. The more striking or exaggerated your mental picture, the bigger are the chances of recall.

Put it on paper: Write the name down as soon as you can. Or write their details on the business card they give you so that you would remember them the next time you see them around. (Just make sure you don't let the person see you writing on their business card.)

Use their name in creative sentences: Mentally construct sentences that are fun and a bit frivolous, to make name recall less stressful. Alliterations, or repeating consonant sounds in succession, are a great way to remember names. For example, to remember Jane who sells kitchen ware, you can repeat in your head: *Jane makes jam and juice in January.*

Be genuinely interested: Remembering names begin with attitude. If you are sincerely interested in a person, then they would make an impact on you. If you adapt the attitude that everyone is interesting, and are a potential ally in business, then remembering names would come as second nature.

The Meet and Greet

An introduction is almost always accompanied by a handshake and conversation. In this module, we would discuss the three steps that make an effective handshake and the four levels of conversation.

The Three-Step Process

A handshake is a part of many social interactions. It's a way to introduce one's self, offer congratulations and even a way to conclude a business deal. A handshake is a gesture of goodwill.

The Three-Step Process to Handshake:

Facial Expression: Start non-verbal's that show openness and sincerity. Maintain eye contact. Smile.

Shake Hands: Your handshake gives an impression. If your grip is too lax, you send the message that you're hesitant and possibly indecisive. If your grip is too tight, you might come across as too brash, even intimidating. Go for a grip that's in between. It sends the message that you're confident. For most occasions, two or three pumps of the hand are appropriate. Longer handshakes can make some people feel uncomfortable. But there are people who do prefer longer handshakes. If uncertain, go with the flow, and follow the lead of the other person. If you feel that it's time to let go, just relax your hand to signal the other person.

Greet the Person: Talk to the person whose hand you are shaking. A simple 'hello' or 'how do you do" is appropriate.

The Four Levels of Conversation

The real art of conversation is not only to say the right thing at the right time, but to leave unsaid the wrong thing at a tempting moment. It requires sensitivity at this stage of a relationship, the context of the conversation and the comfort level of the person you are talking to depend on it.

There are four levels of conversation based on the degree and amount of personal disclosure. They are:

Small Talk: This is commonly referred to as the 'exchange of pleasantries' stage. In this level, you talk only about generic topics, subjects that almost everyone is comfortable discussing. These subjects include the weather, the location you're both in and current events.

The small talk stage establishes rapport; it makes a person feel at ease with you. It's also a safe and neutral avenue for people to subtly 'size up' one another, and explore if it's a conversation or relationship that they'd want to invest in.

If the small talk goes well, you can proceed into the next level: fact disclosure.

Fact Disclosure: In this stage, you tell the other person some facts about you such as your job, your area of residence, and your interests.

This is a 'getting-to-know' stage, and it aims to see if you have something in common with the other person. It's also a signal that you are opening up a little bit to the other person while still staying on neutral topics.

If the fact disclosure stage goes well, you can proceed to sharing viewpoints and opinions.

Viewpoints and Opinions: In this stage of the conversation, you can offer what you think about various topics like politics, the new business model ---or even the latest blockbuster. It helps then to read and be curious about many things, from politics to entertainment to current events.

Sharing viewpoints and opinions require the 'buffering effect' of the first two stages for two reasons:

First, a person needs rapport with another before they can discuss potentially contentious statements, even if they're having a healthy debate.

Second, sharing viewpoints and opinions opens a person to the scrutiny of another, and this requires that there is some level of safety and trust in a relationship. The controversial, and therefore potentially offensive, nature of an opinion exists in a range; make sure that you remain within the 'safe' zone in the early stages of your relationship.

Personal Feelings: The fourth stage is disclosure and acknowledgment of personal feelings. For instance you can share about your excitement for the new project, or your worry about your son's upcoming piano recital. Depending on the context and the level of the friendship, you can disclose more personal subjects. This stage requires trust, rapport, and even a genuine friendship, because of the intimate nature of the subject.

Different people have different comfort levels when it comes to disclosing feelings, and there are cases when you'd need several conversations before they would trust enough to open themselves. In some cases, you never get to this stage. Just make sure to be sensitive and test the other person's readiness before opening an intimate topic.

Listening is vital in all stages of the conversation but especially so in this fourth stage. Listen with empathy and understanding to acknowledge that you heard the feeling that they have shared.

The Dining in Style

Conducting business over meals is a great way to build business relationships. Meals make for a more casual atmosphere compared to offices, and are therefore more conducive for a relaxed discussion. In this module, we would discuss some of the etiquette rules when dining with business associates such as understanding place setting, etiquette rules while eating, and ways to avoid sticky situations.

Understanding Your Place Setting

Place setting is the arrangement of the drinking vessels (glasses, mugs), food receptacles (plates, bowls, and saucers), and utensils (spoons, forks, knives) that will be used during a meal.

Place settings differ depending on the menu and the formality of the dining event. The more informal you intend your meal to be, the less rigidly you have to adhere to the rules of place setting.

Here are a few basics to remember:

Solids on the left, liquids on the right.

Plates are always placed on the left, while glasses are on the upper right. This guide can help you find which place settings are yours.

Forks are on the left, knives, and spoons on the right side of the plate.

In general, forks are placed to the left of the plate with the exception of the oyster fork which is placed on the right.

Work your way inwards with the utensils.

The rule for utensils is to work inward toward your plate as the meal progresses. Place settings are organized so that, with each new course presented, the guest can use the outermost utensil(s). For instance, the salad fork would be leftmost, before the dinner fork, as the salad comes before the main course.

Follow the 'rule of three's.'

If you're hosting the dinner, don't clutter the table with too many implements. Set at most three of anything (e.g. three glasses, three forks etc.). If more than three would be used, then the additional implement would come as the new meal is presented.

Using Your Napkin

Here are some etiquette guidelines to using your napkin:

- When everyone is seated, gently unfold your napkin and place it on your lap. If the napkin is large, fold the napkin in half first.

- Your napkin remains on your lap throughout the entire meal. If you need to use your napkin to clean something on your lips, just dab it lightly.

- If you leave the table during a dinner, place your napkin on your chair to signal to the server that you will be returning.

- When you are finished dining, place your napkin neatly on the table to the left side of the plate.

- If you drop your napkin on the floor, discreetly ask the waiter or host for another one.

Eating Your Meal

Basic etiquette guidelines when eating:

- Don't talk business during the meal proper, unless the senior members want to do so. Otherwise, business matters should be addressed either before the meal or after it.

- Take a cue from the host, or the most senior in the table, where to sit yourself.

- Take your cue from the host, or the most senior in the table, when to begin eating.

- Keep elbows off the table while eating. Elbows on the table are acceptable in between meals.

- Don't talk with your mouth full. Chew quietly. Don't slurp your liquids.

- Don't apply make-up or comb your hair while dining.

- Don't pick your teeth at the table.

- If you need something that is not within your reach, politely ask the person next to you to pass it to you. Food is typically passed from left to right.

- Try to pace yourself so that you can finish at the same time as everyone else. When you have finished eating, you can let others know that you have by placing your knife and folk together, with the tines on the fork facing upwards, on your plate.

- Don't forget to thank your host for the meal!

Sticky Situations and Possible Solutions

Here are some awkward dining situations and how to deal with them:

- Having put something in your mouth that doesn't agree with you: Ask the waiter for a paper napkin and discreetly spit the food out. Crumple the napkin and place it under the sides of your plate. Keep the food you had spit out away from the other's view.

- You accidentally spilt food or drinks on a guest: Don't panic. Apologize sincerely first. Use the cloth napkin and water to gently wipe the spill. You may also guide the guest to the wash room.

- A guest commits a faux pas: If you notice that a colleague or a subordinate is using the wrong utensil, the best way to let them know is by using the right one yourself. Don't correct them, it would just cause embarrassment.

- You've noticed a bug in your food: Discreetly send it out to the server. You don't have to tell everyone as it might ruin their appetite.

- You have dietary limitations: If you cannot eat a certain type of food or have some special needs, tell your host several days before the dinner party. This can help avoid awkward situations like not being able to eat what was served because of a health issue or religious conviction.

Eating Out

In the previous module, we talked about etiquette guidelines relating to dining in style. In this module, we will look at basic courtesies to be observed while eating out, including guidelines in ordering in a restaurant, intake of alcohol during a business meeting, paying the bill and tipping.

Ordering in a Restaurant

The following are some basic etiquette rules when ordering:

- As with many places, say 'please' and 'thank you' especially when addressing the waiter or server. For example, say "May I have the tuna casserole?" or "Could I please see your specials?"

- Don't order the most expensive item. When in doubt, follow the lead of the host. If they give an indication for you to do that, then order that.

- If you're the host, cue the server subtly at the start of the meal. You can say "My guests would like to know your specials" or "I'd like my guests to order first". Servers take orders from the first person to the host's right so make sure that you sit yourself to the immediate left of the most senior member of the group.

- Don't order for your associate. If they seem indecisive, offer a recommendation.

- If, after looking at the menu, you see items that you are uncertain about, ask your server any questions that you may have. Answering your questions is part of the server's job.

About Alcoholic Beverages

In general, alcohol is not recommended to be part of a business meeting. Alcohol intake lowers inhibition, which might affect the professional atmosphere at the table. Even if the meal is a social occasion meant to establish a relationship, you'd still want to project your best in front of potential partners and clients.

Depending on your guests, alcohol may be appropriate or even expected. If you do have to drink alcohol, limit it to 1 or 2 glasses.

What are the instances when alcohol is appropriate?

- Dinners are traditionally accompanied by wine. White wine goes with fish and poultry, while red wine goes with red meats.

- During celebratory occasions, such as a deal going through, a toast may be in order.

- There are certain cultures where wine is expected. Germans like to drink wine before a meal; Texans find a beer appropriate with a barbecue lunch.

If uncertain on how alcohol will be handled, take a cue from others at your table. If the boss, client, or interviewer orders a drink, then you can follow suit.

Paying the Bill

Here are some etiquette tips when paying the bill:

Who picks the tab? The host picks up the tab. If you're the one who invited the guests, then it is assumed that you would be the one picking up the tab.

If a client or investor invites you to discuss something that would profit you, it's good form to at least offer to pay the bill. If they insist paying, offer once to at least pay your half and just leave it at that. Never fight over a bill if someone else offers to pay; you can counter once, and then after that simply thank the person paying for the generosity and offer to pick up the tab the next time.

Be discreet in paying the bill: If you can, arrange that the receipt be not brought to your table. You can do this by:

- Requesting that the bill be held at the Maitre D's station. Excuse yourself as the meal is coming to a close, go to the station to review and sign the slip, and pick up your receipt.

- Arranging to pick the check on your way out.

- Arranging to have the check sent to your office.

- Leaving your credit card with the restaurant, and request that the server add the tip to the meal. The server will then run your credit card ahead of time, and return it and the receipt for you to sign at the end of the meal.

If the slip is brought to your table, pick it up and check the total without comment. Put the check *face down* on the tray in a folder with your card or money underneath.

Don't fuss with the check. Don't let the others know how much the meal cost.

Tipping

Tip appropriately. The standard is 15% for moderate service and 20% for excellent service of the pre-tax cost of the meal. In a self-service or buffet style restaurant, a tip of 10-12% is standard.

Deal with bad food or service by talking to the manager. Remember that many get a portion of the waiter's tip, not just the waiter, so you may be punishing the chef for a server's lack and vice-versa.

Keep the tip between you and the staff. There is no need to flaunt how much you gave.

Business Email Etiquette

Email is a convenient and effective medium to conduct business communication. In this module we will discuss etiquette guidelines on how to address an email message, the use of grammar and acronyms in the letter body and top 5 technology tips.

Addressing Your Message

Here are two basic guidelines in addressing an email:

Know when to use the To, Cc and Bcc fields.

There are three common ways to address an email, and each way is most appropriate to specific contexts.

Using the 'To' field.

The 'To' field is used when sending a direct message to someone.

You may send the same email to multiple addresses using the 'To' field. Do so when your email is meant to be addressed directly to all recipients, as in the case of a manager directing his team.

Note though that when you use the 'To' field, all email addresses can be viewed by all recipients. Put multiple addresses in the 'To' field only when every recipient is okay with his or her email address being released to everyone.

Using the 'Cc' field.

Cc stands for carbon copy.

You use the 'Cc' field to send a copy of the email message to people who are not meant to be the direct recipients of the message, but still need to be kept on the loop.

For instance, if a manager has ordered his secretary to send a memo to everyone in the department, the secretary may place all the department employees' email address on the 'To' section, and the manager's email address on the 'Cc' field.

Note that, like the 'To' field, all email addresses entered in a 'Cc' field can be viewed by everyone.

Using the "Bcc' field.

Bcc stands for Blind carbon copy.

When you place email addresses in 'Bcc' field, recipients are 'blind' to other recipients' email address. The use of the 'Bcc' field is most appropriate if the recipients have not given permission for their email address to be released, or if there is reason to keep the email address private.

Because the 'Bcc' field offers privacy that the 'To' and 'Cc' fields do not, you may use the blind carbon copy field for both direct and indirect email messages where privacy of email addresses is needed. If you wish to send an email to many direct recipients, but you don't wish to disclose anyone's email address, just use your own email address in the 'To' field, and use the 'Bcc' field for the recipients' addresses.

Address the receiver by name in the first sentence of your email. *Mary, I received copies of the file.* Use the proper address, like Dr. or Mr. until told to use first names. You may take your cue from the way they sign their email.

Grammar and Acronyms

While online mediums of communication have developed their own vocabulary, it's best to remember that business emails the same formality as any business letter.

Here are some key things to remember with regards to grammar and the use of acronyms in an email.

- Always follow the rules of good grammar. You may refer to English writing style guides for these rules.

- Always use full sentences and words with proper sentence structure. Don't use text-speak. For example use "The reports are due on Monday." instead of "D reports r due Mon"

- Proper capitalization and punctuation are a must! In email, all caps give the impression that you're shouting, and small caps are hard to read. For example: use "The report should include an evaluation report." instead of "The report SHOULD INCLUDE AN EVALUATION REPORT."

- In business emails, avoid text-speak abbreviations such as BTW (by the way), IMHO (In my honest opinion,) and LOL (laugh out loud). Avoid the use of emoticons, as well.

Top 5 Technology Tips

Here are 5 tips when using technology:

Medium is the message: There are some things that are better done face-to-face rather than through the net. An example of this is delivering negative feedback. Don't use technology when a personal approach is much more appropriate and or desirable.

Always re-read your letters: Some statements don't come across well when written. An ironic joke, if people can't see the twinkle in your eye, can end up sounding insulting. Read everything twice before you send it.

Think security: Do not assume privacy when communicating online. Do not use emails to discuss confidential and speculative information.

Think of your recipient's convenience: Since reading from a screen is more difficult than reading from paper, the structure and lay out is very important for e-mail messages. Use short paragraphs and blank lines between each paragraph. When making points, number them or mark each point with bullets.

Also don't attach lengthy documents in your email. Forcing your client to read a long document through a screen is insensitive, not to mention the time it would cost them to download bulk files. If a hard copy is possible, then send a hard copy instead.

Skip it if it's not necessary: Remember that most emails now go into PDA's. Before sending a message in the late hours, ask yourself: how will they react to me sending a text message?

Before you forward a memo you've received to your staff, think if they really need this piece of information. It's nice to keep your staff up to date, but not to the point that you're clogging their inboxes.

Phone Etiquette

This time we will look at telephone etiquette. Particularly, we will discuss how to develop an appropriate greeting, how to deal with voicemail and cell phone do's and don'ts.

Developing an Appropriate Greeting

How to create an appropriate phone greeting:

Say your greeting:

Business telephones should always be answered with a phrase like, "Good morning" or "Good Afternoon." Speak clearly and distinctly, in a pleasant tone of voice. Some trainers recommend smiling before one answers the phone in order to project a positive energy into one's voice.

Identify yourself and the company. It's only polite to tell the other person on the line that they've reached the right place.

"This is ABC Company, Carol speaking." Or "You've reached Marks and Spencer, this is Jonathan."

Inquire how you might be of assistance.

"How may I be of service?" or "How can I help you?" can set the tone.

Dealing with Voicemail

Tips on leaving a voicemail message:

- State your name, affiliation and phone number.

- State your reason for calling.

- State any action plan or action required on your message.

Tips on managing your own voicemail:

- Record your own personal greeting. Include in your greeting your name, the department and or company name so that people know they have reached the correct person.

- Give people information that can help them, to save you time as well. *Example: "Please leave a brief message stating how I can help you, along with your phone number, and I will call you back."*

- Stay on top of your messages. The number of times you check voicemail each day will vary depending on your job function and industry. However, if you have not told people differently, at a minimum you should check messages once a day and return those calls. State when you would be unavailable if you can't respond within 24 hours. Example: *"I'm out of the office today, January 3rd. I will be returning January 5th. I will not check voicemail until I am back. If this is an emergency or you need immediate assistance, please call Bill Withers at 555-555-6789.*

Cell Phone Do's and Don'ts

Here are some cell phone do's and don'ts.

- Don't take calls in the middle of a business meeting or a conversation with another person. Exceptions are when you receive an urgent call, but excuse yourself first before taking it. Likewise, set your ringer to silent or your phone to just vibrate mode when in a social conversation.

- Never talk in intimate settings or places where silence is imperative. Examples of these are elevators, libraries, museums, restaurants, cemeteries, theaters, dentist or doctor waiting rooms, places of worship, auditoriums or other enclosed public spaces, such as hospital emergency rooms or buses.

- Don't talk on a cell phone in a public place. A good rule to keep is the 10 feet rule --- answer calls at least 10 feet away from the next person!

- If you really have to take a call in public, step out or to a secluded area to take that call. You can also set your phone to voicemail when going out in public. If you really must take the call, answer briefly to tell that you're in a public place and that you would return the call as soon as possible.

- Keep business calls within business hours. Just because it's a cell phone doesn't mean that you can call anytime.

The Written Letter

Even in written communication, appropriate tone, content and format must be observed. In this module, we would discuss how to write a 'Thank You' note, a formal letter and an informal letter.

Thank You Notes

Expressing appreciation is always a good idea, whether it's for a gift, an act of kindness, or a business courtesy. You can do this by sending a 'thank you' note.

The formality of your thank you note depends on your relationship with the person you're sending the note to. A thank you note to a senior who gave you a promotion would be more formal than, say, a thank you note to a long-time client for hosting your lunch. Formal ones can be written on the company letterhead, and non-formal ones can simply be a handwritten letter on a piece of stationary.

A thank you note need not be a long letter. Most thank you letters mention:

- Your thanks

- What you're thanking them for

- What their gesture, gift, or action meant to you or the company

Example:

August 14, 2010

Joseph Marvin
Sinclair Enterprises

Dear Joseph,
I would like to express my appreciation for your hard work in preparing the presentation for the Widget account. It was a last minute notice and I knew you pulled in some overtime to get it done. Despite your limited time to prepare, the materials were top-notch and on-target. The presentation went well and we owe it all to you.

Thanks again,
Velma Torres

Formal Letters

A formal style is recommended for most business correspondence. It shows courtesy, professionalism, and knowledge of protocol. As a rule, use a formal style unless invited otherwise or you have already established a relationship with the person you're writing to.

Here are some basic rules when composing formal letters:

Stationary*:* Formal letters are written in plain white (or shades of white like cream) 8 1/2-by-11 inch paper. Stationary that bears the company letterhead may also be used.

Content: A formal letter usually contains the following sections:

- Sender's full name and address

- Addressee's full name and address

- Date the letter is sent (or assumed to fall into the hands of the receiver)

- Formal Salutation e.g. *"Dear + Formal Address"*

- A Subject Heading e.g. *"Re: Job Opening for Quality Control Officer"*

- Letter Body

- Formal Closing e.g. *"Respectfully yours, Sincerely yours,"*

- Name and Signature of the Sender

Lay-out on Page: There are two commonly used lay-outs for a formal letter: the block and the semi-block. In the block format, all text is aligned to the left margin and the paragraph is not indented. In the semi-block format, all text is aligned to the left margin but the paragraphs are indented. Both formats are considered appropriate for business correspondence.

Tone: Formal letters are formal in tone. Words are spelled out and the sentences follow grammatically correct sentence structure. Comments are organized in a clear and concise manner, and avoid unnecessary information. Slang is avoided.

Informal Letters

An informal business letter is a shorter and more straight-forward version of a formal letter. Standard rules on grammar and spelling correctness still apply, but with certain flexibilities.

For instance, contractions, abbreviations, and slang may be permissible as long as the professional tone of the letter is preserved.

The tone in an informal business letter is more relaxed and conversational. Salutations and closings can be more personalized, for instance you may use *"Hey Jim,"* instead of *"Dear Mr. Wentworth;"* and close with *"Cheers,"* instead of *"Respectfully yours,"*

Content can be less technical or academic. Familiarity is assumed but the respect is still there. Example, you can replace *"This letter is in reference to your letter dated July 4, 2009..."* to *"Regarding your message last week..."*

Dressing for Success

A significant part of practicing etiquette is proper self-presentation. The way you look talks to people, not just how you want to project yourself, but also the courtesy you have for the people in your company. In this module, we would discuss guidelines in dressing for success. Particularly, we would talk about the meaning of colors, the meaning of dress codes and guidelines on how to choose the right clothes to wear.

The Meaning of Colors

Here are some guidelines in the use of colors in business attires:

- In general, conservative colors are perceived as more professional and appropriate for business-related situations. These colors include black (which is perceived as the most formal), white, dark-gray, and navy blue. Conservative colors are recommended for formal occasions; you can be more playful during casual days.

- Wear these conservative colors in solid blocks instead of as part of a printed pattern.

- The main suit is recommended to have conservative colors but louder colors can be mixed with the accessories. E.g. the tie and pocket squares for men or scarf for the women.

Some of the common interpretations associated with colors are:

- Red – dominance and power

- Orange – warmth and enthusiasm

- Yellow – optimism and confidence

- Green - vitality and harmony

- Blue - serenity and peace

- A lot of companies use color dress code for building their brand as employees interact with the consumers. Also, when the workforce dresses the same color, it further brings unity among the employees.

Interpreting Common Dress Codes

Dress codes often depend on the company or industry where you work in, and even in the type of job that you do. It is also not unusual for different activities in the same job to call for different dress codes.

Dressy Casual: Dressy casual means dressed up versions of casual looks. For men, it could be neatly pressed slacks and a sports coat. For women, it can be slacks, but also skirts, dresses. This can be matched with solid color t-shirts, mock turtleneck, polo shirt, collared or button down shirts/blouses.

Casual means anything goes but in the business setting, casual is recommended to be interpreted as dressy casual.

- Semi-Formal: Semi formal means a medium between formal and informal. For men, semi-formal can translate to neatly pressed dress pants, slacks, button shirts, & ties. Jackets are optional but preferred. For ladies, it's evening dress, dinner dress (knee length) or some pants suits.

- Formal: Formal means tuxedos, dark suits, and ties for men. For ladies, it's cocktail to floor length dresses, nylons and dress shoes.

- Black tie: Black tie is the most formal dress code. Men wears black tuxedo coat, trousers with satin ribbon, cummerbund and bow tie. Ladies are to wear ball gowns. There are dress codes that state 'Black tie optional'. This means that the men have the option of wearing a regular suit with a tie instead of a tuxedo. Ladies have the option of wearing a cocktail gown or a dinner dress. Long to full-length skirts are preferred.

Deciding What to Wear

Tips when deciding what to wear:

- When attending a work-related social function, try to determine how your host or hostess would like you to dress and go with their response. There is nothing wrong in making inquiries about dress codes beforehand.

- Casual generally means that you can wear whatever you want. But in business, casual carries with it a lot of do's and don'ts. You should dress comfortably but not too comfortable. Business casual means avoiding flip-flops, shorts, cut-off jeans and halters.

- When dressing in the office, refer to the company dress code or if none is written, check the company culture.

- Note the context of the meeting, the seniority of the company, as well as the venue. Obviously, lunch at a burger place is more casual than lunch at a star-rated restaurant. A meeting with board members is more formal than a meeting with your staff. Dress accordingly.

- When in doubt of your client's dress policy, err on the side of conservative. It's better to be overdressed than underdressed.

International Etiquette

Etiquette is heavily influenced by culture; each country and nation has their own set of rules for polite behavior. When dealing with an international clientele, or when conducting business in a foreign country, it's best to be aware of local etiquette guidelines. In this module we would discuss general rules in international etiquette, important points, and ways to prepare.

General Rules

Etiquette is heavily influenced by culture; what may be good manners in one country or to one nation may not be good manners in another. As most businesses today are operating with a global mindset, it pays always keep international etiquette in mind.

- Always take the time to research cross-cultural etiquette when dealing with a foreign client, or when conducting business in a foreign country.

- Awareness of international etiquette is important not just in face-to-face meetings but also in non face-to-face encounters such as sending gifts, conversing over the phone or communicating online.

Areas you need to look at include:

- Religion

- Dress Codes

- Social Hierarchy

- Rules on Meet and Greets

- Use of titles and forms of address

- **Exchanging business cards**

- Valuing Time

- Physical Space

- Dealing with embarrassment

- When uncertain, err on the side of what you presume is conservatism. And be observant; check if people are becoming uncomfortable.

- Etiquette mishaps in international setting can range from merely embarrassing to potentially insulting to the other person. When you realize that you have committed a faux pas, apologize immediately and ask how you can make up for it.

Important Points

Here are some important points when dealing with other cultures:

Some cultures dress conservatively as the norm.

Americans tend to be more relaxed when it comes to dress codes, and even recommends dressing for comfort in certain fields and professions. People from other parts of the world are generally more conservative. The Japanese, for example, dress according to rank. Some Muslim nations find short dresses for women as offensive. If uncertain, err on the side of conservatism.

Some cultures meet and greet people with a kiss, a hug, or a bow instead of a handshake.

A handshake for greeting is mostly universal. However, don't be surprised if you are occasionally met with a kiss, a hug, or a bow somewhere along the way.

Stick to formal titles for business interactions unless invited otherwise.

Approach first names with caution when dealing with people from other cultures. Some cultures are very hierarchical, and with consider it disrespect to be addressed without their title. Some cultures never accept first names in the business setting, and this should be respected.

Some cultures are less time-conscious than others.

Don't take it personally if someone from a more relaxed culture keeps you waiting or spends more of that commodity than you normally would in meetings or over meals. Stick to the rules of punctuality, but be understanding when your contact from another country seems unconcerned.

Understand differences in perception of personal space.

Americans have a particular value for their own physical space and are uncomfortable when other people get in their realm. If the international visitor seems to want to be close, accept it. Backing away can send the wrong message.

Preparation Tips

- It starts with being open-minded.

- Read up!

Possible resources:

- Publications put out by the Department of Trade and Industry (DTI) and local embassies. They usually provide basic facts about demographics and business practices.

- The Economist Business Traveler's Guides have chapters designed to develop awareness with reviews of local etiquette and customs and the 'elusive psychological factors' that can make or break a deal.

- Slim volumes on Simple Etiquette by Paul Norbury Publications.

- Find informants, or experts with good local knowledge of both countries, and simply ask them to talk to you over a good lunch or dinner. If you live near a university or a centre of expertise on a particular country, it can also be helpful to seek guidance from experts who will probably be only too glad to be consulted and share their knowledge.

- For the really serious there is no better way than to spend at least two or three days traveling with at least two representatives selling your company's products or services. Use the time to absorb the atmosphere, methodologies, hospitalities, practices, and styles.

- Take a more specialized course on international etiquette if relating with international clients is a big part of your job description.

In this growing electronic age, we often forget how important it can be to have simple telephone etiquette. Outside the realm of texting and emails, many people still use the telephone as a primary source of communication. Knowing the proper etiquette and procedures for speaking with someone on the telephone can show a great deal of professionalism as well as social knowledge.

- Recognize the different aspects of telephone language

- Properly handle inbound/outbound calls

- Know how to handle angry or rude callers

- Learn to receive and send phone messages

- Know different methods of employee training

Aspects of Phone Etiquette

Many people do not realize they have little or no phone etiquette. When they recognize this, they are often unsure about where to start. One of the first steps to gaining or improving a person's phone etiquette is to know the different aspects of it, such as phrasing and listening skills. Learning this knowledge can be a great starter tool for many people and can help them feel more confident on the phone right away.

Phrasing

When speaking on the telephone, a different set of phrasing is used instead of our everyday talking phrases. Using a more professional group of phrasing portrays to the caller a sense of confidence and a sense that you are there to help them. Using phrases such "Could you", "May I?", "Please", and "Thank you" can help the person on the other end of the line feel more comfortable and feel more at ease with your politeness. Important phrasing sections include introductions, transitions and even call conclusions. Although some of the phrasing can seem uncomfortable at first, but with practice, they can become as natural as our everyday speech.

Examples:

- "How may I help you?"

- "Thank you for calling."

- "Could you repeat that name again?"

- "One moment while I transfer you."

- "May I take a message?"

Tone of Voice

The tone of voice in which we speak can portray a variety of emotions and feelings. When we're sad or angry our voice can lower in tone; and when we're happy or excited it can raise higher. It is generally recommended that when we speak on the telephone, we should speak in our normal tone of voice, if not a few decimals higher. Lower tones of voice can imply sarcasm or disinterest. The speaker should never speak in monotone, which can sound bored and make the caller feel as though the speaker is not sincere. When possible, use inflection in your voice to help stress important points and give the caller verbal hints as to where the conversation is going.

Tips:

- Speak in a normal speaking tone of voice (or higher)

- Avoid lower tones or monotones

- Use inflection when possible

Speaking Clearly

When speaking on the telephone, the two callers cannot read lips or take notice of any sort of body language, so it's important to speak clearly and in a professional tone of voice. Do not speak too quickly, since it can cause your words to sound jumbled or rushed. However, speaking too slowly can make words sound distorted and can mislead the caller from what is trying to be said. As you speak, articulate your words and ensure not to slur any sounds together. When you are finished speaking, pause periodically for signs that the caller has heard and understood you, such as answering the question or a simple "Mm hmm". If in the end they did not catch what you said, calmly repeat the information and try again.

Tips:

- Take deep breaths before each phone call

- Speak slowly – do not rush your phrases

- Pause for understanding from the caller

- Repeat words if necessary

Listen to the Caller

With a telephone in our hand, we can often feel a sense of power and can feel the urge to perform all of the speaking – and forget how to listen. However, we forget that the purpose of the call is the person calling us to begin with. After you give your introduction, pause for a moment to listen for the caller to begin speaking and identify the purpose of their call. Allow the caller to finish speaking without interruptions. Focus on what the caller needs and what they are wanting. When they are finished, reaffirm what they are wanting, which is sometimes referred to as active listening. Let the caller know what you can do for them and how you can help with their needs.

Using Proper Phone Language

Every environment we enter requires a different form of 'language'. For instance, we wouldn't enter a team meeting with the same type of language we may use in the break room. The same is true for the telephone. Telephone language is different than our everyday language and can take some time to get used to its flow. But with the right tools, it can be easy to adapt in no time.

Please and Thank You

Using good etiquette is a way to show respect and consideration to those we interact with. Some of the basic essentials of proper etiquette are phrases such as "Please" and "Thank you". When asking the caller for something, such as their name or account number, always follow with "please". After the customer has given something to you or says something polite, follow with "thank you" to show your appreciation for their help. Using "Please" and "Thank you" when speaking with a customer allows the operator to remain professional while still showing courtesy and respect.

Examples:

- "May I have your name, please?"

- "Please hold for one moment, Mr. Smith."

- "Thank you for your time today."

Do Not Use Slang

Slang is typically defined as a type of language that consists of words and phrases that are regarded as very informal and are used in everyday speech. Common examples include "Yeah", "Y'all", "I guess so", and "ain't". Slang is not appropriate to use on the telephone and should not be used, even if we know the caller. Slang language implies inconsideration and disrespect to the caller and can make them feel as though you do not want take your time to help them. It is important to always use professional and courteous language in order to convey to the caller that you are there to help and can get the job done.

Avoid Using the Term "You"

When speaking with someone on the telephone, it can be easy to get lost in speaking with the caller and letting them know what they may need to do on their end. However, it is important for the operator to avoid using the term "you" excessively. When we continuously use the term 'you', in reference to the caller, it sends the message that everything is their responsibility and that the person on the other end of the line is not there to help them. If we continuously tell them they have to complete a task before we can help them, the company not only looks unprofessional, but unwilling to do business with them.

Avoid phrases such as:

- "You will need to call back tomorrow."

- "You have to take your bill to the other office."

- "I need you to come into the office for that."

Emphasize What You Can Do, Not What You Can't

When we are speaking with someone on the phone, for any reason, it can be hard to communicate what the caller wants or needs from the operator. Sometimes the operator is quick to tell the caller that they cannot complete a certain task or that they cannot help them at all – but this type of attitude does not build relationships. Flatly telling someone you cannot do anything for them shuts the door on negotiations and portrays a negative light on the company. Instead, emphasize what you can do for the caller. Offer 'favors' or alternate tasks you can do for them to help them get what they need. If you're genuinely not able to answer their questions or do something for them, it's alright to let them know that, but offer an alternative action for them, such as finding someone who can help.

Examples:

- "I can help you with that."

- "I'll be happy to transfer you to the department."

- "I can take a message if you'd like."

- "I don't know the answer, but let me find someone that does."

Eliminate Phone Distractions

Distractions can be very common in an office environment. Since employees are not alone or isolated, we learn to adapt to the sounds of other people in the room, telephones or fax machines ringing or even the occasional visitor to our work station. However, if we let these distractions hinder our telephone etiquette, it will cause us to sound unprepared and unprofessional.

Avoid Eating or Drinking

It is a common practice to have something at our desk to sip on or snack on during the day. However, this food and drink should not get in the way of your telephone calls. When someone calls in, be sure to finish chewing/drinking before picking up the phone so your voice is clear and residue free. When you are making a call, do not snack or drink while waiting for the other person to pick up. It never fails that the other party will pick up the line in the middle of your chewing/gulping.

Eating and drinking while on the phone not only distorts our telephone etiquette, but it can also distract us from the task at hand. It's difficult to focus on the caller when we are trying to find the lid to our drink or attempting to wipe our hands of sticky residue from our snack. If possible, keep any food and drinks in a drawer or cabinet until ready to consume them, such as between making calls or when you have a few minutes between incoming calls. But once a call is made/comes to your line, remove the food to somewhere out of sight until you have finished.

Minimize Multi-Tasking

Multi-tasking can be a great tool to have in any office. After all, it's helpful to be able to fill out a form while researching new meeting topics on the internet. However, when speaking on the telephone, less multi-tasking is actually better. Although we are capable of multi-tasking in many different areas while on the phone, it is better to minimize these tasks in order to better provide the caller with our attention and courtesy. When we multi-task, we are dividing our attention among several different areas, which, in reality, doesn't allow us to focus on any area of importance. The customer on the other end of the telephone line requires a great deal of devotion and needs to know that they have our attention, and not only parts of it. It is acceptable to have tools available to you while speaking on the telephone, such as looking for the caller's information in a computer database or completing a hand-written form for them while they speak. But if it does not pertain to the present call or the current caller, put it aside until later.

Remove Office Distractions

Sometimes distractions are all around us and we may not even be aware of it. Office distractions are a common source of our attention stealers and can include simple items such as personal photos, piles of paperwork on our desk, the nearby copy machine or even a recent memo/email hanging on our wall. While some of these items may be helpful to us, such as printed memos or recent paperwork, they can become a distraction when trying to have a conversation over the phone. When speaking on the phone, our attention should be focused on the caller, but seeing random paperwork or hearing the copy machine react can cause a knee-jerk reaction to remember a task we haven't completed or a project we still need to work on, thus taking attention away from the caller. Before you begin taking or making phone calls, take an inventory of your desk and the area around you. Remove any items that can distract you until you are ready to handle them so that they do not grab your attention before then.

Common office distractions include:

- Personal photos or artifacts

- Various paperwork out on the desk

- Memos or sticky notes

- Malfunctioning office equipment (i.e. office chairs, copy machine, computers, etc.)

Do Not Let Others Interrupt You

When we work in an office environment, it's not uncommon to have coworkers around our workstation. Sometimes our coworker is in the same cubicle as we are! This in itself can be a distraction. But the problem with coworkers is that there are always those that want to stop at your cubicle to ask lots of questions or want to chat on their way to the printer, which can distract you. Making and taking telephone calls requires our full attention, and allowing other people to distract us from this not only causes us to lose our focus, but it can make the customer feel less important or even ignored. When a coworker comes by your desk for any reason, do not give them your attention. If you must interact, look them in the eyes, smile, and return to your phone call. This gives them the message that you are busy with a caller and cannot talk at the moment. If they come by again later or if you see them in the office, tell them you're sorry you weren't available but had an important call to tend to and catch up on what they needed.

Inbound Calls

For many companies, inbound calls are a major part of the business. Customer call into the company for orders, consultations and even seeking general information. Inbound calls can seem intimidating at times since many times we don't know who is on the other end of the line. But knowing the right tools, such as a proper greeting and key phrases, can help the telephone operator through any situation.

Avoid Long Greeting Messages

For inbound calls, every company has their own set of greetings or scripting to use when they answer the phone. A good greeting typically includes a salutation, the company name and the operator's name. This lets the caller know where they are calling and who they are speaking to. However, some individuals like to adlib some parts, which can be helpful at times, but can also cause a lengthy greeting message. Long greeting messages may seem as though they are offering information to the caller, but instead they can deter interest and cause the caller to lose interest before the operator has a chance to help them. Generally, an inbound greeting should last between 5-10 seconds. After this time frame, the caller begins to lose focus and interest.

Introduce Yourself

When a person calls into your office, they may not necessarily know who or where they are speaking to. It is important for the operator to find some form of introduction to use with each caller. Every company has something different, but common examples include
"Thank you for calling _____, my name is Jane. How may I help you?"

An introduction should identify where the caller is calling to and who they are speaking with in that location. This type of introduction not only welcomes the caller to the company, but it also lets them know who is there to help them and invites them to get right to their request.

Focus on Their Needs

One of the most important aspects of business is to maintain its customers, and one of the best ways to do that is to focus on the customer's needs. Inbound calls allow patients to call into the company and reach out for help and assistance. So when a customer calls into your line, take the time to focus your attention on answering the call. Focus on what the caller is asking for and what sort of help they need. The caller may speak fast and have a long line of requests or even demands, but the key is listening for what they really want from the call and start from there.

Be Patient

Inbound calls can be lengthy and tiresome for the operator. In these calls, the client is calling into the company and will start making requests right away. Sometimes they can begin talking as soon as they hear a live person on the other end of the line. It is important for the operator to be patient with the caller and be sure to take the time listen for what the caller is really wanting. Never become pushy or pressure the caller to make a decision or state their purpose for calling. Some calming tips include taking deep breaths or silent counting exercises. Keeping your cool while still being able to assist the caller is a great exercise in patience. This will not only reflect well on you, but for the company as well.

Outbound Calls

Outbound calls can be some of the hardest types of calls to make. They require the caller to be well prepared and be able to keep the 'target' engaged while trying to deliver a point. Feeling such as nervousness and a fear of rejection can make these types of calls seem daunting to anyone. But with some helpful techniques and a little practice, the caller will have no problems picking up the phone and dialing a number.

Be Prepared

When making outbound calls, it is important to have all of your information prepared and ready before you even dial the number. Remember, you are asking the caller for a moment of their time, so be respectful and be ready with your information as soon as they pick up. Practice saying any scripting or phrases ahead of time so that you aren't surprised by anything. Review the name of the person you're calling and what their title is. Know what to say if they have any possible questions or if they want to refuse service. By preparing everything you need beforehand, you'll be ready for anything that may come up.

Identify Yourself and Your Company

When making outbound calls, the person on the other end of the line will most likely not have any idea who you are or what you want. Before you begin speaking about your product or service, it is important to identify yourself, your company and the reason for your call. If you do not identify yourself from the start, the recipient will become uncomfortable speaking with you and will lose interest right away. The recipient wants to know that you are calling them for a specific reason and that they are not just a random dial made by the company. Make them feel special by letting them know who you are and where you are calling from, and get right to the point as to why you are calling them today.

Examples:

- "Hello. My name is Sally and I'm calling from Smith Industries. May I speak to Mr. Jones?"

- "Hello there. My name is John. I'm calling from Amy Corp. Is Ms. Petty available?"

Give Them the Reason for the Call

After you've prepared yourself and have identified yourself to the recipient, the next step is to tell the recipient the reason you are calling them. If our introductions runs too long, or we begin our scripting without stating its purpose, the recipient can become bored, confused, or even plain angry. Once they have become agitated, they will be unwilling to listen to anything you try to say and will disengage the call. To hold their attention, keep the information in a steady flow without a lot of pauses or 'filler words' (such as 'um' and 'uh'). Introduce yourself and your company, and then move into the reason for your call and why you would like to speak with them.

Examples:

- "Hello, my name is Pat. I'm calling from ABC Corp about your current cable service."

- "Hello. My name is Kate and I'm calling from Ally Hospital. Do you have a minute to complete a patient survey?"

- "Hello. My name is Jack. I'm calling from Ace Autos. I'd like to speak with you about your recent purchase."

Keep Caller Information Private

Before we can begin to make outbound calls, we should already have a mound of personal information about the customers we intend to call. Since we are the ones doing the majority of the talking, we control much of the information in the conversation. It is important that the caller know that their information will be kept private and will not be 'aired' throughout the office. When a call is made, keep the customer information with you to review while speaking with them. Speak in soft volumes so that employees around you cannot hear the customer's information. Assure the customer that their information will be kept private and will not be shared with anyone. Finally, when the call is over and you no longer need the information, shred any hard copies that were made and delete any digital files that are not needed at the time.

Handling Rude or Angry Callers

One of the hardest, and somewhat scariest, situations a telephone operator can handle is a rude or angry caller. Every company has them and any person that answers a company phone will encounter them at some point. Many times they can come out of nowhere and it can be difficult to keep the caller focused on what they need/want. But depending on how the operator responds can be the difference between saving and losing that customer.

Stay Calm

Staying calm with an angry or rude called can be one of the hardest tasks a phone operator must do. Our natural reflect to anger or rudeness is to become defensive and lash back. However, if we show our emotions, especially negative ones, it only makes the caller angrier. Remember that the customer just wants to be heard and wants to have their problem resolved. So even if the customer starts speaking rudely or becomes angry with you, using your favorite tip or trick to help you stay calm and you'll be able to help the caller once they have begun to cool down.

Tips for staying calm:

- Never take what the caller says personally

- Take deep, relaxing breaths

- Empathize with the customer

- Speak in calm, assuring tones

Listen to Their Needs

When we encounter rude or angry callers, our first instinct is to stop listening to what they have to say due to their poor attitude. However, this is not the key. The caller may be upset, but they still want to be assured that someone will hear their complaint and help them get what they need. As the telephone operator, it is important to listen to what the caller has to say and try to identify what they are seeking. Many times the upset caller will tell us exactly what they need, but will mask it with harsh words and raw emotions. It is your job to put these feelings aside and let the customer know you can still help them get what they need.

Tips:

- Empathize with the caller's needs

- Remember that their needs/concerns are important too

- Identify what the caller is asking for

Never Interrupt

When a person is interrupted while they are speaking, it can cause them to become irritated or frustrated. But when a caller is angry or rude, interrupting them will only make the caller angrier, causing the situation to worsen. Although it may sound counter-productive, the best method to use with callers such as these is to let them speak until they begin to slow down and eventually finished with their rant. During this process, listen empathetically and continue to acknowledge their concerns. Once the caller has finished speaking, or to least pauses for a continued response, then you can begin to offer ways you can help the caller and what you can do for them. In many cases, the customer just wants to know their complaints or problems are heard and acknowledged by someone in the company. Once they feel like someone has heard their concerns, they will be more open to accepting some sort of solution available.

Identify What You Can Do for Them

When a customer is angry or upset, the last thing they want to hear from the company is what *can't* be done for them. This can cause them to become angrier and more upset. Once you have identified why the caller is upset, it is time to offer a real solution. By identifying what you can do for the caller, rather than what you can't do, you are assuring them that you are there to help and can help them resolve the problem they are having. Give them realistic options that can actually be done, such as speaking with a manager, filing a complaint with customer service or receiving help with the product/item/service. If you're able to solve the problem, do what you can to do so. If the caller needs to speak with someone else, take the time to ensure they reach the appropriate person and can go to the next step of reaching a solution.

Handling Interoffice Calls

When handling calls with the outside public, there is a set of guidelines and policies that the telephone operator follows. But when the calls are within the company, or within the same office, these policies and guidelines can shift a bit and become a whole new set of guidelines all their own.

Transferring Calls

Transferring a call to another telephone number may seem like an easy task, but it still requires a bit of skill in any office environment. Many times, when a caller is transferred, they feel as though they are being ignored and simply 'dumped' onto someone else. So if you have a caller on the line that needs to be transferred to somewhere in the department or the company, first notify the caller as to why you are transferring them. Once they understand why, let them know where you are transferring them to and the name of the person to speak with, if known. This lets the caller know that you are trying to help them by getting them to the correct place.

When possible, 'warm transfer' the caller to the extension. Warm transferring allows the telephone operator to call the department they are trying to reach, speak with an agent and give them information about the call. Once the agent is ready, the operator transfers the call directly to them.

Tips for transferring calls:

- Tell the caller why they are being transferred

- Let them know who/where you are transferring them to

- When possible, introduce the call before transferring

Placing Callers on Hold

Just the same as transferring a call, placing a caller on hold can make them feel ignored and that the telephone operator does not want to help them. In order to assure the caller that we are there to help them, we must take precautions when placing them on hold. When handling calls from within or outside the office, always ask the caller if they are able to hold and wait for their answer before doing so. Let them know why you may need to put them on hold, such as if you need to search for more information or find the person they are trying to reach. When you return, be sure to thank them for their patience while holding and let them know what you have found for them. If, for some reason, the caller cannot or will not hold, offer to take their contact information and give them a call back when you have the information/party they are searching for.

Tips for placing callers on hold:

- *Always* ask permission to place the caller on hold

- Check back periodically if the caller is on hold for a long time

- Remember to thank the caller for waiting when you return

- If the caller does not want to hold, offer to take a message

Taking Messages

Although many departments do not require employees to take message for each other, the occasion can arise where an employee receives a call from someone looking for another person and wants to leave their callback information. When taking messages for someone in the office, it is similar to the process of taking a message from an outside caller. First, make a note of what day and time the call came to you. Then obtain the caller's information, such as name and their title, if they have one, and ask them for the best callback they want to leave with you. Finally, note what the caller wants from the other party, such as requesting a callback, simply leaving information for the other party, or if the message is urgent and they need to speak with them right away. Ensure you have all the information **you need before disconnecting with the caller.**

Tips for taking messages:

- Note the date and time of the message

- Get the caller's name and title (if they have one)

- Verify a good callback number

- Note what the message is for

End the Conversation

Sometimes ending a call with someone can be an awkward feeling and can leave both parties unsure if the call is over. The key is to remain professional while letting the caller know that the conversation is over, which means you are about to hang up. Begin by reviewing the information from the call, such as if you took a message for them or will need to connect them to another party. Once the caller has understood that you have everything you will need, offer a salutation or parting phrase, such "Thank you for calling today" or "It was a pleasure speaking with you". This alerts the caller that you are wrapping up and they may offer a farewell first. Always end with a professional "Good bye" or "Have a good day/evening/night". Avoid using slang terms such as "bye-bye" or "Alright" when dismissing callers since these can cheapen your sentiments and sound unprofessional.

Samples phrases for ending a conversation:

- "Is there anything else I can do for you?"

- "Thank you for calling today."

- "Have a good day/evening."

- "I'm glad I was able to help you today."

Handling Voicemail Messages

Voicemails are a great tool to have in this age of technology, especially since the employee may not always be at their desk or may be busy taking calls from another customer. It is important to understand how to retrieve and deliver these messages efficiently so that critical information isn't lost and the chance to build a professional relationship isn't missed.

Ensure the Voicemail Has a Proper Greeting

When establishing your own voicemail, it is important to have a proper greeting message for your callers to hear. For your personal voicemail, record your own message in your own voice. Include your name, title and department when possible. Many callers already feel as though the call is impersonal once they reach the voicemail and they want to be reassured that they have reached the right person before they leave their information. If you are going to be away for an extended period (i.e. vacation, business travel), it is helpful to include this information on your voicemail greeting so that callers can know to expect a callback once you return.

Voicemail tips:

- Record your own greeting

- Avoid automated greetings

- Include your name and department

- Give it a personal touch

Answer Important Messages Right Away

A voicemail can contain several messages at once from numerous sources. Although they can seem overwhelming at times, it is important to determine which messages are urgent and need to be answered right away. Every department is different and will have a different definition of urgent calls, but urgent generally refers to calls that cannot wait too long to be answered or they can cause damage in some form or fashion. This include messages from angry or upset callers, a call from a customer needing answers right away or messages that have gone unanswered for an extended period of time. Urgent calls should typically be answered within 24 hours of receiving them. If you do not have the answers/resources they need, give them a call to let them know that you did receive their message and that you are currently seeking the information they need and will call them back as soon as you have it. If possible, give an estimated time frame for your return call.

Ensure Messages are Delivered to the Right Person

This can seem like a simple task, but there are many times a message is delivered to the wrong person or delivered to someone that is not able to relay the message, so it is never answered. If you receive a voicemail on your personal line for someone else, take note of the caller's name, the employee's name and if the caller mentions what department they are in. If the employee is in your department, then pass the message along by hand and let them know you received it by mistake on your line. If they are in a different department or area, speak to human resources or a company courier as to how you can have the message safely delivered to them. If you are checking a department voicemail that covers several different employees, the process should be similar. Ensure that you record the caller's name and information, if there is a certain employee they are trying to reach and the purpose for their call. If you cannot return the call, it is important to deliver the message to someone who can so that the message does not go unanswered.

When Leaving a Message for Others

Leaving a voicemail message for someone can sometimes feel like an art form. Many voicemail machines only allow a certain amount of time to leave a message, so it's important to only leave the essential information with enough details for the recipient to know why you called. When on a voicemail, leave your name and title. Also leave the date and time that you called and the reason you're calling. Finally, be sure to leave a good contact number where you can be reached and the best time of day to contact you. Try and limit your message to one topic at a time and do not overload the voicemail with various topics.

Tips:

- Leave your name, title and department

- Leave the date and time you called

- Include the best number and time of day to reach you

Methods of Training Employees

While having good telephone etiquette is beneficial, it will not do any good if it is not taught to the rest of the team. It is important to the company's success that every employee is properly trained and able to demonstrate telephone etiquette before being let loose on the telephone. Every employee learns differently, so it's helpful to have several methods available to allow employees to adopt these skills.

Group Training

Group training, sometimes referred to as classroom training, is a method training employees that involves one or two trainers that are responsible for training a group of new hires, typically in a separate room or training area. When training for telephone etiquette, group trainers will set up an area where multiple employees can listen to recorded calls, review anonymous employee evaluations, and review different techniques and procedures, such as a classroom setting. In this process, the company is able to train several employees at once and allows for these employees to gain some experience before leaving their training stages.

Common techniques used in group training:

- Role playing

- Simulations

- Audio visual aides

- Current employee examples

One-on-One Training

One-on-one training typically involves the employee being trained an only one, sometimes two, trainers. This method is more popular when training a current employee or an employee that is just coming into the department, rather than a new hire. These types of training sessions are usually a little more informal to allow the employee and the trainer to become comfortable with each other. In one-on-one sessions, the training can be more customized to the employee and can focus on areas that the employee may have trouble in while offering individualized goals and benchmarks for the employee to work towards.

Common activities used in one-on-one training:

- Direct questions/answer sessions

- Identifying strengths and weaknesses

- Offer individualized support

- Creating performance goals

Peer Training

Although peer training is a method that is not used as often as other methods, it is still a helpful tool when training a small group of employees. In most cases, peer training is used for training a very small group of employees (2-4 preferably) and can include new hires as well as current employees. Peer training involves a member of the staff, usually a team or floor leader, which will train fellow employees in a certain area. For new hires, they can train with a peer trainer after going through some sort of initial company training. But current employees can also train with a peer trainer if they are being introduced to new areas of phone etiquette or if they are new to the department (such as an internal transfer). Peer training can be advantageous to many employees since they can learn first-hand from someone who is doing similar work and can simplify any areas of confusion the employee may have.

Job Shadowing

Job shadowing is defined as a type of employee training designed for a new employee, or an employee wanting to become familiar with the job area, observes and follows an experienced employee in the department. Job shadowing differs from peer training in that job shadowing allows for more observations and questions/answers rather than engage in any direct form of training. The employee is able to experience the trainer's approach to telephone calls and the steps and actions necessary to perform the job that the group or company trainer might never think to mention. This method can include observation methods such as listening to active calls (the Y-method), observing employee actions and even learning to work some of the equipment involved (telephones, computers, etc.).

Correcting Poor Telephone Etiquette

Poor employee skills can decrease productivity and damage company costs. The key is to address and handle the problem before it can affect the whole team. Poor telephone etiquette is no exception. Many employees may not realize that their etiquette may be inadequate, so it is important that there are several tools available to help them get back on track.

Screening Calls

Many companies that offer a telephone service have taken advantage of some sort of call monitoring service. The service records each employee call and allows them to be played back at a later time for review. This process, known as screening calls, can be a great tool for reviewing employee phone calls and checking for correct telephone etiquette. A manger or supervisor can review as many calls as needed to review an employee's performance and determine if any poor telephone etiquette was a small occurrence or a consistent problem. After the manager/supervisor has reviewed the calls, it is best to bring the employee into a secluded meeting to review the calls together. From here, the employee can hear how their calls sound to others and identify areas they need to improve on. This process is also a helpful tool for the manager/supervisor and the employee to create and set future performance goals.

Employee Evaluations

Individual employee evaluations are another great tool for assessing and correcting any instance of poor telephone etiquette. An employee evaluation is typically created with several points or guidelines in place that an employee is expected to follow and meet certain criteria. Employee evaluations can be done through a number of methods, but the main goal is to use the criteria form and assess an employee's telephone etiquette skills and mark areas that are excelling and which areas will need improvement. The evaluator should meet with the employee to discuss any results of an evaluation so that they can know which areas are not meeting expectations and can set future performance goals.

Methods of employee evaluations:

- Individual call screenings

- Call re-enactment/role playing

- Direct monitoring

- Secret shoppers

Peer Monitoring

Peer monitoring is a tool of assessment that is growing in popularity. Peer monitoring allows employees to work together to help improve areas of skill and technique. This process allows an employee's peer, typically a team leader or floor manager, to work with an employee to evaluate and assess their telephone etiquette skills. Some common methods include direct monitoring by sitting with the employee, screening calls together and even completing written evaluations. Often times, because the monitoring is completed by a peer (instead of a manager or supervisor), the employee may feel less threatened and more at ease to accept terms of advice or criticism. However, the peer monitor must be able to deliver any positive or negative feedback necessary and not let the employee relationship hinder that process.

Customer Surveys

Another method of evaluating employee telephone etiquette is to employee customer/client surveys. A very common method of using customer surveys is to enable 'secret shoppers' to call and complete a survey on their experience. Secret shoppers are a well-known service that allows anonymous evaluators to call into a business and act and respond like a typical customer. The telephone operator does not know the caller is grading them or that their skills are being evaluated at that moment. At the end of the call, the secret shopper completes the evaluation and returns it to management. From here, the manager can meet with the employee and review how the call played out.

Another common method of customer surveys is by using customer follow up calls. While these calls typically focus on the company/service as a whole, they can be tailored to focus on the customer's experience with the telephone operator. They can be asked if the operator was friendly or helpful, or if the operator needed improvement in any areas. Once again, these evaluations can be completed and returned to management so they can be reviewed with the employee.

Chapter 11 – Performance Management

Performance Management is not a company's way of employing "micro-managing" techniques that stunt the professional growth of its employees. But rather, it is a strategic approach to ensuring the efficiency and effectiveness of an organization. Whether at the organizational, departmental or employee level, the goal of performance management is to make sure all business goals are being met in a satisfactorily manner.

By the end of this chapter, you will be able to:

- Define performance management.

- Understand how performance management works and the tools to make it work.

- Learn the three phases of performance management and how to assess it.

- Discuss effective goal-setting.

- Learn how to give feedback on performance management.

- Identify Kolb's Learning Cycle.

- Recognize the importance of motivation.

- Develop a performance journal and performance plan.

The Basics

The effectiveness of an organization in terms of whether or not it is meeting its mission or goals can be determined by engaging in performance management. According to the U.S. Office of Personnel Management, performance management consists of five components: "Planning work and setting expectations, continually monitoring performance, developing the capacity to perform, periodically rating performance in a summary fashion, and rewarding."

What is Performance Management?

The phrase "Performance Management" was coined in the 1970s by Dr. Aubrey Daniels, a clinical psychologist. At the time, he used it to describe technology and the importance of managing behavior and the result of the behavior. Effective management would ensure proper behaviors are being executed, which would in turn produce favorable results. He later associated this approach to the interactions of people whether in a formal or informal setting.

With the proper training, management can manipulate the conditions of the workplace (e.g. policies and procedures, available skills to train and motivate employees) in order to measure the true success of the business – that is the financial standing of a company as well as the individual success of its employees.

How Does Performance Management Work?

The drive to implement a performance management system is not sufficient. Management as well as employees must put forth the effort necessary to make it happen. With "all hands on deck" and the observation of the following, organizations can build a successful program.

- Clearly identify the job's purpose as well as the duties associated with it.

- Determine goals and how to measure outcomes.

- Rank job priority.

- Characterize the standard of performance for critical aspects of the position.

- Discuss employee performance and provide feedback. This should at least be done on a quarterly basis.

- Keep track of performance records.

- If necessary, create an improvement plan to better employees' performance.

Tools

It is unrealistic to expect employees to perform at an optimal level without providing them with the tools to succeed. The following tools are crucial to the achievement of the system.

Model of standards: Creating a model that clearly defines employee performance standards helps the company and employees avoid ambiguities in what is expected. It also enables employers to provide their employees with specific feedback, which is greatly beneficial because it potentially increases job satisfaction.

Whether in writing or delivered verbally, performance standards are enforceable. It is, however advisable that they are captured in writing to avoid questions in the future.

There should be a set standard for every aspect of one's position. For example, an employee who is a Customer Service/Sales Representative may be expected to take and sufficiently answer the service questions of 10 customers an hour. This employee may also be required to upsell products to 50% of the clients he talks to.

There are several factors to keep in mind when developing this model. Performance standards should:

- Be realistic in terms of whether or not it can be attained as well as whether or not employees have adequate training.

- Be measurable with regard to quantity, quality, time, etc.

- Be clear in defining the proper method for gathering performance information and how it measures against the standard.

Annual Employee Appraisal Document: While employers monitor employees' performance throughout the year and provide feedback and coaching during that interval, employers are also responsible for conducting an employee appraisal, which is generally done on an annual basis. The appraisal allows the employer to summarize the employee's performance, gauge job satisfaction, as well as prepare for the future.

Coaching: Once the standard has been set and performance feedback has been provided to the employee, it is critical that the employer offer some type of coaching. The purpose of coaching is to strengthen areas of improvement as well as enhance areas where the employee is currently successful. In order to accomplish this, coaching must be done in a positive manner. The words used must build and not destroy. Diplomacy is important when providing coaching. Coaching promotes employee motivation as well as continued success.

A Performance Management system is only as good as its evaluation process. It is not enough to implement an effective program that covers all the basics, but you must be able to measure its success via assessments and performance reviews. This will in turn allow you to see where modifications need to take place (e.g. in the performance management system itself, performance of the company as a whole or specific employee performance).

Three Phase Process

Kurt Lewin, also known as the "founder of social psychology", introduced a three-phase theory of change that goes hand-in-hand with performance management. The process includes the following:

Phase One: Unfreezing: This phase is extremely important as you aim to understand change and how it takes place. This phase is crucial because it includes coming to the realization that change needs to happen. It also requires one to leave that which has been comfortable in order to make this change possible.

In order for someone to decide whether or not they are willing to change, they must weigh the advantages and disadvantages of this being done. This concept is what Force Field Analysis is based on. Force Field Analysis considers the different factors that work for and against the change that one must understand in order to make a decision.

Phase Two: Change: In Lewin's model, he pointed out that "change" is not a one-time event that takes place, but rather the inner-transition that takes place as a response to the outward changes that are taking place.

Due to the uncertainties of "what will happen next", this phase is considered one of the more difficult ones to achieve. And because of this, it is important for employees to have access to training and coaching to help ease the transition.

Phase Three: Freezing: Also known as "refreezing", this phase is the establishment of new norms and gaining stability after the institution of change. This phase can sometimes be misleading. It seems to be a long-term state, when in fact it is one that can change to "Unfreezing" within a matter of days. So, although this stage cannot be viewed as the "last", having the ability to successfully make it to this point is a great accomplishment. This could allude to the fact that it is becoming easier for someone to adjust to change, which is crucial because it happens regularly.

Assessments

There are a variety of assessments that can be utilized to determine skill, knowledge, and ability. These assessments can be administered when the individual is a prospective employee or an actual employee.

Types of Assessments

Pre-Screening: A Pre-Screening Assessment can be used to find out information on a prospective employees skills and knowledge before committing to hire them and this can save the employer costly mistakes down the road.

360-Degree Review: As its name implies, this type of assessment takes a comprehensive look at an employee with regard to their work performance. This information can be attained by involving a diverse pool of individuals, with varying levels of interaction with the employee (e.g. supervisor, peers, clients, etc.)

Knowledge: This type of assessment generally takes on a questionnaire format. It allows the employer to ask specific questions on topics relating to the business, usually in the form of multiple choice questions.

Performance Reviews

According to Entrepreneur.com, a performance review is defined as "An analysis of an employee's work habits undertaken at a fixed point in time to determine the degree to which stated objectives and expectations have been reached."

While each company has its own ideas of what a performance review should include, here are steps that should be taken with regard to all performance reviews:

- **Preparation:** Both the employer and employee must be adequately groomed for the review. This may involve reviewing any notes, engaging in a one-on-one discussion with the employee beforehand or simply making the employee aware of the review in advance.

- **Prioritize the meeting:** To show the employee that this review is a top priority, there should be a formal agenda that is adhered to. There should also be as few interruptions as possible.

- **Encourage positivity:** When speaking to the employee, invoke positive responses by communicating in a positive manner.

- **Clarity:** Be sure the purpose of the meeting is clear from the beginning.

- **Expectations:** Review the job description, why it is needed, and the standards of performance.

- **Explain employee's performance:** Discuss the employee's actual performance, whether it fell below, met or exceeded expectations. Give specific examples.

- **Employee feedback:** Allow the employee to express their concerns or suggestions.

- **Goal-setting:** Discuss goals for areas that require improvement. If there are no "areas for improvement", create goals to enhance the knowledge and skills of the employee for personal development as well as bettering the department / company as a whole.

- **Follow-up:** Determine the appropriate method and or time for follow-up.

- **Closing:** The meeting should end positively. Review the contributions the employee is making to the company. Inform employee that you are willing to help in any way necessary.

Goal Setting

Every successful business plan requires goals and objectives. Goals show the strengths and weaknesses of plans and procedures. Implementing regularly evaluated goals allows leaders to understand where performance is and what needs to be improved. When managing performance, make sure that you implement SMART goals.

SMART Goal Setting

People often fail to reach their goals. This usually indicates that the wrong goals are being chosen. SMART goals will improve the chances of achieving both personal and business goals.

SMART goals:

- **Specific:** Goals should have specific instructions.

- **Measurable:** It should be clear when goals and objectives are met.

- **Attainable:** Impossible goals are not motivating.

- **Realistic:** Goals need to be something people are able to work towards.

- **Timely:** Goals need specific timeframes.

Specific Goals

Goals need to be specific. Employees need to understand exactly what they are expected to do. It is not enough to simply ask for improvement. This is a general goal. Specific goals explain who is involved and what goal should be achieved. It can also identify a location, requirements, and reasoning behind the goal.

Example:

- **General goal:** Improve performance.

- **Specific goal**: Meet with your mentor once a week.

Measurable Goals

Goals need to be measurable in order to be effective. They specify how much or how many. Measurable goals allow employees to identify when they have accomplished their goals.

Example:

- **General goal**: Increase sales.

- **Measurable goal**: Increase sales 7 percent over last year's.

Attainable Goals

Goals must always be attainable. Employees need goals that challenge them but must still be within reach. When goals are seen as unattainable, employees will give up on them without even trying. The measure of a goal should always be within reach.

- **Unattainable goal**: Reduce turnover by 60 percent.

- **Attainable goal:** Reduce turnover by 10 percent.

Realistic Goals

Employees need realistic goals. It is important that employees are able to achieve their goals. The goals need to relate directly to employee abilities, and it is important to make sure that they have the tools necessary to meet them. Breaking larger goals down to smaller achievements will make them more realistic.

Example:

Realistic Goal: The production department currently makes 200 cars a week. With new training, they will create 225 a week.

Timely Goals

Goals should always have a time frame. General goals do not establish a time frame. Time frames encourage employees to move forward. Having specific dates will also determine when goals are reevaluated.

Example:

- **General goal**: Increase sales.

- **Timely goal**: Increase sales within six months.

Monitoring Results

Once goals are established, it is important to monitor their results. This will determine how effective a plan or strategy is. Use a basic evaluation to determine what changes need to be made in a plan and reevaluate your goals.

What to evaluate:

- Were the goals and objectives achieved?

- Were they achieved in the established time frame?

- What is the feedback from employees and leadership?

- What are the financial gains or losses?

Establishing Performance Goals

Performance goals require strategic action. To be effective, these goals should not be handed down to employees. It is important to include employees in the goal setting process and encourage them to meet their individual performance goals. This will improve individual and company performance.

Strategic Planning

A strategic plan determines where employees are, where they want to be, and how they will get there. It should embrace the values of the organization and align with the following company information. The organization must create a strategic plan before creating performance goals.

Company Strategic Plan:

- Vision

- Mission

- Philosophy

- Goals

- Objectives

Employee performance goals need to consider the company's strategic plan. Individual performance goals must be SMART goals that include strategies and actions for employees to take.

Example Goal: Stay informed about innovations in the industry, it can help improve productivity by 10 percent this year.

Examples of Actions:

- Attend training classes

- Meet with a mentor

- Communicate consistently

Job Analysis

A job analysis determines what is required to do a specific job. It will help determine which skills and attributes an employee needs to complete a job successfully. A job analysis will help determine who to hire, how to train, and what compensation a job should receive. Job analyses are instrumental in determining performance. Research a position to determine the following information:

Job Requirements:

- Responsibilities
- Tools or systems used
- Reporting requirements

Employee Requirements:

- Training/Education
- Skills
- Aptitudes
- Necessary certification

Setting Goals

Performance goals need to be SMART goals. They need to address behavior, competency, and results. Remember to involve employees in their performance goals.

Examples of Goals:

- **Behavior**: Employees have complained about distance. Communicate with employees in person every week, rather than just sending emails.
- **Competency:** New equipment is being installed. Perform all the training within three weeks.
- **Results:** Sales are down. Increase sales by 5 percent this quarter.

Motivation

Performance is related to motivation. Motivation is the job of every leader. There is not a single method for motivating employees. People have different personal motives, and leaders must meet the needs of individuals.

Motivating Tips:

- **Lead by example**: Motivate yourself before you can motivate others.
- **Meet with individuals**: Communicate with employees directly to find out what motivates them.
- **Reward employees**: Find motivating rewards for individuals.
- **Delegate**: Do not micromanage employees.
- **Inform**: Inform people about how they are making a difference in the organization.

- **Celebrate**: Pay attention to achievements and celebrate with employees.

360 Degree Feedback

360 degree feedback is useful for evaluating performance. It provides evaluations from different sources to paint a clear picture of how well an individual performs. Identifying strengths and weaknesses will allow employees to continually improve how they perform.

What is 360 Degree Feedback?

360 degree feedback is an alternative method of reviewing employees. Rather than a traditional review, employees are given anonymous feedback from supervisors and peers. Managers' feedback also includes direct reports and reviews from employees. Individuals also evaluate themselves in 360 degree feedback. Together, these evaluations will help improve performance by:

- Identifying and enhancing strengths

- Identifying areas that need development

- Helping Employees set goals

- Creating action plans

Vs. Traditional Performance Reviews

360 degree feedback provides a better picture of performance than traditional reviews. Supervisors perform traditional performance reviews. Traditional review can have a negative impact on performance, if employees feel it is not fair. This can damage trust between managers and employees. Traditional performance reviews also do little to encourage cooperation between employees because coworkers do not influence scores on traditional reviews. People in positions of authority also benefit from 360 degree feedback. Traditional performance reviews do not always give an accurate description of employer/employee relationships.

The Components

360 degree feedback evaluation forms are typically done on a scale of 1 to 10. There is a place for comments on the evaluation form. The scores from supervisors, peers, employees, and direct reports are averaged and compared with average company scores. HR typically handles the reporting to make sure that the feedback remains confidential.

Example:

Computer Skills

1_____2_____3_____4_____5_____

Comments:

_____

Competency Assessments

Competency assessments are essential to performance management. These assessments make it easier to hire and promote the right people. They also help assess performance and the different competencies that employees need to improve. It will also identify the top performers.

Competency Assessment Defined

Competencies are a set of skills and essential knowledge that are necessary to perform a job well. The competencies for every position should be defined before hiring. They are important to the hiring and guide the interview process. A competency assessment assesses the skills of employees and compares them with previously established core competencies. A supervisor or HR professional decides the score of each assessment. The performance is based on chosen indicators and separate level for each rating. Each company has its own competency assessment levels, but most assessments include the following ratings:

Sample Rating:

- Excellent

- Meets expectations

- Needs improvement

- Not applicable

- Have opportunities to advance

Implementation

There are several steps that you need to take before you implement competency assessments. Successful implementation requires you to complete all of the steps.

Steps:

- **Identify Competencies**: Ascertain which competencies are needed to perform a job and the skill level of each competency.

- **Develop Assessments**: Create a fair method of assessment that concentrates on targets. Company goals will determine the targets.

- **Practice Assessments**: Practice using assessments, just like any other skill.

- **Assess Employees**: Use the standards and assessments to review employees.

- **Plan**: Use action plans to help employees develop.

Final Destination

The final destination will provide a pool of trained professionals with strong performance. Each company will have its own final destination that depends on the goals and needs. Reaching the stage of final destination may mean completely overhauling the competency program. It could also mean placing more attention on action plans and training. It all depends on the competencies required for each role. Identifying the goals of the organization and the competencies of each position will allow your organization to reach the final destination.

Kolb's Learning Cycle

Kolb's Learning Cycle states that learning is based on experience. The learning cycle has four basic elements: experience, observation, conceptualization, and experimentation. It is important to be familiar with the learning cycle to effectively manage performance, and guide employees to greater achievements.

Experience

Kolb describes the importance of concrete experience. Concrete experience is direct experience that involves the senses. It is not simply knowledge about a subject. Hands-on training is an example of concrete experience that employees learn at work. Experience and conceptualization are the two ways that employees take in knowledge.

Observation

Kolb defines observation as reflective observation. It is what the concrete experience means to the person learning. Watching is the way that knowledge is transformed into meaning for an individual. This is where the connotations are created as learners see different perspectives. An example would be watching a trainer perform a task again or considering a task recently performed. Experimentation is another way to transform knowledge.

Conceptualization

Abstract conceptualization is a way to gather knowledge on a subject without direct experience. This involves a basic understanding of a situation by applying logic. An example of this would be reading a training manual. Abstract conceptualization is having the knowledge about something.

Experimentation

Active experimentation is the final part of Kolb's Learning Cycle. Here, people learn by doing. They transform knowledge by acting on it. An example of this would be using a new computer program. Active experimentation involves taking risks based on the knowledge people have gathered. It is important that employees be allowed to take risks when learning.

Motivation

Every employee needs to be motivated in order for performance management to be successful. While employees must take some responsibility in motivating themselves, management can help motivate and develop individuals. Practicing basic motivational techniques will improve performance as it boosts morale.

Key Factors

Motivation is more than being satisfied. Motivation is what causes employees to go the extra mile and commit to a project or company. Fredrick Herzberg identified the key factors that drive motivation in employees across different fields. Pay and work conditions were tied to satisfaction. Poor pay and work conditions adversely affect productivity, but positive pay and work conditions do little to increase motivation.

Motivators:

- **Responsibility:** Employees should have a sense of ownership in their work.

- **Nature of the work:** The nature of the work can help motivate people.

- **Recognition:** Employee efforts need to be recognized.

- **Achievement:** People need to feel like they are achieving something worthwhile.

The Motivation Organization

People perform better when they believe in their company. When the values of an organization match the personal values of employees, an organization will be highly motivated. This is why socially responsible companies are able to easily attract talent. They speak to an individual's internal motivators. Businesses that address internal motivations are more likely to be high performing.

Internal Motivations:

- Family

- Environment

- Success

- Community

- Personal time

Identifying Personal Motivators

Each person has a different set of motivators. Some people respond better to verbal praise and others need rewards. It is important to motivate employees on a personal level. This is easier to do in small organizations. Large companies will have to rely on each manager to identify personal motivators.

Techniques to Identify Personal Motivators:

- Observation: Observe how individuals respond to different motivators and take notes.

- Communication: Get to know each employee, and identify personal motivators.

- Surveys: Have employees fill out surveys that identify what motivates them.

Evaluating and Adapting

Like everything else, it is essential to evaluate and adapt motivation techniques. This should include the following steps:

- Surveys: Surveys will show the level of engagement and how motivated employees are.

- Review mission: Compare the mission, policies, and procedures to internal motivators. Are they aligned?

- Development: Examine the number of employees who have advanced within the company.

- Goals: Whether or not company goals are met is an indication of motivation.

Adapt motivation techniques as necessary to improve performance and engage employees.

The Performance Journal

Performance journals create evaluations that are more accurate by allowing employees and manager to keep track of performance throughout the year. Both managers and employees can keep journals. This will help guide and develop employees who challenge themselves and improve performance.

Record Goals and Accomplishments

It is important to record your goals and accomplishments. Even minor accomplishments need to go in the performance journal. Seeing your accomplishments will encourage you, and seeing your goals will motivate you to continue working towards them. Comparing goals and accomplishments will help you focus on what you need to do to improve performance.

Employee Records:

- **Accomplishments:** Include recognitions and awards.

- **Challenges:** Include requests for training or other help to meet goals.

Employer Records:

- **Accomplishments:** Details include documentation and notes.

- **Evaluation:** Include performance gaps and direct reports.

Linking with Your Employees or Managers

It is important that employees and managers connect for performance management to be effective. Relationships on every level must remain professional. When employees and managers do not trust each other, performance suffers. It is possible for managers to link to employees' performance journals and see any information that employees choose to share with them. This helps managers see things from an employee's perspective and create accurate evaluations. It also makes employees part of the evaluation process.

Implementing a Performance Coach

A performance coach will help people meet their needs to improve performance. In most organizations, managers act as performance coaches. How well managers coach performance affects the quality of employee performance. Managers must communicate effectively with each employee and motivate that person to excel. This requires a combination of encouragement, praise, and correction. Assess and coach employees in the following areas.

Coaching Assessments:

- Assess skills and knowledge: Provide any necessary training.

- Assess the tools: Make sure that the individual has everything necessary to complete his or her job.

- Assess the processes: Improve procedures to help employees, or instruct them in using different procedures.

- Assess motivation: Motivate people on a personal level.

Keeping Track

Coaches need to keep track of employee progress. This will help them create strategies that will challenge employees and help them grow. There are several ways to keep track of performance.

- Traditional Evaluations

- 360 Feedback

- Journals

- Performance log

A performance log is where you can make notes of any observations regarding performance. This will help you become a better coach.

Creating a Performance Plan

A performance plan is essential to performance management. It is a strategic plan that each individual needs to follow to become high performing employees. Managers must create a plan with every employee they work with. There is always room for improvement.

Goals

Establish professional goals that reflect the needs of the organization and individual. Make sure that employees have the tools to reach these goals and provide them if they do not. This will improve productivity and performance.

Setting Goals:

- Determine what employees need to accomplish.

- Make SMART goals.

- Allow employees to develop the goals with you.

Example:

- Enroll in a speaking class within three months to facilitate meetings by the end of the year.

Desired Results

The results of a performance plan are not strategies. They are what employees are expected to achieve, and this should be made clear in the performance plan. Employees are responsible for achieving the desired results. For example, a desired result may be to consistently meet sales goals. The ability or inability to meet desired results determines the level of performance. An individual who cannot meet desired results will need coaching in that area.

Prioritization

It is important to prioritize goals. Employees should focus on the top three goals. The goals given priority need to align with the company goals and the top competencies of each position. These usually influence productivity and cost. A nonessential goal such as filing at the end of each day does not take priority. Make sure that goals do not conflict with each other.

Example of Prioritizing Goals:

- Train to use the new software within two months.

- Call clients every week to increase customer satisfaction.

- Meet monthly sales goals with social networking, cold calling, and scheduled meetings.

Measure

Performance must be measured. This is not always easy because some tasks may be subjective. There must be fair standards and measurement established for each position. You will need to consider the job requirements and employee competencies that you previously established. It is also helpful to make the measurements cost specific, when possible. Create a rating scale for each measure. It can be numbered or not.

Measurement Example:

- The total number of customer complaints.

- Percentage of wasted product.

- Met personal goals

Evaluation

Compare the measurements against performance to evaluate employees. It is also important to include whether or not employees achieved their goals and met desired expectations. This information is normally included in an employee evaluation form. Formal reviews are typically done every year, but frequent informal reviews are more effective. Meet with employees regularly to evaluate performance. Use the same criteria as a formal evaluation to help direct and improve performance.

Chapter 12 – Coaching and Mentoring

You are in your office looking over your performance report and it happened again. Your low performing employee failed to meet quota this month even after you spoke with them about the importance of meeting goals. This employee has a great attitude and you know they can do better. You just do not know how to motivate them to reach the goal. Money used to work, but that has worn off. You are baffled and you know being frustrated makes matters worse. What do you do?

This workshop focuses on how to better coach your employees to a higher performance. Coaching is a process of relationship building and setting goals. How well you coach relates directly to how well you are able to foster a great working relationship with your employees through understanding them and strategic goal setting.

An easy-to-understand coaching model taught in this workshop will guide you through the coaching process. Prepare yourself to change a few things about yourself in order to coach your employees to better a performance.

At the end of this chapter, you should be able to:

- Define coaching, mentoring and the GROW model.

- Identify and set appropriate goals using the SMART technique of goal setting.

- Identify the steps necessary in defining the current state or reality of your employee's situation.

- Identify the steps needed in defining options for your employee and turn them into a preliminary plan.

- Identify the steps in developing a finalized plan or wrapping it up and getting your employee motivated to accomplish those plans.

- Identify the benefits of building and fostering trust with your employee.

- Identify the steps in giving effective feedback while maintaining trust.

- Identify and overcoming common obstacles to the growth and development of your employee.

- Identify when the coaching is at an end and transitioning your employee to other growth opportunities.

- Identify the difference between mentoring and coaching, using both to enable long-term development through a positive relationship with your employee.

Defining Coaching and Mentoring

Before getting deeper into the subject of coaching, it is prudent to discuss mentoring and what it tries to achieve. Understanding the difference between coaching and mentoring will help you be clear on your coaching objective. Many times, these two concepts are misunderstood.

The goal of this module is to define both concepts and introduce a coaching model that will allow you to focus on improving performance. Let us begin by defining what coaching is.

What is Coaching?

A coach tutors or instructs a person to achieve a specific goal or skill. In baseball, a batting coach only focuses on the mechanics of hitting the ball. They spend time instructing the hitter how to change their swing to improve their performance. They give exercises and goals to the hitter that target the swing of the bat.

In the office environment, you may see similar coaches helping others improve a skill. They may be sales coaches or customer service coaches. No matter what the area of focus is, a coach specializes on improving one or two areas of development at a time.

Here is a recap of the characteristics of a coach:

- Trainer

- Instructor

- Tutor

- Focus on one or two skills at a time

- Their interaction is planned and structured

What is Mentoring?

Mentoring has a different purpose and goal. Mentoring is the act of guiding, counseling, and supporting. This is vastly different from coaching. It is fundamentally teaching. However, the objective is slightly different.

Mentorship is more voluntary in nature and is less formal than coaching. The mentor and protégé endeavor on a broad development goal like becoming a leader. Mentoring encompasses many complex areas of development.

In your matching activity, we learned that coaching scenarios include the following:

- Sales

- Customer service

- Production work

- Behavioral issues like tardiness

Likewise, we learned that mentoring scenarios include the following:

- Networking

- Political strategizing

- Negotiation

- Managing

In this workshop, you will learn how to effectively coach; however, later, there will be a discussion on how to transition from a coach to a mentor. It should be a manager's goal to develop their people in a way that furthers their career. Mentoring does this. For now, we are going to focus on coaching people for specific goals. The next lesson discusses an easy-to-remember coaching process.

Introducing the G.R.O.W. Model

Having a consistent and uniform approach to coaching enables you to coach more effectively with strategy and direction. Using a coaching model will also instill confidence in your employee, because they see a methodical approach. When we approach coaching haphazardly, we become disorganized and this creates frustrating coaching sessions.

The GROW model helps you organize your coaching process in a flow that identifies the goal first and ends with putting a plan together. Here are the details of the GROW model:

- **Goal setting**: a goal has to be set in order to give direction and purpose to the coaching session. Ambiguous goals are usually never achieved. Setting the goal first shapes your discussion with your employee and sets the tone.

- **Reality check**: both you and your employee must come to terms on the current state or level of performance or any issues that are causing breakdowns. Getting to the bottom of the problem begins with identifying it and claiming. From there obstacles are better identified.

- **Options developed**: here you and your employee explore action steps that will help them improve their performance. Usually goals options that are prefabricated by an employee's manager result in poor buy-in and missed goals. Allow your employee to explore options they develop.

- **Wrap it up with a plan**: once you nail down an option or two, it is time to strike it down on paper so to speak. If it is not written down, it won't happen. Creating a well-defined plan is essential in order to know the direction you need to go and to demonstrate success or failure.

GROW is simple yet powerful. Following the GROW process consistently will develop a natural process for you. Coaching should be natural. This puts you and your employee at ease, making the process more valuable and rewarding. Let us unpack the GROW model over the next few modules and see how to incorporate it into our daily work lives.

Setting Goals

Without a goal, your chances of successfully coaching your employee to better performance are low. Defining specific, measurable, attainable, realistic, and time driven goals will plot a marker in the horizon that acts as your beacon. Without it, you are navigating blindly, causing frustration for both you and your employee, because you never seem to make any improvement. It becomes a constant cycle of failing to meet the goal and talking to your employee about it. This repeats repeatedly without a well-defined goal.

This module will discuss setting **goals** with an easy-to-remember technique. This is the first component or the "G" of the **GROW** method of coaching. Let us explore what this is and how to develop it.

Goals in the Context of GROW

The first step of the **GROW** model is the key step in the process. Setting the goal gives you and your employee direction and purpose. You will find it very difficult if you were handed a bunch of tools and materials and told to build something without a clear vision or goal of what is to be built.

The same holds true for developmental goals. It is not good enough to tell your employee they must improve in sales or build widgets faster. These types of goals create more confusion because they do not know where to start. Back to the building analogy, you may end up building a stool when what was really needed was as birdhouse. Clear goals are the cornerstone of the **GROW** model.

Here are some benefits to establishing goals upfront in the process:

- Both you and your employee have a better chance of starting in the right direction together.

- Coaching time is more efficient once goals are discussed upfront.

- You are able to plan ahead of the session and prepare targeted questions.

- The coaching session is direct and avoids meandering.

- You will come across more clear, instilling confidence in your employees.

Now, since we established the importance and benefit of goal setting early in the coaching process, let us look at identifying appropriate goal areas.

Identifying Appropriate Goal Areas

When coaching, it is a temptation for you to talk more because we have plenty to say. However, in order to gain information and identifying appropriate goal areas, you must listen more. Remember, you have two ears and one mouth. Listen twice as much as you talk. Your objective here is to "catch" as much information as possible to help you determine what specific areas you can leverage and achieve results. Many times, allowing your employee to achieve even the smallest of goals begins a positive reinforcement of coaching. At some point before your actual coaching session, you want to engage in a brief discussion with your employee to determine their personal goals.

Here are some questions you should ask while during your pre-coaching meeting. Remember to write down their answers for your reference later:

- What goals are you working on right now?

- Where are you in relation to those goals?

- What do you think is keeping you from reaching this goal?

- How will you know you reached that goal?

Asking these open-ended questions starts a conversation about your employee, which is what you want to achieve. Allowing your employee to speak more enables you to gather more information. Asking questions about their goals reveals their desires and this is something you can tie in to your coaching goal. Maybe an employee is furthering their education by going to college at night. Understanding this, you may be able to motivate your employee to achieve better performance, leading them to make more incentive they can use to fund their educational needs.

Furthermore, understanding where they are in relation to their goals reveals needs that may need support from you. Helping your employee with their personal goals builds a great working relationship. Finally, determining what roadblocks are preventing them from reaching their goals will provide insight into their personal circumstances. Granted, you may not solve all of your employee's problems, but demonstrating empathy goes a long way and helps to form goals for you that take into consideration your employee's personal situation. Remember, your employee does not care how much you know until you show how much you care. Listen more and talk less.

One final note, at first you may find asking questions challenging. This is normal. Give it time and do not give up. You may even have to let your employee know that you are interested more in their personal goals as a way to help them reach goals at work.

Setting SMART Goals

Writing goals can be a daunting task if done without a particular format or process. After you have your pre-coaching meeting with your employee, you are ready to meet again with your employee and write a clear goal, starting the GROW process. Having a clear format and goal development process will enable you build an effective goal. SMART is the technique you want to use when building the goal with your employee. It outlines your goal in an easy and clear format that your employee will find useful.

SMART stands for the following goal characteristics:

- **Specific**: What needs to be done? The goal must be clear. It cannot be a general statement like be better at sales or be more organized. Use action verbs like increase sales or use a calendar. Next, we need to put some measurement in place.

- **Measurable**: Place some form of measurement that is easily verifiable to the goal. For example, continuing with the last example, increase sales by 3 percent or use a calendar two times a week. When you have a number incorporated to the goal, it makes it easier to check progress and hold your employee accountable.

- **Attainable**: Make sure the goal is not too much at one time to complete. Setting huge goals will lead to failure because the employee will see it as impossible. In addition, assess your employee's attitude. Use the information gained from your questions to help make this goal relevant. Irrelevant goals are not done. Make the goal manageable yet challenging.

- **Realistic**: Take in to consideration any learning, mentoring that has to take place or habits that have to be broken first before you set your employee's goal. If you are asking your employee to do something better, make sure they have the basics down first. Assess them, determine any gaps, and set you goals according to their skills and abilities.

- **Timely**: Always set a time limit or timeframe. Do not allow your employee's goal to wander aimlessly. Set follow up meetings and keep them. Your employee looks forward to these meetings especially when they are moving towards the goal. Do not set too much time between intervals. This may send the message to your employee that they have time to make the adjustment. You want to set short specific timeframes.

SMART goals are easy to do, but require a commitment on your part to use it consistently. Now that you have an idea how to develop your goal, we are going to see why understanding the reality is essential to the coaching process.

Understanding the Realities

In the last module, you plotted a marker in the horizon as a beacon, guiding your employee to a specific, measurable, attainable, realistic, and timely goal. This is a great start, but there is also a need to know where your journey began. Placing a marker at the starting point of your employee's coaching journey enables both you and your employee to determine and measure progress. The goal in the offing may never seem to get any closer, because you have no point of reference to gauge your progress.

In this module, you will learn how to place that stake in the ground, marking the beginning of the coaching journey. Examining the current **realities** is the second component or the "R" of the GROW model. Let us delve into this concept to learn more about it.

Getting a Picture of Where You Are

Framing the reality of the situation for your employee is an important step to accepting the coaching process. It is easier for you to outline your employee's performance problem, but this does not create the most receptive environment. In order to gain acceptance of the problem it is best to let the employees come to the realization themselves. Neglecting to do this could result in a non-responsive employee. They may feel apprehensive or defensive and shut down. They may go along with your coaching, but their attitude is that of just getting the coaching session over with in the least amount of time. Involving your employee is easy if you are willing to ask questions, listen, and guide your employee to where they are in their performance. Here are four simple questions you can ask:

- What is happening now?

- How often is this happening?

- When does it happen?

- What is the affect?

These questions help you to guide your employee to a place where they can see their performance affect the organization. When they realize the impact on their own more buy-in is created. In addition, more information may be obtained on why your employee is not performing at the level they should be achieving.

The realization of the problem marks the starting point. It also serves as a marker on performance. For instance, an employee may discover that they are not reaching production goals because they are taking extra time doing something incorrectly. Knowing this, you are able to refer to this issue when improvements occur.

Identifying Obstacles

When coaching, obstacles will arise and you need to be prepared to handle them with efficiency. The last thing you want to happen is your employee handing you an obstacle you cannot address because you are not prepared to handle the problem with a consistent response.

Using the IRA steps to obstacle identification and removal is vital to the coaching process. Here is the breakdown of the process.

- **Identify the obstacle**: Have a frank discussion with your employee and determine what is blocking their performance. Waiting for them to give you the information voluntarily will probably not happen.

- **Root out the cause**: Many times underlying emotions or problems may be the cause of the obstacles. Ask probing questions and jot down answers. You might realize they have a fear that must be addressed.

- **Antidote given**: A remedy to the situation is needed in order to get past this obstacle. Brainstorm with your employee on ways to remove the obstacles. In some cases, you may have to try several different antidotes. Be patient if the cause is genuine.

No matter what the perceived obstacles are, do not let it stifle you coaching objective. Rarely, you may encounter an employee that throws obstacles constantly your way in an effort to derail you. Identify this and address it with that employee, documenting every conversation.

Exploring the Past

Exploring your employees past performance and development is a great way to develop the reality of today's performance. Of course, you want to avoid belaboring a past mistake to the point where it makes the session ineffective. On the other hand, focusing on previous achievements helps to encourage your employee.

Here are some things to focus from the past:

- Goals that were met

- Great behaviors

- Great attitudes

- Problems solved

Using the past helps to recap where your employee is at today. It is like telling a story but the end has not yet been determined. Use this time to speak positively to your employee. Avoid being negative or emphasizing the consequences to failure. This will leave an impression on your employee that could hinder their success.

Setting a positive environment opens the door for the next part of the GROW model. Developing options is an essential step both you and your employee must take in order to continue toward meeting your development goals. Let us explore what this entails.

Developing Options

This module discusses how to explore **options** that will enable your employee to move towards the goal that was set before them. This is the next component or the "O" in the GROW model. This is the pivotal step in the coaching process. If done correctly, you will engage your employee and create a desire for them to improve. If done incorrectly, your employee will disengage and they probably will fail again. It is the coach's job to create this participative environment. Let us look and see how.

Identifying Paths

Many times, we feel that we have to outline the specific actions and employee has to take in order to reach the stated goal. While this may make you feel better, the likely hood of this action becoming meaningful to your employee is close to nil. Let us quickly review what we have done so far. You established what the goal is. There is usually very little wiggle room when it comes to a performance goal. It is the plain, unchangeable business reality. Next, we established the current state of affairs with respect to your employee's performance. This historical and factual reality is also unchangeable.

Now, let us take it from the employee's perspective. How in control do they feel? Would they shut down if we, as their coach, solely determine the action steps they are going to take? They might. It is imperative to keep the employee engaged. If not, the rest of the coaching session is just a one-way discussion, leaving your employee powerless in his or her own development.

When you allow your employee to participate in the development of their options, you get B.I.G. results. B.I.G. results stand for the following benefits:

- **Buy-in** by your employee, because the options developed was a collaborative effort

- **Innovation**, because more creativity is possible when two work at it

- **Growth**, because the options developed will have more meaning and lasting commitment

Choosing Your Final Approach

Deciding on which option to implement could be frustrating. The best thing to do is to implement a consistent method to determining the best possible option. The APAC section of the B.I.G. template is designed to help you come to a quick decision on which option to implement. Here is how it works.

After you have brainstormed your options with your employee, assess the pros of each option. Determine the benefits and possible rewards to selection that option. Write those benefits in the template. Next, assess the cons for each option. Here are some things to consider:

- Resources needed

- Cost

- Time

- Return on investment

- Disruption of the business

All of these factors could rule out an option. Once you identify the cons place those in the corresponding area on the template. Next, determine the top five options that are feasibility to implement. Use a rating scale from 1-5 and place that in the rating column. Now, you are ready to rate the relevancy of the options identified as feasible. Rate the relevancy of the options to the goal. Here are some things to consider when rating this category:

- Does this option build new supporting skills?

- Does this option meet the time requirement of the goal?

- Is this option measurable?

Once you determine the relevancy, you are able to multiply the feasibility rating with the relevancy rating. The highest number is possibly your best option. Remember to gain consensus from your employee on this option.

Structuring a Plan

Since you have your employee's attention, it is best to begin the planning process. Structuring a plan as soon as possible sends the message to your employee you mean business when it comes to implementing the option. For example: your SMART goal may be to increase the sales attempt rate from five percent to seven in 30 days. Next, you and your employee may have agreed to focus on asking open-ended questions during a sales call as their option, giving them more information to help them attempt better. When are they going to start asking those questions? How many are they going to ask? These are action items you want document in a preliminary plan.

The **3T** questioning technique helps you document three major milestones. Basically, you ask, "What are you going to do:

- Tomorrow?

- Two weeks from today?

- Thirty days from today?

You may need to guide your employee when answering the first question. Remember the more time you let pass from the time you coach them and the time you implement your first action step, you could be losing precious information discussed in your coaching session. Here is an example of how the earlier scenario could be developed:

Coach: "You said you wanted to ask more open-ended questions to help you attempt better sales. Great, what steps are you going to take tomorrow to begin that process? "

Employee: "I can try asking an open ended question on every few calls."

Coach: "Do you think you can ask a question on every third call?"

Employee: "Okay, I will try to ask on every third call."

Coach: "Let's look ahead two weeks from now. Do you think you can increase the frequency to every other call?"

Employee: "That sounds fair."

Coach: "Great, now, let's shoot to ask questions on every call 30 days from now. What do you think?"

Employee: "I believe I can do this or get really close."

Coach: "Let's write this down on paper and put a final plan together."

Once you get to this point, you are ready to begin drafting your final plan. Let us see what this involves.

Wrapping it All Up

In the last module, your goal was to get your employee participating in the coaching process by identifying actions steps together. It is time know to solidify what has been said and established as actions steps or simply stated—wrapping it all up.

In this module, you are going to learn how to finalize your employee's plan in a way that motivates them to take action immediately. **Wrapping** up the coaching session is the final component or the "W" in the GROW model to coaching. This step is crucial, because it should set things in motion quickly, which is your goal. Let us see how.

Creating the Final Plan

When creating a development plan, there must be consistent steps outlined, allowing your employee the opportunity to learn, apply measure, and assess their development. The LAMA process is designed to approach the planning activity in a consistent and efficient manner.

Each component of the LAMA process is time sensitive and is anchored by your overall SMART goal, meaning the entire process should be complete by the goal day you set. Here is the breakdown of LAMA and a description of each of the components:

- **Learn**: some form of learning should take place. It could be a variety of activities. Mentoring with a peer, reading a book, taking a course, are some examples of learning opportunities you may implement.

- **Apply**: implement what was learned soon after learning is completed.

- **Measure**: agree on a method of measuring when and how the new learning is used on the job. You can perform observations, or have your employee track it on a worksheet you developed. The idea is to monitor the use of the new knowledge.

- **Assess**: review the impact of the new skill on the performance metric being improved. Any success should be attributed to the new skill and encouraged.

As mentioned earlier, each component must have a start and an end date. The assessment date should correspond to the SMART goal date. If you are SMART goal timeframe is greater than 30 days, you should plan more assessment dates and coach according to the performance results.

Since you now have a basic idea how to create that final plan, let us look at how to determine the first step.

Identifying the First Step

The first step to any development activity is to learn. Allowing the employees to learn something new is essential to their overall development. There are many benefits to making learning a deliberate practice in coaching process.

Here is a summary of benefits:

- Employee feels valued with the investment you are making in them

- You demonstrate that you care which helps to foster a better working relationship

- You give a chance for a role model to become a mentor to your employee

- New skills learned could be shared with other employees

Now you understand some of the benefits to learning. Let us look at ways you are able to motivate your employee.

Getting Motivated

Motivating your employee is an essential part of coaching. Many times, motivating by money alone is not enough. Employees prefer to have a great working environment and a good relationship with their manager. It is the manager's job to create this environment. Here is a helpful way to create the supportive and motivating environment your employees need to thrive.

The process is called the five B's now this process requires you to re-think the way you manage. If you find yourself challenged by this topic, seek out additional resources that will help you develop the skills and behaviors necessary to foster a motivating atmosphere.

The five B's are the following:

- Be consistent in your coaching. Coach all of your employees. Do not reserve coaching for only your "problem "employees.

- Be respectful with your employees. Being a manager does not give you the ability to insult or berate your employees.

- Be caring and watch your employees' behavior for signs of personal issues. The goal is to guide them when they are experiencing problems both in and outside of work. Of course, you are not going to get personally involved, but you want to lend and empathetic ear and guide them to resources that my help them.

- Be flexible and find ways to reward you employees with non-monetary items. Perhaps some downtime away from their desk doing something else or cross training is a possibility.

- Be a cheerleader and celebrate even the smallest of successes. Give recognition the way your employees prefer. Some may like public recognition while others prefer low-key ones. Find out what your employees prefer and use it strategically.

Taking the time to motivate your employees is a worthwhile investment. Make sure you plan it and implement it without fail or else your coaching efforts will be in vain. Next, let us look at the importance of trust in the coaching environment.

The Importance of Trust

In your coaching session with your employees, you will discover many times things about your employee that are personal and sensitive topics. This is normal and demonstrates trust in you. As their coach, establishing and maintaining trust is the most essential ingredient to the entire process. If your employee determines that your purpose of improving their performance is to further your career, then they will not trust you. Without trust, whatever you say and do will be subject to skepticism.

This module discusses the meaning of trust, its relationship to coaching and building trust. Building trust must be a sincere desire in you. It requires an investment in time and emotion. Anything less will not foster a trusting relationship between you and your employee. First, let us begin by defining what trust is.

What is Trust?

In the next couple of lessons, we are going to discuss trust. Coaching should be a place where you and your employee can discuss things openly. Having a trusting relationship with your employees is essential to the coaching process. Without trust, you will seldom get to the root cause of issues that could be hindering their performance.

Trust is built over time and is accomplished through your actions. Trust, in the realm of coaching, could be defined as the ability to instill confidence, and reliance in you by being fair, truthful, honorable, and competent in what you do as a manager. Lacking in any of these areas could hinder you instilling trust into your employees.

Let us look at how trust works in coaching.

Trust and Coaching

Effective coaching is done in a trusting environment. There is no doubt about this. In order for you to be able to inspire your employees to perform better, they have to trust you. Your coaching session is the only opportunity to demonstrate to them that they can trust you because you use the coaching session as a tool for building up employees and not tearing them down.

Avoid using your coach session as a venue to deliver reprimands, sanctions, bad news, etc. This is not the place for that kind of information. In addition, avoid using coaching when only negative things need to be addressed. Coaching should be a purposeful event that happens regularly and is void of negative information. This is not to say you cannot discuss performance issues. It just has to be presented in a way that speaks of development than of punishment.

When coaching, we should avoid being a DOPE, or

- **Degrading** your employees

  o Using negative words like stupid, lazy, slacker, etc.

- **Ostracizing** your employee

  o Using coaching sessions only as a means for disciplinary action

- **Punishing** your employee

  o Using sessions to deliver sanctions or firing them

- **Evaluating** your employee

  o Telling employees that they are the worst performer,

  o Why can't they be like the other good employees, etc.

Make coaching a haven for encouragement and development and not a place for stress and discouragement. Without trust, you will not be able to coach well. Next, let us look at how to build trust.

Building Trust

Building trust takes practice and dedication to being sensitive to your employee's needs. Here are eight steps to building trust with your employees in and out of the coaching session:

1. Maintain positive body language

2. Listen to them intently and speak less

3. Always respect your employees

4. Keep things confidential

5. Keep your promises

6. Be honest and transparent

7. Be confident

8. Tell them you believe in them

Next, let us learn ways to provide feedback in a positive yet serious manner.

Providing Feedback

We discussed the importance of establishing trust and its relation to the coaching process. Although building trust is a personal investment you must make, you are still required to provide both negative and positive feedback.

Understanding how to structure feedback is essential in balancing trust with the need to discuss desired and undesired behaviors with your employee. In this module, you are going to learn techniques for delivering feedback well. Let us begin.

The Feedback Sandwich

Initiating the feedback process could be a stressful situation if done incorrectly. However, as managers, we have to make tough discussions with our employees. In the world of giving feedback, time is the essence. You want to be comfortable when giving feedback. When you are comfortable, your employee will be comfortable.

The Feedback Sandwich is a method of introducing feedback to your employee surrounded by praise. It starts the conversation by briefly reviewing a positive aspect your employee is currently demonstrating. It could be a good attitude; a well-executed sales pitch, etc. Be careful not to spend too much time praising at the beginning, because your "meat" of feedback message will be diluted. Remember, the reason why you are speaking to your employee at this time is to deliver feedback.

Next, deliver the opportunity for growth in a positive tone. Avoid accusing your employee, but remain focused on the message you must deliver. In the next lesson, we will discuss how to structure constructive criticism. For now, remember this is the largest part of your dialogue.

Finally, close the feedback session on a positive note. Praise the employee on a strength they have or tell them you are confident they are going to adjust and be successful. This helps the employee overcome the embarrassment that is associated with receiving feedback.

To review, you want to structure your feedback sandwich by starting with Praise, then delivering the opportunity for growth and closing with praise again. This is easy to remember if you recall the acronym **POP**.

Here is a sample delivery:

Praise: *John, your sales attempts this month are doing well because you are asking good probing questions up front and I appreciate your work.*

Opportunity for growth: *Here is something I noticed. When a customer says, "No" to your attempt, you immediately stop selling and abandon the sales attempt. This is where you should use more questions. As a result, your sales percentage is one of the lowest on the team.*

Praise: *I know you are capable of asking more questions because you build good rapport with our customers.*

Providing Constructive Criticism

Providing constructive criticism is a skill that requires you to focus on four key areas.

First, focus on one issue at a time. Avoid addressing multiple issues. This will only cause confusion and frustration. Identify the issue and set plan on how you are going to address this.

Second, focus on being timely. Once you identify an issue, make sure you do not wait too long to deliver the critique. The more time passes the less affective it will be. Your employee may even forget what they did.

Third and most importantly, focus on observable actions or behaviors. Avoid generalities. For example, do not say, "You have an issue with time management." This statement is lacking an observable action or behavior. Instead, you might want to say, "I notice you spend extra time talking to other employees on your way to meetings, making you late to most of them." The observable behavior is "talking to other employees." With this behavior identified, you are now able to focus on the next point.

Fourth, focus on a plan to change the behavior. Depending on the extent of change that must happen, your plan may be a simple adjustment. However, if it is complex, then use your SMART goal writing technique to help your employee set successful goals.

Now let us learn how to encourage growth and development.

Encouraging Growth and Development

Encouraging growth and development is really providing opportunities to learn. When we give opportunities to our employees, we send the message that we value them and are willing to invest time, effort, and sometimes money into their development.

As managers, we should foster an environment of learning. Here are some ways you are able to provide learning opportunities for your employees:

- Develop a peer mentorship process

- Use your internal training department

- Send your employee on lend to another department to learn something new

- Start a book of the month club where your employees read, on company time, a few pages at a time

- Use your team meeting as a venue for team learning

- Send your employees to seminars if your budget allows

A good approach is to create a menu of opportunities for your employees to learn. Remember that learning styles vary among adults. Therefore, try different approaches.

Overcoming Roadblocks

It is common to encounter roadblocks during the coaching process. Roadblocks manifest in many different forms. Roadblocks, however, should not spell and end to the coaching process. You should expect roadblocks to occur. It is natural for it to happen because we are expecting behavior change, which that in and of itself is a task for your employee.

In this module, we will discuss ways to overcoming roadblocks. Some of the things you will learn are identifying common roadblocks re-evaluate goals and focus on progress. Roadblocks are not dead ends. They are warning signs that will help you identify when you need to intervene and get your employee back on track.

Common Obstacles

Coaching takes two people to accomplish. The manager must be just as engaged as the employee. Lack of zeal and honesty creates roadblocks that will hinder your employee's ability to reach their goals. Here are some common obstacles we as managers create:

- Do not have enough time to coach properly

- Lack of confidence in coaching

- Fear of confrontation

- Feels awkward

- Fear of failure in coaching

- Afraid employee will not respond

Now, from the employee's perspective, here are some common obstacles they may encounter:

- Home/life issues are blocking progress

- Fear of losing their job

- Lack of confidence reaching the goal

- Denial there is anything wrong

- Poor relationship with the coach

Obstacles come in many different forms. However, the root of the obstacles typically comes from a personal deficiency in their life situation. Maslow's theory of needs outlines basic needs we all must have in order to reach higher order needs. Here is brief overview of the needs.

- Physical need

- Safety need

- Social need

- Esteem need

- Growth need

The basics of all needs are the physical and safety needs. If a person is lacking in either of these areas, they will find it difficult to progress further into the higher needs. For example, if you know your employee is having issues at home, their physical or safety need may be at risk, creating an obstacle to reaching a goal, which is a higher order need. When faced with a needs issue, try your best to acknowledge the need and guide them to a qualified resource to assist them with this issue.

Let us look at how to re-evaluate goals and realign the employee back to achieving the goal.

Re-evaluating Goals

As time passes from the original coaching session, you want to check in on your employee and see where they are at, in respect to the goal that was set. It is at this point, where you may want to re-evaluate the goal and determine if it is still SMART.

There are several things you want to take into consideration when re-evaluating goals. First, re-evaluating does not mean that you have to change it. Re-evaluating is an opportunity to check on the goal and to determine how your employee is doing in achieving this goal. Here are some steps you want to take when re-evaluating a goal:

- Revisit the starting point. You want to review where you began. This way you are able to see if progress has been made and your employee is moving towards the goal.

- Determine what has been accomplished. Look at what the current performance level is and compare it to the starting point determined earlier.

- Review the amount of time left in respect to the goal date. You want to see if the amount of improvement is aligned with how much time has passed or how much time is left before the goal date is reached.

- Determine if the time remaining before the goal date is adequate to fulfill the goal. Here you want to see if there is still enough time to improve and reach the goal.

- If not enough time is left to accomplish goal by goal date, then set a new goal and goal date based on how much improvement has been accomplished and the time it took to get there.

- If there is still enough time, set smaller goals to help the employee move towards the established general goal.

In overcoming roadblocks, you may need to be more flexible. Perhaps the goal originally seemed like a viable goal, but when put into practice it becomes apparent that you will not be able to reach it. Do not become frustrated. Be flexible and understanding of your employee if you have to reset a goal.

Focusing on Progress

If you find yourself with an employee struggling with reaching their goals, you may be tempted to pull them over and discuss how they are missing the mark and the related consequences.

Focusing on the negative aspects will only create more obstacles. Remember the hierarchy of needs mentioned earlier? Well, if you start making the coaching session feel more negative, the employee may feel that their job is threatened. If this happens, they will become more fearful and this adds to the roadblocks.

Instead of focusing on the negatives, focus on the progress. Tell your employee that you see progress and that you believe that they are able to make their goals. Speaking positively expands the employee's belief about themselves. Use encouraging phrases like the ones here:

- I know you are not quite there yet, but you managed to improve this much in such a short amount of time.

- Your progress is steady and you are showing promise that you will reach that goal.

- You showed definite improvement since our last discussion. I am confident you are going to hit this goal.

It is easy to speak into the positive aspects of progress. The benefits of focusing on progress could reap the following:

- Increased communication between you and your employee

- Build trust

- Increase motivation

- Goal is reached

- Build good relationship with your employee

- Employee's confidence is boosted

You see if you speak positively, then positive things come out, but if you speak negatively, and then you will get a negative reaction.

Reaching the End

Identifying the end of the coaching process for a particular goal is a vital step that helps both you and your employee acknowledge you have both reached the end. Failing to acknowledge the achievement of a goal could result in disappointment for your employee. Many times, they are anticipating the end and perhaps expect some form of celebration or kudos. No matter how you do it, as a coach, you must know when your employee has reached their goal and acknowledge it.

In this module, you will learn to recognize success, transition your employee from this coaching goal to another and wrapping it up. Let us begin by discussing how to know when you have achieved success.

How to Know When You've Achieved Success

Determining if success is achieved is a crucial element to the coaching process. If you fail to recognize success, you could hurt your coaching program. Your employee worked hard to reach their goals and it is your job to recognize when it has been achieved.

Taking inventory of your employee's accomplishments helps you to determine how well your employee has achieved success. This inventory could also help you determine if your employee is ready to move into the next level of their development.

Here are some areas to review when taking inventory:

- Review the goals and compare them to how well your employee achieved them

- Review where your employee is at the beginning of the coaching process and how far they have progressed

- List the behaviors you employee demonstrated during the coaching progress

- List your employee's strengths

- List your employee's weaknesses

- List your expectations and compare them to how well your employee meets or exceeds your expectations

- If applicable, determine if your employee is ready of the next level of their development

If you noticed, there are two levels of success. The first level deals with the immediate goal. During the course of developing your employee, you probably set various goals. You may use this inventory to determine if they are successful in one goal and then move on to the next goal.

On the other hand, you may use this to help you determine if your employee has achieved overall success and is ready to move on to more development in other areas like management.

Transitioning the Coachee

Transitioning is moving your employee to the next level of development. You may also transition your employee to the next developmental goal. In any case, it is a good practice to make a clear transition. Making it clear tells the employee they achieve success and are ready to take on new challenges.

Failure to transition may frustrate the employee over time. Transitioning closes a door and opens the next. Below are the steps to making a good transition:

- Make a statement of success. This is a purposeful announcement you make to your employee as a way to mark the transition. Here is a sample:

"John, you have accomplished a great deal over the last year. Today marks the beginning of a new phase of development for you."

- Overview of accomplishments given: here you review what your employee has accomplished and how well they did and that you are proud of them

- Verify your employee agrees. You want to ensure that you and your employee are on the same page. They may not quickly understand that you are about to move them into another level of development. Use open-ended questions to help you determine if your employee is in fact ready to transition. If they are not ready, then set goals to help them address those concerns and coach them through it, using SMART goals and the GROW coaching process.

- Engage the employee with the next level of development. You should have a plan in place that outlines the transition. Share this plan with your employee and have them engage it as soon as possible. Perhaps you may have to hand them off to another manager for development, then walk the employee over to that manager and introduce them.

If your purpose is to transition your employee to the next development goal, then follow the steps like before this time engage your employee to the new goal instead. Always make sure your employee is ready for the next level of development.

Wrapping it All Up

Wrapping it all up is just a matter of organizing your employee's coaching file and transitioning the file to the next manager for reference. Even if you do not plan to transition your employee over to a new manager, wrap up the coaching file and keep it accessible for future use.

Here are some things you want to do so you can wrap this coaching file up:

- Have all your coaching documents related to your employee placed in a file folder. If it is electronic, do the same.

- Use the wrap up worksheet and place that as the first page of the coaching file. The Wrapping it up worksheet outlines the following:

- Employee's profile (i.e. name, years at organization, job title, etc.)

- List of achievements

- List of positive behaviors

- List of areas for further development

- List of goals your employee would like to achieve

- Your overall assessment

- Your recommendation

- Brief outline of the next events

Your employee's coaching sessions are now transitioning into something else. Let us look at what mentoring is and how to leverage that is a form of development for your employee.

How Mentoring Differs from Coaching

Earlier in this workshop, we defined the terms coaching and mentoring. We learned that both concepts vary greatly in terms of the goal each sought to achieve. In this module, you are going to learn the practical differences and blend the two for a balanced development program. In addition, we will discover how to integrate the GROW module when you are mentoring your employee and finally, you will learn how to focus more on building relationships. Let us start by comparing the practical differences between coaching and mentoring.

The Basic Differences

There are differences between coaching and mentoring. Each typically has goals to accomplish, but the methods are vastly different.

Coaching has the following characteristics:

- Interaction is usually not voluntary

- The interaction usually is for a set amount of time.

- The interaction is structured and meetings are typically confined to scheduled meetings

- Coach does not necessarily have to be an expert on the coaching topic

- Generally, the interaction is short-termed and focus usually in one or two areas of development

- The focus is on a particular job function developmental issue

- The goal is to produce a more immediate change or result

- Coaching is typically targeting specific opportunities for improvement

Mentoring has the following characteristics:

- Interaction is usually voluntary

- Relationship is usually long-term over an extensive period of time

- Interaction is less structured with more causal than structured meetings

- Mentor is usually regarded as an expert in their field and is a resource to the protégé

- Career development is the overall goal of mentoring

- The goal is to develop areas that the protégé deems necessary for their development for future roles

- Mentoring targets the entire career path of a protégé

Let us see how we can blend the two models for an effective development program for your employees.

Blending the Two Models

Depending on the type of working environment you have and the overall goal of your employee, you may want to combine the characteristics of coaching with mentorship. What you decide to use depends on the current work environment, the type of advancement opportunity your employee has and the time you or someone else have to give to develop the target employee.

There is no right or wrong answer when determining which characteristic you want to combine. Simply pick the ones that will help you achieve maximum results. For example, you may want to blend the more casual approach to meeting with your employee with a targeted area of development. On the other hand, you may want to blend the relationship-building aspect of mentoring to the planned meeting intervals.

The approach you determine is considered the best for you environment. Here is a list of benefits you realize when you combine coaching with mentorship:

- Increased flexibility

- Allows you to supervise your employee while acting autonomous

- Allows your employee to determine what they want to develop

- Your employee will feel more empowered in their development

- You can enlist the help of other managers in the development of your employee

- Greater satisfaction for both you and your employee

In essence, blending the two models provides more flexibility with the monitoring you need to ensure your employee is on the path to career development.

Adapting the GROW Model for Mentoring

Adapting the GROW model to mentoring is very easy to do. When coaching, the GROW model is used as a guide for the coach to structure their dialogue with their employee. The coach develops the goal and guides the employee to reach a goal the coach selects.

In mentoring, the GROW model is used as a guide to questioning the protégé on when development path they want seek. Here the mentor asks open-ended questions that form the basis of the mentoring program. Here are some questions you can use when you want to use GROW for mentoring purposes:

- **Goal**: What are your career goals? What do you want to accomplish in the next year?

- **Reality**: Where are you in relation to your career goal? What are you lacking that you need to have in order to reach that career goal?

- **Options**: What are activities you think will help you develop those missing skills? How do you want to go about developing the skills necessary to advance your career?

- **Wrap it up**: What is your plan? How do you want to go about this?

Focusing on the Relationship

When you coach, the relationship is hierarchal, meaning that you are driving the process and the employee must respond. Mentoring is not meant to be set up that way. Mentoring is a shoulder-to-shoulder type relationship. In coaching your focus is on reaching goal with a targeted development plan.

On the other hand, mentoring is sharing and guiding your protégé. It requires less structure but more relationship building. Being a mentor to someone creates a special relationship where the mentor watches over the protégé, guides them, and corrects them in different situations. There is not a set intervention. It is constant awareness, looking out for pitfalls and political traps that are common in the work environment.

Mentors also become more involved in the protégé's life, demonstrating caring, understanding, and guiding them through it from the employment perspective. Deep personal issues should be taken care of by professionals; however, guiding them to that professional level is a mentor's job.

Here are some behaviors that help to foster a good relationship between a mentor and a protégé:

- Demonstrate caring by listening for issues that are not readily disclosed to you. Perhaps you over hear a conversation where your protégé is struggling with something. Demonstrate care by encouraging your protégé to discuss it with you.

- Demonstrate understanding by acknowledging and empathizing with your employees situation. Take the time to fully grasp what is going on and acknowledge it is real and that you would feel the same if you were in their shoes.

- Demonstrate listening by giving your undivided attention and avoid interruptions when talking with them like answering the telephone or looking at email. Notate and mirror things back to your protégé to demonstrate you are listening.

- Demonstrate respect by keeping the relationship professional at all times. Avoid degrading your protégé or using causal language in front of others. Show you respect your employee as if they were an equal.

Keeping an eye on the relationship is just as important as keeping focus on the goal. The mentor-protégé relationship is delicate because the employee must see the value of the relationship. If they do not see a relationship, then the purpose for mentoring is gone.

We are near the close of this workshop, and it is time to wrap this class up. Let us here some words from the wise before we do close this session.

Chapter 13 – Employee Motivation

Employee Motivation is becoming ever more important in the workplace as time goes on, and everyone agrees that a motivated workforce is far more likely to be a successful workforce. The happier and more professional an employee is, the better the results they will deliver for you. Of course, every employer wants to make sure that they have a workforce who will do their best, but this does not simply mean making the job easy for their employees. In fact, part of the problem of motivation is that where the job is too easy, employees become complacent.

There is therefore a challenge for all employers and management in delivering the right balance between a confident, motivated workforce and a workforce which is driven to attain goals. It can be described as a mix between the pleasure of a comfortable working environment and the fear of failure, although in honesty it is more complicated than that equation suggests. Regardless of how it is characterized, it is important to get the right balance in order to ensure that you have a motivated workforce. This manual is designed to show participants the way to get the best out of a confident, motivated set of employees, and to show them how to motivate that group.

By the end of this chapter, you will:

- Defining motivation, an employer's role in it and how the employee can play a part

- Identifying the importance of Employee Motivation

- Identifying methods of Employee Motivation

- Describing the theories which pertain to Employee Motivation – with particular reference to psychology

- Identifying personality types and how they fit into a plan for Employee Motivation.

- Setting clear and defined goals.

- Identifying specific issues in the field, and addressing these issues and how to maintain this going forward.

A Psychological Approach

The importance of psychology in achieving and maintaining Employee Motivation is essential. A message can be repeated over and over to a group of employees but unless they believe it and believe in it, the words are empty. The following are some of the key psychological theories which aid employers in their end goal of producing a motivated workforce.

Herzberg's Theory of Motivation

Herzberg's theory is that Employee Motivation is affected both by the employee's level of satisfaction and dissatisfaction and that, importantly, these two elements are independent of one another. That is to say that although an employee can be satisfied by the elements of their job which are intrinsic to the job itself, such as achievement and recognition, while at the same time being dissatisfied by the elements which are secondary factors of the work – pay and benefits, job security and relationships with co-workers.

This was described by Herzberg as the Motivation-Hygiene Theory. Elements which are done because they are essential to the job were considered the "motivation" part of the theory. They were done because they *had* to be done; therefore the worker was "motivated" to carry them out. Carrying these tasks out was considered to be the motivation of the employee, because they were required or compelled to do them.

Having work to do demand that the worker rise to – and meet – a challenge, their motivation was set in stone.

The "hygiene" element, rather than a reference to personal hygiene and cleanliness as one might assume, was actually a reference to the upkeep of personal determination. They were things that needed to be constantly maintained because they were not intrinsic to the job. Herzberg's assertion was that the opposite of satisfaction was not Dissatisfaction, but rather an absence of satisfaction. Similarly, the opposite of dissatisfaction was an absence of dissatisfaction rather than simply satisfaction. In terms of motivating employees, it is important to encourage satisfaction on the one hand, and avoid dissatisfaction on the other.

Maslow's Hierarchy of Needs

Abraham Maslow's pyramid detailing the hierarchy of human needs is actually a more general listing of things on which every human should be able to rely on, but is applicable to the issue of Employee Motivation. In any job, from the most basic to the most specialized, the employee should be able to rely on their employer and their co-workers to uphold their access to the most basic needs – those which are essential and without which a human's health will suffer. The absence of access to these needs is the basis for everything else. As we go up the pyramid the needs become less essential but arguably more decisive.

A sense of security and of belonging is also important to any employee. Knowing that one's physical safety is ensured allows a person to do their job without fear. Security is not merely a physical concept; it also refers to the security of a person's job and the conditions that allow them to do that job. Giving a person tasks to do is an essential part of motivation, but providing them the environment in which to carry out those tasks is no less important for motivation. Allowing a level of interaction and encouraging a team ethic will further a person's intent to do their job and do it well.

In the upper two echelons of the pyramid, the needs are now more refined and specific. It is possible to do a job without self-esteem, but it is undesirable. Encouragement and positive feedback are important factors in ensuring that an employee does their job to the best of their ability. Without these factors, the likely outcome is a drop in performance and a reluctance to carry out further tasks completely and reliably. Self-actualization needs such as creativity and spontaneity allow the mind to work to its optimum level, and actively motivate the employee. These theories fit in somewhat with Herzberg's – that there are certain things which must be guaranteed as an absolute base, and then others which guarantee the effort of an effective employee through their desire to be part of something good.

The Two Models and Motivation

Abraham Maslow's theory on the hierarchy of human needs was an influence on Frederick Herzberg's later theory regarding the factors which motivate workers. While Maslow considered the needs of a person to all be on the one hierarchical list, Herzberg felt that there were two very separate elements of the plan. To look at Maslow's list, one would feel that as the requirements as set out in the pyramid were met, the level of satisfaction would rise while, at the same pace, the dissatisfaction would drop. It was Herzberg's contention that this is not the case. Herzberg felt that satisfaction and dissatisfaction were actually wholly separate and that both needed to be attended to.

Herzberg and Maslow created two separate theories, and while much of what is set out in the hierarchy of needs is backed up by the theories in the "two factor" theory, it is expanded upon and honed. While to look at Maslow's model one would feel that as long as certain needs were met, satisfaction would rise and dissatisfaction fall in equal measure, Herzberg holds that one could have a high level of satisfaction from carrying out their tasks in an efficient manner and meeting their targets, yet if they were constantly worried that they could lose their job for reasons separate to performance, they would not be as motivated as they could be.

There is, however, something to be said of Maslow's hierarchy, in that the pyramid as he set it out could be split into sections. In this case, the top sections (and particularly the peak) would correspond somewhat to Herzberg's "motivation" factors and the lower sections to his "hygiene factors. Herzberg's theory is not a contradiction of Maslow's, but at the same time is not a direct application of it. There are certainly differences between the two. They both have their part to play in employee motivation, however, and they have a lot more in common than to separate them.

Object-Oriented Theory

Motivation is not all about philosophical needs, of course. A lot of people work better when they have the concrete facts in front of them – something to work towards, something to avoid. Different things motivate different people, and in any given team or workforce there will be a mix of these people. As Herzberg's Theory suggests, what will motivate each individual will be a mix of satisfaction and non-dissatisfaction. This is similar to the old theory of the "carrot and whip" – based on the hypothesis of riding a horse and using the carrot to encourage it to speed up, and the whip to prevent it from slowing down too much. Then there is also the idea of the plant – seeing a worker as a "plant" who, given the right mix of the already-discussed factors, will flower beautifully. The carrot, the whip, and the plant are united into the heading of "Object-Oriented Theory".

The Carrot

The "carrot" as a theory takes its lead from horse-riding and dates back to the middle of the 20th century. The idea is that a cart driver would tie a carrot to a long stick and dangle it in front of the horse or donkey which was pulling his cart. As the donkey moved forward towards the carrot, he would pull the cart and driver forward, ensuring that the carrot always remained beyond his reach until such time as the driver slowed down and stopped, at which point – should he so desire – the driver could give the carrot to the horse as a reward for doing what it has been encouraged to do.

For the employer, this can perhaps be read in a number of ways. Looking at how the "carrot" theory works, it is quite easy to assume that the "carrots" offered to employees should be continually moved beyond their reach, and this assumes that the employee is as stubborn and witless as a donkey. This would be a rash assumption to make, and continually moving the point of reward away from the employee could be seen as a disincentive. Not delivering on a promise is always likely to annoy workers rather than stiffen their resolve to meet the new goals.

It could, however, also be argued that the carrot on the stick is something which should not just hang there within easy reach. The employee will need to keep testing themselves, but as long as they meet their challenges they will be rewarded at the end of their efforts. In the theory detailed in the first paragraph, there is a defined end point. The important element of the theory is that if someone has the promise of a reward at the end of their work, they are likely to keep striving for it. If that reward is continually denied them even at the end of their work, however, do not be surprised if it ceases to work.

The Whip

In different cultures it is known by different names, but the second part of the "Carrot" theory is the Whip. There is a long history of terms and sayings attached to the idea of having an element of threat involved in motivating a group of employees, or anyone for that matter. "Spare the rod and spoil the child", for example, is an old proverb meaning that if you never punish someone for transgressing, they will come to believe that they can transgress as and when they wish. In the old "Carrot" theory, the way it works is that if the employee tired of chasing after a carrot that never seems to get any closer, simply slows down, a quick smack with the whip will make it speed up again.

The theory of motivation by threat of punishment is one which needs to be handled very carefully indeed. Not only is it absolutely illegal in many places to physically discipline workers, but other forms of threat can have a detrimental effect on the workforce. An employer, team leader, or manager with a reputation for flying off the handle when things are not to their satisfaction may get results from some people, but this method can lead to a culture of fear within a company or department, and stifle performance in order to simply get the work done.

It is left up to the person providing the motivation to decide to what extent and in what way they will use the "whip". There can be initiatives which combine the carrot and the whip – for example, in a one-off situation over the course of a day or so, the person or people who have performed worst in the team can be required to buy coffees or any other small reward for those who have performed best. A "forfeit" system can also be applied, but it is dangerous to apply anything too humiliating in this situation. The limits of the system need to be clearly defined. If it is something so meaningless that it won't be taken seriously, the whip ceases to be a motivation. If it is too stringent it becomes the whole focus and can infringe upon performance.

The Plant

An element of objected-oriented motivation which, is essentially separate from the above, but not incompatible with them, is known as "Plant" theory. Take as your example a simple house plant. In order to ensure that a plant flourishes it is important to give it the best combination possible of different nourishing elements. Most plants will require sunlight, warmth, water, and food in order to grow in the way you would wish. By the same token, employees will be motivated by a combination of factors.

The average employee will require motivation in many of the forms discussed by Maslow and Herzberg, and because humans are not all the same it will be a matter of judgment to ensure that each employee gets the right amount of each factor. This can be something as simple as getting the balance of "carrot and whip" motivation right. It is important, in many managers' eyes, to get the balance right between the arm around the shoulders and the boot up the backside. Making an employee feel valued and supported without letting them become coddled is important, as is ensuring that they know they have to perform without making them feel like they have a gun against their head.

Taking three of Herzberg's essential elements of motivation as an example, some employees work best with the prospect of challenge in their work, while some will work better with the goal of recognition. Others, equally, will want simply to get through as much work as they can while doing the work to a high level of quality. It is important to take into account the differing "buttons" that need to be pressed in each staff member to ensure that they do their job as well as possible. It is many people's view that the team which will work best is the one that has a combination of people who work well under different motivations. This way, tasks within the team can be assigned in a balanced way and ensure the best performance from every individual, and consequently the best performance from the team. The "Plant" theory, as applied here, is about knowing which plant requires which type of nourishment in which measure. By getting the balance right you can ensure the best "greenhouse" arrangement.

Using Reinforcement Theory

The concept of reinforcement theory is an old idea, which has been used in many different settings for many different purposes. If you have a pet dog, the chances are that you have used reinforcement theory in training it to behave the right way – a treat for sitting, rolling over and walking when you ask it to, and a punishment for climbing on the furniture or going to the toilet in the house. It is not, however, limited to dogs, although the way it is applied changes depending on whom the theory is being practiced on. For humans, something as crude as a piece of candy to reward a good deed will not be as effective, but the concept of rewarding good practice and punishing bad holds firm. Reinforcement theory has been established as successful and coherent, and it is a valid method of ensuring the best performance.

A History of Reinforcement Theory

We are all conditioned to act in certain ways based on certain stimuli. This is something that is visible in most things we do. From something as simple as waking up and getting out of bed when an alarm goes, to calling the fire department if we see a fire, our responses to certain situations are more or less instinctive , as we are not automatons, we do have some leeway in exactly how we respond. The knowledge of how we respond to stimuli was articulated in 1911 by E.L. Thorndike in what he called the "Law of Effect". Essentially, this lays down that in a situation where normal results can be expected, a response to stimuli which is followed by something good will become more "right" in our minds, while a response followed by something "bad" will become more "wrong".

To take this theory and apply it practically, as children we are still learning and our parents will usually use positive and negative reinforcement to apply lessons. Practically, if we eat up all our vegetable when we may not necessarily want to, we will be given a pudding after dinner. If we push our sister over, we may be sent to our room or to sit in the corner and think about what we have done. These reinforcement steps may be applied as often as possible until we always eat our vegetable and refrain from pushing our sisters over.

Behavioral conditioning is a subject which some consider controversial and even cruel, but there is a strong body of opinion which suggests that it is absolutely necessary. B.F. Skinner responded to arguments that human drives needed to be respected by saying that people learn behaviors based on what resulted from them. If somebody is of a mind to transgress because they enjoy transgression, but find that the result of their conduct is reduced freedom, they will become less likely to transgress so often. The thought of transgressing can become painful when associated with the idea of what will result. This theory is known as "behaviorism".

Behavior Modification in Four Steps

Once we have accepted that there is a truth to the theory of reinforcement, it is important to look at how the theory can be applied in terms of ensuring the desired behavior. The message of reinforcement theory is that it is possible for you to modify behavior in yourself or in others by associating undesirable behaviors with undesirable outcomes. In order to be fully "scientific" and guarantee the desired results from a program of behavior modification, it is worth following a strict pattern and recording the results faithfully. By referring to the results it is possible to see what patterns of modification work best. The following is a trusted four-step pattern for behavior modification:

1. Define the behavior to be modified.

2. Record the rate at which that behavior takes place.

3. Change the consequences which result from that behavior.

4. If this does not succeed in preventing the behavior, change the consequences to a greater or lesser extent.

By working through this model as often as is necessary it is possible to change the behavior of an individual from being detrimental to being positive in most cases. The form that this pattern might take practically in a workplace is as follows. *Person A has a tendency to leave their work station and go and speak to their friend, Person B. Person A is perfectly capable of delivering good work when they keep their mind on it. The distraction is infringing on Person B's work, too, and they do not have the willpower to refrain from chatting with Person A. In order to ensure that both people's work is as good as it can be it is necessary to stop Person A from behaving in this way.* Thus we have defined the behavior to be modified.

It is then necessary to see how often this happens. If it happens three times a day outside of scheduled breaks, and goes on for ten minutes at a time, then half an hour is lost to this behavior in a given day. If it is allowed to continue, this can build into hours lost in a given week – in fact, in a five day week, five "person hours" are lost to this behavior – half an hour each day for Person A and half an hour for Person B. As yet, nothing is being done. There are numerous things that could be tried here. Simply telling them to return to their workstation is one. If this works in reducing the amount of time lost, then a positive result has been achieved.

However, this may mean that Person A simply changes tack and goes to chat with their friend when you are not in the vicinity. Most offices now, however, have software which records the amount of time an employee stays away from their work station. By checking the time lost in a given day, and tallying the times that Person A and B were both inactive, it is possible to record how much time is lost when you are away from your desk. This can then be addressed in a number of ways. One way may be to stagger the lunch breaks of the members of the team, ensuring that Persons A and B cannot take lunch together as they would prefer. By checking how this affects the conduct of Person A you can see if this is working. As time goes on you can apply a number of different methods and settle on the one that works best.

Appropriate Uses in the Workplace

As things stand, it is really up to the employer, line manager or other supervisor to decide how to apply reinforcement and behavior modification in the workplace. The above example is one case where it can be helpful, but behavior modification is not limited to cases of deliberate transgression (although if the transgression is deliberate it will be more likely to build a clear, causal link in the mind of the individual). Behavior modification can also be used to aid a situation where an employee is working less effectively than they might for reasons other than rule-breaking. People have different ways of going about their jobs, but if one or more employees have a technique that is hindering their results, then behavior modification can form part of their coaching.

Reinforcement theory can also play a part in rewarding employees. If the members of a team have risen above and beyond what is expected of them, it is usually within the capability of a company to deliver some form of reward such as a team lunch. The knowledge that they can have a leisurely two-hour lunch break on the company if they consistently hit targets and exceed expectations is something that will remain in the minds of employees. They will be encouraged to continue the good work by the knowledge that their ability to exceed expectations has been noted and rewarded, and may be rewarded again.

Using Expectancy Theory

While there are a number of theories which focus on needs as a driver of motivation, Victor Vroom's Theory of Expectancy rather thrives on the outcomes. To clarify, while Herzberg and Maslow make the case for motivation being something that is dependent on need, Vroom suggests that the best motivation is to concentrate on the result of work as being the ultimate goal. He splits the process down into three sections – effort (for which motivation is essential), performance, and outcome. The theory is that if the employee is sufficiently motivated to achieve the results, their performance will be better as a result, and the outcome will to some extent take care of itself as a result of improved performance – which will itself be a result of greater effort.

A History of Expectancy Theory

Victor Vroom is a much-respected professor and researcher in the business world, and works at the Yale Business School as well as serving as a consultant for some of the world's most successful companies. This elevated status is due in no small part to his expectancy theory of motivation, which addresses the reasons why people follow the path that they do within corporations. His proposition was that behavior results from choices made by the individual where the choice exists to do something else. The underlying truth in this theory is that people will do what works out best for them. The important element is the outcome.

Vroom worked on this theory with fellow business scientists Edward Lawler and Lyman Porter. The theory dates back to 1964 and is still widely used by professors. While the process is characterized as **Effort, Performance, Outcome**, and more specifically as **E>P** (increased effort leads to a greater performance) and **P>O** (increased performance brings a better outcome), he takes notice of the fact that greater effort will not happen all by itself. What makes a satisfactory outcome for one individual may not necessarily work for another.

Clearly the theory has convinced many, as Vroom has been much in demand since the theory was unveiled, and major companies such as American Express have taken great care to solicit his opinions. While the Expectancy Theory may seem simple and largely self-explanatory, Vroom does make specific reference to elements which can easily be ignored, and without which the theory would not work. It is therefore beneficial to take not only the three factors above, but Vroom's three "Variables".

Understanding the Three Factors

The core variables in the theory of expectancy are Valence, Expectancy, and Instrumentality. The meaning that these variables have is as follows:

Valence – the importance that is placed by the individual upon the expected outcome. If the outcome for a project's successful completion is that the individual will be rewarded with more important projects when they would actually rather be rewarded with time off, they will place less value on the outcome, and their motivation to perform well will suffer, leading to reduced effort. Ensuring that the valence of a task is at a suitable level is a significant motivation

Expectancy – the belief that increased effort will lead to increased performance. Expressed in more simple terms, this means that if you put in more effort, the results will be better. This obviously depends to some extent on having the resources, the skills, and the support to get the job done. While effort is undoubtedly important it is not quite accurate to say that more effort will always mean better results. More effort on its own may well simply be wasted effort, if the person doing the work is using the wrong tools, is the wrong person or is working with people who have limited interest in reaching the same outcome.

Instrumentality – this is the belief that if an individual performs up to a certain level, they will be rewarded with an outcome that will be beneficial to them. It is one thing to tell an individual that, should they meet their performance targets, they will be rewarded with a beneficial outcome, and another to convince them of that. The important factors in Instrumentality are:

- an understanding that performance equals outcome (so the reward depends upon the satisfactory performance)

- a sense of trust that the people who promise the reward will deliver

- trust in the capacity of the people judging the performance and the outcome

Therefore, the Theory will only work in practice if the individual recognizes that they need to perform, and trusts the people in control to judge their performance and deliver what is promised.

Using the Three Factors to Motivate in the Workplace

The three factors of the theory of expectation as set out above all have their part to play in the workplace. Along with what has been learned from Herzberg and Maslow's theories, we can take their insistence on the needs of an employee and put them in a goal-oriented context by applying Vroom's theories.

Firstly there is the issue of valence. Does the motivation exist to complete a task well if the outcome is uninspiring? Surely not, therefore to ensure the maximum motivation, it is ideal to offer something which will be coveted. This is perhaps the most important level of the E>P>O equation. The effort will rise to meet the outcome. How this is used in the workplace will depend on what the company can deliver.

Then there is the issue of expectancy. Effort will only lead to performance where the conditions exist to make it so. In the simplest terms, you might be able to deliver a fine reward to someone who can build a kennel for your dog. But if you only hand them two planks of wood and a broken screwdriver, you may as well offer them a trip around the world for all the good it will do. You cannot expect someone to meet their goals if you do not present conditions which make this possible. All the effort in the world will not make it happen.

Finally there is the issue of instrumentality. This is important in workplaces where big rewards have been offered before, and in those where it is done for the first time. There is little point in a small-income business to offer a sports car as an incentive for better performance, as there is little likelihood of them delivering it. Equally there is limited reason to offer a chocolate bar as the reward for a project which will make a company a million dollars, as it just seems like a slap in the face. Equally, if rewards have been offered before and the task completed only for the company to express their regrets and fail to pay out the reward, the chance that people will trust enough to put the effort in again is greatly reduced.

Personality's Role in Motivation

In any organization, there needs to be a mix of personality types. The importance of personality types is decried by some as a kind of fad science, but it is difficult to run an office or any other workplace when everyone has the same "soft skills". The reason for this is perhaps best explained by the old saying "too many cooks spoil the broth". Where everyone has the same personality type and a problem arises, there is likely to be conflict as everyone tries to take the same role in solving it. The different personality types are not explicitly defined, and therefore there is no hard-and-fast list, but there is a set of soft skills which all workplaces require, and these are best met by different types of people.

Identifying Your Personality Type

You probably have an idea of your own personality type. A personality type is defined by the aspects of your character that emerge when around others or when doing important work. These character aspects are, as often as not, described as "soft skills". You may have been described as "maternal", "skeptical", "humorous", or any number of other things. These are issues which do not relate directly to your work but can aid or restrict your ability to do it, and can aid or restrict others. It is considered beneficial to have as many different types of personality in a workplace as possible.

There are countless tests that can be done to detect a personality type, and many different ways the results can be expressed, but there are certain things which hold true in all personality tests. Perhaps the best way in the workplace to detect a personality type is to judge your reaction to a problem which affects a whole team, or a group within it. Are you immediately looking for a way of overcoming the problem? Are you instinctively worried by what happens, and do you look to other people to help out? Do you comfort people who are stressed out by the problem? Or do you perhaps sit on the fringes, making comments and playing for laughs? Strange as it may sound, all of these elements are worthwhile in a team. The person who immediately looks for the solution is a "problem solver"; the second type is a "consensus seeker". The third is considered a "nurturer" while the last listed is a "humorist". All of these are classic personality types.

Equally, all of these people, and others, play a major part in making up a workplace.

- Without the problem solvers, an organization would be in trouble if things deviated from the plan as laid out.

- Without consensus seekers, it would be easy for a problem solver to become too autonomous, solving the problem to their satisfaction without being particularly concerned for how others felt about the solution.

- Without the nurturers, people would feel that a problem could too easily become a crisis.

- Without the humorists a bad situation would depress everyone.

Reason and etiquette dictate how much we allow our personality to take control of us, but most people will avoid becoming too "cliché" in how they behave. What is your personality type?

Identifying Others' Personality Type

Most people know, or have an idea of, what personality type they conform to most. When meeting new people – and the workplace is one arena where this happens perhaps more than any other – it can be difficult to get a handle on what other people's personality types are. The only way to really get a firm sight of what kind of personality you are dealing with is to speak to people and to monitor how they conduct themselves. One way of doing the latter is to hold "ice-breaking" or "getting to know you" games and sessions. By playing certain games and by monitoring people, you can find out a lot about what kind of person they are.

There are countless games designed to find out about people, one of which is the "stranded on a desert island" game. This basically takes the shape of a hypothetical shipwreck where the team is stranded on a desert island after their ship has run aground. There is a list of things which have been left on the ship, and limited time before the tide comes in and takes it away, so you have to prioritize what you will rescue, from the small, seemingly insignificant things to the larger items which may seem to have more practical use. Different people will wish to rescue different things, and will make their reasoning known. This game is beneficial because not only does it show what people's priorities are, it will also show a lot about their personality when you step "outside the game".

There will initially be a team of people sat there with lists which differ hugely. The whole team will, though, need to decide what they as a team rescue from the ship. In doing this, team members will make their points and some ground will be given on some items. From this you will be able to work out who is a dominant character, who is pragmatic, who is light-hearted, and so on. Some people will concede points quickly whereas others will try to make their point – whether they do so in a bullish way, a more structured way or however else. You will also find that in many situations two or more people will vie for the "Alpha" role, while others will value their less confrontational part. From games such as this you can learn a lot about someone else's personality type.

Motivators by Personality Type

The different personality types have different ways of motivating the people around them as well as themselves. Someone who emerges as a conciliatory person is likely to motivate others by speaking to them one-on-one and allowing them to see where they excel as well as where they can improve. Being able to put bad news in a good way, as well as being able to share good news discreetly in a way, can be very valuable.

Other people, who may have a more dominant personality, will have a different way of motivating positively or negatively. They will generally tend to prefer delivering criticism one-on-one, as doing it in the open will de-motivate others, but good news will be delivered loudly and shared throughout the team, as a way of spreading the joy and motivating other people to try to achieve the same, and gain the same kind of acclaim.

Depending on someone's personality type, they will have vastly different ways in which they can contribute to the team's motivation. Indeed, it is becoming common practice in many workplaces to have what are known as "champions" to take control of certain aspects of the team. This empowers people in non-management roles to play a significant part without pressuring them with the responsibility of the concrete performance of the team. By assigning people the correct champion's role, you can enable them to get the best out of themselves and others, and not let a talent go to waste.

Setting Goals

It is universally accepted that a business will get nowhere without having targets and ambitions to which to aspire. There is a phrase often used which describes people as "goal-oriented". The meaning of this phrase is that the individual seeks to achieve goals and defines their success by the reaching of these goals. If they fail to meet it, they consider that they have failed overall, no matter the quality of the work they have done to get there, or any obstacles overcome. Though this seems a little negative given the numerous ways in which a person can fail to reach their goals, it does not mean that having goals and aiming for them is not a valuable way to work.

Goals and Motivation

Anyone in a job will have some targets to meet with regard to their performance. The extent to which they achieve that, the number of times they do so, and the quality which they apply is all considered worthwhile material for target setting and attainment. Some companies set business-wide goals, while others set individual goals for each of their employees. Whatever the case, these goals are used in a number of ways, and are considered an important part of every job.

One way in which goals feed motivation is the obvious one of performance-related pay. While just about every job will come with a basic salary, the importance of ensuring that work is done to a satisfactory standard means that bonuses and top-up payments are paid out for achieving and surpassing goals. This feeds into people's need to be financially rewarded for doing a satisfactory job, one of the major motivations for working. If you feel that you are undervalued in your job, one complaint you may have is that it does not pay well enough. Therefore it is important for your employer to motivate you by paying you well enough, and for you to ensure you are well paid by meeting goals.

Another way in which goals aid the motivation of employees is that they introduce an element of competition. In most offices these days you will see a "results" board which carries the names of team members and their performance in set categories. Depending on how seriously you take competition, you may feel that being top of the list is the important thing – or that being ahead of a specific individual is more important. Regardless, no one wants to be last, and the public displaying of goals can make sure that people do their level best to perform – after all, as Herzberg contends, recognition is a major element of motivation.

Setting SMART Goal

It is one thing to set goals, and another to set meaningful goals. Anyone can set themselves an easily achievable goal, and meet it without really trying. This is not beneficial for motivation; by the same token it is non-beneficial to set goals for someone else that they simply cannot attain. The result of doing this is that they will fail to meet these goals and be discouraged. Rather than striving to meet them next time, they are as likely to exhaust themselves through futile effort or to let their frustration overcome them and fall ever shorter. It is important, to set intuitive goals which, though achievable, are not in any way guaranteed. This increases the challenge while keeping the real possibility of success.

Managers are now using an acronym to sum up the criteria that goals need to meet in order to be worthwhile, and calling them SMART goals. The acronym has various meanings, but for the most part the elements fall into the following categories:

Specific: Goals need to be definite and defined. They need to be on a level where only people who are prepared to work hard will achieve them.

Measurable: Goals need to be something which can be assessed and plotted against previous months and fellow staff members. They need to be worthwhile, and to constitute something that people will be proud to achieve

Achievable: There is no point in setting goals arbitrarily and unilaterally. Setting goals which a member of staff cannot achieve is counter-productive, and may have the opposite result from that intended

Realistic: As mentioned before, there is no point setting goals that cannot be achieved or which are too easy to achieve. They should not be set in regard to a minor element of the job, and achieving them should have tangible benefits.

Timed: Setting a goal of selling 100 units is relatively meaningless unless you specify a time period. Also, during the time period it should be possible to check in and see if the candidate is set to meet their goals or miss them.

Evaluating and Adapting

Based on what we have seen above, the importance of goals is not only in setting them in the first place, but in learning from the experience of achieving or missing them. Sometimes what looks like a realistic goal can be difficult or impossible to reach in the current situation and either the goals need to be re-set or the employee needs to be retrained or coached. Sometimes the goals will be achieved easily and ahead of schedule with a minimum of effort, in which case they may well need to be revised upwards or the employee's methods scrutinized. What is certain is that realistic and accurate goals can be used to evaluate an employee's performance and to see where changes can be made.

Based on an employee just narrowly missing their goals a few months in a row, it may be possible to find out one factor which is holding them back and preventing them from achieving what they are capable of. It may also be that they are hitting all but one of their targets, but just failing on the final one. In these cases, a target or goal can be used as a way of motivating the employee. If they can just hit that last target, then they will be rewarded. There are ways that they can improve their performance on that front, so they know what they need to do in order to hit it. This can be a very useful tool in ensuring that people take their training to heart and are motivated to apply it.

What can be said for certain is that misapplied targets and goals can have a detrimental effect on employee motivation from either side. Too easy and the employee becomes complacent, too hard and they become frustrated. This is why it is necessary to set SMART goals for an employee, and to fine-tune them if they cease to be SMART.

A Personal Toolbox

Motivating yourself and others is something that takes no small amount of effort and can sometimes seem like a fruitless endeavor, as motivation initiatives do not always take hold immediately (or at all, in some cases). It is also worth mentioning that, although there are many resources on the Internet for managers and team leaders seeking to motivate their employees, not all of these will work in a specific situation. It is well worth reading the best books and the best sites in order to promote ideas, but the best motivational strategy will always take some account of the exact situation where it is used, so it is worth honing yours somewhat.

Building Your Own Motivational Plan

A dedicated and specific motivational plan pertaining to the circumstances in which you are trying to motivate workers is a smart move. There are countless motivational plans and structures already in existence, but one of the reasons that these motivational plans have been successful is that they were designed for specific situations. Therefore, they may not work as well in your situation. They will most likely be beneficial, unquestionably, but they could be more so if you tailor the plan to your specific needs.

A good motivational plan will take account of a number of things: the identities and personality types of the people to be motivated; the time available to implement the plan; and the resources available to push the plan forward. Recognition of the parameters within which you must work is important. Few motivational plans are "one size fits all" in nature – and the ones which are will be of limited success because, they have to be less specific than they should be. A plan can be as intricate or as simple as you want to make it, but remember that the time you invest in it will be repaid by the results you get from using it.

This does not mean that you need to start from scratch and construct your own motivational plan from the ground up. There are some templates you can use, and a number of example plans on the Internet which can be taken as a guide from which to build. In these cases, it is important to look at the elements which are transferable and those which are not. The ones which are not should then be replaced by elements which are relevant to the situation in which you wish to implement a motivational program.

Encouraging Growth and Development

Development is something that is demanded by just about every section of our society today, and the workplace is absolutely no different in this respect. An employee who is new in the workplace will not offer the same skills and understanding as someone who has been there for five years, but will certainly bring some of their own qualities including a fresher outlook. The employee will change with time, and this is to be encouraged. It is also to be encouraged that they have some input while they are new. The benefits of this are twofold. Firstly, the new member of staff is encouraged to feel part of the team, and an important part at that. Secondly, the business benefits from a fresher outlook on things.

In order to encourage a new member of staff to grow as part of the business, it is worth listening to them and finding out where they see themselves fitting in. This will help in encouraging their development as a member of staff and as a person, and it will not solely benefit them. The more integrated a team is, the more smoothly it will work. The better people work together the more motivated they will feel to continue. A lack of personal motivation for the job is one of the main reasons that people look to find work elsewhere, and a business is never helped by losing its more able members.

The importance of growth and development in a business does not lie solely with its newer members. The fact is that you can teach an old dog a new trick, and the processes of development need not have an absolute end. Some people are of the opinion that once you cease developing it is time to give up. There is some truth behind this assertion, as development is a necessary by-product of challenge, and once a job has ceased to present challenges, it is difficult to retain your motivation.

Getting Others to See the Glass Half-Full

A major part of motivation in the workplace has to do with ensuring that people are not discouraged by situations which are anything other than favorable. The very definition of a challenge is that it is a situation which presents some risk of failure. For many people the fear of failure can be troubling. The challenge is in getting the fear of failure to represent as something different – the desire, the need for success. Fear of failure should not be a de-motivating factor. It would be surprising for most of us if we were not to some extent scared of failing – no one wants to fail, and this fear can provide the impetus for us to make sure we succeed.

More than anything, turning a bad or potentially bad situation into a good one relies on outlook. The way that this is normally verbalized is by asking whether you are a "glass half-full or a glass half empty" person. This is in some ways just a more simplified way of separating optimists from pessimists. Optimists look at a glass of water which contains exactly half its capacity and say that it is half-full, while pessimists look at it and say that it is half-empty. The more people you can get to maintain a "half-full" mindset, the better for staff motivation.

There are various ways to get people to see the glass half-full. Most common among these is in knowing the fact that challenges come with consequences and rewards. If you do not meet the challenge, you fear the consequences. If you do meet the challenge, you eagerly anticipate the rewards. The challenge is part of the job, so there is really no point in shrinking from it for fear of the consequences. Keeping the rewards in mind is a way of seeing the glass half-full, and makes it far more likely that you will live up to the challenge and have a chance to share in the rewards.

Motivation on the Job

The importance of motivation in any workplace is clear to see. Without motivated employees, any manager or team leader will find it a lot harder to get results out of their team. One can produce a fairly reasonable standard of work without having great motivation, but to exceed expectations and achieve great results it is essential to have superb motivation. Without something to concentrate on as the reward, the reason you do the job and the reason you *want to* do the job, it is difficult to produce quality results, because an absence of enthusiasm will always result in flaws.

The Key Factors

Over the course of this workshop we have looked at various factors in motivation, and philosophies of motivation as put forward by great minds of the business world. The key factors of motivation are diverse, and can come from anywhere. You may feel more motivated by the prospect of the punishment of failure than you do by the rewards of success. Even if you are motivated by the trappings of success, there are several different elements that can be covered by this – a higher salary, a promotion, the recognition of co-workers. Human motivation is something personal and cannot be second-guessed.

The inherent factors in motivational tools are that they fulfill a priority for the person concerned and that they can be relied on. If you want to provide motivation to a group of workers, it is essential that you allow for the fact that different workers will be motivated by different things. A company can spend as much money as it likes on tools for the job and on office facilities, but if the employees are not motivated on a personal level there is simply no point. Giving the employees reason to come in in the morning and do their job to the best of their ability is the only way you can guarantee the optimum level of performance.

Many of the factors that need to be considered with a view to motivating employees are those listed by Herzberg, Maslow, and Vroom. Employees need to feel secure first and foremost. They wish to feel secure in their job, and also in their personal life. If they are well enough remunerated they will be able to meet their rent or their mortgage payments. Employees also need to feel that they are valued and respected. But as well as how an employee feels, it is also important to consider what they covet. As often as not this will be a higher salary, better benefits, and the chance to take part in occasions which recognize brilliance.

Creating a Motivational Organization

An organization is only ever as strong as its employees, and a group of employees will only be as strong as its weakest members. In order to produce the best results over and over again there is nothing more important than ensuring that motivation is high throughout the organization. This means that a company needs to have a policy for motivation if it wants to have the best results. Good motivation from top to bottom is not something that can be achieved simply by flipping a switch, nor by decree from one boss. Good motivation is achieved by team members knowing that their work is appreciated and will be rewarded, and that they are valued within their organization.

Ensuring that this is the case entails a process of selecting the right people for the right jobs. Someone can be an excellent worker in terms of their knowledge of the procedures and tools required to perform operations, but if they are liable to have a corrosive effect on team morale then their position has to be considered. It is all well and good to be able to carry out your duties, but if when you are not carrying them out you insult team mates and create a hostile atmosphere then the overall effect will be negative for the company. To ensure a motivational organization it is essential to prioritize the appointment of staff that can work with others, provide encouragement or advice, and contribute to a positive working environment.

This is a question which comes down to balance. If you have an organization which has its fair share of problem solvers, consensus builders, nurturers, and humorists among others then you will have a far greater chance of creating the motivational environment that you are looking for. This is something that should be checked for at the recruitment stage. It is important to get people who can do the job, and it is also hugely important to get people with whom you and other people can work. A motivational organization is one in which the employees naturally complement one another as personalities and as workers.

Creating a Motivational Job

Ideally, any employee in a company will be able to reply to the question "Do you like your job?" with a "yes", a smile, and a list of reasons why. We have all heard, or read, or have been that person who is never done complaining about their job when not in the office, so it would appear that there is still some work to be done before we are all doing our perfect job. If perfect is not possible, then, we are looking for jobs which make us feel motivated, and as though we feel it is worth going to work tomorrow. Jobs like that do not grow on trees, but when you are a manager it is up to you to put the right job description together in order that potential employees feel that they want to do the job.

Everyone has their own perfect job. The idea of a perfect job is that it will be one that the employee will be happy to show up for, and which they would consider doing even if they weren't being paid. Although the simple truth is that most of us only countenance doing our job because we know that there is a pay check waiting at the end of it, it should be a target for everyone to have a job where they require little extra motivation beyond that which already exists – a target for employers and employees. If you have a happy workforce you are much more likely to have good work done.

So while people will generally find it very hard to ever get hold of their perfect job, having a good motivational job is something worth aiming for. The perfect motivational job is one which combines as many of the business philosophers' essential factors as possible. It will present challenges for the employee, but ones which are achievable for a diligent worker. Achieving these challenges will be met with financial and social reward and the confidence of maintaining a place in the business while also being recognized as a strong worker. In the best motivational jobs, an understanding will exist between the employer and the employee that each knows what the other is looking for, and can provide it.

Addressing Specific Morale Issues

Motivation in a job is linked intrinsically to morale. As interesting and challenging as work may be, if there is a problem with morale then it can very quickly run through the business and lead to underperformance. There are many reasons why morale may be low, and they range from the banal to the very serious. It is only by knowing the nature of the problem causing low morale that morale can be restored and the performance of the business resurrected to a high level. Low morale can affect an individual, or it may go wider than that. It can end up affecting an entire team, department, or company. Depending on what causes it each situation may require a different solution.

Dealing with Individual Morale Problems

Every employer has seen at least once in their time as the head of a team or company an employee who is suffering from low morale. Morale is the mental state of being confident in one's purpose, and is therefore most relevant in the workplace. Low morale is usually not difficult to identify, as it is usually visible in an individual's entire bearing, and then in their work performance. There are so many different factors which can affect morale that second-guessing the reasons why a particular staff member is unhappy can be very difficult. How you deal with the issue of an employee's low morale can easily govern how well they perform and how their morale goes from there.

On identifying an employee with low morale it can be a tricky situation to address. Everybody has their low days and these can happen for any reason, even for no reason. Sometimes people just "wake up on the wrong side of the bed". If you are concerned that it may be something more than that – if the colleague is showing signs of visible distress or appears not to be "switched on" for a prolonged period – then it is worth asking them how they are. This can be something as simple as stopping on your way past to ask "Are you OK?" in a relatively conversational tone. Generally people will not want to make a big deal of it, but it is important to ensure that they are looked after and aware that the help is there if they need it.

If the problem of low morale continues over time, it will clearly become detrimental to the employee and the employer. From a point of view of employee motivation as well as a sense of camaraderie, it is vital to ensure that every avenue is explored to ensure that the morale is lifted and the employee satisfied. It may be that they are concerned about their ability to do the job, and it may be something entirely unconnected to the job, but whatever the case it is essential that the employee should be able to see that there is available support there for them. If this support is not forthcoming, the morale problems can continue and spread. If it is, however, the team morale can be raised as a result.

Addressing Team Morale

Ask any sports coach, and they will tell you that a team assembled expensively from the finest players on the planet can be beaten by a team of scrappers from an amateur league if the professionals are short on team morale. Some of the most extravagantly gifted sides around rarely win anything because they fail to operate as a team. Meanwhile, sides who have players of limited ability can win trophies, as long as everybody works together and sacrifices their individual gratification for the collective good. In short, team spirit is vital to team performance. The way that people work together is governed by how they relate to one another.

In many workplaces, a team will be made up of ten or more people. This means that there are several different dynamics within the team, including those between each individual member, between groups and so forth. Having good team morale depends on ensuring that the separate team members are well-enough disposed towards one another to be able to work with them. If there is conflict within a team, it is certain to affect morale for some of those involved, and those who are on the outside watching it. For a team manager, the challenge is to ensure that this is avoided.

A manager can affect team morale being proactive or reactive, and can contribute to its building, or its destruction. It is essential in cases of team conflict to be even-handed and fair. Even if one does not feel this way they must be seen to be impartial. Favoritism must be avoided at all costs, and you need to be prepared to be unpopular in the short-term. It is much better to put your personal loyalties aside in order to ensure that individuals within the team are not alienated. Petty conflicts can be over in days, but a reputation for bias sticks for good.

What to Do When the Whole Company is De-Motivated

A motivated workforce is absolutely essential to a successful company, and if there is an absence of motivation in just one part of the company it can affect results negatively. If that lack of morale spreads, or a lack of morale arises generally within the organization, then things will be much worse. The worst of all is when an entire company becomes de-motivated, and this can happen for a variety of reasons. The implications of this happening are that people will lose interest in their work, the company's results will drop, and people will begin to fear for their future employment.

An entire company can become de-motivated for a range of reasons. Perhaps the most obvious of these is that a company seems set to go bust, leading to mass unemployment of its members of staff. While in some cases this may galvanize the workforce to work harder in order to ensure the company's survival, market forces dictate that when a company is facing bankruptcy or liquidation it will be extremely difficult to turn things around without outside investment and a lot of luck. The mere prospect of unemployment can be enough to de-motivate the majority of a workforce. Other reasons why an entire workforce may become de-motivated include the loss of an important member of staff or an unpopular change in working practices.

When an entire company loses its motivation for any reason, this falls under the heading of "emergency" and action is required immediately to prevent it from becoming terminal. It falls upon the leaders of the company to sit down with the employees under their jurisdiction and speak seriously with them, offering complete honesty and answering all questions. Being realistic is absolutely essential in this respect. Just saying "there is no problem, everything is going to be OK" will convince no one. Admitting that there is something wrong and outlining how it will be overcome will encourage employees and even those who are initially unconvinced will have the chance to see how it will work. Nothing short of this kind of urgent action will prevent a workplace-wide loss of motivation from becoming terminal.

Keeping Yourself Motivated

Maintaining personal motivation is something essential as an important member of a company, particularly in the case where you are responsible for the motivation of others. As a team leader or manager you will be looked to for reassurance and guidance in a job, and if you give the impression that you are merely going through the motions, your lack of motivation can become contagious. Even if you are responsible solely for yourself, personal motivation remains vitally important. Motivation is what keeps us from giving up and refusing to get out of bed in the morning. Any way we can improve on our level of personal motivation is valuable.

Identifying Personal Motivators

What constitutes a motivation for one person may not be the same for others. Personal motivators are different between people, because the very definition of personal requires that you see things differently from the next person. The importance of identifying your own personal motivators is clear. Without a clear, identifiable set of personal motivating factors, it can be easy to fall into either an unmotivated condition or to rely on other people's motivations to keep you going forward. There are times when we cannot rely on other people to give us the motivation we feel we need, and when you are on your own you need to motivate yourself.

Identifying your own personal motivators is something that takes some self-knowledge and some thinking time. What is it that you want to take from your job? Are you happy to keep cashing the pay checks, or do you wish to advance further in the company? Why did you apply for the job in the first place – and are you close to satisfying that goal? Ask as many questions as you can ask yourself, and as many answers as you can give to those questions, the better your own personal motivation.

One motivation that works well for a number of people is surpassing themselves. Keeping a record of personal achievements attained while in your current job and attempting to do better every month is a challenge that is never completed. If this fails to motivate you, then look at other things which reward performance. Often, people are most motivated by the recognition of their achievements by others, and by setting an example to other members of staff. Whatever works for you is a valid means of self-motivation. Make sure that you have as many motivating factors as you can think of, because the more things you want to achieve, the more you will achieve.

Maximizing Your Motivators

As far as motivation in a job is concerned, it is a matter which requires regular evaluation and frequent updating. There are countless potential motivators for individuals, and as long as they work for you they are valid. What some people struggle with is ensuring that they continue to work. Particularly if you have been in the same job for a long time, it can be easy to lose the urgency and motivation that drove you to your best results when you started. Think of yourself ten years ago and the principles you held which you believed to be as solid as a rock. Do you still feel the same way now, or has life given you a different outlook?

Constantly giving some thought to what motivates you and why will enable you to get the best out of your motivators. When you started in the job, it may have been about the money, but maybe you have enough money now. In this case, it can help to think of something that you want to do which will require more money – taking a break to travel for a while, building a new house, or whatever suits your means. This is a way of maximizing an old motivator which may have ceased to be that effective. Maybe one of your motivations has been recognition. In this case, seeking to mentor a newer member of staff can be beneficial. While you may have achieved almost all there is to achieve in this job, someone else could maybe do with the benefit of your experience.

Taking the factors which have motivated you in the past and updating them for the future is one way to maximize your motivational factors. In addition, it helps to look at your home life as it relates to your work life. If there is something you really need or really want in your home life, and your job can help you achieve it, then this may be all the motivation you need. Pushing yourself to achieve as much as possible will eventually pay off, especially when other people have ceased to push you because they know how good you are

Evaluating and Adapting

We all have things which motivate us – when we are kids, when we are young adults and when we are mature adults – and all that changes is the nature of our motivations. Even once we have retired, we will often find that there are things that we need to do and need to achieve before we can truly rest. In fact, one thing that motivates a lot of people is the need to keep their minds active. Research has proven that people who remain active through their middle and early old age keep syndromes such as dementia at bay for longer than those who do not. This makes it all the more important to remain motivated.

It is sometimes too easy to just let things pass you by through complacency, especially when you have already achieved enough to make you more or less immune from being fired. While it may be nice to remain in a job even when on auto-pilot, there is no denying that it is disadvantageous for keeping the challenge in a job and for motivation. Should you want to make a move into another part of the company or another job, it is always useful to have a results sheet which shows continuing improvement and achievement. To this end it always helps to have a record of achievement and keep testing yourself against it

In the end, the person who can best judge how well you are doing is you. Any manager to whom you answer will probably have other people to manage as well, who may require more careful handling than you. The only way you can ensure you remain motivated is to motivate yourself – so if you find that your motivation is beginning to wane, look at other reasons to stay in the job and work harder. There are always reasons to push yourself, and it is a matter of finding the one which does it for you, no matter how often that changes.

Chapter 14 – Delivering Constructive Criticism

Constructive criticism can be a helpful tool when used with the intent of helping or improving a situation in the workplace. However, it can be one of the most challenging things not only to receive, but also to give. It can often involve various emotions and feelings, which can make matters delicate. But when management learns effective ways to handle and deliver constructive criticism, employees can not only learn from their mistakes, but even benefit from them.

By the end of this chapter, you will be able to:

- Understand when feedback should take place

- Learn how to prepare and plan to deliver constructive criticism

- Determine the appropriate atmosphere in which it should take place

- Identify the proper steps to be taken during the session

- Know how emotions and certain actions can negatively impact the effects of the session

- Recognize the importance of setting goals and the method used to set them

- Uncover the best techniques for following up with the employee after the session

When Should Feedback Occur?

One aspect of delivering constructive criticism is in knowing the right time and opportunity to deliver it. Some instances can be addressed on the employee's next annual review, while others should be addressed right away. If it is done too soon, it could make the employee doubt their abilities and affect their job performance. If delivered too late, then the employee may ignore it altogether and dismiss any help at all. Identifying key situations can help decide when feedback needs to be done.

Repeated Events or Behavior

An employee that displays repeated negative behaviors or patterns should be addressed in order to either stop or further prevent it in the future. Before addressing the problem, the employee should be monitored to ensure the event or behavior is reoccurring, not a onetime incident. Once it has been identified, the employee should be addressed in private. Privately, a resolution can be found to end the behavior and prevent it from happening further without embarrassing the employee in front of other coworkers.

Examples:

- An employee is constantly tardy to meetings, although they contribute throughout the session.

- An employee turns in their reports in the incorrect format, but they are always on time.

- An employee works hard during the day, but takes long breaks and lunches.

Breaches in Company Policy

Situations such as tardiness, improper dress, and poor performance are examples of a breach in company policy. Problems such as these should not wait until the employee's next review, but should be addressed right away. If not properly handled, the employee's behaviors can start to affect others in the office and disrupt the work flow. Employees should be reminded of the company policy, including guidelines to follow and possible consequences for misconduct.

Examples:

- Excessive tardiness or absences

- Consistent violation of dress code policies

- Disruptive behavior to other employees

- Continued unsatisfactory job performance

When Informal Feedback Has Not Worked

Informal feedback includes actions such as a helpful reminder, a discussion in passing or even an email or memo. Many managers will try one of these methods (or another) to address a problem with an employee and keep the constructive criticism to a minimum. But when informal methods do not work, and the behavior continues the manager needs to then find a form of formal feedback to speak with the employee. Formal feedback, as the name suggests, usually involves a more planned or structured approach, such as a meeting or review. These actions normally allow more direct contact with the employee and can better address the problem, as well as a solution.

Example of formal feedback:

- Private meetings or discussions

- Personal follow-up after a particular incident

- Employee review or appraisal

Immediately After the Occurrence

One of the best times to deliver feedback is immediately after the incident happens. This way, the behavior or problem can be addressed right away. If a problem is ignored and allowed to continue, it can not only affect the employee, but coworkers as well. The longer the behavior goes on or the more time that passes after an incident, the value, and effect of the feedback decreases. Formal or informal feedback can be used, as long as it effectively resolves the problem.

Tips:

- Speak with the employee privately.

- Address the problem – don't criticize the employee.

- Find a solution and how it can be implemented.

Preparing and Planning

Management generally finds it easier to deliver any form of constructive criticism once they have prepared what they want to say and how they want to deliver it. The key is to decide what problems or situations you want to address and how you can provide the employee the information they need to succeed. Careful preparation, clear information delivery, and a sense of sensitivity toward the employee will not only result in better employee performance, but possibly a better relationship between management and employees.

Gather Facts on the Issue

Before you can begin to address any situation, you have to gather the facts. It's best to make a quick list of what you'll need to cover and what information you'll need to do that. This can include employee performance stats, memos; emails exchanged, or even notes containing your own personal observations. If needed, include information from company policies or training guides. The more facts and information you gather beforehand, the more prepared you'll be when the time comes meet with the employee.

Hints:

- Review the reason for giving the constructive criticism

- Find what the employee may need to improve or change in the future

- Gather information that supports why you have addressed the problem (i.e. performance stats, behaviors)

Practice Your Tone

The point of constructive criticism is to help the employee and encourage them to improve and be successful. However, the tone of your voice can speak louder than the words you use. If your tone is hard or comes across as disapproving, the employee may interpret the meeting as a form of criticism or discipline and then ignore or dismiss any helpful advice or action plan. On the other hand, if the tone is too light and amicable, the employee may interpret the action plan as friendly advice and not take the need for improvement seriously.

Points to remember:

- Remain neutral – your focus is to help the employee.

- Watch for angry or accusing tones – these can counteract the help being offered.

- Practice what you want to say beforehand. Look for tones and pitches that can either help or harm.

Create an Action Plan

Once the problem has been addressed, an action plan will help the employee to make the proper adjustments and improvements they need. Change can be hard for anyone, so the employee will need proper support from management to succeed. Make realistic goals the employee can achieve and focus on the areas of work the employee has control to change (their duties or department). Once a plan has been made, allow ample time for it to be put in place and monitor the employee to see how they are doing. It may also be helpful to schedule a follow-up meeting to check on their progress.

Tips:

- Give specific feedback and improvements that need to be made.

- Focus on goals the employee can achieve to correct the problem.

- Form an action plan that helps achieve those goals.

- Follow-up as needed.

Keep Written Records

Written and documented records are often important when delivering constructive criticism. Written records not only help track the behavior or actions that need to be corrected, but also help document the actions that will be taken to correct the situation. Document employee behaviors and reactions to keep in employee files and add to the action plan. The action plan can be a form of documentation once it has been written and can also be added to the employee's and manager's work files.

Example of written records:

- Exchanged emails/notes/memos

- Log of employee behaviors or actions

- Action plan with improvement ideas and strategies

- Signed forms signed by the employee (acknowledgement of feedback, actions plan, etc.)

Choosing a Time and Place

Choosing a time and a place to deliver constructive criticism can play a key role. The location should allow for the parties to speak in private and away from other coworkers. Many factors can affect what would be the best time, such as if the employee is tired or getting ready to go to lunch. Also the manager should consider how they are feeling before setting a time. If they are angry or uncomfortable with the subject, they may need more time to prepare.

Check the Ego at the Door

One of the first steps in delivering constructive criticism is to remove the emotions involved. This includes the manager's emotions and the possible ego they can bring with them. When preparing to speak with an employee, leave opinions and emotions at the door and deal with the subject at hand. Don't let something such as your personal opinion of the employee or your knowledge of the subject affects how you resolve the problem.

Tips:

- Focus on the issue, not the person.

- Remain open to suggestions or questions.

- Don't harp on an issue. Say what has to be said and move on.

Criticize in Private, Praise in Public

Constructive criticism shouldn't be done in a public setting, such as the employee's cubicle or the break room. Confronting an employee in front of coworkers or in a common area can cause embarrassment or anger, which counteracts the purpose of offering help and creating solutions. A private meeting allows both parties to speak and go over every aspect of the issue. The employee can feel free to ask questions and not feel as though they are being attacked in a group setting.

Ensuring that the conversation takes place in private and only between the relevant parties not only eliminates unnecessary gossip, but shows respect for the employee and their future success. On the other hand, praising the employee in a public setting can not only boost morale for the employee being praised, but also for all employees who witness it. This allows employees to see firsthand that the company they work for not only discusses changes that must be made with employees, but also appreciates the things that employees are doing right!

It Has to Be Face to Face

When delivering constructive criticism, the best method is always to speak face to face with the employee or other parties. Even though we live in the electronic age and rely on technology too often communicate with others, a traditional face to face meeting is always best when delivering news or criticism to someone. Emails or written letters are usually one sided and portray accidental tones. Phone calls can cause intimidation and usually do not allow the employee to speak in private if the phone call is made on an office phone. Speaking with the employee live and in person leaves no room for implied tones or pressures and allows them to speak openly. After the initial meeting, it is acceptable to follow up in an informal method, such as email or phone call.

When meeting face to face:

- Meet in a private setting where everyone can be comfortable.

- Keep a respectable distance, but remain close enough to speak without raising your voice.

- Speak directly with the employee and turn your focus to them when they are speaking.

Create a Safe Atmosphere

The last thing an employee wants to feel is that the manager's office is a place of discipline or criticism. Don't make employees fear coming into your office. Establish trust and open communication with your employees and ensure them that you are available to them. Ensure employees that they can approach you with any questions or concerns they may have. This allows you to create a safe atmosphere and environment where you can deliver the constructive criticism you need without making employees feel as though they are in a torture chamber.

Benefits of a safe atmosphere:

- Employees are more open to approaching you with problems or concerns.

- Allows you to deliver news or criticism to employees without frightening them.

- Employees feel more at ease hearing constructive criticism.

During the Session

After thoroughly preparing the information and process needed, the manager is ready to successfully deliver the needed constructive criticism. Remain businesslike and focus on the problem at hand. After both parties have had a chance to speak and express their position, both parties can move toward the corrective action and solution.

The Feedback Sandwich

The purpose of the feedback sandwich is to offer coaching and support while softening the blow of the initial criticism. It's referred to as a 'sandwich' because the manager should start with a compliment before introducing the criticism. Then follow up with another positive statement. This technique allows the employee to hear the necessary criticism, but also gets to hear the good points of their performance too. The feedback sandwich can be an effective tool to use, but if used in excess or without sincerity, the compliment process can seem cheesy and employees may only focus on the negative.

Step to the Feedback Sandwich:

- Prepare and outline what you want to say or address

- Identify the positive and make a compliment

- Present the criticism and facts

- Add another positive statement and encouragement

- Follow up with the employee periodically

Monitor Body Language

Body language can be a good indicator of how someone is feeling and how they are accepting what is being said. When the manager is speaking, gestures such as furrowed brows, eye rolling, or certain standing positions can make the employee feel uncomfortable and dismiss what is being said. The manager should not only monitor their own body language, but pay attention to gestures the employee may be making, such as squirming in their seat, fidgeting, or not making eye contact. Based on the employee's body language, the manager may need to change tactics and approach the subject in a different way.

Common body language gestures:

- Eye rolling

- Fidgeting

- Looking away or not making eye contact

- Certain stances, such as leaning away, slumped shoulders, or crossed arms

Check for Understanding

After the manager has delivered the constructive criticism and is preparing to put the action plan into play, they must check for understanding from the employee. Allow the employee to ask questions and add input to the solution. Ensure that the criticism is understood clearly and that it is meant to help the employee grow and succeed, not to single them out or make them feel like a target. Reassure the feedback is for their benefit and that they understand the information is provided to make positive changes in the future.

Practice Active Listening

Active listening is where a person makes a conscious effort to hear what the other person is saying. This requires your full attention, so try to ignore distracting noises or situations around you. Don't dwell on responses or answers you want to make when the person stops speaking, as this can take your attention away from the message. Some tips you can include are saying the other person's words back to yourself and using body gestures such as head nodding to acknowledge what is being said. When they are finished, follow up with questions or comments to show you've taken in the information.

Keys to active listening:

- Pay attention to the speaker. Try not to let your mind wander.

- Show you are listening by using body language, such as nodding your head or smiling.

- Provide feedback and ask questions.

- Allow the speaker to finish talking. Don't interrupt with counter arguments.

- Respond respectfully and offer opinions or comments.

The end of the session is the key part that allows the manager and the employee to come together to make a plan of improvement or change. If the action plan is only made by one party, the terms can be one-sided and won't address the roles in which both parties need to take. While this can be a delicate subject to approach, with the correct planning and outline, a plan can be formed and implemented in no time.

Set Goals

When creating an action plan, one of the most important steps is to create goals to help the employee improve or make changes. Ask the employee what they want to accomplish and find ways to work together in reaching these goals. Set goals that are realistic and can be achieved by the employee in a reasonable amount of time. Then outline a plan and a sample timeline depicting what actions should be taken to achieve these goals. Offer ways you can help the employee reach these goals.

Common goals managers and employees make:

- Improve training or skill sets
- Decrease absences or tardiness
- Increase general job performance
- Reduce errors and future mistakes on trouble areas

Be Collaborative

Working together to correct a problem not only helps make the appropriate changes, but it can strengthen the team bond between the manager and employee. Knowing they will always have support from management encourages employees to work harder and come to you sooner rather than later if they have a problem. Allowing employees to be a part of the solution will make them feel as though they are contributing and will feel more willing to make the necessary changes and improvements.

Tips:

- Make sure you and the employee realize what needs to change or improve.
- Address what actions should be taken to achieve these changes.
- Ask the employee for input and what actions they can take to help.
- Form a plan together that both parties can agree to.

Ask for a Self-Assessment

One of the more difficult parts of delivering constructive criticism is asking the employee to perform a self-assessment. While the manager may have plenty of comments or opinions about the employee and their performance, a self-assessment may seem like a graded paper the teacher gives in school. Employees are more likely to recognize their own mistakes when they are not just being *told* to recognize them, but that they can *see* it for themselves. Ask the employee to take the time to analyze their skills and abilities and what actions they have recently taken. By forming skillful questions the employee can think over not only what helps them recognize their mistakes, but also perceive the criticism as a means to benefit their growth as a worker. Once they have finished their self-assessment, they are not only ready to own up to their shortcomings, but they are more willing to learn from them.

Always Keep Emotions in Check

After you've checked your ego at the door, be sure to check on your emotions also. To effectively deliver constructive criticism, you must eliminate any personal emotions or feelings. Emotions can make you susceptible to bias and can make what you have to say seem one-sided or narrow-minded. View the situation from a business-like point of view. To a certain extent, the employee's feelings should be taken into consideration when delivering the information. You might not be able to save them from a little embarrassment, but outright humiliation can and should be avoided.

Tips:

- Consider the employee's feelings (put yourself in their shoes)

- Don't confuse the employee with the mistake

- If you are feeling angry or upset before confronting the employee, take additional time to think it over and calm yourself

Setting Goals

Now that you are ready to put your action plan into play, together you and the employee need to set goals that can be achieved to improve the employee's future performance. What kind of goals should both of you set? What areas should be included? These are some of the questions you can face when planning goals, and knowing how to outline their future path with the employee will ensure you'll be able to effectively answer them when the time comes.

SMART Goals

Goals are usually one of the most valuable tools when planning success, but they are often not used to their full potential. Goals that are created to help the employee achieve and be successful are often referred to as S.M.A.R.T. goals. S.M.A.R.T. goals are used to outline what steps should be taken and how to follow through with it. Employee success rates are generally higher with these goal plans since they are specific to the individual person.

The five steps to outlining S.M.A.R.T. goals are:

SPECIFIC: In order for you to achieve a goal, you must be very clear about what exactly you want. Often creating a list of benefits that the accomplishment of your goal will bring to your life, will you give your mind a compelling reason to pursue that goal.

MEASURABLE: It's crucial for goal achievement that you are able to track your progress towards your goal. That's why all goals need some form of objective measuring system so that you can stay on track and become motivated when you enjoy the sweet taste of quantifiable progress.

ACHIEVABLE: Setting big goals is great, but setting unrealistic goals will just de-motivate you. A good goal is one that challenges, but is not so unrealistic that you have virtually no chance of accomplishing it.

RELEVANT: Before you even set goals, it's a good idea to sit down and define your core values and your life purpose because it's these tools which ultimately decide how and what goals you choose for your life. Goals, in and of themselves, do not provide any happiness.

TIMED: Without setting deadlines for your goals, you have no real compelling reason or motivation to start working on them. By setting a deadline, your subconscious mind begins to work on that goal, night and day, to bring you closer to achievement.

The Three P's

Goals can't be achieved over night; they take time to plan, make reviews, and then take action. The Three P's are helpful tools that aide you and your employee in achieving goals that you've prepared together. Each step of the Three P's, purpose, planning and partnering, can help you manage and strive toward your goals by outlining key steps, and tips to remember.

The Three P's:

Purpose: Decide what the purpose is of your goal. Do you want to improve job performance? Maybe decrease errors? The purpose of your goal is what you are willing to work for and go after.

Planning: Outline your goals and the steps needed to achieve them. Long term goals can be broken down into smaller, short term goals to make the process easier.

Partnering: No matter how self-disciplined you perceive yourself, it is always best to seek help when planning and pursuing your goals. Get support from your coworkers and management. Don't be afraid to rely on others for help.

Ask for Their Input

Setting goals is not a one way street when working with another employee. Both parties should know the purpose of the goal and realize what efforts will need to be made to accomplish them. If one person decides on the terms of a goal, it may come across as an order or demand rather than a mutual plan. As a manager, let the employee know what you want to see in regards to achievements and accomplishments, but also ask them what they want to gain from it. Have them input ideas and plans they feel will help them succeed. Ask them to come up with things they can do to achieve their goals and then ask what you can do to be a part of it. When goals are made as a team effort and the employee feels they have your support, they will be more willing to work for it and succeed.

Be as Specific as Possible

Goals that are specific and precise will work better than goals that are generalized and vague. For example, when planning goals with an employee, the phrase "I'd like to see you do better on your reports each week" doesn't specify a purpose or needed action. Instead, something such as "I'd like to see you improve your editing and proofreading skills before you turn in your next report" expresses a specific action that needs to be taken, and a tentative time line. Goals sound more 'doable' when they outline what specifically needs to change and improve. When they are presented with unspecific needs or information, they can seem like a guessing game.

Tips:

Name a specific action or topic that needs work

If you have multiple topics, break them up individually. Accomplishing three smaller tasks is easier than one large one.

If possible, give a time line in which actions should be done. Remember to be flexible.

Diffusing Anger or Negative Emotions

Unfortunately, constructive criticism is often accompanied by some form of anger or negative emotion, such as denial or embarrassment. The goal of constructive criticism is to help the employee grow and improve, not to hurt their feelings or downplay their work. Therefore, it should be delivered in the correct manner and without negative undertones. When criticism is delivered correctly, emotions can generally be set aside and both parties can focus on the issue.

Choose the Correct Words

Much like our tones, our words can send the wrong message when used in the wrong context. Words that can portray blame or negative criticism are generally rebuffed and can create someone to become defensive. Avoid the 'you messages' that place the blame or problems on the other person. Start sentences with "I" and express how their actions affect you and the company, rather than just criticizing their behavior. The correct phrasing can make all the difference when trying to deliver sensitive constructive criticism.

Incorrect vs. correct word examples:

- Don't start a sentence with "you"; begin with "I"

- Avoid words such as "angry", "outraged," or "furious"; words such as "confused" or "disheartened" will help to keep the mood calmer.

- Express understanding rather than fury or disbelief.

Stay on Topic

Sometimes we can have a lot of ideas and topics going through our head at once, or we try to multi-task between different areas, which can ultimately make us lose focus on what is important. When delivering constructive criticism, it is important to stay focused and stay on topic. Keep eye contact with the employee and avoid trying to do tasks on the computer or fiddle with paperwork. Deliver one topic at a time and completely finish with it before moving on to the next one. Trying to combine several topics into one speech can overload the employee and make them miss the main points. Also, be sure to leave past occurrences in the past. Bringing up problems from the past can distract from recent mistakes and can confuse the employee as to what he's supposed to be talking about today.

Tips:

- Avoid words such as "however", "although", and "but" since they can lead to other thoughts and topics.

- Keep eye contact with the employee. This will help you to focus on them and the issue at hand.

- When speaking with the employee, stop any previous task you were working on. Do not try to combine them.

Empathize

Before a manager can even begin to deliver constructive criticism to an employee, they must first stop and put themselves in the employee's shoes. Remember what it was like to be in their place? Remember how vulnerable and defensive you felt? Think of how the employee would respond to what you have to say. Help your employee feel at ease by empathizing with them and letting them know you are there to help. Criticism that is delivered with empathy in mind is more likely to be accepted by the employee and can even strengthen business relationships.

Try to Avoid "You Messages"

When we're angry or upset, our self-defense mode normally wants to find blame somewhere else, or on "you". This is especially common when trying to deliver constructive criticism. Phrases such as *"You were late yesterday"* or *"Your poor attitude is affecting everyone"* can appear unprofessional and make it appear as though you are insulting the employee. Instead, focus on how it makes others feel, such as *"I felt disappointed when you were late yesterday because we went over some important topics in the meeting"* or *"Our customers were very upset when you greeted them in an unfriendly manner."* The employee will begin to see that you are trying to portray how their actions affect others instead of feeling as though you are blaming or attacking him.

Common "You messages" to try to avoid:

- *"Your job performance has been lagging lately."*

- *"You've been late every day for the past week."*

- *"Your disruptive behavior is starting to affect your coworkers."*

- *"You've been slacking off on your duties."*

What Not to Do

There are always helpful tips for what you're supposed to do when delivering constructive criticism, but there are often times that people don't tell us what we *shouldn't* say. Managers can learn all the right things to say and feel they may have everything they need, but knowing what sensitive topics and negative phrases to avoid can be just as crucial.

Attacking or Blaming

Constructive criticism is meant to attack the problem at hand, not the person. Blaming or attacking the employee doesn't resolve the issue, but can actually make matters worse. This can cause the employee to become defensive or even resentful, which in turn makes them lose their trust and respect for you as well as their job. When addressing the employee, remove thoughts of blame or personal attacks and focus on the actual problem at hand. Even though the employee has made a mistake, that doesn't mean they *are* the mistake or that it is a reflection on their character.

Tips:

- Avoid starting sentences with "You" – these sentences always end in blame.

- Separate the problem from the person – i.e. being tardy doesn't mean the person is lazy.

- Avoid words with negative connotations, such as "angry", "frustrated", or "disbelief".

Not Giving Them a Chance to Speak

Generally, people have an inner need to be heard and feel as though others understand their point of view. If a person (or employee), feels as though this need is not met, they can become angry and resentful. Arguments can start since both parties try to talk at the same time, hoping to make the other one listen to them. One simple way to avoid this complication is by allowing the employee a chance to discuss the issue and add their input. After you speak, give them a chance to respond without interrupting. Be open to hear their opinions and concerns as well.

Tips:

- Allow time for one person at a time to talk uninterrupted for several minutes.

- Let the employee know they can express whatever they are feeling, positive or negative.

- Keep an open mind to receive the employee's feedback as well.

Talking Down

When delivering constructive criticism, it is important not to let the tone of the conversation become derogatory, or 'talking down'. Talking down not only insults the employee, but it dehumanizes them and makes you forget you are talking to a real live person. Using angry words or attaching a character label to the employee, such as jerk or idiot, will only put the employee on their defense and create arguments and conflicts. As a manager, when you are speaking with an employee, keep in mind that there is a person in that chair and that they deserve to be treated with respect. They are there for you to unleash your anger or frustrations on.

Remember:

- Avoid attaching character labels or name calling.

- Be aware of the tone of voice you are using – how do you sound to others?

- Approach the employee using a one-on-one level – treat them as your equal.

Becoming Emotional

If your emotions tend to control your actions or responses, then take a few extra minutes to review the situation before delivering constructive criticism. These emotions can make it seem too easy to unleash on the employee and you may not be able to restrain yourself. Becoming emotional can not only make you seem unstable or bias, but it upsets the employee and can make them try to become emotional in retaliation. Before you can begin to address another employee's behavior, you need to step back and take a few minutes to gain your composure and focus on the topic at hand. Going into a meeting with your emotions fully loaded will not get you the results you need.

Helpful hints:

- Avoid trying to personally attack the employee.

- Do not let emotions control the mood in the room – yours or the employee's.

- Plan ahead – decide what you want to say and ensure that you've gained your full composure.

After the Session

Constructive criticism should not be done without a proper follow-up. Schedule some sort of follow-up meeting to check on the employee's progress and see if they have any additional questions or concerns. Make yourself available to the employee and let them know how they are doing. If goals were met and the employee has improved, congratulate them. If not, go back to the drawing board and see what other actions need to be taken. Don't leave the employee in the dark about their progress or shortcomings.

Set a Follow-Up Meeting

Follow-up meetings are important in letting an employee know how they are doing after you last spoke with them and created an action plan together. Review the employee's performance stats and determine if things have improved or if the action plan needs to be remade. Feel free to praise positive achievements in public, but remember to provide any additional constructive criticism in private.

Remember:

- Once a follow-up meeting has been scheduled, keep the appointment.

- Praise the employee in public, but give criticism in a private meeting.

- Encourage the employee to keep up the good work

Make Yourself Available

Once the employee is given the action plan and sent back out to the workplace, it is important to let them know they are not alone in their journey. Assure the employee your door is always open and that they are free to approach you with any questions or concerns. Periodically check in with the employee to see if you can be of any help. They may not need you at the moment, but they'll appreciate the gesture and know that you are there to help when they do.

Tips:

- Be open to listen to the employee and their needs.

- Maintain an open door policy – make sure your employees are aware of it.

- Always be approachable – remain interested in your employees and avoid becoming too distant.

Be Very Specific with the Instructions

When creating an action plan or setting up goals, instructions need to be specific and action-oriented. Vague instructions such as "Do better on the next report" don't address the problem, corrective action, or possible timeline needed. A better response would sound something like *"I'd like to see you improve your proofreading skills before you complete your next report"*, which not only provides a specific problem that needs to be corrected, but gives a tentative time in which it needs to be completed. Let the employee know exactly what needs to change and ways to make it happen. General or vague instructions can often be misinterpreted and can cause the employee to exhibit regression rather than progression.

Specific instructions include:

- A set problem to be fixed or corrected.

- Steps or actions that should be taken.

- A possible timeline in which the task should be completed.

Provide Support and Resources

As part of making yourself available to the employee, also make available any additional support or resources they may need, such as other managers or training resources. As a good manager, don't forget to offer plenty of encouragement and personal support. An action plan would not be able to succeed if the employee does not have the support and resources needed to work it. Ensure the employee can always use you as a resource and if they need something they cannot find or get on their own, you will do your best to provide it to them.

Example of additional support and resources:

- Emotional support and encouragement

- Coworker and other management support teams

- Additional training times and materials

- Additional reading material – including manuals, brochures, pamphlets.

One of the most important business tools is being able to provide feedback and constructive criticism to your employees. As a manager, part of your job is to ensure every employee performs to their highest potential. You provide guidance, feedback and the occasional criticism to help them succeed and continue to improve. Don't lose sight of the reason for giving constructive criticism – which is to help the employee grow. After the session, don't lose focus of what you set out to accomplish together. Remember the action plan, the goals set and don't forget to follow up!

Focus on the Future

Past event and past performances are just that – in the past. One of the points of constructive criticism is to move forward and look to the future for improvements. Focus on what can be done or be changed now, rather than what did or didn't happen before now. This is the time for you and the employee to create a plan of action and potential goals the employee can do to change what is currently wrong. Plan on future strategies that are solution oriented. Forget what may have happened before and look toward a better tomorrow.

Measuring Results

When conducting a follow up session, decide how improvement and growth should be measured. Based upon the tasks being completed, different forms of evaluations can be done. Decide what task your employee was in charge of doing and review what they were supposed to be working on. In many cases, written evaluations can be helpful, but sometimes managers choose to drop in and witness the employee at work. However you decide to complete it, the employee deserves to have their results and progress re-evaluated periodically and told how they are measuring up.

Sample ways of measuring results:

- 'Secret Shopper' surveys

- Personal, one-on-one meetings

- Written evaluations or reviews

- Personal monitoring and observance

Was the Action Plan Followed?

Think back on what action plan you and the employee decided upon. Review the tasks that were outlined together, as well as goals and objectives that were set. Analyze if the employee is on track with the plan and what tasks they completed at a certain point in time. Did they follow the plan or stray from it? Did they maintain their timeline goals? Are they showing improvement that would come with completion of the action plan? These are all points that should be evaluated before confronting the employee directly. Once you have had a chance to review their progress on your own, schedule a follow up meeting and see if and where they are having trouble meeting their goals. Discuss any roadblocks they may have hit or resources they can use to get back on track.

Points of the action plan to review for improvement:

- What plan of action was decided upon?

- What goals were set?

- What specific tasks were outlined for improvement?

- Was there a timeline in place? Was it reasonable?

If Improvement is Not Seen, Then What?

After the employee has had time to work their action plan and you've held a follow-up meeting, what do you do when you find there hasn't been any improvement? First, the manager and employee should attempt to rework or rethink their action and goal plans. Do corrections or alteration need to be made? Does the employee need a different course of action? As a manager, provide additional training and support (previously mentioned) to give the employee an extra boost. Ask what you can do to help them be more successful. After a new plan of action has been made, release the employee out on their own again. Let them know you will meet on a regular basis to review their progress and how they are doing on the job.

Helpful tips:

- Identify several areas that are lacking improvement and how that can be changed.

- Provide additional support and opportunities.

- As a last resort, outline the possible consequences for a lack of improvement over time.

Chapter 15 – Conflict Resolution

Wherever two or more people come together, there is the possibility of conflict. This course will give participants a six-step process that they can use to modify and resolve conflicts of any size. Participants will also learn crucial conflict resolution skills, including dealing with anger and using the Agreement Frame.

At the end of this chapter, you should:

- Understand what conflict and conflict resolution mean

- Understand all six phases of the conflict resolution process

- Understand the five main styles of conflict resolution

- Be able to adapt the process for all types of conflicts

- Be able to break out parts of the process and use those tools to prevent conflict

- Be able to use basic communication tools, such as the agreement frame and open questions

- Be able to use basic anger and stress management techniques

Conflict is always negative.

This statement is false. Although conflict is often unpleasant, it can be a catalyst for positive changes.

Conflict is always violent.

This statement is false. When managed properly, conflict can be peaceful and productive.

Conflict is inevitable.

This statement is true. Conflict occurs whenever two or more people interact. In fact, it's even possible to have an inner conflict with yourself.

Anyone can experience conflict.

This statement is also true. Conflict happens to everyone, so it is important to be prepared.

An Introduction to Conflict Resolution

People often assume that conflict is always negative. This is not true! People are inherently different, and conflict simply happens when those differences come to light. Viewing conflict in this way can help us maximize the possible positive outcomes of the problem at hand. Equipped with a conflict resolution process, people can explore and understand those differences, and use them to interact in a more positive, productive way.

What is Conflict?

The Random House Dictionary defines conflict as, "to come into collision or disagreement; be contradictory, at variance, or in opposition; clash."

Some examples of conflict can include:

- Two sales representatives are arguing over who gets the latest customer

- A team of employees is upset with their manager over a recent scheduling change

- A group of managers cannot decide who gets the latest project assignment

(Although we are going to focus primarily on workplace conflicts in this workshop, the tools covered can also be used in personal situations as well.)

Conflict can also be healthy. Think about how conflict will increase motivation and competitiveness in these scenarios.

- Two companies vie for the top market share of a particular product

- Several sales teams work to get first place

- Six hockey teams work towards winning a championship

These types of drivers can result in greater success, whether "success" means a better product, better teamwork, better processes, lower prices, trophies, or medals.

Remember, everyone experiences conflict, but how you deal with it, is what matters.

What is Conflict Resolution?

The term "conflict resolution" simply means how you solve conflicts. Although there are many processes available, we have developed one process that you can adapt for any situation. You will even be able to use these tools to prevent conflict and to help others work through conflict.

Some common conflict resolution terms include:

- **Mediation**: It is a process to resolve differences, conducted by an impartial third party.

- **Mediator**: In impartial person who conducts a process to resolve differences.

- **Dispute Resolution**: The name given to any process aimed at resolving differences between two parties.

- **Apparent Conflict**: A situation where the conflict is in the open.

- **Hidden Conflict**: A situation where the conflict is not in the open.

Understanding the Conflict Resolution Process

Conflict can come in many forms, and our process will help you in any situation. Below, you can find a brief overview of how we are going to spend most of this workshop.

Although we have outlined the various conflict resolution phases in a particular order and with a particular grouping, that doesn't mean that you have to use all the phases all the time. Near the end of this workshop, we will look at some of the steps as individual tools.

Create an Effective Atmosphere

- Neutralize Emotions
- Set Ground Rules
- Set the Time and Place

Create a Mutual Understanding

- Identify Needs for Me, Them, and Us

Focus on Individual and Shared Needs

- Find Common Ground
- Build Positive Energy and Goodwill
- Strengthen the Partnership

Get to the Root Cause

- Examine Root Causes
- Create a Fishbone Diagram (for complex issues)
- Identify Opportunities for Forgiveness
- Identify the Benefits of Resolution

Generate Options

- Generate, Don't Evaluate
- Create Mutual Gain Options and Multiple Option Solutions
- Dig Deeper into the Options

Build a Solution

- Create Criteria
- Create the Shortlist
- Choose a Solution
- Build a Plan

Conflict Resolution Styles with the Thomas-Kilmann Instrument

There are five widely accepted styles of resolving conflicts. These were originally developed by Kenneth Thomas and Ralph Kilmann in the 1970's. We have even designed our conflict resolution process so that it can be used in conjunction with these styles.

Although we promote the collaborative style throughout this workshop, there are instances where it is not appropriate (for example, it may be too time-consuming if the issue is relatively insignificant). Understanding all five styles and knowing when to use them is an important part of successful conflict resolution.

Collaborating

We will use this approach during this workshop. With the collaborating approach, the parties work together to develop a win-win solution. This approach promotes assertiveness (rather than aggressiveness or passiveness).

This style is appropriate when:

- The situation is not urgent

- An important decision needs to be made

- The conflict involves a large number of people, or people across different teams

- Previous conflict resolution attempts have failed

This style is not appropriate when:

- A decision needs to be made urgently

- The matter is trivial to all involved

Competing

With a competitive approach, the person in conflict takes a firm stand. They compete with the other party for power, and they typically win (unless they're up against someone else who is competing!) This style is often seen as aggressive, and can often be the cause of other people in the conflict to feeling injured or stepped on.

This style is appropriate when:

- A decision needs to be made quickly (i.e., emergencies)

- An unpopular decision needs to be made

- Someone is trying to take advantage of a situation

This style is not appropriate when:

- People are feeling sensitive about the conflict

- The situation is not urgent

Compromising

With the compromising approach, each person in the conflict gives up something that contributes towards the conflict resolution.

This style is appropriate when:

- A decision needs to be made sooner rather than later (meaning the situation is important but not urgent)

- Resolving the conflict is more important than having each individual "win"

- Power between people in the conflict is equal

This style is not appropriate when:

- A wide variety of important needs must be met

- The situation is extremely urgent

- One person holds more power than another

Accommodating

The accommodating style is one of the most passive conflict resolution styles. With this style, one of the parties in conflict gives up what they want so that the other party can have what they want. In general, this style is not very effective, but it is appropriate in certain scenarios.

This style is appropriate when:

- Maintaining the relationship is more important than winning

- The issue at hand is very important to the other person but is not important to you

This style is not appropriate when:

- The issue is important to you

- Accommodating will not permanently solve the problem

Avoiding

The last approach in the TKI is to avoid the conflict entirely. People who use this style tend to accept decisions without question, avoid confrontation, and delegate difficult decisions and tasks. Avoiding is another passive approach that is typically not effective, but it does have its uses.

This style is appropriate when:

- The issue is trivial

- The conflict will resolve itself on its own soon

This style is not appropriate when:

- The issue is important to you or those close to you (such as your team)

- The conflict will continue or get worse without attention

Creating an Effective Atmosphere

When people are involved in a conflict, there is typically a lot of negative energy. Anger, frustration, and disappointment are just a few of the emotions often felt. By establishing a positive atmosphere, we can begin to turn that negative energy around, and create a powerful problem-solving force. This creates a strong beginning for the conflict resolution process.

Neutralizing Emotions

Before beginning the conflict resolution process, both parties must agree that they want to resolve the conflict. Without this crucial buy-in step, achieving a win-win solution is close to impossible.

Once participants have agreed to resolve the conflict, it is important to neutralize as many negative emotions as possible. This means giving the participants in the conflict time to vent and work through the feelings associated with the conflict.

Key steps for the people in conflict include:

- Accept that you have negative feelings and that these feelings are normal.

- Acknowledge the feelings and their root causes. Example: "I feel very angry about the way George spoke to me in that meeting."

- Identify how you might resolve your feelings. Example: "If George apologized to me, I would feel a lot better."

- This can generate ideas about what the root cause of the conflict is, and how to resolve it. Example: "George and I haven't been getting along very well since the merger. I wonder if he might be having some stress and anxiety."

Setting Ground Rules

Ground rules provide a framework for people to resolve their conflict. Ground rules should be set at the beginning of any conflict resolution process. They can be very brief or very detailed – whatever the situation requires.

Ground rules should be:

- Developed and agreed upon by both parties.

- Positive when it is possible. (For example, "We will listen to each other's statements fully," rather than, "We will not interrupt.")

- Fair to both parties

- Enforceable

- Adjustable

- Written and posted somewhere where both parties can refer to it (for more formal dispute resolution processes).

If the parties are using a mediator to help them resolve the conflict, it is important that the ground rules be developed by the parties and not the mediator. The mediator's role is that of a guide and mentor, not a judge or supreme ruler.

Some examples of ground rules include:

- We will listen to each other's statements fully before responding.

- We will work together to achieve a mutually acceptable solution.

- We will respect each other as individuals, and therefore not engage in personal insults and attacks.

Participants can use the ground rules throughout the conflict resolution process to monitor and modify their behaviors. Ground rules give participants an objective, logical way of addressing personal attacks and emotional issues.

An example: "Joe, I feel like you have cut off my last several statements. We agreed at the beginning of this that we would listen to each other's statements fully before answering."

If the conflict is being mediated, this also gives the mediator a fair way to give participants feedback and help them work with the conflict. Since the same rules are being applied to everyone, it can help the mediator maintain fairness and avoid bias.

Choosing the Time and Place

The right time and place is often a key part of resolving conflict. Trying to solve a major team issue five minutes before the end of the shift just isn't going to work – people are going to be focused on going home, not on the problem.

When possible, choose a quiet place to discuss the conflict. Make sure that there is lots of time allowed. Minimize distractions if possible: turn cell phones off, forward office phones to voice mail, and turn off computers.

If you are mediating a conflict resolution meeting, be conscious of the needs of both parties when scheduling the meeting. Make sure that the time chosen works well for both of them. Choose a location that is neutral (one that they are both comfortable with or that neither has visited before). Removing distractions will enable both parties to concentrate on the matter at hand: resolving the conflict.

Creating a Mutual Understanding

There is an old story about two girls arguing over an orange. They both wanted this single orange to themselves. They argued for hours over who should get it and why. Finally, though, they realized that they could both win: one wanted the rind for a cake, while the other one wanted to make juice from the inside of the orange.

This model of win-win situations and mutual gain is our preferred outcome for any conflict. In this module, we will explore how creating mutual understanding can lay the groundwork for a win-win solution.

What Do I Want?

To begin, identify what you personally want out of the conflict. Try to state this positively.

Examples:

- I want a fair share of all new customers.

- I want a better working relationship with my manager.

- I want changes to the schedule.

You can create two versions of your personal needs statement: your ideal resolution and your realistic resolution. Alternatively, you could frame your statement into several steps if the conflict is complicated.

Another useful exercise is to break down your statement into wants and needs. This is particularly valuable if your statement is vague. Let's take the statement, "I want changes to the schedule," as an example.

Want	Need
More input into the scheduling process	To work less than 30 hours per week
A more regular schedule	More notice for schedule changes

This will give you some bargaining room during the conflict resolution process, and will help ensure that you get what you need out of the solution. In the example above, you may be willing to give up a more regular schedule if more notice for schedule changes is provided.

What Do They Want?

Next, identify what the person that you are in conflict with wants. Try to frame this positively. Explore all the angles to maximize your possibilities for mutual gain.

These framing questions will help you start the process.

- What does my opponent need?

- What does my opponent want?

- What is most important to them?

- What is least important to them?

What Do We Want?

Now that you have identified the wants and needs of both sides, look for areas of overlap. These will be the starting points for establishing mutual ground.

Here is an example. Joe and George are in conflict over the current schedule. As the most senior members of the assembly line team, they both alternate their regular duties with that of supervisor. Although taking on the responsibility gives the supervisor an extra $250 per shift, the supervisor also has to work an extra hour per shift, and has additional safety responsibilities.

Joe and George both work Monday to Friday, and as a regular assembly line team member, their shifts are from 8:30 a.m. to 4:30 p.m. As supervisor, they are expected to work from 8 a.m. to 5 p.m.

	Joe	George
WANTS	To have at least two supervisor shifts per week.	To have at least two supervisor shifts per week. To leave by 4:30 p.m. on Fridays.
NEEDS	To leave by 4:30 p.m. on Mondays and Wednesdays to pick up his children. To ensure that the foreman position is covered by someone from Monday to Friday, 8 a.m. to 5 p.m.	Not to have more than three supervisor shifts per week as it will require him to pay extra taxes. To ensure that the foreman position is covered by someone from Monday to Friday, 8 a.m. to 5 p.m.

From this simple chart, we can see that Joe and George have the same goal: to ensure that the supervisor position is covered by someone during regular working hours. Thus, this is a logistical conflict rather than an emotional one. We can also see from the chart that there seems to be some good starting ground for a solution.

When working through the wants and needs of both parties, be careful not to jump to conclusions. Rather, be on the lookout for the root cause. Often, the problem is not what it seems.

Focusing on Individual and Shared Needs

So far, we have talked about laying the foundation for common ground, one of the key building blocks for win-win solutions. This module will look at some techniques on building common ground and using it to create partnerships.

It may not seem like we have progressed very far in resolving the conflict. Indeed, most of these primary steps are focused on information gathering and problem solving. For minor conflicts, having these steps in your toolbox will simply help you keep all possibilities in mind during the conflict. For major conflicts, these steps will help you ensure you achieve the best solution possible for the situation.

Finding Common Ground

We have already talked about finding common ground when exploring each side's wants and needs. With these tools, you should be able to find common ground even before the conflict begins.

In our earlier example, with Joe and George in conflict over the supervisor schedule, they both wanted to ensure that the position was covered during their hours of responsibility. Other possible areas of common ground could include ensuring the safety of the assembly line team, continuing to work with each other, or continuing to work for the company. Try hard enough and you'll find something in common!

You should continue to try to find common ground throughout the entire conflict resolution process. It will help you understand your adversary's position and better position you to help create a win-win solution. These positive gestures will build goodwill, and help you make the shift from being two people in conflict to being two people working to solve a problem.

Some examples:

- "I think the company needs a more unified sales team, too."

- "I would really like us to win first place this year, too."

- "I agree that we can get this conflict resolved and build a better widget."

Building Positive Energy and Goodwill

There are often many negative emotions associated with conflict. No wonder – conflict makes many people upset and anxious, and often results in negative feelings like anger and disappointment.

If you are able to turn that negative energy into positive energy to help build goodwill with the person that you are in conflict with, resolving the conflict will be much easier. Ironically, the more negative the situation, the more important this step is.

Let's say that the person that you are in conflict with is very angry with you. Although they have agreed that they want to resolve the conflict, they are cool towards you and putting in minimum effort towards resolving the problem.

You may think, "Why should I bother?" This is a very important question indeed. How much energy and time are you will to spend on this conflict? Is it worth resolving? (We will explore these questions more in the next module.)

Consider, however, the power that your approach has. You have two basic options: to match your adversary's demeanor, or to be a positive influence. Both will likely take as much energy, but which will yield greater results?

Here are some ways to build positive energy.

- Have a good attitude. The preparation steps we discussed earlier should help you identify the positive things that will come out of this conflict. Try to focus on these things instead of the negative aspects of the conflict.

- Frame things positively.

- Create actionable items.

- Try to keep emotions out of your statements. State feelings and opinions in as objective a manner as possible. Label your thoughts as thoughts by starting sentences with, "I think…"

- Take a break when you need it.

- If you say, "I see where you're coming from," make sure you mean it. If you can't see where they are coming from, ask them to tell you more. Often, sharing information can break down even the toughest person's defenses.

- Invite the other person to step into your shoes. Tell them a story, outline consequences, and explain how you feel in an objective manner. Share as much information as you can.

Strengthening Your Partnership

Making the transition from opponents to problem-solving teammates is one of the most powerful conflict resolution tools. We have already discussed ways to build common ground to help bridge the gap between you and the person having the conflict. These tools are a great start, but there are some additional things that you can do to maintain and strengthen that partnership.

In 1965, Bruce Tuckman, developed a four-stage model showing how teams grow and develop. This model can be applied to one-on-one human interactions, too.

Stage	Explanation	What You Can Do to Help
Forming	Team members are just meeting, unsure of their role and themselves.	Encourage team building through non-conflict laden tasks and activities. Involve the team in task planning and goal setting.
Storming	Team members discover differences and butt heads; conflict can interfere with progress.	Continue with the plan; evaluate and adjust as necessary. Support the team through conflict and help them resolve it.
Norming	Team members start to discover similarities too. Performance typically improves, but social interaction may also cause it to drop.	Keep the group focused on the goal; encourage social activities outside of team time.
Performing	Team members are now comfortable with each other and work together well.	Continue to offer resources and support to the team. Monitor performance, as teams can change stages at any time (particularly when members join in or drop out).

Getting to the Root Cause

Building a positive foundation and gathering information are key steps to resolving conflict, but it is going to be difficult to solve the problem if we don't know what the problem is! In this module, we will learn how to delve below the current conflict to the root of the problem. This phase is important for long-term resolution, rather than a band aid solution.

Examining Root Causes

Once the groundwork has been laid, it is important to look at the root causes of the conflict.

One way to do this is through simple verbal investigation. This involves continuously asking "Why?" to get to the root of the problem. An example:

- I was very upset when Sharon vetoed my idea at the meeting.

- Why <were you upset>?

- I felt that my idea had real value and she didn't listen to what I had to say.

- Why <didn't she listen to what you had to say>?

- She has been with the company for a lot longer than I have and I feel that she doesn't respect me.

Now we have progressed from a single isolated incident to the root cause of the incident itself (and probably many more past and future incidents). Resolving this root cause will provide greater value and satisfaction to all involved.

Paying attention to the wording of the root cause is important, too.

- Watch out for vague verbs.

- Try to keep emotions out of the problem statements.

Creating a Cause and Effect Diagram

Another way of examining root causes is to create a cause and effect diagram (also known as a fishbone diagram) with the person that you are having the conflict. To start, draw a horizontal arrow pointing to the right on a large sheet of paper. At the end of the arrow, write down the problem.

Sales Team and Marketing Team cannot decide on their main approach for this year

Now, work together to list possible causes. Group these causes. Draw a line pointing to the large arrow for each cause and write the cause at the top.

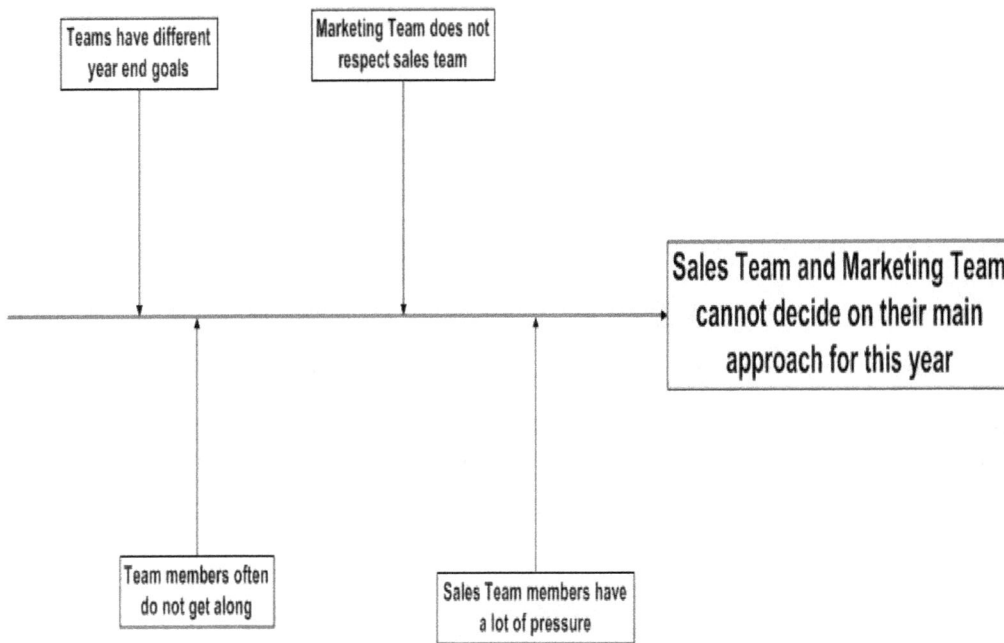

Now, write each cause on a line pointing to the group arrow. (Sticky notes work well for this.)

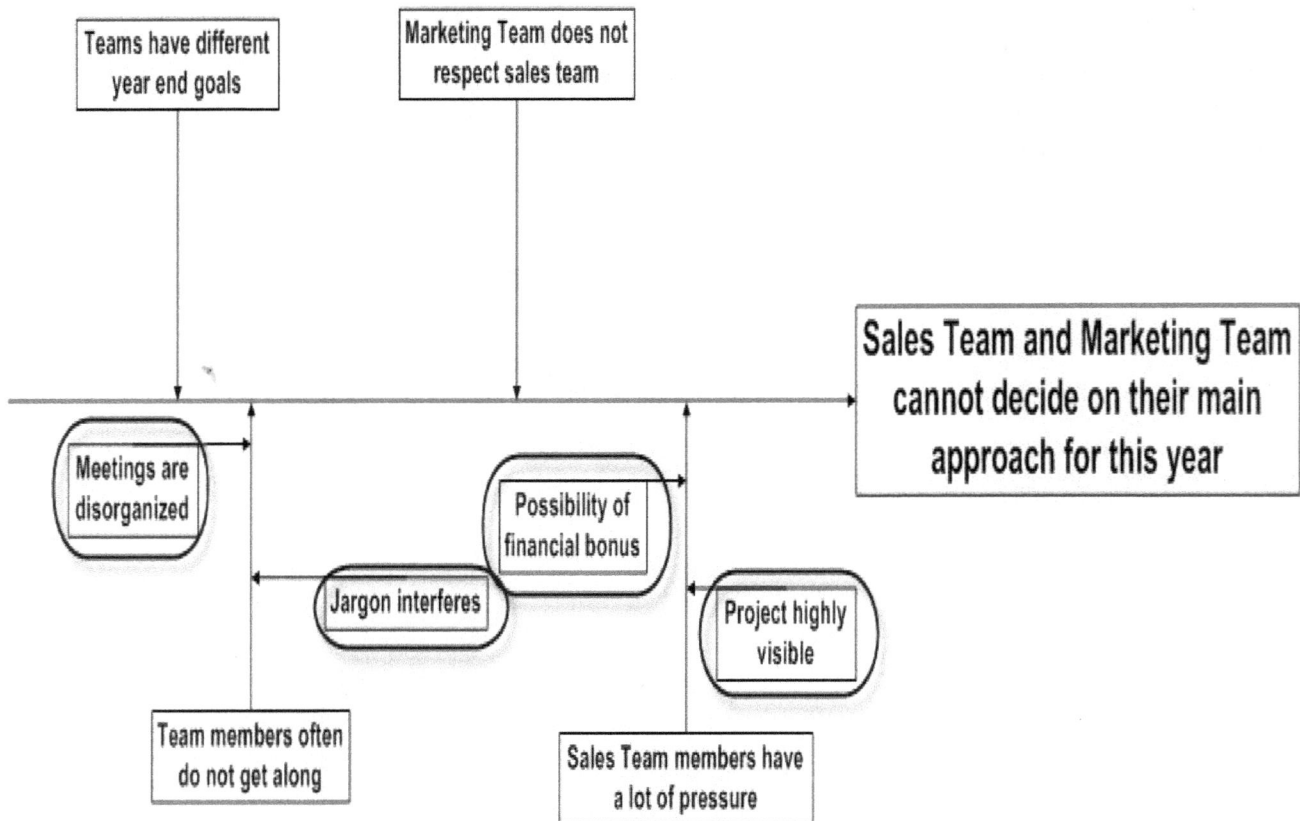

Now the people in the conflict have a clear map of what is happening.

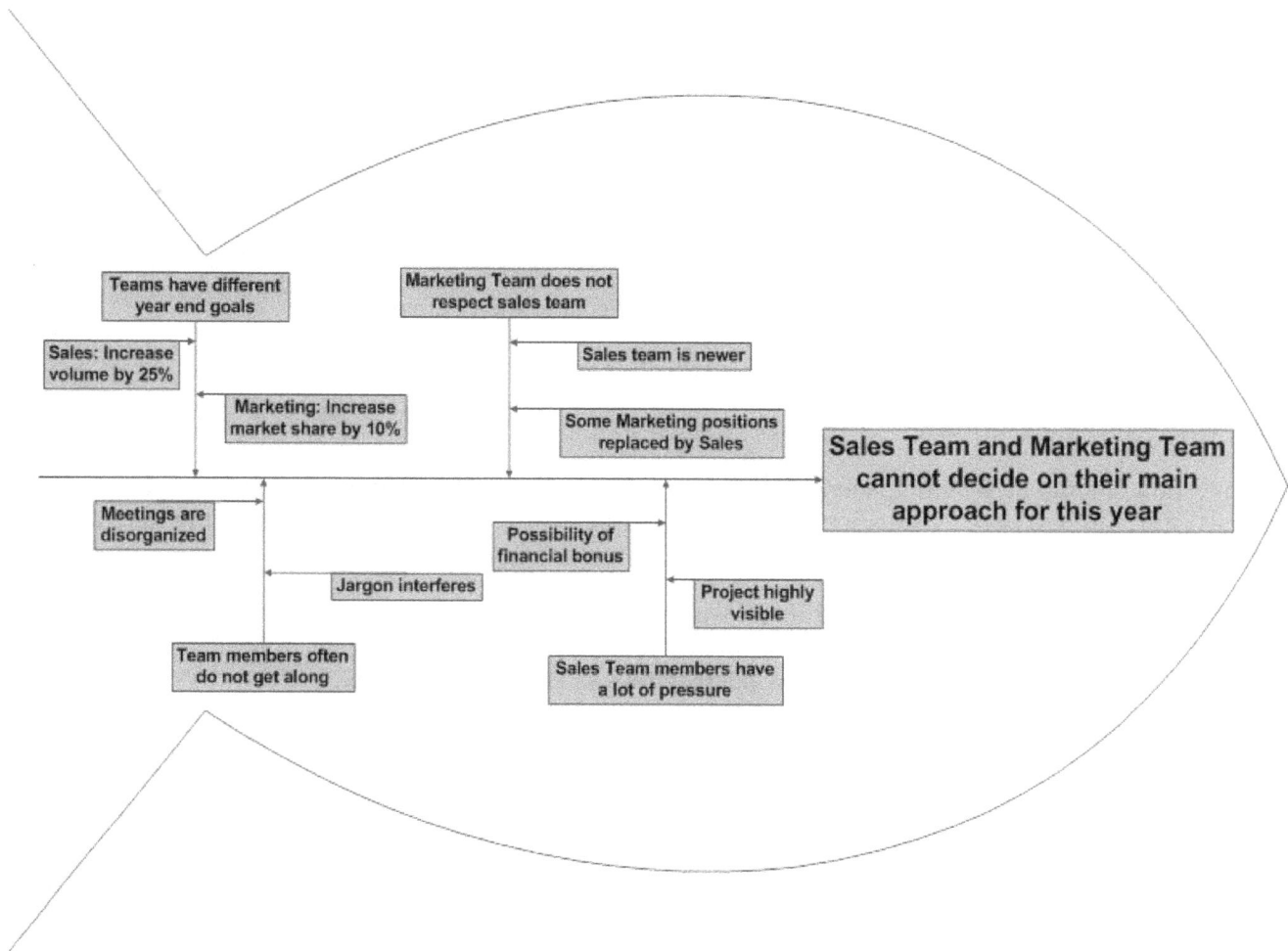

Although this technique can be time-consuming, it is excellent for complicated conflicts or for team conflicts where there may be more than one root cause. The drawing should be updated as new causes are discovered.

The Importance of Forgiveness

Forgiveness is a key concept in conflict resolution. Forgiveness does not mean forgetting that the conflict happened, or erasing the emotions that it created. It does mean accepting that the conflict happened. Accepting and working through how it made you feel, accepting the consequences that it had, and letting those actions and consequences exist in the past.

Successful conflict resolution should give the participants some feeling of closure over the issue. Participants should feel that the conflict has been resolved to their satisfaction, and that it will not likely reoccur. These accomplishments should help participants put the conflict behind them and move forward, to more things that are positive.

These goals should be kept in mind during the resolution process. Ask yourself, "Will resolving this help provide me with closure? Will this action help me accept what has happened and move on?"

Identifying the Benefits of Resolution

There is no doubt about it – conflict resolution can be hard work. Effective conflict resolution digs deep into the issues, often exploring unfamiliar territory, to resolve the core conflict and prevent the problem from reoccurring.

However, this process can be time-consuming and emotionally difficult. You and the person that you are in conflict with may arrive at a point (or several points) in the conflict resolution process where you wonder, "Is this really worth it?"

When you arrive at these stalemates, look at why you are resolving the conflict. It can also be helpful to explore what will happen if the conflict is not resolved.

- What relationships will deteriorate or break up?

- If this is a workplace conflict, what is the financial cost to the company?

- What will be the emotional cost to the participants?

- Who else will be affected?

These questions should help participants put things into perspective and evaluate whether or not the conflict is truly worth resolving. In most situations, resolving the true conflict is well worth the effort in the long term. Visualizing the benefits can provide the motivation to work through the rest of the process.

For complex conflicts, there are some additional ways to stay motivated. It's OK to break the resolution sessions into parts, with a different goal for each session. It's also OK to take breaks as needed – a walk around the block or a glass of water can do wonders to refresh the mind and body.

Generating Options

Once you have a good handle on the conflict, it's time for all parties in conflict to start generating some options for resolution. In this stage, it's all about quantity, not quality; you want as many options to choose from as possible.

Generate, Don't Evaluate

To begin, generate ideas for resolving the symptoms of the conflict. Then, move on to the root cause and expand your list of ideas.

Don't be afraid to throw out wacky ideas or to ask, "What if?" Remember, this stage is about what you can do, not what you will do.

It is very important not to censor yourself or the person that you are having the conflict. Record all possible ideas into a list or brainstorming diagram. If you have created a cause and effect diagram, you can record ideas for resolution right on the diagram. (Once again, sticky notes are ideal for this initial, idea-generating phase.)

At this stage, all your work to build common ground and positive relationships will really start to pay off. As you and the person you are in conflict with start to generate options, the positive energy will build, increasing your creative output exponentially.

If you are having trouble thinking of solutions, use these questions to jump-start your creativity.

- In an ideal world, how would this conflict be resolved?

- How do we not want this conflict to be resolved?

- How might others resolve this conflict?

Creating Mutual Gain Options and Multiple Option Solutions

Once you have a good list of options, look over the list, and perform some basic evaluation.

- Cross off options that are an absolute no-go for either party.

- Highlight options that provide gains for both parties.

- Look for options that can be combined for an optimal solution.

- Make options more detailed where appropriate.

- Continue brainstorming and generating ideas.

What if your entire list of options gets crossed off? Then it's back to the drawing board! If you are having trouble coming up with ideas, consider taking a quick break, moving the brainstorming meeting elsewhere, and/or involving outside parties.

Digging Deeper into Your Options

Once the list has been narrowed down, dig deeper into each option and identify the following:

- The effort for each option (perhaps on a scale of one to ten)

- The payback for each option (also on a scale of one to ten)

- Your estimation as to its likelihood of success

- Other options that could be used to complement it

- Each party's preference for it (expressed as yes/no, or a percentage in favor)

At this point, we are still gathering information and exploring options, so try to make the list as long as possible. For simple conflicts, three to five options is usually sufficient, but with more complex issues, five to eight options may be necessary. If the team involves more than two people, you will likely need eight to twelve options.

Building a Solution

Once the possible solutions are laid out, it's time to move on to choosing a solution and laying the groundwork for a resolution. This module will explore how to create criteria and how to use those criteria to create a shortlist of options, and then to move on to a solution.

Creating Criteria

For the moment, set aside your list of options. It's time to create a framework to evaluate those options. Try not to think about the different options as you create the criteria. Focus instead on the wants and needs of both parties.

Criteria should explore what you want and do not want from the solution. You can also prioritize your criteria by what is necessary to have and what you would like to have (also known as needs and wants). Identify any items on the list you would be willing to make a compromise with.

Criteria	Want?	Need?	Shared with Opponent?	Compromise On?

The best approach is for each party to take a few moments to write down their individual criteria, and then come together and combine the lists to create a final set of criteria. Although it is important to work together on this list, it is also important that the wants and needs of both parties be respected.

You may ask, why create criteria after creating options? Wouldn't it make more sense to create a list of criteria and then generate a list of options?

Logically, this approach does make more sense. However, it can be difficult to come up with creative options when you already have a framework in mind. Therefore, we recommend brainstorming first, and then creating criteria second.

Creating a Shortlist

Once the criteria have been created, bring out the list of solutions. Eliminate any solutions that do not match the must-have criteria that you and your partner identified. At the end of this process, you should have a small, manageable list of potential solutions.

You may find that there are no solutions left after this process. There are two options in this case. One is to re-evaluate your criteria and re-evaluate the solutions, to ensure there really are no options left. Another is to go back to the drawing board and work on additional solution ideas.

Choosing a Solution

Now, choose a final solution. Remember, you can often combine multiple options for even greater success!

Here is a checklist to evaluate the chosen solution.

- Is it a win-win solution for everyone involved?

- Are all needs provided for?

- Are all criteria met?

Building a Plan

Now, let's create a plan to put the solution in action. The complexity of this plan should vary with the complexity of the situation. For simple conflicts, you may frame an agreement like this: "Janice and I will take turns taking new customers, and we will make sure that we let each other know when this happens."

With complex situations, such as those involving a group of people or multiple option solutions, a detailed action plan may be appropriate. It is important that each party take responsibility for implementing the solution, even if it is determined that one party is at fault.

For example, let's say that the conflict resolution process has determined that communication issues between Janet and Susan are causing most of the conflict over new customer assignment. Although Janet and Susan are going to work on this problem by improving communication and keeping fairness in mind, the remainder of the team will be responsible for supporting Janet and Susan and following up to make sure no further issues arise.

The action plan should also include a list of things to do if the conflict is not actually resolved after implementing the solution. Typically, the parties will re-evaluate the cause and effect diagram to ensure their analysis of the root cause was accurate. They may also want to examine their criteria and explore other solutions.

The Short Version of the Process

So far, we have explored the six phases of the conflict resolution process in depth. As we discussed earlier, these phases can be adapted for virtually any type of conflict. In this module, we will work through an abridged version of the processes that can be used easily to successfully resolve conflicts. We will also look at some individual steps that can be used as conflict resolution and prevention tools.

Evaluating the Situation

To begin, we will combine all the groundwork into a single step.

- **Phase One** (Creating an Effective Atmosphere): Take a moment to calm down and deal with your emotions. Look at the possible positive outcomes of the conflict.

- **Phase Two** (Creating a Mutual Understanding): Quickly evaluate your wants and needs, and those of the other party. Try to identify the real issue.

- **Phase Three** (Focusing on Individual and Shared Goals): Identify common ground.

This information can be gathered in just a few moments, and it will help you identify the most appropriate conflict resolution approach. (Remember the five approaches that we looked at in Module Two.) Although we promote the collaborative approach, there are situations where other approaches are more appropriate and beneficial.

Choosing Your Steps

Now, let's work through phases four and five. Think about the current conflict. Is it really the root cause or is it just a symptom of a larger problem? (Most often, it's just a symptom.) How could the problem be resolved?

Make a short list of possible solutions, even if it's just in your head. Now we're ready to move on to the next phases.

Creating an Action Plan

Once you have some ideas on how to resolve the conflict, do a quick evaluation. What do you want and need out of the solution? What might the other party need? Use these to sketch out a solution. (Remember, if you're going to propose a solution, the other party is going to want to know what's in it for them, so make sure you have something to offer.)

Have a backup plan, too, in case your approach doesn't work. This could be a different solution, a different way of presenting your original solution, or even a proposal to move to a more complex resolution process. Simply have some ideas in your back pocket in case your original approach doesn't work.

Using Individual Process Steps

In this workshop, we have outlined the various conflict resolution phases in a particular order and with a particular grouping. That doesn't mean that you have to use all the phases all the time. Most of the items we have discussed can be used individually as conflict prevention or resolution tools.

Here are some examples.

- A new person has joined your team. She is very quiet and the team (yourself included) is having a hard time getting to know and like her. You use some of the tools we discussed today to build common ground with her and improve teamwork.

- Lately, team status meetings have gotten out of hand. People talk over each other, argue constantly, and often leave the room. You suggest implementing ground rules for these meetings.

- One of your colleagues often behaves very aggressively. You find it very difficult to communicate with him because you find him so intimidating. You use emotional neutralization techniques to focus on your message and reduce the impact of his behavior.

Additional Tools

To help wrap up this workshop, we would like to share some additional tools that can help you resolve conflicts.

Stress and Anger Management Techniques

There is no doubt about it – dealing with conflict can be hard on the mind and the body. Being well equipped with some stress and anger management techniques can help you stay calm during the conflict resolution process. Nothing is going to get solved when either (or both) parties are angry and upset.

Here are some tips to help keep you cool during the conflict resolution process.

- Deep breathing has beneficial mental and physical effects.

- Coping thoughts can help you stay calm, too. Some examples: "I feel like he is just trying to push my buttons. I'm stronger than that!" or, "I'm not going to let myself get upset – that won't solve anything. Instead, I am going to focus on getting this conflict solved."

- Make sure to take breaks as needed. If the person you are in conflict with becomes emotional or stressed, encourage them to take breaks as well.

- After the conflict is over, talk about it with someone appropriate.

The Agreement Frame

The Agreement Frame can be used in any situation to explain your viewpoint in an assertive, non-confrontational way, without watering your position down. It is designed to encourage discussion and information sharing between all parties. Although it can be used in many situations, it is particularly effective in conflict resolution.

The Agreement Frame takes one of three forms:

- I appreciate, and…

- I respect, and…

- I agree, and…

Here is an example of the Agreement Frame in use.

Person A	Person B
The best way to resolve this conflict is for you to resign your position immediately.	I respect your opinion, and I think that there might be some other viable options.
What options were you considering?	I think that if I issued an apology to the team for the misunderstanding that we would be on our way to resolving the conflict.
I think that option is too low-key for this situation.	I agree that it might not be a strong enough statement, and I may need to have team meetings to address the underlying issues.

Remember, the words "but" and "however" are conversation-stoppers. Try to avoid using them with the agreement frame.

Asking Open Questions

When possible, use the five W's or the H to ask a question.

- Who?

- What?

- Where?

- When?

- Why?

- How?

These questions encourage discussion, self-evaluation, and open conversation. Some useful questions for conflict resolution include:

- What happened?

- Why do you feel that way?

- When did this problem start?

- How does that make you feel?

- Who else is involved?

Chapter 16 – Change Management

Change is a constant in many of our lives. All around us, technologies, processes, people, ideas, and methods often change, affecting the way we perform daily tasks and live our lives. This workshop will give any leader tools to implement changes more smoothly and to have those changes better accepted. This workshop will also give all participants an understanding of how change is implemented and some tools for managing their reactions to change.

By the end of this chapter, you should be able to:

- List the steps necessary for preparing a change strategy and building support for the change

- Describe the WIFM – the individual motivators for change

- Use needed components to develop a change management and communications plans, and to list implementation strategies

- Employ strategies for gathering data, addressing concerns and issues, evaluating options and adapting a change direction

- Utilize methods for leading change project status meetings, celebrating a successful change implementation, and sharing the results and benefits

- Describe the four states of Appreciative Inquiry, its purposes, and sample uses in case studies

- Use strategies for aligning people with a change, appealing to emotions and facts

- Describe the importance of resiliency in the context of change, and employ strategies the change leader and individual change participant can use to foster resiliency

- Explain the importance of flexibility in the context of change, and demonstrate methods the change leader and individual change participant can use to promote flexibility

Preparing for Change

A simple definition of change is "to cause to be different". The idea of change management on a personal level has been studied for more than one hundred years. But it is only since the mid- 1980's that change management has been explored within the context of business applications.

Today's change management initiatives have become a business discipline, driving bottom-line results through changes in systems and behaviors. Managing change has therefore become a critical skill, both for leadership -- and for workers in an organization.

Defining Your Strategy

It is critical to manage change by creating and implementing a strategy that defines an approach consistent with the unique needs of the organization. The strategy serves as the guiding framework, providing direction and shaping decision making throughout the change process.

A simple way to gather data for the strategy is to set up interviews and ask questions regarding the different aspects of the change. Below are some typical questions:

Aspect	Question
The Situation	What is being changed? How much perceived need for the change exists? What groups will be impacted? How long will the change take?
People and their Roles	Who will serve as a high-level sponsor? What functional groups should be represented to lead the effort?
Issues for Analysis	What will happen if we do/don't do this? How universal is the change? Are there exceptions or deviations to consider?

From the answers to the questions, the strategy document is created, serving as a "blueprint" for the initiative. A strategy document should discuss important components of the change. The components are listed below, accompanied by sample wording.

Strategy Component	Sample Language / Notes
Description of the proposed change vision, and its goals	Transform the business processes and the technology by which the organization manages the human resources and payroll functions
The reasons(s) why the change is necessary	These changes will allow the organization to save time and money and provide more responsive HR and payroll services to our employees
Critical success measures and key performance indicators	Risks have been proactively identified and addressed Employees are prepared to perform their new job on Go live day with a 95% success ratio
Project stakeholders and stakeholder groups and their involvement	The current Phase: Senior management The Pre-Implementation Phase: Senior management, subject matter experts, change champions
Key messages to communicate	Pre-Implementation Phase: The business requirements, business case staffing, and the projected timeline
Roles and Responsibilities	Communications Team Lead: Develop project communications and presentations Change Management Team Lead: Direct overall team activities; Provide team with change management expertise; Manage Project Team Effectiveness, Capability Transfer, & Leadership Alignment activities
Target time frame to achieve goals	(This can be a graphical time line, a paragraph, an embedded spreadsheet, etc.)
Focus Areas	Leadership Alignment: Align leaders to the project vision and enable them to champion the effort Organizational transition: Design new employee roles, jobs, and organization structures to support the new processes and technology

Building the Team

To effectively implement a team positioned for success, leaders must select members who display a high degree of skill in six key elements:

- Commitment

- Contribution

- Communication

- Cooperation

- Conflict management

- Connection

The team must represent all of the needed functional groups and roles necessary to manage the change initiative. By formalizing the team and providing funding and other resources, it sends a message of accountability and responsibility, and illustrates the investment the organization has made in the change.

Identifying the WIFM

For change to be successful, people must desire to support and participate in the change. Simply building awareness does not generate desire. Showing everyone what is in it for them will produce a great starting point and help generate support. The beginning of the change process is very important and showing the affected parties how the change will improve their environment will initiate the process on the right foot.

What's in it for Me?

In order to answer the question "What's in it for Me?", or WIFM, change management leadership must create energy and engagement around the change. This builds momentum, and instills support at all levels of the organization. Factors that influence WIFM are:

- The nature of the change

- The organizational context for the change

- An employee's personal situation

- What motivates the person as an individual?

The next exercise provides data input that can be used to discover what's in the change for employees at Contemporary Chemical.

Building Support

Effective communications are essential for building support throughout the organization.

Whoever communicates with people impacted by a change must have a clear understanding of the overall nature of the change, its reasons, and how it aligns with the vision for the organization. He or she must understand the risks of not changing, the timing for the change, and what people will be most impacted by the change.

Communications options are many, including email, presentations, postings on the organization's intranet, flyers and circulars, banners, online or phone conferences, and special social events.

Beforehand, communicators should identify and segment audience groups, craft messages appropriate for each audience, and determine the most effective packaging, timing, and methods for communicating.

- Executive sponsorship

- Coaching by managers and supervisors

- Ready access to business information

Understanding Change

Change is constant and will always occur, and understanding its components on an individual level can help us relate it to an organizational level. Change is important to understand, as it affects many facets of an organization. Its effect on the individual is of great importance as it will filter through and influence all levels of the organization. Organizational change can create fear and uncertainty, it is important to understand these influences; what is expected when they do occur, and preparing for them when they happen.

Influences on Change

Typically causes of change can be split into two categories: Internal and External.

No organization is an island and external forces are always influencing and interacting with its existence. Individuals and organizations may have very little ability to influence such external factors such as politics, culture, economy, societal changes, or technology. It is important to understand that if the change is the result of an external factor, accept the change, and then modify any internal processes or items that are affected by the external influence.

Internal factors are very numerous, as almost any item or event can influence change within an organization, but some of the more influential ones are employees, policies, organization structure, managerial, and financial. With internal causes of change we have the most ability to control and prepare the outcomes of such events. The benefits of this are numerous as we can prepare with education, communication, training, and support. These tools will help mitigate any negative outcomes which may occur as a result of the change.

Common Reactions to Change

Denial: If a change is announced some people may feel that the change is not necessary. They may be reluctant to listen or deny any facts or information presented to support the change.

Resistance: With any change there will always be people who resist the change. Resistance is very common and stems from a fear of the unknown. Not knowing how an event is going to turn out can be a scary event for those who go through the change.

Anger: When change occurs and the norm is uprooted, people can experience anger. People may lash out and become uncooperative during this time. Humans are creatures of habit, and when that changes people can become angry.

Indifference: People just may not care, or the change may not have an impact on their routines or work. Be wary of this, as the change may be intended to have an impact, if the individual is indifferent about it the change then they may not understand or accept it.

Acceptance: Changes generally occur for the better and have a positive influence on those involved. Even with positive change acceptance may not happen right away, but should occur quicker as opposed to when the change is perceived to be negative.

Tools to Help the Change Process

Preparing for the change is very important as with preparation comes more chance of success. These tools will help facilitate the change process and provide it the best chances for success.

Communication: Keep the lines of communication open before, during and after the change as on the fly changes may be needed. This will help with any unforeseen events that occur during the change. It will also help to learn for the event which should make future changes occur even smoother.

Education: Educate all parties the reasons for the change, and what the expected outcomes will be. People want to know why a change is occurring. It will also help to stop and clear up any rumors that may have been spread.

Training: Make sure all parties are trained and up to date with any and all material required for the change. A very important step if the change involves adding or removing any pertinent in the business.

Flexibility: When change is planned for not all events can be foreseen. Be flexible and ready to modify or update the current plan to account for any unforeseen events.

Affected Parties: It is especially important to have the individuals that are involved in the change participate in the change process. They may be able to shed light into the subject from an expert's point of view.

These tools will help battle any negative reactions when they occur, and with more preparation the change should be smoother.

Leading and Managing the Change

Every change begins with a leadership decision. Making the decision to institute changes is not always easy. Being prepared, planning well, and being surrounded by a good team will make that decision a lot easier.

Preparing and Planning

Begin by putting yourself in a positive frame of mind. You are likely to experience higher than normal levels of stress and knowing this beforehand will give you the ability to be prepared mentally and physically. You will be the anchorperson and foundation, and with your steady hand will guide your team through the stressful events. Be a reassuring and active force throughout the whole process.

It is impossible to prepare for every contingency, but planning for the known is a must. Add time or extra room to the schedule for the unknowns. When you encounter an unexpected event your schedule should not be put off by much if you have built in some leeway. It will provide that buffer that gives you and your team the ability to deal with the unknowns and keep rolling with the change process.

Delegating

Surround yourself with people that you can delegate to and be confident in their abilities and skills. Be precise and specific with your directions as when the change process begins you will be depending on these individuals and their talents. Communicating and providing feedback are the keys to successful delegation; make sure your team understands this. If communication fails or there is not accurate feedback the chances of a success are lessened.

An issue that sometimes arises when delegating is micro-managing. Keep an eye out to not micro-manage as you can quickly lose track of events and it will take time away from your main duties. Delegating is a skill that takes time as you must first learn the strengths and weakness of your team and know what tasks you can and cannot hand out. It may not be possible to always delegate, but when it can be done it will provide a great resource.

Keep the Lines of Communication Open

Always be available during the change process. Before the change prepare your friends and family that you may not be available for social events. Reassure your team that you are there for them and you are here to provide them with the necessary resources to lead them through the change. Stress to them that you are available and focused on keeping the communications lines open.

Always be aware of rumors, they will happen before during and after the change. Do not ignore any rumor, put out honest and clear communication as soon as possible. Reassure your team that if they hear a rumor to seek out more information from a reliable source. Remind them that spreading rumors helps no one and will causes more harm than good.

Coping with Pushback

Not everyone will agree on the change. Keep in mind that these types of feelings are normal as people generally do not enjoy change and are sometimes made nervous by it. You will likely encounter pushback and resistance by a number of team members. Provide facts and data to show why the change is happening and reassure them the need and benefits of the change. These types of individuals are best suited to be educated about the change with information.

If you are encountering an extreme case of pushback, provide them with some choices that still fall within the spectrum of the intended change. They should then feel more involved in the process and it will help alleviate the negative mindset they may be experiencing.

Gaining Support

It is vitally important to make sure that all stakeholders and employees are on board with a change.

Gathering Data

In order to continue increasing awareness and to build desire to support the upcoming change; the change management team must reach out to the organization at large. The force field analysis, developed by German social psychologist Kurt Lewin helps a change management team to:

- Identify pros and cons of an option prior to making a decision

- Explore what is going right -- and what is going wrong

- Analyze any two opposing positions.

Addressing Concerns and Issues

If concerns or issues arise, then steps must be taken to ensure awareness is continually raised and that desire to support the change is increased. Strategies that can help the change management team responsively address employees' concerns include:

- Engaging employees, providing forums for people to express their questions and concerns

- Equipping managers & supervisors to be effective change leaders and managers of resistance

- Orchestrating opportunities for advocates of the change to contact those not yet on board

- Aligning incentive and performance management systems to support the change.

Evaluating and Adapting

Change is not exempt from Murphy's Law. And even if something isn't going wrong, change management team members must constantly be observing, listening, and evaluating the progress and process during a change. Below are several tools to help the team accomplish this.

A feedback form is used to gather information from those involved in a change to help shape the remaining course of the change project. Instead of a paper form, feedback can be obtained through online surveys

(Zoomerang.com or Survey Monkey.com), an in-house questionnaire on the intranet, a few questions sent by email, or a focus group. The questions will vary depending upon the subject being queried.

Open Feedback:

Please feel free to share your suggestions and comments

The compiled results of the feedback forms can be used by the change management team members to modify the project plan and/or the communication plan or to work with specific individuals or groups that may be providing roadblocks to success.

Making it All Worthwhile

Once a change initiative is underway, it is critical to sustain the change with reinforcement.

Leading Status Meetings

The leader must make sure that the project and communication plan remain on track. They need to identify, and explore any issues from employees or stakeholders that have emerged, and review and consider any feedback gathered to date.

Acting as a facilitator, the leader helps to bring about learning and productivity. Communication will be a byproduct of this by providing indirect or unobtrusive assistance, guidance, and supervision.

He or she listens actively, asks questions, encourages diverse viewpoints, organizes information, helps the group reach consensus, and understands that the individual needs of team members will affect teamwork.

The LEAD model provides a simple methodology for facilitating a participative meeting:

- **Lead with objectives**: When clear objectives are stated up front, group energy is channeled toward achieving an outcome. The objectives shape the content of the meeting.

- **Empower to participate:** In the Lead model, the facilitator is empowered to encourage active participation.

- **Aim for consensus:** Getting the team to consensus will have members more likely to support and carry out the decisions of the team.

- **Direct the process:** How the meeting progresses will influence the quality of the decisions of the team, and influences the commitment of team members.

Leaders must differentiate between process and content. *Content* includes the topics, subjects, or issues; *process* is about how the topics, subjects, or issues are addressed.

Celebrating Successes

Because communications from managers and supervisors have been shown to have a significant impact on employees during a change initiative, it is appropriate that they be actively involved in celebrating success with employees as a result of positive performance. Celebrations can occur on three levels:

Level 1 - One on one conversation: In a private meeting, a supervisor should attest to the fact that due to the employee's effort, a change was made, and how it is succeeding. He or she should extend verbal thanks to the employee.

Level 2 - Public recognition: Public recognition officially acknowledges outstanding performance and points out a role model that helped make a successful change happen. Supervisors should carefully consider who receives recognition, and not alienate group members who participated in the change but who many not have distinguished themselves as significantly.

Level 3 - Group celebrations: Fun or engaging activities are used to celebrate key milestones by a group. They include buffet or restaurant lunches, dinner events, or can include group outings to sports, amusement, or cultural events. It is important that these types of celebrations try to include the involvement of the primary change sponsor in some way.

The exercise below that draws upon experiences from the change management class is an example of a group celebration that might precede a lunch, dinner, our outing.

Sharing the Results and Benefits

In order to sustain the impact of a change, it is important for everyone who is involved in the process to know what results are occurring. This occurs across a number of dimensions.

Ongoing feedback is needed from employees at all levels. Feedback tools such as the Feedback at Contemporary Chemical form in the Evaluating and Adapting section of Module 6 remain a good method for gathering ongoing input. Using an electronic delivery method improves throughput.

Using Appreciative Inquiry

Appreciative inquiry is a model for change management developed by David L. Cooperrider, Ph.D., a professor at Case Western University. The name combines two definitions:

- **Appreciate**: to look for the best in something, and to increase something in value.

- **Inquiry** means to seek understanding using a process based on provocative questions.

Based on the meanings of the two words, AI theorizes that organizations are not problems to be solved. Rather, each organization has been created as a solution, designed in its own time, to meet a challenge, or to satisfy a need within society.

A guiding principle in appreciative inquiry is the concept of the positive core, or what gives life to an organization. Below is a list of elements that make up a positive core.

Achievements, strategic opportunities, cooperative moments, technical assets, innovations, elevated thoughts, community assets, positive emotions, financial assets, community wisdom, core competencies, visions of possibility, vital traditions and values, positive macro trends, social capital, and embedded knowledge.

The Four Stages

The four stages in the Appreciative Inquiry model are known as the 4-D cycle. They are:

Stage 1 Discovery: Mobilizing the whole system by engaging all stakeholders in the articulation of strengths and best practices. Identifying "The best of what has been and what is."

Stage 2 Dream: Creating a clear results-oriented vision in relation to discovered potential and in relation to questions of higher purpose, such as "What does the world call us to become?"

Stage 3 Design: Creating possibility propositions of the idea organization, articulating an organization design that is capable of drawing upon and magnifying the positive core to realize the newly expressed dream.

Stage 4 Destiny: Strengthening the affirmative capability of the whole system, enabling it to build hope and sustain momentum for ongoing positive change and high performance.

While each AI process is unique in an organization, change efforts typically progress sequentially through the 4-D cycle. Positioned in the center of the diagram below, the organization's **Affirmative Topic Choice** is entered, surrounded by the four phases.

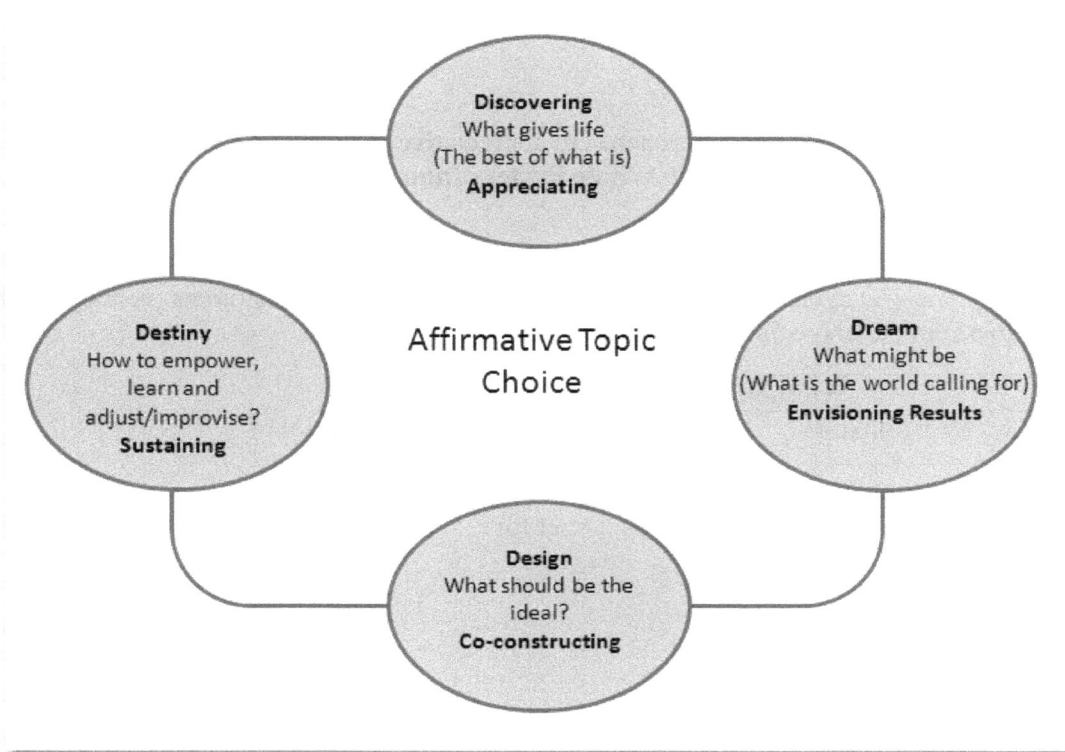

Various types of questions help elicit feedback and ideas during the process:

- What's the biggest problem here?

- Why do we still have those problems?

- What possibilities exist that we have not yet considered?

- What's the smallest change that could make the biggest impact?

- What solutions would have us both win?

Topics emerge from interviews with people throughout the organization in several ways.

- Preliminary interviews are held within the organization at its best levels

- A cross-section of people throughout the organization are engaged in inquiry

- People are challenged to shift deficit (negative) issues into affirmative (positive) topics for inquiry.

The Purposes of Appreciative Inquiry

Appreciative inquiry is conducted in organizations for several reasons.

- It allows the performance of people from across the whole system to participate in an inquiry; all stakeholders (employees, customers, vendors, and interested community members) are involved in the process.

- It leads to the design of appreciative organizations that can support stakeholders fostering a triple bottom line; people, profits, and planet.

- It serves as a catalyst for the transformation of an organizational culture.

Examples and Case Studies

Over the past twenty years, there have been many approaches to appreciative inquiry. Two key methods of the appreciative inquiry used often in organizations are **Whole System Inquiry** and the **AI Summit**.

Whole-System Inquiry

Whole-System Inquiry follows the 4-D cycle to involve all stakeholders (employees, customers, vendors, and interested community members) in the appreciative inquiry process.

Cycle Phase(s)	Methods
Discovery	Interviews by facilitators Interviews of each other
Dream, Design, and Destiny	During these three phases, small groups gather to: • share stories • capture best practices • launch teams to address innovation or other issues that have arisen

The AI Summit

The AI Summit is a full-scale meeting process that concentrates on the discovery and development of an organization's positive core. The process participants then use this knowledge to design strategic business processes (marketing, customer service, leadership, human resources development, new products). Cross sections of diverse stakeholders participate.

Typically a four-day event, each day focuses on one of the cycle phases.

Day	Cycle Phase(s)	Focus	Participants
1	Discovery	Perform a system-wide inquiry into the core	• Hold appreciative interviews • Capture, reflect on interview highlights
2	Dream	Imagine the organization's greatest potential for positive influence and effect in the world	• Share dreams captured during the interviews • Create and present dramatic enactments
3	Design	Create propositions that reflect a boldly alive positive core in all strategies, processes, systems, decisions, and collaborations	• Create provocative design statements, incorporating the positive core
4	Destiny	Invite action inspired by the discovery, dream and design days	• Declare intended actions publicly and ask for support • Use self-organized groups to plan next steps

Roadway Express

In 2000, Roadway Express, a leading transporter of industrial, commercial, and retail goods decided to drive down costs and increase business by creating an organization that expressed leadership at every level. At facilities around their network, drivers, dock workers, and office workers and professionals at all levels would join senior management at annual strategic planning sessions, learn the business, and create new levels of partnership between the unions and the company. Appreciative inquiry was chosen as the change methodology.

At many AI Summits, Roadway looked to increase employee leadership empowerment to increase net profit margins of 5%. At a Summit held at a Winston-Salem, NC terminal, a team of short-haul drivers generated twelve cost-cutting measures. For example, if each of 32 drivers made only one extra delivery per hour, that would result in 288 additional daily shipments.

In first quarter 2003, Roadway reported that their fourth quarter revenues were up 25.7 percent versus the same quarter one year earlier. During the AI Summit process, Roadway stock increased from $14 per share to $40 per share.

When Roadway merged with Yellow to form the new YRC Company, the AI Summit was selected as the vehicle to propel the merger integration to a higher level. As of 2005, more than ten thousand people at YRC had participated in at least one AI Summit. A new electronic and virtual architecture called the Core Strength Network has allowed employees to spread innovation and best practices throughout the organization. Now using virtual meetings with the Network, the company has redesigned the dock in Akron, allowed drivers the opportunity to become successful salespersons, and encouraged one terminal to become the highest margin facility in the company. New software called Ovation.Net is now taking the online knowledge sharing and collaboration to the next level.

British Airways

In 1999, David Erich, V.P. of Customer Service for British Airways North America wanted to engage employees to make changes to increase work satisfaction and to provide the level of customer service for which the airline is known worldwide. In North America, it was found that best practices were not being identified, shared, or replicated across the 22 stations. Mr. Erich undertook a whole-system appreciative inquiry process to transform the organizational culture.

After several preliminary briefings and meetings where more than fifty line managers and organizational development professionals learned about appreciative inquiry and checked with colleagues in two other companies, a full-scale appreciative inquiry initiative was launched.

During a pivotal core team meeting where affirmative inquiry topics were being selected, the issue of the cost and frustrations of delayed and lost baggage emerged. However upon further exploration by the facilitators, it was determined that the ability of customer service agents to provide an exceptional arrival experience would be a more positive focus. Three other topics agreed to were happiness at work, continuous people development, and harmony among work groups.

Two initiatives would be required in order to effect positive change with the four topics: management commitment and the involvement of the entire workforce. This meant that a whole-system involvement would be needed to achieve the goals.

With the agreement of the core team to steward the process, volunteers signed up for roles including:

- Conducting interviews

- Naming and branding the initiative

- Speaking about AI to groups

- Writing articles or being interviewed for in-house communications

- Serving as the AI coordinator at the station.

A cross-level, cross-functional steering team that included an AI consultant was formed to oversee the issues and team progress. The process was given a name, "The Power of Two", and the AI initiative took off at British Airways.

Typical of the questions that were asked were:

- Describe your most memorable arrival experience, as a customer or, as airline personnel. What made it memorable for you? How did you feel?

- Tell me a story about your most powerful service recovery. Describe the situation. What was it about you that made it happen?

- Who else was involved and why was he or she significant?

- What tools did you use or what did you do that others might be able to do when in a similar situation?

The Imagine Chicago project

A third case involves a non-profit community organization in Chicago. Imagine Chicago was founded by Bliss Browne in 1992 to help people imagine and create a positive future for Chicago and its children. Its first project was a city-wide appreciative inquiry process in which 50 at risk youths interviewed more than 150 adult community builders in Chicago to learn about the highlights of their lives as citizens -- and their hopes and plans for the city's future.

During a five-month period, several different strategies were used:

- Provide training to citizen leaders about the appreciative inquiry process

- Learning to ask positive questions

- Team formation and organization strategies

- Brainstorming strategies to determine project focuses

- Action planning

- Implementation and sustaining strategies.

IMAGINE Chicago's AI work involved three core processes:

1. Dialogue -- across cultural, racial, and generational boundaries

2. Curriculum development -- frameworks and organizers to understand, imagine and create projects that build community

3. Network formation -- to link individuals and organizations committed to developing a positive future for Chicago and its children.

As a result of the AI project consisting mainly of intergenerational interviews, Imagine Chicago leaders discovered that commitments of the adult community citizens were rejuvenated, a new sense of shared civic identify was cultivated, and young people felt a greater commitment toward making a difference.

Bringing People to Your Side

Leadership in change management involves aligning people with an organization's issue or need, allowing them to see that they are working together toward an important cause.

A Dash of Emotion

Emotion is defined as a state of feeling. Because change in organizations doesn't happen without people, human elements and emotion cannot be downplayed. As an organization works with the appreciative inquiry process, six essential conditions come together in an organization. They liberate personal and organizational power, resulting in a transformation for the people in the organization.

1. **Freedom to be known in relationship**: The nature of the appreciative inquiry process leads people to feel encouraged to shine as individuals, not just as someone performing a role.

2. **Freedom to be heard:** Through the interview process, individuals gain the freedom to be heard.

3. **Freedom to dream in community**: People feel more free and in a safe place to share dreams as they dialogue together.

4. **Freedom to choose to contribute:** People feel empowered in an appreciative inquiry environment, and assume commitments they might not otherwise undertake.

5. **Freedom to act with support:** The awareness that others care about their work makes individuals comfortable experimenting with new ideas.

6. **Freedom to be positive:** Suddenly, the environment validates the fact that it is acceptable to have fun. People feel positive and proud of their work experiences.

Plenty of Facts

A fact is something that is demonstrated to exist, or known to have existed. As opposed to the "people" component, emotion, facts are straightforward, and necessary to measure progress. As a change management project shifts into the launch or in-process stage, the change management team must make sure that measurement is ongoing. Two types of measurements are described below.

- **Audits and performance measurement systems:** Audits and measurement systems provide data to determine the adoption rate of change. They help to determine:

- How many employees are using the new processes or systems?

- Individual or group proficiency levels

- Who is not engaged with the process, or is struggling, and why?

Formal, quantitative assessment instruments and a review of performance data provide this information. The results allow the change management and/or project teams to develop and implement corrective actions, make modifications to the program, or use positive results to propel to the project forward.

- **Accountability Systems:** Enhancements should be made to performance evaluation and compensation systems in order to maintain the accountability and credibility of the change. This is important in order to maintain ongoing reinforcement of the changed systems or processes.

Building Resiliency

Resiliency is the capacity to absorb high levels of change while maintaining a level of performance and displaying minimal dysfunctional behavior.

People who are resilient do two things to reduce their susceptibility to dysfunctional behavior during change: They increase their capacity to absorb shock, and they reduce the amount of effort necessary to successfully implement any one change.

What is Resiliency?

Resilience isn't an absolute characteristic; rather it is a combination of traits of varying degrees in people. Resilient people, whom psychologist Daryl Conner terms O-Type, perceive more opportunity than non-resilient people do. They approach life as meaningful, and as a guiding beacon through the challenges of change. Their optimistic view lets them see each new day as providing a new set of opportunities and choices; they view disruption as a necessary part of adjusting to the challenges of change.

In contrast to O-Type individuals, D-Types perceive danger; they are individuals who use defense mechanisms such as denial, distortion, and delusions to deflect change and are reactive. The opposite O-Type individuals are proactive, and understand when to ask for help.

Why is It Important?

When resilient people are confronted with ambiguity, anxiety, and a loss of control that accompanies change, they tend to grow stronger from the experiences, rather than allowing themselves to be depleted. Resilient people are more likely to make a quicker and more effective adaptation to change. They are winners, rather than losers, critically important in organizations. Resilient people are necessary to foster success during a change.

While no person is specifically O-Type or D-Type, people with O-Type characteristics tend to exhibit a high degree of resilience. This allows them to understand that the future contains constantly shifting variables, display willingness to explore paradoxes, and stay the course during periods of significant disruption.

People shift between sides on a resilience continuum, depending upon the characteristics being exhibited, and the change being experienced.

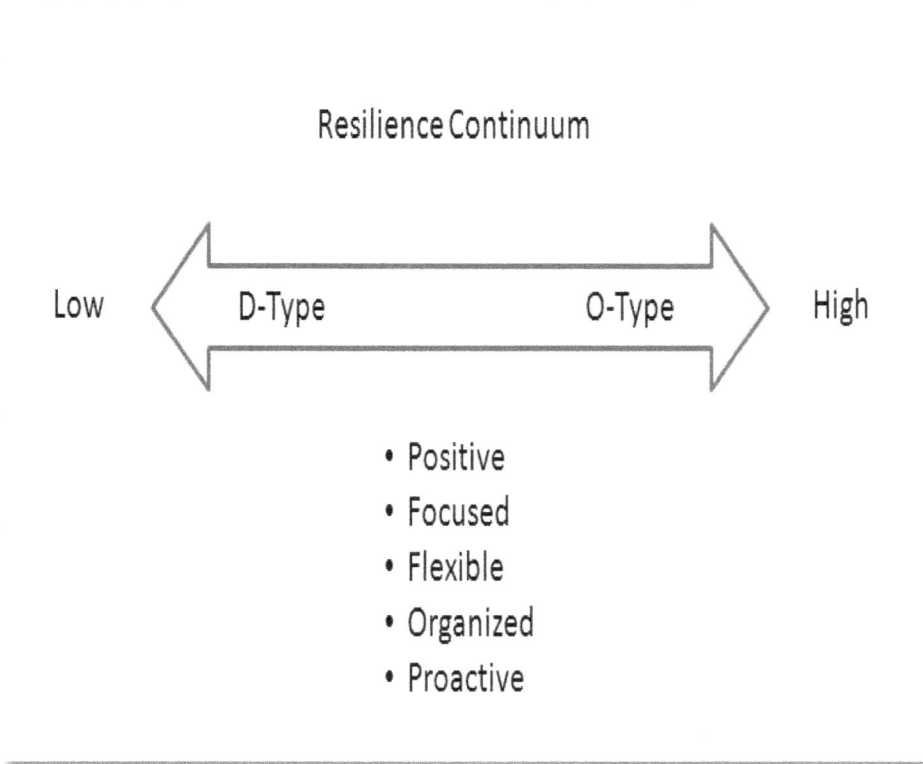

Resilience Continuum

Low ⟵ D-Type   O-Type ⟶ High

- Positive
- Focused
- Flexible
- Organized
- Proactive

Five Easy Steps for the Leader and the Individual

One can practice behaviors and steps to become more resilient. Below are some steps leaders and individuals can take to foster resilience?

Step 1: Develop a more Positive world view and self-concept

- Notice what you say to yourself in an unfamiliar situation

- Find specific opportunities during challenges you face

- Practice turning minuses into pluses

- Take a time out during a period of frustration

- Look for a positive person to serve as your coach

Step 2: Maintain a Focused sense of purpose for long-term goals and priorities

- Explore your value system and identify your personal sense of direction on which you can rely to make choices

- Set new priorities when faced with the disruption of change

Step 3: Use Flexible thinking to explore multiple approaches for addressing uncertainty.

- Switch sides when discussing a topic about which you feel strongly

- Rather than assuming your first answer is the solution, suspend judgment if you are in the middle of a change

- List three positives and three negatives about a new idea or concept

- Be willing to work in an unfamiliar role to learn a different point of view

- Identify a person who is a strong flexible thinker, and ask for some coaching

Step 4: Use Organized, structured approaches when managing ambiguity

- Learn to quickly sort information and find patterns in new situations

- Use a planner or planning software to keep to-do lists, track plans, commitments, and next steps for each change initiative

- Break down complex or ambiguous situations into manageable chunks

- Find a coach who has strong organizational skills.

Step 5: Experiment proactively with new approaches and solutions

- Choose a small project and experiment with a new approach

- For a challenge you face, define the worst-case scenario; list how you would address each risk

- Find someone you perceive as a successful risk-taker and discuss your objections and concerns about a change

- Try to view a risk associated with a change you are facing as a "win-win" situation; determine what you can learn by assuming the risk

- Find a coach who excels at proactive experimentation.

Building Flexibility

Being flexible on personal and social levels is critical for individuals involved in or leading a change to be able to make shifts as necessary during a project.

What is Flexibility?

There are two dimensions of flexibility; flexible thinking, and social flexibility.

Flexible Thinking: People who think flexibly can generate a broad range of thoughts and possible responses without feeling compelled to decide on one response right away. They have a tolerance for ambiguity plus a high level of creativity. This allows them to tackle a problem from many directions.

Flexible thinkers enjoy new or complex ideas, are open to varying perspectives, and devise creative solutions in order to adapt to change. At a personal level, people who think flexibly supplement their own knowledge with the talents of other people, knowing they themselves cannot have all the answers. They are facile at building networks to freely exchange support and information.

Social Flexibility: People with a great degree of social flexibility have a clear sense of their individual strengths and weaknesses. Their self-concept is not easily threatened as they reach out to others, looking for collaboration and working to build social networks. They have no problem reaching out to see where others can add value and asking others for support.

Why is it Important?

Flexible people are team players, a critical need during a change management initiative. Flexibility allows one to brainstorm more efficiently, bringing a wider range of ideas to a project team. The broad range of solutions brought to the table by a flexible thinker encourages a strong change solution -- and avoids the potential for inferior solutions that may be generated by people with low levels of social flexibility.

Five Easy Steps for the Leader and the Individual

The following five steps can benefit either a leader or an individual who is dealing with change on a personal or an organizational level.

Personal Level	Social Level
Swap sides in a discussion on a topic about which you feel strongly.	Identify colleagues who have a different view than you, and ask their opinions.
Suspend judgment during a change. Don't assume that the first answer is the best or only one.	If a colleague presents an idea that seems off-base to you, take a step back and try to see the rationale from your colleague's point of view.
Practice thinking of paradoxes (both/and) rather than contradictions (either/or). Try to generate both positives and negatives about a new idea or concept, rather than focusing exclusively on one or another. Listen to others.	Ask colleagues or friends for their opinions about your thoughts regarding a change; listen completely to their answers and avoid passing judgment on their contributions.
Offer to work in a role that's unfamiliar to you so you can approach a situation from a different point of view.	Pinpoint a skill you want to learn; ask someone to help you learn it.
Find someone who is strong in flexible thinking to serve as your coach.	Identify someone who is adept with social flexibility and ask for coaching.

Chapter 17 – Networking Inside a Company

Networking is unavoidable in modern society. Many people focus on external networking, but the networking process must be used with the company in order to be truly effective. By following the information outlined in this publication, you will be able to network effectively and reap the rewards that come with making connections within the organization.

At the end of this chapter, you should be able to:

- Define networking

- Understand networking principles

- Use networking tools

- Avoid common mistakes

- Understand how to build relationships

- Manage time successfully

The Benefits of Networking at Work

It is easy to overlook the need to make connections within your own organization. The benefits of networking at work, however, are valuable to any career. These benefits include the shared knowledge and increased opportunities. Networking within the organization will also improve your professional image.

Gain Connections

Never underestimate the importance of making connections at work. The personal relationships that you create at work will grow your network in more ways than one. You are directly connected with your coworker, but you are also indirectly connected with the members of your coworker's network. Every connection that you make increases your chances of being referred for new opportunities and greater responsibility.

Shared Knowledge

Networking at work provides the ideal opportunity for shared knowledge. Knowledge sharing is a two-way street. When your connections share knowledge, you will learn how to avoid the mistakes they made and benefit from their experience. Additionally, the information that your connections provide will help inspire new ideas.

Sharing your own knowledge provides its own benefits. When you are able to share valuable information with contacts, you can develop your reputation and expertise. In turn, you can create opportunities for yourself.

Increase Opportunity

Networking in the workplace helps increase opportunity. By having many people in your network, your reputation will quickly spread beyond your immediate peers. As your network develops, word of your skills and expertise will reach superiors and other departments. You will be viewed for your entire skill set rather than by your job description alone. Opportunities that may develop because of your connections include training, mentoring, lateral moves, and promotion.

Improve Image

Creating a network allows you to fine tune your professional image as you connect with others. You can share your successes with your network and conduct yourself in a way that people admire. This provides you with the perfect opportunity to improve your professional image among your peers and superiors. If you take advantage of all the opportunities that networking provides, your professional image will be everything that you want it to be. There are a few tips to improving your image:

- Be helpful

- Be professional

- Share knowledge

Networking Obstacles

Like every endeavor in life, you will face obstacles in your networking. Fortunately, you will be able to navigate and avoid many of these obstacles by correctly defining networking and swallowing your pride. Additionally, the ability to identify difficult personality traits and cultural barriers will provide you with opportunities to avoid miscommunications and facilitate functional relationships

Confusion About The Definition Of Networking

There is some confusion over the definition of networking, which is why many people fail to network effectively. Some people assume that networking is simply meeting new people and collecting their contact information. Others equate networking with socializing. The problem with both definitions is that neither results in true business connections. In true networking, developing contacts and relationships results in new knowledge and greater influence.

By understanding what networking truly is, you will be able to focus your energy appropriately and develop beneficial relationships. We will explore ways to achieve this definition in the following modules.

Personality Traits

Each person has a unique personality. Unfortunately, different personality traits will clash with each other. If you do not know how to handle different personalities, you will encounter obstacles in your networking attempts.

Personality examples:

- Extroverted and playful: These people require more attention and verbal approval than some other personalities.

- Assertive leaders: This type of personality requires loyalty and recognition of achievements.

- Meticulous planners: Meticulous people need the space to complete the tasks, and their perfectionist habits require understanding.

- Peacemakers: Peacemakers work to avoid and settle conflict. They require a calm work environment and appreciation for their efforts.

These are just an overview of personalities. You probably want to research different personalities on your own.

Cultural Barriers

You are likely to encounter cultural barriers in the modern workplace. A diverse work environment provides numerous benefits. A blend of different cultures, however, is likely to result in the miscommunications and conflict. You need to be aware cultural barriers and develop sensitivity towards different people and customs.

Barriers:

- Language: Overcome language barriers with translators and listening carefully. It is also advisable to learn other languages.

- Stereotypes: Monitor your thoughts and feelings to identify any prejudices or stereotypes that would keep you from developing relationships with people from different cultures.

- Cultural Norms: Take the time to understand what normal and respectful behavior is in other cultures. For example, some cultures find making eye contact rude and others do not approve of emotional displays.

Personal Pride

In many instances, personal pride is a benefit. It creates confidence and showcases your talent. In networking, however, personal pride can become a barrier to success. Pride can prevent people from networking effectively. Many people develop relationships but fail to call upon people in their network for help because of their pride. Remember that definition of networking. If you allow your pride to prevent you from using your network, there is no point in having one in the first place.

Networking Principles

Now that you know the basic definition of networking and how to avoid common obstacles, it is time to learn the basic networking principles. Networking requires you to build relationships. You need to listen to the people in your network, offer value, and build trust. As you master the basic principles of networking, you will begin to see your network develop.

Relationships

Networking requires building true relationships. Like any other relationship, networking requires time and energy. If you are not willing to put the effort into building new relationships, there is not point in networking. We will delve deeper into relationship building later, but here are some common sense methods to building relationships.

- Communicate with your contacts – Communication is necessary for any relationship.

- Avoid constantly asking for help – While your contacts are resources, being needy is very off-putting.

- Personalize conversation – Get to know your contacts and take interest in their lives.

Listen

It is easy to underestimate the importance of listening when networking. While networking requires selling yourself, it is more than a sales pitch. You need to listen in order to build relationships and network effectively. Do not just allow the other person to talk, actively listening will ensure that you truly understand what the other person is saying.

Tips for Listening:

- Keep eye contact.

- Avoid fidgeting or checking your phone.

- Ask pertinent questions, but do not interrupt

- Pay attention.

- Rephrase what is said.

Offer Value

As we have already stated, networking is a two-way street. You cannot simply expect your contacts to support you and share their knowledge if there is no value in it for them. You must show new contacts that you are an asset. Offering value requires you to understand your networks.

How to Offer Value:

- Identify the needs of others.

- Determine how your expertise meets these needs.

- Offer to help.

Do not over complicate offering value. It can be something as simple as helping a coworker install a new program or sharing notes from a missed meeting.

Build Trust

Trust is needed for every functional relationship, and networking is no different. Your contacts need to feel that you can be trusted. Building trust with new people takes time, but it is not that difficult to accomplish if you pay attention to your behavior.

Steps to Building Trust:

- Be honest – Trust is easier to build when people are honest.

- Act with consistency – Be a mindful employee every day, not just when the boss is around.

- Be helpful – Do not be seen as a self-serving coworker who is willing to do anything to succeed.

How to Build Networks

Now that you understand the principles of networking, it is time to address building your network. The guidelines to building networks require using basic common sense. They may seem too simplistic at first glance, but they are essential and must not be overlooked.

Meet New People

Telling you that you need to meet new people to build a network may seem like pointing out the obvious, but this step is often over looked. If you are passive about meeting people, you will never be able to build you network. Meeting people requires action; do not simply wait for people to come to you. Here are a few tips to help you expand your social circle in the workplace:

- Introduce yourself to people – This may be difficult for shy personalities, but it is unlikely that you will be introduced to everyone, particularly in larger organizations, so you must do it yourself.

- Invite people to join you for lunch – This extends to other events.

- Attend groups and functions – These groups and functions may be official or unofficial. Just take the time to meet new people.

Be Polite

It is easy to forget manners in our fast-paced society. Being polite, however, will help you stand out and improve the way that other people view you. It makes you appear more personable and trustworthy. You do not need to be Miss Manners to be polite. Simply exercise common courtesy. Here are a few steps that you can take to being polite.

- Make a good impression: Dress appropriately and address people respectfully at work.

- Pay attention to people: Do not pay attention to your phone or anything else while people are talking to you at work.

- Be considerate: Help other people when you can.

- Think before acting or speaking: Consider the implications of your words or actions, and avoid the workplace dramas.

No matter how hard you try to be polite, you will accidentally offend someone. It is unavoidable. The only way to move past it is to apologize promptly.

Follow up

After meeting new people, it is important to follow up with them. This part of the networking experience can be awkward, so it must be approached carefully. There are different ways you can follow up with people: email, phone, face-to-face, etc. It is possible that you will have to briefly remind your contact of your last encounter, so be prepared to give a few details, Do not, however, spend too much time on this. It is important that you move forward, show the value in your relationship, and prepare the next step. There are different ways to accomplish this early on in the process.

- Suggest an article or book based on the previous meeting.

- Continue your conversation if possible.

- Extend an invitation.

Once you have followed up with your contact, it is up to the other person to respond.

Allow Relationships to Develop Naturally

All relationships have a natural development that should not be rushed. While it is important to follow-up with people, you must avoid appearing desperate or clingy. You will not be able to develop a relationship with everyone, and it is important that you are able to take no for an answer. As a general rule of thumb, you should only contact people three times before they return communication. If they do not contact you, it is best to leave them alone.

Even if your contact has followed up with you, it is important that you do not become an overbearing stalker. This requires common sense. Consider the frequency that you would be comfortable with new people contacting you. Allow this to guide you in developing new relationships.

Recognize Networking Opportunities

You cannot build networks unless you are able to recognize networking opportunities around you. It is imperative that you take advantage of the formal networking, informal networking, and workday opportunities that you encounter. Additionally, it is not possible to predict every network opportunity. You should always be prepared to network.

Formal Networking

Formal networking opportunities will vary with each organization. This type of networking takes place at organized social events. This ranges from professional and social groups that your peers are part of, to meetings and social functions. When you engage in formal networking, you need to appear polished and professional. It is essential that you do your homework before attending a formal networking event. For example, you should learn about the type of activities that a young professionals group at your organization participates in before going to a meeting.

Informal Networking

Informal networking happens much more frequently than formal networking. These opportunities occur every day, so you need to be aware of them. Informal opportunities occur with email interactions, coffee breaks, lunches, and group discussions. Since informal networking is not scheduled, it requires you to take initiative. For example, invite someone to join your group for lunch. Informal networking is a low-pressure way to extend your network and improving your relationships.

Workday Opportunities

You need to recognize that there are numerous networking opportunities within the workplace. Some of these may be available in programs at your organization. For example, you can greet new employees or join a mentoring group. You can also make your own workday opportunities. Bring coffee for your coworkers or keep snacks in your workspace. Remember to take the initiative when the company does not provide you with the opportunities that you would like to see.

Always Be Ready to Network

You never know when a networking opportunity will occur, so you must always be prepared. There are a few steps you can take to improve your readiness and increase your network:

- Pay attention to the people around you – Pay attention to potential opportunities.

- Look the part at all times – Keep your professional appearance.

- Make personal gestures – This helps endear you to others.

- Pay attention to changes in the industry – Maintain you expertise.

Common Networking Mistakes

Before going any further, it is time to point out the common networking mistakes that people make so that you can avoid them. We have already addressed meeting people and following through, but these remain common mistakes. Creating expectations that are too high and failing to remain professional are also common mistakes that should be avoided.

Not Meeting New People

As we have already discussed, it is not possible to expand a network without meeting new people. It is easy to consciously accept this fact while failing to act upon it. There are many reasons why people fail to follow this basic rule. Some people struggle with this because of their personalities. Others have a list of excuses that they use: there is no time; they don't know where to go, etc. In reality, people will prioritize what they find important. If they believe that networking and meeting people is important, they will make an effort to do it.

Not Following Through

Following through is just as important as meeting people. Sometimes it is easy to get caught up in the meeting new contacts at the expense of following through, and may people believe that mass communication is effective enough to establish networks. It is essential, however, to follow up with each contact individually. There is a very brief window of opportunity to follow through with contacts. If you do not follow up with new contacts quickly, the contact will forget about you or conclude that you are not interested in pursuing a relationship.

High Expectations

Another common mistake is placing high expectations on networking. While it is important to place reasonable expectations on the networking, you should not make the expectations too high. There will be a learning curve as you network, and placing unreasonably high expectations on your efforts can lead to avoidance. If you feel like your efforts at networking are not fruitful, you will not attempt to improve your networking skills. Networking typically takes a great deal of time and effort before you actually see results. Be patient, and examine and adjust your techniques before giving up on networking altogether.

Being Professional

Professionalism needs to be balanced in networking. On the one hand, people confuse being professional with being distant and cold. This will not encourage people to join your social network. Networking requires a warm and friendly tone to attract others to you. On the other hand, being too familiar will make people feel uncomfortable. Take the time to get to know new contacts. Do not take liberties. It is important to maintain a level of decorum in your professional networks.

Develop Interpersonal Relationships

As we have already discussed, networking is actually relationship building. Developing and maintaining intrapersonal relationships takes the time and effort, but they are worth the payoff. Interpersonal relationships require being genuine, participating in dialogue, maintaining boundaries, and investing time. By following the information outlined in this module, you will find it easier to develop interpersonal relationships.

Be Genuine

When developing relationships, it is essential that you be genuine. Many people are prejudiced against networking because they feel that it requires being fake and manipulative. In reality, however, interpersonal relationships require people to be genuine. Build relationships on common interests and passions. It is better to stop your efforts to connect with someone than build a relationship on false pretense. Identify your interests and passions, and be prepared to discuss them with others. This will not only show that you are genuine but also give insight into your strengths and skills.

Dialogue

We have already addressed the importance of listening and communication. Developing strong interpersonal relationships requires successful dialogue. This demands an understanding of all that dialogue entails. Dialogue is a two-way method of communication that promotes understanding. It incorporates active listening and polite conversation.

Steps to Dialogue:

- Listen actively and without interrupting.

- Be respectful even when you disagree.

- Resist the urge to argue when you respond.

Maintain Boundaries

All relationships require boundaries, and networking relationships are no exception. It is essential that you establish your own boundaries and respect the boundaries that other people have. If you do not establish boundaries, you will find yourself the stressed and overworked. You must create personal boundaries that fit your individual needs. There are steps anyone can take to help establish and keep personal boundaries.

- Establish time in your schedule for yourself and protect it.

- Communicate your boundaries.

- Learn to say no, and explain why.

- Prepare an appropriate response for people who violate your boundaries.

Invest Time

Like any other relationship, the relationships in your network require you to invest time. Given the busy schedule that most people have, it is easy to overlook networking contacts, particularly at work. It is not enough to simply run into people at work, you need to set aside time to reach out to your individual contacts. This typically requires carving time out in your schedule. Take time to make calls, send emails, and meet with your contacts. You do not have to carve out large chunks of time. Simply make the effort to invest in your contacts.

Online Networking Tools

Taking part in the networking requires using the appropriate tools. Fortunately, the internet provides a number of online networking tools that will assist your networking activities. Commonly used networking tools include popular social networks, blogs, chat rooms, and email. Implementing these tools will allow you to easily keep up with your contacts.

Social Networks

There are numerous social media networks. Three networks that are commonly used in business are Facebook, LinkedIn, and Twitter.

Facebook

Originally created for college students, Facebook has become a tool commonly used by business professionals. The site uploads comments, images, and video. You connect to people on Facebook by friending them, which gives you access to their page.

Twitter

Twitter is called a microblog. Tweets or statements uploaded are limited to 140 characters each. You connect to people by following them, and hashtags are used to label the content of tweets and create trends.

LinkedIn

LinkedIn is unique because it is a professional social network. Users create profiles with their areas of expertise and work history, similar to a resume. Linking with professional connections allows you to endorse them and them to endorse you.

You must be careful about what you post on social media. With each social network, you run the risk of over sharing. If you have any doubt that something is inappropriate, do not post it.

Blogs

Blogs are useful tools that showcase your expertise in different areas. They can also be used for networking.

Tips to Network with Blogs:

- Limit post to topics that you understand well.

- Link posts to social media and other sites.

- Comment on blogs written by other people to begin a dialogue.

- Share blog posts from other people.

- Interview contacts for blog posts.

Chat Rooms

Chat rooms are a bit more difficult to navigate than social networks are. They are online networks where people talk about specific topics. Chat rooms, however, are helpful for meeting new people who are interested in similar subjects. There are numerous chat rooms with a variety of topics. You simply choose one that you are interested in and find a conversation thread that looks promising. You can ask your coworkers if they frequent any chat rooms. People behave better in some chat rooms than others. If you find a chat room is not conducive to dialogue, leave it and find one that is more suitable.

Email

Most people are familiar with email. Email can be used for work or personal use, and it is the most commonly used networking tool. It allows you to maintain contact with people in your network without being intrusive. There are a few tips that will help you email coworkers effectively when attempting to network:

- Have a point, and place it in the subject line.

- Individualize emails, and avoid mass emails when possible.

- Be brief (keep emails close to 150 words).

- Make offers (do not simply send requests).

Emails are easy to use; so do not make them your only method of communication. It is important that you connect with people in different ways.

Time Management

Making networking a priority requires time management skills. When it comes to time management in networking, it is important to prioritize contacts and schedule activities. Connecting online and organizing activities for groups will also help you manage your time while developing relationships within your network.

Prioritize Contacts

Some contacts are more useful or more interested in developing relationships than others. When managing your time, you need to prioritize your contacts. Begin by creating a list of your contacts. Next, prioritize them according to the following information:

1. Is interested in connecting with you

2. Has useful connections

3. Has useful knowledge

Begin with your high priority contacts, and work your way down the list when connecting with people. It is more important to reach your high priority contacts first since they are more likely to be active parts of your network.

Create Group Activities

A good way to manage your network is by organizing group activities. Schedule some time each week to meet with your contacts outside the office. This is a great opportunity to expand your network and keep in touch with your contacts. These activities should be casual meeting times to get to know people outside of the workplace. Group activities do not have to be grand affairs. Consider fun activities that many people in your group will enjoy such as games, dining, bowling, movies, etc.

Connect Online

Connecting online is essential to networking. We have already discussed the different online tools. It is essential, however, that you use these tools regularly. It is not enough to simply join social networks and start a blog. You need to update regularly to keep your connections interested, and you need to comment and dialogue on other social networking sites and blogs.

Schedule time to connect online each day. You do not have to use each online tool daily. Divide your time between the tools that are most important and will reach the maximum number of people. For example, you may want to blog once a week, email daily, and update social media three to five times a week.

Schedule Your Networking Activities

Networking activities need to be scheduled or you will forget about them. A good rule of thumb is to schedule out a week in advance and make adjustments at the end of each day. Your schedule needs to include time for online networks, group activities, and private meetings. Remember that the weekly schedule is not set in stone, but creating it makes networking a priority so that you are less likely to neglect your networking activities.

Maintaining Relationships Over Time

Once you have built your network, it is essential that you maintain these relationships for the long term. It is easy to forget about established relationships as you pursue new ones to grow your network. Ignoring established connections, however, can cause individuals to feel betrayed and unwanted. This will not help your reputation with their social circle in the office.

Contact Networks Regularly

Contacting networks regularly may seem like a no brainer, but it is a rule that is all too often ignored. It is not enough to contact people with group messages or invite them to group activities. You need to reach out to individuals regularly. Send personal emails, talk on the phone, meet for coffee, or enjoy an activity together. It is not essential to connect this way on a daily or even weekly basis. Going for months without any personal contact, however, will send the message that you do not value the relationship you have already developed.

Be Honest

Any functional relationship requires honesty. This is particularly true in the workplace where people tend to be more competitive. Never lie or misrepresent yourself to your contacts. The internet makes it much easier for lies to be discovered, and you relationship will be irreparably harmed. Practicing honesty, however, does not require over sharing. You need to reveal what affects your coworkers such as new data, news, and ways you can assist them. You are not obligated to share your personal life in any detail.
Never over promise or make sweeping statements. No one likes to admit not knowing something, but providing false information is much worse. If you are not sure about something, tell your contacts that you will discover the facts and get back to them. This will give you a reputation as a good source of information.

Give Personal Attention

Contacting people in your network is important, but it is equally important to provide them all with personal attention. This is where active listening comes in handy. By paying attention to what your contacts say, you will understand their needs and interests. Rather than sending a standard form email, you will be able to send information that you know will the receiver will appreciate. You will also be able to offer the assistance when your contact needs.

Always respond as soon as possible when you are contacted. Even if you need to look something up first, respond and say that you will have an answer soon. This lets the contacts know that you see them as priorities instead of afterthoughts. Going a step further to provide personal attention will serve to improve your networking relationships.

Limit Networks to a Manageable Size

The definition of a manageable size will vary with each individually. For example, someone who has no family ties may have more time to socialize than someone who does not. Outside clubs, hobbies, etc. will also affect the time that you have to devote to managing your networks. Not keeping your network to a manageable size will result in networking failure. You will not be able to give any of your network personalized attention. There are a few factors you need to consider when reviewing your network:

- Is everyone in the network committed to growing the relationship? – If the answer is no, you need to develop the relationships further or remove them from your network.

- Do you personally know everyone in the network? – Again, remove people you do not know unless you feel that there is hope for developing the relationship.

You should review your contacts periodically to keep your network to a manageable size. Additionally, you need to be particular about who you choose to network with in the first place. If you do not see a future for a relationship, do not waste time pursuing it.

Chapter 18 – Networking Outside a Company

Everyone knows that networking is important to long-term business success. The networking process itself, however, can be confusing. Learning effective networking techniques will help you develop relationships that will benefit you both personally and professionally.

At the end of this chapter, participants should be able to:

- Identify and avoid obstacles

- Implement networking principles

- Use online tools

- Prioritize contacts

- Manage networks effectively

The Benefits of Networking Outside of Work

The term "networking" is frequently tossed around the business world. It is easy to talk about networking, but implementing it is another matter, particularly when you have to go beyond the confines of the workplace. Fortunately, you will improve your networking skills when you create a solid network and position yourself for success. Networking outside of your company takes time and energy, but the reward is certainly worth the effort.

Create a Solid Network

Creating a solid network requires you to make connections. It is not enough to simply meet people; you need to meet the right people, people who are likely to develop a professional relationship with you. This requires you to search for connections carefully.

Where to find possible connections:

- **Referrals**: Ask friends, peers, or family to introduce you to like-minded people. You never know who you might meet.

- **Join groups:** Professional societies offer numerous opportunities to meet new people and make connections.

- **Attend events:** Networking events can be intimidating, but they are essential. You may not make useful connections at every event, but you will not make any connections staying home.

Meet Strategic Alliance Partners

Strategic alliance partners are made when two companies work together on a joint venture. The partnership may be formal or informal. When two separate businesses begin to work together, however, tension is inevitable. This is why you need to carefully screen potential strategic alliance partners.

This is where networking is indispensable. Since strategic alliance partners need a mutually beneficial working relationship, so you need to get to know your partners ahead of time. You may choose to partner with someone you already know or work with someone new. There are strategic alliance partner networking groups to help you make valuable connections. Like any connection, you need to consider the characteristic that you need in a partnership before you look for one. What strengths do you need to see? Build relationships and make a list of contacts you would be interested in partnering with in the future, and meet with them to assess interest.

Generate Leads

Networking is invaluable when it comes to generating business leads. People are always more comfortable doing business with individuals they know and trust. You can generate leads from networking events as well as from social networking sites. We will go into more detail about the methods later. Networking to generate leads is time consuming, but it is very effective.

When using networking to generate leads, your focus should be on offering value and selling yourself. Meet with different prospects. After meeting individuals who may become leads, follow-up and connect with them. As you build relationships, you will develop new leads.

Position Yourself

Networking can be used to help you position yourself in your industry. People will contact you once you build a reputation as a reliable expert. Your reputation will develop as people in your network share your strengths as well as the strengths of your company. For example, your network may share an expert article that you write. As the article is shared, you will gain exposure, and your reputation will grow.

Networking Obstacles

Like any other endeavor, you will run into obstacles when you network. When you are aware of the common obstacles ahead of time, you are more likely to avoid them or address them correctly. Common obstacles to avoid include time constraints, fear of rejection, networking in the wrong places, and saying the wrong thing.

Time Constraints

Networking requires the consistent investment of time and energy. The normal time constraints of everyday life can quickly become an obstacle. To avoid this obstacle, it is important that you make networking a priority and schedule for it. The time that you set aside to meet and follow-up with contacts needs to be realistic. You will never attempt to invest the necessary time if your schedule is ridiculous. No one has hours to invest every day. For example, schedule 30 minutes each morning to send emails and make phone calls. Failure to invest the necessary time will damage your relationships as well as your networks.

Saying the Wrong Thing

People often say the wrong things in social settings. A misplaced word or phrase can have disastrous effects on your network. The best way to address this obstacle is to speak carefully. Prepare yourself before every meeting. Make a list of topics to avoid and topics that are suitable, and stick to it. While you are in a social setting, mind your manners.

- Avoid alcohol: Drinking too much can result in questionable behavior

- Do not criticize: Overly critical attitudes will affect you negatively

- Be courteous: Treat everyone, even the competition, with courtesy

Unfortunately, miscommunications are inevitable given enough time. If you accidentally say the wrong thing to someone, apologize immediately.

Where to Go to Network

People are often confused about where they should network. A common obstacle is limiting network locations. Someone who only networks on social media will lose the opportunity to connect in person. The same is true for only meeting people in person. Another obstacle is networking in the wrong location. While it is important to make sure that you do not limit your networks, you should make sure that you choose networks that relate to you and your goals. For example, joining professional associations that focus on your interests and goals. This will provide you with a useful pool of connections. The same holds true for social media networking.

Fear of Rejection

Encountering rejection is inevitable when you are networking. Sometimes the fear of rejection will become an obstacle. Fear is a stifling emotion, which can lead to the failure to try. It is possible to be controlled by fear and not even know it. A sign of fear is avoidance. People will make excuses to avoid unpleasant tasks. If you find yourself making excuses about networking, consider the motivation behind the excuses.

Networking Principles

There are four basic networking principles that can help guide you as you expand your personal and professional network. Developing new contacts, organizing contacts, following-up, and building relationships will lead to a stable network of connections on which you can rely.

Develop Contacts

Developing contacts sounds easy, but the first step is often the hardest. At this stage, it is important that you meet people. Meeting people requires the practice of interpersonal skills. When you do meet people, whether in person or online, avoid launching into sales pitch. You sell yourself by meeting their needs, not by talking about yourself incessantly. A contact who is interested in you will provide you with his or her contact information.

Tips to Make Contacts:

- Listen

- Be polite

- Find common interests

Organize Your Contacts

Collecting contact information alone will not help build your network. If your want to build a strong network, you will need to organize your contacts. This will help you keep better track of them.

Organization:

- **Central location:** List all of your contacts and their information in a central location. You can use any method you choose: Outlook, phone, address book, spreadsheet, etc.

- **Categorize:** It is important that you categorize your contacts. The way you do it is up to you. For example, you could label customers separately from peers.

- **Make notes:** Once you have categorized your contacts, make notes. For example, you could note the last time that you spoke with the contact along with the topic.

Follow-Up

Following up with contacts is essential for building a strong network. Follow-up requires you to provide individual attention. Mass emails are not sufficient to establish relationships with contacts and grow a network. It is important that you follow-up with people quickly. A general rule of thumb is to follow-up with new contacts within 24 hours of the first meeting. After this, it is useful to follow-up with contacts at least once a month. If you fail to follow-up with contacts in a timely manner, they are not likely to remember their earlier conversations with you.

It is important to know when a contact is not interested in becoming part of your network. If a contact does not respond to you after three attempts to follow-up, move on and focus your energy on other people.

Maintain Relationships

Over time, you will build relationships with your contacts. You need to maintain your relationships with your contacts. If you do not focus on maintenance, your network will slowly fade. There are a few steps that will help you maintain relationships:

- **Communicate regularly:** Connect with contact regularly, even after you consider them part of your network. Call, text, email, or use social network; make an effort to communicate.

- **Individual attention:** This advice is given to help develop contacts, but it is as equally important after a contact is made. Let each contact know that he or she is valued.

- **Limit your network:** It is not possible to give thousands of people individual attention. Limit the size of your network so that you will be able to maintain relationships with everyone.

Why Network

There are various reasons to network. Networking affects your reputation and your social circle. Engaging in networking can result in jobs, partnerships, and support. The benefits include an increase in trust and visibility. Networking can also provide an inside advantage when it comes to your professional and personal life.

Gain Trust

When done correctly, networking helps people gain trust. The more people trust you, the more likely they are to want to do business with you. There are a few steps that anyone can take to gain trust from contacts. These steps are common sense, but their importance cannot be overemphasized.

Gaining Trust:

- **Be honest:** Trust is easily gained when people have a reputation for being honest and sincere.

- **Act with consistency:** This requires acting with integrity at all times, even when no one is watching.

- **Be helpful:** Remember that it is your goal to meet contacts' needs. Develop a reputation for being helpful.

- **Be Visible**

Networking can help increase your visibility in the market place, where it doesn't hurt to stand out. Job listings tend to draw piles of applicants, and many of them are qualified. In this competitive atmosphere, it is essential that you stand out from the rest. There are a number of ways to increase visibility. Your circumstances will determine which actions will be effective for you.

Increase Visibility:

- Volunteer

- Speak at events

- Write content

- Share expertise

- Ask questions

- Share news (blog, social media, newsletters, etc.)

Be an Insider

Networking can help make you an insider. People in your network will be able to guide you to new opportunities. Remember that not every job you want will be advertised. The right connections can provide you with insider opportunities. If a connection feels that you would be perfect for a job, he or she will recommend you. You may be offered it before it is ever posted. You should expect to do the same for your contacts should the opportunity present itself.

Gain Advantage

Networking will help you gain an advantage as your visibility increases. You will be able to stay in the forefront of the decision makers' minds. There are steps to take to ensure that you will have a positive relationship with the decision makers:

- Dress appropriately

- Watch your tone and body language

- Be helpful

- Be engaged (at work and in the community)

How to Build Networks

It is important to consider the different ways to build networks and engage in the different methods of networking. There is physical networking, which includes networking events. Social networking sites and network referral lists are also beneficial in building strong networks.

Physical Networking Groups

Never underestimate the importance of physical networking. We are more likely to remember people we meet in person. There are a variety of physical networking groups, and you will be able to choose the ones that you feel are best for you.

Common Networking Groups:

- Community service clubs

- Professional associations

- Business organizations

- Social organizations

Physical network groups are very useful when making new contacts and developing relationships.

Attend Networking Events

Physical networking groups will result in the need to attend networking events. It is important to carefully choose the events you attend. Attending too many events will cost you your focus. Once you choose the event, there are some steps that you can take to improve your networking success. First, you need to work the room, do not limit your socialization to people you know. Make sure that you speak to at least one person you do not know.

Be prepared to talk about relevant topics in an educated way. Gauge conversations carefully. If you are not connecting with someone, excuse yourself. Additionally, do not cut a useful conversation short just to meet new people.

Social Networking Sites

Love it or hate it, the internet has changed the way that people communicate. Social networking is an essential method of communication. There are a number of different social networks to examine. We will examine the main three sites (Facebook, Twitter, LinkedIn) later. Other popular social networking tools include:

- YouTube

- Pinterest

- Tumblr

- Instagram

- Google+

Create Networking Referral Lists

Once you have established contacts, it is a good idea to consider creating referral lists. This list should be made up of trustworthy people you can benefit from and who can benefit you. The people on the list are typically linked to your area of expertise either directly or indirectly. For example, a lawyer who specializes in your field could be included on the list. When you place people on the referral list, you are willing to refer others to them. This will have an impact on your reputation, so it is essential that you choose people you trust. Before creating a referral list, it is a good idea to consider the type of positions you want to include in your referral network.

Online Networking Tools

Various online networking tools are available for your use. Given the number of networking tools available, you are sure to find something that will help you build and maintain your network. Internet tools that are commonly used include: social networks, blogs, chat rooms, and email. Each one of these tools will make your connections in cyberspace easier to monitor.

Social Networks

Facebook, LinkedIn, and Twitter are the three networks commonly used in business. Each one has its own strengths.

Facebook

Although it was originally created for college students, Facebook is now a tool that many business professionals use. The site allows users to upload comments, images, and video. You connect to people on Facebook when you make friend requests that are accepted. Friending people gives you access to their profiles.

Twitter

Often called a microblog, Twitter provides brief communication. You upload tweets, but they are limited to 140 characters each. You connect to other people by following them, and they can follow you. Most of the communication is public. You can label conversation topics using hashtags.

LinkedIn

LinkedIn is a professional social network. Like a resume, profiles include areas of expertise and work history. Once you link with professional connections, you can publically endorse them, and they can endorse you.

NOTE: Do not post anything on social media you do not want shared. With each social network, you run the risk of over sharing. If you have any doubt that something is inappropriate, do not post it.

Blogs

A blog provides a platform that allows you to showcase your expertise and attract contacts. Blogs are useful networking tools because entries can be shared. The comment section also allows you to communicate with connections.

Tips to Networking with Blogs:

- Limit post to topics that you are comfortable with

- Link blog posts to social media and other sites

- Begin a dialogue by commenting on blogs written by other people

- Share your connections' blog posts

- Interview contacts as experts for your blog

Chat Rooms

Chat rooms require more direct interactions than most social networks do. Many chat rooms are online meeting places where people discuss different topics. They are helpful for making contacts because most of the people you meet in chat rooms will share your interests. There are numerous chat rooms available to join. You simply need choose one that has a topic you are interested in and find a conversation thread that looks promising. You should ask your peers and contacts if they frequent any chat rooms. Remember that people behave better in some chat rooms than others. If you find a chat room where people do not communicate respectfully, leave it and find one where people are better behaved.

Email

Email is a familiar networking tool. Probably the tool that is most often used, email is useful for both personal and professional use. Email is beneficial because it allows you to maintain contact with the people in your network without invading their privacy. There are a few tips you need to remember when using email:

- Have a clear topic, and include it in the subject line

- Send individualized emails, when possible

- Be brief (keep emails around 150 words)

- Be helpful (don't simply ask for things)

While emails are effective, they should not be your only method of communication. It is necessary to connect with people in different ways.

Develop Interpersonal Relationships

Interpersonal relationships will develop overtime, since networking is intertwined with relationship building. Building new relationships requires a great deal of effort, but the payoff is worth the energy. Developing interpersonal relationships requires deliberate action, integrity, and boundaries, all which take time to implement.

Be Specific

Interpersonal relationships require acting with specificity. Many are prejudiced against networking because they feel that it lacks sincerity; no one likes to feel like a number. Choose to build relationships with specific contacts and be genuine in your interactions. It is best to build relationships on common interests and passions. If you choose to build friendships with specific people you enjoy interacting with, the relationship will develop naturally.

When you meet new contacts, be prepared to discuss your interests and passions. This will help you identify like-minded people and build strong relationships.

Keep Your Word

People are unlikely to build relationships with individuals they do not trust. It is imperative that you do everything that you can to ensure that your prospects see you as trustworthy. In order to do this, you must always keep your word. This may sound simplistic, but it its importance cannot be overstated. It is necessary to take extra precautions to make certain that you are able to keep your word.

- **Do not over commit:** Something will be left undone if this happens.

- **Manage your time carefully:** Consistently being late gives the impression that you do not pay attention to promises.

- **Make reasonable promises:** Do not make promises you cannot keep.

Maintain Boundaries

Every relationship needs boundaries; this is also true of networking relationships. For relationships to be successful, you need to establish your own boundaries and also respect the boundaries that other people have created. If you fail to establish boundaries, you will find that people will become intrusive. You need to create personal boundaries that fit your individual needs. These are steps anyone can take to help establish and keep personal boundaries.

- Put time in your schedule for yourself and protect it

- Communicate your boundaries to others

- Learn to say no, when necessary

- Prepare a response for anyone who violates your boundaries

Invest Time

All relationships demand that you invest your time. Given the busy schedule that most people have, taking the time to reach out to individuals, is often overlooked. It is not enough to simply run into people at events, you need to set aside time to reach out to the individuals with whom you want to build relationships. To make sure that you take the time that is necessary, schedule it. Take time to make calls, send emails, and meet with your contacts. You do not have to carve out large chunks of time, and it does not have to be a daily endeavor. Simply make the effort.

Common Networking Mistakes

If you are aware of the common networking mistakes, you will have a better chance of avoiding them. Common mistakes include taking before giving, making assumptions, reaching too high, and assuming that tools alone will build connections. Always monitor your interactions with others to prevent making these all too common errors.

Taking Before Giving

As we have already established, you need to offer value in new relationships. Give other people a reason to pursue a relationship with you. Prove that you are an asset. You should try giving before taking. When you take before giving, you appear selfish.

Giving does not have to be a grand gesture. You can offer something simple. For example, provide a referral for a service or provide expert advice. The important thing to remember is that you need to give before you take.

Assumptions

Making assumptions is not advised when making new contacts. Assumptions are often wrong, particularly in the early phases of the relationship. A common assumption is that people should automatically care about your needs and make an effort to help you. If you make this assumption, you are likely to face disappointment and also strain your relationship with your contacts. You may ask your contacts for help, and they may or may not choose to help you. If you place expectations on people, however, you will only serve to make them uncomfortable and alienate them.

Reaching Too High

Another common goal is reaching too high. Basically, this is making unachievable goals. While it is a good idea to have networking goals, they need to be realistic. There are two ways people typically reach too high when networking. One goal is trying to expand the network too quickly. The other mistake is attempting to network with people at the top of the profession too soon. Networking is long-term, and it requires realistic goals. For example, collecting the information of five contacts at an event is less likely than collecting the information of two contacts. Additionally, you are unlikely to connect with the CEO of a Fortune 500 when you first begin. Reaching too high will damage your networking effort. If you are not able to achieve a goal, you are unlikely to continue making an effort.

Assume Tools Create Connections

Knowing what networking tools can improve your networking skills. A mistake is made, however, when too much faith is placed in the tools. The tools themselves do not guarantee anything. The effect that tools have on networking is directly related to the skill and effort of the individual using them. For example, a blog is an online tool, but it will not generate any new contacts if it is poorly written or rarely updated. Additionally, tools are no substitute for connecting with individuals in person. Tools are useful, but they are only as effective as the individual using them.

Time Management

Because time is such an obstacle to networking, time management needs to be addressed. Time management for networking can be improved by prioritizing contacts and scheduling activities. Connecting with people online and organizing activities for groups will also help you manage your time as you develop relationships within your network.

Prioritize Contacts

Prioritizing contacts will help you focus your attention on people who are likely to become close contacts. You must remember that not every contact will have the same level of interest in the relationship. This is why prioritizing contacts is necessary. There are four steps to helping prioritize your contacts.

1. Make a list of contacts

2. Note people interested in connecting with you

3. Note people who have useful connections

4. Note people who have useful knowledge

The people who meet these criteria are your priority contacts. Arrange your list beginning with highest priority contacts, and work your way down.

Create Group Activities

Group activities are effective for network management. By meeting with the members of your network in a group setting, you will find it easier to keep in touch with different contacts. It also allows the members of your network to meet and expand their relationships with each other. Your group activities should be informal and enjoyable. You do not have to spend a great deal of money on a group activity, but they should reflect the tastes of your contacts. Common activities include:

- Movies

- Dining

- Bowling

- Sports games

Connect Online

Networking requires people to connect online. Many of these online tools should be familiar since we have already covered them. You must, however, use these tools regularly. It is not enough to simply join social networks and start a blog. You must update regularly to maintain the interest of your connections, and it is equally important that you comment on other social networking sites and blogs to establish dialogue.

You should schedule time to connect online each day. You do not have to use all tools daily. Divide the bulk of your time between the tools that are most important and will reach the maximum number of people. For example, you may want to blog once a week, email daily, and update other social media several times a week.

Schedule Your Network Activities

You need to schedule your networking activities, or you will forget about them. Individual schedules will vary. A good rule of thumb is to make out a schedule at least a week in advance. Then you make adjustments to your schedule at the end of each day. When making a schedule, it is important to include time for online networks, group activities, and private meetings. You need to remember that your weekly schedule is not set in stone. It may be altered, but creating it helps you make networking a priority for you, making it less likely that you will neglect your networking activities.

Manage Personal and Professional Networks

As you create your personal and professional networks, you will have the responsibility of managing them. Your networks will thrive as long as you remember to be responsive and give back while you stay in-touch with your contacts. It is also beneficial to separate your personal activities from your business ones. As you learn to manage your networks, you will reap the rewards.

Be Responsive

You must be responsive in your professional and personal relationships. Do not ignore people; always respond in a timely manner. Ignoring requests for career help gives the impression that you are not invested in the individual asking you for help. If you do not have the time to fully address an issue, schedule a meeting for a better time. The most important thing you can do is respond to requests from your network.

Give Back

Part of networking is giving back. When people ask for your help, find a way to give it. There are many ways you can give back to the people in your network.

Example:

- Provide advice

- Offer career help

- Share expertise

- Reference people in a blog post

- Provide a recommendation

Separate Personal and Business Activities

Establishing boundaries between personal and business life is important. Separating personal and business activities will reinforce these boundaries. For example, use one social networking site for personal use and another for business. Some people have a personal and a professional Facebook site, while others only use LinkedIn for professional use and Facebook for personal. There are also privacy settings that limit what people see on your sites. You will have to determine the best method for separating your personal and business activities. Once you discover the method that works for you, stick with it.

Stay Physically In-touch

We have already addressed the importance of staying connected. This requires staying physically in-touch whenever possible. This is easier to do when people are local. However, it is still important to make connections with people who are not local. This requires a little more effort. When you travel, you should make the time to reach out to people you know. Even if visits are infrequent, people will appreciate the attempt to reach out to them.

Chapter 19 – Servant Leadership

Servant leadership can seem like a contradicting term, but it is becoming a very popular tool in many businesses. Servant leadership is a philosophy that involves focusing on others (i.e. your employees), and focus on their success, and in turn build better professional relationships that can benefit both manager and employee. Servant leadership shows that managers can be great leaders while boosting their employee's confidence and further their success at the same time.

At the end of this chapter, you should be able to:

- Define servant leadership

- Know the characteristics of servant leadership

- Recognize the barriers of servant leadership

- Learn to be a mentor and a motivator

- Practice self-reflection

What is Servant Leadership?

Servant leadership is a business philosophy that emphasizes the act of the leader, such as a manager or supervisor, focusing on the growth and development of their employees and ensuring their success. In doing so, the leader succeeds when their employees do. In a business team, servant leadership can not only help employees achieve and grow, but it can also benefit their leaders and the company as a whole.

A Desire to Serve

It is a leader's responsibility to guide their followers on the right path. But to become a better leader, it's not enough just to take the wheel and steer – you must also be willing to serve your followers and assist them in their own journey. A servant leader should have a desire to serve their employees, which includes taking the time to identify your employees and how they perform or being beside them as they face challenges. Take the time to assist in their growth and help them work toward achieving their goals. Don't be afraid to give yourself into their processes and become part of their evolvement.

Knowing to Share the Power

As a leader, it is a common feeling to absorb the 'power' of the position and a have a sense of superiority. But a servant leader does not save this power only for themselves because they learn to share it with their team of employees. Employees under a servant leader should feel some of the servant leader's power and pull, which can make them feel more empowered in their place on the team and in their own abilities. Sharing the power allows employees to feel like their contributions matter and that their input is valued.

Share the power by:

- Delegating

- Asking employee opinions

- Working together on challenges or projects

- Taking a census, when possible

Putting Others First

One of the main principles of servant leadership is the act of putting other's needs ahead of your own. As a leader, we can sometimes think in the 'ME' mentality and want to focus on our own agenda and needs. But in servant leadership, the leader must focus on his tea of employees first before focusing on themselves. The leader should focus on what the employee needs or wants, how they can achieve this and how it will make them successful in the long run. A leader should strive to develop relationships and even friendships with their employees and deliver feedback when possible. They must be able to set their own ego aside and realize that without their team of employees, no one can be successful.

Helping Employees Grow

Once again, as a leader, we can focus on our own goals, responsibilities and even our own challenges. But as a servant leader, the needs of the employee should come first and the main goal should be to help them succeed and grow in the company. A good leader knows that a chain is only as strong as its weakest link, so everyone benefits when every employee is encouraged, mentored and motivated. Sometimes this may mean you'll have to share in successes as well as failures, but every goal set and worked together is another stepping stone for the employee and helps them work toward their ultimate target.

Help employees grow by:

- Encourage goals

- Give feedback when possible

- Listen to their questions and requests

- Offer help but don't complete things for them

Leadership Practices

There are many different types of leaders and each one has a different method and approach to handling conflict and success. However, many leaders often blend different style types together in order to find the right mixture for their employees. A leader must be able to recognize their own characteristics and styles, as well as the employee's personality and attributes in order to determine what style of leadership will work best.

Democratic Leadership Style

Democratic leadership is a type of leadership that utilizes the input and opinions of the team as a whole, rather than just the opinions of a select few. Many decisions are often based on some sort of vote or census from the team and then discussed with everyone. Every team member is allowed to have their voice heard and give their thoughts regarding projects, job duties or general work environment. Employees will feel as though their input is valid and will feel more appreciated in their work. While the democratic leadership can be helpful in big groups, it can be difficult to navigate when making quick, immediate decisions or if a decision must be made against the group conformity.

Characteristics of democratic leadership:

- Uses voting practices

- Employees help shape decisions

- Employees feel more valued

332

- Not optimal for immediate decisions

Laissez-Faire Style

Loosely translated, laissez-faire is a French term that means 'allow to do'. It has grown into a work style that generally allows employees a lot of freedom to perform as they want in order to reach a goal or complete a task. Leaders can still provide support, advice or input if requested but will typically leave the employee to their own means. Many employees enjoy this type of freedom and work better when they feel as though they are not being watched. However, some employees need motivation or help with time management and may not function well in a laissez-faire environment. Also, employees that do not have the necessary knowledge or skills to complete the job will need more instruction from the manager and will require the leader to regain control of the team and become more active in leadership.

Characteristics of laissez-faire leadership:

- Allows a lot of freedom among employees

- Do not get involved in work flow

- Some employees may lack motivation

- Managers could lose control of the team

Leading by Example

As a leader, especially a servant leader, it is your responsibility to work to inspire your employees and encourage them to reach and succeed for more. One of the best ways you can do that is to show them the way – leading them by your example. Commonly known as "practice what you preach", when you lead by example, you demonstrate to your employees that their success is possible; you show them that they can achieve their goals and can strive for what they want. Employees will still need the guidance, motivation and even structure as they grow, so it's important that leaders still work alongside their employees and be accessible to them when needed.

To lead by example:

- Remember that employees look to you

- Inspire and motivate employees

- Give feedback – both positive and negative

Path-Goal Theory

The path-goal theory is a leadership theory written by Robert House that a leader should change their leadership style based on the situation at hand. It recognizes that not all employee or all problems are the same and may require different approaches. The path-goal theory not only focuses on how the leader can help lead their employees, but is also based on what the employees need/want, such as more structure, types of feedback or simply time to work on their own. This theory claims that the leader should want to help their employees identify and achieve their goals, assisting them along their growth path, and in the end offer rewards or incentives for their achievements; and in order to do so, the leader must be flexible in their approach and leadership style.

Types of leadership under the path-goal theory:

- Supportive leadership – focuses on building relationships

- Directive leadership – communicate tasks, goals, and expectations

- Participative leadership – work directly alongside your employees

- Achievement-orientated leadership – set goals and tasks for your team to complete

Share the Power

For some leaders, learning to share the power can be one of the hardest obstacles they face. After all, leaders are supposed to have a sense of power and use it when they can! But a servant leader knows that when they share the power with their employees, learn to be empathetic and share successes with employees, they in turn gain more power in the end and become an even better leader.

Being Empathetic

Being empathetic toward employees can seem like an easy concept, but many leaders actually do not practice empathy with their team, which can lead to unhappy employees. Empathy should not be confused with sympathy – empathy allows you to put yourself in someone else's shoes and see how they feel. By being empathetic, leaders are able to share the power by metaphorically getting on the employee's levels and understand the problems and challenges they face and how it affects the work they do. It shows the employee that their leader listens to their problems and recognize their efforts, which in turn can actually boost their confidence and create a desire to work harder for their leader.

Be more empathetic:

- Use active listening

- Understand personal challenges or obstacles

- Do not mistake empathy for weakness

Learn to Delegate

Many leaders have a problem with proper delegation. Many leaders fear delegating tasks because they fear the employee may not complete the task the right way, so the leader develops the old attitude that "if you want something done right, you've got to do it yourself". However, this type of thinking can be harmful to the servant leader and their team of employees. A leader must learn to delegate to not only ensure that they are not doing all of the work themselves, but delegating also instills a sense of trust among the employees when they know that their leader can trust them to do something right.

Tips for delegating:

- Assign the right task to the right person

- Give clear instructions

- Ensure understanding before releasing

- Follow up

Their Success is Your Success

This element of servant leadership is the easiest to comprehend: a leader knows that when their employees succeed, they succeed as well. There is no 'I' in team. Once again, a chain is only as strong as its weakest link, so if one link breaks, the whole chain falls apart. But if every link is strong and capable, then the chain can withstand almost anything. A leader must work with their employees by coaching them, guiding them, offering advice and help when needed in order to help them meet deadlines, achieve their goals and grow professionally. As employees succeed and become an asset to the company, leaders will feel the success as well because they will have the satisfaction of knowing that the employee reached success with their help and will continue to do great work under their guidance.

Know When to Step In

As a servant leader, it is a natural desire to want to serve our employees and to assist them in every challenge that they face. It's natural to want to hold their hand at times until they have finally reached their goal. But a leader must also know when they need to step back from the employee and when is the right time to step in and help. Employees should possess the right knowledge and skills to work a task or complete a project. Of course the employee will face challenges or have trouble in some area, but the employee must first try to work out the problem themselves. Although a leader may observe the employee and see when they are challenged, the leader must know that it is appropriate to stand back while the employee works through the problem. Only when the employee cannot progress further or is at a point in which they do not have any skills or knowledge of, the leader can step in and offer help or guidance. It can be a hard balance between letting the employee work on their own to learn more and doing everything with them every step of the way, but a servant leader can find an equilibrium somewhere in between and benefit both the employee and the leader.

Characteristics of a Servant Leader

There are many qualities and characteristics that define a servant leader, including good listening skills, empathy, power of persuasion and great communication skills. Although a servant leader may develop or follow different leadership styles, they must all possess some of these main qualities and characteristics in order to become a great servant leader to their employees.

Listening Skills

Great listening skills can be an important tool in any position. Leaders must be able to listen to their employees and actually hear what they are saying and what they are needing. Active listening is a common tool used in improving listening skills because it involves listening without distractions and then periodically repeating back what is heard for clarification. Good listening skills also include being able to remove distractions, never interrupting while someone is speaking, and paying attention to non-verbal communication, such as body language, tone and gestures. A servant leader knows that improving their listening skills can improve communication with employees, which in turn can lead to better professional relationships.

Improve your listening skills by:

- Actively listen

- Avoid interruption

- Give your undivided attention

- Notice non-verbal communication

Persuasive Powers

Some leaders confuse power and authority with the ability of persuasion. But persuasion is a powerful tool that can be used without, well, power. Persuasion is the art of using your knowledge and expertise in order to enlighten and encourage others. It does not use force or backhanded coercion. A servant leader can use persuasion to build unity among the team and conformity when making big decisions. Of course persuasion should always be back by facts and research, so a servant leader should never use persuasion that is based on false information or personal choices. Persuasion builds trust, so leaders must learn to use it effectively.

Help improve your powers of persuasion by:

- Know your facts and do your research

- Aim to educate

- Knowing when to listen to the other side

Recognizes Opportunities

Sometimes when a leader recognizes an opportunity for growth and expansion, it is often referred to as foresight. Generally, a servant leader can recognize an employee's potential or certain skill set and can see an opportunity for them to set a goal or complete a task. Sometimes the leader can simply observe how an employee works and find a good fit for them. Communicating with each employee allows the leader to get to know each employee and build a personal relationship with them. Other times, simple work evaluations can be done in which the leader takes notes about the employee and creates an outcome from their findings. Whatever tools the leader uses, it is always important to listen to their intuition as well and always keep their eyes open.

Common tools to identify opportunities:

- Observe the employee

- Keep open communication with employees

- Perform formal and informal evaluations

Relates to Employees

Being able to relate to an employee is similar to being able to be empathetic, but requires a little more emotional involvement. A leader should be able to relate to an employee by remembering how they got to the position they are in and what leader helped them along the way. Leaders can relate to their employees because they used to be one. When employees need help, or struggle with a task, their leader should be able to relate to their sense of need, rather than criticize or judge them for it. When it's time to delegate tasks, ensure that you are assigning duties and not barking orders or demands. Allow the employee to work on their own as much as possible and let them work on their own confidence level. In the end, employees will feel closer to your equal and less like just another one of your employees.

Barriers to Servant Leadership

We've covered a lot of qualities and characteristics that make a great servant leader, but it is just as important to recognize what can hinder someone as well. Servant leaders are meant to encourage growth and promote confidence in their employees, but delivering excessive criticism, demanding action from employees and simply refusing to engage with them can create the complete opposite effect.

Excessive Criticism

Constructive criticism can be a helpful tool in management when it is used correctly. However, simply delivering criticism to employees without any form of evaluation or redemption is damaging to the employee and the confidence they carry at work. Excessive criticism can cause employees to feel as though they cannot perform their job correctly on many levels, which can lead to a lack of confidence and decreased productivity. A servant leader should review any form of criticism before they deliver it to the employee and determine if it will ultimately be helpful to them and what is the best way to deliver the feedback so it is constructive – not destructive.

Think before delivering criticism:

- Is this helpful?

- Can it be worded more effectively?

- How will the employee perceive this?

- Can I offer any positive notes with it?

Doing Everything Yourself

Learning to delegate is an important step in becoming a great servant leader. When a leader delegates tasks (and not demand action), it shows their confidence in their employees that they will complete the job right without much interference from management. But when a leader decides to simply do every task by themselves, it can not only create a very large workload for them to do, but it loses the faith of the employees and can weaken professional relationships. As a servant leader, learn to delegate and assign tasks to avoid the workload 'burn out' and show faith and trust in your employee's abilities and skills.

Remember to delegate:

- Show trust in your employees

- Give clear instructions and expectations

- Give employees a chance to ask questions

- Follow up to ensure the task is completed

Sitting on the Sidelines

A servant leader knows when it is time to step in to help an employee and when it is the right time to step back and observe from a distance. However, if a leader constantly sits on the sidelines, refusing to participate and but still giving orders, they will lose the loyalty of their team and any respect as a leader. A servant leader is involved in their employee's successes and their challenges because they care about their achievements and growth. But a leader who simply sits on the sidelines and does not work alongside their employees shows that they only care about their own agendas and interests. By not participating in the workplace, this leader relays the message that they hold all the power themselves and have no problem telling their employees what to do, but won't actually put in much of their own effort. While employees may work for this type of leader for a short while, they will eventually feel unvalued and under-appreciated, leading them to move on to other areas.

Demanding from Employees

A servant leader knows how to delegate properly and make requests to employees without a sense of demand or threatening. However, many leaders feel that as a leader, they are entitled to demand what they need from their employees and expect them to blindly follow. A demanding leader will not only intimidate their employees to get what they want/need, but they will also demand more from them over time – such as more work to meet a deadline, more duties assigned to them to complete or more time spent at the office for various tasks. But this type of leader is actually not leading at all, but trying to build a herd of followers.

Some employees may follow for the time being, but many employees will not tolerate all of the demands and seek to move on somewhere else.

Building a Team Community

A good leader knows that every member of the team brings a unique talent and aspect to the group. Every employee should work together and complement each other's skills in order to get work done efficiently. But a leader but also be aware of any challenges a team may face, such as clashing personalities, and be prepared to step in and remedy any situation.

Identify the Group Needs

The servant leader knows the purpose of their team and has most likely started defining goals for the group. However, it is important for the leader to also identify the needs of each group member and the group as a whole. Every member is different and every member needs something different from the leader. Some may need further coaching; some may need more independent work while others will simply need periodic feedback from management.

As a group, the needs may be a little more complex. The group will need to have some sort of goal or charter that defines what they are working toward. The group will need to establish what tools or supplies are needed and what days/hours will need to be worked to accomplish their deadline. Identifying the group needs can seem like one of the easier aspects of building a team, but if overlooked, it can weaken the foundation of the group and crumble before the project is finished.

Complement Member Skills

When building a team, it is important to identify every team member and what skills or talents they will bring to the group. Many teams often feature members that are good in various areas, such as bookkeeping, research, public speaking or presentations, so that each member can excel in their area while contributing to the whole team. Rather than have a few members try and handle all aspects of the project, bring on several members that can divide tasks and duties more evenly and will work best as a group. One the leader has gathered all of the team members for the group; it's important to start building relationships among members, so try using some team building activities or begins a Questions and Answers session.

Common team building exercises:

- Great Egg Drop

- Survival Scenario

- Two Truths and a Lie

- The Great Escape

Create Group Goals

Essentially, the group goal should outline why the team was created and what ultimately needs to be done. Once your team or group is assembled, one of the main tasks is to create goals that the whole group can work toward. They can be work oriented, such as setting productivity goals or ultimate deadlines, or can be goals based on group members, such as working together to finish a subproject or goals that aim toward allowing members to get to know each other. The group goal should be created with every member in mind and should include input from each member. Goals that are created together are achieved together.

Tips for created group goals:

- Determine what the ultimate outcome needs to be

- Identify every member's part in the goal

- Take input and opinions from every member

- Create a charter or outline for everyone to see

Encourage Communication

Communication can be a scary thing for newly built teams, or even teams with new members. It is important for a leader to not only encourage communication among team members, but with leaders and management as well. To increase communication among members, encourage employees to get to know one another and build a working relationship. Employees that are more comfortable with each other will communicate better. For leaders and management, host small meetings or gathering to speak with teammates and allow them to give their ideas and inputs, or just talk about problems they are having. Let employees know how to reach you so they can communicate with you when needed. Encourage communication in any way possible so that employees always know how to reach each other and their leaders.

Tips for encouraging communication:

- Welcome input and opinions from team members

- Encourage team members to build relationships

- Schedule small, regular meetings or gatherings

- Stay in contact – whether by phone, email, text, etc.

Be a Motivator

Motivation is an important tool to use in the workplace because it keeps employees uplifted and inspired to keep moving forward. But every employee responds to different methods of motivations, so the leader must be able to know what makes their employees tick and what works for them. Employees work best in an environment where their feel their leader is behind them and gives them a good reason to do great work.

Make it Challenging

It can be difficult for a leader to make the workplace a challenge because they may not be aware of what their employees can handle at one time. But a servant leader should be aware of the term 'grow or go' that is often used in the workplace. 'Grow and go' is a concept that means if a team leader or other management does not challenge the employee or make a stimulating workplace (i.e. 'grow'), the employee may 'go' elsewhere. This could mean they leave the company entirely, or it can refer to their sense of confidence and willingness to work. A servant leader can help keep the workplace interesting by helping the employee grow in their own area, as well as others, by allowing them to expand their job duties or take on additional projects. Never feel threatened by those that want to take on more, but welcome the challenge they seek in new opportunities.

Provide Resources

Sometimes the simplest form of motivation is ensuring the employee has everything they need to succeed. This can refer to physical resources, such as supplies, team members or training materials. Resources can also include personal support, such as encouragement and feedback. After all, employees cannot do their job right if they do not have all the resources that they need. As a leader, let your team know that you are a valuable resource they can use, especially if they need something they cannot acquire on their own.

Common types of resource to provide:

- Physical supplies, such as paper, pen, computers, scanners, etc.

- Additional training materials or class time

- Emotional support and encouragement

- Coworker and other management support teams

Ask for Employee Input

Sometimes a leader can struggle with finding ways to motivate their employees, but the simple solution is to just ask the employees what they want. Seek out the employee's input on various topics, such as how they like to be rewarded, what drives them to do better, or simply ask what their leader can do to make their job easier. Most employees are eager to share what make them happy and will feel valued while giving their thoughts and opinions. Now that the leader knows what makes their employees happy and productive, they can use the information find better ways of keeping them motivated.

Methods of gaining employee input:

- Add a suggestion box

- Hold open discussion meetings

- Invite employees for one-on-one sessions

Offer Incentives

Bonus and incentive programs are a popular motivation tool for many employees. Incentives can come in many forms, such as monetary bonuses, gifts, special titles or even manager recognition. Some employees may not respond to certain types of incentives, so a leader should recognize different forms of incentives and know which ones are best for their team. It is important to know the difference between an incentive and a bribe for good work. Employees want to feel rewarded for the work they have not – not like they are being coerced with a small gift to work harder.

Tips creating incentive ideas:

- Determine what forms of incentives motivate the team

- Gain employee input about existing incentive programs

- Develop clear performance goals for all employees

Be a Mentor

Being a mentor can sometimes be lost in terms such as 'manager' or even 'coach', but mentors are a valuable tool to many workplaces. Mentors can be helpful to new employees or to employees who have begun to lose confidence in their work. A good leader must also take on this mentor role and ensure their employees are getting the boost they may need.

Establish Goals

One of the best tools a mentor can give their employee is the ability to establish and set goals for themselves. Start by asking the employee what they want to achieve and how they want to reach it. Individual goals can include work issues, such as increased productivity or decreased distractions, or can be more personal, such as working to decrease personal absences. When working with a team, leaders should ensure each member has their own set of goals, and then establish goals for the team as a whole. This ensures that everyone has a goal to work toward on their own, as well as a goal to work with the rest of the team. Goals help everyone stay focused and can make them feel valued as an individual and as a group.

Tips for helping set goals:

- Ask the employee what they want to achieve

- Outline a path that can help get them there (there may be more than one)

- Determine a reward or incentive for when the goal is reached

Know When to Praise or Criticize

As a leader and a mentor, it can be difficult when to determine an employee should be criticized or reprimanded, or when open praise will be an effective tool. Praise and compliments are a great tool for building confidence in employees, but too much can lose its luster. Employees that are over praised may begin to lose faith in what their mentor is saying and lose the desire to work hard for that well earned praise. On the other hand, employees that are over criticized or chastised may lose self-confidence and pride in their work, causing them to create more errors and low productivity.

Praise and negativity should be based on the individual employee, not the group. If you must criticize, always do so in private and use phrases that are not personal attacks. With every negative point, offer a positive note as well to counterbalance. Let the employee know that you are there to help them, not attack them. Additionally, use praise and kudos when an employee has shown a change in their productivity, such as meeting a goal or over-succeeding on a quota. Do not use praises for everyday tasks and accomplishments or they will lose their value and will no longer feel like something special.

Create a Supportive Environment

In order to mentor and bring together a team of employees, a leader must be able to create a supportive environment for them to work in. After all, employees do not want to feel like the workplace is a place that should be feared and only generates criticism or humiliation. A servant leader should act as a mentor by creating an environment that is safe and supportive to employees, where they do not fear you or other employees. Visit with employees periodically and build a sense of comfort and trust so that communication is always open. Let employees know you are available if they need you and take the time to speak with them if you are approached. Your employees will appreciate the support and in turn will feel confident that they are not alone in the office.

Benefits of a creating a supportive environment:

- Employees are happier working together

- Employees feel comfortable approaching you with their problems or ideas

- Employees are more receptive to feedback

Create an Open Door Policy

Whether you are mentoring a new employee or an entire new group, one of the first things to establish is an open door policy for the office. Let your employees know they can come to you with any problems or concerns they are having – or even with positive ideas they want to share. Seeing someone as a leader can be intimidating or downright scary, so assure employees that you are there for them and want to support them in their goals and challenges. Give them ways to reach out to you, whether it in your office, by phone or by email, but also establish simple boundaries, such as best times to contact or following a chain of command with management. Your employees will value your time and feel as though you are there for them – not just for the job.

Tips for creating an open door policy:

- Ensure everyone is aware of the policy

- Be open to listen to the employees and their needs.

- Always be approachable – avoid becoming too distant.

- Establish boundaries that allow employees to reach you, but by appropriate means/times

Training Future Leaders

As a servant leader, one of the best qualities you can possess is the ability to instill servant leadership into another leader. Training future leaders takes many processes and cannot be completed overnight. Take the time to teach great values for a leader, such as a desire to serve, the ability to be empathetic, and the knowledge of how to motivate employees.

Offer Guidance and Advice

It can be very frightening and intimidating for a leader in training to begin to learn all they need to know to become a great servant leader. The amount of information and training can feel overwhelming and make the trainee question if the decision is right for them. But as their leader and their trainer, it is up to you to help them through these challenges and help them achieve their goal. Offer guidance when needed and give advice on areas they may not be familiar with yet. This can include training materials they can take with them, personal one-on-one time or even personal advice that you found helpful. Share stories of when you were training to be a leader and let them know that you are empathetic to their needs. Sharing personal experience can be a great ice breaker and it lets your trainee know that you've been where they are now.

Identify Their Skill Sets

When training future leaders, one aspect of their training is to identify their skill sets and what talents they possess. While basic leadership skills, such as organization, strategic thinking, and problem solving skills, are necessary for a leader in training, it is also important to identify other skill sets they may also possess to enhance their leadership. Many candidates possess skills sets such as enhanced sales abilities, great communication skills, extended computer knowledge or good public speaking skills. The training leader should take the time to identify these skills in their trainee, which can be done in several different methods, including formal evaluations, direct observations, or simply speaking with the trainee one-on-one.

Methods of Feedback

Feedback is a very important tool during training. Not only will the trainee learn to receive feedback and gain knowledge about how they are doing, but they will learn how to give feedback to others and use when they are a leader on their own. Provide feedback to the trainee as they learn and let them know what areas they are excelling in and which areas need more work. Give praise when appropriate and allow time to set goals and targets. When training on how to deliver feedback, go over several different methods of feedback, such as informal versus informal methods, and tools that can be used in the process, such as surveys or evaluations. Different methods of feedback can be effective on different types of people, so it is important to know the different ways of delivering feedback so it can have the most effect.

Common types of feedback:

- Formal vs. informal

- Employee evaluation

- Feedback sandwich – using both negative and positive feedback

- The 3x3 method – utilizing three pieces of feedback in one

Establish Long Term Goals

When leaders are first brought onto a team or training area, one of the first things they do is establish a goal. Typically, these goals are short term, such as a goal to during their training session or a goal to achieve in the next few months after training. But when training future leaders, it is important for them to be able to set goals that are long term and require more time and work to achieve. Together, the trainer and trainee should establish long term goals and outline ways that goal can be reached within a certain amount of time. The goal should be realistic and reachable. Outline milestones and progress points you want to see while they work toward the goal. Of course, let your trainee know that you are there to help them when needed and your door is open to them. Remind them that they are not going to have to go on their path all alone.

Tips for making long term goals:

- Establish what the trainee wants to accomplish

- Set a realistic time frame

- Outline progress points or milestones to reach

- Schedule periodic meetings to check on their status and progress

Self-Reflection

When the day is done and the employees have gone home, where does that leave you – the servant leader? While it is important to take care of your employees and help them grow to succeed, you cannot forget to help yourself grow and pay attention to what you want to gain or achieve. A servant leader has to have a desire to serve not only others, but themselves.

Keep a Journal

It may sound elementary, but keeping a journal of your goals, desires, progress and even current projects can not only be therapeutic, but can help you keep track of where you've been, where you are at now, and what you want to reach in the future. It can be a great tool for tracking different ideas, opinions or general feelings during training or working with employees. Don't be afraid to record any problems or frustrations you may be facing because the goal is to obtain honest self-reflection. Makes notes of areas you are doing well in and identify areas in which you think need more work. While you may be training and teaching others, don't forget to take the time to note your own challenges and achievements.

Types of journals:

- Handwritten or paper journals

- Web blogs

- Audio journals

Identify Your Strengths and Weaknesses

You spend all day evaluating your employees and future leaders to determine their strengths and skills and what areas they need more help with. But have you ever stopped to evaluate yourself? As a servant leader, it is important for you to identify your own strengths and weaknesses. Of course you have common leadership traits, but what other strengths do you bring to the table? On the other hand, what are your weaknesses that you need to address? What areas do you need to request help with? A good tool for this exercise is a simple written evaluation of yourself, but you can also use formal job assessments that identify job strengths and weaknesses, and of course a one-on-one conversation with a colleague can be a real eye opener.

The goal of this exercise is to be honest with ourselves. We cannot gain knowledge or seek help if we do not identify that there is a problem. If there is an area we excel in and identify as a strength, don't be afraid to 'hone' those skills and share them with others.

Identify Your Needs

A servant leader has the desire to serve their employees and help them in their areas of need. But a leader cannot forget to identify their own needs as well. Sometimes we have to admit when we are in need of something and not be afraid to seek help. You may be a leader, but you are not invincible. Maybe you need more help developing training courses? Maybe you need more help learning computer programs? Or maybe you just need help getting the office organized or in order. Some needs may be more personal, such as a need for personal growth or a need for some time to yourself. Whatever your need turns out to be, it is important to not bury them inside and try to solve them all yourself. Don't be afraid to reach out to others and request help with meeting your own needs.

Creating Your Own Goals

As a leader, one of the first exercises you stress to employees is to establish goals for them to work toward. This practice is the same for you. When you begin a new segment at work, whether it is training a group of leaders or creating a new team to work with, you should take the time to create goals of your own to work on. Periodically check in on these goals to see if you are moving on the right path or identify areas you still need to work toward. Don't be afraid to create long term goals as well that may take more time to accomplish. When you finish, determine if you can achieve these goals on your own or if you will need help from an outside source to do so. Don't be afraid to reach out to others for help achieving your own goals and desires.

Tips for creating your own goals:

- Make them realistic

- Make goals for work and for personal life

- Set tentative timelines

- Identify if you will need help in certain areas to reach your goals

Chapter 20 - Leadership and Influence

They say that leaders are born, not made. While it is true that some people are born leaders, some leaders are born in the midst of adversity. Often, simple people who have never had a leadership role will stand up and take the lead when a situation they care about requires it. A simple example is parenting. When a child arrives, many parents discover leadership abilities they never knew existed in order to guide and protect their offspring. There are countless war stories of simple GI's and sailors who rose to a challenge on their own in the heat of battle.

Clearly, leadership potential exists within each of us. That potential can be triggered by outside events, or it can be learned by exploring ourselves from within. This training takes the latter approach. Once you learn the techniques of true leadership, you will be able to build the confidence it takes to take the lead. The more experience you have acting as a genuine leader, the easier it will be for you. It is never easy to take the lead, as you will need to make decisions and face challenges, but it can become natural and rewarding.

Leadership is not telling others what to do. Leadership is inspiring others to do what needs to be done. Many people around the world who are in leadership positions are not leaders. Dictators call themselves leaders but they are not – they are tyrants. There have been many presidents of the United States, but few were real leaders. Genuine leaders take a stand and motivate others to join them in a noble purpose. One such leader was Abraham Lincoln, who ended slavery in the United States. Another was John F. Kennedy, who inspired a nation to go to the moon within a decade, and it did. General Patton had a completely different but no less effective leadership style. What is it that makes a leader, and what separates the good from the great? This workshop will explore different leadership theories and examine what makes a great leader.

Influence is subtle, yet incredibly powerful. You can order someone to do a task, but you cannot order them to do their best. It simply does not work and usually has the opposite effect. You can influence people to do their best by providing a strong, motivating example in addition to positive reinforcement. Leadership addresses tasks, while influence addresses attitudes and awareness. Influence is the soul of leadership.

By the end of this chapter, you will be able to:

- Define "leadership"

- Explain the Great Man Theory

- Explain the Trait Theory

- Understand Transformational Leadership

- Understand the people you lead and how to adapt your leadership styles

- Explain leading by Directing

- Explain leading by Coaching

- Explain leading by Participating

- Explain leading by Delegating

- Kouzes and Posner

- Conduct a personal inventory

- Create an action plan

- Establish personal goals

The Evolution of Leadership

As long as there have been leaders, there have been those who tried to determine how and why they were successful. Leadership itself has not evolved, but our understanding of it has. It is important to understand why very different leadership styles can be effective, why the same leadership techniques will not work in every situation, and which leadership style fits your personality best. Everyone has leadership potential within them, but understanding these concepts will help you maximize your leadership ability.

Defining Leadership

Simply speaking, "leadership" is defined as "the ability to lead." Unfortunately, this is not very helpful. A better definition comes from the BNET online Business Dictionary: *"The capacity to establish direction and to influence and align others toward a common goal, motivating and committing them to action and making them responsible for their performance."* Although this is more descriptive, it is not substantial. It does not tell us what leadership actually *is*, but rather what it *does*.

Characteristics of a Leader

The mark of a true leader is not a position or title held, but it is how many people are willing to follow them. Santa Clara University and the Tom Peters group outline the following leadership characteristics:

- Honest

- Competent

- Forward-looking

- Inspiring

- Intelligent

- Fair-minded

- Broad-minded

- Courageous

- Straightforward

- Imaginative

Leadership Principles

The United States Army offers 11 Leadership Principles:

- Be tactically and technically proficient

- Know yourself and seek self-improvement

- Know your soldiers and look out for their welfare

- Keep your soldiers informed

- Set the example

- Ensure the task is understood, supervised and accomplished

- Train your soldiers as a team

- Make sound and timely decisions

- Develop a sense of responsibility in your subordinates

- Employ your unit in accordance with its capabilities

- Seek responsibility and take responsibility for your actions

You will notice that none of the above actually tells you *how to lead* in a practical manner. They don't address what to do or say in any given situation. That is because there is no real formula to being a leader. Leadership must come from within and it is based on your personality. In this training, you will learn how to develop your innate leadership abilities and build the confidence required in being a true leader.

A Brief History of Leadership

Historical Leaders

Throughout the centuries, there have been leaders. We are social animals who bond together, but we look for order against the chaos of life. We look to be organized to accomplish tasks as a society that we cannot perform individually. As a result, someone inevitably ends up in charge.

Leaders in the past have generally belonged to one of three categories: Political, Military or Religious.

- Political: Around 1790 B.C., Babylonian ruler Hammurabi created the codified laws, which unified his empire in what was seen as a fair order as all people were subject to the same rules.

- Military: Sun Tzu was a military general in China from 500 B.C. He wrote the Art of War, and although he was a great military leader, his book is actually about how to *not* use armies except as a last resort, focusing more on wise political policies and strategies to prevent war.

- Religious: It may be said that religious leaders have had the greatest impact on their societies, with results that last for centuries.

Modern Leaders

With the rise of the industrial revolution, a new kind of leader emerged: Economic. The so-called Captains of Industry found they could build an empire based on modern technology instead of swords. Oil Barons, railroad magnates, and factory owners built large fortunes without the benefit of armies; it was often at the expense of the people they employed. This gave rise to Union leaders and various movements designed to promote justice where abuses were perceived to exist.

The Industrial Revolution also increased the number of Scientific Leaders, as scientists now had easy access to a wide range of new materials for their work. Psychiatry and Psychology came into prominence with studies on the workplace, in regards to improving productivity and the effect on the workforce.

Studies have shown consistently that workers are more productive when they are in a "positive work environment." The attitude and influence of the boss is a major factor in this productivity. If employees feel they are listened to, respected, and treated fairly, they are happier in their work and perform better than those who feel they are disrespected and unappreciated. Which kind of work environment would *you* prefer?

Three Theories of Leadership

The Great Man Theory

The Great Man Theory was abandoned in favor of the theories of behavioral science. It's easy to be inspired by stories of great men and women who did great things in their lives. Alexander the Great conquered the known world. Genghis Khan then ravaged most of it. Abraham Lincoln freed the slaves. Harriet Tubman saved hundreds from slavery in the Underground Railroad. Mother Theresa aided and comforted thousands in Calcutta who were abandoned by society. Theory goes that these people did great things because they were simple great people determined by fate and fulfilling their destiny.

The Trait Theory

It has often been said, *"Great leaders are born, not made."* Trait Theory takes this saying literally. If you have the ability to lead, you were born with it, with no way to learning those skills. This theory expands on the Great Man Theory by defining what makes great leaders "great."

Today, we recognize that true leadership seems to come from a combination of both theories – and more. As we have seen, there are wide varieties of leadership qualities. Everyone has some ability in at least one or more of these areas. This means that under the right circumstances, anyone can rise to a leadership role and be successful based on the leadership style that best matches their personality if they know how to use that ability to properly address the situation at hand. Other leadership skills can indeed be learned, developed, and mastered.

Transformational Leadership

In 1978, James MacGregor Burns introduced the idea of transformational leadership as he researched political leaders. Burns theorized that "transformational leadership" is actually a process where leaders interact with their followers and inspire each other to advance together. His characteristics and behaviors demonstrated the differences between "management" and "leadership." People and organizations are transformed due to the leadership style and abilities of the leader, who is able to convey a vision and guide the transformation.

Bernard M. Bass, in 1985, added to Burns' transformational leadership theory buy shifting the focus to the followers. It is not the individual traits and vision of the leader that matter as much as it is their ability to influence the feelings, attitudes, and commitment of their followers. As we mentioned before in productivity studies, if followers feel they can trust a leader (or better yet, if they admire a leader who can stimulate a sense of loyalty and respect) the followers go beyond what was originally expected of them and will do so happily. As a result, productivity and unity increases. The followers are transformed by a charismatic, motivational leader.

Summary

Through all of the studies, we have seen that there are a variety of attributes and abilities associated with leadership, and these vary from leader to leader. Some leaders are great orators, others great writers. Some leaders are very quiet, but the force of their logic or passion wins the day. The difference between a good leader and a great leader is partly the number of leadership skills they have developed. The other part is their ability to apply those skills properly to those who would follow. We will address these issues in the next section.

Situational Leadership

Now we get to the nuts and bolts of leadership. The definitive leadership style research comes from Paul Hersey and Kenneth Blanchard, which they expressed in their Situational Leadership Model. The Hersey-Blanchard model addresses the key to practical leadership development: the attributes and styles of the *followers*.

Not everyone is on the same intellectual, maturity, compliance, or motivational level. Different people are motivated by different things, and this must be taken into account if one is to be a great leader. Communications experts consider it critical to tailor your message to your "target audience." It is the followers that you want to motivate and influence and you cannot do that if you don't know whom you are trying to motivate or influence.

The Situational Leadership model addresses four types of leadership styles, based on the follower:

- Telling

- Selling

- Participating

- Delegating

The goal is to develop followers to the Delegating level as seen below:

Situational Leadership: Telling

Telling is the lowest level of leadership style. Most new employees require direct instructions, so this is called the "Telling" or "Directing" style. The follower is characterized by low competence and high commitment, being unable to comply, with possible feelings of insecurity.

The leader must focus highly on tasks, rather than a relationship with the employee, as a relationship does not yet exist.

When an employee can't do the job because they are unknowledgeable, the leader must spend much more time working with the employee, offering clear instructions and regular follow up. The leader must be encouraging and motivational, offering praise for positive results and correction for less than positive results. The idea is to motivate the follower to rise to the next level of ability.

Situational Leadership Model

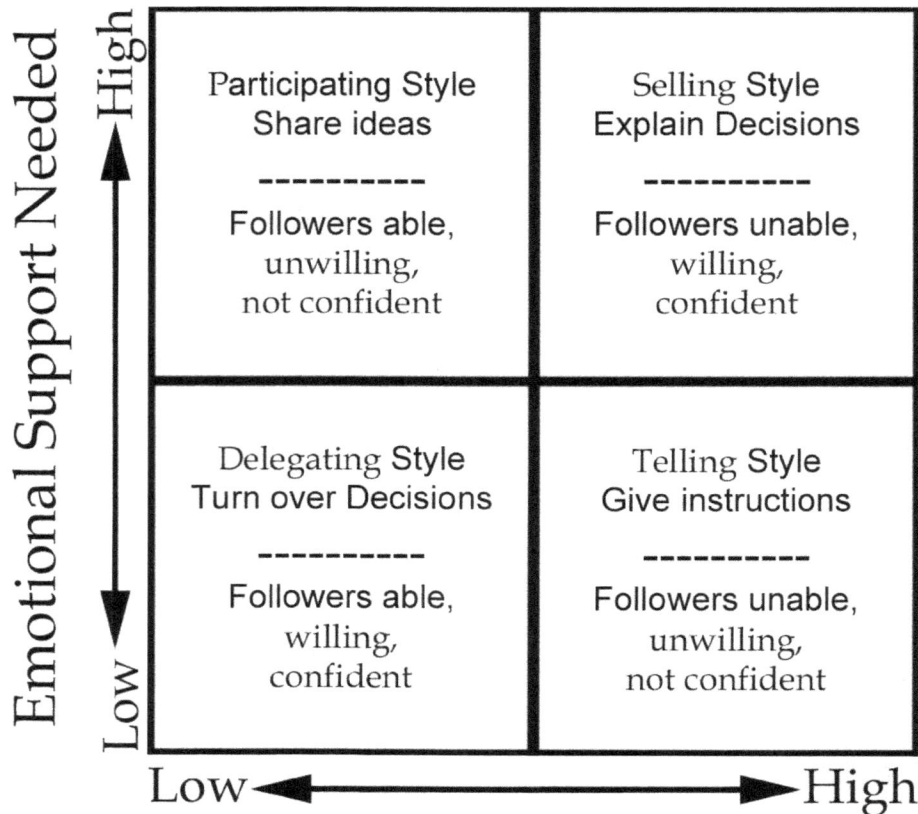

Emotional Support Needed (High ↕ Low)	**Participating Style** Share ideas ---------- Followers able, unwilling, not confident	**Selling Style** Explain Decisions ---------- Followers unable, willing, confident
	Delegating Style Turn over Decisions ---------- Followers able, willing, confident	**Telling Style** Give instructions ---------- Followers unable, unwilling, not confident

Low ◄─────────────► High

This is a very leader-driven stage.

Situational Leadership: Selling

Selling addresses the follower who has developed some competence with an improved commitment. The follower is not convinced yet, but is open to becoming cooperative and motivated.

The leader must still focus highly on tasks and this still requires much of the leader's time, but the focus now also includes developing a relationship with the employee. Build upon the trust that has begun to develop and the encouragement that has been demonstrated. The leader must spend more time listening and offering advice, scheduling the follower for additional training if the situation requires it.

The goal is to engage the follower so they can develop to the next level. There is less "telling" and more "suggesting" which leads to more encouragement, acting as a coach. It is recognition that they have progressed and motivates them to progress even further.

This is a very leader-driven stage.

Situational Leadership: Participating

Participating addresses the follower who is now competent at the job, but remains somewhat inconsistent and is not yet fully committed. The follower may be uncooperative or performing as little work as possible, despite their competence with the tasks

The leader must participate with and support the follower. The leader no longer needs to give detailed instructions and follow up as often, but does need to continue working with the follower to ensure the work is being done at the level required.

The follower is now highly competent, but is not yet convinced in his or her ability or not fully committed to do their best and excel. The leader must now focus less on the tasks assigned and more on the relationship between the follower, the leader, and the group.

This is a very follower-driven, relationship-focused stage.

Situational Leadership: Delegating

Delegating is the ultimate goal: a follower who feels fully empowered and competent enough to take the ball and run with it, with minimal supervision. The follower is highly competent, highly committed, motivated, and empowered.

The leader can now delegate tasks to the follower and observe with minimal follow up, knowing that acceptable or even excellent results will be achieved. There is a low focus on tasks and a low focus on relationships. There is no need to compliment the follower on every task, although continued praise for outstanding performance must be given as appropriate.

This is a very follower-driven stage.

A Personal Inventory

In 2002, Jossey Bass published a book by James Kouzes and Barry Posner called *The Leadership Challenge (Copyright © 2000-2012 by John Wiley & Sons Canada, Ltd, or related companies. All rights reserved.)* Building upon the Hersey-Blanchard model and other transformational leadership models, they went to the heart of what skills are required by the leader to stimulate such a transformation. What abilities are able to influence followers and bring them to accept the leader's vision as their own?

An Introduction to Kouzes and Posner

James Kouzes and Barry Posner asked thousands of people to rank list of characteristics associated with leadership, including the seven top qualities that motivated them to follow willingly. They gave this survey to over 75,000 people over a 20-year period.

In their book, *The Leadership Challenge (Copyright © 2000-2012 by John Wiley & Sons Canada, Ltd, or related companies. All rights reserved.)* the authors identified five abilities that were crucial to successful leadership:

- **Model the Way**: You must lead by example. You can't come into work 10 minutes late every day if you want your employees to arrive on time.

- **Inspire a Shared Vision**: If you capture the imagination, you will inspire creative thought and increase loyalty. The vision doesn't need to be grandiose, but it needs to be communicated effectively for others to adopt it as one of their own.

- **Challenge the Process**: Don't continue doing something just because "We've always done it that way." Situations change, and sometimes a policy or procedure never worked well in the first place. Think outside the box.

- **Enable Others to Act**: Truly empower people to act on their own within their level of authority. The famed Ritz-Carlton hotel empowers every employee at all levels to spend up to $1000 on behalf of a guest (who is informed reimbursement will be required for whatever request they make).

- **Encourage the Heart**: A positive attitude is infectious. If the leader appears passionate or excited about the vision, others will catch the enthusiasm as well.

A Personal Inventory

The results of the Kouzes/Posner study, with the most important quality at the top:

Creating an Action Plan

Now that you understand the various concepts, it's time to plan how to put them into action by incorporating them into your life.

Set Leadership Goals: In leadership, as in life, you will never come to the end of your learning, but you want to rank in priority order those qualities you want to develop.

Address the Goals: Determine how you will accomplish your goals. Do you feel you need to learn more about teamwork so you can better lead a team? Join a team sport. Do you want to communicate better? Take a creative writing class or join Toastmasters and get some public speaking experience. Toastmasters are also great if you are shy and want to feel more comfortable in social situations.

Seek Inspiration: Learn about a variety of leaders, including their styles with dealing with challenges. Read books and conduct research on the internet or at libraries.

Choose a Role Model: Based on your research, choose a role model that fits your personality. You might choose a dynamic leader like Teddy Roosevelt, or an intellectual leader like Albert Schweitzer or Albert Einstein. Read several biographies and find videos on his or her life.

Seek Experience: Take a leadership role on a social group or club. Gain experience working with people on many levels.

Create a Personal Mission Statement: Imagine your legacy. How do you want to be remembered? What do you want people to think of you? What type of leader you determined to be? Write a statement that defines who you will become.

Modeling the Way

Remember that the best leaders are examples of what they want their followers to be. George Washington rode into battle with his troops. You cannot lead from the rear, and sending your followers out to take the heat and face the challenges while you remain in an ivory tower will eliminate any possibility of respect.

By definition, a leader is in the *lead*, right up front, ready to take the heat if something goes wrong. If something does go wrong, a true leader never blames his followers even if in fact they failed. A true leader takes the blame, and then addresses how to correct the problems that arose.

Determining Your Way

Once you have chosen your role model, study what qualities made them successful. Learn about what challenges they faced and how the challenges were met. Learn about the ideas and philosophies that drove them and made them successful. Study again the Hersey- Blanchard model and see how different situations called for different styles of leadership.

Since there is no leader in history who has not had failures, pay particular attention to how your hero deals with adversity. George Washington nearly lost the American Revolution through major hesitations in leadership and in fact, he lost New York to the British general William Howe, but he learned from his mistakes and the rest, as they say, is history.

Being an Inspirational Role Model

Leadership is neither for the timid nor for the arrogant. Confidence is often resented or misinterpreted for arrogance. People who lack self-confidence often feel intimidated by a true leader. This should never hold you back. If you have honesty, integrity and deal with everyone fairly, then others will see that. Be willing to listen to criticism, but also consider the source. If you are too afraid of what others might say about you, or you ignore legitimate complaints insisting on respect solely because of your position, you will lose the respect and cooperation of your followers and peers.

President Theodore Roosevelt said it best:

"It is not the critic who counts; not the man who points out how the strong man stumbles, or where the doer of deeds could have done them better. The credit belongs to the man who is actually in the arena, whose face is marred by dust and sweat and blood, who strives valiantly; who errs and comes short again and again; because there is not effort without error and shortcomings; but who does actually strive to do the deed; who knows the great enthusiasm, the great devotion, who spends himself in a worthy cause, who at the best knows in the end the triumph of high achievement and who at the worst, if he fails, at least he fails while daring greatly. So that his place shall never be with those cold and timid souls who know neither victory nor defeat."

Influencing Others' Perspectives

You may have heard that perception is reality. You must always present an honest, caring, dedicated attitude to inspire others. To inspire loyalty, you must have a track record of honesty and fairness. If any of your followers do feel they have been wronged, for whatever reason, you need to address the issue immediately. People talk, and a problem ignored is a problem that grows.

Believe it or not, the most powerful influence you can have is often not trying to influence someone. When people believe you are open to their suggestions and believe they have been heard, they will work harder even if they disagree with the methods or goals. That is the power of listening. Simply listening to others makes them feel empowered, even if you don't accept their suggestions. If a follower feels there's no point talking to you, they won't, and they will disengage themselves from your vision and will only follow your directions begrudgingly.

If you are seen as going the extra mile, your followers are more likely to go the extra mile. If you hide in your office and people never see you, you will be perceived as out of the loop, uninformed, uninterested, and therefore unworthy to lead. Many a successful corporate executive makes it a point to be seen by their employees every day. If an employee is to be commended for something, it is done publicly, often right in the middle of their workplace while they are surrounded by their coworkers. That sends a powerful message to everyone.

Inspiring a Shared Vision

The key to true leadership is to inspire a shared vision among your followers. Before you can convey a vision, however, you have to develop it. You must be clear in your vision, live it before others can see it, and model it from your behavior.

Choosing Your Vision

What do you want to accomplish, and what do you need to do to get there? Determine attainable goals and focus on them. King Arthur sought the Holy Grail. Lewis and Clark mapped much of the United States. NASA took us to the moon. What is your vision?

Your vision will provide a sense of direction for you and your followers. In the military, focus is on "the mission." Whatever the mission is, everyone is dedicated to it. Let your vision be like a lighthouse on a hill, guiding ships to safety and warning them away from the rocks.

Communicating Your Vision

Communication is more than just the words you say or the memos you write. Remember, actions speak louder than words. Take every opportunity to communicate your vision in words and deeds. One of the best ways to communicate a vision is to sum it up in a simple catch phrase.

Post your slogan, catch phrase and mission statement in prominent locations. When you send out emails, list it in quotes below your signature block. Hold meetings occasionally or hand out "Visionary Awards" to people who exemplify your vision. Above all, lead by example.

Identifying the Benefit for Others

Answer the question, "What's in it for me?" as if you were one of your own followers. The answer might not always be obvious. Certainly, performance bonuses and awards work, but most followers enjoy being part of a larger, successful organization. Everyone loves a winner. When the home team wins at the stadium, you would think the fans in the stand were the players by the way they share in the victory and excitement.

We are social creatures who like to feel like we belong. We crave acceptance. If you can get your followers to accept your vision as their own, and excite them about being part of it, they will often excel beyond what you (or they) thought possible. Be sure to reward loyalty and performance above and beyond the call of duty.

Challenging the Process

Far too often, we cling to what is familiar, even if what we cling to is known to be inadequate. Most large groups are governed by the law of inertia: if it takes effort to change something, nothing will change. As a leader, you must search out opportunities to change, grow, innovate, and improve.

There is no reward without risk however, so you must be willing to experiment, take risks, and learn from any mistakes. Ask questions, even if you fear the answers. Start with the question, "Why?" Why are things the way they are? Why do we do things the way we do?

Think Outside the Box

A *paradigm* is an established model or structure. Sometimes they work quite well, but often they are inadequate or even counterproductive. Sometimes it is necessary to "think outside the box" and break the paradigm. Don't be afraid to ask the question "Why?" Ask questions of your followers, employees, customers, former leaders. Answers and ideas can be found in the least likely places. Often the lowest ranking persons in an organization can tell you exactly what is wrong because they see it daily from their vantage points.

Developing Your Inner Innovator

Innovation is more than just improvement on a process or procedure; it is a total redirection or restructuring based upon stated goals and research. While it can be helpful to adapt an outdated procedure or task to today's standards, often the procedure itself is the problem, not the manner in which it is implemented. Innovators reverse engineer policies and procedures based on the new vision and goals, working from the target backwards, rather than from the status quo looking forward.

To be sure, not all innovative strategies will be feasible or cost effective. Requiring an entirely new computerized network and infrastructure, for example, may cost hundreds of thousands of dollars and produce little improved efficiency over the old one. However, if you don't start thinking "outside the box," you will miss many valuable solutions that can and will work.

Note that change should never be made simply for the sake of change. Change can be exciting, but it can also be unnerving and difficult for employees. Constant change causes frustration. Moreover, if you seem to change too many things too often, you will lose respect, as your followers perceive you don't really know what you are doing, so be sure to plan your innovations carefully. There should be solid evidence that a new way of doing things is likely to work before you invest money and everyone's time.

Keep focused on the goals and be willing to break the rules if they need to be broken. Just make sure they really need to be broken and you don't break something that needs to keep working! With proper research and planning, you can dare to be bold!

Seeing Room for Improvement

A strong vision does not lend itself to mediocrity. A drive to excellence always seeks improvement. If you accept 95% efficiency as a goal, the efficiency will inevitably slip to 90%. If that's considered "good enough," it will become hard to keep it above 85% and so on. A vision is a goal that is strived to achieve.

Goals must not be unrealistic or unattainable, or the followers will simply give up trying altogether, becoming dispirited and demoralized in the process. If 95% of people fail to meet a standard, then that standard is likely too high and must be changed. On the other hand, the bar must not be set so low that little or no effort is required to meet it.

Based on your vision, set high goals that are attainable but with some degree of difficulty, and reward those who meet the goals. If a large number of followers are meeting the goal, raise the target. If only a very few are meeting it, lower it somewhat.

Investigate any potential bottlenecks that might be stifling progress and resolve them. Talk to your followers about possible solutions. The people who actually do the work are far more likely to be able to tell you why they are having difficulty accomplishing a task than their supervisors.

Lobbying for Change

To lobby for change, you need to influence people and excite them to your vision. You may need to persuade a reluctant boss or fight a corporate culture that doesn't understand what you are trying to do. In that case, you need to demonstrate why your requested change needs to occur.

Do your research, and always enter a meeting by being prepared. Study the situation and present all of your findings in a short report, preferably with simple charts or graphs. Give them something they can easily understand. Have the details ready in case you are asked a question, but don't overload people with facts. Show as clearly as possible how your plan will effect positive change.

If you are lobbying your own followers, the same is true. You may want to revolutionize a cultural change. Perhaps you are a shop manager and people are unmotivated. You may need to bring about change slowly, rather than with one big dramatic gesture. On the other hand, you may need to shake things up in a big way. Whatever the situation, you can successfully lobby for change if you attack the problem with a plan, sound reasoning, and infectious enthusiasm!

Enabling Others to Act

As mentioned before, you cannot do your followers' work for them. Besides, if you do their work, what are they getting paid for? You have your own work to do. This is the ultimate goal of the Hersey-Blanchard situational Leadership model: to develop your followers to the point where you can delegate tasks without a lot of oversight.

To be a true leader, you must enable others to act responsibly and not encourage bad worker habits by compensating for them or overlooking them. At the same time, you cannot berate a follower for trying hard but making an honest mistake. The goal of a leader is to empower others to work. To the extent that you can do this is the extent that you will be successful.

Encouraging Growth in Others

A positive attitude is essential to encouragement. No one likes to fail and many take it very personally. While failure should never be rewarded, an understanding attitude and positive outlook can work wonders. A child only learns to walk by falling down many times. The focus is not on the fall, but on getting up. The goal is to walk…then to run.

Meeting with an employee one-on-one is important to positive motivation. Here again, you must use the power of listening. Avoid blame when something goes wrong and focus on the reason for the failure. You may learn someone needs more training, more self-confidence, or more freedom. You may learn someone does not have the tools needed to be successful. You will never know if you don't ask questions and listen – or worse, if you berate someone for a failure.

If someone is willfully defiant, then feel free to be stern and resolute. Take disciplinary action if necessary and document the conversation. If you allow someone to be defiant or lazy out of a misplaced concern for his or her feelings, you will be performing a great injustice against the rest who are working hard. In most cases, people really do want to do a good job and they have a sense of pride when they meet a challenge.

Creating Mutual Respect

You will never be worthy of respect if you don't give respect. Respect should be given to everyone at all levels unless they deliberately do something to lose that respect.

You need to build respect in other ways as well. Be visible to your followers. Show them you are available and interested in knowing everything about what they do. Develop and demonstrate your knowledge of the organization and details of the product, service, or operation. If you are perceived as being knowledgeable and can answer questions, you will not only earn respect, but will motivate others to learn as well.

The Importance of Trust

Respect inevitably leads to trust. Do what you say and say what you mean. Under-promise and over-deliver can help manage expectations. If you are given a task you know will take you one hour, say you "should" have it done in two hours. You never know when you'll get a phone call that eats into your time or when an emergency may pop up. If you get done in less than two hours, you will be perceived as a hero. If not, you can call and apologize that it will be "a little later" without much trouble because you said you *should* have it done. You didn't promise that you *would* have it done. If people feel they can rely on you, they will trust you.

Also let people know that you are not asking them to do anything you would not do yourself, or have done in the past. Work hard and be seen working hard. If you come in early and see others who are there early as well, stop by and simply mention that fact positively. A simple word of recognition will go a long way to earning respect. Without respect, you will never have loyalty and without loyalty, you cannot trust your followers. Without mutual trust and respect, you cannot accomplish great things.

Remember: while your people need to be able to trust you, you need to build them up to the level where you can also trust them.

Encouraging the Heart

One of the worst developments in the workplace was the creation of the term "Human Resources." Formerly known as the "Personnel Department," the focus was on dealing with people as *persons*. At a time when industry was supposedly focused on making the workplace more humane in order to increase job satisfaction and productivity, it took a major step backwards.

No one wants to be considered a "human resource." A resource is something you use as long as it is functional. When the shelf life expires or is no longer as effective as it once was, you throw it away without a thought. It would be a glorious thing if every Human Resource department was abolished and the name Personnel made resurgence.

Employees, workers and followers are not robots. Human beings have intellect and emotions. Failing to deal with them on those levels will ultimately backfire. You cannot program loyalty.

Sharing Rewards

If your followers are going to share in the work, make certain they share in the rewards. If you are going to get a bonus for a successful task, share at least a portion of it with your followers. More than one employee has felt betrayed by leadership when the boss gets a big bonus and those who do all the work get nothing. You don't need to give them half or divide it all up among all your followers, but you should at least throw them a party, provide a free lunch, or give everyone a pair of movie tickets or a lottery ticket. Do something to show they didn't work hard only to see you take all the credit.

Celebrating Accomplishments

Set both personal and team goals and milestones. Nothing motivates someone like public recognition. Although some may seem somewhat embarrassed by a public display, inside they are proud they have been recognized. There has never been a recorded study that quotes an employee who was honored in public with them saying that they never wanted that to happen again. Celebrate team milestones as well. It breaks up the routine of the workday, gives a well-deserved break, and motivates people to work harder when they return to work refreshed.

Making Celebration Part of Your Culture

You don't need to decorate the office each day or have morning pep rallies, but the workplace should never be dreaded by employees. People spend most of their waking lives at work, with substantially less time for family, friends and activities they would much rather be doing. By the very definition, they come to "work" and you have to pay them to be there. People have to feel motivated by more than just a paycheck.

Be sure to have a welcoming environment where people feel respected. Celebrate special occasions to break up the routine, but don't make celebration itself the routine of no work will get done.

Basic Influencing Skills

The best leaders are able to influence others to do something and think it was all their idea. Don't worry about taking credit for every good thing that happens on your watch. As the leader, you get credit whenever your followers succeed because you created the environment that allowed their success.

The Art of Persuasion

Aristotle was a master of the art persuasion, and he outlines his thinking in his work, Rhetoric, where he identifies three important factors: ethos, pathos, and logos.

Ethos (credibility) persuades people using character. If you are respectful and honest, people will be more likely to follow you because of your character. Your character convinces the follower that you are someone who is worth listening to for advice.

Pathos (emotional) persuades people by appealing to their emotions. For example, when a politician wants to gain support for the bill, it inevitably is argued, "it's for the children!" Babies, puppies, and kitties abound in advertising for a reason. Although a car is neither male nor female, they are sometimes called "sexy" in car commercials. Pathos allows you to tie into emotional triggers that will capture a person's attention and enlist their support, but it can be easily abused, leading to a loss of Ethos, as described above.

Logos (logical) persuades people by means persuading by appealing to their intellect. This was Aristotle's favorite and his forte', but not everyone reacts on a rational level.

Of the three, Ethos must always come first. Ideally, you want to appeal to Pathos, back your arguments up with Logos, and never lose Ethos. President Bill Clinton appealed to people using Pathos, saying often, "I feel your pain," but there were serious questions raised about his Ethos, and he often did not back up his appeals with Logos. There is no doubt that he was a successful, but there is also no doubt that he was not as successful as he could have been.

The Principles of Influence

Robert B. Cialdini, Ph. D. once said, "It is through the influence process that we generate and manage change." In his studies, he outlined five universal principles of influence, which are useful and effective in a wide range of circumstances.

Reciprocation: People are more willing to do something for you if you have already done something for them first. Married couples do this all the time, giving in on little things so they can ask for that big night out or a chance to watch the game later.

Commitment: You cannot get people to commit to you or your vision if they don't see your commitment. Once you provide a solid, consistent example, they will feel they have to do the same.

Authority: If people believe you know what you are talking about and accept your expertise, they are far more likely to follow you. Despite the rebel cry, "Question Authority," when people need help with something, they will seek out an authority figure. If you place a man in a tie next to a man in jeans and a ratty T-shirt, people will invariably ask the man in the tie for advice on a technical subject first simply because he *looks* like an authority.

Social Validation: As independent as we like to consider ourselves, we love to be part of a crowd. It will always be a part of us, that school age desire to be accepted, no matter how many times our parents tell us, "If everyone jumped off a cliff, would you join them?" People will always jump on a bandwagon if their friends like the band.

Friendship: People listen to their friends. If they know you and like you, they are far more likely to support you. A pleasant personality can make up for a multitude of failures. More than one leader has been abandoned at the first sign of trouble because they were not very well liked.

Creating an Impact

As mentioned before, communication is accomplished with more than just words. The more of the previous leadership skills you develop, the more you will make an impact. In addition, the bigger the impact, the greater the positive change you can create.

Impact is created by a number of intangible factors:

- A confident bearing, tempered by a kindly manner

- A strong sense of justice, tempered by mercy

- A strong intellect, tempered by the willingness to learn

- A strong sense of emotion, tempered by self-control

- A strong ability to communicate, tempered by the ability to listen

- A strong insistence on following the rules, tempered by flexibility

- A strong commitment to innovation, tempered by situational reality

- A strong commitment to your followers, tempered by the ability to lead

Above all: maintain a strong personal commitment to your vision.

Setting Goals

A vision without specific, targeted goals is just a wish or a hope. Without targeted goals, how will you ever know if your vision is being accomplished? A vision needs a project roadmap with milestones, but how do you determine what those goals are? First, we will discuss goals themselves, then how to determine what your goals should be and how to support them.

Setting SMART Goals

SMART goals are:

Specific: The vision itself is general while the goals are specific targets to be met. Specific goals answer the questions of who, what, when, where, why and how questions as specifically as possible.

Measurable*:* Goals must be measurable in terms of progress and attainment. They must be tracked according to the amount of time or money spent, or results achieved as appropriate.

Attainable*:* A goal which cannot be met, is not a goal, it is an ideal. If you know you need certain infrastructure in place to accomplish your vision, you should break down your goals into attainable steps you can monitor as each step is put into place.

Realistic*:* A goal may be attainable, but not with the resources at hand. In that case, you need other goals to build up to the level where the attainable goal becomes realistic. A goal may be possible, but you need the right people with the right amount of time and support to make it happen.

Timed: All goals need to be accomplished within a given time frame. Deadlines may indeed be missed, but without any timetable, there will be no sense of urgency and no reason not to put it off until "later."

Each goal should lead to the "next step" in the overall plan until the ultimate vision is reached.

Creating a Long-Term Plan

Also called Strategic Planning, the long-term plan is the road map that guides you to the ultimate realization of your vision. As discussed in the previous module. A goal may be possible, but not attainable or realistic – now. You may be missing a quality person for a key position, you may lack the funds, or time to achieve the higher-level goals, so lower level stepping stone goals must be planned.

If your goal is to unify a modern computer network throughout your organization, but you only have a few outdated computers and older shared printers, your ultimate goal will be possible and attainable, but not realistic. If you do not have the money for the new equipment and do not have a strong IT person on staff, your goal will be unattainable. If you need everything done in a week, your goal cannot be timely, as it will take much longer. Intermediate goals, however, can make your ultimate goal realistic, attainable, and timely.

You might first want to increase your revenue through increased sales, a fundraiser, long-term business loan, or by other means. You can make a goal to hire a network guru for a reasonable cost who can analyze your current systems and determine what needs to be upgraded according to modern networking technology. That analysis will provide you the information to set new goals of buying, configuring and implementing the equipment, then adding the infrastructure to network it all together. In the end, the goal that seemed impossible will become a reality, according to your original vision.

Creating a Support System

Once your goals are established you need a way to ensure they are set into motion. Duties must be assigned and documentation must be established to support and track progress. A Gantt Chart is a great way to track milestones over a period of time. You need to establish the tools necessary to track progress or development as appropriate. These might include a simple checklist for some tasks and complicated advanced software tracking systems for others.

Monitoring and oversight are the keys to achieving all goals.

Chapter 21 – Public Speaking

According to a survey by the Sunday Times of London, 41% of people list public speaking as their biggest fear. Forget small spaces, darkness, and spiders – standing up in front of a crowd and talking is far more terrifying for most people.

However, mastering this fear and getting comfortable speaking in public can be a great ego booster, not to mention a huge benefit to your career. This workshop will give you some valuable public speaking skills, including in-depth information on developing an engaging program and delivering your presentation with power.

By the end of this chapter, you will be able to:

- Identify their audience

- Create a basic outline

- Organize their ideas

- Flesh out their presentation

- Find the right words

- Prepare all the details

- Overcome nervousness

- Deliver a polished, professional speech

- Handle questions and comments effectively

Think about the most effective presentation or speech you have ever heard. Keep it in mind while reading the chapter to help identify practical applications for the tools and techniques that we discuss.

Identifying Your Audience

The key to effective public speaking is preparation. The better you prepare, the more confident you will feel.

Preparation begins with identifying your audience. What do you know about your audience? What do they care about? What's important to them? Do they have any misconceptions about your topic? These are the kinds of questions you should ask as part of your preparation. Sitting down and listing the questions, and your answers to them, will give you a basic structure for your speech, around which you can add things and take them away as you see fit.

Holding the attention of an audience and speaking to what interests them is the most important thing about any public speech. It is not merely about what you say, but also how you say it. If you have a message you wish to get across, then think of how that message will communicate itself best to the audience you are speaking to.

Performing a Needs Analysis

Preparing for a speech should begin with thinking about the wants and needs of the audience. What are they interested in? What do they care about? No matter how entertaining a speaker you are, people will not give you their full attention unless you are talking about something that is meaningful to them.

You should try to let the audience know early in your speech that you are going to try to address their concerns. Too often a speaker starts out with a lengthy discussion about the history or background of a topic. That is usually not what the audience cares about! They want to know how this topic will affect their lives.

A needs analysis measures what skills employees have -- and what they need. It indicates how to deliver the right training at the right time. The results answer the following questions:

- Where is the *audience* with the problem or need for change?

- What *tasks* and subtasks does an expert perform to complete a work process?

- What *gaps* exist between experts, average, and poor performers of a work process?

- How do we translate the needs into objectives to promote a strong learning *outcome*?

The method can be simple observation, careful note taking, and asking questions.

Question	Methods
Audience?	Interview key stakeholders and listen to their concerns about the problem Define who needs help to overcome the problem Identify and describe the audience and the work
Tasks?	Observe the work being done by recognized experts Take careful notes and ask questions where needed Document the proper performance of the work tasks
Gaps?	Observe other workers doing the tasks. Compare results with the performance of experts. Document identified skill gaps.
Outcome?	Develop a complete list of tasks for performing the work completely and correctly.

Creating an Audience Profile

- **Education:** If your audience is well-educated, you can use fairly sophisticated vocabulary. If they're not, you need to keep things simple.

- **Familiarity with Topic:** What do people know about the topic already and what do you need to explain?

- **Familiarity with Jargon:** Avoid any specialized vocabulary unless you think that everyone in the audience will understand it. If you have to use a technical term, explain it.

- **Interest in the Topic:** What do people care about? What's important to them?

- **Possible Misconceptions:** Which incorrect ideas might you need to correct?

- **Attitude:** Are people hostile, supportive, curious, worried? The attitude of your audience will affect the tone of your speech.

One of the most important elements of written or spoken language is the register in which it is delivered. Experts say that there are three registers of language, titled R1, R2, and R3. R1 is the level of language used most commonly by politicians, lawyers, and found in the upper-market range of newspapers. R2 is the most commonly used by people in everyday conversation with acquaintances and people they have just met (outside a framework of formality).

R3 is the register that may be used between close friends and is heavily based in slang. Considering how educated your audience is, and how formal you wish the speech to be, will govern the choice of register.

The audience's familiarity with an interest in the topic will also be of importance. You may be seeking to educate your audience on the topic in hand, or to communicate your own ideas to an audience who is already familiar with the topic. Deciding between these will help shape your speech – if they are familiar with the topic then it does not hurt to include some jargon, as this may even make your speech that little bit more dynamic – if you don't need to keep explaining things, you can communicate ideas more effectively.

The mood and opinion of your audience is also important. It will influence the tone and content of your speech, as a nervous or worried audience will require an element of comfort or reassurance, while a celebratory audience will want to share a positive, electric atmosphere and possibly hear some congratulations.

One person speaking to a large crowd is in a unique position – they have the attention of many people and the power to get ideas across that will change mindsets and behavior on a large scale. It is therefore important to consider how you phrase things, and that you correct any persistent misconceptions of which you are aware.

Identifying Key Questions and Concerns

If you have a good understanding of your audience, you can probably predict the key questions and concerns they are likely to have. You may not be able to give the audience the answers they would like to hear, but at least you should be ready to discuss the things they care about most.

Many speeches these days are followed by a question and answer session which allows the audience to raise any issues they do not feel have been fully dealt with by the original speech – but it is better for the audience if the original speech deals with those concerns, as it shows that they have been thought through rather than addressed "on the hoof".

Predicting questions and concerns should be straightforward. If you are in a position to address a larger group of people, then the chances are that you have knowledge of the issues that affect them and how these can be addressed. It is also possible to take a sounding from people "on the ground" as to what is concerning them. It may well be that you share those concerns and have given some thought to addressing them.

If you can speak intelligently and emotionally about the issues that concern your audience, they will have a lot more trust that you can help provide solutions to problems, and that their position is understood and respected.

It may help before delivering a speech or presentation to make a list of the five most searching questions you expect people to have. Your presentation should then concern itself with answering those questions as well as delivering your own standpoint.

When delivering the speech it is helpful to pay tribute to the fact that these concerns exist, by saying something along the lines of: "And before I go any further, I would like to raise an issue that I know has been foremost among the minds of many here…". As the audience is giving you their attention, it is simply reasonable that you make clear that they, too, have yours.

Creating a Basic Outline

The main advantage of creating an outline is that it helps you to organize your thoughts. The audience gets more out of a presentation when it is well-organized. They also are more likely to think that the speaker knows the subject thoroughly and has given some thought on how to present it.

In this module we will be considering a hypothetical presentation about a project that has just been completed, but the general approach we will consider is applicable to just about any type of presentation.

Often this approach is seen as being similar to creating a body. You start with the skeleton – the basic outline, the bare minimum of the speech in something like the shape that it will eventually take – and progress by adding meat to the bones, and layering the rest on top of that.

At key points of the presentation, specific issues will need to be confronted, and by allotting them a place in the basic outline you will be able to ensure that these are prioritized and addressed correctly.

Outlining the Situation

Almost every project addresses a problem, an opportunity, or both. An effective way to introduce your speech is by outlining the situation that your project addresses. This approach forces you to get to the point right away.

In outlining the situation, try to avoid giving too much history or background. Most people won't care about that sort of information. If you start out by discussing something people don't care about, it will be hard to recapture their interest.

Provide only the background information people will need to understand the situation. Your audience in many cases may already know the background. Covering old ground will simply lead to a "here we go again" feeling in the room.

So instead of beginning with a history of the problem, the nature of the problem can be covered in a few sentences, and followed with a statement of what you as a group decided had to be done about it. It is beneficial to make reference to situations and occasions with which the audience is familiar. In doing this you will keep their attention by recognizing that their opinions mattered and were taken into account.

The introduction of a presentation is where you will often take and hold an audience's attention, or lose it for good. It is wise, then, to keep an introduction brief and informative, and set the scene for the rest of the presentation.

In an introduction, there are just a few essential elements to keep in mind. First of all, you should introduce yourself in your capacity with regards to the project. Even if everyone there knows you, it helps to explain exactly why *you* are delivering the presentation. You should then give a brief overview of what the presentation seeks to address.

This will stop anyone in the audience from thinking "When are they going to get to the bit about x?", and allow all present to concentrate on the presentation itself.

Identifying the Task That Had to Be Performed

Your task description will be the organizing principle for the rest of your presentation. Most of what follows will be an account of what you did to complete the task.

One way to come up with a simple, clear task description is to imagine you are writing it for a teenager. How would you describe what you did to someone who knows very little about your work? This can obviously be tweaked depending on the audience, but it is worthwhile remembering that the audience to which you speak will all have their specialties in certain fields. Something that is perfectly evident to you may not be perfectly evident to many in your audience.

This does not mean that a lot of your speech should be taken up by lengthy explanations of what you do. Think of it in a similar way to a film. In most films we have periods of what the directors like to call "exposition". They lay down the "back story", telling us why what we are watching had to happen.

Film reviewers are very quick to criticize films which have lengthy spells of exposition, as all we really need are the essential details. We can piece the rest together for ourselves. Take the same approach to explaining the task that you were dealing with. Give the important details, and assume a basic level of understanding.

The result of having these brief explanations is that your wider presentation will then be set in a certain context, and it is in this context where the things you say will make sense. When you have completed the first draft of the presentation or speech it helps to then read over it and see if it would make sense to someone who is coming to the presentation without the information that you have.

Any terms which give space for confusion can then be explained a little bit better so that the audience can follow the presentation. If any remaining confusion persists, then a question-and-answer period can pick that up.

Listing the Actions You Took

If a presentation contains a list of actions, it's a good idea to present the list on a slide or a flip chart. People have a hard time keeping more than three or four items straight in their head unless they see them displayed.

As you go through your list in your presentation, you can point to each item on your chart or slide. This will make it easier for people to follow along. It will also help people see where you are in your presentation, and how much longer it is likely to go on.

It is important to do this for a number of reasons:

- Firstly, if people are confused as to what exactly will be dealt with – and when – they are liable to lose concentration, and any key points you make in the presentation will resonate less as a result of people wondering what is next.

- Secondly, there will be people in your audience who, although they are keen to listen closely to the presentation, will still wonder when their particular area of interest will be dealt with. We change how we listen depending on our familiarity with the topic.

- Thirdly, if people are concerned about the length of the presentation, their minds will begin to wander as it passes the point where they would have hoped for it to finish.

Making the audience aware of the structure of your presentation in advance may seem to some like an invitation for them to tune in and tune out as the topics suit. However, having a table of contents allows people to keep concentration.

In the areas where they are less informed than in others, they will listen in order to further inform themselves. In their areas of expertise they will listen not more closely, but differently – giving themselves a chance to contribute after the presentation if necessary.

A good structure does not just help the writer and deliverer of a presentation, but the audience too. It is easier to maintain concentration if one is aware of what they should be concentrating on and this will mean that you carry the audience with you over the course of your presentation, allowing them to be better informed, reassured, and prepared at the end of your presentation than they were at the beginning.

Revealing the Results

Revealing the results of a project involves answering a few basic questions:

- Did the project achieve its goal?

- Were there any unexpected consequences?

- What's next?

The first question may seem like an obvious one with an obvious answer. Simply put, either it achieved its objective or it did not. However, any project will have stages of success and stages of failure. In deciding whether a project achieved its goal it is important to refer back to the questions and the brief as set out in the introduction to the presentation.

There was a plan to achieve something – did it succeed? If so, did it come through on, or ahead of, schedule? Was any outside help required? And if it failed, did it fall some distance short or was it close enough to be termed a "deferment" rather than a straight failure?

As for unexpected consequences, these can arise in any project. In preparation for a project, it is common to look ahead at potential problems and decide how these can be avoided or addressed. However, the best laid plans can still always run up against unforeseen problems – and, for that matter, unforeseen benefits.

These can change the shape of a project and lead to the redrawing of an entire brief. Often the kind of on-the-spot management that is required to handle such a situation can be the difference between success and failure, and any conclusion should deal with these circumstances, how they arose, and how they were dealt with.

At the end of the presentation, it is safe to say that the audience will be better informed as to the extent of the success or failure of a plan. Their minds will then, naturally, turn to the matter of where things will go next. Assuming that the business itself has not been wound up, there will be follow-up work to do, and getting on with that work will be the priority.

The question of "What next?" can be answered with reference to the presentation you have just delivered. Everyone will now be clearer on the consequences of the previous months, and now is the best time to lay down the next plan.

Organizing the Program

The key to creating a well-organized speech or presentation is to keep your audience in mind. Start with something that will capture their attention and give them a clear idea of your topic.

Organize the body of your presentation in a way that will be easy for your audience to understand. Plan to review your main points briefly and then wrap things up on a positive note, perhaps giving your audience a "call to action."

The essential thing to remember is that you are giving your presentation for the benefit of your audience. That means you need to organize it in a way that will make sense to them. The most important thing to keep in the forefront of your mind is that you are not making the speech for yourself, but your audience.

Think of how politicians do things. When they are campaigning they will speak to groups as diverse as different occupations, different ethnicities, and different ages. How they will speak to each changes between speeches. Then, when they are speaking to a cabinet meeting of fellow politicians, the language and the issues will be different again. Keep this in mind when giving a presentation.

Making Organization Easy

Some thoughts on the basic parts of a presentation:

Opening. Some speakers like to start a presentation with a joke. Sometimes this works. It starts on a light note and puts the audience at ease. Buy many people do not tell jokes well. If a presentation starts with something that doesn't work, the audience will start to question your ability as a speaker. Other ways to start include asking a rhetorical question, giving people a surprising statistic, or telling a brief anecdote that is related to the topic of the presentation.

Body. The next two activities will address the body of a presentation.

Review. Many speakers skip this step, but it can be worth including. Chances are that some members of the audience didn't get the few key points you want them to take away from the presentation. Restate these key points briefly for the sake of those who were "tuned out" the first time you made them.

Closing. Restate the main point of your presentation. In some cases, you may want to give people a "call to action."

Obviously, the longer a presentation goes on the more chances there are to lose the attention of your audience. However, making a presentation too short can leave people uninformed and dissatisfied with the body of the presentation. It is therefore essential to structure your presentation correctly, allowing enough time to give it a powerful opening which will draw listeners in, a strong middle which will hold that attention and give them all the facts, and a closing section which reinforces what they were told and gives them an idea about what action needs to be taken to back it all up.

All these parts need to be present, and each needs to be weighted correctly according to the amount of time you have available to you. It may well be the case that in order to attend a presentation people are taken away from doing their "normal" job.

Such demands on a person's time will reflect in how they view the presentation and how much of their attention they give it.

The amount of time you give to each section of a presentation will therefore be governed by how much time you have overall and how much of that time will be necessary to get all of your substantive points across. If your presentation is in danger of running over time, it will be necessary to trim it in places, beginning with any extraneous detail.

Remember that most presentations will be followed up by a pick-up session of sorts, where individual questions can be dealt with. The presentation itself is where larger issues are raised and answered.

Organizational Methods

It's important to realize that most people will be able to remember only a few key points from a presentation. Don't overwhelm the audience with facts that they will forget as soon as they walk out the door. Focus on a few key points.

It's a good idea to write your key points on a flip chart or show them on a slide. That will help your audience understand how your presentation is organized. If you return to your flip chart page or slide when you move on to a new key point, the audience will be able to see where you are in your presentation.

As well as this, at the close of a presentation you can then go, one by one, through the key points that you have made. Making a point coherently consists of three steps: introduction, substance, and reinforcement. If you want the audience to leave your presentation with a certain point locked in their minds, then it is essential that you address all three of those steps.

Whichever way you choose to organize the body of your presentation, it is important to keep the elements of it down to a manageable number. Taking one of the above as an example, we will look at how a "Problem/Solution" style of presentation can best be cut down into a few manageable steps.

An organization may have any number of problems which it wishes to address. If there are, say, fifteen problems that it wants to get to the bottom of it, covering all of these in a presentation results in the problem that fifteen of anything is a large number to remember.

In order to ensure that the presentation does not result in an audience being bemused by the sheer number of problems, it is advisable if you can to find a category for each problem, whether it be "time", "manpower", "finance" or another suitable category.

Your intention should be to find a few category headings which can cover a few problems each. If these problems require more time, this can best be covered by a meeting where the attendees are all people who have experience in the specific field where problems exist.

Any presentation will benefit from this kind of organization. One thing worth remembering is that the "rule of three" is adhered to by most people, if not consciously then certainly subconsciously. Therefore if you can keep concentrated discussion to around three headings – or a maximum of five – then you will be able to retain attention much better than if you have a numbered list which never seems to end. You can always, after all, emphasize the key points at the end of the presentation.

Classifying and Categorizing

Categorizing information is one way that people make sense of complex topics. A speaker can help people come to grips with complex topics by breaking them down into a few categories.

If participants have trouble thinking of things to consider in a health insurance plan, you can make a few suggestions:

Cost:

- Payroll deductions
- Copayments
- Cost of prescriptions

Coverage:

- Hospitalization
- Emergency room visits
- Coverage when traveling
- Annual physicals
- Routine doctor's visits

Choice:

- Referral requirements
- Network restrictions (doctors)
- Network restrictions (hospitals)

One key benefit of doing this is that you can take a highly complicated topic and break it down into smaller areas, which benefits members of your audience who may specialize in a certain area. The areas in which they do not specialize will not be a signal to turn off, but an opportunity to learn more about that specific area, allowing a "joined-up" process to have greater success within the organization. The areas in which they do specialize are an opportunity for them to listen, evaluate, and potentially contribute suggestions which may benefit everyone in future.

Additionally, the introduction of smaller topic areas allows the brain to process information in more manageable "chunks". Rather than trying to make sense of a topic which seems monolithic in size and importance, cutting it down into smaller pieces allows the individual to mentally breathe in between those sections.

Think of it as being like a journey. If you were to travel from one tip of Africa to the other in one go, you would be exhausted and unwell at the end of it. If, on the other hand, you include stopping-off points and rest breaks, you will allow yourself to recover and galvanize yourself for the journey ahead.

This approach applies in the healthcare example detailed above, but also in several other areas. A broader topic can be split down into more specific topics, which in themselves can potentially be split into more, even hyper-specific areas depending upon the audience you are dealing with. It is also essential not to overdo this.

By splitting down a topic repeatedly you can end up with so many chunks that the constant changing leads to a presentation losing its momentum. A balance between over-complication and over-simplification is essential. If you get it right in the middle, the presentation will flow naturally.

Fleshing It Out

Audiences are often a little skeptical about a speaker's message, especially if the speaker is addressing a controversial issue. You can build credibility with an audience by using reliable sources of information and backing up your statements with citations to trusted authorities.

You need to think about your presentation as though it was going to be written down on paper and distributed throughout the audience and their bosses. Throwaway lines which you assumed would just pass over people's heads will end up being the bits that certain people remember – so be sure to keep a close eye on what you say and how you say it.

Often, people make the mistake of believing that the more they say, the better their speech is. Others, feeling that brevity is the soul of wit, keep what they say to a minimum. As with so many things, the truth lies somewhere in between and the key to making a presentation as powerful and as well-received as it can be is to say enough, and make what you say mean enough.

There is no point in fleshing out a presentation with extraneous detail which no-one will remember, and at the same time you should avoid leaving out anything remotely important so that your message is strong, coherent, and memorable.

Identifying Appropriate Sources

The Internet supplies us with an endless stream of information, but how reliable is it? One way to evaluate reliability is to compare data from several different sources. One way to check for bias (especially with controversial topics) is to compare statements by people who have opposing views.

For people who wish their words to be given attention and taken seriously, balance is of vital importance. Maintaining that balance relies on good research and not allowing your opinion to be mistaken in your mind for fact. There is so much information available for research, and your task is to separate the redundant, excess information from the important data.

For example, many people use the popular online encyclopedia Wikipedia for research. This is not a bad idea; the site is filled with information which is well cross-referenced and constantly updated. In terms of freshness, online encyclopedias such as this cannot be beaten by the traditional, paper-based form of encyclopedia, which in turn are incredibly inconvenient for the purposes of cross-reference. So if there is this much convenience to an online encyclopedia, and so much information therein, we should be looking to use it for all of our research needs, should we not?

Well, in fairness, using an online resource like Wikipedia can be a very good way to do substantial research, but it is important to make sure that any facts and figures you use from a Wikipedia article are cited and backed up by other sources.

You will find the citation reference in square brackets next to the information in the article body. This links to the table of references, which can be used to find the source that, the statistics or other information were drawn from. The more sources you have for information – and the more views you listen to from both sides of a debate – the better for any research that you do. Even if you disagree with the information and opinions given by a certain source, it can after all be used as a jumping-off point for a counter-argument.

Establishing Credibility

It is extremely important to be sure of your facts. If you make even one factually incorrect statement, some people will doubt everything you say. This is something that holds true wherever you are, including in some of the highest courts in the land.

A lawyer will be much in demand if he or she can take one small inaccuracy in a witness' statement and turn it to the advantage of his or her client by using it to paint the witness as unreliable. In terms of a presentation, the stakes may not be as high, but all the same it is wise to make sure that you have authority behind what you tell people. This begins with how you present yourself.

It is often said that you cannot judge a book by its cover, and the truth is that that it absolutely correct. Some fine minds are to be found behind faces which appear, to many people to suggest docility.

But if you want to keep the audience's attention on what you are saying, it is advisable to appear businesslike and efficient at all times. You should be tidily dressed, and should be aware at all times of what you have just said, what you are currently saying, and what you will say next. If this involves referring to flash cards on occasion, then there is no problem in doing so – much better to have the information to hand than have it disappear from your mind.

It is also worth bearing in mind the fact that the audience have not come to be told things they already know. If they had, then any one of them could be giving the presentation. It is much better to think about things from another angle.

You know what they think, so some of this presentation can be about what you think. The bits of the presentation that they remember may well be the moments when their opinions were challenged and potentially changed. Doing this will involve arguing a point and backing it up with sound reasoning, facts and figures, and the impact it has on an audience can be genuinely impressive.

You should use whatever is at your disposal to make your points in a presentation as efficiently as possible. Known statistics, testimonies from respected individuals and documentary evidence are all extremely helpful when it comes to making your point effectively.

Each person in the audience may have a different "convincer". The more complete your presentation is, the more people you will convince. Unless you are preaching to the converted, do not assume that you will carry all before you with the same arguments that sounded right to you.

The Importance of Citations

Some groups or individuals are so trusted that citing their statements can be the deciding factor in getting people to agree with you. Some examples:

- The Centers for Disease Control

- The Congressional Budget Office

- The Census Bureau

- The Journal of the American Medical Association

The point that unites these groups listed above, and others like them, is that they are considered to be a leading authority in their specific field. When it comes to discovering information on any subject, going right to the leading authorities to find it out is always a sensible move.

If you are giving a presentation, going to a leading authority in the area you wish to discuss is very wise indeed. Sometimes in a presentation you will find that some of your listeners are skeptical and will challenge the statistics you mention. If you can mention that those statistics have come from a leading authority, and cite that they are up to date as well, then you will advance your case much further.

It has become common practice to begin sentences in presentations, essays and speeches with the phrase "Everybody knows that…" or "It goes without saying that…" when often this is very far from being the case.

This is a rhetorical device which can be used appropriately and inappropriately. In the first case, if it is something everyone does know, then it prevents you from having to go over well-worn explanations. In many other cases, however, it may be used because the speaker has not been able to source direct proof for an assertion and simply wants their audience to accept it. After all, if "everybody" knows something, not many people will happily be the one to disagree.

When it comes to backing your points up, it is best that you go to the experts.

The more evidence you can back up a statement with, the more confidence you can have in asserting it. Furthermore, the fact that the information comes from a trusted source means that you can immediately trump skeptical listeners who wish to make your presentation seem less informed than it is.

Putting It All Together

Once you've outlined your speech and lined up some solid evidence to back up your ideas, it's time to put all the pieces together. Whether you plan to write out your speech word for word or just speak from notes, you need to have a clear idea of what you want to say — the actual words, not just the ideas.

It is generally recommended not to have everything you want to say written down but rather a series of prompts. If you appear to be reading from a script, then there is less chance of you getting your point across with the power that you want it to have.

Nonetheless, you should refrain from improvising too much as there are clear disadvantages to this process, not least of them the fact that this is filled with risks such as momentarily being lost for words.

This makes you appear less competent, and people will be less likely to take you seriously. The general impression is that you should have in mind the body of what you want to say, and any additions which occur to you can always be included. Therefore, you do not have to worry about deviating from a pre-written speech, while also avoiding the dangers of having nothing to say.

Writing Your Presentation

Most of the time it's a bad idea to read a presentation word for word. It's boring and it makes it difficult to build a rapport with the audience. Any presentation is a kind of social occasion. If you just wanted people to hear what you have to say, you could print copies of your presentation and hand them out.

Effective speakers try to make a connection with their audience. Reading a speech word for word creates a barrier between the speaker and the audience and eliminates spontaneity. Your audience should feel like you're having a conversation with them, not lecturing them.

If you are constantly referring to notes this makes it impossible to maintain any kind of eye contact with your audience, and you may as well record the speech and play it to them. Speaking from notes does not have the same problems connected with it – it simply allows you to have prompts from which to elaborate.

The main benefit to making a speech is that you allow your words to come alive. Some of the most impressive speeches are made by speakers who have minimal notes and have thought long and hard about what they want to say and how they want to say it. This allows them to maintain a rapport with their audience, and gives the words more resonance. Also, if you are reading from a full speech, this makes it more difficult to respond to questions which may arise in the course of your presentation. Allowing your brain to do most of the work sharpens your reaction times and gives you greater credibility.

If you wish to write out any part of your speech or memorize it word for word, the best thing to do is write down what you will say in the first two or three minutes of the speech. From here you can usually gain the confidence that you require to give the rest of your speech more freely. By this point, you will have gained the confidence of your audience, who will be happy to hear what you have to say, and you will be "warmed up" – making the rest of the speech far more coherent and convincing.

Adding a Plan B

It is almost inevitable that at some point you will encounter unexpected problems in giving presentations. How you handle these problems, will determine whether your presentation is a success or not.

Some people get very flustered when something goes wrong. They may become irritated or angry. The audience picks up on this emotion and starts to form a negative impression of the speaker. Skillful speakers treat unexpected problems humorously. If their projector doesn't work or they trip over a cord, they make a joke out of it.

This puts everyone at ease and starts to build a rapport with the audience. This is one element which separates comfortable public speakers from speakers who are less professional.

The importance of having a Plan B is recognized by everyone who has a Plan A. The thing that many people forget about plans is that they are not always going to be carried out in the conditions for which they were planned.

Things can go wrong without notice. Even if you have planned out every seemingly foreseeable eventuality there is always the danger that, for example, the power will go off in the middle of the presentation. How you react to these problems is almost as important as the quality of your speech.

Good public speakers will always be ready for the possibility of unforeseen problems. This does not mean that, should you spill something over your notes or have a momentary lapse of memory, you should launch into a stand-up comedy routine. It is much better to simply go into the speech you have planned with the awareness that you may need to "fill space". One way in which people do this is to make light of the problem and – if you can think of a way to do so – make the unexpected problem into part of your Plan B.

For example – and this is a very specific example – if the power should cut out during a speech on the importance of energy efficiency, you can turn this into a jumping off point by saying "...and this is a good example of the importance of what I am talking about. Thank you very much for that illustration". Of course, sometimes the fates will throw problems at you that are not so easily turned into a joke, but thinking on your feet will win you points.

Often, it is enough simply to know that you may encounter such problems and to have an attitude those things are in the lap of the gods. Having the confidence to turn them into something that can drive a presentation forward is the mark of a good speaker.

Reviewing, Editing, and Rewriting

Here are some things to look for in reviewing the first draft of a presentation:

Content and Organization:

- Does the opening provide a good idea of what the presentation is about?

- Are the main ideas arranged in a logical order?

- Are opinions backed up with facts, statistics, and authorities?

Language:

- Have you come with clear, effective statements of your main ideas?

- Have you eliminated jargon as much as possible?

- Have you used vocabulary that the audience will understand?

Length:

- Have you devoted an appropriate amount of time to each part of your presentation?

- Is your entire presentation an appropriate length?

Very few first drafts are good enough to be "the draft". Unless you have immense clarity of thought and eerie foresight, the chances are that you will make a reference later on in your speech that either contradicts something you said before, or has a meaning that is not immediately clear to your listeners going on the basis of what you said before.

The first draft of a speech is about getting all your ideas on to the page and ensuring that they are coherently presented. The further drafts will be about ensuring that the speech flows like it should, and sounds like a complete document rather than a series of thoughts.

Writing a speech that takes all of the important factors into account first time is not impossible, but does take an inordinate period of time, and the final document can often sound like pages of research.

Getting the balance right between informative content and something that will hold the attention of your audience generally requires you to revisit the speech after you have written it. You could sit to write with a reference book in front of you, checking every fact, figure and quote before you commit it to paper. However, this approach almost always leads to a speech that has very little life in it.

The best bet is to write a draft of the speech that sounds like something you would say. The latter drafts of it will then take into account the details that you have checked, and any amendments you have made as a result of a read-through.

It may be that in the original draft you have given more time to one section than you have to another, equally important section. By adding and subtracting elements, you will have a speech that sounds coherent and impressive. By sitting and working on a first draft that takes everything into account and has all of the important facts and figures checked, you will have a speech that sounds like a research document.

Being Prepared

Preparation serves several important purposes:

- It boosts your self-confidence.

- It reduces the chances of something going wrong.

- It creates an impression of you as a competent, diligent person.

- It makes it easier for you to give a polished, professional presentation.

It is often said that those who fail to prepare, prepare to fail. The reason for this is that only by preparing properly will you eliminate the obvious potential errors that can turn what would be an excellent speech into a mess.

By taking the time to prepare, you can look ahead to the presentation and get an impression for how it should and will go. It will also allow you to take into consideration what difficulties may arise, and have a strategy for dealing with each of them.

Some people can walk into a room and hold the attention of their audience by speaking "off the cuff" for half an hour or more. These people are naturally gifted, and quite rare. Usually, they make a living as stand-up comedians, as comedy is one of very few fields where the act of preparing a routine is not hamstrung by the necessity for getting every fact right and every detail nailed down.

This does not mean that delivering a presentation cannot be an enjoyable process. In fact, the right amount and the right kind of preparation can ensure that the presentation is enjoyable, informative, and useful both for you and for your audience.

Checking Out the Venue

Here are some things to look for when checking out the venue for a presentation:

- Adequate seating.

- Good sight lines. Some chairs may need to be moved so that everyone can see the speaker or the screen.

- Projectors or other equipment. If you will be using the site's projector, be sure it works, and check to see if it is compatible with your laptop. Will you need an extension cord?

- Lighting. What combination of lights will allow the audience to see you, their notes, and the screen if you plan to use slides?

- Speaker's accommodations. Is there a podium if you plan to use one? Is there a place for you to put handouts?

- Miscellaneous. Where are the restrooms and emergency exits?

Sometimes a lot of preparation goes into a presentation, taking into account the way the speaker moves, sounds and sees the audience, as well as the visual aids the speaker will use during the course of the presentation.

A great deal of preparation should ensure that things go smoothly, but the level of presentation needs to be matched by the quality of preparation. Think for a moment how you would react if you had written a 30-minute presentation which called for frequent reference to a visual slideshow, and when you arrived at the venue you found that they did not have a projector.

If you can have access to the venue before you deliver the presentation, this should allow you to carry out a study of the room and get all the information you need. If you can have access for long enough to do a "dry run", so much the better, as this will allow you to foresee any problems and either amend your speech or make alternative arrangements.

It is essential that you take nothing for granted when seeking to deliver a presentation, because it will be you who is in the unenviable position of explaining and dealing with any problems that happen during the live presentation.

If you cannot get access to the venue prior to your presentation, then you should at least be able to get a floor plan of the venue and a checklist of items you will have available to you, as well as knowing whether the venue will support any equipment you bring with you.

If you have written into your presentation a very clever ten-minute scenario that requires you to walk among the audience, you will need to know that the layout of the room allows this. If you have included a short film in your presentation, it will be entirely useless if most people cannot see the film because a pillar is in their way.

Then, before you deliver your presentation, you should look around the room and ensure that nothing there will distract people from what you are saying, and visualize how you will deliver your speech in this room.

Gathering Materials

If you are going to use handouts, be sure you have enough. Handouts serve several purposes:

- Listeners like to take notes. Listeners like to have something to take away from your presentation as a reminder of what you said. Many listeners will take notes on any scrap of paper that is handy. By providing your listeners with handouts, you can reduce the time they spend taking notes because they will already have the main information you are presenting.

- The less time they spend taking notes, the more time they can spend focusing on you.

- Handouts help reinforce your main points. People listen selectively. As hard as you try to emphasize a particular point, some listeners will remember some other point you made that was probably less important. Handouts will help you drive home your main message.

- Handouts make listeners happy. People like to take away something tangible from a presentation, something more than their recollection of what you said. Giving people handouts makes them feel as if they "own" the information they have just heard.

When you write your speech, it is beneficial to condense what you are saying into its key points. This is beneficial for the sake of having visual prompts for what you are going to say, but can actually serve a dual purpose. If you condense a speech into its key points and other useful information, then in this form or in a slightly amended one it can make an excellent handout.

As wonderful as your speech may be, remember that it will be experienced slightly differently by however many people hear it. All of these people may take something slightly different away from the room, so if you have absolutely concrete points that you would insist on them remembering, ensure that these are available on the handout.

By giving everyone a handout you also ensure that they feel as though they have participated in the presentation. Rather than simply demanding that they sit there, listen and remember everything you have said, you give them what is in effect a souvenir of the occasion (in fact, *souvenir* is by origin a French word for "to remember").

This will be something they can refer back to after the event, particularly if they annotate the handout themselves with their own thoughts or something specific that you said during the presentation. Additionally, this allows them to sit and listen to the presentation as you deliver it, without having to constantly write and refer back to detailed notes during the speech.

A 24 Hour Checklist

Presentation:

____   Do you know what you're going to say in the first two minutes?

____   Do you know how you're going to introduce your topic?

____   Have you prepared clear statements of your main points?

____   Do you know how you're going to close your presentation?

____   Have you prepared answers for the questions that are likely to come up?

Slides and handouts:

____   Have you proofread your slides?

____   Do you need to add any slides?

____   Should you delete any slides?

____   Do you have enough handouts for everyone?

Logistics:

____   Do you know where you're going and how you're going to get there?

____   Have you gathered all the equipment and other materials you need?

____   Have you called a contact person to make sure the room will be ready?

Overcoming Nervousness

It's OK to be nervous. In fact, it's probably a good thing. If you are very calm before a presentation, you may be underestimating the difficulty of your assignment. If you're calm because you consider the topic an easy one (a "no brainer"), you may not project enough interest in your subject.

If you're not nervous, you may have a hard time projecting the energy and enthusiasm that you will need to win your listeners' attention. Nervousness can be a tool to communicate enthusiasm.

Channel your nervousness by forcing yourself to speak clearly and to make eye contact with your listeners. It cannot be stressed too often that the element of balance is important in delivering a speech.

Come across as too relaxed and you will sound a little bit bored. If you are bored, then the audience will expect to be bored as well, and they will need very little excuse to start mentally running through other things that they have to do later on that day.

Conversely, if you come across as too nervous, they will wonder why you are giving the presentation rather than someone "competent". Also remember that although eye contact with your audience is good, staring at them will just make them apprehensive – or worse yet, amused.

A Visit from the Boss

Suggested responses to statements from the boss

- I know you're going to do a great job on this presentation. *Thanks. I'm ready to go.*

- This is a very important presentation. Are you ready? *I've spent a lot of time preparing. I think it will go well.*

- You might run into some strong opposition in this meeting. *I've thought about the objections people might have and I've prepared responses.*

- Do you think you can handle this presentation? *I know what I'm going to say and what kinds of questions people will have. I'm ready.*

Sometimes even the best bosses have a tendency to put pressure on you when they would swear they are simply trying to help you. Words of encouragement may well feel as though they are loaded with other meanings.

To a nervous presenter a phrase like "I know you're going to go out there and give a great presentation" seems to be silently followed with "I know this because if you don't, I'm going to fire you at the first opportunity". This may not be what was meant, but nervousness does not always follow a logical path.

Should your boss deliver any of the above phrases of encouragement, leave aside for the time being any other meaning that they may have had. Accept their words of encouragement, and allow your boss to see that you have prepared well for the speech, and anticipate that you may run into some opposition.

As part of your preparation, you will have included your responses to any difficulties that you anticipate. Allow them to remain at the back of your mind. If you go into a presentation on the defensive, then you will find it very hard to win the approval of your audience and may even appear paranoid.

Nervousness can be energy. If it is appropriate, you may even refer to how nervous you feel and ask the audience to be gentle with you.

The work of your presentation has already mostly been done. What you are doing now is merely its culmination, so remember that you know what you are talking about, you know what you will say, and you have every right to say it.

Preparing Mentally

Some advice for participants on mental preparation:

- Like an athlete preparing for a big game, you need to keep yourself positive as you prepare for your own important contest. Think of all your successes in life – all the worthwhile things you have done. Remind yourself that you have prepared for this presentation, that you know what to expect.

- Think about similar experiences you have had. How have you responded in similar situations in the past? If you're like most people, your feelings of anxiety will gradually go away as you work your way through your presentation. You have probably been through things like this in the past – an initial period of nervousness and anxiety that lasts only a short time.

In so many cases, the anticipation of an event is the most emotionally charged part of it. The "athlete" analogy is a good one. If you allow yourself to think too much about the bad things that might happen, it becomes almost a self-fulfilling prophecy. Do not go into the meeting or conference room with a sense of foreboding and a strategy of damage limitation. All that this will do is invite problems – problems which do not need to be there.

You have already done most of the work – actually delivering the presentation is no more than the final ten per cent. Once you are in the "zone", momentum will take you to the end.

What many people actually do, and it is something that can be destructive if you allow it to be, is anticipate being nervous. The more you think "Oh, the nerves are going to get to me", the more they will. Accept that nerves are a part of public speaking, and channel those nerves into making your speech come alive.

Anyone who claims not to have been nervous the first time they spoke in public is almost certainly lying. It is something that is very hard to pre-imagine accurately, and in most cases, the nerves dissipate after the first few minutes. Accept that you will be nervous, and concentrate on delivering a good presentation. You will learn to love those nerves.

Physical Relaxation Techniques

Deep breathing:

- Sit up straight, cross your legs at the ankles or keep your feet flat on the floor.

- Take a long, slow breath in through your nose. Pretend that you are breathing into your abdomen.

- Allow your abdomen to expand.

- Exhale slowly and evenly through your nose. As you exhale, allow your abdomen to go in.

- Continue to breathe in this way for five to ten breaths.

Progressive Relaxation

- Tense a group of muscles so that they are as tightly contracted as possible.

- Hold them in this state of extreme tension for a few seconds.

- Relax the muscles as you normally would.

- Consciously relax your muscles further so that you are as relaxed as you can be.

Appearing Confident in Front of the Crowd

A speaker who fumbles around with his materials gives an impression of poor organization and lack of interest. The audience suspects that such a speaker hasn't put much effort or thought into preparing for the presentation.

Allow yourself enough time to organize all your materials before you begin your presentation. Being well-organized can also improve your self-confidence.

Remember that there is no reason for the people in the audience to feel anything but well-disposed towards you. Even if they may not agree with what you have to say, as long as you do not say it confrontationally they will accept your right to say it.

One of the most famous strategies to deal with nervousness when addressing an audience is to picture them all in their underwear. However, this is more a joke than a serious strategy. Those who have seriously tried it have found that it distracted them more than anything. It is much better simply to look out into the audience, smile in a relaxed way, and introduce yourself.

The chances are that many of your audience will smile back, and you can then address parts of your speech in their direction in order to feel supported.

The most important thing to remember in order to deliver the most confident presentation you can is to have an awareness of your surroundings. If you move around, bear in mind the positioning of things in the room. If you walk into something, pass it off with a brief joke about people planting things to put you off your stride, and simply allow your speech to flow.

Delivering Your Speech

A few simple steps can help you improve the delivery of your presentation:

- Start off strong by preparing an opening that will capture the audience's attention.

- Learn how to use visual aids effectively.

- Check the volume of your voice.

- Practice beforehand – to check running time, but not to the point where it is automatic.

As long as you have the confidence to use the room to your advantage, and have your ideas straight in your head, the presentation really will take care of itself for most of the time. You will find that, simply through saying it and hearing it often enough, your speech will evolve to a point where you can make slight adjustments on the spot as and where necessary without it becoming confusing.

Starting Off on the Right Foot

The opening of a presentation has two purposes:

- To capture the audience's attention.

- To introduce the subject of the presentation.

The opening should be very brief, in most cases one to two minutes. In that short span of time, you need to present yourself and your topic in a way that will make your audience want to pay attention. In planning your opening, go back to your analysis of your audience.

An effective opening convinces your audience that what you are going to say will be worth their time and attention. If you lose them in the first two minutes, there is not much you can do to get them back with you. In some ways the presentation's most important element is its introduction.

There are many things you can do to catch the audience's attention. Taking into account that a presentation is generally a quite formal setting, this number is maybe slightly reduced in terms of what you can do to catch the audience's attention and keep your job. However, if you work on getting the opening right, you will find that your presentations receive the attention they deserve, and that you will be able to hone them to the point where you become a very skilled presenter.

It is worth opening with a bold statement. The statement may be controversial – to the extent that it is something you believe and that some in the audience may disagree with. "Controversy" in this case is more to do with slight differences of opinion than saying something which will offend people. But it is fine to open with a statement along the lines of "X is something which is absolutely essential to the running of a business", where "X" stands for something that, up to now, many people may not have agreed was essential. Follow this up by saying "I know, many of you may not agree with me, but this is what I plan to prove to you here and now".

Making a statement which requires backing up will draw the attention of the audience, as they listen in to see how you will back it up. You will also have introduced your subject, and can then follow up with a few lines about how opinions have differed on the subject, but people with more years in the business than you have had very positive, complimentary things to say about it. In some cases, it may be beneficial to write the opening statement for your presentation after you have written the rest of it, as this allows you to make your statement chime with what you are going to say.

Using Visual Aids

Visual aids are able to:

- Clarify data that may be difficult for the audience to grasp from a verbal presentation alone. Charts and graphs are especially helpful for this purpose.

- Highlight your main ideas.

- Help your audience remember your main ideas. Many studies have shown that an audience remembers the main points of a presentation longer if the speaker uses visual aids.

- Signal transitions between major sections of your presentation.

- Shorten meetings. If handled properly, visual aids can shorten meetings by allowing the speaker to spend less time clarifying and repeating the main points of the presentation.

One study has shown that presentations that include visual aids are more persuasive than presentations that do not. There is some dispute over whether the use of visual aids is simply a gimmick to cover for the fact that a presentation does not say very much – an accusation of style over substance – and there are certainly cases where this happens.

But the coherent use of visual aids will make a presentation more memorable to the audience and will allow the presenter to make his or her points more completely. Getting it right can be difficult, but if you do get it right the pay-off can be huge.

Try to avoid simply copying the visual aids you have seen used before. If you have seen them, then the chances are that your audience will have seen them too. If they were successful then, the audience will be prone to think back to that presentation and either ignore yours or constantly compare the two.

If they were unsuccessful, then it is unlikely that they will suddenly have become more effective. It is best to think of visual aids after you have written the presentation, as this will allow you to think of a coherent uniting factor between the elements you wish to illustrate.

If you can think of a visual aid that can be used interactively, then so much the better. One obstacle which presenters find they run into is the difficulty of saying something that has not been said before, or in a way in which it has never been said.

By achieving this, you will create a situation where your audience will refer back to your presentation as "remember the time when …" Having this kind of memorable impact can make your presentation a lot more effective. It should, however, not be all that people remember. Over-reliance on visual aids will simply lead to your broader message falling on deaf ears.

Checking the Volume of Your Voice

The more people there are in a room, the louder you will have to speak. People make noise unintentionally by moving around in their seats or shuffling papers.

If you find that you have to shout to make yourself heard in the back of the room, then you need a microphone. Overall, though, conference rooms tend to be built in order to allow a presenter's voice to carry. The difficulty of getting your voice to just the right volume for a presentation is made by the fact that there are multiple rows of people viewing the presentation. In this case, it is important to take account of the seating arrangements.

Before you say anything else in a presentation, it may be a good idea to ask, in the voice you intend to use for the presentation, whether everyone can hear you clearly. The element of balance is again important here.

Speakers who are too quiet will have the obvious disadvantage that their listeners genuinely cannot hear them, as well as the fact that they will appear nervous and not in command. This does not excuse going too far in the opposite direction, which will lead people to consider you brash and over-confident, and either consciously or subconsciously give less weight to your views.

Shouting distorts the voice, and it is a simple fact that something which is shouted will not be heard as clearly as something of a similar length which is spoken powerfully from the middle of the chest. Also bear in mind that if you plan to move around the venue, you will need to make adjustments at times to ensure that your voice carries the extra distance.

If you are facing away from the audience, keep your statements during this time to a minimum, and try if possible to turn to face them during this period. If a microphone will be necessary, ensure that one is available, and tested before use – microphones can have a distorting effect which will make any presentation less worthwhile.

During the course of a presentation, you need to be aware of how things are going. Are people starting to lose interest? Do they need a break? Do you need to do something different to change the pace?

When it's time to wrap up your presentation, you need to remind people of your basic message. You hope that a week from now, if someone asked the members of your audience they would be able to recall what your presentation was all about.

This is something that depends greatly upon the audience, but as you have no control over their reactions your job is simply to ensure that you get your message across as persuasively as you possibly can.

You will probably be given an allotted time to deliver your presentation, and it is a good idea to take this time and look at all the elements you need to cover. By doing this you can then divide the allotted time into shorter spells in which you can cover the topics in hand.

Adjusting on the Fly

Here are some adjustments you could make if the audience seemed to be losing interest:

- Ask questions.

- Have a member of the audience come to the front of the room and help you with a demonstration.

- Conduct an informal poll ("How many people think that…?").

- Introduce a brief, interesting digression (go off topic for two or three minutes).

- Use a brief anecdote (preferably one that has something to do with your topic).

Each of the above adjustments has the advantage of offering a change of pace, and if your audience has given the appearance of losing interest these can turn that around by reminding the audience that there is a reason for them to listen.

Some audiences react to different things than others, and you will normally be able to tell what it is that your presentation lacks by reading the faces of your audience. If they look slightly pained and confused, it may be that you are speaking from a vocabulary with which they are unfamiliar. If they simply look bored, then it may be that you are not telling them anything new.

Involving the audience is something which, done carefully, can get a presentation right back on track when it has been threatening to lose their attention. From something as simple as not wanting to be called up to the front and exposed for their failure to pay attention, to something as enjoyable as the ability to participate in a genuinely interesting diversion, this will cause people to sit forward and become more interested in proceedings.

It may also be that you have been speaking excessively formally, and have appeared distanced and humorless. Obviously, a lot has gone into this presentation and you may well consider it to be "no laughing matter", but a certain lightness of touch can make the presentation flow better and involve the audience more. It is wise to avoid disrespectful humor, but some light self-mocking can go a long way to getting the audience on your side.

Gauging Whether Breaks Are Required

When you tell people to take a break, tell them exactly when you plan to start again. Fifteen minutes is a typical length for a break. The shorter presentations – those under an hour, will generally not require a break, but if the presentation edges towards an hour and a half it may well be that offering a break in the middle can be the wisest thing to do.

Although people will sit for upwards of two hours in a movie theater, there is a clear difference between a movie and a presentation. Atmospherically, dynamically and in many other ways it is much easier to sit through a film of a certain length than it is to sit through a presentation of the same length.

If you do give a break to the audience at a presentation, it is essential to specify that you will begin the presentation again at a set time and impress upon them the importance of their being back at the right time.

If people stay out beyond the allotted time for a break then it simply results in the recommencing of the presentation being delayed, and gives a very bad impression. If there are some stragglers who take a little bit more time to arrive back, then it is beneficial to simply have a short, informal conversation with the people who have arrived on time or stayed in the auditorium during the break.

This can be a good way of gauging how the presentation is being received, and allow you to get an impression for what your audience is like.

Wrapping Up and Winding Down

Sometimes a speaker will end a presentation with a question and answer session. If you do this, don't end the presentation with your answer to the last question. It might have little to do with your main point. Instead, after you have answered the last question, say something like:

"That's all we have time for. If there is one thing I hope you will remember from this presentation, it's..."

Doing this will end the presentation in a neat way, and pull together the strands of the previous period of time. It will also allow you to reinforce the central point of your presentation. As people leave, thank them for attending and say goodbye to them.

If people leave the presentation on a positive note they are more likely to remember what has gone before in a positive light. Whatever else you do, you should ensure that if people have follow-up questions after the event they can address them to you in whatever way is possible.

Questions and Answers

The way you respond to questions will have a major effect on what kind of rapport you are able to build with the audience. If you answer questions thoughtfully and respectfully, people will feel that you are taking them seriously. If you give flip, dismissive answers, people will feel that you don't have time for them.

People may ask questions which are not a hundred per cent serious, but even then you should not be dismissive, simply take the question in the spirit it was intended and take the opportunity to display a sense of humor.

Questions may well be an opportunity for you to get information into the presentation that you could not address due to overall time constraints. When someone asks a good question, begin your response with a sentence along the lines of *"That's a very good question, and I am glad you asked me that. I think the most important thing here is that..."*

If someone asks a question which you find either you cannot answer or which is difficult, do not simply say "*I don't know*" but say *"That's a good question. I have to admit I hadn't covered that issue – what do you think?"* This way you will not lose respect, but will allow discussion to flow more freely.

Ground Rules

At the end of your presentation you say, "Does anyone have any questions?" And no one does. What do you do? You could try waiting for 20 seconds or so and then say, "Well, one question people often ask is…" Come up with your own question to show people what kinds of questions you expect.

NOTE: The question you come up with should be an easy one so people will get the idea that they don't have to ask something very complicated or difficult.

If the presentation is longer than an hour, it is beneficial to allow questions at regular intervals. This is because the longer people are sat in silence, the less interest they will show in whatever is at hand.

However, most presentations will be shorter than that, and it is advisable to hold off questions until the end. If you have an hour in total for the presentation, you should look to wind down at the 45-minute mark and take questions in the last fifteen minutes.

This will allow you to answer questions and look for feedback on those answers. An open question-and-answer session will enliven matters with more group participation. It will give everyone a chance to participate – in a way which will reinforce what they hopefully have learned.

Answering Questions That Sound Like an Attack

At some point, someone in your audience might ask a question that sounds like an attack. How should you respond to a hostile question?

- Don't confront the person. Don't say, *"No, I think you're wrong."*

- Affirm the person. Say,

    "That's an interesting point, but here's another way to look at."

    "I can see why you would feel that way, but I was trying to make the point that..."

    "Point taken; I might have been too sweeping in my generalization."

Everyone in the room will be waiting to hear how you respond to the challenge. If you keep cool and say something positive before you proceed to your answer, you will impress your audience with your professionalism and your command of the situation.

Agree with the person as far as you can. State your disagreement in a non-confrontational way. *"I think we agree on XYX, but not on ABC."*

Answering hostile questions with an equally hostile response will simply make the whole process tense. As you are the person at the front of the room, and the person asking the question is sat with a number of other people, it will simply set you against a larger group of people, making the atmosphere needlessly confrontational.

Additionally, if you answer a hostile question by showing good grace and considering the question on its positive merits, you will increase the likelihood of the initially hostile individual backing down from their confrontational position, whether through embarrassment for their unnecessary hostility, or because they were impressed by you looking to answer their question fairly despite the fact that it could have been taken as an attack.

It should be clear that you are not a teacher to the group of people, but some of the principles of teaching remain intact. Among these, the fact that you are in a position of some responsibility and importance should prevent you from allowing yourself to have a pop back at the person.

Dealing with Complex Questions

Listen

- Listen attentively to the question.

- Make eye contact with the questioner.

- Nod or give other indications of encouragement.

- Don't interrupt.

- Paraphrase when appropriate. If a person asks a long, rambling question, you might want to paraphrase it before you respond. Say something like, *"Let me be sure I understand you. You are asking..."*

Analyze

- Before responding, make sure you understand the question.

- Try to determine the intent of the questioner. Is he genuinely asking for clarification, or is he trying to disprove or challenge you? Watch facial expression and body language. Listen for tone.

- Ask yourself; is there a broader issue behind the question that I need to address?

Affirm

- Make eye contact with the questioner again.

- Say something like, *"That's an interesting point,"* or *"I'm glad you brought that up."* An affirmation of this kind is especially important if the question was asked in a challenging way.

Answer

- Don't duck a question or give a vague answer.

- If you don't know the answer, say so. You might want to tell the questioner that you will call him the next day with an answer.

- Give an honest answer. If the audience gets the impression that you are trying to put one over on them, you might as well pack up and go home.

The question and answer session traditionally comes at the end of the presentation, so if you shine during this section, people will remember that very clearly, as they will surely remember you negatively if you duck questions or give fraudulent answers. Ending on a positive note is hugely important in a presentation, and if you can do that you are most of the way to being a good public speaker.

Chapter 22 – Facilitation Skills

Facilitation is often referred to as the new cornerstone of management philosophy. With its focus on fairness and creating an easy decision making, facilitation can make any organization make better decisions. This workshop will give participants an understanding of what facilitation is all about, as well as some tools that they can use to facilitate small meetings.

At the end of this chapter, you should be able to:

- Define facilitation and identify its purpose and benefits.

- Clarify the role and focus of a facilitator.

- Differentiate between process and content in the context of a group discussion.

- Provide tips in choosing and preparing for facilitation.

- Identify a facilitator's role when managing groups in each of Tuckman and Jensen's stages of group development: forming, storming, norming, and performing.

- Identify ways a facilitator can help a group reach a consensus: from encouraging participation to choosing a solution.

- Provide guidelines in dealing with disruptions, dysfunctions, and difficult people in groups.

- Define what interventions are, when they are appropriate, and how to implement them.

Recall the last time you had a group meeting. The group meeting can be at work, at church, at civic groups or even within the family.

Think about the way the meeting was ran, the person (or people) who steered the discussion, and the tools and techniques used to engage the participants and accomplish all the meeting's goals.

The following guided questions can help this process:

In your group:

Did you feel that everyone's contribution is welcome?

- What are your indicators?

- What did the facilitator (this maybe you) say or do to make the group feel welcome or unwelcome?

Did you feel that the decisions your group made are reflective of everyone's position, or at least the best compromise of everyone's position?

- What are your indicators?

- What did the facilitator (this maybe you) say or do to make surface everyone's point of view and incorporate it in the decision-making process?

Which of these two do you think is prioritized more in your group: getting the tasks in the agenda accomplished, or making the most of the knowledge, creativity, and relationships in the group? What makes you say so?

Understanding Facilitation

Groups are powerful resources in any organization. When you tap into groups, you don't just get the best of individual members, you also get the best of group interaction. The result is a more dynamic, creative and empowered team.

To get the most of groups, you need facilitation skills. In this module, we will discuss what is facilitation, what is a facilitator and when is facilitation appropriate.

What is Facilitation?

Facilitation is a manner of handling group meetings in a way that takes the focus away from just one leader, and instead distributes leadership to all members of the group. There is premium on democracy, group involvement, and cooperation. The focus is not just on getting things done, but also in feeling good about it.

Consultant Dave Sibbet defines facilitation as *"the art of leading people through processes towards agreed-upon objectives in a manner that encourages participation, ownership, and creativity from all involved."*

Facilitation is often contrasted with presentation, which is delivering information or decisions to a group. Facilitation is group-centered while presentation is leader-centered. For this reason, facilitation is incompatible with an autocratic management style.

Example of the difference between facilitation and presentation:

FACILITATION: *"How do you think the company can solve this problem? Does anyone have any ideas?"*

PRESENTATION: *"This is how we will solve the problem…"*

What is a Facilitator?

Group-centered meetings require an individual or individuals in the case of larger groups to manage the process. This person(s) is a facilitator.

A facilitator is a person who helps groups to arrive at their objective by ensuring that everyone's contribution is heard and the processes being used are both productive and empowering to all. Facilitators work primarily through leading and blocking techniques, basically directing traffic within a group discussion. Facilitation can also involve managing group member's emotions, defusing tensions and encouraging team cohesiveness. In some cases, facilitators help in setting and revising meeting structure, and managing conflicts.

To be effective, facilitators have to be neutral to the discussion, not partial to any members, and acceptable to everyone involved. They should not take a position in any of the issues raised, nor should they advocate a solution --- or attempt to directly solve the problem. Having an objective "third party" facilitator ensures that group members would feel safe about voicing out their opinions.

Knowledge of group process and an appreciation of democratic management are pre-requisites to becoming an effective facilitator. Sensitivity and keen observation skills are also non-negotiable.

When is Facilitation Appropriate?

In general, facilitation has something positive to offer every group process, whether we're talking about a working group or a recreational group.

Facilitation is most appropriate:

When you want to encourage group motivation, commitment and confidence. A facilitated process is a great way to get employees engaged and empowered; it sends the message that all team members' opinions, suggestions, and feelings are valued, and will at least be taken into consideration before making a decision. When a discussion is facilitated, group members can take pride in the results, because the bulk of the ideas came from them.

More so, a facilitated process promotes ownership of a task or an issue among group members. Because results depend directly on the team members' effort and performance, teams are more likely to invest in the process and carry a task through.

When you want to make the most of group knowledge, experience and diversity. Facilitation is ideal when you have people of different backgrounds, expertise and or work style, and you want to create something that integrates all these differences. For example, brainstorming sessions always work best if participants are from diverse disciplines. Facilitation can ensure that all members have their say, and that cross-fertilization of ideas (members building on other members' ideas) can happen.

When there is more than one answer to a question, or one side to a story. Facilitation is appropriate for discussion of issues that allow a healthy debate and multiple perspectives. A discussion where the solution is clear from the very beginning, or where no other viable alternative exists, is not recommended for facilitations. Similarly, a conflict situation where only one position will be tolerated is not for facilitation.

When a person in power wants to just be a participant. Facilitation is recommended when a leader wants to level off with his members when discussing an issue. For example, a discussion on a sensitive policy change is best handled by a neutral facilitator; so that members don't feel intimidated or threatened by their boss' position, and boss' can be guided in seeing things from their employees' point of view. Facilitation is also advisable when a person in power wants a fresh perspective, and he's worried that he'll influence output if he leads the discussion.

When you want to learn about your group's process, or challenge an inefficient process. Facilitation can be a way to identify roots of unproductive discussions, and teach alternative ways of tackling an issue. For example, meetings that often monopolized by one person can be restructured by simply adding a facilitator. Once that group experiences a facilitated discussion, they might be inclined to have more democratic meetings even after the facilitator leaves.

When there are psychological blocks that need to be addressed in an issue. A discussion might seem clear cut, with decisions final. However if there are underlying tensions and reservations, calling in a facilitator will be a good idea. Facilitators are experts in not just managing what was said, but what was left unsaid as well. He or she can surface psychological blocks to an issue and bring it to discussion.

Facilitation is least appropriate:

When discussing issues where the only solution is administrative adjudication. Some issues are not meant for discussion but for an executive decision, an example of this is the termination of an employee. Also, if two parties are at a stalemate and the only way to resolve the issue is for the leader to directly interfere and make a judgment call, then mediation is more appropriate than facilitation.

When the goal of a meeting is merely to inform a group. Facilitation is not recommended in situations when group members don't have the information or sometimes authority, to get the task done. The same goes when group members are in no position to contribute to the issue for ethical or legal reasons. In these cases, information can only flow from the leader down to the members and not vice-versa.

When participants take turns in arriving at the meeting. Group-centered discussions require continuity, which is why it should only be appropriate to situations where all or a significant number of group members are available for meeting at the same time. If a group is always changing members in the middle of a discussion, or only one "clique" or coalition in a group is present, it is difficult to conduct effective processes.

In crisis situations when quick decisions have to be made. Facilitated discussions take significantly more time than non-facilitated discussions, and arriving at a consensus is not always guaranteed. If quick decision-making and immediate action is required, facilitation is not recommended.

Process vs. Content

Facilitators are process experts; they are as interested in the "how?" as much as the "what?" To produce quality output, you must arrive at it functionally. In this module, we will discuss the difference between process and content, and which among the two should be a facilitator's focus.

About Process

Process refers to the way a discussion is happening, independent of the subject matter or issue being talked about. Basically, process talks about how a group works together. It includes how members talk to each other, how they identify and solve problems, how they make decisions, and how they handle conflict. It takes into account group dynamics, non-verbal messages, and situational elements.

Process elements include:

- **Meeting Flow**. How does the meeting begin? How do they transition to another item in the agenda? Who keeps the ball rolling? Are there topic jumps? How does the meeting end?

- **Participation**. How many people contribute to the discussion? What is the quality of their contribution? Are there highs, lows, and shifts in group participation? How are silent people treated?

- **Communication.**, How do group members communicate with one another? Is the verbal communication congruent with the non-verbal communication? Who talks with whom? Who interrupts whom?

- **Roles**. What roles do each member of the group play? Are these roles self-assigned or assigned by others? Are the roles productive? How do the members of the group respond to these roles?

- **Power/ Influence**. Who has high influence? Who can move the group into a particular action whether positive or negative? How do they exert this power? Is the group democratic, authoritarian, or permissive when it comes to discussions? Are there shifts in power/influence? Are there rivalries? Do there seem to be coalitions and alliances?

- **Problem-Solving Process**. Is the problem stated in clear workable terms? Does it seem clear to everyone what the issue is? How does the group arrive at solution? Is this method acceptable and fair to all members?

- **Decision-Making Process**. How are the best interests of all participants represented in the decision making process? Are there self-authorized decision-makers? Does the group arrive at a consensus? Is the way of deciding acceptable to all members of the group? How are people who disagree with the majority treated?

- **Group Atmosphere**. What is the general feeling in the group? How are feelings handled? Are they encouraged and validated? Is this group capable of care? Are there significant emotional attachments between members?

About Content

Content refers to the subject matter of a discussion: the actual words or ideas that were spoken independent of contextual variables like non-verbal cues and procedural variables. It refers mainly to the literal meaning of words and makes no reference to connotations, subtexts, and insinuations behind messages.

In a meeting, content is the agenda topic, the suggestions put forward by the staff members, the solutions they arrive at. Content in a facilitated discussion should *all* come from the group and not the facilitator.

Example: The content of the meeting may be "how to change the company's image to that it will appeal to a younger market." In contrast the process element in the same meeting is brainstorming to solicit as many options as possible.

A Facilitator's Focus

Which between process and content should a group facilitator attend to?

Ideally, a facilitator should attend to both process and content. After all, process and content feed one another. Good meeting processes create better content; keeping to relevant content makes for a great discussion process. A productive discussion can only happen when the content is on track and the meeting flows in a functional way.

However, facilitators are primarily process experts; they manage information flow and treatment. They are not encouraged to provide content input in any way. While some knowledge of a meeting's topic can help a facilitator manage a meeting better, a facilitator should not put forward personal opinions and suggestions, or make judgments and decisions for the group. They're also content neutral; they should never take sides in a debate.

When a facilitator adds to the content of a discussion, the facilitator's role is confused from neutral guide to biased participant or a trainer/ coach. If a content expert is needed (one whose task is to clarify technical issues in a discussion e.g. a lawyer for union issues, or an Organizational Development consultant), they can be included as participant in the group for expert reference.

Here is an example of a facilitator focusing primarily on process instead of content:

Imagine that a group discussion is stuck. The group can't seem to generate a good, viable idea for their project. A content expert in this situation can provide a range of alternatives they can try--- after all he or she has specialized knowledge in this area. But a facilitator is a process expert. Instead of giving suggestions, a facilitator would seek to identify why idea generation is not proceeding well. Maybe the group is tired? Maybe the problem needs to be re-defined? In these cases, a facilitator can encourage a working break to get the thinking juices flowing, or ask the group to re-define the problem to encourage a different perspective, respectively.

Laying the Groundwork

A facilitated approach is not just a technique; it's an attitude and disposition to doing things that should be shared by the whole organization. To best benefit from group facilitation, you need to set the stage for it. In this module, we will discuss choosing a facilitated approach, planning for a facilitated meeting and collecting data.

Choosing a Facilitated Approach

In an earlier module, we discussed about the situations where facilitation is appropriate and situations when facilitation is not appropriate. These factors can be a guide if facilitation is the best approach to managing a meeting in your organization.

If your organization has decided that facilitation is appropriate, the following are some steps you should take:

Orient the participants about what facilitation is, and what it can do for them. If a team is new to the facilitated approach, they might find difficulty with the process. For example, individuals from a hierarchal organization might feel uneasy contributing when there are senior members in the group. In situations where there's conflict, the group might even expect the facilitator to adjudicate the issue or at least offer an opinion. It's important then to level everyone off with what facilitation is (and what it isn't) before you start implementing it in your group. If there are significant reservations about changing to a facilitated approach, surface them so that they may be addressed.

Make sure that facilitation has the administration's support. The incentive to make the most out of a facilitated discussion can be nullified if the people who make decisions still prefer a top-down, autocratic approach. While it's not guaranteed that ideas and proposal produced by facilitated teams will get approved, administration should at the very least communicate their openness to the team's efforts.

Choose the right facilitator. Facilitators can be from within the organization or a freelance professional.

It is important that you pick a facilitator who is not part of the problem-context or the solution, and is generally perceived as unbiased with no conflict of interest. They must also possess the right attitude and disposition in handling people's contribution.

Planning for a Facilitated Meeting

The following are some things you can do in preparation for a facilitated meeting:

Set the venue. Facilitation works best if the venue is conducive to a comfortable discussion. Chairs arranged in a circle are always better than a classroom set-up, to emphasize equality among all members. Privacy is a must. If you need to use materials like flip chart paper, markers, and nametags, prepare them beforehand.

It also helps to prepare not just the venue of the meeting proper, but the surrounding areas as well. It's not unusual for facilitators to invite meeting participants to break out in smaller discussion groups, or even "take a walk" to blow off steam. As such, preparations for these activities should be made before the meeting.

Set aside time. Facilitated meetings should not be rushed; minding process is the reason why it works well. The length of a facilitated meeting depends on the agenda and the number of participants, but the recommended duration is 30 minutes to one hour.

Prepare a Facilitation Plan. As a facilitator, never go blindly into a meeting. While an experienced facilitator would likely have enough skills enough to "wing it", it always pays to be prepared.

Make sure you know what the objective of the meeting is, expectations of the group and/or the organization from you, and the profile of your participants. Decide ahead how you are going to begin and end the meeting, and how you plan to manage the meeting itself. For this process, it helps if you research and gather relevant information beforehand (more on this later), and prepare a Facilitation Plan (see the next page).

Make plans for documentation. To better be able to follow up, and identify process issues in a group, it always helps if a meeting is documented. Typically, groups assign a secretary to take minutes of a meeting. However, traditional minutes usually deal with just content. For best results, consider assigning a process observer: someone to document process elements in a group.

Prepare Psychologically. Lastly, it's important that you take the time to prepare internally if you're going to facilitate a meeting. Being a facilitator can be a mentally, sometimes even emotionally, demanding job. You want to make sure that you are in a relaxed frame of mind before you facilitate. Deal with personal issues that can interfere with the process, and note your biases and assumptions about the group or the subject of the meeting.

Below is a sample template for a Facilitation Plan:

Participants:	
Beginning Time:	**Ending Time:**
Meeting Topic(s):	

Meeting Objectives:
    A.
    B.
    C.	

Icebreaker or Opener:	
Discussion Questions:	**Discussion Method:**
Summary/ Integration:	
Evaluation:	

Collecting Data

The more information a facilitator has about the group she will be facilitating, the more effective he or she can be.

The following are some tips in collecting data as preparation for facilitating a meeting:

Communicate ahead with the person who invited you to facilitate the meeting to understand what is expected from the meeting and what is expected from you as a facilitator. If there are presenters and content experts in the meeting, it's also best to meet with them beforehand to ensure that you are both on the same page.

Ideally, you should also be able to interview or survey participants ahead of time. This can give you time to understand the dynamics of the situation, as well as establish rapport. Ask about the group's history, their view of the meeting subject, and how the group normally accomplishes things. It also helps to know ahead if there are reservations about inviting a facilitator.

Request documentation about the group's previous meetings e.g. minutes or progress reports. They will give you an idea of where the group is at the moment.

If there's a sensitive issue involved, know as much as you can about the situation – and even the personalities involved. For instance, knowing that there's underlying tension about a specific topic will tell you to approach it cautiously. Similarly, knowing who the participants in conflict are can guide you when dividing participants into working groups. Note though: always triangulate your information gathering method so that you don't get just one side of the story.

Understand the subject matter of the meeting. While facilitators are not content experts, you must know enough about the topic to be able to track the discussion. For example, familiarize yourself with the terms and language of the group. You lose precious time by having to ask the group to explain terms to you.

Tuckman and Jensen's Model of Team Development

Groups are not stagnant entities; they change. Initial uncertainty and ambiguity give way to stable patterns of interaction, while relationship between members wax and wane. To be an effective facilitator, you must be sensitive to the changes happening within groups.

In this module, we will discuss one of the most widely-used theories of group development: Tuckman and Jensen's Model of Team Development. We will also discuss how a facilitator can best respond to groups depending on what stage of development they are in.

Stage One: Forming

The initial stage of group development is the forming stage. It is commonly referred to as the orientation stage or the *"getting-to-know-you"* stage, as group members still don't know much about each other or about the organization. If the organization itself is new, then there might not be any existing structure or rules in the group yet.

During the forming stage, members tend to feel tensions and uncertainties. After all, group members are dealing with people they hardly know, and this initial unfamiliarity may leave them feeling uncomfortable and constrained. Often, members are on guard, carefully monitoring their behavior to make certain they avoid any embarrassing lapses of social poise.

Without the benefit of a long and solid relationship with the group, involvement and commitment to the organization may be low. There may also be extreme dependence on leaders, dominant personalities and other group members.

The forming stage is characterized by many tentative and testing behaviors: explorations of the boundaries of both rules and tasks.

During the forming stage, it is important for the facilitator to:

- Establish rapport among group members

- Encourage members to be comfortable with one another

- Make everyone feel accepted in the group

- Establish rules and guidelines for both task and relational behavior

- Encourage the group to be comfortable with the organization

Stage Two: Storming

A natural offshoot of uncertainty and ambiguity is the need to clarify expectations, establish patterns, and put a structure into place. Clarity, patterns, and structure are what make a group stable. However with many different personalities and perspectives to reconcile, these things don't always evolve smoothly. The natural formation of sub-relationships within the group can also add to the pressure. Enter the second stage of group development: the storming stage.

The storming stage of group development is characterized by conflict, whether overt fighting or subtle tensions. This happens when at least two people disagree on a way of doing things or a way of relating. Conflicts in groups also occur when particular members assert control or dominance in some form, and other members resist. Coalition-building and fractionalization of the group can happen as members take sides on an issue.

The emotional atmosphere in groups during the storming stage can be characterized by tension, anger, frustration, and discounting of other people's responses.

A facilitator guiding a team in the storming stage should remember that conflict is normal, even necessary element, in group development. Conflicts are signs that there are processes that need streamlining, or issues that require a definite response. When conflicts surface within groups, facilitators can help the group see an opportunity to set a structure (which is the next stage.)

During the storming stage, it is important for the facilitator to:

- Defuse tensions

- Promote positive communication in the group

- Identify problems areas

- Facilitate conflict resolution processes

Stage Three: Norming

The third stage of group development is the norming stage.

If the conflict areas during the storming stage are addressed properly, the result should be the establishment of norms.

Norms are rules or standards of behavior within a group. They can be explicit (such as a company policy) or implicit (unspoken expectations). Norms help groups to meet their goals. At the very least, norms help the group maintain some degree of stability so that tasks can be done.

During the norming stage, group members develop greater cohesiveness and possibly intimacy. There is greater security in opening up to others and suggesting new ways of doing things. The norming stage is a period of clarity in terms of the group's identity, dynamics, and direction.

If you're a facilitator handling a group in the norming stage, it helps to:

- Practice skills in identifying possible solutions

- Define roles and expectations

- Manage change

- Help the group to reach a consensus

Evaluating new systems and protocols, and making revisions if necessary are also part of the norming stage.

Stage Four: Performing

When groups are able to successfully implement a new rule or system, they can begin a period of optimum productivity. With stability in place, there is room for creativity, initiative, stability, open relationships, pride, learning and high morale. Group energy is no longer taken up by set-up matters, and can be channeled fully to the work. The group goes into the height of task success: the performing stage.

The relationships among group members also become more relaxed and involved. Because the task details are already clearly defined, and there is no need for vicious power struggles, there is more room for closeness and deeper relationships among members.

To get to the performing stage is the goal of all organizations. As a facilitator, your task is to guide the group towards this stage. One important thing to remember though is that optimal productivity often occurs later in a group's life, and a period of storming and norming are pre-requisites to it.

At this stage, the role of the facilitator is to help maintain the group in the performing stage. Tasks include providing support and motivation in each task, and reinforcing best practices.

What happens if the group gets new members or encounters new tasks? What if a new issue comes about threatening peak performance? In these cases, the group can go back to earlier stages. For example, if new groups members make pre-existing rules obsolete, or a new conflict area is spotted, then the group returns to the storming stage to hash out a new system. It is said that in the life course of a group, it will return to the storming stage regularly. See figure in the next page.

An effective facilitator can point out that that re-accomplishing developmental tasks characteristic of earlier stages (e.g. establishing rapport) may be needed to adapt to new changes.

An Illustration of Tuckman and Jensen's Stages of Team Development:

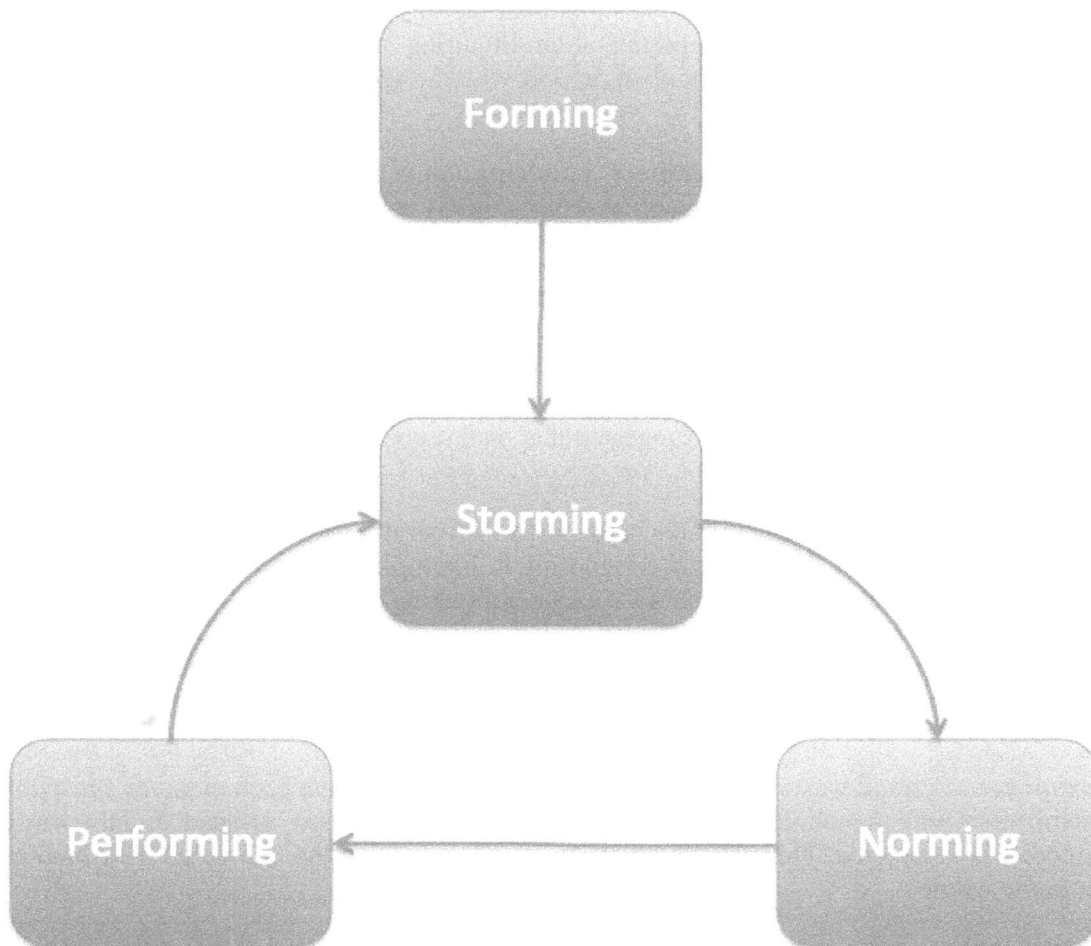

Building Consensus

The aim of facilitated discussions is to create participatory groups: one where the goal is cooperative rather than competitive decision-making. All members should have equal input in the process, and equal opportunity to voice opposition to an idea or conclusion. In this module, we will discuss the key facilitation skills needed to build consensus: encouraging participation, gathering information, presenting information, synthesizing and summarizing.

Encouraging Participation

Consensus is more likely to happen if members feel encouraged to contribute. The following are some of the ways a facilitator can encourage participation in small groups:

Provide preparation guidelines in the meeting agenda. Participants are more likely to contribute, if they feel confident that they have something to add to the discussion. It's helpful then to send out a meeting invitation with guidelines what to review and study in preparation for the meeting. It is also better if you can also send out guide questions ahead of time.

Before starting a group meeting, check on everyone's comfort level. Some people are at ease being in meetings; others have difficulty. There are also situational factors, such as an uncomfortable seat or a poorly ventilated room, which can hamper group participation. Inquiring if group members are comfortable before starting a meeting can help a facilitator establish rapport with the group, and address hindrances to group participation.

State at the start of the meeting that members' participation is not just welcome, but is integral to the process. Sometimes, all it takes is for the facilitator to explicitly say that members are allowed and encouraged to participate for the discussion to be a lively one. These guidelines can be made part of the orientation process.

Acknowledge responses. Show that you have heard and understood a contribution. You can do this in non-verbal and verbal ways. Non-verbal ways include eye contact, nodding, and leaning forward towards the speaker. Verbal ways include praising ("I'm glad you brought that up.", "That's a good point."), clarifying (If I may reiterate what you just said, you suggested that, is this correct?), and requesting for more information ("Tell us more.", "Please go on.").

Avoid discounting responses. Similar, make sure that you're careful not to give a response that might be interpreted as devaluing a contribution, or even ignoring it. Examples of discounting responses are "That was said already." , "That's irrelevant." , "That's it? Is there anything else?"

Solicit group members' responses. You can encourage participation by directly asking everyone their opinion on a subject matter. Example: "Can I get everyone's opinion about this proposal?" or "Let's share all our ideas. We won't react until we've heard them all."

Build on responses. A good way to encourage participation is to integrate each member's response with that of other members or with the whole group. Similarities and differences are surfaced, and the way each point relates to another is verbalized. This way, the discussion is moving and the individual contributions are seen as relevant to the whole.

Ways to do this include:

- **Universalizing** – Helping the group see that their concerns are shared. Example: "Who else has felt this way?"

- **Linking** – Making verbal connections to what individual members say and feel. Example: "Bill thinks that there should be another meeting to prepare for the conference. This seems to be similar to what April was saying a while ago." Or "Michael believes that the group should outsource all customer communication. Jonathan, on the other hand, feels that an in-house customer care staff will serve the company better. It seems we have two different but equally valid approaches to this problem."

- **Redirecting** – To promote the involvement of all in the discussion. Example: "What do you think about that?" or "What do you think about Mark's idea?"

Intentionally keep silent. Intentional silence can also be a way to encourage participation, especially if a group is eager to contribute and needs no prompting.

Thanking the Group. Lastly, affirming the group for their participation, and each member for their contribution, can encourage greater involvement in the succeeding meetings.

Gathering Information

The following are some of the ways a facilitator can gather information during a discussion.

Go-round. In this technique, each member of the group gets a turn to speak without getting interrupted. Sometimes, the amount of time each member is allowed to speak is limited to encourage fairness. In go-rounds, each member gets to speak. Note that this method may not be applicable if you have many participants.

Break Out Groups. In this technique, the facilitator divides the participants into smaller groups (anywhere from dyads up, depending on the size of the group and the subject to be discussed) and then later allots time for a representative from each group to share their point of view. This method is applicable when there are too many participants to do an efficient go round, or some discussion is necessary, but that discussion is more effective in smaller teams.

BRAINSTORMING. Brainstorming is a method of gathering information that involves getting as many ideas from the group in limited time. During brainstorming, participants can verbalize any idea they have, good or bad, and a documenter logs it in a flip chart. Only when all the ideas have been exhausted, or there are already enough ideas for consideration, does the group check out each idea one by one. For best results the time for brainstorming is limited.

FISHBOWL Method. This method is best when an intense discussion of a subject is needed, but the group is too large for the time allotted. In the fishbowl method, a sample of the group discusses the topic, while the rest function as observers. Ideally, the discussion sample should represent the diversity in the group.

Presenting Information

In order for a discussion group to reach a consensus, it is important that they are well-informed of the facts of the issue, as well as the positions of the different parties concerned. In this sense, an effective facilitator is one that can guide group members in presenting important information to the plenary.

The following are some tips in presenting information in groups.

Separate presentation from discussion time. Assign a time particularly for presentation of information. Going back and forth between discussion and presentation can disrupt group process and may even make for ineffective decision-making. For best results, place the presentation time on the agenda, and assign presenters before the meeting proper.

If there are more than one side to an issue, or more than one option in consideration, make sure you assign equal time for each. Process can be helped if each party feels that they are being treated fairly. Being given equal time as another party can facilitate this. And even if there are no conflicting parties in the group, giving each subject or each proposal the same time as the others can ensure that decisions that would be made at the end of the meeting are not biased in any way.

Use a multi-media guide if possible. When presenting information, it helps to know that information can be presented in visual (the use of colorful presentations, hand-outs, demonstrations, flipcharts, videos, etc.), auditory (descriptive narratives and reports) and bodily/kinesthetic (activities to learn key points) ways. Use the method that fits the learning style of the group and the subject of the presentation.

Note that the use of projected visual aids may require a darkened room, making the meeting less conducive for group interaction.

Synthesizing and Summarizing

A synthesis is an integration of key points or key process movements in the discussion. An example of synthesizing is listing issues that have been resolved and issues that are still up for discussion. A summary, on the other hand is a short recap of what has been discussed or what has happened. Syntheses and summaries are not just conducted at the end of each meeting, but also during the discussion proper.

Synthesizing and summarizing key discussion points is facilitative during a meeting. There are many reasons for this. First, synthesis and summaries show that the discussion is on track and following the agenda. It can also clear confusing discussions, and help members see where the group is at any moment. These processes also give the group a sense of accomplishment --- the synthesis and the summary is usually an indication of movement in the discussion.

The following are some ways a facilitator can synthesize or summarize during a group discussion:

- Let the group summarize or synthesize for themselves. Example: Ask group members "What have we discussed so far?", "What did you learn from this discussion?" or "What have we decided about this situation?"

- Ask a group member/ group members to provide a synthesis or summary.

- Offer your tentative synthesis/ summary and seek for the group's clarification. For example: "This is what we have discussed so far….Did I miss anything?"

- Refer to the agenda or published documentation in a flip chart paper. "So far, we have discussed Topic A and B. These are our resolutions…"

Reaching a Decision Point

The steps outlined in the previous module are just ways to set the stage towards consensus-building. When it comes to the actual decision point, it helps that a facilitator knows ways to guide a group towards optimal decision-making. In this module, we will discuss ways to identify options, create a short list, and choose a solution. We will also use a way of deciding not often considered by many, called the multi-option technique.

Identifying the Options

The following are some ways groups can identify options during decision-making. Some of these ways are also the ways of gathering information discussed earlier.

Brainstorm. Brainstorming is the process of coming up with as many ideas as you can in the shortest time possible. It makes use of diversity of personalities in a group, so that one can come up with the widest range of fresh ideas. Quantity of ideas is more important than quality of ideas in the initial stage of brainstorming; you can filter out the bad ones later on with an in-depth review of their pros and cons.

Round Robin. Ask each member of the group to suggest one option for consideration. All members must contribute an idea.

Facilitated SWOT Analysis. Some teams create each option as a group, and they do so by conducting a facilitated analysis of the organization's strengths, weaknesses, opportunities and threats, as they relate to the problem.

The most import thing about these processes is that they are conducted in a consultative fashion.

Creating a Short List

There are many criteria a facilitator uses to help a group create a shortlist. The following are just some of these ways:

- **Costs and benefits.** An ideal solution is one that has the least costs and most benefits.

- **Disagreeing parties' interests**. An ideal solution has factored in the impact on all parties concerned and has made adjustments accordingly.

- **Foresight**. An ideal solution doesn't have just short-term gains but long term ones as well.

- **Obstacles.** An ideal solution has anticipated all possible obstacles in its implementation and has made plans accordingly.

- **Values.** An ideal solution is one that is consistent with the mission-vision of the organization and or its individual members.

Choosing a Solution

There are many ways a facilitator can guide a group in creating a shortlist. The following are just some of these ways:

Decide on a criterion (or criteria). Ask the group to come up with the criteria to be used to evaluate each option. These criteria could be costs and benefits, consistency with the values of the organization, feasibility, etc. Once criteria are set, the facilitator can guide the group into weighing each option according to the criteria.

Survey which options members like. A facilitator can also conduct a quick survey of what each group members like in the list. You can select the solution either by strict consensus or by majority vote.

Survey which options members don't like. Similarly, a facilitator can ask the group which options from the short list are no-no's and eliminate them from the list.

Using the Multi-Option Technique

When coming up with solutions to an issue, you are not limited to choosing one best one. You can also pick several solutions to a problem, and follow through on these many solutions simultaneously. This process is called the multi-option technique.

For instance, in addressing a problem about lagging sales, approaches can be related to poor advertising, poor market selection, or a problem in the product itself. A group following the multi-option technique will assign a person or team to follow through on each option. One team can create a better advertising campaign; another team can look for a better market; while another team can improve the product. In succeeding meetings, each team will report their results as separate teams.

The solutions followed through in a multi-option technique are not necessarily complimentary to one another, although groups have the option to follow through on only complimentary ideas. But if the group wants to see two opposing scenarios with different assumptions, they can do so.

How can a facilitator conduct the multi-option technique? The group can brainstorm several options, and the facilitator can help the group select which of the many options they want to pursue further.

Dealing with Difficult People

Group process can get hampered by the presence of difficult members. A skilled facilitator should know how to deal with difficult people, so that the discussion will remain on track and the group atmosphere will remain pleasant and conducive to participation. In this module, we will discuss how to address disruptions, common types of difficult people in groups and how to handle them, and how to let the group resolve issues on their own.

Addressing Disruptions

Disruptions in groups can be in any form. They can be from the members, or from the environmental factors.

The following are ways to deal with disruptions in groups:

- **Refocus the discussion on the agenda.** This intervention is similar to the intervention on keeping the discussion on track. If a disruption occurs, gently remind the group of the topic.

- **Identify the intention behind the disruption and address it.** Don't focus on what was said. Instead, focus on why the person said it. Example: repeated interjections can mean that a member does not feel like he or she is being listened to.

- **Reiterate rules.** You may refer to ground rules set at the beginning of the session.

- **If no rule against the disruption exists, then take it as an opportunity to set one.**

Common Types of Difficult People and How to Handle Them

The following are some of the common types of difficult people in groups and how to handle them.

Type of Difficult Person	Description	Typical Behavior	Ways to Deal with Them
Dominating	These are members who monopolize the conversation and even overtly block other members from making a contribution.	*"I am the only one with experience in this matter. Let me tell you what to do."*	Solicit other members' opinion. *"We appreciate your experience and we'll take what you said into account. But let's see what others think too."*
Aggressive	Members who resort to personal attacks.	*"You just don't know what you're doing!"*	Reiterate the ground rules. *"We have agreed that there will be no personal attacks."* Get back on topic. *"Remember all comments are useful as long as they relate to the topic."* Re-state their position in objective terms

Quiet and Non-Participative	Group members can be quiet for a variety of reasons: they can be shy, intimidated, or uncomfortable joining in the topic.		Establish eye contact and invite them to join in. *"We'd like to hear from people we haven't heard from before. Could you give us your take on this issue?"*
Overly Talkative	Members talk too much.		Remind them of the time limit. Tell them you can only discuss one point at a time. Ask them for key summary points.

Helping the Group Resolve Issues on Their Own

The following are two ways a facilitator can help groups resolve issues on their own:

Ignore. For cooperative teams, natural facilitators will emerge if the facilitator doesn't make immediate interventions.

Promote direct feedback. Ask the group members what they think about the situation or a particular person's behavior. Example: "Mike, can you tell Bob the effect on you when he interrupts you?"

Addressing Group Dysfunction

All groups have the potential to be dysfunctional: incapable of achieving goals. This is because each person is different, and each group has their own unique history. A facilitator must know how to recognize signs of group dysfunction, and be skilled to address them. In this module, we will discuss three ways to address group dysfunction: setting ground rules, restatement and reframing issues and keeping the discussion on track.

Using Ground Rules to Prevent Dysfunction

One of the best ways a facilitator can anticipate problems in a group discussion is to set ground rules. Ground rules orient participants with what is expected from them. Moreover, they set boundaries of acceptable and unacceptable behavior during the discussion. For best results, ground rules must be set in a consultative fashion, with the rules, and sometimes the consequences of violation of rules, negotiated among members of the group and agreed upon by consensus.

When setting ground rules, it is important to both verify if the rules are understood, and if they are acceptable. Make sure too that a documentation of the ground rules is available for everyone, either as a hand-out or posted in a flipchart paper for everyone to see.

Ground rules in a group meeting can relate to:

- **How to make the most of the meeting.** For example: practice timely attendance, participate fully.

- **How to make a contribution to the discussion.** For example: do the members raise their hands and ask the facilitator for permission to speak; use I-messages.

- **How members should treat other members**. For example: "don't interrupt whoever is speaking, listen actively to whoever has the floor, accept that everyone has a right to their own opinion, no swearing or any aggressive behavior.

- **Issues relating to confidentiality.** Example: all matters discussed in the group shall remain within the group. This is also the moment for the facilitator to reveal if the minutes of the meeting will remain solely for his or her reference, or will it be given to an authority in the organization.

- **How violations of ground rules would be addressed.** Example: the use of graduated interventions from warning to expulsion from the group.

Restating and Reframing Issues

The way an issue or problem is phrased can influence group members' attitudes towards it. After all, different words have different meanings and connotations. A simple example is the difference between the words "problem" and "challenge" in reference to a situation, or "victim" and "survivor" in reference to a person.

Restatement is similar to paraphrasing; it is changing the wording of an issue, but the main idea is the same. For example: simply changing "this suggestion seems to have made some members of the group angry", to "there seems to be a strong concerns about the suggestion" can lessen the antagonistic nature of the statement.

Reframing is similar to restatement, except reframing goes deeper. In reframing, a facilitator changes the way a problem is conceptualized in order to facilitate a consensus or support a conflict resolution. In some cases, the problem is reframed in order to support the position of two parties in contention. The meaning may or may not change, but the spirit of the statement remains the same. For example, instead of saying "we're here to talk about how to approach salary cuts," a facilitator can say "we're here to talk about how the company can provide employee security despite limited funds."

In group facilitation, simply restating or reframing an issue can lessen the adversarial nature of a position, or invite a fresh way of looking at things. When the issue is phrased in neutral or workable terms, it becomes conducive to a reasonable discussion.

How can a facilitator successfully re-state or reframe an issue? The main skill necessary for these processes is active listening. An effective facilitator must be sensitive to what each party needs and be able to incorporate these interests when phrasing an issue. Having an appreciation of the language of the group, and their unique perspective, are also important in this process.

Some of the ways of restating and reframing includes:

- Changing "hot buttons" or value-laden words into neutral ones.

- Reminding the group of larger goals/ smaller goals the entire group is working on.

- Changing a problem into workable terms.

- Approaching an issue from another perspective.

Getting People Back on Track

A group discussion can go off-topic for many reasons. Sometimes, the purpose of the meeting wasn't really clear. In other times, the discussion naturally led to an interesting issue not part of the agenda. And in other times, there are individuals who initiate and maintain off-topic discussions.

Regardless of the reason, the following are ways to get a discussion back on track:

Review the agenda. A facilitator can create check points in the agenda and constantly refer to it as the discussion progresses. For example: "Let's take a moment to take a process check. Are we still following our agreed upon agenda?"

Reflect to the group what is happening, and reintroduce the correct topic. Example: *"I appreciate the participation and enthusiasm. But it seems that we have gone off the agreed upon agenda. I believe the topic under discussion is..."*

Offer to put the off-topic on a "parking lot" for possible later discussion. For example: "You raised a good point Mary. Maybe we can look at that later it today, or set a separate meeting for it."

Ask the group if they are finding the discussion helpful to the goal. This intervention is recommended for unstructured meetings, where a foray into an off-topic is not necessarily a negative thing. For example: "I noticed that there has been a long debate in the group about this idea. Is this discussion helpful for everyone?"

Ignore the off-topic discussion and reintroduce the correct topic. If you feel that acknowledging a topic detour will just result in more dysfunction (e.g. it will provoke a long, defensive response), then it may be best to just ignore it. Instead, summarize the last thing that was said related to the topic, and ask a question that continues from it. For example: "If I may get back to what Louis was saying earlier. He said....Does anyone agree with his observation?"

About Intervention

In general, facilitators neither inject themselves in issues nor direct the flow of discussion; they merely go where the group wants to go. There are occasions, however, when stronger responses are needed to make the group more functional and productive. In this module, we will discuss what these stronger responses are, why they are necessary, and when is it appropriate to use them.

Why Intervention May Be Necessary

Facilitators are part of a group for a reason: to help the group achieve their goals in the most democratic and cooperative way possible. Ideally, groups should have cooperative members with knowledge, skill, and personality to assist this process. However, in the real world, groups are much more complicated. Indeed, even well-meaning group members can create dysfunctional teams. For this reason, intervention may be necessary.

An intervention is an injection of one's self in the process in pursuit of a specific goal. Interventions are what separate a facilitator from a mere participant--- the participant's statements are contributions, whereas a facilitators' statements are interventions.

Technically, anything that a facilitator does, both verbally and non-verbally, in the course of his or her role in a group is an "intervention." However, the term intervention is usually reserved to relatively stronger interference in a group's natural way of doing things.

The following are some of the reasons why intervention may be necessary:

To help the group achieve their goals. If an on-going dynamic in the group is keeping the entire team from reaching their objective, then it's time to intervene. For example: if a coalition exists in members, decision-making might get skewed to one side of the issue.

To protect group process. If the integrity of the chosen methodology in getting results is being compromised, then a facilitator must intervene.

To prevent the escalation of an issue. Generally, facilitators should let the group handle things on their own. But some hot issues are better nipped in the bud, or they might blow up into a larger issue can create serious damage.

To sample "skills" to the group. In some occasions, group members lack the skills to deal with a group issue, e.g. two conflicting issues. In these cases, intervention may be necessary to expose the group on more functional processes.

When to Intervene

The following are some situations when intervention may be necessary:

- The group is stuck. This means that the process is not producing results, or the process is not progressing to the next level.

- The group is about to move on to the next agenda without realizing that an important aspect of the discussion is unresolved or unaddressed.

- The group continues to follow a negative pattern despite soft interventions. (We will discuss levels of interventions in the next section.)

- Something unethical is going on in the group, like a personal attack or subtle/blatant intimidation.

- Group process is being hampered by a dominant person or clique.

- Group members are misunderstanding each other.

- The facilitator perceives tension and suspiciousness in the group.

Levels of Intervention

There is a guiding principle in medicine that goes: don't prescribe strong medicine when a milder one will do. Similarly, interventions in facilitation range from non-directive to directive, subtle to explicit, non-intrusive to very intrusive. It helps to know what the levels of intervention are in order to decide what response to give to different situations in a group.

The following are the different levels of intervention:

No intervention. Unless there is a pressing concern that requires a facilitator's intervention, the first level of response is to do nothing. By not responding to a concern, a facilitator is effectively letting the group take care of the problem, and implement their own solution. Note though that even if a facilitator is not directly responding to the problem, he or she may be actively gathering information about the group and how they process their own issues.

Reflective Technique. The first few levels of intervention are geared towards increasing awareness within the group that a problematic situation is in place. One way to do this is to objectively state what you notice is going on. Note that you are not supposed to voice out your opinions or evaluations of the group dynamic; merely bring to awareness something that the group may not have noticed. The group is left to confirm or refute the facilitator's observations. Either way, the result may be further clarification.

Example: "I noticed that four of you had been very quiet since we started."

Solicit the Group's Observations. As much as possible, let the group members identify themselves what is happening within the group. One way to do this is to solicit feedback through general leads. Example: *"Jane. What can you say about what is happening right now?"*

If general leads are not working, you can use direct leads. Example: "Jane, what can you say about the way the discussion about (subject) is going?

Interpret observations. This becomes necessary when the group has difficulty seeing the implications of what is going on in the process. NOTE: always phrase your interpretations in tentative fashion, as if seeking confirmation from the group if your observations are correct or incorrect.

Example: *"I'm noticing that the energy is low? Are we focusing on the right issue? Or is there something else that we have more energy for?"*

Suggest solutions. If the group seems to be stuck, suggest a way to deal with the problem. Note: suggest only process changes. And always get the approval of the group. Example: "We seem to be stuck, would you like to try a different approach?"

Restructure the process or an aspect of it. Change the group process by re-organizing the structure of dialogue (dyads, small groups, etc.), using problem solving processes, inserting a "process break" or changing the original agenda.

Confront. This is directly mentioning the problem, or the difficult individual. Note that confrontation is a very strong intervention, and must be used only as a last resort, when all other softer interventions have been exhausted.

Example: *"I noticed that you are always encouraging the other members of the group to leave the meeting prematurely. And twice now it has disrupted the process. May I know what the reason why you're doing this is?"*

Intervention Techniques

In the previous module, we introduced intervention and the different levels of intervention. In this module, we will focus on particular intervention techniques: use of processes, boomerang it back, and **ICE** it.

Using Your Processes

As process experts, the best way a facilitator can intervene in an unproductive or dysfunctional group is by introducing a process that would directly address the problem or issue.

For example, if a group's problem is the monopoly of the floor by certain members, a facilitator can introduce the round robin discussion to ensure that everyone gets their turn to speak.

If the problem is the lack of information about the issue in contention, the facilitator can make presentation part of the agenda.

If the problem is a lack of understanding between management and staff, the facilitator can break the group into pairs of management and staff.

Boomerang it Back

To "boomerang" an issue back is to present an issue back to the group for them to resolve. The reflective technique (discussed in the previous module) is one of the basic ways of mirroring an issue to a group.

Another way to do this is to rephrase a group's concern into a question addressed to the group. For example, when a group member says "maybe we are just too tired to think of a new idea for this project", a facilitator can simply say *"do you think you are too tired?"*

Or if a group member asks a facilitator a question, the facilitator can just bounce the question back. Example: if a group member asks "should we continue this project?" the facilitator can simply reply *"What do you think? Should you?"*

ICE It: Identify, Check for Agreement, Evaluate How to Resolve

Another way to intervene is to use the ICE technique.

ICE stands for:

- Identify

- Check for Agreement

- Evaluate How to Resolve.

When you ICE it, you surface what the problem is, verify with the group its accuracy (or at least their agreement), and then start the process of looking for solutions.

Example: "What do you think is going on in the group right now? So, if I understand correctly, this is what is happening? Is this correct? How do we go about addressing this problem?"

Chapter 23 – Goal Setting and Getting Things Done

Everyone has dreams and goals. Achieving personal and professional goals, however, requires planning and action. Learning how to manage time and set realistic goals will increase your chance of success in every area of your life. Following the advice in this course will help increase your productivity and help you achieve your dreams.

At the end of this chapter, you should be able to:

- Overcome procrastination

- Manage time effectively

- Accomplish important tasks

- Self-motivate

- Create SMART goals

Before reading through this chapter, review the following questions and note your responses.

- How would you describe your goal setting and time management process?

- Have you ever taken a course in goal setting? What was the focus?

- Where do you feel your skills are weak?

- What do you hope to learn from this course?

Overcoming Procrastination

We all procrastinate from time to time. Procrastination occurs when we avoid tasks that we find unpleasant. Even if we perform other work-related tasks instead of the ones we dislike, we are guilty of procrastination. Unfortunately, procrastination will hinder our long-term success. With the proper skills, you can overcome procrastination.

Eat That Frog!

Mark Twain has a saying that applies to procrastination:

If the first thing you do each morning is to eat a live frog, you can go through the day with the satisfaction of knowing that that is probably the worst thing that is going to happen to you all day long!

Brian Tracy named his course on time management "Eat that Frog" because of this saying. The frog is anything that you do not want to do. Basically, you should complete your dreaded tasks first. Getting them out of the way will provide you with a sense of accomplishment and keep you from procrastinating. Always begin with the task that is the hardest and most significant, and you will be less tempted to procrastinate on other activities.

Just Do It

When you dislike a particular task, it is easy to procrastinate. Whether you spend time checking email or looking at Instagram, you are procrastinating. You need to do more than identify when you procrastinate. You need to discover why.

- Discover your obstacles: What do you choose over your tasks?

- Discover ways to remove obstacles: Ask for support, and take action. For example, you could turn off the Internet and your phone.

- Reward yourself: Make the task fun, and use small rewards as incentive.

Once you have identified your frogs and obstacles, the only answer is take action. Make the tasks that you want to avoid part of your daily routine. Schedule the tasks into your calendar. Once they become habit, you will find them easier to accomplish. Once you have scheduled the time to accomplish your tasks, you must follow through. Resist the temptation to procrastinate with your favorite time waster. Just do it.

The 15 Minute Rule

Lack of time is a common excuse for not completing a task. We often overestimate the time that it takes to complete tasks, but the 15 minute rule allows you to accurately time your tasks. When you follow the 15 minute rule, you set a timer for 15 minutes and work on a task. You should stop working on the task when the time is up. You will be surprised by how many tasks you complete within the 15 minutes. When you are not able to complete a task within 15 minutes, schedule 15 minutes the next day for the same task. This allows you to make consistent progress. You will also be able to better estimate how long a similar task will take.

Chop It Up

The size of a project can also contribute to procrastination. It is easy to become overwhelmed by a large project. The key to overcoming procrastination is to chop up the large project into smaller tasks. Rather than looking at the entire project, focus on the single task. This will prevent you from becoming overwhelmed by the enormity of the work you must complete. For example, you could break a large report into different tasks such as brainstorming, outlining, writing, etc. This technique will create a sense of achievement with each step and improve motivation, allowing you to stay focused as you reach the end of the entire project.

Procrastination can happen at any time. It is not enough to identify that you are avoiding a project. You need to take active steps to remove the temptation to procrastinate. By taking control of your schedule and work environment, you will be able to reduce the amount of time that you spend procrastinating each day. In turn, you will be able to improve your productivity and accomplish your goals.

Remove Distractions

We are bombarded with distractions every day. These distractions are temptations to procrastinate. By removing as many distractions as possible, you will be on track to overcoming procrastination.

Distractions to Avoid:

- **Office clutter**: Clean up your space at the end of each day, both at home and in the office. This will help to keep you focused, and you will not be tempted to clean during a project.

- **Email notification**: Establish specific times to check email. Automatic notifications are distracting and cut into the time you spend on each project.

- **Telephone calls**: Do not take all calls. Choose a time to return calls and texts.

- **Environment**: Remove distractions such as books, magazines, etc., from your workstation.

Start Small and Build

A habit of procrastination does not happen overnight. Equally, it is not possible to stop procrastinating overnight. Expecting an immediate change will only lead to disappointment. You need to start small and build in order to end procrastination once and for all. Begin by creating a daily "to do list" for your personal life. Include the daily tasks that you have trouble completing such as laundry or cleaning the kitchen. When you have stability in your personal schedule, it will be easier to address procrastination at work.

Create a daily schedule for work once you have broken down your larger tasks into smaller ones. As your productivity increases, you will be able to build upon your schedule. You will soon find that you are finishing tasks ahead of schedule.

Reward Yourself

People tend to procrastinate because they do not find certain tasks to be pleasant. Procrastination becomes its own reward. Overcoming procrastination requires that you implement a reward system for completing tasks. Otherwise, you will revert to bad habits. Rewards should match the tasks completed. For example, taking 10 minutes on Facebook could be a reward for returning your phone calls. Similarly, going to a movie could be a reward for completing a report on time. When choosing rewards, you need to stay away from anything that you already have planned. For example, if you already have plans to go out with friends on a weekend, the outing will not serve as a reward. Using the appropriate rewards will improve motivation and help prevent procrastination.

Set Realistic Deadlines

Schedules and deadlines will help you stay focused and avoid procrastination. When setting deadlines, however, you must be realistic. Deadlines that are not realistic will actually contribute to procrastination. If you do not have a chance of completing a task on time, you will avoid it. If you are creating your own deadline, you should consider how long similar tasks have taken. Be honest, and allow time for interruptions and emergencies. Do not create a schedule based on the best-case scenario. You are setting yourself up for failure. If you are assigned a deadline, determine if it is realistic. If the deadline is not realistic, you should attempt to negotiate a more realistic date. This negotiation should be done as quickly as possible to prevent complications later.

Four P's of Goal Setting

You need goals to get things done. However, not every goal is effective. The way that you word your goals will determine whether or not you reach them. When establishing goals, it is important to remember the **Four P's** of goal setting. They need to be positive, personal, possible, and prioritized.

They Need to Be Positive

When you are creating goals, remember to make sure that they are positive. This means that you focus on what you want to achieve rather than what you want to avoid. For example, you would write, *"I will achieve a promotion."* rather than *"I will no longer work at this horrible job."* Staying focused on the positive will help improve your outlook and remove any negativity. This, in turn, will improve your chances for success. Reaching your goals will automatically help you avoid your present circumstances. When creating positive goals, remember to be as specific as possible.

They Need to Be Personal

When creating goals, they need to reflect your dreams and desires. Goals that are not personal are ineffective. Your goals should be about you and only you. For example, *"My boss will appreciate me."* is an ineffective goal because it is not about you. It is possible to be a wonderful employee and still be unappreciated. A better goal would be, *"I will find a supervisory position where I am appreciated for my talent."* If your goals are not personal, you will never achieve them. Making goals personal places the burden of responsibility on you, but it also means that other people do not determine when you reach your goals.

They Need to Be Possible

When creating goals, you need to make sure that they are possible. When you set impossible goals, you set yourself up for failure and disappointment. Creating possible goals demands that you be honest with yourself. Some goals may require continued education or experience to achieve while others will remain out of reach. For example, it is not possible for someone to become a famous singer without any talent whatsoever. You need to assess your talents and determine what you can achieve with hard work and what will be impossible for you to accomplish. Once you have determined which goals are possible for you to achieve, success will be within reach.

They Need to Be Prioritized

Brainstorming goals can become overwhelming. You will probably have more goals than you can handle. This is the time to prioritize your goals. Begin by numerically ranking your goals and choosing the five goals that are the most important to you. Choose these goals based on your passions, and make sure that they cover all areas of your life: professional, health, personal growth, finances, etc. All of your time and energy should be spent working towards these goals.

You should place your other goals on the back burner. It is not possible to focus on 20 goals at the same time. In fact, you should avoid the other goals at all cost. You risk becoming side tracked with less important goals if you continue to entertain them. You will need to reprioritize your goals periodically. For example, you can reprioritize after you achieve one of your top five goals.

Improving Motivation

Goals can be inspiring, but that inspiration can fade in the reality of everyday life. In order to achieve your goals, it is important that you find ways to motivate yourself. You cannot constantly rely on external motivation. Implementing different methods of motivation such as remembering peak moments, writing down goals and gamification will help keep you stay focused and positive as you work towards your goals.

Remember Peak Moments

Positive memories are powerful motivators. Remembering peak moments creates the sense of achievement and encourages us to seek out that same feeling again. Peak moments are not relegated to work accomplishments. They are any strong memories that create positive feelings. For example, completing a marathon may be a peak moment. Getting married or having a child can also be peak moments. Looking back over your peak moments will show you how much you already have, and how far you have already come. They will encourage and motivate you to keep moving forward and reach your goals.

Write Down Your Goals

Knowing your goals is not enough to keep you motivated; you have to write them down. Writing down goals creates a visual reminder of where you are going. When you are writing down your goals, remember to:

- Use the present tense or the present perfect tense: This will help you visualize reaching your goals.

- Use "I" statements: An "I" statement reinforces that they are personal goals. They are your responsibility.

Example:

- I am graduating with my Master's degree.

Once your goals are written down, you should display them someplace where you will see them regularly.

Use Gamification

Gamification uses the process of game dynamics to blend intrinsic and extrinsic motivation. Unlike online games that can become obstacles to productivity, gamification will actually help you achieve your goals. This system allows you to earn points towards rewards by accomplishing tasks. The points you earn provide incentives to complete more tasks and earn more rewards. You can create your own life game by taking a few steps.

Create Your Own Game:

- **Identify tasks:** List the tasks/chores that you need to accomplish.

- **Assign points**: Assign a number of points to each task. Tasks that you typically avoid should be given more points to provide greater incentive.

- **Assign rewards:** Determine how many points are necessary to earn each reward. Higher point counts should be given to rewards that are more valuable. For example, an outing to a coffee shop could be 20 points, while purchasing game, book, etc., could be 120 points. The rewards will depend on what motivates you.

- **Keep score:** Find a method to keep track of your points that works for you. You could use a spreadsheet or list them in an app on your phone.

You will probably have to adjust your game to find the most motivating rewards system. Once you have made the necessary adjustments, you will have fun reaching your goals.

Track Your Progress

Tracking your progress will help you see your accomplishments and which areas require more effort. Additionally, seeing the improvements that you make will motivate you to continue your hard work. Over time, you should see yourself consistently reaching more of your daily goals. There are different ways to track progress. You may choose to do it by hand, use a spreadsheet, or use an online tool such as Joe's Charts. No matter the format you use, charting requires you to complete a list of daily goals. At the end of each day, you check off the goals that you accomplished. Do not expect to always reach all of your goals. The purpose of tracking progress is to show you the areas need more of your focus.

Example:

Goal	Mon	Tues	Wed	Thurs	Fri	Sat	Sun
Exercise	X		X	X		X	
Journal		X			X	X	X

Time management is the key to getting things done. It is easy to become sidetracked by unimportant tasks that do not help you reach your goals without the proper time management. By following the following strategies, you will be able to navigate your time wisely. They will help you achieve your goals while decreasing your stress level and making your life easier.

Urgent/Important Matrix

In order to manage time, you need to determine the difference between urgent and important tasks. Urgent tasks are tasks that need to be done quickly, and important tasks are related to specific goals. Most tasks will be a combination of the two, such as urgent/important or urgent/unimportant. You need to place priority on important tasks, completing tasks that are both urgent and important first.

Unfortunately, we are often trapped performing urgent tasks that are not important. They may be important to the people around you, but they are distractions and interruptions that do nothing to help you meet your own goals. Important tasks should take priority because they are focused on specific goals. The urgent/important matrix below will help you identify which tasks are urgent and which ones are important.

The Urgent/Important Matrix:

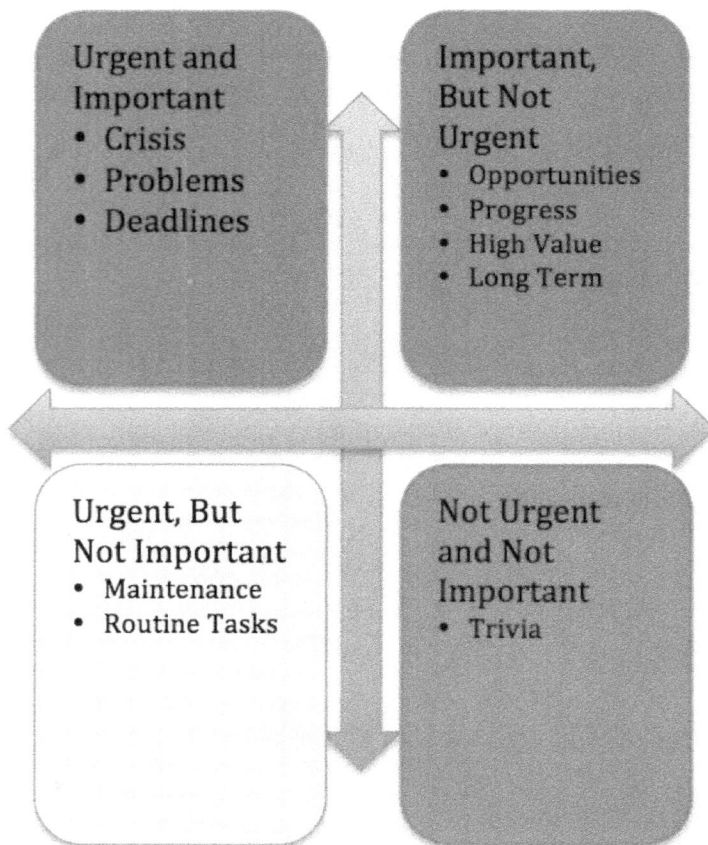

Urgent and Important	Important, But Not Urgent
• Crisis	• Opportunities
• Problems	• Progress
• Deadlines	• High Value
	• Long Term
Urgent, But Not Important	**Not Urgent and Not Important**
• Maintenance	• Trivia
• Routine Tasks	

The 80/20 Rule

Many successful individuals recommend following the 80/20 Rule. The 80/20 rule states that only 20 percent of our actions are responsible for 80 percent of our successes. This means that it is necessary to discover the

20 percent of our actions that are the most effective. Focus on these actions once you discover them and make them your priorities.

The 80/20 Rule should be linked to your goals. Once you prioritize goals, you should spend your most of your time working on the 20 percent of activities that you know will move you forward.

Utilize a Calendar

Calendars are essential to effective time management. Calendars are familiar tools, but they are not always used effectively. When using a calendar to manage time, it is important that you only use one. Given the different calendar options, it is easy to try to integrate different calendars, but you risk scheduling mistakes. You can choose from physical calendars, mid tech options like day-timer, and high tech apps for your phone. Find the calendar that works for you and stick with it.

Calendar Rules:

- Keep the calendar with you: Leaving the calendar behind means that you may forget to list something on it.

- Only list appointments and day events: Appointments require specific times. Events include birthdays, anniversaries, etc.

- Avoid notes: Do not clutter your calendar. Have a separate section for notes.

- Include phone numbers: While you should avoid clutter, phone numbers and addresses may be useful.

Create a Ritual

Rituals can help improve time management. Rituals are repetitive actions, which do not need to be scheduled. For example, you do not think about brushing and flossing before bed or making coffee with breakfast. By creating rituals that are connected with goals, you will not have to schedule certain tasks. For example, if you get up at the same time every morning and exercise for 30 minutes, you will create a ritual. This ritual will become a habit over time.

You will not create a ritual overnight. For the first few months, you will have to be disciplined in your efforts. It takes time to create a habit. How long it takes a habit to form will vary according to each individual. There is no magic number. You will have to continue your quest until your ritual is complete.

Tips for Completing Tasks

It is easy to begin tasks, but completing them is much more difficult. Life will always find a way to distract us from our tasks. Given how easy it is to procrastinate and avoid tasks, most people have a list of tasks waiting to be completed. As this list grows, stress levels increase. By following a few simple tasks, you will improve your chances of completing tasks and staying on track and reducing stress levels.

One Minute Rule

Everyone hates doing small, mundane tasks. They may seem unimportant, but over time, they will pile up, which will diminish focus and waste time. For example, if you do not take the garbage out regularly, it will overflow. This makes a simple task much more difficult. Implementing the one minute rule eliminates this difficult situation and protects your focus.

According to the one minute rule, if a task will only take one minute, you should complete it immediately. Examples of tasks that follow the one minute rule include: filing papers, putting clothes the in laundry hamper, and taking out the garbage. A single minute will not put you behind schedule, and following the rule will save you time in the long run.

Five Minute Rule

Schedules only help people focus and manage time when they are done correctly. A common mistake that people make when creating schedules is to make them too strict. It is not possible to plan the day down to the minute. When creating a schedule, you should follow the five minute rule. The five minute rule is simple: allow at least five minutes between scheduled tasks. This time is set aside so that you can complete small tasks that you have been avoiding or neglecting. The five minutes do more than provide time to complete small, seemingly unimportant projects. They also provide a buffer between scheduled activities, which will help keep you on schedule in case a task runs longer than you expected.

Break Up Large Tasks

Many tasks have multiple steps. These tasks may be overwhelming when you look at the complete picture. By breaking these tasks up into their basic steps, you will be able to remain focused as you work. Additionally, you will feel a sense of achievement as you complete each step in the process. An example of breaking up a large task would be cleaning out a garage.

Example:

- Sort through everything

- Remove unwanted items

- Organize the remaining items

- Put away items in their appropriate locations

Breaking down a task into manageable steps will make them much easier to manage. Additionally, you will be more likely to complete a project when you break it down into smaller tasks.

Utilize Technology

Technology has made completing tasks much easier. Computer software and online programs help you manage tasks, create reminders, and track your progress. Besides computer programs, there are countless apps now that help you make lists, keep track of schedules, and complete tasks. No matter which smartphone you have, there are apps to keep you on track such as Reminders, Outlook, and Todoist. You can make schedules, create lists, reply to email, etc. wherever you are. Find the technology that fits your lifestyle. If you try to use an app that you do not like, you will abandon your efforts completely. Before trying an app, ask your friends for recommendations and look up reviews online. You may also want to begin with free apps. With a free app, you have not lost any money if you do not find the app useful.

Increase Your Productivity

Improving your time management strategies will help increase your productivity. By improving your productivity, you will find it easier to reach your goals. Increased productivity takes time. However, as you begin to implement different strategies, you will discover which methods are effective and improve your personal and professional productivity.

Repeat What Works

There are numerous programs, hints, and tips available to help you improve productivity. The key to improvement is discovering what works and repeating actions with the appropriate tools. This requires researching and trying different strategies to determine which ones fit best with your workload and habits. For example, not everyone can use the same technology to keep a schedule. Once you determine which resources and strategies are effective, it is important to keep repeating them. There is no reason to change your routine once you have determined what works for you. Over time, the repetition will increase your productivity and help you move forward.

Get Faster

It may seem obvious, but the faster that you become, the more productive you will be. Practice and effort will help increase your speed on tasks that you perform regularly. For example, you can work on getting faster at typing, reading, walking, etc. No matter the task, just try to increase the speed a little bit at a time. There are numerous ways to help you get faster and improve your productivity.

Ways to Improve Speed:

- Games

- Tasks

- Apps

- Computer programs

Choose the method that fits best with your life and interests.

Remove "Should" from Your Dictionary

The words that you use have a greater impact on your life than you may realize. We have already discussed remaining positive by avoiding negative language. It is also important to avoid uncertainty in your language. For example, the word "should" needs to leave your dictionary. This word implies feelings of guilt because you do not plan on actually following through. For example, someone who says, "I should start exercising every morning" is not likely to start exercising. The decisive word "will" indicates a decision has been made. Saying, "I will start exercising" is making a commitment to follow through with an idea. Making this simple shift in vocabulary will commit you to action and improve your productivity.

Build on Your Successes

Success itself can become a cycle if you start small and build on your achievements. Once you have a single success, you will find the motivation to work towards more. You should start with a small success and build. Begin with the goal that is easy to reach. For example, you could begin by blogging every day for a week. Move on to another achievable goal. These successes will provide a foundation to build on as you attempt to reach more goals and success. By moving from success to success, you will be able to increase productivity in both your personal and professional life.

"To Do" List Characteristics

"To do" lists are staples in modern life. If "to do" lists are not done properly, they are useless. Too often, people create lists that they never come close to completing. There are characteristics that effective "to do" lists share. If your "to do" list includes these basic characteristics, you will find it easier to accomplish the tasks that you established.

Focus on the Important

The main mistake that people make when creating to do lists is making them too long. It is not possible to place every little task on a "to do" list. For a list to be effective, you must focus on the important tasks. The best method for making a "to do" list is to create a list of everything you want to accomplish and then cut that list down to a manageable size. You may want to use the urgent/important matrix to determine which tasks should make your list. Remember that an important task will align with your goals. If a task is not important enough to make the list, do not attempt to squeeze it in later. You do not want to split your attention. Focusing only on the important tasks will help you complete your to do list and reach your goals.

Chunk, Block, Tackle

When creating a "to do" list, you should keep chunk, block, and tackle in mind. The first part of this strategy should be familiar. You need to break up a large task into smaller ones.

- **Chunk:** Break projects into tasks that are 15 minutes or fewer.

- **Block:** Block out time to complete each chunk.

- **Tackle:** Tackle each specific task individually rather than looking at the entire project.

Implementing chunk, block, tackle, will motivate you to complete the project because you will feel a sense of accomplishment as you complete each chunk. When creating your to do list, include the project chunks that you have created rather than listing the project as a whole. You should also include the time estimate for each task.

Make It a Habit

You need to make "to do" lists regularly for them to be effective. Creating "to do" lists should become a habit for you. They should become second nature; you should not need to think about them. The best way to accomplish this is by creating your "to do" list at the same time each day. If you are an early riser, you may want to create your list first thing in the morning. On the other hand, many people prefer creating their lists at the end of the day so that it is ready in the morning. When you create a new "to do" list, you should transfer any unfinished tasks from your current list to the list for the next day. If you create your list at the same time each day, it will become a habit over time. Once creating the list becomes a habit, it will become faster and easier to revise your "to do" list every day.

Plan Ahead

"To do" lists will not help you reach your goals unless you implement them. Until they are executed, lists are just reminders of what you still need to accomplish. The key to using lists is to plan ahead. Take the time to prioritize and schedule your list each day. Place time estimates next to each task, so you can place them in your schedule.

How to complete the list:

- Make a schedule: Schedule the tasks on your "to do" list each day.

- Set a timer: Set a timer or an alarm for each task.

- Stay focused: Do not be sidetracked by unimportant tasks.

If you plan your day around your "to do" list, you will find yourself completing more of the tasks that you have assigned yourself and getting things done.

Smart Goals

If you cannot achieve your goals, there is a chance that you are not creating the correct goals. Whenever you create goals, you will find that following the rules for SMART goals will be easier to achieve. SMART goals are specific, measurable, attainable, realistic, and timely. When you combine the elements of SMART goals, you have a greater chance of success.

Specific

Goals need to be specific. You will not be able to reach you goals if they are broad and general because planning will be too difficult. For example, "Improve my life" is too broad. You cannot work towards this general goal. Specific goals explain what is necessary to complete a goal and guides you as you try to reach the goal. Specific goals may also identify location, requirements, and the reasoning behind the goal.

Example:

- **General goal:** Make more money.

- **Specific goal**: Earn a promotion with a pay increase.

Measurable

Goals need to be measurable in order to be effective. A measurable goal specifies the when a goal is accomplished by answering, "how much?" or "how many?" It provides measurable results. Without measurable goals, it is difficult to realize when the goal has been reached.

Example:

- **General goal:** Work on a book.

- **Measurable goal:** Write 10 pages a day of a book.

Attainable

Goals must always be attainable. It is important that you create goals that are challenging, but they still need to be within reach. When goals are unattainable, you will give up on them without even trying. The measure of a goal should always be attainable.

- **Unattainable goal**: Earn $1 million in the next three months.

- **Attainable goal:** Earn a $2 an hour raise with my next review.

Realistic

It is important that you set realistic goals. Realistic goals are directly related to your abilities. For example, a goal to reprogram the computer is not realistic if you do not have the education or experience to accomplish the task. Additionally, you need to make sure that you have access to the tools necessary to meet your goals. If a goal seems unrealistic, break it down into smaller chunks to know for certain.

Example:

- **Unrealistic Goal:** Run a marathon. (without training)

- **Realistic Goal:** Complete a marathon after training for a year.

Timely

Always create goals that have specific time frames. General goals do not establish any time frames, which means that you may continue to pursue goals that you should relinquish. Timely goals encourage you to move forward in order to meet the deadline you have established. Once a time frame has been reached, you should take the time to reevaluate the goal.

Example:

- **General goal:** Complete a computer training course.

- **Timely goal:** Complete a computer training course within the next month.

Mistakes Will Happen

No matter how well you prepare or what precautions you take, mistakes will happen. Mistakes are an essential part of life. Without them, it is not possible to fully grow and learn. When mistakes do occur, the key is to bounce back, learn from them, and move forward. If you learn from your mistakes, you are less likely to repeat them. You will also be able to guide others away from making the same mistakes you have.

Accept It

There are two ways to handle mistakes. You can deny the mistake or blame others, or you can accept it and take responsibility for your actions. Becoming defensive and making excuses will not help you grow or improve your relationship with other people. In fact, refusing to accept responsibility can eventually breed contempt between you and those around you, particularly if you are blaming them for your errors. Accepting is always the better option. It is the mature decision and a sign of integrity.

How to Accept Responsibility:

- Make an appropriate apology: Apologize for mistakes. Do not, however, grovel or become overly emotional.

- Reframe: Explain the mistake and the process that led to it. It honestly explains exactly what went wrong. Reframing may improve the way everyone views the error.

Bouncing Back

Never allow mistakes to paralyze you. Living in fear of making another mistake will stunt your personal and professional growth. Everyone makes mistakes, but successful people are able to bounce back. You will make mistakes, but you must be sure to get back on track when they occur. Keep a positive attitude in the face of mistakes. See them as opportunities for growth.

You must persevere and focus on the future. Never live in the past. The ability to bounce back after making a mistake shows that you are strong and resilient. Bouncing back will make it easier for you to regain trust after suffering the setback of making a mistake.

Adapt and Learn from Them

Mistakes are opportunities to adapt and learn. In order to learn from a mistake, you must look at the situation honestly. It is imperative that you show others you are able to adapt and change in the face of mistakes. This skill will help you preserve your reputation. You will also be able to provide valuable advice and prevent those around you from repeating your errors. This ability transforms your mistake from a liability to an asset.

Ask yourself the following questions:

- What went wrong?

- How did it happen?

- When did it happen?

- Why did it happen?

- How could it have been prevented?

Once you have the answers to these questions, you will be able to adapt your actions in the future.

If Needed, Ask for Help

Overcoming your mistakes will require the help of your support system. An effective support system will include trust, diverse views, and mutual respect. The members of your support system can offer you advice and guidance. They will also provide valuable feedback that will show you how mistakes occurred and ways to avoid repeating the same errors.

Your support system will only be able to help you when you ask for it. You cannot expect people to automatically know when you need them. When you do ask for help, remember to follow basic etiquette.

- Ask: Do not demand that people help you or manipulate them with guilt.

- Be straightforward: Do not be dramatic or minimize the help necessary.

- Be thankful: Always thank friends who are willing to help you succeed.

Chapter 24 – Office Politics for Managers

Office politics, or work politics, are the strategies and procedures that employees use to function and advance in a work setting. It is important for managers to learn and understand the office environment and the employees that make it tick. Since the manager interacts with several aspects of the workplace, one should learn how to effectively work with colleagues, supervisors, and upper management in order to help keep the department functioning as a whole.

To effectively deal with office politics, you must first accept the reality that they exist in every environment. Once accepted, the manager can learn the different ways to successfully manage employees as well as build the support they need to grow.

- Understand the purpose and benefits of office politics.

- Setting boundaries and ground rules for new employees.

- Learn to interact and influence among colleagues.

- Learn how to manage various personality types in the office.

- Determine how to gain support and effectively network.

- Recognize how you are a part of a group and how you function.

New Hires

Once new employees are brought onboard, they are often given vital information and skills needed to succeed in the group. While this information can help them get started, the new hire will need to learn the inner workings of the office and the environment they are now a part of in order to thrive and be successful. As a manager, you can help new employees realize how the office functions and what they can do to fit right in.

Company Core Values

Learning a company's core values is a common first step during an employee's first orientation. Having this information allows the employee to build a base knowledge of the company and how it works. Some important points to include are:

- What the core values are.

- How these values are enacted.

- What kind of results and productivity are valued.

Building Relationships

Building key relationships with new hires ensures they will feel confident in what they do in the office and that they can come to you if they need assistance. Establishing a connection from the beginning and throughout the duration of the person's stay with the company helps them to establish their own ground while learning the politics of their environment.

Keys to building better relationships among employees:

- Create self-awareness: Identify how you appear to others.

- Establish roles as manager and employee.

- Encourage communication between colleagues as well as management (i.e. open door policy).

Encourage Respect

As a manager, it is important to encourage respect and etiquette among employees. Not only should you respect your workers, but respect from them is just as crucial. Any new hire is especially encouraged to respect their new coworkers and managers and establish a relationship from the beginning. An equal amount of respect should be shown to each employee and etiquette guidelines should be established.

Respect includes consideration for:

- Other people's privacy

- Employee's physical space and belongings

- Different viewpoints

- Philosophies and beliefs

- Personality

Setting Ground Rules

When a new employee is hired, they are expected to come into the workplace and learn to work with peers and contribute to the team. Setting ground rules before they are released to the group is a key step to ensuring they can work with others while knowing what is, or isn't, expected of them. While most of this information can be found in an employee manual or handbook, a review from the manager can make the information easily accepted and allows for any questions that may arise.

Ground rules should touch on various topics of the office, including:

- Dress code and attire

- Behavior and tolerance

- Chain of command (i.e. for complaints, questions, etc.)

- Productivity guidelines (i.e. deadlines, processes, quotas)

It's About Interacting and Influencing

As stated before, office politics exist in every office environment. Offices are normally made up of a wide range of people and personality types. They key to maintaining good politics is to know how to interact with each other and influence the employees under your management.

Dealing with Different Personalities

Good relationships among employees can build the base for a better team. Different personalities have different strengths and weaknesses, which can be paired together to complement each other. Knowing the different types of personalities and how to deal with them can make any office situation easy to manage. You'll learn more about types of personalities in modules five and six.

Common office personality types:

- Complainer
- Gossiper
- Bully
- Negative Ned/Nancy
- Information Keeper
- Know-it-all
- The Apple Polisher
- Nosey Neighbor

Build a Culture of Collaboration

When companies grow, the group culture grows and cliques can begin to form. With so many conflicting visions, a company can lose sight of its original purpose. The goal for a manager is to form a collaboration that features every person's talents and visions.

Tips:

- Listen and observe your employees
- Be diplomatic
- Keep private matters private
- Don't get emotional – keep a professional standing

Be Nice to Everyone (Not Just Those Who Can Help You)

It's important to be nice to everyone in the office. As a manager, people should feel free to approach you with their problems or concerns. If they feel as though you've picked favorites or excluded others, it could not only affect their performance on the job, but yours as well. Treating everyone equally is the best way to help prevent cliques and out casting in the office.

Useful Tips:

- Stay neutral
- Don't get involved in office gossip or hype
- Watch for red flags among employees
- Monitor how you approach employees and delegate tasks

Be a Team Player

A team player believes that they can (or the group can) get ahead by working hard and participating toward advancing the goals of the team. They know to put the team's needs ahead of their personal needs and usually follow the path needed to get the job done right the first time. As a manager, you are an important part of the team and an influential team member. Following our previous exercises, we've learned it's important to identify your team's differences and similarities in order to have the team run not only smoothly, but successfully.

Characteristics of being a team player:

- Do not make pre-judgments about your team members. Base your observations on their current work habits and behaviors.

- Provide encouragement and motivation to your employees.

- Show empathy for another worker's problems or needs.

- Keep an open mind about every member. Respect their values and opinions.

- If problems should arise with an employee or among the team, take care of it right away. Allowing them to go unsettled can cause problems among the team.

Dealing with Rumors, Gossip, and Half - Truths

While every manager likes to believe everyone in their office gets along, unfortunately, this is not always the case. When people come together, problems such as rumors and gossip can arise and spread quickly. If these issues are not addressed and resolved from the start, they can grow larger and cause disruptions among coworkers. You have the ability to instill confidence and trust with your employees.

Its Effects on Morale

Although office conflicts are normal, frequent gossip, rumors or even informal comments can demoralize any employee. Negative comments that spread throughout the office cannot only be hurtful, but can cause doubt and fear among employees and affect their job performance. Employees can start to fear coming to work, question their job security, or simply make them withdraw from the group. In turn, the morale of the group drops and the team no longer works together.

Reinforce the Truth with Facts

When a piece of gossip or a rumor is heard in the office, our first instinct should be to stop it from spreading any further. One of the best ways to accomplish this is by discrediting the information and reinforcing the truth with the facts. Since gossip is often started through a lack of communication or a lack of knowledge, a little education or open communication can go a long way in helping it stop.

Example methods:

- Pull groups together to talk about the incident.

- Open the door for communication. Speak with your employees and answer any questions employees may have.

- Hold weekly meetings to address any recent "word around the office". Address any concerns or problems employees may have. Also use this time to offer facts and information that can stop the gossip and alleviate any doubts or negativity.

Do Not Participate

One of the best ways to end gossip or rumors is to simply not share it with others. Gossip feeds on those willing to send it down the grapevine and has trouble moving on when it hits a brick wall. Participating in the rumor mill not only perpetuates it, but you discredit and even belittle yourself. As a person in a management position, any participation in office gossip can portray you in a negative way and may you appear to be a non-team player.

Deal With it Swiftly

Refusing to pass on a rumor or piece of gossip won't end its cycle through the office. When something like this approaches you, speak openly with the person who told it to you and let them know you don't intend to share the information with anyone else. Also tell them why you believe the information could be hurtful if passed along any further. This shows you will not participate in that kind of behavior and help shed some light for the other person to see how negative their actions are as well. Follow up with other employees and have the same discussion with them. If needed, have a meeting with the office and address a group of employees at once. The quicker these problems are approached, the sooner the grapevine will stop and work can continue.

Office Personalities

Every employee is unique in their job skills and office presence. That also means every employee has their own office personality. While many are tolerable and even upbeat, some can have negative effects on other employees. Managers should understand these different types and know how to handle them in the workplace.

Complainer

The complainer in the office is typically the employee who always finds something to complain about on the job, whether it includes the amount of hours they work, the assignments they get, or simply the type of coffee in the break room. They love to circulate bad news and feed off of the misery of others. They were most likely a model employee, but then probably had too many confrontations with coworkers or negative comments from upper management.

Tips when handling a complainer personality:

- Try to keep their views in perspective.

- Direct their negativity toward more positive views.

- Instead of listening to their opinions, form your own.

- Don't let their cynical views blur your vision of the office.

Gossiper

The primary mission of the office gossiper is to know and share the latest scoop of the office; and if they don't know it, they'll simply make it up. They have a need to feel important and think that since they hold the key to the best information, this puts them on top. A gossip will purposely seek those who are willing to listen and feed on the attention. While they believe this type of behavior makes them more likable and popular, it can actually have the opposite effect, making them untrustworthy and undependable.

Tips when handling a gossiper personality:

- Avoid engaging in their gossip or rumors.

- State that you are not interested in what they may have to offer.

- Do not pass on information they may have passed onto you.

- Avoid discussing any personal matters near them, unless you want the entire office to know.

Bully

There are several types of office bullies with several different characteristics, but their behavior is generally the same. Bullies look to dominate and control their work area. They often insult or downplay their coworkers or their performance in order to distract from theirs. Bullies have their own 'growl' that they use to make employees fear them and comply with what they say. Only when they feel like they have control and power will they feel happy.

Tips when handling a bully personality:

- Don't try to challenge them. This only feeds their bully persona.

- Don't take their remarks personally. Chances are it's really not about you.

- Avoid trying to please them. They can normally not be satisfied so easily.

- When addressing their behavior, do it privately and calmly.

Negative Ned / Nancy

Negative Ned and Nancy typically do not trust anyone with authority or power. They have the "they're out to get me" attitude. While they believe that they are always right, they hold back on answers but are quick to let out ''told you so" when things go wrong. This personality always sees the down side of any situation.

Tips when handling a negative Ned/Nancy personality:

- Stay positive, but stay realistic.

- Avoid trying to simply find a solution since they will dismiss them.

- Stick with the facts.

- Avoid arguing with them or trying to correct them.

As we've stated, every employee is unique and brings his own personality to the office. Some of these personalities can have negative effects not only on fellow coworkers and management, but even the whole office. Here we discuss more personality types a manager could encounter and ways to handle them in the workplace.

Information Keeper

Information keepers are similar to know-it-alls, except that they tend to keep the information to themselves, rather than blasting it all over the office. Their power comes from within, in which they know the information needed and wait for others to seek them out. They thrive on gathering information on all subjects and departments, even if they are not an active part of it.

Tips when handling an information keeper personality:

- Realize it's alright to ask for their help, but don't let them control the situation.

- Don't try to correct them or get them to change their mind.

- Stick to the topic at hand – don't wander into other categories.

- Don't try to compete with them.

Know-It-All

The know-it-all is the person in the office that is very skilled in their area and makes a great expert on the subject, but makes a poor coworker. Whether you've asked for their help or not, they are more than willing to show off what they know and what they can do. Their arrogance can make them hard to work with, but their expertise is a key asset to the office.

Tips when handling a know-it-all personality:

- Keep them focused on the task or information needed.

- Don't be afraid to ask for their help, but keep it work related.

- Avoid trying to compete with them.

- Don't argue or correct them if something is incorrect. Offer to speak with them privately.

The Apple - Polisher

There are often many names for the apple-polisher type – such as boss's pet, brown-noser, or frankly just the office 'suck up'. Since they fear rejection, an apple polisher will be overly nice and polite to feel accepted. They love to give praise since they think it gets them ahead. They always volunteer for projects, even if it hasn't been asked yet. They usually put their relationship with the manager above their relationship with their peers, which can make then unlikable in the workplace. In extreme cases, the apple-polisher can become a 'snitch' if they feel it would put them on the good side of management.

Tips when handling an apple-polisher personality:

- Always speak with this person in private.

- Find what the employee really needs – not just what they are willing to take.

- Avoid giving flat out rejection.

- Thank them for their effort and willingness to help, but remind them they don't have to do it all to be a great team member.

Nosey Neighbor

The nosey neighbor type is the one in the office that always wants to know everyone else's business. They constantly ask personal questions and can appear in your office several times a day. While this employee can be annoying, they often believe they are just being helpful or even friendly. It is not easy to deflect this type of person since if they are not handled with care, they can intensify and try harder to become closer.

Tips when handling a nosey neighbor personality:

- Answer their prying questions with as few facts as needed.

- Remain friendly but don't feed into their need for information.

- Avoid talking about your personal life at work.

- When asked personal questions, try to shift their focus back to work related matters.

Sometimes it can seem hard to gain support behind your office projects, but don't throw in the towel so early. Some of the key aspects of gaining support are building relationships with the staff, making allies that can give you a boost, and not being afraid to show others what you have to offer. Using honest and 'good' politics cannot only gain support for any project you may be carrying, but will propel your career forward without burning bridges behind you.

Gain Trust Through Honesty

A manager that instills confidence and mutual trust creates an office environment that holds to high standards and clear ethics. Although office politics can make some people think of terms like deception and trickery. Keep in mind that honesty and trust will provide a more powerful and lasting benefit to the employee and propel their career further. Don't lie or cover up recent mistakes you might have made. Be open about steps you've had to take to correct situations. When asked for statistics or reports for your project, offer them freely. It's important to build trusting relationships that people can depend on to gain support over time. Relationships built on dishonesty and misguidances do not hold up.

Helpful tips:

- Be polite an honest with coworkers.

- Be open with others and don't be afraid to 'tell it like it is" rather than beat around the bush.

- Don't use deception and lies, or 'bad' politics to get ahead.

Be Assertive

Being assertive can often be misconstrued as being mean or just being a jerk. But belittling, intimidating or trying to control those that could very well help you will cause trouble in the office and will cause you to lose others' respect. Being assertive requires one to be confident without being aggressive. Don't be afraid to say what you want or need, and as long you do it tactfully and respectfully. If your answer is no, don't give up right away. Regroup and rethink what you need to do in order to go for your goal.

Helpful tips:

- Be confident, but not arrogant.

- Don't be afraid of rejection or criticism.

- State what you want or intend to gain. Don't beat around the bush or use smoke and mirrors.

Blow Your Own Horn

One of the best ways to gain support for your cause is to let others know what you have accomplished or what you can bring to the table in the future. Be cautious of the fine line between blowing your horn and downright bragging or being boastful. When speaking with those who can potentially give the support you need, subtly add in some of your recent successes or a good comment made on your last evaluation. Once they see your value and potential, you will have more people on your side next time you present your case in a staff meeting. Keep your comments truthful and realistic. Be sure not to just make up great things to say – those that want to back you will most likely check their facts first.

Make Allies

Don't underestimate the power and value of having allies not only in your department, but other departments as well. To win them over, take time to learn how you can help and contribute with your time. Staying on good terms with different department heads can put you right in the middle of the networking movement in the company, and allow you to tap into every department when needed. This also allows you to not only build credibility, but strong office alliances that will prove very helpful.

Helpful tips:

- Alliances are not built overnight. Be committed.

- Offer your time to help other departments and managers. If you want them to do it for you, be willing to do it for them.

- Don't underestimate the little guys. Many alliances start small.

Conflict Resolution

While conflict is bound to happen in any office, managers are still responsible for creating a work environment that allows its employees to work comfortably together without fear or hostility. Cliques, disagreements, and plain arguments can develop which can affect the entire office. As a manager, it is your responsibility to identify these conflicts and make sure they are resolved as soon as possible.

The Importance of Forgiveness

Conflict causes stress and emotional pain. Once a conflict has been resolved, it is important to forgive all parties involved. Those who do not forgive can be caught in a circle of anger and resentment, affecting not only their work performance, but others as well. Forgiveness allows a person to let go of the blame and pain and feel the weight come off of their shoulders.

Forgiveness benefits:

- Enables one to feel more empathy toward the other party.

- Provides the parties to repair any damage to their relationship.

- Allows employee(s) to feel less like a victim and more of an active role in the resolution.

Neutralizing Emotions

When a manager attempts to ignore or push aside emotions in a conflict, it can not only make the original conflict worse, and it makes the manager part of the conflict as well. The negative emotions are soon pointed at the manager and can create more problems than intended. In any case, before a conflict can begin to be resolved, the manager must first neutralize the emotions. Once this is done, the problem can be looked at objectively and settled more calmly.

Tips on handling emotions:

- Remind the employee(s) of their positive attributes, which draws attention away from the negative emotions.

- Offer solutions you can personally provide, such a change in assignments, or a one-on-one meeting.

- Above all, acknowledge the parties' feelings. Some employees just want to be heard.

The Benefits of a Resolution

Resolving a conflict can make any work environment feel powerful. Employees feel as though they can go on about their day rather than feel the stress of conflict and arguments. Although, conflict can never be eliminated from the office, employees and managers can learn how to manage conflict and keep these frustrating instances to a minimum.

Common benefits of resolving conflicts:

- Requires the employee(s) to take ownership in their own actions

- Allows people to listen to each other and consider different point of views.

- Enables employees to play a part in their own resolution, rather than being done completely by management.

The Agreement Frame

The Agreement Frame is used to explain the employee's viewpoint during a conflict in a firm way, without offending the other party and without demeaning their own position. The Agreement Frame is meant to encourage open discussion and conversation between all parties involved.
Employees should start the conversation with "I agree…and…" I appreciate…and…", "I respect…and…", "I believe…and…" or even "I think…and…" These phrases allow the employee to acknowledge how the other party is feeling but also lets them interject with their own opinions as well. When used correctly, the Agreement Frame can be a great tool for resolving any conflict.

Remember:

- Allow both parties to speak and encourage using the previous key phrases.

- Make employees focus on what they want in the solution

- Using words such as "but", "although", "however", "nonetheless", etc. are negative adverbs and can distract from the final solution. Avoid using them while employees are speaking.

Ethics

Ethics is a set of standards used to judge from right and wrong. In the workplace, it can refer to the act of fair competition, acting honestly and treating coworkers and management respectively. Every day managers will need to make ethical decisions that will affect their employees as well as themselves. That's why it is very important that the manager understands their company's ethical obligations so that they can not only meet the requirements set forth, but to also display appropriate behavior for their employees and coworkers.

Benefits of an Ethical Environment

An office that creates an ethical environment is an office where employees can feel safe and trusted. Employees that work in this type of environment are proven to work harder and increase productivity over time. When workers know they're management follows a code of ethics, they are more inclined to go above and beyond for them and excel in their work.

Additional benefits:

- Enables open communications between management and employees.

- Employees are more likely to report misconduct.

Lead by Example

Since good ethics are first noticed at the top, management must lead by example. Employees may sit through seminars or see a poster in the break room about good ethics, but they are truly learning ethics from the people that surround them, including management. So as a key tool in this learning process, it is important that, as a manager, you are up to speed on the company's code of ethics and how to carry them out.

Remember:

- Managers are to uphold the ethical standards for the entire company.

- Employees look to you for guidance. Give them an example worth following.

Ensuring Ethical Behavior

Now that you are leading your employees by example in your ethical behavior, how do you ensure the ethical behavior in others? Many companies use various types of ways to first instill their ethics and then ensuring they are carried out, such as training programs or handbooks. Some use bribes and rewards that are given when good ethical behavior is seen. The opposite method is also used, in which employees are quickly disciplined when they display unethical behavior. This effect is normally done in a semi-private way to 'make an example' of the employee and discourages others from committing the same act or acts. Both methods should be used with caution, since they can actually *lead to* unethical behavior. As a manager, it is up to you as to how you can effectively ensure ethical behavior in your workplace.

Example methods:

- Reward programs

- Discipline plans

- Training sessions – including posters, handbooks and manuals

Addressing Unethical Behavior

Unethical behavior is never fun to catch. One of the main problems after witnessing such behavior is how to address it properly so that the behavior can be corrected. Employees can have a hard time exposing unethical behavior if it is not clearly defined or runs a risk or retaliation of some sort. Managers can face the same problems at times, so it is best for the company to create some sort of policy or procedure on how to report any witnessed behavior. With clear instructions outlined, employees and managers don't have to hesitate reporting the unethical behavior.

Key points to addressing the unethical behavior:

- Speak directly with the employee, preferably in private.

- Use empathy and understanding, but remain firm that the behavior was inappropriate.

- Adhere to the company policy and the consequences stated.

- Carry out such consequences and remind the employee (if still in your employ) that this type of behavior is unacceptable.

Sometimes, as a manager, we can feel like we are on our own little island doing our job as intended. But don't forget to look up and see your team of employees that are there to work for and with you, as well as partners in upper management. No one can manage everything by themselves, and will need to reach out from time to time. Sometimes we find that we may need to reach out to those we've just met, or even someone we thought we'd left behind.

Never Burn a Bridge

Whether you left another company to come to this one or you are moving departments, there is always a bridge behind you that is moving you forward. Our natural instinct is to let out our frustrations on the people you no longer have to see, but burning that bridge behind you won't erase the past and could harm your future. You never know when or where you'll need to face the company or person again. You'll want to ensure if you do meet again or if you ever need their assistance (a reference perhaps), that you'll be in their favor.

Tips:

- Leave with notice, if possible.

- Do not leave in anger – keep all negative comments and frustrations to yourself.

- Thank the manager or HR for your time at the company. They will remember your gracious attitude when they are called for a reference.

Take the High Road

"Taking the high road" simply means to make a decision based on moral, or to act ethically. When faced with a difficult decision, the manager should 'take the high road' to either resolve the problem or correct what they might have done wrong. The key to doing this is to have certain boundaries and use them when needed. Acknowledge the position someone else may hold, even if you do not like it or agree with them, and then use your boundaries to express your side with being negative or unethical. Even if the situation is not any better, it certainly did not get worse.

Helpful tips:

- Take a deep breath and think about what *should* be done, rather than what is currently *being* done.

- Think about the kind of person you want to exhibit to those around you – show it in your actions.

- Remember that we all have disagreements and make mistakes. How would you want the other person to treat you in you were in their shoes?

Trust is a Two-Way Street

Employees want to trust their manager and depend on them for their needs at work. It is important for the manager to build trust between themselves and their employees, especially since this may help repair any trust deficiencies made somewhere else. When managers show trust in their employees and believe in their hard work, employees will continue to strive to do well for their managers and show their trust in return.

Tips to help build trust:

- Show confidence in your employees.

- Be honest and tell the truth, even if it makes you look bad or puts you at a disadvantage.

- Demonstrate that your words are consistent with your actions – make due on your promises.

Don't Hide in Your Office

Office employees count on their managers to be leaders and want to know that they are there to face tough office situation when they arise. Some managers try to find the benefit of staying in their office, perhaps to gain focus or ignore non-office related chatter, but in reality it is actually hurting the team they are trying to focus on. When the manager spends most of their time behind a closed door, employees begin to feel neglected and can start to resent their manager. Make it a point to come out of the office and speak with your employees and how they are doing on the job. Your employees will respect you more as a coworker and an ally then the stuffy manager that hides behind closed doors.

Social Events Outside of Work

While socializing outside of work can generally sound like a great idea (the team that plays together stays together), there comes a time when employees and managers should respect each other's boundaries and know when to spend time apart. Also, employees and managers must spend some time away from the stress and hustle of the office and should not take their job with them when they go out.

How to Decline Politely

Managers can't, or don't want, to necessarily attend social events with their employees, whether it's because of the late nights, difference of interests or simply a lack of time. Even though there is nothing wrong with this, it is important to offer a polite decline rather than just giving your employees the cold shoulder. When asked to attend an event or gathering, thank the person for the invitation and simply state that you cannot attend for whatever reason. The employees may laugh or mock it a little at first, but they will grow to respect you and your reasoning. To avoid losing touch with them altogether, you can plan and offer your own events to invite your coworkers to that are more your style or that can fit into your schedule. It won't keep them from doing their own thing, but it does allow the chance for them to spend time with you and socialize outside of work.

Common reasons to decline a social event:

- Family responsibilities

- Lack of time/schedule permitting

- Lack or difference of interests

Rules When Attending

When a group from the office is planning to get together outside of the workplace setting, it is always best to instill a set of spoken or even unspoken boundaries. Things such as client information or personal employee information should not be brought to the table. If time permits, gather the group before and discuss what sort of boundaries need to be set, whether personal or professional.

Common rules and boundaries set:

- No talking about the office (client, salaries, assignments, coworkers).

- Pictures should be kept to a minimum and not posted on a social networking site without the subject permission.

- The event does not prevent the employee from coming to work the next day.

Meeting New People

When meeting new people outside of work, things can either feel natural or turn awkward real fast. Sometimes we're unsure of ourselves outside of work and are unsure of the identity we put out there. After all, out here you're not just the manager and coworker; you're Joe/Bob/Susan/Anne, etc.

Situations like these can go back to our grade school days and remember how you made new friends, plain and simple:

- Approach people calmly and say something about yourself. Ask them to return the favor.

- Keep introductions short. They don't need to know your entire resume in one conversation.

- If you encounter someone who is rude or being a jerk, smile politely and simply move on.

Conversation Dos and Don'ts

One of the general social event rules is to have an understood list of topics that should not be discussed when out with colleagues. As stated before, information such as company client list or employee salaries should rank high on the do not discuss list. Other topics can include employee evaluations or assignments, office meetings or even other coworkers. Some offices choose to just eliminate office talk altogether.
You can't control what employees talk about when they are out, but you can influence the conversation at the events you choose to attend. Let your group know what subjects are off limits or would be inappropriate. Clarify any misunderstandings before they have a chance to rise.

Chapter 25 – Meeting Management

You are on your first project and you have to organize and manage the project kick-off meeting. What do you do first? Do you create the agenda or the invitation list? How do you run a meeting? What preparation do you need? All of these are valid and real questions you, as the meeting manager, must address. There is no doubt about it. Meetings require skill and technique in order for the meeting to achieve its purpose. Disorganized and poorly managed meetings waste time and hurt your credibility as a meeting manager. Consistently leaving a poor impression with the attendees will haunt you if left unchecked.

This training course is designed to give you the basic tools you need to initiate and manage your meetings. You will learn planning and leading techniques that will give you the confidence to run a meeting that will engage your attendees and leave a positive and lasting impression. This is a hands-on workshop and your participation will help make it a valuable experience. Use this time to begin the process of developing your skills along with other participants who share the same desire to improve their meeting management skills.

Before we begin, let's get to know each other better. Since we will be spending most of today working with each other, it is worth the time to share some things about ourselves now, making it easier to engage in the course.

By the end of this chapter, you will:

- Planning and Preparing

- Identifying the Participants

- How to choose the time and place

- How to create the agenda

- How to set up the meeting space

- How to incorporate your electronic options

- Meeting Roles and Responsibilities

- Use an agenda

- Chairing a Meeting

- How to deal with disruptions

- How to professionally deal with personality conflicts

- How to take minutes

- How to make the most of your meeting using games, activities and prizes

Planning and Preparing

The first step in making your meeting effective begins with your planning and preparation activity. Determining the purpose of your meeting, the people who should attend, and the place of the meeting will form the foundation on which you will build your agenda, decide what materials you need, and identify the roles each attendee hold in the meeting. In addition, planning and preparing for your meeting helps to reduce the stress that may result from managing a meeting, because you will avoid unexpected incidents and issues that could derail your meeting.

This module is part one of your planning session, which focuses on important factors that could affect the success of your meeting. These factors are the people, place, and purpose of the meeting. Let us take a closer look to see how we can organize this to your success.

Identifying the Participants

Determining your meeting participants is an important planning step. You should not approach this casually. Who attends your meeting could help or hinder the meeting dynamics. There is a tendency to invite everyone you know in an effort to cover all angles. This is overkill. Before you think about whom to invite, think about the purpose of the meeting. This will help you determine who should be invited. Be specific when determining the purpose of the meeting. For example, if you are meeting to resolve a problem, invite only those who are capable of providing solutions to the problem. Avoid inviting a high-ranking manager, who could thwart solutions before they are developed.

On the other hand, if your meeting is to come to a decision on a policy or product, do not invite people who do not have the power to enact those changes. Having people who cannot contribute to the meeting will exclude them and affect the meeting environment. Identifying the purpose of your meeting first will help to determine who should attend. Here are some common reasons to call a meeting:

- Problem solving

- Decision making

- Conflict resolution

- Project initiation

- Planning

- Brainstorming

Once you determine your meeting purpose, you can list all the names of the participants you wish to attend. Once this list is created, then determine what each participant will contribute to the meeting. If a participant is deemed a non-contributor, they should be removed from the list. When all non-contributors are removed, you should have a good list of participants for your meeting.

Choosing the Time and Place

There are several considerations you must address when planning the time and place of your meeting. For instance, the time of day is essential if your meeting is meant to be a brainstorming session or problem-solving meeting. Setting these types of meetings right after lunch or late in the day could be a frustrating experience. Humans after lunch are usually lethargic and meetings at the end of the day are plagued with participants looking at the clock in anticipation to leave work and go home.

Meetings that require energy and high level of participation are best scheduled between 8 and 9 AM in the morning. Most workers are not engaged in their daily work yet so you will have their attention and energy for use in your meeting. The next best time for a meeting is around 3 PM. This gives your participants enough time to recuperate from their lunchtime meal. It also gives you at least an hour of cushion before your participants start thinking about going home. Meetings that are low key could be scheduled anytime during the day. Just remember not to schedule them to close to lunch or the end of the workday.

The location is also important to your meeting dynamics. Try to schedule your meeting in a well-lit spacious room. If you can get a room with windows, do so. Dark and cramped rooms will bog down your meeting. Some people get claustrophobic and are distracted by their surroundings. A couple of other things to consider are the need for privacy or if you intend to have an outside visitor attend. If the meeting topic is of a sensitive nature, then getting a room with more privacy will make participants more comfortable to discuss the issue. Furthermore, if you plan to have an outside visitor attend your meeting, get a room that is closes to the main entrance. This way your visitor does not have to search the halls of your organization in search of your meeting.

Creating the Agenda

Creating the agenda can be easy if you know what to do in advance. The **SOAP** technique helps to collect the topics, organize them, and select the ones that will contribute the most to your meeting.

Seek topics from your participants: send an email to the list of participants you created, asking for agenda topics. Give a brief explanation of the purpose of the meeting and an idea of what you are looking for in terms of topics. Do not make this the formal invitation. When you make the request, make sure you ask the participants for the time they need to discuss their topic, and provide a deadline to get their topic to you so it can be included on the agenda.

Organize topics into a list: once you receive the topics, organize them into a list along with the time and the name of the presenter. This will give you the ability to scan through the list, narrowing it down to the topics you will select for the agenda.

Assess which topics are relevant to the meeting purpose: with your list organized, determine which topics are the most relevant to the purpose of the meeting. Scratch out those topics you do not intend to use.

Pick the number of relevant topics that will fit into your meeting time: review the time of the remaining topics. Select the enough topics to fill the time of your meeting minus ten minutes. Give yourself ten minutes for meeting overrun. If you go over, you will end on time. If you do not, then you get to adjourn your meeting early, making everyone happy.

Remember to contact the presenter that had their topic removed from the agenda, explaining the reason why it was not put on the agenda and recommending that topic be saved for another meeting.

Gathering Materials

Each meeting you hold will require both basic and special materials. Your job as the meeting manager is to determine what you need and acquire them in advance, avoiding last minute surprises.

The **SHOWS** acronym stands for stationary, handouts, organizer, writing tools, and special requests. Let us break down each letter so you get a better understanding of what this means.

Stationary: this is all the paper you will need at the meeting. It includes, note pads, sticky notes, index cards, envelops, tape, paper clips, folders, and flip chart. Each meeting is different. You do not have to bring everything on this list. Determine what is going to take place at the meeting and materials needed for each activity or presentation. It is also wise to consult with the people on your agenda to see if they are going to facilitate activities that require stationary.

Handouts: many times you or your presenters will need to distribute handouts. There could be a worksheet or an outline from an electronic presentation. In any case, you should consult with your presenters and acquire any handouts they may use. Determine if the handout they are giving you will be the most up-to-date version. If not, have them send it to you when they finalize it. Remember to set the expectation to have it a day or so in advance, giving you time to print and file it in your handout organizer.

Organizer: when it is time to meet, the last thing you want to do is show up with a stack of handouts. Using an organizer like a portable accordion file or Pendaflex is an easy way to file your handouts and other stationary materials in one container. The filing system will allow you to file the documents in an orderly fashion, making distribution of the materials more professional. You want to avoid shuffling handouts around in front of your participants when it comes time to distribute them.

Writing tools: this includes pens, markers, highlighters, and dry erase markers you may need for your meeting.

Special requests: from time to time, your presenters may make a special request. An example could be a poster. Ask your presenters ahead of time for special requests.

Sending Invitations

Many times invitations are sent without much thought. We figure the sending mechanism, whether it is Outlook or any other type of electronic program, will do the job effectively. It is wise to use an electronic tool for your invitation; however, there is more thought that should go into it. The three "P" approach gives a consistent and clear method of structuring your meeting invitation. Here is the breakdown:

Purpose: the purpose of your meeting must be stated up front. It is not enough to put in the subject line: "Planning Session." The vagueness of your purpose could result in low attendance. Be specific with your purpose. Instead of "Planning Session," you could state, "Planning our budget for the first quarter." In addition, you should attach your agenda, which gives more detail of the discussion topics.

Place and Time: determine ahead of time where and when the meeting will take place. Avoid sending out invitations with a to-be-determine (TBD) message. The more effort you place on getting the details done in advance the more your attendees will take you seriously. In addition, provide clear instructions on the exact location.

Pact: create a sense of binding agreement by setting expectations so you get the most responses as soon as possible with a level of commitment. For example, state, "Please respond to this invitation within 48 hours." Also, set a cancellation policy by stating, "If you need to cancel, please call, or email me as soon as possible." You could also include a statement that states, "Upon acceptance of this invitation, you are expected to attend." Finally, you could also include a statement like this, "This meeting is a planning session, and your participation and idea-sharing will be greatly appreciated."

Structuring your invitation with clear and concise information and expectations sends the message that you are seriously managing this meeting. You do not want to be famous for holding boring and inefficient meetings. This is something that takes a long time to correct.

Making Logistical Arrangements

There are several areas where you should be planning the logistics.

Physical space: consider the space in which you plan to hold your meeting.
- Is it on site or off site?
- Do you need to make reservations?
- Does it need to be set up?
- Do you have to contact you facilities department to remove or add partitions?
- Do you need furniture moved?

Travel: identify who will need to travel to your meeting.
- Do they need travel arrangements?
- Do they need transportation to and from the meeting location?
- Do you have to make security aware of their presence so they are not held up at the door?

Food: determine if you need to organize meals.
- Is your meeting starting early in the morning and you need to serve a light breakfast?
- Is your meeting all day?
- Are you going to cater food?
- Are you planning to have lunch at a local restaurant?
- Do you need to make reservations?

Audio and visual: later there will be a discussion on electronic options; however, if you plan to use electronics like a presentation or video.
- Do you have to get this placed in the meeting room?
- Are you savvy enough in troubleshooting technical problems or do you need a technical assistant?
- Do you need a projector, screen, computer, etc.?
- Do you need a sound system set up so everyone can hear the presenters?

Signage:
- Do you need to get signs, posters, special handouts made up for your meeting?

Setting up the Meeting Space

You are now ready to set up the meeting space. There are many things to consider that will determine what needs to be included in your set up. In the last module, you planned for the things you need. In this module, you are going to put it all together. Although this may seem like a trivial step, you should not take it for granted. The difference from an okay meeting to a remarkable meeting could be the small details. Let us begin with the basics.

The Basic Essentials

Having a predefined list for setting up your meeting is a useful tool and we are going to discuss the setup of your meeting using a handout over the next three lessons. In the first section, you will see a simple list of items comprising of the basic essentials in setting up the meeting space. The list consists of the following items:

- Sufficient number of tables and chairs

- Power strips for laptops and other electronic devices

- Audio and visual set up

- Whiteboard with markers and eraser

- Lectern

- Water

- Verify the room temperature is comfortable

- Microphone for large meetings

- Projector

- Laptop

- Verify room is located in quiet and private area

Make sure you get to the meeting place early enough, giving you time to set up the room without the participants seeing you do it. Getting "caught" setting up the room gives the impression that you are unprepared, which could affect your meeting environment.

The Extra Touches

Extra touches make your meeting more meaningful to your participants. Your handout from the last lesson outlines some items you can incorporate in you meeting set up. Let review some of the extra touches:

- Name tents already printed and set up on the tables

- Table with name tags for each participant already printed

- Projector on with a welcome message illuminating on the screen

- Signage outside the meeting room professionally done

- Keepsake or logo item at each place setting

- Music before meeting starts and during breaks

- Folder with all meeting materials inside (i.e. agenda, handouts, etc.)

- Candy or mints at the tables

- Posters or visual aids posted around the meeting room (professionally done looks better)

- Video playing relevant materials on the screen before meeting starts

- Coat rack during winter months

When it comes to adding the extra touches, be sure to gauge the audience and meeting purpose and plan accordingly. You do not want to create a celebratory experience when the meeting is about cutting costs, etc. Otherwise, going the extra mile helps to make your meeting more effective by creating a personalized environment.

Choosing a Physical Arrangement

The types of activities that are involved in your meeting could help you determine the physical setup. However, before you think further on this topic, let us review some basic setups.

- **Conference style seating:** this is the basic long rectangular or oval shaped table. This type of setup is good for short meetings with less than 30 participants. You would use this for small training sessions and close interactions.

- **U-shape seating:** this is a setup where the tables form a U shape. This is effective where face-to-face interaction is desired. This set up also accommodates larger groups.

- **T-Shape seating:** this design sets up the tables in a T shape. This is also used for face-to-face and large group meetings; however, this shape allows for a leaders to sit at the cross point.

- **Classroom style seating:** this type of seating is best when learning is going to take place and the participants need to take notes. This style can be used for both large and small groups.

Knowing the various styles of seating arrangements helps to determine which to use based on the activity. Below are some suggestions:

- Planning meeting: conference style seating

- Product sales training: classroom style seating

- Strategy sharing meeting: T-shape style seating

- Project update meeting: U-shape style seating

The physical arrangement of the meeting room should always focus on providing a comfortable set up where all participants are able to view the presenter, other participants, screens, and flipchart and whiteboards.

Electronic Options

Advancements in technology have made meetings more effective by providing ways of communicating and storing meeting information. Although many new tools are available to help give your meeting that cutting-edge-feel, there are many things to consider when determining electronic options. It is not always imperative to use new technology at your meetings, but having an understanding in advance helps to expand your choices. In this module, you will learn about the latest meeting tools available to you, things to consider and reaching a decision.

Overview of Choices Available

Electronics in meetings bring a wealth of advantages if used properly. Technology has increased the reach of the meeting room into the virtual world. You are capable of connecting with participants anywhere in the world. Technology also expands your ability to disseminate and record information. This lesson presents an overview of the various tools you can employ in your next meeting.

- **Presentation software:** programs like Microsoft Power Point help to organize your materials into one file. Once the information is in the presentation program, you can make handouts that you can give to your participants as an agenda.

- **Electronic whiteboard:** an electronic whiteboard is an efficient way to write and record ideas all with one source. The electronic device acts like a normal whiteboard, but uses special electronic markers. This electronic device also records the items written on the board for referencing later.

- **Web meeting programs:** programs similar to Microsoft Live Meeting allow you to conduct your meeting via the Internet. Voice, images from your desktop, and a web cam view of the meeting room and the individual.

- **Video conferencing**: this dedicated line uses cameras and television screens to connect two or more remote sites into one meeting.

- **Telephone conferencing:** this is a dedicated telephone line where many participants call in and participate in the meeting.

There a many variations of the electronic tools listed in the lesson that you can use. You can have your company purchase these programs or use a pay-as-you-go product from an online vendor. Choosing the type of electronic tool depends on the audience, distance and technological capabilities of the meeting place.

Things to Consider

The most important thing to consider when dealing with electronic meeting tools is your ability to use and troubleshoot them. Many things could affect the performance of the tools. You must be comfortable enough with the technology to deal with the unexpected. In order to avoid embarrassing issues during the meeting, you should test all systems and make sure your Information Technology (IT) department supports them. In fact, you should always run your technology plans with your IT. They may need to do some backend things to help support your video or web conferencing tool. Before you try using a new tool, get some training and practice. Understanding your electronic tool could take some reading and practice. Test the program with someone you know. Practice using the tool in smaller, more personal meetings before you decides to do it in a larger meeting with outside guests.

Avoid using technology just for the sake of using it. Use it only when it is necessary. Make sure that the participants who will need to use the tools to participate are capable of using it themselves. The last thing you want is someone telling you in the middle of the meeting that they do not know how to launch the program. Here is a quick list of things to consider if you plan to use technology:

- Is the complexity of adding the technology outweighing the potential glitches?

- Are you capable enough to handle any issues that may arise during your meeting?

- Is your audience capable of handing the technology?

- Will you have adequate support from your IT department?

- Are there any costs that you have to consider?

In any case, using technology requires knowledge. If you desire to use technology in your meetings, learn the system and practice, practice, practice. Finally, do not get carried away with technology. It becomes obvious when technology is being used just to dazzle the audience. This is distracting and reduces the effectiveness of your meeting.

Making a Final Decision

This assessment allows you to determine quickly if you need to use technology or not. When making a decision determines the following:

- Am I proficient with the technology?

- Am I able to acquire someone who is proficient and can assist me with the technology?

- Will there be people connecting to my meeting from remote locations?

- Is there a large number of graphics that will be presented?

- Are the participants capable of using the technology?

- Does the meeting room support technology?

- Do you have IT support available?

- Do you have the budget to support the technology?

If you answer "no" to any of these questions, determine the risk of going ahead with the technology. If it is too risky, avoid using the technology, unless you must like in the case of remote conferencing. Just make sure you get the training you need well in advance or get someone to be there as a technical helper if technology is unavoidable.

Meeting Roles and Responsibilities

Establishing clear roles and responsibilities in your meeting helps to manage the meeting effectively. When roles are established, the participants have a clear understanding of what is taking place because the person in a specific role has a job to fulfill. Assigning roles also alleviates the task you have to manage. This way you can focus on the role you are to manage within the meeting time. Remember that you do not have to do it all. Get others involved.

In this module, you will learn the role of the Chairperson, Minute Taker, and the Attendees. Finally, you will learn how to vary the roles for large and small meetings. Let us begin first by identifying the role of the Chairperson.

The Chairperson

The meeting chairperson is responsible for directing the proceedings of the meeting. They are time managers, referees, and enforcer of the rules when they are broken. The chairperson does not necessarily have to be you all the time, but when you do defer the chairperson's duty to someone other than you, make sure you are confident the chairperson you choose can handle the role. The chairperson must be able to lead the meeting and be firm throughout the meeting.

Here are additional responsibilities of the chairperson:

- Be aware of the rules of the meeting if present

- Keep to the aim or objective of the meeting

- Remain fair with all participants

- Start the meeting

- Transition from agenda topic to the next

- Introduce the next presenter

- Handle disruptions

Some of the qualities a chairperson should possess are as follows:

- They should have some level of authority

- Demonstrate flexibility

- Remain impartial

- Display maturity

The role of the chairperson is essential if the meeting is to have some form of control. If you are the chairperson, make sure you do not take on additional roles. You want to remain focus on the tasks associated with the role of the chairperson. If you select another person to be the chairperson, it is a good practice to meet with him or her in advance of the meeting to coordinate the agenda and set expectations. You want to avoid miscommunication during the meeting, which could hurt the credibility of both your chairperson and yourself.

The Minute Taker

Taking minutes requires some basic skills. For instance, a good minute taker will possess great listening skills, and attention to detail. Furthermore, they should have excellent writing skills and communication skills. The person you select must be able to maintain focus and not be carried away with the meeting, missing crucial meeting information. It is best to select someone who is not directly involved in the meeting, allowing them not to participate. Here is a list of tasks the minute taker should handle:

Before the meeting
- Determine what tool to use for recording the minutes (ex. Laptop, paper, recording)
- Become familiar with the names of the attendees and who they are
- Obtain the agenda and become familiar with the topics

During the meeting
- Take attendance
- Note the time the meeting begins
- Write the main ideas presented in the meeting and the contributor of that information
- Write down decisions made and who supported and opposed the decision
- Note follow up items
- Note items to be discussed in the next meeting
- Note the end time of the meeting

After the meeting
- Type up the minutes immediately after the meeting (if manual notes or recordings were taken)
- Proofread the minutes and correct any errors in grammar and spelling
- Save or send the document to the meeting owner

Using a template helps to keep the minute taking consistent. Remember to meet with the person you choose to be your minute taker before the meeting to go over the template.

The Attendees

The attendees are not excluded from assuming a role or having a responsibility in the meeting setting. Of course, you cannot force the responsibility on to your attendees, but you can attempt to influence them. The attendees are the biggest success factor of your meeting. If they feel that they accomplished something in the meeting, they will applaud you. However, if they walk away feeling they wasted their time, this could affect your credibility. The following are responsibilities your attendees could assume:

Prepare
- Be prepared to contribute to the meeting
- Be prepared to arrive early and avoid being late
- Be prepared for the meeting by jotting down ideas and questions ahead of meeting
- Be prepared by reading the agenda before the meeting
- Be prepared for a long meeting by getting enough rest the night before

Participate
- Ask questions
- Take notes
- Share ideas

Productive
- Avoid carrying side conversations
- Remove distractions like cell phones and PDA's
- Keep to the allotted time if on the agenda

Setting up expectations is the best way to communicate the role of the attendees. This is accomplished in either the meeting invitation, or separate email to the attendees. In any case, it is worth the time. Remember that all participants play a vital role in the meeting. Your job is to remind them of their role and the responsibility that comes with that role.

Variations for Large and Small Meetings

Large meetings present very different dynamics than smaller meetings. Managing a larger meeting requires more resources and assigned roles. If you are chairing the meeting yourself, you will need to rely on others to ensure all things are well executed. Here is a list of additional roles you may want to add when managing a large meeting:

- An extra minutes taker for better accuracy

- A person to distribute all the materials related to the meeting

- A person to greet attendees

- A person to run the audio and visual equipment

- A person to manage the hospitality aspect of your meeting

- A co-chairperson

- A person managing the presentations

On the other hand, in small meetings, you can assume multiple roles. For example, you can be the chairperson, technical person, and the minute taker in a small meeting. Small meetings are less formal and you can leverage the informal environment to multitask. You may need an assistant if the meeting is comprised of important people. In any situation, careful planning and assessing the risk of working with less roles will help you to determine what roles need to be filled. When in doubt, get more help. Err on the side of caution.

Chairing a Meeting

Chairing the meeting is a leadership role. You must be ready and able to stand up and kick off the meeting without sounding nervous or uncomfortable. Your ability to communicate early in the meeting sets the tone of the meeting. Chairing a meeting effectively takes time to develop and requires practice.

This module is part one of two modules that teaches how to effectively chair a meeting. The first part, will teach how to start your meeting on the right foot. Next, we will discuss the role of the agenda and finally, we will discuss how to use the parking lot. All these techniques are designed to make you a more effective chairperson. In fact, you will get an opportunity to practice commencing a meeting. Do not worry. This is a safe learning environment where you will not be forced to do something you are not comfortable doing. However, remember to use your action plan if you need more practice chairing a meeting. Let us start this module from the top, which is getting off on the right foot.

Getting Off on the Right Foot

Opening your meeting effectively requires both a technique and a flow. The **SIGNALS** flow gives you an easy model to follow when opening the meeting. Here is a breakdown of the acronym:

- **Salutation** is opening the meeting by welcoming and greeting your participants

- **Introduction** is where you introduce who you are

- **Guest mentioned** is where you introduce those attendees that are special guests

- **Need-to-know** is a list of things like logistics, bathroom location, fire exits, general meeting format that is shared with the attendees

- **Agenda** is where you discuss the purpose of the meeting and give a brief overview of the agenda

- **"Laws of the meeting"** is where you discuss how the meeting is going to run. This includes policies on electronic devices, participation, and handling conflict.

- **Segue** is the part of your introduction that links this part to the next topic, which in this case will be the role of the agenda.

Practicing your opening is the best way to become better at it. Over time, you will develop your own style, which will be comfortable to you. In any case, you will need to do it in order for you to learn it.

The Role of the Agenda

The agenda is an entity that plays a vital role like the chairperson or minute taker. Is should not be ignored, because if it is ignored, your meeting will experience time and participant management problems. Many times meetings run over or are cut short leaving topics unaddressed that were on the agenda. Consistently missing the agenda time and topics is a sign of poor meeting management. Here is a list of items the agenda accomplishes when handled as a role at the beginning of the meeting:

The agenda communicates:
- Meeting topics
- Presenters
- Time allotment for each speaker

The agenda provides focus by:
- Stating the meeting objectives clearly
- Outlining the meeting in increments of time
- Providing a checklist of things to accomplish in the meeting
- Allowing the attendees to see both the beginning and the end of the meeting, avoiding them becoming distracted when they are left wondering when this meeting end will

Here is a sample introduction of how to introduce the agenda as a role at the beginning of the meeting:

"The agenda today will help us meet today's goal of deriving a good sales strategy. We have four presenters who are going to discuss how to present the new product, handle objections, gain commitment, and close the sale. The agenda will be our guide so we can stay on track and finish on time."

Simply handing out the agenda does not communicate its role. You must introduce it like any other person that has a role in the meeting.

Using a Parking Lot

Using a parking lot in your meetings provides a place where topics that cannot be answered during the meeting are noted for follow up later. Sometimes the topics in the parking lot may be answered during the course of the meeting, but this is unusual. The parking lot is simple to implement. You could create a physical place by using piece of flip chart paper with sticky notes. Perhaps you prefer electronic documentation. You can collect parking lot topics onto a spreadsheet. Whatever you choose, you need to have a basic format. Here are some things to consider:

- Take a few moments to share with the attendees how the parking lot works
  - Meant for topics that require follow up after the meeting
  - Hold questions that can be answered later in the meeting

- Provide brief instruction on how to register a parking lot issue
  - Provide the question or topic, name, and contact information, on a sticky note or verbally to the minute taker
  - Chairperson will review parking lot topics to determine if the topic requires follow up after the meeting.
  - Follow up communication will be sent to all the members of the meeting

The parking lot is helpful in managing your time. It gives you the ability to move off a topic that requires more research and time to develop. Remember to check the parking lot at the end of the meeting and always be sure to follow up when you say you will.

Keeping the Meeting on Track

In order to keep your meeting on track, you should set clear expectations on how time management will be used in the meeting. Setting expectations up front avoids surprised and indignation from the presenter, because they are not caught off guard. In addition, as a chairperson, you must feel comfortable interrupting the presenter when necessary. Many times the presenter would like to be told their time is up. This way they do not have to worry about time. The **STOP** technique helps to keep your meeting on track by doing the following:

Set expectations: letting your presenters and attendees know you intend on managing the agenda vigorously removes the element of surprise. When you neglect to set time management expectations, you are subject to an array of reactions from the presenter and attendees. It may be taken as rude behavior. It does not have to be that way. Let the presenter know that you will give them a signal at five and two minutes remaining. In addition, set expectations for questions and answers. Telling attendees to write their questions down to be asked at the end of the presentation avoids unnecessary interruptions, potentially side tracking the conversation.

Time the presenter: using a timer is the best way to manage the time of your meeting. Keep to the allotted time for both the presentation and the question and answer activity. Always provide a warning time so the presenter does not have to stop abruptly.

Overcome fear of interrupting: perhaps you do not have a problem with this, but there are many who see interrupting someone as rude and find it difficult to do. The best way to overcome this is by setting those expectations upfront. This way you know the presenter is expecting an interruption. The same holds true for questions being asked. If left unchecked, you could lose a lot of time by allowing excessive questions. Use your parking lot to hold questions that require more thought in answering. Call time on questions and answers so you can move to the next topic.

Politely warn people time is nearing: avoid being harsh and rigid. Treating others with respect is the best way to keep the meeting moving and with plenty of participation. You do not want them to shut down because you are becoming a tyrant.

Dealing with Overtime

Going into overtime presents several problems. Once the meeting extends beyond its original end time, you will begin to lose the attendees' attention. This is particularly obvious in large meetings. No matter what size meeting you are dealing with, the goal to dealing with overtime is to acknowledge it before it happens. Look at the agenda and determine if you will need to go over. If you do, then do the following to mitigate the effects of going into overtime:

- Determine your constraints
  - Is the room or venue available for overtime
  - Do attendees have to travel and cannot stay

- Warn attendees in advance that the meeting will over run

- Determine how much more time will be needed

- Communicate the extra time to the attendees

- In a small meeting, gain consensus to go into overtime

- Give choices
  - In a large meeting, provide a brief break at the normal end time so those who have to leave will do so during the break and not the meeting
  - In a small meeting, allow those who need to leave to do so

- If overtime is not an option, determine what agenda items will be missed and plan an alternative way of getting the information to the attendees
  - Follow up email
  - Topic saved for next meeting

If you do not manage overtime, then you will see frustration build among the attendees. Have a plan in place so you know what to do once you determine if your meeting is going to run longer than expected.

Holding Participants Accountable

In a meeting, it may be difficult to hold participants accountable. Participation, questioning, and preparedness could easily be overlooked. Holding your participants accountable involves communication.

Here are three basic steps you can take to holding your participants accountable:

Step 1: Set your expectations: in advance, perhaps in your invitation you should outline what you expect from the participants in this meeting. You may need them to bring questions, or help by providing information. You may want them to participate with vigor. In any case, you must outline what you expect of them before you can hold them to a standard or expectation.

Step 2: Clarify the consequences: let the participants know how you plan to hold them accountable. Perhaps you can warn that you will be calling on everyone for answers. You may also leverage their manager if applicable. You may say that you will be sending the meeting minutes to their supervisors where they can see if they participated or not.

Step 3: Follow through: if you said you would do something, then you have to do it. Do not get into the habit of making empty threats. People will respect you and will naturally be accountable to you because of your work ethic.

Most participants do not want to be on the "bad" side. They want to contribute. Your ability to assert yourself and communicate with clarity your expectations, consequences and determination will make this an easy process with practice.

Dealing with Disruptions

Disruptions in the meeting are bound to happen. Personal technology keeps participants constantly connected to the outside world. Frequent disruptions could impede the effectiveness of your meeting and become distracting to those who are focused on the meeting. Furthermore, poorly managing disruptions will reflect on the chairperson or meeting organizer. The key to mitigating disruptions is to plan for them and setting expectations.

In this module, you will learn how to deal with participants constantly running in and out of your meeting, cell phones, off topic discussions and conflicts. The goal is to reduce the affect. It is very difficult to avoid these distractions. It is human nature. Let us begin the module with a lesson on how to deal with participants constantly leaving the meeting.

Running in and Out

Constant disruptions caused by attendees running in and out of your meeting will affect the experience for the other attendees. We often take it for granted that attendees will stay in the meeting and not leave. Therefore, we do not discuss this issue very often at the beginning of the meetings. Addressing this form of distraction is best done proactively. Using the **SIT** technique helps your set the expectation regarding running in and out of the meeting. Next, incorporating frequent breaks lessens the changes of participants leaving the room, and finally giving timely feedback to those who break the rule is necessary in order to stop frequent violators. Let us review each step in more detail.

Set expectations: tell your participants at the beginning of the meeting what you expect of them when it comes to staying in the meeting room. Tell them the effects of constantly running in and out of the meeting on the presenter and other participants. Let all the participants know that if they need to leave the room to do so only if it is an emergency and if it is a severe problem, that they should leave the meeting. They will be more of a distraction if they stay.

Incorporate frequent breaks: at the beginning of your meeting, tell the participants they will get a five-minute break every hour the meeting lasts. Establishing this up front let the participants know when to expect a break and wait until then to call people back, etc.

Timely feedback given to those who break the rules: when you have a person still running in and out of your meeting, it is best to address that with them as soon as possible. If you have a problem participant, quietly leave the room and wait for them outside. Speak with the participant in a respectful manner and tell them that their behavior is disrupting the meeting. Ask if they are experiencing an emergency and if they need to leave. If they are not in an emergency, tell the participant if they could wait until the scheduled breaks to do what they have to do.

Cell Phone and PDA Ringing

Most people know to silent their cell phones and PDA's when entering a meeting. However, they may forget every so often. Your job as the meeting manager is to remind them. Here are a couple of steps you can take to remind your participants to turn off those phones.

- Place signs in the room instructing participants to silence their cell phone and PDA's. They can be humorous and light-hearted. In any case, you will get your message across.

- Make an announcement at the beginning of the meeting instructing the participants to turn off their cell phone or PDA now. The signs are a back-up in case you forget to do this.

- Since the participants will most likely looking at the agenda, place a reminder there too. This way you have several areas where the participants can get the message.

One cell phone or PDA going off in the middle of the meeting could lead to a disruption that could last a couple of minutes. You can reduce this type of disruption by almost 100 percent by just mentioning it at the beginning of the meeting and providing reminder signs.

Off on a Tangent

This is by far the most difficult to manage in a meeting. The biggest challenge is to redirect without offending the participants. Using the **EAR** technique helps to do this in three simple steps.

- **Engage the conversation by becoming contributor for a moment.** The goal is not to carry the conversation, but to gain some control by getting the meeting floor. Once engaged you are able to go to the next step.

- **Acknowledge that the topic is valid and worthy of discussion.** This should be a short and affirming statement. This avoids embarrassment of those who carried the conversation when it is time to redirect.

- **Redirect the participants back to the conversation.** This brief statement ends the last discussion and starts up the previous one that was on topic.

Here is a sample **EAR** script:

Participant on a tangent: *I think pizza for breakfast is the best! There is now doubt about it.*

Meeting manager: *I am willing to try pizza for breakfast. It can't be that bad.*

Meeting manager: *Perhaps you represent a large number of pizza lovers that enjoy the same thing you do. I won't knock it until I try it.*

Meeting manager: *Now, let's get back to the problem of employee morale in the call center. Who has some ideas they can share?*

Granted the topic was embellished, but this last script demonstrated the steps clearly. Using EAR will help you master the meeting room every time the conversation goes astray.

Personality Conflict

Sometimes a meeting could result in conflict. This may be true of meetings where new teams are storming together and forming the team. Conflict could arise when two participants with opposing views clash. In any case, conflict in a meeting has to be managed. There is an acceptable degree of tension, which is normal in debates. However, when the tension turns in to outright conflict, the focus turns from the meeting to the spectacle that is the conflict. Your job as a meeting manager is to diffuse the conflict and restore order in the meeting. Allowing conflict to go unchecked could fester into a bigger problem for everyone in the meeting. The news of the conflict will spread quickly and how you managed, it will be scrutinized. Here are three steps to take when conflict arises.

Step 1 Stop: Stop the conflict by intervening and making a statement that acknowledges the conflict. Do not become frustrated yourself. Avoid taking sides. Never yell. Be professional and calm. Simply state that the discussion has turned personal and that it needs to stop.

Step 2 Drop: instruct the parties in conflict to drop the discussion for now and regain their composure. There is no need to carry on if the discussion is counterproductive.

Step 3 Roll: roll into a break. Even if you just got back from one, take a break and send the participants away for a moment. Call on the parties in conflict and hold a brief expectations meeting. You are not there to resolve personal conflict. However, you must manage the conflict because it is your meeting. Tell the persons in conflict that they must immediately stop the behavior. Restate the need for the meeting and that healthy debate is always welcomed. Have them agree to behave for the remainder of the meeting.

The meeting room is no place to try to resolve the deeper issues of the conflict. On the other hand, if the participants are all a part of a team that will meet regularly, then this issue has to be addressed in a coaching session and not in front of spectators.

Taking Minutes

Earlier in this course, we discussed the important of the minute taker. In this module, you are going to learn the details of how to take meeting minutes. First, we are going to discuss the purpose of the meeting minutes. Second, we are going to discuss what to record throughout the meeting and finally, we are going to review a template that will help facilitate the minute taking process.

What are Minutes?

Minutes record major points, decisions, and follow up actions that are a result of the meeting. Meeting minutes also help to keep the meeting on track, because it uses the agenda as its outline. Meeting minutes serve as historical data that can be referenced in case a dispute should arise. They are also used to set the topics for discussion in the next meetings. Many times people who could not attend a meeting ask for the minutes so they can be updated on the latest developments in the meetings.

The minute taker should not have a major part in the meeting themselves. They must focus their attention on what is being said instead of participating. With this said, the act of taking minutes does not require that every word that is said must be recorded.

When taking notes, avoid becoming bogged down with writing full paragraphs. Outlining your points will make your note taking more efficient. When you are done taking minutes, immediately proofread and send them to the chairperson and distribute to all the meeting participants. File your minutes for referencing later.

What do I Record?

Many times people think taking minutes is a daunting task because there is a belief that every single word must be documented. If this was the case, then all you have to do is use a recorder and you are done. Recording everything will only make the minutes useless. The idea is to record information about who attended this meeting, the results and follow up action items. Here is a list of items that should be recorded in the minutes:

- Date, time and place of meeting

- The goal or purpose of the meeting

- The chairperson's name

- Action items assigned to someone for completion after the meeting

- Decisions made during the meeting

- Attendees present and not present

- Items that did not get resolved

- Items to discuss in the next meeting

- Items that were on the agenda that did not get discussed in the meeting for one reason or the other

- The meeting end time

Keeping to this short list will make taking minutes more efficient and useful.

A Take-Home Template

Using a template for your meeting minutes brings consistency to your technique. When you have a template, you can share it with some else, increasing the likelihood of getting similar results. Templates can be either electronic or printed. Incorporating a template for taking minutes also saves, you time by reducing the amount of time formatting the document for distributing to the meeting attendees.

Making the Most of Your Meeting

Many times, meetings can be seen as boring events that people have to attend. That does not have to be the case. You can incorporate various elements into your meeting, which could make your meetings more interesting. Making the most of your meeting does not have to involve a lot of preparation. It just requires creativity and imagination. Let us learn some ways we can make our meetings fun.

The 50 Minute Meeting

The reason why meetings usually last an hour is that our computer program that sets up the meeting usually has 30-minute increments of time. We are forced to schedule meetings to last at least an hour. On a daily basis, we attend more 1-hour meetings than any other kind. When you have several meetings in a row that last an hour each, you will find that you do not have time to check your emails or do other things in between because the next meeting starts right on the hour. The 50-minute meeting is an effective way to space out meetings, allowing us time to do things in between meetings. Conducting 50-minute meetings takes discipline in time management. Here are four steps to make the most of your 50-minute meeting:

Step 1 Have an agenda: We discussed the importance of having an agenda. The agenda is the document that outlines what will be discussed in a specific amount of time. With an agenda, you will have the group agree on what topics for discussion. Send out your agenda ahead of time so your participants get an idea of time spent on each topic.

Step 2 No side conversations: Set the expectations with your participants that side-conversations are not allowed and that you expect them to be fully engaged in the meeting. Blackberries, iPhones, etc. are not allowed and express that you will hold them accountable if you see people looking under the table at such devices.

Step 3 Summarize actions steps: At the end of the meeting, summarize any action steps that resulted from the meeting. You should have action steps at the end of the meeting. If not, rethink why you held the meeting in the first place.

Step 4 Send out summary notes: This is the meeting minutes. This should be done as soon as possible after the meeting. Sending out the meeting notes is a great way to solidify those action items with the people responsible for doing them.

Using Games

Using games in meetings helps to increase productivity. Many games could be used in meetings. We recommend you research the bookstores and find a resource that outlines appropriate games you can use. Remember to think about the meeting purpose before you use a game. If the meeting is about budget cuts, then you do not want to use a game in that type of meeting. Meetings that form new teams or launches a new product is best suited for games. Furthermore, determine how much time the game will take to complete versus the entire time you will be in the meeting. You do not want to play a 15-minute game in a 50-minute meeting.

Here are some Do's and Don'ts when it comes to using games at meetings:

Do's

- Do use games from a book or legitimate resource

- Do use games for meetings that are meant to form new teams

- Do gauge the amount of time the game takes to play against the entire meeting time

- Do practice the game before you use it

Don'ts

- Do not use games in serious meetings

- Do not spend too much time on the game

- Do not make up a game of your own (unless you are confident you can pull it off)

Giving Prizes

Prizes in meetings should be used to reinforce positive behaviors. The prizes do not have to be extravagant. They could be pens, desk decorations, t-shirts, etc. When giving prizes away, be clear on how to win the prizes. Unclear instructions will lead to outbreaks of conflict when someone feels cheated. For example, if you announce that a person will get a prize for coming back from break on time, almost 95 percent of the time you will have some stay in the room and not go to break to win the prize. Make it clear that they have to leave the room. Perhaps you can up the challenge by stating that the person coming back to the meeting who is the closest to the break end-time without going over will win.

Here are some ways you can leverage prizes in your meetings:

- The most participation

- The first to arrive at the meeting

- Volunteering for something in the meeting

- Creative solution

- Who can recap the action items the best

There are no limits on how to use prizes at your meetings.

Stuffed Magic

Simple magic tricks can help reduce stress and create a fun meeting environment. Before you start doing magic tricks in meetings, you will need to practice them at home. Magic tricks work well only when they are done right and with confidence. The setting up of the magic trick is the most important aspect. Do not be eager to do the trick or make an announcement. Be calm and natural. Incorporate it into the meeting seamlessly. You do not want to stop and announce you are going to do a trick. When participants are taken in by the trick without knowing, the effects are greater.

Research books and the Internet for magic tricks you can use. Practice the tricks and use them in the appropriate meeting settings. Try to avoid tricks that could embarrass others. You want to create an environment that is safe and offending someone could hurt that environment.

Creating the Program

We will look at the beginning steps to follow when creating a plan to improve your Presentation Skills. The first thing to look at is to perform a Needs Analysis. This will help you to understand your audience and provide you with the answers to a few basic questions. A basic outline and some minor research would then be utilized to help create the basic program that will assist you in developing greater Presentation Skills.

Performing a Needs Analysis

A needs analysis measures what skills employees have -- and what they need. It indicates how to deliver the right training at the right time. The results answer the following questions:

- What is the **audience** with the problem or need for change?

- What **tasks** and subtasks does an expert perform to complete a work process?

- What **gaps** exist between experts, average, and poor performers of a work process?

- How do we translate the needs into objectives to promote a strong learning **outcome**?

The method can be simple; observation, careful note taking, and asking questions work.

Question	Methods
Audience?	Interview key stakeholders and listen to their concerns about the problem. Define who needs help to overcome the problem. Identify and describe the audience and the work.
Tasks?	Observe the work being done by recognized experts. Take careful notes and ask questions where needed. Document the proper performance of the work tasks.
Gaps?	Observe other workers doing the tasks. Compare results with the performance of experts. Document identified skill gaps.
Outcome?	Develop a complete list of tasks for performing the work completely and correctly.

Example: Although the call center reps are empowered to assist customers, several are not solving callers' product problems. Instead, they are passing them on to the Escalation Desk, creating a bottleneck -- and unhappy customers. The needs analysis identified a task called "Resolve customer complaints". Some of its subtasks are:

- Answer call

- Listen to customer's problem

- Express empathy for the trouble

- Open a new support ticket

- Resolve complaint per the list of allowable resolutions

- Document resolution in the call notes

- Close support ticket.

Writing the Basic Outline

To develop the outline, group the tasks that fit together logically, and create headings that reflect the goal of the subtasks.

Handling a Call

- Answer call

- Listen to customer's problem

- Express empathy for the trouble

- Open a new support ticket

- Resolve the complaint per the list of allowable resolutions

Documenting Call Resolution

- Document the resolution in the call notes

- Close support ticket

Add headings for an introduction and workshop objectives at the beginning -- and a wrap-up and evaluation at the end, and your basic outline is complete.

Researching, Writing, and Editing

Researching: The needs analysis has likely produced much of the supporting content required to build the program. However, if information gaps exist, return to your expert performers (also termed subject matter experts) and ask questions.

Writing: If you're using a word processor, create a template so your material is consistent from the beginning. Assign a preliminary time length to each module based on the total time available for the presentation. (You'll validate it later.) When writing, aim for brevity. The more you say, the less the audience remembers.

Make sure to validate your finalized content before you move on to editing.

Editing: As you edit, write for the ear, not for the eyes. Make sure sentences are twenty words or less and only convey one thought. Use simple, familiar words. Make sure that you have provided the definitions of any terms important to the learning experience. Try to spice up your module titles.

Choosing Your Delivery Methods

Now it's time to determine what methods you will use to deliver your presentation. We will be beginning by covering basic delivery methods. Once we have a good foundation and grasp on the basic methods we will delve into more advanced methods.

Basic Methods

Lecture: If you must lecture occasionally, use strategies to make the delivery more interactive.

Discussion: A discussion facilitated by the presenter can be rich in interactivity.

Small Group learning experiences: A small group experience provides direction toward specific learning goals, and provides a high degree of participant involvement.

- **Dyads (Groups of 2).** Using pairs provides unlimited options for simple interactive experiences. You can say, "Turn to the person on your right and…" Using dyads manages the attention span, the extent of influence, and the focus of the goal. The learning experience is relatively intimate.

- **Triads (Groups of 3).** Trios expand the focus and experience opportunities. A measure of intimacy is still retained, but multiple viewpoints can be contributed. Triads are useful for producing definitions, establishing priorities, or providing an ongoing support system.

Case Study: The case study method is the presentation of detailed information about a particular situation, often problem solving. Case studies can be very creative exercises, and they are well-suited for small groups. Here are six guidelines for developing a case study:

1. Determine the principle you wish to have the case emphasize

2. Establish a situation that demonstrates the principle

3. Develop appropriate symptoms

4. Develop the characters

5. Write the case

6. Provide questions to guide the learners as they process the case study to solve a problem.

Advanced Methods

After you feel comfortable with basic delivery methods, you can begin to explore some of the more challenging ways to present and facilitate learning experiences.

Role play: Role playing allows participants to act out a behavioral role. This exercise -- done with small groups or the large group -- allows members to expand their awareness of varying points of view, and provides an experiential learning opportunity. A role play can be used in several ways; to solve a participant problem, clarify or sharpen an issue, or demonstrate a skill approach to a task. Importantly, it gives people an opportunity to practice a skill or approach in a safe environment and use the experience later on the job.

Here are several tips for managing a role play exercises:

- Obtain volunteers, rather than making assignments

- Use role play later in the training session, when participants know each other better

- Select low-threat situations, such as a work group holding a staff meeting.

Problem solving: Problem solving experiences are increasingly popular in training presentations because they allow participants to gain "real world" experience that often provides direct transfer back to the job.

There are three phases to a problem solving exercise:

1. Defining the problem and generating data about it

2. Generating potential solutions

3. Selecting an implementing a solution.

Below are several of the many proven methods that are available to help participants with each phase.

Phase	Method	Description
Defining the problem and generating data about it	Pareto Analysis	Vilfredo Pareto, a mathematician and economist coined the "80/20" rule. A Pareto Analysis allows you to group and analyze data for a problem such as defects in a model of kitchen faucet.
	Force Field Analysis	Kurt Lewin defined driving forces and restraining forces that influence the solution to a problem.
Generating potential solutions	Brainstorming	Brainstorming allows a group to generate a large volume of ideas about a problem, or potential solutions. Later, the results must be condensed to a workable number of ideas, typically through grouping, and then voted on.
	The Delphi Technique	Originally used by the RAND corporation, the Delphi technique allows the anonymous generating of ideas which are then filtered.
Selecting and implementing a solution	Ranking	Participants rank options on a given scale, with or without criteria.
	The Journalist's Six Questions	Use "who, what, when, where, why and how" questions to generate data.

Basic Criteria to Consider

A training presentation may use any combination of delivery methods as long as the net result is to achieve learning outcomes -- and consider organizational requirements and constraints. The four-step process below will help you select the best training delivery options to meet your training needs.

1. List all possible learning methodologies that could be used to achieve the session objectives

2. Identify possible delivery options for the learning methodologies

3. Identify the organizational, presenter, facility, and resource parameters and their impact on the delivery options.

4. Recommend your delivery strategies.

At a bank, the outcome of the process might look like this:

Objective	Delivery Strategy	Expansion/Notes
List the five key customer support principles at the bank	Lecture only the principles, using the flip chart or PowerPoint for emphasis, and then add interactivity	Find a lead-off story Develop a group problem-solving exercise to provide follow-up practice
Demonstrate a performance problem with a customer support team in a bank	Role play	Use triads Find extra space
Generate ideas for improving customer support service	Brainstorming	Procure additional flip charts for groups

Verbal Communication Skills

Communication skills are needed to be able to provide an excellent presentation. Without being able to verbalize your ideas and opinions there is very little chance of having a successful presentation. We will begin by looking at listening and hearing skills, asking the correct questions and finish with communicating with more power.

Listening and Hearing: They Aren't the Same Thing

Hearing is the act of perceiving sound by the ear. Assuming an individual is not hearing-impaired, hearing simply happens. Listening, however, is something that one consciously chooses to do. Listening requires concentration so that the brain processes meaning from words and sentences. Listening leads to learning.

This is not always an easy task. The normal adult rate of speech is 100-150 words per minute, but the brain can think at a rate of 400-500 words per minute, leaving extra time for daydreaming, or anticipating the speaker's or the recipient's next words. Listening skills, however, can be learned and refined.

Asking Questions

Three types of questions are useful in a presentation; open questions, clarifying questions, and closed questions.

Open Questions: Open questions stimulate thinking and discussion or responses including opinions or feelings. They pass control of the conversation to the respondent. Leading words in open questions include: *Why, what, or how.* A statement such as *"describe the characteristics of the car"* is really an open question. Examples of open questions include:

- Describe the style of the leader of the meeting.

- How do you feel when you hit a home run?

Asking questions is both an art and a science. Your questions in a presentation should be:

- Clear and concise, covering a single issue

- Reasonable, based on what participants are expected to know

- Challenging, to provoke thought

- Honest and relevant, eliciting logical answers

Clarifying Questions: A clarifying question helps to remove ambiguity, elicits additional detail, and guides you as you answer a question. Below are some examples:

- You said you liked apples more than oranges, why is that?

- What sort of savings are you looking to achieve?

Closed Questions: Closed questions usually require a one-word answer, and shut off discussion. Closed questions provide facts, allow the questioner to maintain control of the conversation, and are easy to answer. Typical leading words are: *Is, can, how many, or does.* Below are several examples of closed questions:

- Who will lead the meeting?

- Do you know how to open the emergency exit door on this aircraft?

Phrasing: To evoke an answer, your question should use phrasing that is:

- *Clear and concise*, covering a single issue

- *Reasonable*, based on what participants are expected to know

- *Challenging*, to provoke thought

- *Honest and relevant*, directing participants to logical answers.

Directing Questions appropriately: Should you direct your questions to individuals or to an entire group? When you direct a question to an individual, you:

- Stimulate one participant to think and respond

- Tap the known resources of an "expert" in the room

If you choose to direct your question to the group instead, you:

- Stimulate the thinking of all participants

- Provide participants the opportunity to respond voluntarily

- Avoid putting any one person on the spot.

The following exercise provides practice with questioning concepts and techniques.

Communicating with Power

It's been said that you have between thirty seconds and two minutes to capture your participants' attention. It's critical to engage people from the beginning.

Voice: 38% of the message received by a listener is governed by the tone and quality of your voice. The pitch, volume, and control of your voice all make a difference in audience perception.

Characteristics	Description	Tips
Pitch	How high or low your voice is	Avoid a high-pitched sound. Speak from your stomach, the location of your diaphragm.
Volume	The loudness of your voice must be governed by your diaphragm	Speak through your diaphragm, not your throat
Quality	The color, warmth, and meaning given to your voice	Add emotion to your voice. Smile as much as possible when you are speaking

Command: Selecting a good opener is an important way to take command of an audience. Making judicious use of certain types of remarks will endear you to the audience from the moment the program starts.

- A dramatic story

- A reference to a current or well-known news story

- A personal experience

- A rhetorical question

- A historical event

- Adventure, either past or present.

More Tips

- Did we say practice? And practice again?

- Smile

- Stand up straight and tall

- Rivet your participants with eye contact

- Dress like your audience, or one level above it.

Non-Verbal Communication Skills

Understanding your body language and other physical cues is very important when you are presenting material in front of an audience. Your non-verbal communication skills are just as important as your verbal skills. Combined they make up the complete communication package that you use when you are presenting your material.

Body Language

Non-verbal communication is the process of communication through sending and receiving wordless messages. It is the single most powerful form of communication. Nonverbal communication cues you in to what is on another person's mind, even more than voice or words can do.

One study at UCLA found that up to 93 percent of communication effectiveness is determined by nonverbal cues. Another study indicated that the impact of a performance was determined 7 percent by the words used, 38 percent by voice quality, and 55 percent by non-verbal communication.

Body language is a form of non-verbal communication involving the use of stylized gestures, postures, and physiologic signs which act as cues to other people. Humans unconsciously send and receive non-verbal signals through body language all the time.

Your words represent only 7% of the message that is received. Your body language represents 55%. But your body language must match the words used. If a conflict arises between your words and your body language, your body language governs.

Gestures

Gestures are an important tool for a presenter. The challenge is to make gestures support the speaking, reinforcing ideas. Below are several basic rules for the use of gestures:

- Make most gestures above the waist. (Those below the waist suggest failure, defeat, and despair.)

- Hold your forearms parallel to the waist, with your elbows about 3 inches from the side.

- Make your hands part of your forearm, opening them, with your fingers slightly curved. (Limp hands may indicate a lack of leadership.)

- Use both hands to convey power.

Gestures of direction, size, shape, description, feeling, and intensity are all effective when speaking.

The Signals You Send to Others

Signals are movements used to communicate needs, desires, and feelings to others. They are a form of expressive communication. More than 75% of the signals you send to others are non-verbal.

People who are excellent communicators are sensitive to the power of the emotions and thoughts communicated non-verbally through signals.

Types of Non-Verbal Signals: Other than gestures already discussed, signals include:

- Eye contact

- Posture

- Body movements

They all convey important information that isn't put into words. By paying closer attention to other people's nonverbal behaviors, you will improve your own ability to communicate nonverbally.

Intervals of four to five seconds of eye contact are recommended.

It is also important to use a tone of voice to reinforce the words in your presentation. For example, using an animated tone of voice emphasizes your enthusiasm for a participant's contribution in a debrief session.

As a presenter, your words should match your non-verbal behaviors. If they do not, people will tend to pay less attention to what you said, and focus instead on your nonverbal signals.

It's Not What You Say, It's How You Say It

Tone of Voice: We are all born with a particular tone of voice. While most people are not gifted with a radio announcer's voice, we can learn to improve our tone of voice. The idea is have your voice sound upbeat, warm, under control, and clear. Here are some tips to help you begin the process.

- Make sure you are breathing from the diaphragm.

- Stay hydrated by drinking lots of water and avoid caffeine due to its diuretic effects

- Stand up tall; posture affects breathing, which affects tone.

- Smile; it warms up the tone of your voice.

- If your voice is particularly high or low, exercise the range of your voice by doing a sliding scale. You can also expand the range of your voice by singing.

- Record your voice and analyze the playback.

- Practice speaking in a slightly lower octave. Deeper voices have more credibility than higher pitched voices. It will take getting used to pitching your voice down an octave, but it will be worth the effort.

- Get feedback from a colleague or family member about the tone of your voice.

Overcoming Nervousness

Nervousness is normal when giving a presentation. After all, public speaking is the top fear in the top ten lists of fears. Nervousness can strike at different points in a presentation:

- At the beginning

- If you feel the audience has slipped away from you

- If your memory betrays you.

This module will provide you with concrete strategies for overcoming presentation jitters.

Preparing Mentally

Visualization is the formation of mental visual images. It is an excellent way to prepare your mind before a presentation. There are several types of visualization:

Receptive Visualization: Relax, clear your mind, sketch a vague scene, ask a question, and wait for a response. You might imagine you are on the beach, hearing and smelling the sea. You might ask, "Why can't I relax?", and the answer may flow into your consciousness.

Programmed Visualization: Create an image, giving it sight, taste, sound, and smell. Imagine a goal you want to reach, or a healing you wish to accelerate. Jane used visualization when she took up running, feeling the push of running the hills, the sweat, and the press to the finish line.

Guided Visualization: Visualize again a scene in detail, but this time leave out important elements. Wait for your subconscious to supply missing pieces to your puzzle. Your scene could be something pleasant from the past.

The process for Effective Visualization

- Loosen your clothing, sit or lie down in a quiet place, and close your eyes softly.

- Scan your body, seeking tension in specific muscles. Relax those muscles as much as you can.

- Form mental sense impressions. Involve all your senses; sight, hearing, smell, touch and taste.

- Use affirmations. Repeat short, positive statements and avoid negatives such as "I am not tense"; rather, say "I am letting go of tension."

- Use affirmations. Repeat short, positive statements that affirm your ability to relax now. Use present tense and positive language. As an example:

- Tension flows from my body

- I can relax at will.

- I am in harmony with life.

- Peace is within me.

Visualize three times a day. It's easiest if you visualize in the morning and at night while lying in bed. Soon, you will be able to visualize just about anywhere, especially before a presentation.

Physical Relaxation Techniques

People who are nervous tend to breathe many short, shallow breaths in their upper chest. Breathing exercises can alleviate this. You can do most breathing exercises anywhere. Below are some exercises that will assist you in relaxing.

Breathing Exercises: Deliberately controlling your breathing can help a person calm down. Ways to do this include: breathing through one's nose and exhaling through one's mouth, breathing from one's diagram, and breathing rhythmically.

Meditation: Meditation is a way of exercising mental discipline. Most meditation techniques involve increasing self-awareness, monitoring thoughts, and focusing. Meditation techniques include prayer, the repetition of a mantra, and relaxing movement or postures.

Progressive Muscle Relaxation (PMR): PMR is a technique of stress management that involves mentally inducing your muscles to tense and relax. PMR usually focuses on areas of the body where tension is commonly felt, such as the head, shoulders, and chest area. It's a way to exercise the power of the mind over the body.

Visualization: Visualization is the use of mental imagery to induce relaxation. Some visualization exercise involves picturing a place of serenity and comfort, such as a beach or a garden. Other visualization exercises involve imagining the release of anger in a metaphorical form. An example of this latter kind of visualization is imagining one's anger as a ball to be released to space.

Appearing Confident in Front of the Crowd

In addition to everything we've discussed, below are some tips for maintaining your confidence when you're "on".

- Get a good night's sleep

- Practice your words along with your visuals

- Have a full "dress rehearsal"

- If you are traveling to a new site out of town, try to arrive early in the evening and locate the site. That way you won't be frazzled in the morning, trying to locate the venue.

Creating Fantastic Flip Charts

Information written on flip charts enhances the learning process. During a presentation, the use of flip charts serves to inform participants, record information, and focus attention on a topic. They represent a simple, low-cost learning aid -- with no requirements for power or technology, and no worries about burned-out bulbs or darkened rooms. Flip charts add versatility to a presentation, and allow the presenter to use creativity to enhance the learning process.

Required Tools

At a minimum, you will need a flip chart easel, several pads of flip chart paper, a few sets of colored markers, and masking tape for posting the results of exercises. Also handy are several packages of sticky notes to flag specific pages, and a straight edge. You may want to plan to cover up information that you will reveal at a given time during the presentation and then have some pre-cut paper available, sized appropriately for the text.

If you are bringing pre-written charts to an off-site presentation, you will also need some type of container to protect the pages.

The Advantages of Pre-Writing

There are many good reasons to pre-write your flip chart content.

- **Confidence**: You are in control of the material for your presentation – design, organization, and appearance. This also helps reduce nervousness.

- **Appearance**: Your material has a specific "look and feel" that is not necessarily easy to achieve when prepared during a session.

- **Time**: With your charts ready ahead of the presentation, the time during a presentation is used for learning activities, not writing, which keeps your back to the participants.

Tips:

- Always print; never use handwriting

- Consider using a straight edge to stem tendency to write "downhill"

- If you are using charts in a sequence, number them.

Using Colors Appropriately

Good use of color can make the difference in the dynamics of a presentation -- and participants' acceptance of the content. Conversely, the effect of a great chart can suffer from the poor use of color. According to the Optical Society of America, blue, black, and green offer the greatest visibility, and blue is the most pleasing color. Avoid purple, brown, pink, and yellow for any type of general printing.

The use of two or three color combinations can be very effective. Here are several rules.

- Red and orange should only be used as accent colors for bullets, underlines, or arrows, or for key words when everything else is in black or blue

- Avoid orange and blue together

- Never use yellow.

When creating your charts, take some time to think about the colors you are using, and how they can enhance the understanding of your topic.

Creating a Plan B

Paper is not permanent, even if you are presenting at your own location. And if you're flying with your materials or shipping them, packages do occasionally get lost or damaged. You will need a backup plan in case something happens. Below are some tasks for creating your Plan B.

- Keep documents on your computer organized by course, reflecting the content and order sequence of each flip chart.

- Make paper handouts of the most critical information on the charts.

- Take pictures of the chart pages, and have the camera or images with you on site.

- If you have time to re-create some of your charts, enlist a volunteer to help you reconstruct the most critical ones.

- If you will be returning to the site, consider leaving a set of your charts with a trusted colleague until you return.

- As time permits, duplicate your charts in PowerPoint. Although you will probably continue to use flip charts, having them available in PowerPoint becomes a backup.

Creating Compelling PowerPoint Presentations

Microsoft PowerPoint is a commanding tool for creating visual screens for a presentation. Visuals created in PowerPoint and projected on a screen are often easier to see in a large room than information displayed on a flip chart. Using PowerPoint offers the following benefits:

- Allows you to add emphasis to important concepts, helping to increase retention of information

- Adds variety to your presentation

- Makes it easier to display images, charts, or graphs possibly too complex for a flip chart.

Also, PowerPoint files can easily be shared with participants or others after the session.

Required Tools

To create and use a Microsoft PowerPoint file to support your presentation outline, you will need:

- Microsoft Office PowerPoint software for Microsoft Windows or Macintosh OS

- A Windows or a MAC computer equipped with the minimum hardware and software specifications for your version of PowerPoint

- An LCD or DLP projector

- A projection screen

Optionally, you may wish to add the following to your toolkit:

- Storage media such as a USB memory stick or CD-R disc

- An extension cord

- A laser pointer for emphasis during the discussion of a PowerPoint slide.

Tips and Tricks

Use the following suggestions to enhance the benefit of your PowerPoint presentation.

Overall Appearance

- Display only one major concept on each slide

- Use short phrases or bullet points rather than paragraphs

- Limit each line of text to no more than 7-8 words

- Allow only 7-8 lines of text per slide

- Use images sparingly; one or two per slide

- Leave a good amount of blank space in your presentation

- Create a title for each slide

- Use effects, transitions animation, and sound very sparingly.

Fonts and Color

- Use simple sans serif fonts such as Helvetica or Arial for readability

- Select a point size of 32 or larger for titles, and 20 points for body text

- Use colors that work well together, such as yellow or white on a dark blue background.

- Check the readability and visibility of your fonts and color choices with the lighting in the room in which you will present.

Preparation

- Make sure to match your slides to the purpose of the presentation

- Develop a template and stick to it for a consistent look and feel

Computer

- Check your equipment, computer settings, and room lighting in advance

- Before your presentation, turn off screensavers, instant messaging, and email notifications

- Make sure that your computer's power management console will not automatically shut the system down after a set amount of time.

Creating a Plan B

While technology allows you to make great enhancements to a presentation, it also offers more opportunities for technical trouble. Here are some suggestions to keep your presentation moving along, even if the technology isn't.

- Make one or more backup copies of your PowerPoint file on the computer on which you plan to show the presentation.

- Before the presentation, download and install the free Microsoft PowerPoint Viewer available at www.microsoft.com. In the event that your PowerPoint software won't run, you will still be able to use the viewer to show your PowerPoint slides.

- Copy your PowerPoint file onto a USB Drive. That way, if you have a computer problem, you can move the file to another one, if available.

- Bring sufficient printed copies of your presentation for participants. If logistics prevent that, plan to have at least one copy available for photocopying on site.

- If all else fails, write your key points on a flip chart.

Wow 'Em with the Whiteboard

A whiteboard is the name for any glossy-surfaced writing board where non-permanent markings can be made. Unlike the predecessor chalkboard, there is no chalk dust, and markings remain longer than they would on a chalkboard.

Whiteboards have been around since the 1970's, and are now vastly improved and more affordable compared to early models. The use of a whiteboard helps to promote interactivity during a presentation.

Traditional and Electronic Whiteboards

Traditional Whiteboards: Traditional whiteboards are attached to the wall, or are available in free-standing frames. Unlike pre-written flip chart paper sheets, whiteboards cannot easily be moved from site to site. However, they are usually larger, and are useful for recording the results of small group exercises or spontaneous information arising in a discussion. Traditional whiteboards cost less than $100, or up to $1,000. A traditional whiteboard requires a set of wet or dry erase whiteboard markers, a whiteboard eraser, and whiteboard cleaning solution.

Electronic Whiteboards: An electronic whiteboard looks like a traditional whiteboard, but is a unique combination of hardware and software. The surface is connected to a computer and a projector. A projector beams the computer's desktop onto the board's surface, where users control the computer using a pen, finger, or other device. Uses include:

- Operating any software that is loaded onto the connected PC, including web browsers and proprietary software

- Using software to electronically capture text or marks written on the whiteboard

- Translating cursive writing to text

- Controlling the PC.

Because the markings on the whiteboard are digitized, the resulting electronic information can be stored, printed, or shared in real time with participants in other locations. Electronic whiteboards cost more than $1,000.

Using Colors Appropriately

Colors on a whiteboard are often more vivid than those on a flip chart. Otherwise, most of the same rules apply:

- Blue, black, and green offer the greatest visibility, with blue the most pleasing color.

- Avoid purple, brown, pink, and yellow for any type of general printing.

- The use of two or three color combinations can be very effective; however orange should only be used with red as an accent color. Never use yellow, and avoid orange and blue together.

Creating a Plan B

Traditional Whiteboards: When using a traditional whiteboard, have extra markers on hand, because they tend to dry up easily.

If your presentation is longer than one day, plan to make a backup of your work from the computer to a USB flash drive in the event that they are erased overnight.

Electronic Whiteboards: If you are working with an electronic whiteboard and encounter technical issues, you can show a previously created PowerPoint presentation through a projector. Plan to carry at least one copy of the PowerPoint handouts for duplication if needed. You can always quickly jot down key points on a flip chart.

Regardless of which type of whiteboard is used, key content should be available in a handout master or on flip chart pages as a backup.

Vibrant Videos and Amazing Audio

Audio and video are very much a part of our everyday lives, so they are accepted --and even expected media in a presentation. They are attractive options for a presentation because they provide learners with more dimensions by which to receive information. While video and audio both represent a one-way communication to participants, the opportunity to use them as part of learning exercises or in the ensuing discussions adds value to the presentation.

Video

There are three main ways to obtain video material:

- Creating your own media using a small personal video camera

- Purchasing off-the-shelf video designed for training presentations

- Hiring a professional video production company.

Your media budget, the amount of available preparation time, your comfort and skill level with video, and the type of presentation will all influence the direction.

Audio

Audio can be used as a standalone option, as part of the video, or even created by the participants, such as an exercise to write and sign a song.

Required Tools

For video with audio you will need some type of player, depending upon the media type:

- A DVD-ROM or Blu-ray player if you are using a video disc

- USB memory stick

- A laptop or PC with software to play digital video

You will also need a projector and a projection screen. Speakers are optional, but recommended for more than the smallest room and group.

Although today's cameras are light-sensitive, you may also need some simple lighting, such as a handyman light from a hardware store. If you want more than the onboard audio built into the camera, get a simple lavaliere or handheld microphone.

Finally, especially if budget is an issue, consider using one or more personal video devices -- such as smartphone. You'll also need a handful of inexpensive ear buds. You can pass the iPods around the room at certain times, or have participants up to view and listen to the material. While perhaps less formal than the others, this solution, is much more portable if your presentation is delivering off-site.

Tips and Tricks

Purchased Off-The-Shelf Video

- Check reviews of the media online

- Shop around for the best prices

- Preview the work before you purchase

- Test the video in conjunction with the exercise with a colleague before the presentation.

Personally created video

- Plan by creating a simple outline that matches your presentation content

- Create a storyboard using PowerPoint, a word processor, or paper before you record

- Check your equipment thoroughly

- Do a practice run before your final recording.

- Transfer the recording immediately to a computer for backup.

Professionally produced video from a production company

- Create an outline. (The storyboard may be provided by the production company.)

- Carefully create a request for proposal, and interview several companies

- Preview finished samples of each company's work

- Ask for a client list, and check with several of them

- Plan to dedicate an in-house resource person to work with the production company

- Manage costs through a preproduction meeting, trimming, if necessary, where it makes sense

- Maintain frequent two-way communication during the project

- If all proposals come in nearly equal, trust your instincts based on the relationships you have formed with the prospective companies

Creating a Plan B

Regardless of the method you use for your audio and video, it is essential to have a backup plan in the event that something goes awry with the technology.

- Have one or two backup copies of your media, perhaps on a USB flash drive and a DVD

- Test everything before the presentation

- For higher-end productions, have a technician on standby if possible

- Record and back up the audio track separately; if the video fails you will still have the audio

- Create a handout with the key concepts contained in your video

- Capture screen shots directly from the video (if permissible by copyright) and add them to a PowerPoint file

- If sequence isn't an issue, and you have access to a technician later, adjust your agenda to utilize the video later in the program.

If, for any reason, none of the above is feasible, consider substituting a role play between you and the selected participants. Above all, today's participants understand the "gotchas" when technology is involved, and will probably be empathetic as you carry on your presentation as if it was no big deal.

Pumping it Up a Notch

Bringing it to the next level is something you can accomplish after feeling comfortable with all of the previous topics discussed. You can add the little touches that will produce a lot of value during your presentation.

Make Them Laugh a Little

Humor is a popular way to liven up a presentation. It makes the audience align with you, and sends a signal that you are in charge. Handled properly, humor enriches a presentation.

When considering humor, make sure that whatever content you choose meets four criteria:

- You think the joke or lines are funny

- You can repeat the piece confidently and comfortably

- Your choice is not offensive to anyone (gender, race, age, disability, politics)

- Your audience will understand and appreciate what you are saying.

- A joke should have a punch line, delivered with all you've got.

Here are some tips for collecting and using humor:

- Jot down jokes as you hear them in everyday life; classify them as your collection grows

- Deliver any humor verbally only, and keep things light

- Match your humor to the demographics of the audience

- Research and consider using local humor if you're working off-site

- Don't be afraid to poke fun at yourself.

If a joke or delivering humor with words isn't within your comfort level, consider sharing a lighthearted cartoon, doing a simple magic trick, or doing something else that is unexpected and evokes a reaction and some emotion from the participants.

Ask Them a Question

Questions can be used in many ways, and at just about any time during your presentation.

- As an opener

- To check whether the desired learning is occurring, or to extend the learning experience

- To diffuse a difficult or uncomfortable situation

- To fill a long pause

- To get a feel about the mood in the room.

As we learned in module four, Verbal Communication Skills, you can use open, clarifying, or closed, questions, depending upon your needs.

Encouraging Discussion

Much of the discussion during your presentation will be structured to fit with the learning exercises. If a remark or question is made during a discussion that is off topic or something that should not be dealt with at the time, you can always add it to the parking lot, and return to it during the wrap-up to bring closure.

Dealing with Questions

Q&A Sessions: If time permits in your presentation, you may choose to hold a general question-and-answer session. Since as the presenter you are in control, you can decide when to stop the discussion. In a large room, be prepared to repeat each question. If no questions arise, be prepared to ask one yourself.

You can use an open question to begin the session: "What questions do you have?"

Restating Negative Questions: If a question is phrased negatively, restate it. For example, "Why have so many of his staff displayed chronic absenteeism?" can be restated as "Let's explore what we can do to reduce absenteeism in the team."

Off-topic: Don't forget about the parking lot if you receive an off-topic question.

Leveraging experience in the room: There may be situations when you wish to redirect a question to one of the participants. Again, you are in charge, so call upon someone and keep the discussion moving on afterward.

476

Chapter 27 – Negotiation Skills

Although people often think of boardrooms, suits, and million dollar deals when they hear the word "negotiation," the truth is that we negotiate all the time. For example, have you ever:

- Decided where to eat with a group of friends?

- Decided on chore assignments with your family?

- Asked your boss for a raise?

These are all situations that involve negotiating! This workshop will give participants an understanding of the phases of negotiation, tools to use during a negotiation, and ways to build win-win solutions for all those involved.

By the end of this chapter, you will be able to:

- Understand the basic types of negotiations, the phases of negotiations, and the skills needed for successful negotiating

- Understand and apply basic negotiating concepts: WATNA, BATNA, WAP, and ZOPA

- Lay the groundwork for negotiation

- Identify what information to share and what to keep to yourself

- Understand basic bargaining techniques

- Apply strategies for identifying mutual gain

- Understand how to reach consensus and set the terms of agreement

- Deal with personal attacks and other difficult issues

- Use the negotiating process to solve everyday problems

- Negotiate on behalf of someone else

Understanding Negotiation

Before we get started, let's take a look at two basic types of negotiation. We'll consider the three phases of negotiation and the skills you need to become an effective negotiator.

Types of Negotiations

The two basic types of negotiations require different approaches.

Integrative negotiations are based on cooperation. Both parties believe they can walk away with something they want without giving up something important. The dominant approach in integrative negotiations is problem solving. Integrative negotiations involve:

- Multiple issues. This allows each party to make concessions on less important issues in return for concessions from the other party on more important issues.

- Information sharing. This is an essential part of problem solving.

- Bridge building. The success of integrative negotiations depends on a spirit of trust and cooperation.

Distributive negotiations involve a fixed pie. There is only so much to go around and each party wants as big a slice as possible. An example of a distributive negotiation is haggling over the price of a car with a car salesman. In this type of negotiation, the parties are less interested in forming a relationship or creating a positive impression. Distributive relationships involve:

- Keeping information confidential. For example, you don't want a car salesman to know how badly you need a new car or how much you are willing to pay.

- Trying to extract information from the other party. In a negotiation, knowledge truly is power. The more you know about the other party's situation, the stronger your bargaining position is.

- Letting the other party make the first offer. It might be just what you were planning to offer yourself!

The Three Phases

The three phases of a negotiation are:

1. Exchanging Information
2. Bargaining
3. Closing

These phases describe the negotiation process itself. Before the process begins, both parties need to prepare for the negotiation. This involves establishing their bargaining position by defining their BATNA, WATNA, and WAP (see Module Three). It also involves gathering information about the issues to be addressed in the negotiation.

After the negotiation, both parties should work to restore relationships that may have been frayed by the negotiation process.

It is essential to pay attention to all the phases of negotiation. Without the first phase, the exchange of information, and the establishment of bargaining positions, the second phase cannot happen in any meaningful sense because no one knows where they stand. It sets a scene for demands to be manageable and reasonable. Negotiations are, after all, about the art of the possible. Without the third phase, anything that has been decided during phase two cannot be formalized and will not take hold – leading to the necessity for further negotiation or an absolute breakdown in a relationship.

Skills for Successful Negotiating

Key skills include:

- Effective speaking

- Effective listening

- A sense of humor

- A positive attitude

- Respect

Without the above factors, negotiations will be difficult if not impossible. The necessity for negotiation arises because neither party will be able to get everything they want. Knowing that there must be concessions, each party in the negotiation is required to adopt an attitude of understanding that they must get the best deal possible in a way which is acceptable to the other party. The importance of effective speaking and listening is clear; it is necessary to establish what you are looking for and what you are prepared to accept, while understanding what the other parties will be happy with.

A sense of humor and a positive attitude are essential because they allow for a sense of give and take. Negotiations can become fraught, and having the ability to see the other side's point of view while being sanguine with regard to what you can achieve will be essential. Of course you will want as much as you can get – but the other side needs to achieve what they can, too. Seriously uneven negotiations will simply lead to further problems along the line. An atmosphere of respect is essential. If you do not make concessions while demanding them from your counterpart, it makes for a negotiation which will end in dissatisfaction.

However important a sense of understanding for your "opponent" may be, it is also necessary to have the confidence to not settle for less than you feel is fair. Good negotiators understand the importance of balance. Yes, you will have to make concessions, but the point of making concessions is to secure what you can get – so you need to pay attention to your bottom line and ensure you are not beaten down to a minimum. Knowing what is realistic, and ensuring that you can get the best deal, relies on being ready to insist upon something that the other side may not be willing to give initially. Emotional intelligence, persistence, patience, and creativity can all play a part here.

Getting Prepared

Like any challenging task, negotiation requires preparation. Before you begin a negotiation, you need to define what you hope to get out of it, what you will settle for, and what you consider unacceptable. You also need to prepare yourself personally. The key to personal preparation is to approach the negotiation with self-confidence and a positive attitude.

Without this preparation, you will end up giving more than you get from negotiations. It may be unavoidable that you will have to give up more than you would ordinarily be willing to, but finding the balance between acceptable concessions and getting the best deal for yourself relies on you being ready to go into negotiations with the strongest bargaining position you can.

Establishing Your WATNA and BATNA

In most negotiations, the parties are influenced by their assumptions about what they think are the alternatives to a negotiated agreement. Often the parties have an unrealistic idea of what these alternatives are, and they are unwilling to make concessions because they think they can do just as well without negotiating. If you do not have a clear idea of your **WATNA (Worst Alternative to a Negotiated Agreement)** and **BATNA (Best Alternative to a Negotiated Agreement)**, you will negotiate poorly based on false notions about what you can expect without an agreement.

Often the parties in a negotiation need to decide how likely a particular outcome will be. If your WATNA is something that would be difficult for you to accept, but the likelihood of it happening is small, you might not feel compelled to give up much in negotiations. Realism is essential in this situation. If you could have the ideal situation, the "blue sky" scenario, negotiations would not be necessary. In order to focus on the negotiations with a sense of purpose, your WATNA is important. What is often referred to as the "worst case scenario" is something that any sensible person will think about before embarking on any initiative. What if it goes wrong? How will we deal with that? How you feel about the WATNA will dictate how flexible you need to be (and therefore will be) in negotiations.

The BATNA is almost more important than the WATNA. If you look at your situation in the absence of a negotiated agreement, and find it almost unthinkable, you will be pressed to enter negotiations in the hope of getting a satisfactory agreement. The word "satisfactory" is important here. Is the WATNA better than satisfactory? Is the BATNA worse? Generally, people only enter into negotiations because they feel they have to. They arrive at this conclusion based on analysis of their WATNA and BATNA.

Identifying Your WAP

In any negotiation, it is important that you keep your **WAP (Walk Away Price)** to yourself, especially if it is significantly less than your initial offer. If the other party knows that you will be willing to take a lot less than you are offering, then you will be negotiating from a position of weakness. If the other party knows, or has an idea of your WAP then it stops being your WAP and simply becomes your price. Establishing a WAP in your mind, and ensuring that those negotiators on your side of the bargain (and only they) know it, allows you to take your strongest possible bargaining position. The other party will try to argue you down from your proposed price, so you will need to remain firm. If they want to pay less, then you may be prepared to agree on a lower price in return for concessions.

The opposing party will then have to consider what is acceptable to them. Rather than push too hard and lose out on a deal which would be beneficial to themselves, they will have their own areas where they are willing to make concessions. However, if they know that you have set a WAP that would save them money, they will simply hold firm at that price. They have no incentive to make concessions to you. In many ways, negotiation is about keeping as much to yourself as you possibly can until you can no longer maintain that position.

Once you have set your WAP, it is essential to keep to it. A walk away price becomes absolutely meaningless if you are not prepared to walk away should it not be met. You should give the impression to opponents in negotiation that you could walk away at any time. They will, after all, not be prepared to stop once they get a price which is satisfactory to them – they will look to wring a bit more value out of the deal for themselves, testing you to see what you will give up. A warning against setting your WAP unrealistically low is that the other party will not take you seriously if you are a pushover in negotiations. They will seek to test you at every turn.

Identifying Your ZOPA

In the negotiation for the used car, both parties should feel good about the outcome. Even though the parties might have hoped for a better deal, both got a better price than their WAP.

This negotiation demonstrates the importance of keeping your WAP to yourself if you want to negotiate the best deal. Your range in this situation falls between the price that you would ideally, realistically get and the WAP you have set. In an ideal world you could demand a million dollars and expect to get it. In a realistic world, you need to be realistic in negotiations.

You should arrive at your ideal realistic price by seeing what the accepted market value for what you are offering is. By adjusting for your specific negotiating position (whether you are approaching it from a position of need, etc.), you can find your best realistic price. Then think about a price at which it would no longer be worthwhile to strike a deal.

Your co-negotiator will have done the same. What he hopes to pay and what you hope to get are just that – hopeful. The **ZOPA (Zone Of Possible Agreement)** is the area in which the final price will sit, and within that ZOPA you will ideally end up with a price closer to their WAP than yours. If you hint at where your WAP is, the other party will be less likely to come to an agreement that is substantially better than that.

Personal Preparation

One way to relieve some of the tension you may be feeling before a negotiation is to remind yourself that there is nothing to be afraid of. As long as you understand your position, there is no danger that you will "lose" the negotiation. During and before negotiation you should always be:

- Polite - It never reduces your argument

- Firm - Removes Perceptions of Weakness

- Calm - Facilitates Persuasion and Compromise

- Do not take things personally

Knowing your position before entering negotiations means that you are sure of your "red lines". Things that you are not prepared to consider that would make your position worse than it is now. Many people get pushed into a deal which is unsatisfactory to them because they have failed to prepare for the negotiation in this way. If you go into negotiations with vague ideas, that vagueness will become a weakness in your negotiating position.

The important thing about your position in negotiations is that you should be the only one who knows what it is. Many people compare negotiation to a game of poker. When playing poker you should always be careful to keep to yourself what kind of hand you have. If your opponent knows your position, they will squeeze you to its very limits, confident that you have no strong impetus to push back.

When a negotiator knows that their "opponent" has a weak or compromised position, they will instinctively know that they are negotiating with someone who is working from a position of desperation. They will believe "that's what he's decided he is willing to settle for, because he needs this deal. Does he need it enough to give me a little bit more leverage?", and will negotiate from that standpoint.

Laying the Groundwork

In the previous module, we looked at the importance of establishing your bargaining position. In this module we consider other aspects of preparation: setting the time and place, establishing common ground, and creating a negotiating framework. Even at this early stage it is important to have certain principles in place. If you allow them to be compromised, then you will already have put yourself in a position where you can be considered as prey for hostile negotiators. Getting the groundwork in place may seem like a formality, but it is the first stage of negotiations, and therefore as much a part of the arrangements as any other.

Setting the Time and Place

Setting the time and place can give you an advantage in a negotiation. People feel most comfortable conducting a negotiation on their home turf. Most people have a particular time of day when they feel most alert and clear-headed.

Environmental factors can interfere with negotiations, for example:

- A noisy setting

- Frequent interruptions

- Crowded conditions

- Lack of privacy

If you are conducting a negotiation at your own site, you have control over most of these things. If you are negotiating at the other party's site, ask the other party to remedy these conditions as much as possible before negotiations begin.

In sport, every game takes place at a venue, and in most cases one of the parties involved will be the "home team". In the vast majority of cases, where the parties are evenly matched in terms of talent and preparation, the team that wins will be the home team. They are playing in familiar surroundings, where things such as climate and ambient noise are to their advantage. The away team spends the early part of the game acclimatizing to their unfamiliar surroundings.

In political negotiations leading on from a war (or trying to prevent one), there is a tendency to hold the discussions in a neutral venue, where both parties are equally unfamiliar with the surroundings, meaning that neither has the advantage and allowing the negotiations to be even-handed. In business, it is rare to have the opportunity to hold negotiations in a neutral venue, and frequently there will be a "home side".

The time of negotiations is also important. Human beings are always in some part at the mercy of their "biorhythms" which cause the body and the mind to function differently at different times of day. Some people, as you will know, tend to be "morning people" while others are more comfortable the longer the day goes on. If you want to build in an advantage in negotiations, it is worth making sure either that the negotiations are held at your home venue, at your most comfortable time of day, or both. Sometimes there will be debate about the setting for a negotiation – and often, this is where the first negotiations and concessions will take place.

Establishing Common Ground

Sometimes the parties in a negotiation begin by discussing the issue on which they are farthest apart. It might seem like they are working hard, but they are not working effectively.

It is often more effective to begin by discussing what the parties agree on and then move to an issue on which they are close to agreement. Then they can take on progressively tougher issues until they reach the issue on which they are farthest apart. This gradual approach sets a positive tone for the negotiation. It also helps the two parties get into a pattern of thinking about issues in terms of shared interests.

Momentum is an important thing in negotiations. If the meeting is continually stalled by disputes over the smallest of issues, the outcome is likely to be less desirable for both parties as the goodwill which is necessary to drive negotiations forward will be extremely thin on the ground. For this reason, having an agenda which is stacked in favor of positive items at the beginning is a way that will work best for both sides. Concessions will have to happen in the end, but if both sides are in a positive frame of mind it creates a positive dynamic in which to negotiate.

Creating a Negotiation Framework

Both sides in a negotiation bring their own frame of reference based on their experience, values, and goals. For a negotiation to proceed, the two sides have to agree to a common framework. They need to agree on what issues are being addressed. Sometimes the way these issues are stated will influence the course of the negotiation. Each side would like to frame the issues in a way that furthers its goals. From this it is possible to see how involved negotiations can get. Sometimes people will use a phrase to describe preliminary negotiations: "talks about talks" – and this is a fairly interesting phrase, as it sheds light on just how much is up for debate in the average negotiation.

Before starting negotiations, it is essential to agree on which issues are up for negotiation and which are non-negotiable. Those issues which are non-negotiable are taken off the negotiating table and the parties endeavor to move forward with what they can negotiate on. It can also be decided what form of words will be used in the program for negotiations – making clear to both sides what matters are off limits, and why.

Without establishing a framework, negotiations can be extremely disorganized and lack direction. It helps to remember that trying to get a negotiated settlement between two parties who have their differences calls for a great deal of patience and acceptance on both sides that there will be some "medicine" to take – you don't want to take it, but it is necessary – and therefore it is important to make the pill as sweet as possible. Setting a positive framework for negotiations is all about sweetening the pill.

The Negotiation Process

Preparation ▸ Opening Position ▸ Bargaining ▸ Movement ▸ Closing

Preparation:

- Identify your key commitments

Opening Position:

- Outline Your Opening Position

- Decide whether this will be High Ball or Low Ball

- Ensure that this position is realistic in light of the facts available to both sides

- Allow for movement within whatever opening position you adopt

- Confirm all agreements reached and positions offered

Bargaining

- Question for Information

- Challenge other side for justifications of their position

- Examine and Test their commitment

- Present Your Key Commitments

- Explore Key Commitments

- Summarize Arguments and Seek Acceptance

- Look for Signals of Possible Movement

- Identify and Highlight Common Ground

Movement

- Be Prepared to Concede

- Begin with those of Low Priority and seek High Priority Items

- Never Concede on More than possible by your Brief

- Use your Concessions Wisely

- Don't just give these away expect and receive something in return

- Use Conditional Argument

- All Movement Should be realistic and contained within your brief

- It Should be always towards the other sides position and not away from it

- Be prepared for larger movements at first as it can build trust within the negotiation

- Continue with smaller movements

Closing

- Emphasize the benefits to both parties

- Carefully introduce the consequences of not reaching agreement to both parties and losing what has been agreed so far

- Timing is Essential

- Take Care when making a Final Offer. Be sure that it is consistent with your brief.

- A Small Traded Offer is often better. A small move by them in return for an extra movement by you.

- Ensure that all agreements are understood and accepted before finalization

- This should be well documented and signed at the close of the negotiations

- These should be then forwarded to both parties post negotiations

Phase One — Exchanging Information

The first phase in a negotiation involves an exchange of information. Both sides state their positions on the issues being addressed in a non-confrontational way. The tricky part of this phase is deciding what to reveal and what to hold back. The "poker" metaphor for negotiating is a very good one, because it describes exactly the way that negotiating parties will want to "allow" each other to think. The information you share with your negotiating counterpart will allow them to read a certain amount about your position. You cannot negotiate blindly, after all. However, too much information given away can really come back to bite you.

Getting Off on the Right Foot

Before you actually get down to work, it's a good idea to engage in a little small talk with the other participants in the negotiation. This will help set a positive tone. You might find that you have some things in common (such as hobbies or favorite teams) with the other participants.

If you rush right into the negotiation without some initial pleasantries, the other party may feel that you are being pushy and aggressive. For some people, this is a desirable negotiating style. However, it is advisable to have as many strings as possible to your bow when it comes to negotiations. Being "human" and easy to relate to is far less likely to persuade the other party that you are someone who needs to be kept in check, and may work to your advantage.

Obviously when it comes to introductions and preliminaries it is an idea not to get too informal. Apart from anything else, this will feel quite artificial when all parties are fully aware that there are issues to be debated here. Formality also lends itself to details being correct – how many negotiations, you have to wonder, have foundered at an early stage because one participant forgot the name of a counterpart or made an accidentally offensive remark due to ignorance of a critical detail?

Projecting an image of relaxed friendliness with an element of restraint is your best way to introduce yourself. By no means should you give the impression that you are here to bleed your counterpart dry – this will put them on the defensive and entrench their position, to your disadvantage – but it does help to project self-confidence. If you seem in a hurry to get negotiations completed and an agreement sealed, the impression will be that you want to escape from the whole process with a minimum of losses – which will not make you a formidable negotiating counterpart.

What to Share

At the start of a negotiation, you don't want to give a detailed statement about your position on specific issues. That is a subject for bargaining. If the other party tries to rush you into stating your bargaining position prematurely, say something like, "That's an important question. Before we get to that, let's make sure we agree on the issues we're discussing today."

It may be helpful to think why the other party would be in a hurry to get you to state your position. If they are fixated on that so early in negotiations, the chances are that they have been worrying about it for some time beforehand, and will want to get negotiations over and done with without having to worry about giving away more than they will need to. In such a case, it does you no harm at all to leave them waiting for this information by concentrating on laying down the framework.

In negotiations, one party's opinion on what should constitute the agenda will differ from the other at least in terms of how the issues should be framed. The same issue can be framed in several different ways, and a simple form of words can be quite contentious. Agreeing on the topics for discussion is something that allows both parties to find common ground, while preparing the way for both parties to recognize that they will not complete negotiations without making some movement on some issues.

What to Keep to Yourself

Holding back information can be a tricky business. You don't want to appear secretive or deceptive, but at the same time you don't want to give away your bargaining position prematurely. The best way to deal with this situation is to attempt to set the agenda for the negotiation. Say something like, "Let's get a few general issues settled before we get into specifics." At the start of negotiations both parties will, to some extent, be on the defensive and will want to get an impression of whom they are dealing with before they go any further.

By dealing with matters of agenda first, both parties get an opportunity to "size up" their counterpart and think about what they want to get from the negotiation and what they can get. The major benefit of these early discussions is that the first tentative negotiations can be made without making or breaking the whole process. From here it is possible to have a more realistic idea about who you are dealing with. This can influence how you carry on with the negotiations.

If you walk into negotiations and after preliminary introductions simply say "OK, so this is what we have come for, and we will walk away if we don't get it", then you might as well not be having a negotiation in the first place. Equally, if you hint early in negotiations that you are prepared to settle for a deal which more or less favors your counterpart, you are simply setting the scene for them to take everything you are prepared to offer and more besides. Your success in negotiations depends on knowing what to say, when to say it and when to be silent.

Phase Two — Bargaining

Now we have reached the heart of the negotiation process. This phase — bargaining — is what most people mean when they talk about negotiation. This module explains what to expect when you begin to bargain and what to do if you run into an impasse. It also describes some common bargaining techniques used by experienced negotiators.

What to Expect

In addition to learning about the pressures, targets, and needs that might influence your opponents, you might also want to try to get some idea of their usual negotiating approach.

- Do they typically start out with an unreasonable offer?

- Do they try to rush the negotiation?

- Do they try to frame the issues to their own advantage?

Finding this out can be a process of trial and error, but if you have any contacts in the same business who have negotiated with your opponent you can ask them for a rundown of how the negotiation went. This is something which will be familiar to any sports fan, in that teams and players will "scout" their opponents to exploit any weaknesses and prepare to deal with any strength that might make their opponent formidable.

If an opponent has a reputation for always looking to rush the negotiation, it is possible to use that to your advantage. By remaining firm on your bargaining position you will be able to place pressure on them to get the deal done on your terms. If they want it to be over quickly, they will be less likely to spend time wringing concessions out of you and will have to either spend longer in negotiations than they would ordinarily wish (potentially making them uncomfortable and prone to rash decisions) or make a concession in order to get the arrangement in place quickly.

Finding out – and analyzing – your opponent's pressure, targets and needs is something that should be done if possible prior to your negotiations with them. If they give information in the preliminary stages of a meeting that may be of use to you, then by all means you can duly note that information and bring it into play later in negotiations at a key point. The more information you can find out in advance, the better for you. It will all be useful in negotiation settings.

Techniques to Try

Some of these techniques are what you might expect to encounter when dealing with a street vendor, but that doesn't keep more sophisticated business people from using them. The important thing is to recognize them and be prepared to respond to them if they are used against you in a negotiation. As long as you recognize the technique when it is used, you can actually turn them to your advantage in a pressurized negotiation setting.

One thing that many of the techniques have in common is that they tend to be used more in hope than in expectation. **The Exaggerated First Offer** technique is typically made in the full awareness that that offer will not be met, and the hope that somewhere between the $1000 you will settle for and the $2000 you have asked for, the dealer will make an offer which is as high as you can hope for. Experienced negotiators recognize this technique, and will usually respond with what may be an equally exaggerated counter-offer which undercuts what the car is worth.

The techniques tend not to have a lot to do with realism, essentially trying to create a circumstance whereby a customer feels rushed, belittled, or harried in some way into accepting a situation which is beneficial to the person using the technique. If a customer feels that it is a choice between paying $1,500 today or $3,000 next week, they will usually plump for the former – regardless of how true the pitch was in the first place. As well as this, some negotiators will attempt to flatter you by saying "OK, normally I wouldn't go anywhere near this low, but because I like you, here is what I'm going to do". If you have a firm line to hold to, keep holding it in the face of these techniques and you will hold the power.

Ten Negotiation Techniques:

1. Prepare, prepare, prepare.

2. Pay attention to timing.

3. Leave behind your ego.

4. Ramp up your listening skills.

5. If you don't ask, you don't get.

6. Anticipate compromise.

7. Offer and expect commitment.

8. Don't absorb their problems.

9. Stick to your principles.

10. Close with confirmation.

How to Break an Impasse

The dictionary says an impasse is a noun which describes: "a situation in which no progress is possible, especially because of disagreement; a deadlock".

There are a number of ways to break an impasse in negotiations. Here are a few:

- If the impasse involves money, change the terms: a larger deposit, a shorter pay period, etc.

- Change a team member or the team leader.

- Agree on easy issues and save the more difficult issues for later.

- Change the list of options being considered.

- Agree to adjourn for a fixed period of time to try to come up with other options.

The risk with an impasse in negotiations is that it can become a point where any movement from either party will be seen as weakness. The impasse can become the overall focus of the spell of negotiations, where the actual focus should be that which is set out in the initial framework as agreed in the preliminary stages. Sometimes in politics, negotiations take years to reach their fruition, because sticking points are occasionally unavoidable. In business, it tends not to take that long – but it is essential that you deal with impasses as they occur.

If you want to get around an impasse, the realization needs to be made that it is happening for a reason and that overcoming it will necessitate changing something about the way you are negotiating. If you can see the sticking point, then by all means make that the focus of your change, but failing that it can be a good idea to place to problem on the back burner and deal with something else – something manageable which will enable the momentum to be put back in your negotiations.

About Mutual Gain

In their classic book *Getting to Yes*, Roger Fisher and William Ury argue that most negotiations are not as efficient or as successful as they might be because people tend to argue about positions rather than interests. Once the parties in a negotiation commit themselves to a position, they feel that changing their position represents failure. Instead, Fisher and Ury suggest that the parties in a negotiation focus on their interests. What can we get out of the negotiation that will further our interests? That is the question that should guide a negotiation toward achieving mutual gain.

Three Ways to See Your Options

Positional Bargaining: Soft	Positional Bargaining: Hard	Interest Bargaining
Participants want to be friends	Participants are adversaries	Participants are problem solvers
The goal is agreement	The goal is victory	The goal is an outcome that will satisfy the interests of the participants
Participants trust each other	Participants distrust each other	Participants treat trust and distrust as irrelevant
Participants are soft on the people and the problem	Participants are hard on the people and the problem	Participants are soft on the people, hard on the problem
Participants change positions readily	Participants stick to a position	Participants focus on interests, not positions
Participants state their bottom line	Participants conceal their bottom line	Participants don't have a bottom line
Participants make concessions	Participants demand concessions	Participants invent options for mutual gain
Participants search for one solution	Participants demand one solution	Participants develop multiple options

About Mutual Gain

The key to making the mutual gain approach work is to focus on interests, not positions. Both parties want to create an atmosphere of respect and order in the schools. What options are available to allow them to satisfy their interests?

The answer in this situation may be a compromise. One party wants uniforms, the other does not. The reasons why the first party wants to have uniforms is to avoid a situation where every student wears their own clothes and – potentially – bullying can arise where one person or group act with hostility towards another who have their own individual style. Although individuality is to be encouraged, it has its drawbacks when it leads to marked difference.

One potential answer is to not have a specific uniform requirement – where everyone wears the same clothes – as this has its own drawbacks, making students easily identifiable to outsiders and potentially causing problems for parents with limited financial means. Instead, a dress code can be implemented which requires students to dress in a certain way without necessarily dressing all the same. The dress code can stipulate that the students dress in a modest, reasonable way without necessarily being clones of one another. This allows both parties to get something of what they want, without either side having to give up too much.

Creating a Mutual Gain Solution

Creating a mutual gain solution requires some activities not usually associated with negotiations, for example:

- Brainstorming to "expand the pie" by coming up with a range of options

- Identifying shared values to help create options that will meet the interests of both parties

- Changing the scope of the negotiation — making it larger or smaller

- Identifying issues that can be set aside for future negotiations

One of the problems that arise in negotiations is that parties can feel that they are being marginalized in terms of what they can do and what they can get. They may feel that being in constant opposition means that the negotiations advance at a snail's pace if at all. In order to put in place a mindset where there is a chance for consensus, the parties can look at what unites them rather than what puts them in opposition to one another.

The difficulty in any negotiation arises when there are issues where both parties have a philosophical WAP which is too far from that of the other. There is in this case no ZOPA, and no matter how much negotiation takes place there will be a sticking point. If you can remove the sticking point from the equation at least temporarily, you can get in place a situation where there is space for consensus.

The danger of "ignoring the elephant in the room" is that it will not go away just because it is ignored. It will still be there, and although it is tempting to look at things from a "blue sky" point of view and forget about the clouds forming overhead, you can end up saving up problems for the latter stages of negotiations. What you could look at doing is having someone working away from the negotiating table to find a compromise solution, and bring it back to the table when it looks more palatable to both parties.

What Do I Want?

To begin, identify what you personally want out of the negotiation. Try to state this positively.

Examples:

- I want a fair share of all new customers.

- I want a better working relationship with my manager.

- I want changes to the schedule.

You can create two versions of your personal needs statement: your ideal resolution and your realistic resolution. Or, you could frame your statement into several steps if the negotiation is complicated.

Another useful exercise is to break down your statement into wants and needs. This is particularly valuable if your statement is vague. Let's take the statement, "I want changes to the schedule," as an example.

Want	Need
More input into the scheduling process	To work less than 30 hours per week
A more regular schedule	More notice for schedule changes

This will give you some bargaining room during the negotiation process, and will help ensure that you get what you need out of the solution. In the example above, you may be willing to give up a more regular schedule if more notice for schedule changes is provided.

What Do They Want?

Next, identify what the person that you are in conflict with wants. Try to frame this positively. Explore all the angles to maximize your possibilities for mutual gain.

These framing questions will help you start the process.

- What does my opponent need?

- What does my opponent want?

- What is most important to them?

- What is least important to them?

What Do We Want?

Now that you have identified the wants and needs of both sides, look for areas of overlap. These will be the starting points for establishing mutual ground.

Here is an example. Joe and George are in conflict over the current schedule. As the most senior members of the assembly line team, they both alternate their regular duties with that of foreman. Although taking on the responsibility gives the foreman an extra $250 per shift, the foreman also has to work an extra hour per shift, and has additional safety responsibilities.

Joe and George both work Monday to Friday. As a regular assembly line team member, their shifts are from 8:30 a.m. to 4:30 p.m. As foreman, they are expected to work from 8 a.m. to 5 p.m.

	Joe	George
Wants	To have at least two foreman shifts per week.	To have at least two foreman shifts per week. To leave by 4:30 p.m. on Fridays.

Needs	To leave by 4:30 p.m. on Mondays and Wednesdays to pick up his children.	Not to have more than three foreman shifts per week as it will require him to pay extra taxes.
	To ensure that the foreman position is covered by someone from Monday to Friday, 8 a.m. to 5 p.m.	To ensure that the foreman position is covered by someone from Monday to Friday, 8 a.m. to 5 p.m.

From this simple chart, we can see that Joe and George have the same goal: to ensure that the foreman position is covered by someone during regular working hours. Thus, this is a logistical conflict rather than an emotional one. We can also see from the chart that there seems to be some good starting ground for a solution.

When working through the wants and needs of both parties, be careful not to jump to conclusions. Rather, be on the lookout for the root cause. Often, the problem is not what it seems.

Phase Three — Closing

The final phase of a negotiation is a time for reaching consensus and building an agreement. A little hard work in this phase can ensure that the negotiation achieves it desired results.

Closing a negotiation can mean two different things: First it may be a question of how to bring different ideas to a mutually agreed conclusion. A second possibility view of 'closing' is what means negotiating parties can use to acknowledge or formalize the idea that agreement has been reached.

Recognizing that parties have reached agreement can be quite simple. One can ask the other(s), "Then, have we reached agreement?" The parties can shake hands, make a public announcement, or sign a document. The real issue is that each has to make it clear to other negotiators that a mutually agreed conclusion has indeed been reached.

Reaching Consensus

People have different ideas about what constitutes consensus. When applied to negotiations, consensus usually involves substantive agreement on key issues. Not everyone needs to be completely satisfied to reach consensus, but everyone needs to feel that the outcome of the negotiation is something they can live with. Building consensus is one of the hardest parts of negotiation, because the negotiating parties will potentially have radically different attitudes to what they feel the results should be.

Consensus has different meanings to different people. To some, it is unsatisfactory compromise, with both parties ending on a solution which does not give them everything they want. However, the simple fact is that you cannot please all of the people all of the time. Consensus is about pleasing as many people as far as possible. The best solutions, in reality, are the ones which leave nobody *too* displeased. In an ideal world you could please everyone equally and completely. But this world is not ideal, and the realities dictate that to please one person you will usually have to displease someone else.

This is why you have concessions: if you push for 100%, it is possible to end up with 0%. It is much better, therefore, to have two parties who each have a significant percentage of what they want. Reaching a consensus may have a bittersweet taste for some parties, but it is better to have 50% of something than 100% of nothing.

Building an Agreement

Building an agreement takes a special skill — the ability to translate generalities into specifics. Negotiators should realize that at this stage of the process the bargaining is over. They should try to create an agreement based on a fair and accurate interpretation of the consensus the parties have reached. At the same time they want to be careful they do not inadvertently give something up by not paying close enough attention to the written agreement.

Sometimes in negotiations, there can be a tendency to arrive at certain principle agreements and think that the job has been done. There is more to negotiation than offering a concession here and stipulating a limit there. If you make the mistake of thinking that the negotiation process has ironed out all of the problems in a deal, then you will find that there is a nasty shock waiting for you when you come to formalize the agreement.

It may help to think of the negotiation process as a news broadcast. It is great to have headlines that will make people sit up and take notice, but in order for these headlines to actually have any meaning it is necessary to write the stories. While the basic principle agreement reached in the negotiation room will be the headline, and what sticks in people's minds, it needs to be backed up with details. A good negotiations team will have at least one "details guy (or gal)" who is able to get the small print in place after the negotiators have put the outline in front of them.

Setting the Terms of the Agreement

We are all familiar with what can happen when the terms of an agreement are not clearly spelled out. For example:

Two employees agree on their individual responsibilities for updating their company's website. A week goes by and nothing has happened. Each person was waiting for the other one to take the first step. They had defined their responsibilities but they had not formulated a plan for carrying them out.

For an agreement to be successful, all the essential terms must be clearly stated in writing. It is quite one thing to have an agreement in theory but it will be essentially meaningless without the practicalities. The agreement which emerges at the end of negotiations needs to be backed up with the "how" factor. What emerges from the initial negotiation is what you are going to go, and possibly when. The "how" is the most important of all, though, as without the firm details of how you are going to put everything in place you can agree whatever you want and it will not matter.

Dealing with Difficult Issues

Most people are willing to negotiate in good faith. They don't resort to tricks or intimidation. Every once in a while, though, you might encounter someone who takes a less principled approach. You need to be prepared to deal with people who don't play fair. It is not cynicism to prepare for the possibility that someone will try to bend the rules, especially when those rules are unwritten. It is simply good preparation, and realism. Some people are unscrupulous, but if you know how to handle them it need not be the end of the world.

Being Prepared for Environmental Tactics

Using environmental tactics to gain an advantage in a negotiation doesn't happen that often, but negotiators need to be prepared for it. One rather obvious case is the executive who refuses to come out from behind his desk and forces the other side to sit in visitors' chairs. If this should happen, the best response might be, "I'm sorry, but I need some space to spread out my notes. Is there a conference room available?"

The host of the negotiations is in a position of power. To deny that this is the case would be wholly naïve and counter-productive. However, the way they use this power will differ between hosts. Sometimes you will come up against a host who turns conditions to their advantage, and if you do not at least say something about it you run the risk of your "opponent" feeling that they can do and say anything and get away with it. Even if you merely make a request for an improvement in the conditions, you will make them aware that you have noticed what they have done.

It may be that you feel you can deal with any environmental tactics that are thrown at you. If you show an ability to negotiate competently despite the conditions which have been foisted upon you, this may well win you the respect of your opponent. You should not have to do this, though, and it is sensible to put your opponent on notice that you will not be messed around – politely, but firmly if necessary.

Dealing with Personal Attacks

Any negotiation will be more productive if you are able to focus on problems and not personalities. Unfortunately, the other parties in the negotiation may not take this approach.

There are a number of reasons why negotiators sometimes engage in personal attacks:

- They may think that this type of behavior will give them an advantage in the negotiation.

- They may see any disagreement with their position as a threat to their self-image.

- They may feel that they are not being treated fairly or respectfully.

Sometimes you can avert personal attacks by demonstrating from the very start that you respect the other parties and their positions. A respectful opening sets a positive tone for the negotiation.

If the other party resists your efforts to establish an atmosphere of mutual respect, you might try saying something like, "Let's get back to the issues." If the other party still engages in personal attacks, it may be time to suspend the negotiation. Personal attacks are never helpful, although there may be some people on the opposite side who feel that by acting or speaking in an abusive manner they can intimidate you.

The advice given by many a parent to the child who has been the subject of teasing in the schoolyard does apply here. What someone says something against you; it often says more about them than it does about you. It is wise to take account of the factors which have led to their behavior – it may have come at a particularly emotional point in negotiations, or they may just have been attempting to assert some kind of superiority over you. By maintaining your dignity, you will be held in high regard.

It helps no-one if you respond in kind to personal attacks. All that will do is give the person who attacked you the reaction which tells them that they have scored a direct hit. You will do better by simply requesting to get on with negotiations and ignore unhelpful contributions. It may seem like an attempt to back out of a confrontation, but it is no sign of weakness if you refuse to respond to childishness.

Controlling Your Emotions

Recognizing and controlling emotions is an aspect of "emotional intelligence."

Emotional intelligence is different from what might be called academic intelligence, the type of intelligence that enables some people to get good grades in school and score well on standardized tests. More and more people are realizing that it takes more than just this type of intelligence to succeed in the workplace and in life.

In a negotiation, emotional intelligence involves recognizing how you and the other party are responding emotionally to the discussion. If the emotional temperature in the room seems to be heating up, you may decide that it's time to take a break. There is little benefit to allowing a negative atmosphere to build in a boardroom and turn into something which can torpedo negotiations at a delicate stage.

You will recognize when the emotional temperature is rising beyond where it should be, because discussions will become less focused, voices will be raised and the silences will be all the more silent. At this point in negotiations it might be wise to suggest a short break for everyone to go and have a coffee, or take some fresh air. You can then come back to the negotiations with the atmosphere cleared somewhat and try to make some progress without the risk of people losing their temper.

Deciding When It's Time to Walk Away

It would be wonderful if the atmosphere of every negotiation was warm and friendly, but that's not the way things work in the real world. By their very nature, negotiations involve a kind of adversarial relationship. For a negotiation to proceed, the two parties do not need to have friendly relations, but they do need to keep personal conflicts and unfair tactics from interfering with the process.

It's time to walk away from a negotiation if:

- The other party makes you feel threatened or extremely uncomfortable.

- The other party uses unfair tactics that make it impossible to have an equitable negotiation.

You may feel like walking away is an admission of defeat, and this may inspire you to try and make things work even when the prospect of that happening is becoming more and more remote. However, there are times when the other party simply crosses a line, and you would be well advised to show them that this is not going to be permitted. Calling an end to the meeting, with an invitation to recommence negotiations at a later date, may be the best thing for everyone.

Some negotiators use tactics which are simply and purely threatening to try and ensure that you bend to their will. The reason that many people do this is because it often works. It will, however, only work if it is allowed to work. If people walked away from negotiations every time someone tried to cheat them or intimidate them, then that kind of tactic would die out. It is good to have principles in this regard, because no-one ever got a good deal by making concessions to a threatening negotiator.

Negotiating Outside the Boardroom

Negotiating isn't just something that takes place in conference rooms with powerful forces aligned on either side of a table. People have informal negotiations every day — with their coworkers, merchants, even family members.

Adapting the Process for Smaller Negotiations

Some of the principles of negotiation can be useful in everyday situations. For example:

- Separate the people from the problem. Don't let personalities get in the way of negotiating.

- Focus on interests, not positions. Consider what both parties want and need. Don't let adherence to a particular position narrow the range of options you are willing to consider.

- Expand the range of options. One way to overcome an impasse in a negotiation is to expand the range of the discussion.

- State the terms of an agreement in specific, clear terms.

Even if you are not in a traditional negotiation position, it can be helpful to use the principles of negotiation to bring you a positive outcome in everyday life. Making decisions in the home, you will find that results can be found which are to the benefit of all parties by using these principles. It should be added that you would be ill advised to use these principles for every decision – but where there is some difficulty in reaching a decision, you can reach a positive outcome by taking into account some sound, decent principles which have for years been used to reach positive decisions.

Negotiating via Telephone

The phone can be a convenient vehicle for negotiations, especially when the two parties find it difficult to meet in person. But in many cases an agreement reached over the phone needs to be confirmed through some other method.

For example, suppose you have a phone conversation with a coworker in which you both agree to do certain things within the next week. A week goes by and the other person has not done what he agreed to. You call him and he replies, "I didn't agree to that." It would have been better to follow up the first phone call with an email message that begins, "I just want to confirm what we agreed to do in our phone conversation."

When you arrive at a positive conclusion from a phone negotiation, it can be tempting to just hold on to your belief that you have got the right result, but even if you have recorded the call an unscrupulous counterpart can try to back out of it if they feel they have plausible deniability. Get everything nailed down by following up, and you will be able to put the deal in the record books. It is common sense to keep everything regulated and avoid any difficulties further down the line.

In order to negotiate effectively on the telephone we need to consider a few rules that also apply to face-to-face negotiation:

- Pay attention to particular points.

- Listen Actively. Don't interrupt the other party; don't spend your 'listening time' figuring out how you're going to respond to them when they finally stop talking. The better you listen, the better you can learn, and the more likely you will be able to respond in a way that improves the negotiation's result.

- Don't let the immediacy of a telephone call force you into fast, unwise decisions. There is nothing wrong with requesting more time to think about the terms discussed.

Negotiating via Email

Email can be an effective method of communication, but is has some inherent limitations.

In general, it is appropriate to use email in a negotiation:

- When the topic is clearly defined.

- When the topic does not require extensive discussion

- When the expected response is relatively simple

- When there is little possibility of misunderstanding

It is not appropriate to use email:

- When the topic is complex

- When the topic requires extensive discussion

- When the topic has great personal significance for the parties involved

- When the topic is likely to stir up strong emotions

E-mail has become a very popular way of keeping discussions simple and straightforward both in business and personal communications. However, there are limitations to it and it is important to be aware of these limitations. Keeping communications simple and somewhat informal can be helpful, but it should be remembered that waiting on an e-mail can be frustrating. If multiple communications are required, it is best to keep things face-to-face.

What e-mail does have going for it in a negotiation framework is that it keeps a record of every e-mail sent and received, along with dates and times allowing everything to be official. If you have a relatively simple detail or two to be finalized, e-mail is fine. If you have a situation requiring a full negotiation, e-mail should only be used as a preparation aid and a formal confirmation of things decided in a full, face-to-face negotiation.

Negotiating on Behalf of Someone Else

Negotiating on behalf of someone else presents some special challenges. When you begin such a negotiation, you need to have a clear idea of your Walk Away Price (WAP) and the concessions you have permission to make. You also need to be sure you understand the issues well enough to respond to tough questions that may come up in the negotiation.

If you are assembling a team to assist in the negotiation, you need to select people who have the expertise and the temperament to move the negotiation forward. It is not unlike selecting an army unit, in some ways. When going into battle, you want to have people nearby who will ensure that your interests are protected. It is said that a chain is only as strong as its weakest link, and this is a good principle to take with you into negotiations.

Choosing the Negotiating Team

An essential part of leading a team of any kind is sharing information. Teams need information to thrive. Before the negotiation, hold a meeting with the team to make sure everyone has the information they need to make an effective contribution. You can also use these meetings to:

- Remind everyone of the team's goals

- Ensure that everyone understands his or her role in the negotiation

- Create a "game plan" for the negotiation

You do not want to approach negotiations with a team containing someone who is unaware of their role or of the overall goal. If there is uncertainty in the team, it will spread quickly and it will certainly be picked up on by your counterparts. This can lead to you being hamstrung in terms of your bargaining power, because a team with a clearly defined brief and all its members fully apprised of the plan will be able to pull concessions from one with chaos in its ranks.

Having a team with clearly defined roles and a clearly defined goal is something that will be an asset in any negotiations. The more people you have (as long as they are professional and aware of their position), the more talents at your disposal and the more room for maneuver you will have when it comes to intensive negotiations. What you want is a situation where "two heads are better than one", rather than one where "too many chefs spoil the broth".

Covering All the Bases

Some negotiations are so complex that it is difficult for one person to master all the issues. In these situations it is worthwhile to assemble a team of experts to make sure all the bases are covered. As with any team, it is important that each person knows exactly what he or she is responsible for. What is gained through having a dedicated team designed to achieve the best negotiating muscle can be lost through having people who are unaware of their roles or unclear on what they can and cannot deliver.

It is beneficial to have a team who feel that they can make decisions with an element of autonomy. This will allow them to operate naturally in a negotiation with little fear that they might overstep the mark. However, it is important to have some limitations to their autonomy, as they are not negotiating for themselves. There is a need for balance in these situations. If they feel their hands are tied and they cannot make a decision without referring back to you, they will be powerless in negotiations. If they feel that they have free rein and can do whatever they want, they may make a decision which you would not have made yourself and which damages your position. Finding the point in between where you can be confident that their decisions will benefit you is essential.

As with so many issues, it is important to get the balance right, as complex negotiations have a tendency to break down or end in an unpopular agreement if they are not handled correctly and with a sense of common purpose. If you get your team right, you can ensure at least that you are not the negotiator who ends up with an unpopular deal on your hands.

Dealing with Tough Questions

Here are some possible ways to respond to questions that you decline to answer:

- Suggest (in a friendly way) that the question is irrelevant. For example, you might say, "I'm not sure how that question fits in here."

- Say you don't know the answer. This is the best course of action to take if you really don't know the answer. This approach is better than guessing. As a next step, you might say that you will find out the answer and get back to the questioner within a day or two.

- Say that you would like to wait to respond to the question until later in the negotiation. This is the best thing to do if your answer will reveal too much about your position too soon.

- Reply with a question of your own. This may help clarify the motivation of the questioner. (What is the questioner really asking?)

Each of these approaches is a way that you can take the question in your stride and be seen to be giving it the consideration it deserves, without giving an answer that will put you on the back foot in terms of negotiations. People may ask you difficult questions in order to trap you, or because their own position is uncertain and they want to find a way to clarify it. How you handle such questions will be important, but as long as you show certainty and a desire to be straight with them, you need not lose confidence.

Chapter 28 – Organizational Skills

Good organizational skills can prove beneficial in many areas of life, including personal and business areas. Organization can increase a person's general productivity, project management, and can even affect his memory and retention skills. These skills are not acquired overnight – it will take a lot of hard work and practice. But with a little guidance and the right tools, anyone can learn how to stop hunting for missing things and become better organized.

To effectively learn better organization skills, a person must first learn efficient training tools and tips to help him reach his goal. With this help, everyone can take a better look at their current habits and form a new plan to become better organized in life.

- Examine current habits and routines that are not organized

- Learn to prioritize your time schedule and daily tasks

- Determine ways of storing information and supplies

- Learn to organize personal and work space

- Learn to resist procrastination

- Make plans to stay organized in the future

Remove the Clutter

One of the hardest parts about getting organized is going through and getting rid of the things that cause distractions and take up space. When you find yourself among the stacks and piles of stuff and items, it can seem overwhelming. But by taking it one step at a time, and remembering to breathe, you can begin to de-clutter your life and start on the path to successful organization.

Just Do it

Sometimes we can feel overwhelmed about taking on the task of removing our clutter and tend to make excuses as to why it doesn't get done. We can claim that we don't have the time, or that there is too much to do at once. But as Nike says, we have to "Just Do It" and we have to throw away our excuses and dive in. Make a plan on how you can get started, such as making a 'cleaning calendar' or choosing an area to start on. Stick with your plan until the job is complete, and don't let the same excuses hinder your success.

Helpful tips:

- Make a calendar with time to clean

- Divide the areas that need to be conquered

- Make a list of tasks

- Decide where items go beforehand

You Don't Have to Keep Everything

You know who you are – the person that exclaims *"I have to keep [this] because I might need it later!"*

In reality, we can throw away over half of our saved documents or items without feeling a sense of withdrawal or consequence. The decision to keep everything can drive us to make inappropriate choices with organization and contributes to more clutter. We can break that kind of thinking by examining what we are holding on to and by realizing we can't live by the *'what ifs'* an item may have. Go through your clutter and clarify how it is useful to you right now and get rid of anything that doesn't have a clear purpose. Once you have removed the items you don't need or have use for, you are no longer wasting time on useless clutter, but are developing better organization for the things you did keep.

Ask yourself:

- Am I going to use this in the near future?

- When was the last time I needed this?

- If I keep this, what is it organized into?

Three Boxes: Keep, Donate, and Trash

The most common approach to clearing out clutter is the Three Boxes method. This method forces a decision to be made about each item you touch as you go through your clutter. You don't get to put it aside or come back to it later. Pick up an item, one at a time, and think about which box it should go in. Try not to release the item until a decision is made.

Box 1 – Items to Keep: This box is for items you would like to keep in your area or maybe even put away for safe keeping (such as heirlooms or special gifts). This is not to be confused with the *'things I might need later'* type of thinking. Only keep items that have value and meaning to you.

Box 2 – Items to Donate: This box is for items that you realize you no longer need or want. Items in this box can be donated or sold at a rummage sale, just as long as it leaves the clutter!

Box 3 – Trash: This box is for the things that you do not need or want and cannot be donated or given away. This often includes old papers or documents, mail, or broken items. Once this box is full or complete, remove it from the area right away and don't give it a second look.

A Place for Everything and Everything in its Place

One factor that contributes to our clutter is where we decide to keep it or let it lay. When something is not in its proper place, everything else can seem chaotic and, disorganized. While we are thinking about where things need to go, think about what the item or items are and where it would best be suited. This may require you to refresh your mind and search your office over for every available open space that can be used. But no matter the amount of stuff you plan to keep, once it has found its proper place in your office, it won't stay in the way of you becoming more organized.

Ask yourself:

- What do I need to put here/there?

- Where would this be best suited?

- Will it be in my way/contribute to clutter there?

Prioritize

Organization doesn't only refer to our physical items and physical possessions; it can also include organizing our time and activities. Taking time to label what we want and what we need to accomplish allows us to sort through everything on our plate and find out how to tackle it. Since everything is lined out and identified, regulating our time and energy can seem less overwhelming.

Write It Down

When organizing your priorities, it is important to write them all down and make yourself some sort of 'master' list because it helps you remember everything you want to accomplish or complete later. This list gives you a visual aide to use when making organizational decisions. You don't have to list the items in any particular order, but just list anything that comes to mind. Once you feel you have completed the list (for now), then you can go back and assign their priority order. Common codes such as ABC or 123 can be used to determine each listings priority and how you will proceed with each one.

Urgent/Important Matrix

Sometimes we confuse our urgent priorities with our important ones, which can cause us to be confused about what to take care of first. The Urgent/Important Matrix is a tool that we can use to think about our priorities and how we handle them. Before we can use the matrix, we must write down everything we want to accomplish in a certain period of time, such as daily, weekly, or even further and assign their priority in which we want to get them done (See previous exercise).

The matrix is divided into four quadrants, each ranging in importance, and allows for activities and projects to be plotted in each one based on their need. Using the list you created, you would plot each job in the corresponding quadrant. After all of the tasks have been plotted, we can see all of the things we want or need to do and how urgent or important they are to us. This leads us to make better choices regarding our time management and overall organization.

There are many versions of the Urgent/Important Matrix that can be used for various things. We've included a common version that can be used with everyday activities for this exercise.

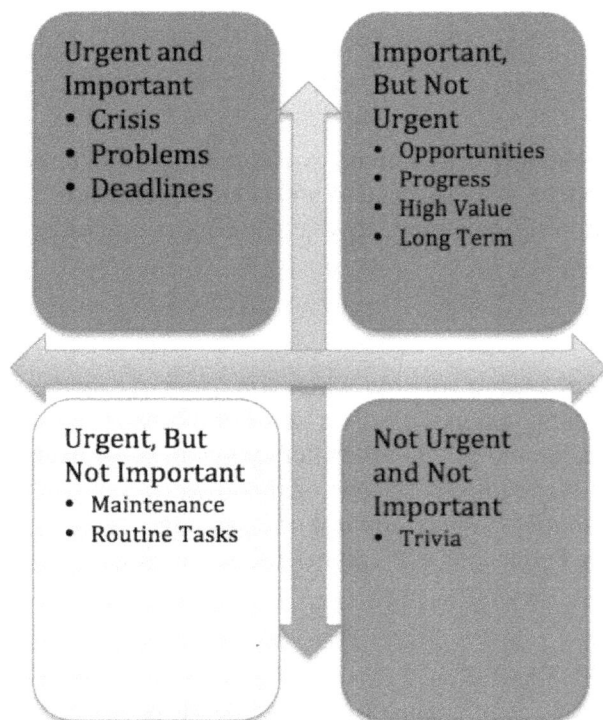

Urgent and Important
- Crisis
- Problems
- Deadlines

Important, But Not Urgent
- Opportunities
- Progress
- High Value
- Long Term

Urgent, But Not Important
- Maintenance
- Routine Tasks

Not Urgent and Not Important
- Trivia

Divide Tasks

Now that you've made a list and categorized all of the things you want to accomplish, it can seem overwhelming or even intimidating to get started. But by dividing your tasks into smaller groups of things to do, we can feel more empowered to get them done. Tasks can be divided any way that is convenient, such as things to do for one particular project or maybe even things to do that involve going through papers. They key is to find what combination works for you.

Helpful hints:

- Sort tasks by each specific project

- Decide what tasks can be done the fastest

- Determine what tasks will need more time

80/20 Rule

Simply put, the 80/20 Rule emphasizes the need to focus on what is important to us, and disregarding the rest. In most cases, 20% of things we have or accumulate are important to us, while the other 80% is usually trivial, if not useless. If the 20% is handled first and focused upon, the remaining 80% practically takes care of itself. For example, using the 80/20 Rule, you can sit down with your daily to-do list and identify the top three or four projects or tasks that *need* to be done (the 20%). Then outline the less important or mundane things that can be done next, or even at a later time (the 80%). By focusing on what is the most important/urgent first, we are more focused and ready to tackle them. Once they are completed, the rest of the tasks seem less daunting and can be done with ease.

The 80/20 Rule is about being organized while doing what you want in your everyday life (and not just more organizing!).

Scheduling Your Time

Your time is valuable, so you should treat it that way. Your schedule can get busy and sometimes it can seem like there are not enough hours in the day. But when that happens, we just need to take a step back, and manage our time effectively. When we schedule our time and resources in a way that benefits us and aides in becoming better organized, there's nothing we can't accomplish.

Have a Master Calendar

It can seem like a good idea to have several calendars for every area of life, but when you use more than one at a time, it's easy to get them confused. With multiple calendars, you can run the risk of double booking events or miss important appointments. Instead, get one calendar and put it somewhere you can see it every day, such as on the refrigerator or hanging by the front door. Write all of your personal and work reminders on it, including deadline dates, appointments, events, and reminders. When you use one calendar for everything you do, you are not only able to manage your time better, but you can get rid of the paper reminders you have posted everywhere.

Setting Deadlines

When scheduling our time, deadlines provide a sense of structure and balance for us. While every person responds to deadlines differently, they are a key tool to better time management. By setting deadlines, you are putting a concrete need in your schedule, and it helps prevent it from being forgotten or lost in the near future. They give us a sense of accountability when it comes to things we either want or need to get done. So whether you write them on a calendar or program them into a mobile device, the next time you plan to do something, set yourself a deadline first and stick to it. You'll find that when you take the time to schedule them, you'll make time for other things.

Tips when setting deadlines:

- Keep your deadlines in arm's reach – write them down where you will see them

- Set periodic reminders – give yourself reminders that a deadline approaches

- Pad your actual deadline a little – give yourself some extra wiggle room

Remove or Limit the Time Wasters

A time waster is something that can distract you or take away from the task at hand. They can occur at home or at work. Removing or even limiting some of these wasters can improve your concentration and help you stay focused on what you want or need to do. They can include personal time wasters, such as checking messages or stopping to talk, or can even be as simple as wasting extra time to go look for that extra file. Practice cutting or limiting one thing that distracts you the most, such as other people or stopping to start another task. Give yourself a set time that you will not let these things distract you or take away from your current duty. You'll be amazed how taking these small steps will improve your time management.

Some common time wasters and distractions:

- Excessively checking email/text/phone messages

- Boredom or daydreams

- Extra time spent away from your work area

- Extra time spent looking for things

- Taking on extra projects

Coping With Things Outside of Your Control

There are many things in life that we cannot control, such as an illness, rude or mean people, and especially the weather. But we learn to cope with them every day and adapt ourselves to them. You can control how you react to certain circumstances and setbacks. When we are faced with something we realize we cannot change or control, the key to dealing with it is to, first, accept it. Once you have accepted that you cannot change the fact that it rained on your moving day or that someone almost rear ended you in traffic, we can learn to cope with them by remembering what we can control. You *can* control what alternative plan you have for moving day and you *can* control how you choose to respond to the rude driver. Focusing on what you can control rather than what you can't will help you feel more empowered and less likely to let other obstacles overcome you.

To Do Lists

Since we can often feel overwhelmed by the amount work we need to do, one of the easiest ways things we can do is create to do lists. Creating a list ensures that tasks are written down in one place and is easily referenced later. You don't have to use a typical to do list, just as long as you can manage the tasks you have written down and prioritize them as needed.

Use a Day Planner

A day planner is a great tool to help you manage your time and stay on top of projects and job lists. It's handy to carry with you and keep within arm's reach. When making your central to do list, your day planner can be used for keeping all of your reminders and notes in one place, which can make it your central source for your information. The key is to update it regularly and to use it every day.

Tips for having a day planner:

- Put contact information in the front of it

- Update it regularly and reference it everyday

- Utilize the 'notes' sections

Finish What You Start

When we complete a task or project, we get a sense of completion and accomplishment, which can make us feel great about ourselves. But when we drop a project or fail to complete it, it can make us feel depressed and bleak. Completing something that you've taken the effort to start also helps you to become more productive and ensures that things are done on time (whether it is your deadline or someone else's). Also, when you complete something all the way through the first time, it saves you from having to come back later and try to finish it then!

Focus on the Important

By now you're keeping several to do lists and endless tallies in your head or even writing some down. Even though you've established your project's priority, sometimes we can lose sight of the big picture and will stray from the main path. It is essential to keep focus on the important aspects of your to do list, whether it's finishing something on time or making sure you get the right data for the report. If you come across a task that does not coordinate with your larger goals, put it aside for now and keep focus on what you need to do to get your things done. If you have to, limit yourself to a few important tasks to focus on first before moving on to the rest. Recognize what tasks are important enough to focus on now, and which ones can wait until a later time.

Remember, anyone can make a to-do list with lots of check marks and bullets, but getting the things done will seem endless if you lack focus and determination.

Do Quick Tasks Immediately

When we make our to-do list, there is normally a variety of chores and tasks to complete. Some are more important than others and some will take more time than others. While looking at your list, make note of things you can do quickly and wouldn't take up much of your time. Do these tasks right away so that you can quickly cross them off of your to do list and give yourself a pat on the back. When you finish these tasks quickly and do them right away, it leaves more room for you to focus on more complicated or lengthy tasks and projects.

Sample 'quick tasks':

- Filing paperwork

- Posting reminders and notices

- Sending follow up emails

Paper and Paperless Storage

We all have those pieces of paper we keep around us, whether it's old receipts, invoices, cards, or old letters. On the other side of the coin, we are living in the 'paperless' age, where everything is done electronically, including utility bills and notifications. Luckily, we don't have to choose between one and the other. A paper and paperless storage system can work for anyone, as long as they work together to keep things organized.

Find a System that Works for You

When deciding whether or not to go paperless, we have to decide what would work best for our situations. Many of us function well with physical pieces of paper in some sort of filing system. Others of us work better in the electronic filing system and keep paperless files, whether on a computer or portable device. Paper storage systems allow you to keep various paper documents in files for easy access and reference and can provide a firm reference if needed to present a hard copy. However, a paperless system allows you to free up more space while managing to keep documents for a longer period of time. So in order to decide what works for you, examine how you store your valuable information.

Ask yourself some of the following questions to help decide what system works for you:

- Where do I keep my information?

- Do I keep physical things or electronic versions?

- If I store paper, do I have the space?

- If I store paperless, do I have the access?

Make It Consistent

Whichever storage system you choose, or whether you decide to use both, keep your methods consistent. If you decide to choose one method over the other, be sure to stick with this method for all of your papers or files. Keep them in one central location so that they are easily accessible. If you decide to use a combination of these methods, keep your paper files and electronic files consistent with matching names for paper folders and the ones on your computer. If file names are different and do not share a key name, documents could be lost or placed in the wrong folder or file. The system you choose to use should help boost your organization, not complicate it.

Make it Time Sensitive

Every piece of information in storage is connected to some kind of time line, such as a printed date, times, or schedules. When we store these items and keep them out of sight, we can often forget what they are for and possibly miss important deadlines. To avoid misplacing or forgetting these time sensitive materials, make your method of organization time sensitive as well. Create bins or folders with dates and reminders on them. Make different categories for them, such as personal, bills, work projects or jobs, to help remind you of their 'shelf life'. By keeping these documents handy or in marked computer files, we can keep track of pressing, time sensitive information without letting the deadlines or due dates slip through our fingers.

Tips for organizing time sensitive information:

- Mark folders/bins/files with dates or date ranges

- Highlight or emphasize deadlines on each material

- Once something has passed a deadline or due date, re-file it to another folder

Setting up Archives

Now that you've sorted all of your files and folders and decided what you need to keep or throw away, the next step is set up various archives for documents that you need to keep for future use, but won't necessarily need every day. Establish a reference system that works for you and can be easily sorted through later when you need to find something. If you're keeping physical files, keep them in a folder or bin that is not in your direct work area. Put it away in the back of a drawer or on a higher shelf than everything else.

If you decide to keep digital files, keep all documents in archived folders and relocate them to another computer if possible. Don't keep them on the desktop along with things you use every day. However you decide to store your materials, setting up archives will help you keep track of files you need to hang on to while keeping them out of your everyday work space.

Organization in Your Work Area

Organization at work is a great tool to help us increase our productivity and keep our tasks and projects in order. However, becoming better organized means more than just keeping your pens and pencils in the right drawer. It's more important to develop good organizing habits and valuable techniques that will keep you on the right track in whatever you have to do at work.

Keeping Items Within Arm's Reach

When in your work space, design your work layout so that everything is within your arm's reach. We waste so much time having to go out of our way to go get a certain file or to stand by the copier. Generally, if you have to leave your work space to get something, you can become distracted or lose focus, which can interfere with your work and your level of productivity. So when you get to work each day, before you do anything else, reorganize your area so you have immediate access to everything, such as your computer, supplies and even files and folders. Taking time to do this at the beginning of the day will not only better organize your work space, but it will save so much time that could have been wasted throughout the day.

Only Have Current Projects on Your Desk

You may have a variety of stacks of papers and projects on your desk, but the key is in knowing what is in them. Keeping your desk more organized by only keeping projects that you are currently working with, in your work area. Projects that you have finished should be filed away in the appropriate place, while projects that you haven't yet started should not be in the work area until you do. Having these projects in sight with your current projects can cause confusion and a lack of focus on unimportant details. Stay focused on current projects by keeping them on your immediate desk area, and don't allow anything else to encroach.

Questions to ask yourself when keeping projects on your desk:

- When does this need to be finished?

- Is it something that can be completed later?

- Has this already been completed?

Arranging Your Drawers

When you are organizing your different drawers at work, think about how each one functions in your everyday routine. What purpose do your desk drawers serve? How often do you use your filing cabinet drawers? Drawers that are within arm's reach, such as your desk drawers, should house items that you use often, but don't necessarily need every day. You want to ensure you have access to everything without a hitch, while not letting things clutter your desk workspace. Keep your filing cabinet drawers organized by a certain filing system, whether it is by color labels or alphabetical sorting. However you decide to arrange and organize your office drawers, be sure to find a method that works for you and will help increase your ease with finding anything you may need.

Organize to Match Your Workflow

Every day you face a variety of tasks or projects to complete, so plan your day accordingly, and plan what you will need to have in order to complete these tasks. If you know you will not need your computer, arrange your workspace to utilize the areas around in and don't bother with turning it on. If you know you will need the copier or scanner all day, organize the supplies and space you will need to accompany that. When you organize your work area to match you current workflow, less time is wasted trying to move between different areas or side step certain supplies, and will increase your productivity throughout the day.

Tips to help organize with your workflow:

- Decide what tools you will need for the day

- Determine if additional supplies are needed

- Focus on that project or set of tasks for the day. Don't try to mix in other things.

Tools to Fight Procrastination

Procrastination is one of the leading causes of disorganization. As we've seen before, we can often make excuses to do it later for find various reasons why something can be put off until later. But once we've compiled our giant to do list and have decided what tasks should be done first, our next step, or steps, is to fight against procrastination and just do them. With the right tools and good habits, you'll be able to say good bye to procrastination sooner, rather than later.

Eat That Frog!

As Mark Twain says, *"Eat a live frog every morning, and nothing worse will happen to you the rest of the day."*

We all have that task we dread doing, whether it's at home doing the dishes or at work sending our email reports. Our normal plan of action is to put it off while completing various other tasks. Then when it's time to complete this unpleasant task, we either find a way to put it off or don't tackle it with full force. But Eat That Frog is a concept that says we should "eat the frog" first, or rather do our least favorite tasks first, and fully complete them before moving onto another project. When this job is out of the way, we spend the rest of our time completing more favorable tasks, and revel in knowing that you don't have to return to the first one.

Eat That Frog Guideline:

1. The Frog – Identify your most important task first.

2. Complete this task first before you move on to anything else.

3. Eat the Frog - Continue with this task until it is completed.

Remove Distractions

Even after you have set your mind to completing a task and checking it off of your to do list, the smallest distraction can make you lose focus and stop working. They can occur at home or at work, and often times we do not even register them as a distraction. When you are preparing to start a project or task, look around and evaluate what is in the area that could distract you. Turn off personal cell phones or devices or put a sign on your door asking for silence and to not disturb. Ensure everything you will need is organized with your workflow to reduce the need to get up and leave your area. When we eliminate these distractions that can make us lose our focus, we will see an increase and production and spend less time trying to complete the same project.

Give Yourself a Reward

Rewards are a great way to keep ourselves motivated. After all, who doesn't want to earn a little treat after a job well done? The key is to only reward the good behavior, such as finishing a small task or completing a whole project. If we jump to the reward too soon, we are only rewarding our negative behavior and are not helping to reduce procrastination. Start with small rewards when working on something, such as taking a break or getting something to snack on. We can reward ourselves with a bigger prize when the entire job is finished, such as going out with friends or doing something fun that we enjoy more.

Tips:

- Only give rewards for work done, not work promised.

- Start with small rewards before working up to bigger ones.

- Keep a visual reminder of what you've accomplished.

Break Up Large Tasks

Sometimes we think we have less to do because we have fewer items on our lists, only to realize they are larger than we realized and could become overwhelming. When we feel defeated by these larger tasks, they can lead to further procrastination. Instead, take this one large task and break it into smaller, more manageable tasks that can be completed more easily. If you have a 20 page slideshow due at work, break the project into separate page tasks, completing one or two at a time until it is all completed. If you have decided to clean out your entire garage, start by retrieving all of your donated items or clearing out trash items. When one task is done, you can move on to the next one until the entire job is done. Don't forget to take periodic breaks and stop to re-evaluate your progress.

Organizing Your Inbox

If your email inbox is cluttered or unorganized, it can make it difficult to find the email or message you need or notice when you have a new one waiting. Many email systems have tools you can use to help sort and organize emails and appointments in order to go through them easier. When your emails are in order, you better able to stay on top of your incoming and outgoing mail and always have the information you may need.

Setting Delivery Rules

Many email systems now allow you to create rules that you can apply to email being delivered to your inbox that can help you better sort and organize certain messages. These 'rules' use filters that you choose and will either flag/highlight an email for you or re-route it to another folder for you to access later. For example, any email from your manager's email address can be highlighted in yellow for immediate attention. Or if you have been speaking with a friend about adopting their new kitten, any email with the word 'kitten' can be re-routed to a folder with her name on it. These filters and rules can help you reorganize your long list of emails and messages into appropriate folders and sections to help you access your information faster and with more ease.

Folder and Message Hierarchy

To better organize email messages, a good folder structure should be in place and ready to use. Once these are established, a folder and message hierarchy system can be put into place. This hierarchy system allows you to sort folders and messages by priority or importance and can be done in several different ways, such as using a color code or relocating items to the top of the inbox for better viewing. Establishing hierarchy among your many emails will help you identify the most important messages first and reduces the risk of you skimming over it to read and handle something less urgent.

Tips to consider when establishing inbox hierarchy:

- Sender of the message

- Urgent topics/subjects

- Upcoming deadlines or projects

Deal With Email Right Away

Your inbox is not meant to be a storage area for your messages. When you receive an email, you don't necessarily have to respond to it right away, but the message should be filed away to an appropriate location to retrieve later. If it needs to be handled at the end of the week, re-file it to another folder that can be reopened later. If the email needs to be addressed by someone else, forward to the appropriate party and remove from your inbox. If the email simply isn't needed, then delete it right away instead of holding onto it any longer. Taking a few more minutes to deal with the email once you open it will not only save you time in the long run, but it will help keep better track of emails that require your attention and which ones do not.

Ask yourself these questions when handling your emails:

- Does this email need immediate action?

- If not, when does it need to be addressed?

- Will you need this information at a later date?

- Does this email pertain to me or my department?

Flag and Highlight Important Items

Important emails should not be forgotten or lost, so you can assign these email a flag or even highlight them in a different color to call attention to them in your inbox or subfolders. Flags can be used to remind you of an upcoming event or project, including meeting or deadlines. Various types of flag categories can be set up, so you can flag some message for a follow up while some can be flagged as an appointment reminder.

If you don't want to individually flag every message, highlights can also be set up to highlight messages from certain sender or that contain key words, such as 'meeting' or 'appointment'. For instance, all emails from your boss can be highlighted in red for urgency, but emails from your best friend can be colored in blue for a later time. Flags and highlights can be used individually if desired or can be used together to work in sync and organize your growing inbox.

Avoid the Causes of Disorganization

Sometimes getting organized means more than just making sure everything has a place or that we check off our to-do list. Often times becoming organized is mainly about avoiding the things that can cause us to become disorganized, especially after we have already started the process of changing our ways. When we make ways to stay organized part of our regular habits, we won't have a need to give in to reasons for disorganization.

Keeping Everything

We are all guilty of trying to keep things that we don't necessarily need. It's usually contributed to the thought of "Well I *might* need it one day". When we keep old or expired items and paperwork, we don't realize that this can actually contribute to further disorganization rather than helping us in the future. Although we feel we have to keep everything, we can actually throw out over half of our saved items or documents without consequence. Avoid building up the clutter, also known as hoarding, by examining what you are trying to hold on to and pin point its purpose in your office area. If it doesn't serve an immediate purpose, throw it out.

How do you determine if it needs to be kept?

- When was the last time I used or needed this?

- What purpose does this serve me?

- If I get rid of this, what will happen?

- Will I need this in the near future?

- If I get rid of this, can I access it later somewhere else (online, office copy, etc.)?

Not Being Consistent

Repetition is the key to learning, and these repeated and consistent behaviors are the key to developing good habits. When in the process of getting organized, we set ourselves to-do lists and actions that we take to keep ourselves organized (such as sorting emails right away or keeping office supplies close by). When we become inconsistent, such as forgetting to turn off our cell phone before starting a project or just throwing the unopened mail on our desk one morning, we are leaving room to become disorganized again. After one slip, it becomes easier to forget what we have learned and begin to fall into our normal pit of excuses or procrastination. Once we have established good organizational habits, it is important to stick to them and be consistent in our actions.

Not Following a Schedule

For many people, not sticking to some sort of routine or schedule can cause them to become disorganized and procrastinate. Ask yourself why you need to follow a schedule, and what is that schedule meant to help you accomplish? A schedule can be simple and flexible, such as creating yourself a to-do list and sticking to it, or schedules can be more definite and set, such as outlining specific tasks and timelines. While schedules are not set in stone, they are supposed to provide a sense of structure when completing tasks, projects, and activities. If schedules are ignored or forgotten altogether, it can lead to wasted time management or prolonged duties.

Bad Habits

Being organized is all about creating good habits that we can stick to in the long run. Unfortunately, we all have bad habits that can steer us away from getting on the right path. Habits such as leaving unused supplies on our desktop 'for later' or keeping every employer newsletter you receive 'to go through'. Sometimes we do not even recognize when we have developed a bad habit that is keeping us from becoming more organized. Take a look at some of your everyday actions and determine if you have, or are developing a bad habit that keeps you disorganized at home or at work. Once we discover the problem, we can work to correct our habits and change them for the better. By making slow, incremental changes, we begin to gain more confidence in ourselves and feel more empowered to kick bad habits once and for all.

Characteristics of a bad habit:

- Doesn't offer an immediate benefit

- Creates more work to do later

- Doesn't make us feel more confident

- Contributes to procrastination or disorganization

Discipline is the Key to Stay Organized

Organization doesn't happen overnight and it is not an easy destination to get to. As we've said before, it takes hard work, discipline, and lots of good habits to keep on the path of good organization. This is why the process can seem overwhelming at first and seem like a real challenge, but it doesn't have to be impossible. With some of the following tips and techniques, we can feel more empowered to stay disciplined in your organization.

Stay Within Your Systems

When we set our minds to become more organized, the first step is finding the right system that will help you reach that goal. Once you find one the system that works for you, the key is to keeping up the momentum to maintain that system. Over time, it is normal to need to re-evaluate or tweak your system in some way.

Develop a more updated system periodically based on your changing priorities, needs and to-do lists. When organizing your home or office, stay within the system that you've adapted so that your routines and actions are consistent and work together.

Learn to Say No

Often times we can become disorganized by taking on too many projects or activities, which can take a toll on our time management. It is important to learn the need to say 'no' when asked to help with a request. While you may feel the need or desire to help everyone that you can, realize that you can best serve others by sticking with the areas in which you have the most to offer and can do the most good. If you over-extend yourself and your skills, not only do many people miss out on the great things you have to offer, but it keeps you from feeling more confident and organized in your life.

Sample phrases for saying No:

- "No, thank you."

- "Sorry but I am already committed to another project."

- "That area is not one of my strengths."

- "Thank you, but I am needed for (project/assignment) right now."

Have Organization Be Part of Your Life

Organization doesn't happen every once in a while or when the occasion arises; it is something that is continued and carried out each day. In order to stay organized over time, we must make organization part of our everyday life. Organization is in everything we do, from daily activities such as sorting out documents, to more long term activities, such as reorganizing a department. When we practice these good habits and helpful tips every day, we are making organization a regular thing in our lives and letting it help us build a better future for ourselves. Don't wait for things or tasks to clutter up your life before you decide it is time to get organized again.

Plan for Tomorrow, Today

If you're waiting for the beginning of the following day to start your organization plan, chances are you are already headed to disorganization. Start today and make a plan for what you want to do in your life, including on a daily, weekly, monthly and even a yearly basis. When you determine what you want (such as becoming more organized!), you can make plans today to reach those goals in the future. Make a to-do list and plan a time to tackle it instead of waiting for the 'urge' to do it comes along. Make plans on how to motivate yourself to keep going and plan rewards for productive behaviors. Set deadlines for yourself and stick to them. When we plan ahead and manage your time effectively, the stress and anxiety of becoming more organized will feel much lighter and a lot less like a chore.

Tips:

- Make short and long term to-do lists.

- Plan ways to execute each list.

- Find ways to keep yourself motivated to stay on task.

- Don't forget to plan deadlines or plan to meet those already in place.

Chapter 29 – Time Management

Time management training most often begins with setting goals. These goals are recorded and may be broken down into a project, an action plan, or a simple task list. Activities are then rated based on urgency and importance, priorities assigned, and deadlines set. This process results in a plan with a task list or calendar of activities. Routine and recurring tasks are often given less focus to free time to work on tasks that contribute to important goals.

This entire process is supported by a skill set that should include personal motivation, delegation skills, organization tools, and crisis management. We'll cover all this and more during this workshop.

At the end of this chapter, you should be able to:

- Plan and prioritize each day's activities in a more efficient, productive manner

- Overcome procrastination quickly and easily

- Handle crises effectively and quickly

- Organize your workspace and workflow to make better use of time

- Delegate more efficiently

- Use rituals to make your life run smoother

- Plan meetings more appropriately and effectively

Encourage participants to write their own workshop objectives in their guide.

Before reviewing this chapter, answer the following questions:

- What are your biggest time wasters?

- What are you currently doing to manage your time?

- What could you be doing better?

- If you came away from this workshop with only one thing, what would that be?

Take a moment to discuss these questions and note answers on the flip chart. Try to come to a group consensus on each item.

Setting SMART Goals

Goal setting is critical to effective time management strategies. It is the single most important life skill that, unfortunately, most people never learn how to do properly. Goal setting can be used in every single area of your life, including financial, physical, personal development, relationships, or even spiritual. According to Brian Tracy's book Goals, fewer than 3% of people have clear, written goals, and a plan for getting there. Setting goals puts you ahead of the pack!

Some people blame everything that goes wrong in their life on something or someone else. They take the role of a victim and they give all their power and control away. Successful people instead dedicate themselves towards taking responsibility for their lives, no matter what the unforeseen or uncontrollable events. Live in the present: the past cannot be changed, and the future is the direct result of what you do right now!

The Three P's

Setting meaningful, long-term goals is a giant step toward achieving your dreams. In turn, setting and achieving short-term goals can help you accomplish the tasks you'll need to achieve the long-term ones. It is also important to make sure that all of your goals unleash the power of the three P's:

POSITIVE: Who could get fired up about a goal such as "Find a career that's not boring"? Goals should be phrased positively, so they help you feel good about yourself and what you're trying to accomplish. A better alternative might be this: "Enroll in pre-law classes so I can help people with legal problems someday."

PERSONAL: Goals must be personal. They must reflect your own dreams and values, not those of friends, family, or the media. When crafting your goal statement, always use the word "I" in the sentence to brand it as your own. When your goals are personal, you'll be more motivated to succeed and take greater pride in your accomplishments.

POSSIBLE: When setting goals, be sure to consider what's possible and within your control. Getting into an Ivy League university may be possible if you are earning good grades but unrealistic if you're struggling. In the latter case, a more reasonable goal might be to attend a university or trade school that offers courses related to your chosen career. You might also pursue volunteer work that would strengthen your college applications.

The SMART Way

SMART is a convenient acronym for the set of criteria that a goal must have in order for it to be realized by the goal achiever.

Specific: Success coach Jack Canfield states in his book The Success Principles that, "Vague goals produce vague results." In order for you to achieve a goal, you must be very clear about what exactly you want. Often creating a list of benefits that the accomplishment of your goal will bring to your life, will give your mind a compelling reason to pursue that goal.

Measurable: It's crucial for goal achievement that you are able to track your progress towards your goal. That's why all goals need some form of objective measuring system so that you can stay on track and become motivated when you enjoy the sweet taste of quantifiable progress.

Achievable: Setting big goals is great, but setting unrealistic goals will just de-motivate you. A good goal is one that challenges, but is not so unrealistic that you have virtually no chance of accomplishing it.

Relevant: Before you even set goals, it's a good idea to sit down and define your core values and your life purpose because it's these tools which ultimately decide how and what goals you choose for your life. Goals, in and of themselves, do not provide any happiness. Goals that are in harmony with our life purpose do have the power to make us happy.

Timed: Without setting deadlines for your goals, you have no real compelling reason or motivation to start working on them. By setting a deadline, your subconscious mind begins to work on that goal, night and day, to bring you closer to achievement.

Prioritizing Your Goals

Achieving challenging goals requires a lot of mental energy. Instead of spreading yourself thin by focusing on several goals at once, invest your mental focus on one goal, the most important goal right now. When you are prioritizing, choose a goal that will have the greatest impact on your life compared to how long it will take to achieve. A large part of goal setting is not just identifying what you want, but also identifying what you must give up in your life in order to get it. Most people are unwilling to make a conscious decision to give up the things in their life necessary to achieve their goals.

Visualization

Emotionalizing and visualizing your goal will help you create the desire to materialize it into your life. One of the best visualization tools is a vision board. Simply find a magazine, cut out pictures that resonate with the goal that you want to achieve, glue them onto a piece of poster board, and place that board somewhere that you can view it several times a day.

In order for visualization to work, it's necessary that you emotionalize your goal as much as possible. Create a list of the benefits you will see when you achieve your goal and concentrate on how that will make you feel.

Prioritizing Your Time

Time management is about more than just managing our time; it is about managing ourselves, in relation to time. It is about setting priorities and taking charge. It means changing habits or activities that cause us to waste time. It means being willing to experiment with different methods and ideas to enable you to find the best way to make maximum use of time.

The 80/20 Rule

The 80/20 rule, also known as Pareto's Principle, states that 80% of your results come from only 20% of your actions. Across the board, you will find that the 80/20 principle is pretty much right on with most things in your life. For most people, it really comes down to analyzing what you are spending your time on. Are you focusing in on the 20% of activities that produce 80% of the results in your life?

The Urgent/Important Matrix

Great time management means being effective as well as efficient. Managing time effectively, and achieving the things that you want to achieve, means spending your time on things that are important and not just urgent. To do this, you need to distinguish clearly between what is urgent and what is important:

- **Important**: These are activities that lead to achieving your goals and have the greatest impact on your life.

- **Urgent**: These activities demand immediate attention, but are often associated with someone else's goals rather than our own.

This concept, coined the Eisenhower Principle, is said to be how former US President Dwight Eisenhower organized his tasks. It was rediscovered and brought into the mainstream as the Urgent/Important Matrix by Stephen Covey in his 1994 business classic, The Seven Habits of Highly Effective People. The Urgent/Important Matrix is a powerful way of organizing tasks based on priorities. Using it helps you overcome the natural tendency to focus on urgent activities, so that you can have time to focus on what's truly important.

The Urgent/Important Matrix:

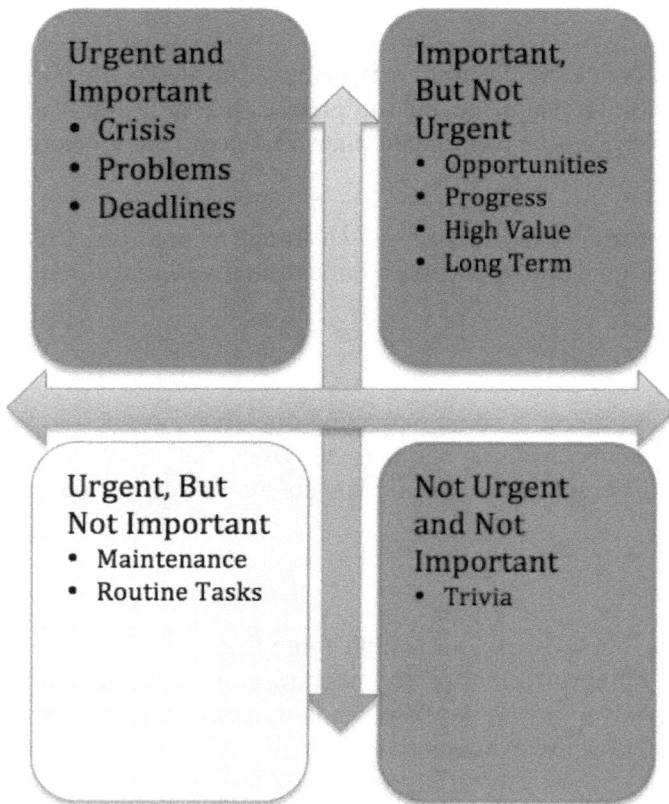

- **Urgent And Important**: Activities in this area relate to dealing with critical issues as they arise and meeting significant commitments. *Perform these duties now.*

- **Important, But Not Urgent:** These success-oriented tasks are critical to achieving goals. *Plan to do these tasks next.*

- **Urgent, But Not Important:** These chores do not move you forward toward your own goals. Manage by delaying them, cutting them short, and rejecting requests from others. *Postpone these chores.*

- **Not Urgent And Not Important:** These trivial interruptions are just a distraction, and should be avoided if possible. However, be careful not to mislabel things like time with family and recreational activities as not important. *Avoid these distractions altogether.*

Being Assertive

At times, requests from others may be important and need immediate attention. Often, however, these requests conflict with our values and take time away from working toward your goals. Even if it is something we would like to do but simply don't have the time for, it can be very difficult to say no. One approach in dealing with these types of interruptions is to use a Positive No, which comes in several forms.

- Say no, followed by an honest explanation, such as, "I am uncomfortable doing that because…"

- Say no and then briefly clarify your reasoning without making excuses. This helps the listener to better understand your position. Example: "I can't right now because I have another project that is due by 5 pm today."

- Say no, and then give an alternative. Example: "I don't have time today, but I could schedule it in for tomorrow morning."

- Empathetically repeat the request in your own words, and then say no. Example: "I understand that you need to have this paperwork filed immediately, but I will not be able to file it for you."

- Say yes, give your reasoning for not doing it, and provide an alternative solution. Example: "Yes, I would love to help you by filing this paperwork, but I do not have time until tomorrow morning."

- Provide an assertive refusal and repeat it no matter what the person says. This approach may be most appropriate with aggressive or manipulative people and can be an effective strategy to control your emotions. Example: "I understand how you feel, but I will not [or cannot]…" Remember to stay focused and not become sidetracked into responding to other issues.

Planning Wisely

The hallmark of successful time management is being consistently productive each day. Many people use a daily plan to motivate themselves. Having a daily plan and committing to it can help you stay focused on the priorities of that particular day. As well, you are more likely to get things accomplished if you write down your plans for the day.

Creating Your Productivity Journal

Essentially, planning is nothing more than taking a piece of paper and a pen and writing down the tasks and associated steps that you need to take throughout the day to ensure that your goal is completed.

To start, get yourself a spiral notebook and label it as your Personal Productivity Journal or your Professional Productivity Journal. (We recommend keeping a separate journal for work and for your personal life, so you can focus on them at separate times, thus maintaining your optimal work/life balance.) Label each page with the day and the date and what needs to be done that particular day. Next, prioritize each task in order of importance. Highlight the top three items and focus on those first. Cross off items as you complete them. Items that are not completed should be carried over to the next page.

Maximizing the Power of Your Productivity Journal

Personal development expert Brian Tracy believes that when you write down your action list the night before, your subconscious mind focuses on that plan while you sleep. By planning the night before, you will also start fresh and focused on the most important tasks for the day. Of course, you will want to review your list in the morning, but you will have a head start on your day.

Always have your productivity journal with you during the day to avoid becoming sidetracked. Crossing off completed tasks will give your subconscious mind a tremendous amount of satisfaction. This will also help to maintain your motivation to complete the remaining items on your action list.

If you find yourself moving uncompleted tasks over into the following day, and the day after that, then you need to ask yourself why that task is on your list in the first place and what value it has in your life. If you postpone a task three times, it does not belong on your action list.

The Glass Jar: Rocks, Pebbles, Sand, and Water

There is a story about time management that uses a glass jar, rocks, stones, pebbles, sand, and water to illustrate how to plan your day. The glass jar represents the time you have each day, and each item that goes into it represents an activity with a priority relative to its size.

Rocks: The general idea is to fill your glass jar first with rocks. Plan each day around your most important tasks that will propel you toward achieving your goals. These represent your highest priority projects and deadlines with the greatest value, often *important, but not urgent* tasks that move you toward your goals.

Pebbles: Next, fill in the space between the rocks with pebbles. These represent tasks that are *urgent, and important*, but contribute less to important goals. Without proper planning, these tasks are often unexpected, and left unmanaged, can quickly fill your day. Working to reduce these tasks will give you more time to work toward your goals.

Sand: Now add sand to fill your jar. In other words, schedule *urgent, but not important* tasks, only after important tasks. These activities are usually routine or maintenance tasks that do not directly contribute to your goals.

Water: Finally, pour water into your jar. These trivial time-wasters are neither important nor urgent and take you away from working toward high return activities and your goals.

If you commit to this approach to planning your days, you will see as time goes on that you are able to achieve more in less time. Instead of finishing things in a mad rush to meet deadlines, each day will be organized and become more productive and profitable. You will also notice yourself spending less time on activities that are of little to no value. And because you have a clear vision for dealing with competing priorities, the level of stress in your life will diminish, which will allow you to become even more focused and productive.

Chunk, Block, and Tackle

Large projects can sometimes be so overwhelming it is difficult to even plan to start them. This time management technique is ideal for taking on these jobs. Simply break down the project into manageable chunks, block off time to work on the project, and then tackle it with a single-minded focus.

- **Chunk**: Break large projects into specific tasks that can be completed in less than 15 minutes.

- **Block:** Rather than scheduling the entire project all at once, block out set times to complete specific chunks as early in the day as possible. This should allow you to ignore most interruptions and focus on just this task.

- **Tackle**: Now tackle the specific task, focusing only on this task rather than the project as a whole. Once completed, you will feel a sense of accomplishment from making progress on the project.

Ready, Fire, Aim!

We've all heard the saying, "Ready, Aim, Fire!" Often in time management planning, it is better to think "Ready, Fire, Aim!" instead. This is because most people aim for the target, and then they keep aiming at the target, but they never seem to fire. They get so caught up with the planning that they fail to take action. This is just another form of procrastination, which we will discuss in a moment. Better to take a shot and see how close you were to the target.

- **Ready**! Do not over-plan each of your actions. By the time you fire, the target may have moved.

- **Fire**! Remember the 80/20 rule and just take action. Even if you don't hit the bull's eye, you'll probably still hit the target.

- **Aim!** Make new plans based on new information. Readjust your aim based on where you hit the target.

Tackling Procrastination

Procrastination means delaying a task (or even several tasks) that should be a priority. The ability to overcome procrastination and tackle the important actions that have the biggest positive impact in your life is a hallmark of the most successful people out there.

Why We Procrastinate

There are many reasons why we tend to procrastinate, including:

- No clear deadline

- Inadequate resources available (time, money, information, etc.)

- Don't know where to begin

- Task feels overwhelming

- No passion for doing the work

- Fear of failure or success

Nine Ways to Overcome Procrastination

Your ability to select your most important task at any given moment, and then to start on that task and get it done both quickly and well, will probably have greatest impact on your success than any other quality or skill you can develop! If you nurture the habit of setting clear priorities and getting important tasks quickly finished, the majority of your time management issues will simply fade away.

Here are some ways to get moving on those tough tasks.

- **Delete it**. What are the consequences of not doing the task at all? Consider the 80/20 rule; maybe it doesn't need to be done in the first place.

- **Delegate**. If the task is important, ask yourself if it's really something that you are responsible for doing in the first place. Know your job description and ask if the task is part of your responsibilities. Can the task be given to someone else?

- **Do it now**. Postponing an important task that needs to be done only creates feelings of anxiety and stress. Do it as early in the day as you can.

Ask for advice. Asking for help from a trusted mentor, supervisor, coach, or expert can give you some great insight on where to start and the steps for completing a project.

CHOP IT UP. Break large projects into milestones, and then into actionable steps. As Bob Proctor says, "Break it down into the ridiculous." Huge things don't look as big when you break it down as small as you can.

- **Obey the 15 minute rule**. To reduce the temptation of procrastination, each actionable step on a project should take no more than 15 minutes to complete.

- **Have clear deadlines**. Assign yourself a deadline for projects and milestones and write it down in your day planner or calendar. Make your deadlines known to other people who will hold you accountable.

- **Give yourself a reward**. Celebrate the completion of project milestones and reward yourself for getting projects done on time. It will provide positive reinforcement and motivate you toward your goals.

- **Remove distractions**. You need to establish a positive working environment that is conducive to getting your work done. Remove any distractions.

Eat That Frog!

"If the first thing you do each morning is to eat a live frog, you can go through the day with the satisfaction of knowing that that is probably the worst thing that is going to happen to you all day long!"

Your frog is the task that will have the greatest impact on achieving your goals, and the task that you are most likely to procrastinate starting.

Another version of this saying is, "If you have to eat two frogs, eat the ugliest one first!"

This is another way of saying that if you have two important tasks before you, start with the biggest, hardest, and most important task first. Discipline yourself to begin immediately and then to persist until the task is complete before you go on to something else. You must resist the temptation to start with the easier task. You must also continually remind yourself that one of the most important decisions you make each day is your choice of what you will do immediately and what you will do later, or postpone indefinitely.

Finally, "If you have to eat a live frog, it does not pay to sit and look at it for a very long time!"

The key to reaching high levels of performance and productivity is for you to develop the lifelong habit of tackling your major task first thing each morning. Don't spend excessive time planning what you will do. You must develop the routine of "eating your frog" before you do anything else and without taking too much time to think about it.

Successful, effective people are those who launch directly into their major tasks and then discipline themselves to work steadily and single-mindedly until those tasks are complete.

In the business world, you are paid and promoted for achieving specific, measurable results. You are paid for making a valuable contribution that is expected of you. But many employees confuse activity with accomplishment and this causes one of the biggest problems in organizations today, which is failure to execute.

Crisis Management

With better planning, improved efficiency, and increased productivity, the number of crises you encounter should decline. However, you can't plan for everything, so in this module we'll look at what to do when a crisis does occur.

When the Storm Hits

The key to successfully handling a crisis is to move quickly and decisively, but carefully.

The first thing to do when a crisis hits is to identify the point of contact and make them aware of the situation. (For this module, we'll assume that point of contact is you.)

Then, you will want to gather and analyze the data.

- What happened?

- What were the direct causes? What were the indirect causes?

- What will happen next? What could happen next?

- What events will this impact?

- Who else needs to know about this?

Above all, take the time to do thorough, proper research. You don't want to jump into action based on erroneous information and make the crisis worse.

You will also want to identify the threshold time: the time that you have before the situation moves out of your control, or becomes exponentially worse. You may also find that the crisis will resolve itself after a certain point of time.

Creating a Plan

Once you have gathered the data, it's time to create a plan. The best approach is to identify the problem, decide on a solution, break it down into parts, and create a timeline.

Below is a sample Action Plan for Quarter One Status Report.

Executing the Plan

As you execute the plan, make sure that you continue evaluating if the plan is working. In the example we just looked at, perhaps after gathering project information, you realize you need more details on a particular item. It would then be appropriate to add that step and make sure you are still on track to meet your timeline.

During execution, it is important to stay organized and on top of events to make sure that your plan is still applicable. This will also help you deliver accurate, effective communication to others affected by the crisis. (In this example, your manager is probably pretty anxious to get that report!)

Lessons Learned

After the crisis is over, take a moment to look at why it happened and how to prevent it in the future. In the example we used, our Quarter One Status Report was not completed on time. (In fact, it sounds like we forgot to start it altogether!) The planning and prioritizing tools that we are discussing in this workshop should help prevent those kinds of emergencies. However, you will likely find that you're always adjusting and perfecting your approach, so it is important to learn from the times where those tools don't work.

You can even be prepared for disasters that can't be predicted, such as illness, fire, or theft. In the case of illness, for example, you could prepare a short contingency plan indicating who will be responsible for your correspondence, projects, and general responsibilities in case you are ill for an extended period. Make sure you share these plans with the appropriate people so that they can be prepared as well.

Organizing Your Workspace

In order to effectively manage your time and to be productive each day, you must create an appropriate environment. By eliminating clutter, setting up an effective filing system, gathering essential tools, and managing workflow, you will be well on your way to creating an effective workspace.

De-Clutter

Removing clutter is itself a time-consuming task, but a cluttered workspace significantly impairs your ability to find things, and you will get the time back that you invest – and more! To retrieve materials quickly, you'll need an effective filing system that includes three basic kinds of files:

- **Working files**: Materials used frequently and needed close at hand.

- **Reference files**: Information needed only occasionally.

- **Archival files:** Materials seldom retrieved but that must be kept. For ease of retrieval, organize files in the simplest way possible. For example, you could label files with a one or two word tag and arrange the files alphabetically.

Once clutter has been eliminated and other materials have been filed, the effective workspace includes only what is essential: a set of three trays to control the workflow on your desk (see the next topic), standard office supplies, a computer, and a telephone. Everything else, except for what you are working on at the moment, can and should be filed where it can be retrieved as needed.

Managing Workflow

How do you process the mountain of material that collects in your paper and electronic in-baskets? The answer is one piece of paper, one electronic message at a time. Many time management experts agree that the most effective people act on an item the first time it is touched.

Although difficult at first, the practice can become habitual, and is made easier with the four Ds:

- **DO**: If a task can be completed in two minutes or less, do it immediately.

- **DELETE**: If the material is trash or junk, delete it. Or, if it's something that you might use later on, file it, and move on.

- **DEFER**: If the task is one that can't be completed quickly and is not a high priority item, simply defer it.

- **DELEGATE**: If a task is not yours to do, then delegate it.

Remember, to take the S.T.I.N.G. out of feeling overwhelmed about a task, follow these steps:

- Select one task to do at a time.

- Time yourself using a clock for no more than one hour.

- Ignore everything else during that time.

- No breaks or interruptions should be permitted.

- Give yourself a reward when the time is up.

Dealing with E-mail

Electronic communication can be managed just as easily and as quickly as paper with the four D's that we just discussed. However, there are some other key ideas that will help you maximize your e-mail time.

- Like other routine tasks (such as returning phone calls, handling paper mail, and checking voice mail), e-mail is best handled in batches at regularly scheduled times of the day.

- Ask your e-mail contacts to use specific subject lines, and make sure to use them yourself. This will help you to determine whether your incoming mail is business or personal, urgent or trivial.

- Once you know the subject of the message, open and read urgent e-mails, and respond accordingly. Non-urgent e-mails, like jokes, can be read later. Delete advertising-related e-mail that you have no interest in, or which you consider spam.

- Use your e-mail system to its fullest potential. Create folders for different topics or projects, or by senders. Most e-mail systems also allow you to create folders and add keywords or categories to messages, which makes information retrieval much easier.

- Many e-mail programs allow you to create rules that automatically move messages to the appropriate folder. This can help you follow your e-mail plan.

- Finally, don't forget to delete e-mail from your trash can and junk folder on a regular basis.

Using Calendars

To manage all of the things that you have to do, it's important to organize your reminders into a small number of calendars and lists that can be reviewed regularly. A calendar (paper or electronic) is the obvious place to record meetings, appointments, and due dates.

People with multiple responsibilities, an annual calendar organized by areas of responsibility (e.g., budget, personnel, schedule, planning, and miscellaneous) may be especially valuable. For each of these areas, one can list the major responsibilities month by month and thereby see at a glance what tasks must be completed in a given month of the year.

Don't forget the Productivity Journal that we discussed earlier. This can be a valuable tool for organizing tasks, identifying patterns, improving workflow, and recording work completed.

Delegating Made Easy

If you work on your own, there's only so much you can get done, no matter how hard you work. As well, everyone needs help and support, and there is no shame in asking for assistance. One of the most common ways of overcoming this limitation is to learn how to delegate your work to other people. If you do this well, you can quickly build a strong and successful team of people.

At first sight, delegation can feel like more hassle than it's worth. However, by delegating effectively, you can hugely expand the amount of work that you can deliver. When you arrange the workload so that you are working on the tasks that have the highest priority for you, and other people are working on meaningful and challenging assignments, you have a recipe for success.

Remember, to delegate effectively, choose the right tasks to delegate, identify the right people to delegate to, and delegate in the right way. There's a lot to this, but you'll achieve so much more once you're delegating effectively!

When to Delegate

Delegation allows you to make the best use of your time and skills, and it helps other people in the team grow and develop to reach their full potential in the organization. Delegation is a win-win situation for all involved, but only when done correctly. Keep these criteria in mind when deciding if a task should be delegated:

- The task should provide an opportunity for growth of another person's skills.

- Weigh the effort to properly train another person against how often the task will reoccur.

- Delegating certain critical tasks may jeopardize the success of your project.

- Management tasks, such as performance reviews, and tasks specifically assigned to you, should not be delegated.

To Whom Should You Delegate?

Once you have decided to delegate a task, think about the possible candidates for accepting the task. Things to think about include:

- What experience, knowledge, skills, and attitude does the person already have?

- What training or assistance might they need?

- Do you have the time and resources to provide any training needed?

- What is the individual's preferred work style? Do they do well on their own or do they require more support and motivation? How independent are they?

- What does he or she want from his or her job?

- What are his or her long-term goals and interest, and how do these align with the work proposed?

- What is the current workload of this person? Does the person have time to take on more work?

- Will you delegating this task require reshuffling of other responsibilities and workloads?

When you first start to delegate to someone, you may notice that he or she takes longer than you do to complete tasks. This is because you are an expert in the field and the person you have delegated to is still learning. Be patient: if you have chosen the right person to delegate to, and you are delegating correctly, you will find that he or she quickly becomes competent and reliable. Also, try to delegate to the lowest possible organizational level. The people who are closest to the work are best suited for the task because they have the most intimate knowledge of the detail of everyday work. This also increases workplace efficiency, and helps to develop people.

How Should You Delegate?

Delegation doesn't have to be all or nothing. There are several different levels of delegation, each with different levels of delegate independence and delegator supervision.

The Spheres of Independence

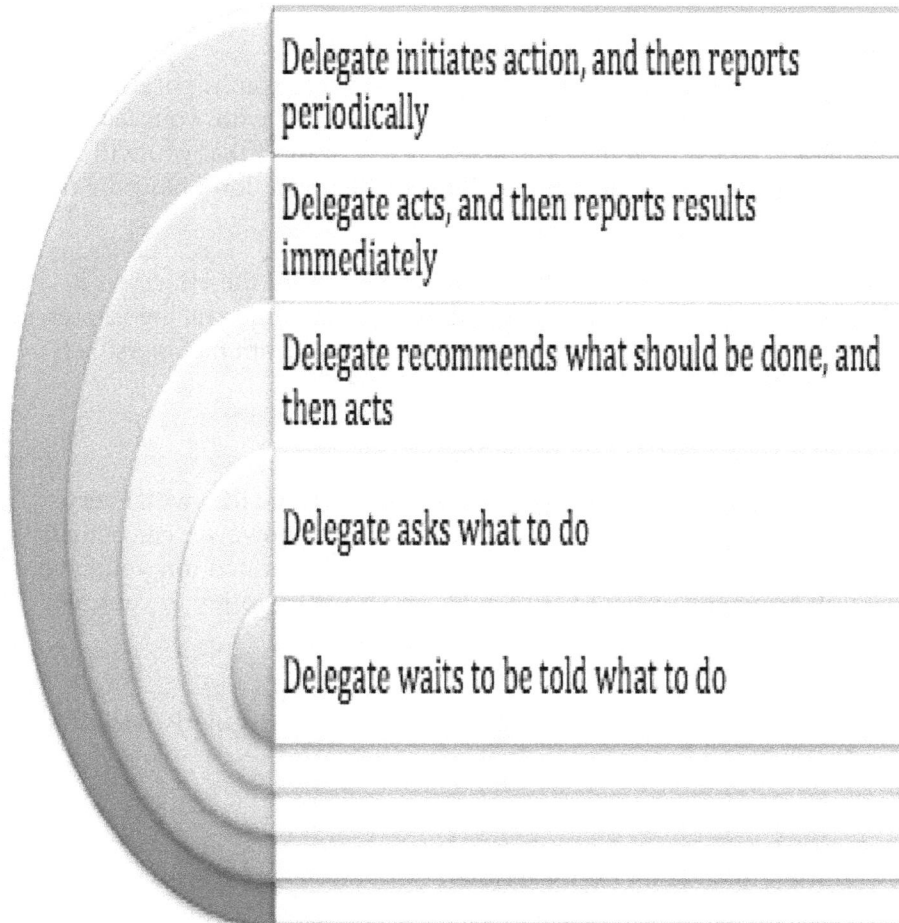

Delegate initiates action, and then reports periodically
Delegate acts, and then reports results immediately
Delegate recommends what should be done, and then acts
Delegate asks what to do
Delegate waits to be told what to do

People often move throughout these spheres during the delegation process. Your goal should be to get the delegate to one of the outer three spheres, depending on the task being performed. Make sure you match the amount of responsibility with the amount of authority. Understand that you can delegate some responsibility, but you can't delegate away ultimate accountability. The buck stops with you!

Keeping Control

Now, once you have worked through the above steps, make sure you brief your team member appropriately. Take time to explain why they were chosen for the job, what's expected from them during the project, the goals you have for the project, all timelines and deadlines, and the resources on which they can draw. Work together to develop a schedule for progress updates, milestones, and other key project points.

You will want to make sure that the team member knows that you want to know if any problems occur, and that you are available for any questions or guidance needed as the work progresses.

We all know that as managers, we shouldn't micro-manage. However, this doesn't mean we must abdicate control altogether. In delegating effectively, we have to find the difficult balance between giving enough space for people to use their abilities, while still monitoring and supporting closely enough to ensure that the job is done correctly and effectively. One way to encourage growth is to ask for recommended solutions when delegates come to you with a problem, and then help them explore those solutions and reach a decision.

The Importance of Full Acceptance

Set aside enough time to thoroughly review any delegated work that was delivered to you. If possible, only accept good quality, fully complete work. If you accept work that you are not satisfied with, your team member does not learn to do the job properly. Worse than this, you accept a new project that you will probably need to complete yourself. Not only does this overload you, it means that you don't have the time to do your own job properly.

Of course, when good work is returned to you, make sure to both recognize and reward the effort. As a leader, you should get in the practice of complimenting members of your team every time you are impressed by what they have done. This effort on your part will go a long way toward building team members' self-confidence and efficiency now and in the future.

Setting a Ritual

For most people, the word "ritual" typically conjures up an image of a boring, repetitive life, with every moment controlled and managed, and no room for spontaneity. Rituals and routines, however, can actually help increase the spontaneity and fun in your life. Because routine tasks are already planned for, you have more energy to spend on the tasks that will bring you closer to your goals and bring more joy to your life.

What is a Ritual?

The Random House Dictionary defines a ritual as, "any practice or pattern of behavior regularly performed in a set manner."

In fact, you can build any type of ritual in three easy steps.

- **Identify the Task.** Let's say you want to build an exercise ritual.

- **Identify the Time and/or Trigger.** For example, perhaps you normally exercise right after work.

- **Identify the Sub-Tasks.** For you, perhaps your ritual involves going to the gym, getting changed, stretching, doing 45 minutes on the treadmill, performing three reps of weights, and doing a lap around the pool to finish things off. Then, you shower and go home.

Remember, a ritual shouldn't be set in stone. Once you establish a ritual, it can be modified at any point in time, depending on what works for you. With our exercise example, you could easily decide to exercise before work or even at lunch and still use the basic task and sub-tasks.

Ritualizing Sleep, Meals, and Exercise

These three items are essential to ritualize. Here are some ideas.

- **Sleep:** Establish a ritual for half an hour before you sleep. This might include filling out your Productivity Journal for the next day, enjoying a cup of tea, taking a warm bath, and/or performing some stretches. All of these activities will help you wind down and sleep better. It is best to try to go to bed at around the same time every night, too.

- **Meals:** Take a half hour each weekend to plan meals for the next week, including lunches and suppers. Then, make a grocery list and get everything you will need. Appliances like slow cookers and delayed-start ovens can also help you make sure supper is ready when you are.

- **Exercise:** Try to exercise for one hour three times a week, or half an hour each day. One easy way is to go for a brisk walk at lunch, or do yoga in the morning before work.

Example Rituals

Here are some rituals that many people find helpful in maximizing their time:

- Instead of checking e-mail, news, and Web sites throughout the day, set aside one or several periods (for example, morning, noon, and at the end of the day). Then, batch and sequence your activities (for example, e-mail, news, and Facebook). You can batch many types of tasks in this way for maximum efficiency.

- Set up a system for maintaining your Productivity Journal. This can be as simple as ten minutes in the morning to update the day's list, ten minutes at noon to update what you have done already, and ten minutes at day's end to evaluate today and create a starting list for tomorrow.

- In the morning, perform your tasks in an organized, routine manner. You can also lay out your clothes and prepare your lunch the night before for maximum efficiency.

Using Rituals to Maximize Time

Once you have been using a ritual for a while, you may find that you have bits of extra time here and there. For example, you may find that by establishing an exercise ritual, you finish five or ten minutes earlier because you know exactly what you're going to do at the gym. At the end of the day, you may find that you have a half hour or more of unexpected time.

This is where the "Trigger" part of rituals can come into play. Instead of setting a specific time of day, you choose a situation or an event that will cause a ritual to come into play.

Some examples:

- During a break at work or at home, read for ten minutes.

- Take one minute to do some deep breathing and stretches.

- Take five minutes to clean off your desk or some other small area.

- Take ten minutes to update your Personal Productivity Journal.

- Set aside one lunch hour a week to do personal errands. Or, make a list at the beginning of each week, and do one a day.

Meeting Management

Meetings are often seen as a necessary evil of office life. Few people look forward to meetings, and with good reason. Too many meetings lack purpose and structure. However, with just a few tools, you can make any meeting a much better use of everyone's time.

Deciding if a Meeting is Necessary

The first thing you need to decide is if a formal meeting is necessary. Perhaps those morning staff meetings could be reduced to a few times a week instead of every day, or maybe they could take place over morning coffee and be more informal. (In the next module, we'll talk about some alternatives to meetings, too.)

If a formal meeting is necessary, divide your attendees into two groups: participants and observers. Let people know what group they belong in so that they can decide whether they want to attend. If you send out a report after the meeting, that may be enough for some people.

Using the PAT Approach

We use the PAT approach to prepare for and schedule meetings.

- **Purpose:** What is the purpose of the meeting? We usually state this in one short sentence. Example: "This meeting is to review the new invoice signing policy." This helps people evaluate if they need to be there. It will also help you build the agenda and determine if the meeting was successful.

- **Agenda:** This is the backbone of the meeting. It should be created well in advance of the meeting, sent to all participants and observers, and be used during the meeting to keep things on track.

- **Time frame:** How long will the meeting be? Typically, meetings should not exceed one hour. (In fact, we recommend a fifty minute meeting, starting at five past the hour and ending five minutes before the hour.) If the meeting needs to be longer, make sure you include breaks, or divide it into two or more sessions.

Building the Agenda

Before the meeting, make a list of what needs to be discussed, how long you believe it will take, and the person who will be presenting the item. Here is an example.

Once the agenda is complete, send it to all participants and observers, preferably with the meeting request, and preferably two to three days before the meeting. Make sure you ask for everyone's approval, including additions or deletions. If you do make changes, send out a single updated copy 24 hours before the meeting.

Keeping Things on Track

Before the meeting, post the agenda on a flip chart, whiteboard, or PowerPoint slide. Spend the first five minutes of the meeting going over the agenda and getting approval. During the meeting, take minutes with the agenda as a framework.

(Although this informal structure will be sufficient for most meetings, more formal meetings may require more formal minutes.)

Your job as chairperson is to keep the meeting running according to the agenda. If an item runs past its scheduled time, ask the group if they think more time is needed to discuss the item. If so, how do they want to handle it? They can reduce the time for other items, remove other items altogether, schedule an offline follow-up session, or schedule another meeting. No matter what the group agrees to, make sure that they stick to their decision.

At the end of the meeting, get agreement that all items on the agenda were sufficiently covered. This will identify any gaps that may require follow-up and it will give people a positive sense of accomplishment about the meeting.

Making Sure the Meeting Was Worthwhile

After the meeting, send out a summary of the meeting, including action items, to all participants and observers, and anyone else who requires a copy. Action items should be clearly indicated, with start and end dates, and progress dates if applicable. If follow-up meetings were scheduled, these should also be communicated.

Alternatives to Meetings

Sometimes, a face-to-face meeting isn't the best solution. In this module, we will explore alternatives to meetings that can help you and your team save time and be more productive.

Don't forget that even if you use a meeting alternative, you should still use the PAT approach that we discussed in the last module, take minutes, and distribute post-meeting notes and action items.

Instant Messaging and Chat Rooms

Instant message applications and chat rooms can be a great alternative to meetings, especially if meeting members are separated by distance.

Some things to remember:

- Make sure you have an agenda and stick to it.

- The chairperson's role in keeping things on track is more important than ever.

- Set some ground rules at the beginning of the meeting to eliminate distractions such as emoticons, sounds, and acronyms.

- Make sure you keep a record of the meeting.

Some applications to try:

- Campfire

- Meeting Pal

- Microsoft Office Communicator

- Windows Live Messenger

Teleconferencing

If more personal contact and real-time sharing is needed, try a teleconferencing system like Adobe's Acrobat.com, Microsoft Live Meeting, or Citrix's GoToMeeting.

Most teleconferencing applications feature:

- Screen sharing

- Collaboration tools

- Interactive whiteboards

- Voice and text chat support

- Meeting recording capabilities (which can serve as minutes)

Again, remember the PAT approach, and remember to keep minutes and action lists.

E-Mail Lists and Online Groups

If your meeting group requires ongoing, interactive communication, rather than periodic face-to-face gatherings, an e-mail list, forum, or online group can be an effective tool.

There are a few options for these online tools. If your organization has the infrastructure in place, you may be able to set up something on site. If your organization doesn't have such an infrastructure, there are many free tools out there, including Google Groups, Yahoo Groups, and Convos.

A few things to keep in mind if you are going to use this sort of solution:

- Having a moderator is essential. These types of tools can quickly get out of control without proper supervision. You'll want to make sure members stay on topic and stay professional.

- Make sure you monitor the time spent on these tools. Setting a daily or weekly update or delivery time might be a good idea.

- Just like a meeting, an online list or group should have a purpose and stick to it.

Collaboration Applications

A more sophisticated electronic tool that can reduce the need for meetings is collaboration applications. Systems like Microsoft SharePoint, Wrike, Pelotonics, Google Docs, and Basecamp can give users interaction and collaboration tools from any location.

These sorts of tools may be most beneficial for project meetings, or situations where users need to peer review each other's work.

Once again, these tools must have their purpose clearly stated, and participants must make sure that these time-saving tools don't turn into time wasters.

Chapter 30 – Team Work and Team Building

For most of us, teamwork is a part of everyday life. Whether it's at home, in the community, or at work, we are often expected to be a functional part of a performing team. This workshop will encourage participants to explore the different aspects of a team, as well as ways that they can become a top-notch team performer.

By the end of this chapter, you should be able to:

- Describe the concept of a team, and its factors for success

- Explain the four phases of the Tuckman team development model and define their characteristics

- List the three types of teams

- Describe actions to take as a leader – and as a follower for each of the four phases (Forming, Storming, Norming and Performing)

- Discuss the uses, benefits and disadvantages of various team-building activities

- Describe several team-building activities that you can use, and in what settings

- Follow strategies for setting and leading team meetings

- Detail problem-solving strategies using the Six Thinking Hats model -- and one consensus-building approach to solving team problems

- List actions to do -- and those to avoid -- when encouraging teamwork

Action Plans and Evaluation Forms

During this course, you will be adding ideas to your personal action plan. The plan uses the SMART system. This means that your goals must be **S**pecific, **M**easurable, **A**ttainable, **R**ealistic, and **T**imely.

Add information throughout the day as you learn new things and have ideas about how to incorporate the concepts being discussed into your work or personal lives.

Defining Success

Success is determined by a wide range of factors. When we are given a project or an assignment we are also usually given a metric to which we can gauge the success of it. Having a strong team will benefit any organization and will lead to more successes than not.

What is a Team?

A team is a group of people formed to achieve a goal. Teams can be temporary, or indefinite. With individuals sharing responsibility, the group as a whole can take advantage of all of the collective talent, knowledge, and experience of each team member.

Team building is an organized effort to improve team effectiveness.

An Overview of Tuckman and Jensen's Four-Phase Model

Educational psychologist Bruce Wayne Tuckman, Ph.D. was charged by his boss at the Naval Medical Research Institute, Bethesda MD with a review of 50 articles about team behavior. From this body of work, Dr. Tuckman conceived his theory of group developmental processes in 1965.

The Forming Stage: Groups initially concern themselves with orientation accomplished primarily through testing. Such testing serves to identify the boundaries of both interpersonal and task behaviors. Coincident with testing in the interpersonal realm is the establishment of dependency relationships with leaders, other group members, or preexisting standards. It may be said that orientation, testing, and dependence constitute the group process of forming.

The Storming Stage: The second point in the sequence is characterized by conflict and polarization around interpersonal issues, with concomitant emotional responding in the task sphere. These behaviors serve as resistance to group influence and task requirements and may be labeled as storming.

The Norming Stage: Resistance is overcome in the third stage in which in-group feeling and cohesiveness develop, new standards evolve, and new roles are adopted. In the task realm, intimate, personal opinions are expressed. Thus, we have the stage of norming.

The Performing Stage: Finally, the group attains the fourth and final stage in which interpersonal structure becomes the tool of task activities. Roles become flexible and functional, and group energy is channeled into the task. Structural issues have been resolved, and structure can now become supportive of task performance. This stage can be labeled as performing.

In 1977 Dr. Tuckman, collaborating with Mary Ann Jensen, proposed an update to the model, termed Adjourning. It describes the process for terminating group roles, task completion, and the reduction of dependencies. This stage has also been called "mourning", especially if the team's dissolution is unplanned. The first four stages are the most commonly used parts of the process.*

Smith, M. K. (2005) 'Bruce W. Tuckman - forming, storming, norming and performing in groups, the encyclopedia of informal education, www.infed.org/thinkers/tuckman.htm. © Mark K. Smith 2005

Types of Teams

The Merriam Webster Dictionary defines a team as a number of persons associated together in work or activity. Teams are formed for many purposes. Examples include project teams, ad-hoc teams, quality improvement teams, and task forces. Sometimes the team is formed to work on a goal as an adjunct to a traditional hierarchy in an organization. At other times, the team is designed to replace the hierarchy.

Several roles help to keep a team operating smoothly.

Role	Responsibilities
Team Leader	<ul><li>Moves the team to accomplish its task</li><li>Provides a conducive environment for getting the work done (location, resources)</li><li>Communicates with the team</li></ul>
Team Facilitator	<ul><li>Makes things happen with ease</li><li>Helps the group with the process</li><li>Enables the group to produce the "how" decisions</li></ul>Note: Facilitators may be members or non-members of the team.
Team Recorder	<ul><li>Writes down the team's key points, ideas and decisions</li><li>Documents the team's process, discussions, and decisions</li></ul>

Time Keeper	• Monitors how long the team is taking to accomplish its tasks
	• Provides regular updates to the team on how well or poorly they are using their time
	• Collaborates with the team leader, facilitator and others to determine new time schedules if the agenda has to be adjusted
Team Members	• Displays enthusiasm and commitment to the team's purpose
	• Behaves honestly; maintain confidential information behind closed doors
	• Shares responsibility to rotate through other team roles
	• Shares knowledge and expertise and not withhold information
	• Asks questions
	• Respects the opinions and positions of others on the team, even if the person has an opposing view or different opinion

The Traditional Team

There are several characteristics common to traditional teams.

- A team gains a shared understanding and purpose among team members, as distinguished from a group.

- Teams require mutually agreed-upon operating principles such as agendas, procedures, and decision-making processes.

- A team is interdependent; everyone works for the good of the team, not for oneself.

- Effective teams distinguish task from process. How they do things (the process) is just as important, if not more important, than what they do (the task).

Self-Directed Teams

A self-directed team is a team that is responsible for a whole product or process. The team plans the work and performs it, managing many of the tasks supervision or management might have done in the past. A facilitator (selected by the team or an outside individual) helps the group get started and stay on track. The facilitator's role decreases as the team increases its ability to work together effectively.

E-Teams

An e-team is a group of individuals who work across space and organizational boundaries with links strengthened by webs of communication technology. Members have complementary skills and are committed to a common purpose, have interdependent performance goals, and share an approach to work for which they hold themselves mutually accountable.

Geographically dispersed teams allow organizations to hire and retain the best people regardless of location. An e-team does not always imply telecommuters, individuals who work from home. Many virtual teams in today's organizations consist of employees both working at home and in small groups in the office, but in different geographic locations.

The benefits of an e-team approach are:

- Workers can be located anywhere in the world

- Virtual environments can give shy participants a new voice

- Members have less commuting and travel time, so they tend to be more productive

- Companies gain an increasingly horizontal organization structure, characterized by structurally, and geographically distributed human resources.

There are a few caveats when using e-teams. They frequently operate from multiple time zones, so it is important to make sure that there is some overlapping work time. In addition, unless a camera is used for meetings, working virtually means that there is no face to face body language to enhance communications. Therefore, intra-team communications must be more formal than with a team whose members meet physically. Care also needs to be taken to make sure no one is left out of the communications loop just because he or she is not visible. E-teams demand a high trust culture.

The First Stage of Team Development – Forming

What makes up a good team? Well, that question is open to interpretation, but we will start with the first step in the team building process which is forming. We will discuss what makes up that stage and how each person in the team fits into the process.

Hallmarks of This Stage

When a new team forms, it concerns itself with becoming oriented. It does this through testing. It tests to discover the boundaries of interpersonal and task behavior. At the same time, the members are establishing dependency relationships with leaders, fellow team members, or any standards that existed when the group formed. The behaviors of orientation, testing, and dependence become the process called Forming.

Members behave independently when the team forms. While there may be good will towards fellow members, unconditional trust is not yet possible.

Work during the Forming stage is categorized as follows:

Tasks	Processes that occur
Introductions	Uncertainty
Coming together	Apprehension
First agenda	Excitement

What to Do As a Leader

Strong leadership skills are essential in the Forming stage. The leader must:

- Provide an environment for introductions

- Create a climate where participants can begin to build rapport

- Present a solid first agenda so that the goals for the team are clear.

What to Do As a Follower

Because the members of a new team may experience uncertainty and apprehension, it's important to help members feel comfortable and that they are a part of the group. In addition, helping team members enhance their listening skills will allow them to focus more clearly on the objectives, thereby helping to maintain interest and enthusiasm for the work of the team.

The Second Stage of Team Development – Storming

We will look at the Storming phase where the team focuses on their objective. This is the reason the team was created, and we will break down where the leaders and followers fit into this stage. Team members will now begin to fill certain rolls and the team is starting to come together.

The Hallmarks of This Stage

In the Storming phase, the team starts to address the objective(s), suggesting ideas. It empowers itself to share leadership. Different ideas may compete for consideration, and if badly managed, this phase can be very destructive for the team. Egos emerge and turf wars occur. In extreme cases, the team can become stuck in this phase.

If a team is too focused on consensus, they may decide on a plan which is less effective to complete the task for the sake of the team. This carries its own set of challenges. It is essential that a team has strong facilitative leadership during this phase.

What to Do As a Leader

Team conflict is normal in this phase, and is a catalyst for creativity. But the leader must address any conflict immediately and directly so issues don't fester. Once you understand two sides to an issue, you can help the team generate a win-win solution. Assertive communication is an important skill during this phase of the group's evolution. It is also important to help team members continue to build trust.

What to Do As a Follower

A mindmap is a diagram used to represent words, ideas, tasks, or other items linked to and arranged around a central key word or idea. Mind maps are used to generate, visualize, structure, and classify ideas, and as an aid in study, organization, problem solving, decision making, and writing.

The elements of a given mind map are arranged intuitively according to the importance of the concepts, and are classified into groupings, branches, or areas, with the goal of representing semantic or other connections between portions of information.

By presenting ideas in a radial, graphical, non-linear manner, mind maps encourage a brainstorming approach to planning and organizational tasks.

The Third Stage of Team Development – Norming

By now the team should be in place and everyone has their role with progress beginning on the objectives. Goals have been set and people are now beginning to work on their tasks.

The Hallmarks of This Stage

As the team moves out of the Storming phase, it enters the Norming phase. This tends to be a move towards harmonious working practices. Teams begin agreeing on the rules and values by which they operate. In the ideal situation, teams begin to trust themselves during this phase as they accept the vital contributions of each member toward achieving the team's goals.

What to Do As a Leader

As individual members take greater responsibility, team leaders can take a step back from the leadership role at this stage. It is an opportune time to provide team members with task and process tools, or even an energizer to keep enthusiasm levels high.

What to Do As a Follower

Because team members have gained some mutual trust, they are freer to focus on process and task. Being a link in a chain is a great way to visualize followers in this stage. If one link is not pulling its weight, or is not as strong as the other links the chance of success is lessened. Everyone needs to work together.

The Fourth Stage of Team Development – Performing

The team should now be well into their work and progress made on their objectives. Communication is going well and team members are sharing knowledge and working well together.

Hallmarks of this Stage

Once teams move from Norming to Performing, they are identified by high levels of independence, motivation, knowledge, and competence. Decision making is collaborative and dissent is expected and encouraged as there will be a high level of respect in the communication between team members.

What to Do As a Leader

Since the team is functioning in a highly independent way in the Performing phase, the leader shifts partially into a support and mentoring role to provide task or process resources to help the team complete its objectives.

What to Do As a Follower

Because the Performing stage implies high interpersonal trust, knowledge, and competence, participants can perform higher level analyses to support decisions toward team objectives.

A SWOT analysis (Strengths, Weaknesses, Opportunities, and Threats) is a simple tool that allows specific ideas to be easily categorized to help support the adoption of a solution to an objective.

Team Building Activities

Teambuilding is an organized effort to improve team effectiveness. All members of the team must be committed to the idea in order for the effort to be effective. Teambuilding can be indicated for any team or for a work team that is considered to be" in trouble". Teambuilding implies hard work that continues on after the initial training session.

The Benefits and Disadvantages

The Benefits:

- Team building improves productivity and motivation.

- Teams will gain and increase ability to solve problems.

- Team building helps break down personal and political barriers and allows for rapport building.

- The process can help level the playing field between outgoing and shy team members.

- Participating in team building can help teams overcome performance problems.

The Disadvantages:

- Team building requires expert facilitation in order to be successful. Not every team leader has innate facilitation skills.

- Activities can be time-consuming for teams with a short-term charter. And if team members are part-time, they may have conflicting feelings about the time the team building takes.

- If several levels of management are on the team, those members may be reluctant to open up.

- Conducting team building activities electronically or by conference cannot be as effective face-to-face sessions.

- Some team building exercises involve touching or physical movement, which can make some people uncomfortable.

Team-Building Activities That Won't Make People Cringe

There are many choices of activities and techniques to foster team building. Which you choose depends upon your assessment of the team, the skill sets of the members, the amount of available time, geographical considerations or constraints, and the team's objectives.

Choosing a Location for Team-Building

A team building session can be intense, and often involves games or other physical exercises. It's important, therefore to select the location carefully to promote the best possible learning outcome. Regardless of whether you hold your team building session on or off site, there are some important considerations to explore.

Making the Most of Team Meetings

They are extremely important in team building and facilitation. It is very important that they are well structured and have a set purpose and time. When a meeting is run well it is a fantastic tool as it provides a forum where a lot of information can be given to a lot of people in a short amount of time. Issues can be addressed and action plans set into play.

Setting the Time and the Place

Giving thought to time and place considerations for a team meeting can go a long way toward producing a more effective meeting outcome. Below are some elements to think about.

- Is the location convenient for participants?

- Quiet. Is the meeting going to be held in an open environment? Near the plant?

- Is this an e-team meeting? Or a meeting with members in remote locations or different time zones?

- What time of day is best?

- Are there time zone considerations for e-teams or remote participants?

- For what other interruptions and distractions can you anticipate and plan?

Trying the 50-Minute Meeting

In some companies, meetings are stacked up on the hour like planes in the landing pattern at O'Hare Airport. The 50-minute meeting concept is simple; instead of a full 60-minute meeting, why not give people time for a bio break, a fresh cup of coffee, and "commuting time" to the next meeting?

50-minute meetings also help manage:

- Overload of information that the mind can absorb at one time

- Wandering attention spans

- Potential health problems from sitting too long

You can't always have a 50 minute meeting, but if you're meeting will run several hours, you could have a connected series of 50 minute meetings. The extra 10 minutes in each hour -- set at a consistent clock time such as 50 minutes after the hour -- could allow for stretches, breaks, or a quick e-mail session.

Using Celebrations of All Sizes

The team just finished a ten-month project to implement SAP in a small manufacturing company. The project delivered on time, and under budget. It's time to celebrate! Celebrations can take many forms. A checklist of elements to consider can help you decide how best to say thanks.

Solving Problems as a Team

One of the most common objectives of a team is to solve a certain problem. It is usually why a team is created. Team members bring a diverse set of skills to the team and this provides a great scenario and the best chance in finding a solution. Because the team is comprised of individuals that bring a unique skill set, it provides the team with a "the whole is greater than its parts" setup which is a valuable tool.

The Six Thinking Hats

In 1999, Dr. Edward de Bono published a book entitled Six Thinking Hats. He theorizes that the human brain thinks in a number of distinct ways -- or states -- which can be identified, deliberately accessed, and therefore planned for use in a structured way, allowing team members to develop strategies for thinking about particular issues.

Six Thinking Hats is a powerful technique that helps teams look at important decisions from a number of different perspectives. It helps them make better decisions by pushing members to move outside their habitual ways of thinking. It helps them understand the full complexity of a decision, and identify issues and opportunities which they might not otherwise notice.

In order to make it easier to clearly identify and work with these states, colored hats are used as metaphors for them. The act of putting on a colored hat allows individuals to symbolically think in terms of the state, either actually or imaginatively.

White Hat: Neutrality: Participants make statements of fact, including identifying information that is absent -- and presenting the views of people who are not present -- in a factual manner. Examples of this the results of this thinking are:

Red Hat: Feeling: Participants state their feelings, exercising their gut instincts. In many cases this is a method for harvesting ideas; it is not a question of recording statements, but rather getting everyone to identify their top two or three choices from a list of ideas or items identified under another hat. This is done to help reducing lists of many options into a few to focus on by allowing each participant to vote for the ones they prefer. It is applied more quickly than the other hats to ensure it is a gut reaction feeling that is recorded. This method can use post-it notes to allow a quick system of voting, and creates a clear visual cue that creates rapid if incomplete agreement around an issue.

Alternatively it may be used to state ones gut reaction or feelings on an issue under discussion - this is more common when using the hats to review personal progress or deal with issues where there is high emotional content that is relevant to discussion. Finally, this hat can be used to request an aesthetic response to a particular design or object.

Black Hat: Negative Judgment: Participants identify barriers, hazards, risks, and other negative connotations. This is critical thinking, looking for problems and mismatches. This hat is usually natural for people to use, the issues with it are that people will tend to use it when it is not requested and when it is not appropriate, thus stopping the flow of others. Preventing inappropriate use of the black hat is a common obstacle and vital step to effective group thinking. Another difficulty faced is that some people will naturally start to look for the solutions to raised problems - they start practicing green on black thinking before it is requested.

Yellow hat – Positive Judgment: Participants identify benefits associated with an idea or issue. This is the opposite of black hat thinking and looks for the reasons in favor of something. This is still a matter of judgment; it is an analytical process, not just blind optimism. One is looking to create justified statements in favor. It is encapsulated in the idea of "undecided positive" (whereas the black hat would be skeptical - undecided negative). The outputs may be statements of the benefits that could be created with a given idea, or positive statements about the likelihood of achieving it or identifying the key supports available that will benefit this course of action

Green Hat: Creative Thinking: This is the hat of thinking new thoughts. It is based around the idea of provocation and thinking for the sake of identifying new possibilities. Things are said for the sake of seeing what they might mean, rather than to form a judgment. This is often carried out on black hat statements in order to identify how to get past the barriers or failings identified there (green on black thinking). Because green hat thinking covers the full spectrum of creativity, it can take many forms.

Blue Hat: The Big Picture: This is the hat under which all participants discuss the thinking process. The facilitator will generally wear it throughout and each member of the team will put it on from time to time to think about directing their work together. This hat should be used at the start and end of each thinking session, to set objectives, to define the route to take to get to them, to evaluate where the group has got to, and where the thinking process is going. Having a facilitator maintain this role throughout helps ensure that the group remains focused on task and improves their chances of achieving their objectives.

Encouraging Brainstorming

Brainstorms are a simple and effective method for generating ideas and suggestions. They allow group members to use each other as creative resources and are effective when a subject is being introduced. The goal is to rapidly generate a large quantity of ideas. Subsequent sorting and prioritizing of the ideas is usually needed to refine the results.

Building Consensus

Consensus is a point of maximum agreement so action can follow. It is a win-win situation in which everyone feels that he or she has one solution that does not compromise any strong convictions or needs. To reach consensus, group members share ideas, discuss, evaluate, organize, and prioritize ideas, and struggle to reach the best conclusions together.

A good test for consensus is to ask the question "can you support this decision?" If everyone can support it, the group has achieved 100% consensus.

Consensus is not always the best strategy. In some cases, reaching consensus does not result in a better decision or outcome. For example, group members are capable of unanimously agreeing on a completely incorrect solution to a problem. But generally, reaching consensus remains a highly desirable goal.

To make consensus work, the leader must become skilled at separating the content of the team's work (the task) from the process (how the team goes about doing the task). But the process should get the most attention. A facilitative leader helps a team to solve its own problem. The problem-solving process is as follows:

1. Identify the problem or goal.

2. Generate alternative solutions.

3. Establish objective criteria.

4. Decide on a solution that best fits the criteria.

5. Proceed with the solution.

6. Evaluate the solution.

Everyone involved in the process should understand exactly which step is being worked on at any given point. When team members sense a problem, they are usually reacting to symptoms of the problem. But they are side effects of the real problem which usually lies below the surface.

Encouraging Teamwork

For every team member that believes and works for the team the chances of success go up exponentially. That is the reason why it is so important in teamwork and team building, as it provides the greats chance of success.

Some Things to Do

- Promote an active learning climate for the team

- Try to relate the team building strategies to the team's work

- Don't be afraid to experiment with new strategies

- Constantly evaluate both your output and your process. In short, ask regularly, *"How are we doing?"*

Some Things to Avoid

- Being aggressive -- instead of assertive

- Failing to let others express their opinions

- Inadequate planning

Some Things to Consider

Encouraging teamwork means making a commitment, and requires practice. The process is not instant and take some time, so be patient. Do not be discouraged by mistakes, learn from them.

Chapter 31 – Virtual Team Building and Management

Virtual teams are growing in popularity since many companies continue to grow and expand in different areas. But sometimes learning to manage a team that we can't physically see every day can be difficult. When we learn how to manage our local teams, as well as our virtual teams, we can form a group that works together to increase productivity and provides a new perspective on any project.

At the end of this chapter, you should be able to:

- Know the keys to establishing a virtual team

- Learn how to hold effective meetings and group sessions

- Learn effective ways to communicate with team members

- Use tools to build trust and confidence among employees

- Know how to handle poor performing employees

- Know how to manage a virtual team during any project

Review the following questions and note the answers before continuing with the chapter.

1. Have you ever been a part of a virtual team? Have you ever had to manage one?

2. What do you think are the benefits of a virtual team? Disadvantages?

3. What obstacles do we face when we try to manage a virtual team

4. What do you hope to learn from this course?

Setting Up Your Virtual Team

One of the key challenges in managing a virtual team is creating one in the first place. The manager must find employees that can work well under minimal supervision and can function with different types of technology. Don't let geographical differences hinder the team you want to create.

Choose Self-Motivated People with Initiative

One aspect of working on a virtual team is the ability to be self-motivated and self-disciplined enough to finish the job without someone looking over your shoulder. When building your virtual team, choose employees that show self-motivation characteristics, such as making goals and having strategies for completing assignments. If looking to utilize current employees, look for employees who have had a proven record for getting assignments done and sticking to what they want to accomplish. If hiring from outside the company, look at the person's resume and see what kind of success they have had and how they reached it.

Characteristics of a self-motivated person:

- They don't fear failure

- They have definite goals

- They make plans

- They are flexible when faced with a problem

Face to Face Meetings at First (Kick-off Meeting)

Even though virtual team members will be working apart from each other, it is important to start the team in the same location, usually through some type of 'kick-off' meeting. At this first meeting, members are introduced to each other and usually exchange contact information. The manager would then usually introduce the goals, assignments, and future projects for the group. This is the time where employees can ask questions, discuss availability, and plan for what they will be doing during the course of the upcoming projects.

If geography is a problem for gathering everyone together, try to find a central location that is a fair distance from everyone involved. In some cases, employees may need to be present by phone or video to be a part of the meeting. Setting up a one-time video meeting or conference may be the only way to get some face time between all participants. Having that initial face time is very important to the overall success of the team.

Diversity Will Add Value

Any manager wants a team of employees that can all work hard and accomplish their goals, but in the same instance a manager needs each employee to be different in their own way and utilize what they have to offer. Each employee is different and has a different set of skills that they excel at. They are able to provide different ideas and opinions that can be shared with others and create a new, unique perspective. When we bring a diverse group of employees together, they are not only able to use their diverse skills to complement each other, but they can ensure their part of the project is done to the best of their abilities, making the overall assignment a great success.

Benefits of a diverse work group:

- Various ideas and perspectives

- Each employee excels at their skill set

- Contributes to the group as a whole

Experienced with Technology

One of the most important aspects of a virtual team member is the need to be experienced with various types of technology. Team members will be in different locations, but will still need to keep in contact. Many ways employees accomplish this is to communicate by phone, email, fax, or even video phone. An employee must know how to operate different forms of technology in order to stay connected to other employees and management.

Assignments and projects are often sent by electronic files in a variety of programs and shared among the group to edit and sent along. If employees do not have a high level of knowledge when it comes to technology, they may not be able to function well on a team that relies so much on it. Current knowledge as well as keeping up-to-date with new and emerging technologies is required for today's teleworker.

When employees are happy and work together, they work harder to accomplish the job. When establishing your virtual team, it's more than just employee skills and abilities – you have to consider how they interact with each other and socialize in a group. Some of these things you may not know in the beginning, but some of them you learn along the way.

Personality Can Count as Much as Skills

Many people can master a certain skill set or become experts in many abilities, but their personality while they do it is what can set them apart. The same thing goes for a virtual team. An accounting team full of employees that can balance a budget is great, but if their personalities don't work together and they don't have personality in their assignments, the experience is not as productive and can even have negative effects. When choosing employees to join your team, look at their personality and how they present themselves. These traits will speak louder than their skills alone.

Avoid negative personality types:

- "Negative Ned/Nancy"

- The "Downer"

- The Gossiper

- The Antagonist

Rules of Engagement

The rules of engagement on any team are an important base to build on. With a virtual team, it can be a crucial part of the team plan. These rules include basic concepts of who to contact and who will be in contact with them. Some organizations have nicknamed it 'the phone tree', in which a chart or graph is created with employee names and channels in which they can use to contact someone else. This is important to establish with your virtual team members to let them know where they can go with any problems or concerns so they don't feel lost when they are in an area by themselves.

Example:

- Who do the employees contact for help?

- Who do they work with on a regular basis?

- Who do they contact with a complaint?

Setting up Ground Rules

Ground rules are guidelines that help form appropriate group behavior. By setting up ground rules at the beginning of your team's formation, it will help stop some problems before they begin. Many ground rules start with employee behavior, such as how to treat each other and some sort of 'code of ethics' but also include basic rules about behavior at work, such as deadlines and basic workplace behaviors. Other areas for ground rules include project deliverables, such as following deadlines and procedures for presenting an assignment. One commonly overlooked set of ground rules are rules for employee work hours, including attendance policies, procedure for calling in sick, and rules for clocking in and out. Although there are many areas to cover when establishing these rules, the team will run smoother when everyone knows what they can and cannot do.

Examples:

- Email usage

- Contact procedure

- Project deliverables and deadlines

- Employee respect

- Employee acknowledgement

- Adhering to employee schedules

Icebreakers and Introductions

Icebreakers and introductions are very important tools to use at the kick-off meeting. Introductions are especially important since it allows employees to get to know each other before they begin working together and are required to communicate back and forth. Icebreakers are a fun way to get each employee to interact in the group. This is often done with a small game or involving everyone in a group activity. In these activities, employees share their name, job title or position, and some sort of fun fact, such as their favorite hobby or vacation spot. Icebreakers and introductions allow employees to relax with one another by talking about themselves and learning things about their fellow team members.

Example Icebreaker activities:

- Talk about favorite foods

- Group people by common job duties

- Compare hobbies

Virtual Team Meetings

Now that you have your virtual team assembled, the next step is to effectively hold virtual team meetings with all of them. Just because your employees aren't at a table in front of you doesn't mean you can't communicate with them and guide them during a project. As with a normal meeting, there will be the issue with setting a good time, ensuring everyone shows up and making sure you deliver all the right information. The key is learning tools that can help you run a successful meeting, in person or virtually!

Scheduling Will Always Be an Issue

Virtual teams have a harder time scheduling meetings because the employees are not in the same location. Some employees are in different time zones, others work different hours while the rest may be constantly traveling. One tip for managing the employees' time schedules is to keep a log or chart of an employee's location, working hours and where they could be assigned later. With this tool, you can determine prime times to hold virtual meetings that won't conflict with someone's schedule.

If different meetings need to be held, plan a schedule with the employees regarding a rotation of employees staying late or coming in earlier to cover meeting times. Many employees are happy to abide by a schedule in which they can give their opinions. Be sure to remind employees of any consequence that can occur for not sticking with the schedule or not participating in the meeting, such as written warnings and disciplinary actions on their employee record. Understand that employees may still be hard to schedule even with adjustments. So have an alternate solution handy in case an employee cannot attend group meetings. Be flexible with employees that attend meetings outside of their normal work hours, offer the next day off or maybe a half day.

Have a Clear Objective and Agenda

An agenda is very important to have in any meeting and is more so in a virtual meeting because it keeps everyone on the same track. Outline what you want to discuss and accomplish from the meeting and jot down ideas on how you can make them happen. Include specific topics that need to be reviewed and events that have happened with the team. Employees need to know there a clear objective to the meeting and that it is not a waste of their production time. Share your agenda with the rest of the team so they can be aware of the purpose of the meeting and what they can contribute.

Tips for sharing your agenda:

- Include it in a mass email so employees can read ahead of time.

- On video calls, have the agenda displayed at all times on the screen.

- For conference call meetings, read over the agenda first and allow employees to take notes.

Solicit Additional Topics in Advance

Soliciting ideas before the actual meeting is an important tool to use when creating your agenda for the meeting. Speak with your employees and ask if they have any additional topics they would like included in the meeting agenda. Sometimes after the employees are aware of the original agenda, ideas or topics are added to the plate, either by management or other employees. However, don't leave these new topics as a surprise for the other meeting attendees.

It is important to share these additional topics with employees before they 'arrive' at the meeting so that they can be prepared and don't feel as though they were blind-sided. When employees know of the meeting topics ahead of time, they are able to research the topic ahead of time and be able to make a meaningful contribution when they participate in the next meeting.

Discourage Just Being a Status Report

Status report type information can be sent through email or other electronic messages because it often does not include much of a response from employees. It is generally one-sided information that is meant to be informative, not discussed in depth. One of the problems of a virtual meeting is that the moderator will do most of the talking and presenting, leaving the other team members feeling as though they are only there to hear the latest status report. The same can go for employees that come to the meeting to share their information and then sit out for the rest of the time. Encourage employees to ask questions and take notes of the information given. Set aside time for employees to share ideas with one another and engage in conversation or debate about the meeting topics. These meeting are meant to be a time of learning and interaction, not just one-sided information sharing.

Communication

Effective communication is a key component to any successful business. It is especially important when managing a virtual team because not only do you deal with traditional communication problems with employees, but virtual teams can face more obstacles trying to keep in touch. Learning helpful tools and techniques for effective communication can take any virtual team a long way.

Early and Often

Early communication means not waiting for a problem to happen before addressing it. Check in with your employees on a regular basis, whether by phone, email, conference, etc. Don't let employees struggle through a problem over a long period of time. Don't wait for them contact you; reach out to them to offer help. Contact each employee often and follow up after any problems they have reported. Keeping in touch with each employee not only cuts down on large problems, but it shows your support in the employee and can boost their morale substantially.

Tips:

- Create a regular schedule to check in with employees

- Find what methods work best for each employee

- Keep track of small problems that arise early to prevent bigger ones later

Rules of Responsiveness

Communication is a two way street and can shut down when one side doesn't contribute or doesn't act on their responsibility. When outlining communication techniques with your virtual team, one aspect to cover is the rules of responsiveness. Determine which forms of response are appropriate in various situations. Do you need a response right away? Is it something they can reply to later? Will you need a short or long response? When sending communication to employees, let them know how soon they need reply and how soon you expect to hear from them. Employees need to understand that the communication you exchange with them is very important and that they need to respond in a timely manner.

Face to Face When Possible

Sometimes communication needs to be made in person or face to face. Communication over the phone or email can often be skewed because there is a loss of tone and body language. Although this can be hard with a virtual team, there are ways the manager and employees can work together. If distance is somewhat small, arrange a time for employees to meet either at your office or theirs. If distance is too great, the next best option is to use some sort of video message system, such as Skype. Although it does not replace in person meetings, it allows the manager and employees to talk 'face to face' and monitor their tone and body language signals. Sometimes long distance communication just can't deliver an effective message – so never underestimate the power of talking in person.

Choose the Best Tool

Every form of communication has an appropriate tool to use with it. Some information can be delivered by informal methods, such as email or telephone calls. Informal methods are great to use when a short or quick answer is needed rather than a longer response. Participants can share information quickly and then continue with their work. Other messages should be delivered more formally, such as face to face talks or even in a group meeting.

Formal methods are better used for in-depth messages and descriptions. The information is often lengthy and may require explanation or presentations. Formal methods also allow participants to ask questions or add their input. To choose the best tool, the manager should determine how urgent the message is, how quickly it needs to be received, and what kind of response they are looking for. Once they determine what is to be shared and what they need in response, they can then choose the best tool for the job.

Poor communication among employees and management has been shown to cause low employee morale and a decrease in productivity. Sometimes employees can feel unsure about approaching you or are not sure what to do when they have a problem. Encourage your employees to engage in two way communication and ask question when they receive new information. When they know who they can come to in a jam, they will feel more comfortable communicating their needs.

Be Honest and Clear

One of the pitfalls about team communication is that we try to hide information from each other. Managers will try to 'sugar coat' a problem within the company or employees won't mention how hard they are struggling with an assignment. When speaking with your employees, don't try to hide facts behind blurred words. If you have to deliver bad news, be upfront and let them know what is going on. If you need to change something they are doing or working on, be clear as to why and the effect it will have on them. When we try to hide facts or information, employees can become skeptical and will eventually lose their trust in you.

Tips:

- Remain honest, even if it is a negative aspect.

- Speak clearly and don't hide the fact behind 'sugar coated' words.

- Ensure the employee is clear about what they hear (Any questions?)

Stay in Constant Contact

Nothing can be more frustrating than trying to reach a manager that has fallen out of touch. Employees need to be able to reach you during regular business hours and should always have a source to contact outside those hours (i.e. on-call, second shift manager). It is especially hard for virtual team members since they cannot always physically contact you and will need some other way to speak to you when needed.

It is important for you to stay in constant contact with your team members and ensure them that you are there for them when they need you. Some examples include sending daily emails to check on progress, or making regular meetings to follow up with employees. Make a note of employees that need your assistance more often and be sure to check up on how they are doing over time. By staying in contact now, you are helping to prevent further problems later.

Don't Make Assumptions

We all know that old saying of what happens when we assume. A common problem in communication is assuming that we have delivered all of the information needed or assuming that the employees will not have any trouble with their work. These assumptions can cause us to leave our team members out to dry and cause them to feel as though you are not there to help them. The employees can begin to resent you and may feel too uncomfortable to ask for further information.

Ask for employees to follow up on any information they receive, especially if they have questions or concerns. Periodically check on each employee's productivity and ask if they are having any difficulties or need another problem addressed. Your team members can benefit from your guidance, so don't assume they will make it on their own without you.

Set Up Email Protocols

Email is one of the most important forms of communication on a virtual team. It allows a person to send a message from anywhere, and at any time. Unfortunately, it can often be misused and can lead to confusion and upset team members. When the virtual team is formed and introduced to using email, introduce employees to the rules and regulations of using email for contact purposes. Outline when it should be used in different situations and stress that is it for company business, not personal usage. Many companies require employees to sign a form acknowledging that they are aware of the email protocols and will abide by them. Again, don't assume your employees know the protocol and follow up with them to check for any questions.

Building Trust

Creating an open and honest environment in the workplace is a key factor to keeping employees happy and productive. On a virtual team, it is just as important to remain open with your team members and keep them in the immediate loop of information. Since they are not always in a central location, it is essential to keep them updated on current happenings in the company and in their department. When the employees feel included, they learn to trust you and will look to you when they have questions.

Trust Your Team and They Will Trust You

Trust is a key component in any relationship, personal or professional. Virtual teams can have additional problems with trust when they are not always in each other's company. They can be unsure about what is being said or if they are doing as well as they should. As a manager, it is important to show your trust in your employees first. Show them that you trust them to complete their work and trust them with crucial information, such as potential job reassignments or even closures. When the employees feel as though you trust them, they can, in turn, learn to trust you. They will instill their trust in you and confide in you when they have concerns or are worried. This trust not only builds a stronger relationship among the employee and manager, but also the entire virtual team.

Beware of "Us vs. Them" Territorial Issues

Often times when management tries to solely run a team without regards to its members, the employees can begin to have that "Us against Them" mentality. They begin to believe that management is only looking out for management or does not value the opinion of the team members. This can cause further resentment from employees and can affect the whole team's productivity. Remind your employees that you are on their side and that you realize that the team works together to accomplish the same goal. Let them know that they are included in many of the decisions made (although not ALL of them), and that their presence on the team is valued. When employees feel as though they are part of the working machine, they are less likely to feel like an opposing force.

Share Best Practices

A form of 'best practice' is loosely defined as a practice that has proved productive in the past and has results behind it to back it up. Sharing best practices with your virtual team can be a great move when faced with some of the same situations. Common forms of sharing these practices including sending them through email or forming some kind of instruction sheet. Some employees may need to be counseled in person or shown how to follow a process step by step. Sharing these practices shows trust among employees and trust that they can continue the chain of success.

Best practices:

- Processes/procedures that have worked before

- Can be shared a number of ways, including email, videos or personal instruction

- Consult with employees regarding alterations/variations if needed

- Follow up with employees to ensure comprehension

Create a Sense of Ownership

One overlooked method of building trust among your virtual team is helping them create a sense of ownership. Employees feel more passionate about their jobs when they feel as though they not only have a part in the team's success, but can feel as though their part is essential to the overall success. Although it can take a good amount of time to help an employee establish their sense of ownership, it can prove beneficial for everyone in the long run.

Tips:

- Ask what you can do to accomplish something

- Encourage every new idea

- Make a plan and put into action

Cultural Issues

Cultural issues in the workplace have been a hot topic for many years. They are more than just demographics and cannot always be detected right away. Even though team members may be from the same office or a similar location, each one has their own unique culture and following. It is important to embrace these differences and acknowledge the cultural issues that may be present. This can help the team build successful relationships with each other and prove more productive in the long run.

Respect and Embrace Differences

Diversity among a group is always a good thing, but under the wrong impressions it can ruin any team. Whether the difference is a type of culture, political opinions, or simply a difference in background, all these factors can change how a person interacts with another person and what kind of view they have. When team members are diverse, it can keep the team from thinking on one path and stop the 'one track mind'. It opens teammates up to new ideas and points of view, which in turn can create new concepts for projects and assignments. Together, they can learn to not only respect their differences among each other, but embrace them to create a whole new work style.

Be Aware of Different Work Styles

Sometimes different work styles on a team can be a good thing because they allow each employee to think on their own and work within a design that works best for them. Other times, it can be a real source of trouble if not properly addressed. Some employees may prefer to work alone even though they are needed on a team project. One employee may be a procrastinator and wait until the last minute to complete their assignment. The key is to learn to be flexible with one another and adjust how you approach each other. No two people work the same way, so any team, especially a virtual one, will need time to adjust to one another and learn what makes the other team member work so hard. When we know how they function, we can work in sync with them without a hitch…most of the time!

Know Your Team Members Cultural Background

On a virtual team, it can be hard to get to know your teammates personally since you are so limited in communication and socialization. Even if the members meet during some sort of meeting or conference, it can be hard to acknowledge a person's cultural background. Some companies have an employee fill out a personal profile that can be shared with other employees, which allows them to better know the person even though they are not in the same office. When we can better understand a person's cultural background, we can better understand why they do some of the things they do and can make them feel more comfortable on your team.

Examples:

- Provide an "All About Me" survey to gather information about employees

- Some information can remain private if desired, such as religion or political views

- Acknowledge cultural instances, such as holidays and rituals

Dealing with Stereotypes

Stereotypes can ruin any team relationship or bond. The sweeping generalization a stereotype can cause people to become confused or view people in a negative light, even if it was unprovoked. Knowledge and understanding are the only tools we can use to deal with stereotypes. Get to know your employees and encourage them to get to know their coworkers. Learn more about the employee as a whole person instead of what their cultural background may have been labeled as. Through observation and interaction, the chances of anyone creating or following stereotypes in the virtual team decreases and employees are able to focus on the task at hand, and not each other.

To Succeed With a Virtual Team

Succeeding with traditional face-to-face teams can be challenging enough, but succeeding with a virtual team can be just as hard, if not more so. Inspiring a team to create and meet goals, maintain motivation and work together are only a few obstacles when managing a team that you cannot see on a daily basis. But with effective communication and a little discipline, any virtual team can succeed.

Set Clear Goals

Setting goals are one of the most elementary processes that can lead to success. After all, you don't know where you're going until you determine what you want! Clear goals are normally set for the team as a whole as well as each individual teammate. The manager works with the team to determine what they want to achieve over a set amount of time (i.e. increased sales, decreased absences) while the employee sets their own goals about what they want to achieve as a member of the team (i.e. decreased data errors, increased personal productivity). Setting goals with your virtual team can help them stay task-focused and can make them feel as though they are making a difference on the team.

Tips for setting goals:

- Determine what you want to achieve

- Define a path that can help you get there (there may be more than one)

- Decide what you will do when you reach that goal

Create Standard Operating Procedures (SOPs)

A Standard Operating System is generally a company's process or procedure that it follows in the workplace. Sometimes a company does not feel the need to document these procedures, since many people may already know it. But creating these procedures and correctly documenting them allows the manager to share them with other employees and create them as a type of guideline and resource. As a manager, review some of the procedure and processes that have worked for you in the past and try to create them into an SOP. Although it can be time consuming, it will be worth the benefits in the end. On a virtual team, these can be especially helpful for employees who may not have experience on the team yet. They will come to you for help and will need to learn procedures if they are to contribute to the team.

Build a Team Culture

Your virtual team is your family. Every member should take the time to know each other and familiarize themselves with someone else's situation. After all, every member of the team is a human being and deserves to be treated with respect and friendliness. If employees are not able to socialize locally, allow them to have a chat room on a private server or virtual community they can come and go in to speak with other employees on a non-business level. If possible, assign projects or assignments in pairs or small groups to encourage further mingling and socializing. When the employees feel as though they are part of a family, they see other teammates as family also and will create their own team culture they can fit into.

Provide Timely Feedback

Positive or negative, feedback is a great tool to help employees at work. On a virtual team, giving timely feedback is important to the team's overall success. Employees need to know how they are doing on assignments and need to know if they need to change anything. Since the manager cannot randomly approach the employee to give feedback as they would in person, it is best to set up regular, scheduled sessions (such as by phone or chat) to alert the employee of any negative feedback that needs to be addressed or any positive feedback that should be shared. This will require the manager to get to know the employee personally so that the feedback sessions are not awkward or uncomfortable.

Dealing With Poor Team Players

When we manage a team, there will always be a time where we have to address a member, or members, that are not working well with the group. No one wants to be the bad guy, but if the employee is not confronted and not given the chance to improve, it can affect the other members of the team and could cause a 'domino effect' for productivity. Learn the techniques of approaching this delicate situation and lookout for your team as a whole – not just one member.

Manage Their Results, Not Their Activities

When a person manages an office, they can see for themselves what an employee is doing or what they are working on. However, on a virtual team, the progress can be much harder to monitor. Because of this, it is more important to monitor the employee's results, rather than the individual activities. If the employee is delivering great work and it's on time, then the process of how they finish it means very little.

For many employees, having this sense of freedom and trust can boost their confidence and improve productivity. However, if an employee is not completing work on time or is not turning in projects, then this is an indication of poor work habits and the manager should investigate into what is causing the problem. Approach the employee and talk to them about their routine schedule. If needed, organize some form of an improvement plan to help them adjust their ways of completing their assignments.

Be Proactive, Not Reactive

It is better to be prepared for any mishap before it happens, which is why it is important to be proactive rather than reactive. If we wait for something to go wrong before we act on it, we cannot think clearly about what to do and it may be too late to fix. The same theory goes for team members. Do not sit back and wait for them to make a mistake before they are taught how to do something correctly. Monitor each employee's progress and notice any minor problems they may have along the way. Speak to the employee early on when they problem starts and try to find a way to guide them on the right path. This will prevent the problem from getting worse and having to use more damage control later. Being proactive will always keep you one step ahead and ready to help the employee succeed.

Check In Often

On the same lines of being proactive, be sure to check in with your employees often. They may not always have the chance to contact you or may not want to admit they need help. Schedule some form of regular communication for informal check in times that best work for you and the employee. Check in can be done by a phone call or simply sending an email. This will help both of you stay on track and allows you to report any feedback that needs to be addressed. Think of it as keeping a close eye on your flock and ensuring that you are there for them if they happen to go astray.

Example forms of check in methods:

- Email

- Phone call

- Recurring group meeting

- Video chat

Remove Them

Sometimes after a manager has tried several attempts to help an employee work well on a virtual team, they come to realize that the particular employee is just not a great fit and will need to be removed. Some employees can be too disruptive to their teammates or are not able to work independently. This can cause problems for the whole team and should be addressed right away. Before you decide to remove the employee, make sure your ducks are in a row and that you have done all you can to help them succeed, such as personal help or extra training. If you have followed all of the correct guidelines and the employee does not show any type of improvement, then you can take the next steps in removing the employee from the virtual team. Some employees may be reassigned to another department in the company while others may need to be fired altogether. Review all of their available options and determine which would be best for the company and the virtual team.

Choosing the Right Tools

Success on any kind of team depends on the tools you use to make it work. After all, you can't build a house without a hammer and you can't change a tire without a jack. But having a lot of tools at your disposal does not necessarily mean you have the right ones to get the job done. The key is in knowing what you want to do and what kind of tool would help you do it.

Communication Software

On a virtual team, communication software is crucial to have and use well. Employees are far apart and cannot communicate in person with each other when they have questions. How do your employees want or need to communicate with each other? For quick and easy questions or comments, text messaging or an instant message program can be the key. But if an employee needs to ask lengthy questions to a coworker or manager, a phone call or tagged email may be the answer instead. Whichever ways the team chooses to communicate with each other, it is just as important to know how to use and work the software, so be sure to ensure every employee has proper training and can come to you with questions.

Examples of communication software:

- Telephones – landlines, cellular or VOIP

- Email systems (AOL, Yahoo!, Gmail, Microsoft Outlook)

- Instant messaging programs (AOL IM, GroupWise Messenger, MSN messenger)

- Video chat room (Skype, ooVoo, Google Voice)

Collaboration and Sharing Tools

Collaboration and sharing tools allow team members across a virtual team to not only share a project they are working on, but also to work with each other by editing and commenting on projects within the same program. It can be a hassle to try and email a project back and forth when one person is trying to suggest a change or add their notes. There are a number of software programs that can be added to the virtual team to help make the collaboration process go more smoothly among team members. Many of these tools allow employees to upload a file for several others to see at once. Others include comment or adjustment features and can save any progress made after each person touches the file. These types of tools can make a virtual team run better and allows them to work as a team rather than several individuals trying to reach the same goal.

Examples of collaboration and sharing tools:

- Adobe Acrobat

- JotSpot

- Microsoft Office

- Novell GroupWise email

- Basecamp

Project Management Software

Project management software is aimed at managing the different aspects of a project, such as budgets, productivity, scheduling, communication, and even employee evaluations. There are many different ways of keeping track of this information, and companies normally take a different approach depending on the situation. Virtual teams generally have some sort of web based management program, such as web application for clocking in and out or keeping track of employee absences.

Other software options can include a program installed on the employee's desktop that can monitor their progress over a period of time and can show the employee what kind of progress they are making. Although we don't want to feel as though we are micromanaging our employees, it is necessary to implement some form of project management software for the team to use. While some may not like the approach to managing their projects, they will feel relieved when the time comes that they will need your feedback and guidance.

Use What Works for You and Your Team

Every manager has an opinion about what methods work and which ones do not for a virtual team. But only you can decide what works for you and your team. You know your employees and you know what would be the best way to communicate with them when you need to. Sometimes this can take some trial and error to see what forms of communication work best for the team as a whole. Some may communicate better by email while others are more comfortable talking on the phone. Many employees communicate using a number of different methods, depending on what kind of response they will need. The best part about having so many tools at your disposal is that you can use a combination of them to achieve what you and your team need to do.

Use the method, or methods, that get(s) what you need:

Email/text messaging/phone calls – short answers and quick information delivery, such as a meeting change or a quick clarification question.

Group meetings/individual meetings/video chats – in-depth and lengthy information given; usually requires explanations or discussions from both sides. This includes discussion of employee progress, business reports, or company changes.

Chapter 32 – Team Building for Management

Your organization's people are its greatest asset, and when they work together as a team they accomplish even more. But teamwork doesn't just happen. Teams have to be created, developed, and continuously nurtured. A solid team building strategy can create an environment of greater collaboration and collegiality, which is good not only for the bottom line for your people themselves. There are many different ways to build a team, and to continue fostering a sense of teamwork. Developing a diverse team building tool kit helps your people grow at every stage.

At the end of this chapter, you should be able to:

- Discuss the benefits of team work

- Understand the importance of intentionally fostering teamwork

- Determine strategies your organization can take to build teams

- Understand the benefits of games and social activities in building a team

- Apply the principles of team building to your own organization

What Are the Benefits of Team Building?

Team building has many benefits, to both the organization and the individual employees that make up the tam. Team building helps to create a sense of cohesion, reinforce shared goals and values, and greater camaraderie. Team building also helps teams be more effective, as they communicate more openly and are more motivated to pursue shared goals. An investment in team building activities is an investment in success.

Better Communication and Conflict Resolution

One of the greatest benefits of team building is better communication. People who have a sense that they are on a team, with shared values and goals, are more likely to be personally invested in one another. This facilitates communication because people want to reach shared goals, and have a shared sense of purpose or vision. Team building helps team members develop strong communication skills, and also helps the team establish communication systems. Improved conflict resolution is another benefit of team building. Clearer communication in and of itself helps to facilitate better conflict resolution. The shared goals and values of a team, along with the increased personal investment and stronger personal relationships that form in a team, also helps to foster an environment in which conflicts are addressed openly and productively.

Effectiveness

Team building helps to create more effective teams. Team building activities create a sense that team members are pulling together toward a common goal or set of goals. This sense of shared purpose tends to foster effectiveness and productivity. Team building also helps the team find greater effectiveness through developing skills in delegating tasks, collaborating, communicating, and creating processes that leverage each team member's skills. A team that has a sense that they are working together, and in which the team members trust each other to honor their commitments, works more efficiently and effectively.

Motivation

Team building activities can be a powerful source of motivation. Spending time together as a team is a chance to reinforce shared goals, set new shared goals, and strengthen relationships with team members. A sense of shared goals and values serves as valuable motivation. When infused with a spirit of healthy competition and camaraderie, team building activities also motivate team members because there is a sense of not just working for one's self but for the good of the entire team. Team building activities help remind your team what they're working for and why, which can be a valuable boost to motivation.

Camaraderie

One of the most powerful benefits of team building is a sense of camaraderie. The reinforcement of shared values and shared goals which goes along with team building helps create a sense of camaraderie and collegiality. Team building activities help to strengthen the interpersonal relationships between team members. Team building gives team members a chance to get to know each other beyond just their work functions, and helps to foster a sense of shared identity. Taking the time to create relationships that go beyond simply interacting over work responsibilities helps team members to invest more in each other emotionally and personally. This creates a sense that team members aren't just pieces of a process, but people with feelings and needs. When team members have a sense of camaraderie, they are more likely to want to collaborate, help each other, and support each other.

Types of Team Building Activities

There is a wide variety of team building activities that you can use in developing your team. Using a mix of games, activities, and social events helps keep your team building plan interesting and engaging. Each team will respond to different activities, so be open to switching up the type of team building you do. Also seek input from your team about which activities they enjoy and find valuable.

Games

Studies show that fostering a sense of play is a great way to foster camaraderie and team work. Using games also infuses a sense of fun and, depending on the game, a sense of friendly competition that can help people open up and form strong relationships. There are a variety of types of games you can use in team building, including:

- Icebreakers or "get to know you" games

- Shared task games

- Problem-solving games

- Interaction games

No matter what type of game or games you chose for a team building session, there are several key components to any effective team building game:

- Focus on learning and remembering names

- Focus on the game itself

- Focus on strengthening relationships

- Cheers and pats on the back

Activities

Group activities can also be a great way to build a team. Activities that are created specifically for team building are one option. Your training department can be a great source of information for team building activities, and there are a variety of excellent books and workbooks to draw from. Activities which are not specifically "team building" activities, but which encourage your team to interact with each other, are also valuable for building your team. Simply engaging in an activity together, whether a recreational activity or a community service activity, can give your team members a chance to take the focus off of work and instead focus on getting to know each other.

Education

Training, development, and education also offer opportunities for team building. When your team builds a new skill together, learns a new technology or process, or otherwise engages in professional development as a group, this reinforces shared goals. Include some education in your training plan about team building specifically as well. Engaging in education about how to function better as a team has clear benefits, as team members build a set of skills together that they can then apply to working with each other. However, any shared learning experience has the potential to create a stronger team. When people learn together, they support each other's development and can find a shared sense of purpose in learning something new or building a new skill. Take time to ask your team what they'd like to learn. You can also focus on the team's strengths and development areas in planning education.

Social Gatherings

Don't underestimate the power of social gatherings to build your team. While it's always important to recognize that family and other commitments can make it difficult for some team members to engage in social time outside of work, gatherings can still be a valuable tool in your team building kit. Whether you have regular team lunches where the topic of conversation is anything but work, an annual holiday gathering, or period get together after work for dinner, drinks, or other fun, social gatherings help to take your team out of their work environment so they can focus on each other. Ask your team what type of gatherings they would enjoy. Be wary of gatherings that center on alcohol, both for liability reasons and because it excludes those team members who do not drink. Vary the type of social gatherings so that those who may not enjoy one type of gathering have other options. Encouraging your team to spend time together as colleagues helps to further foster camaraderie and relationships.

Games

Many studies show that we learn best through play, and that dedicated play time is vital for our mental and emotional health. Games offer a way to bring an element of play to the workday. Games are also a way to help break down barriers by adding a spark of fun. In addition, games require us to think creatively, problem-solve, and work together. All these, plus the bonding element of shared laughter, are valuable for team building.

Games for Introductions

A great place to insert a game into your team building is during introductions. Often called "ice breakers," these games encourage people to think creatively about themselves, and offer their team members a chance to get to know them in a new way. Ice breakers help people get to know others not just by name, but by their interests, experiences, and memories. Ice breaker can be serious or humorous, and can sometimes serve as a launching point for other activities. There are many excellent books and websites with ice breakers out there, so take the time to choose a few you can use. Using different ice breakers means that people can "get to know" even people they have worked with for a long time! Some ideas for ice breakers:

- Three Truths and a Lie: Have each person tell three truths and one lie about him/herself. Then have others see if they can guess the lie

- My Favorite: After introducing themselves, have each member give their favorite of something – candy, music, song, color. "I'm Jane, and my favorite candy bar is Snickers."

- Sort and Mingle: "Sort" team members into groups by category (birth month, for example). Have them get to know each other. Then have them "mingle" with other groups.

Games to Build Camaraderie

Games are a great way to build camaraderie and add an element of play to work. The element of friendly competition helps team members to bond and reinforces shared values and goals. They key when using a game to foster camaraderie is to find a game that includes everyone. Hierarchies in the team (if they exist) should be erased for the game, so that everyone is participating as equals. The focus of the game should be working together and bonding, rather than simply winning. However, having a prize or other reward for the "winners" is also a nice way to foster health competition and collaboration. Some games that can be used to build camaraderie include:

- Scavenger hunts

- Puzzles

- Timed challenges

- Binder clip tag and other "Office Olympics "games

Games for Problem-Solving

Games that center on problem-solving are a fabulous tool for team building. When you give a team a problem to solve, and then add an element of fun, you encourage everyone to work together towards a shard goal. Some of the games that are good for building camaraderie also focus on problem-solving, because working together to solve a problem is an excellent way for people to bond. Scavenger hunts, treasure hunts, and puzzles offer a chance to solve problems while also building a sense of camaraderie. You can choose a "real life" problem as the focus of your game, or you can give your team a somewhat silly challenge that requires them to use critical thinking, creative thinking, and problem-solving skills. Word games are an excellent choice for problem-solving. Hands-on challenges help to promote problem-solving while also giving rich chances for laughter and interaction.

Games to Stimulate Interaction

Another way that games can help build teams is in stimulating interaction. Some of the ice breaker games can be adapted to stimulate interaction rather than just introduce people to one another. Games that require team members to work together also stimulate interaction in a way that regular work duties do not. Even better are games where team members must interact with many people as part of the game – the Sort and Mingle, for example. Games that stimulate interaction may give people on a team who don't interact much beyond the necessities a chance to interact in new ways. It's also useful, when using interaction games, to focus on getting people to interact with others outside their normal circle. When people are "forced" to interact, they often find that they have much in common with people they might not have sought out.

More Team Building Games

Never underestimate the power of play as you build your team. Games can be used to break the ice, to stimulate interaction, and to focus people on common goals. Games also add an element of levity and fun to work relationships, which can make it easier for people to interact and find camaraderie. Games can also be used to foster trust, motivate your team, build communication, and help strengthen conflict resolution skills.

Games to Build Trust

When many people hear "trust building games," they think of the classic game from high school theater where one person falls back and trusts the others to catch them. And while such games do build trust, there are other ways playing games together can help build your people's confidence in each other. Games that build trust are useful in helping your team build confidence in each other and in themselves. By allowing your team to take risks in carefully controlled environments like trust-building games, you empower them to feel safer taking risks and trusting each other on the job. Some trust-building games to try include:

- **Mine Field:** A course of "mines" is laid out (with cups, cones, etc.). Then one person is blindfolded and guided through the maze by a team mate's spoken directions.

- **Eye Contact:** Have each team member make eye contact with a partner for 50 seconds without looking away.

- **Willow in the Wind:** The old classic! Have one team member stand in a circle of colleagues, then let the others push and roll him or her around the circle, trusting they will not let him or her fall.

Games to Motivate

Games can be a great way to motivate your team. Studies show that healthy competition can motivate teams toward goals. When using a game to motivate your team, find a way to incorporate skills they use (or should be using) on the job into the game. Learning to use these skills to win a game can be a powerful motivator to use them in the daily job. You can also use these games as part of training on new skills and procedures, as a way to make learning fun and engaged. As with many of the other types of games, there is overlap – a motivational game may also build communication and conflict resolution, stimulate interaction, or promote camaraderie. Practicing skills in the relative low-stakes environment of a game helps your people be less afraid to make mistakes and take risks, which will make them more comfortable using the new skills in actual situations.

Games to Build Communication

Communication-building games are a worthwhile investment. Games that build communication can also help to build trust and promote interaction, as well as building a sense of camaraderie. Games also give your team low-risk ways to try new communication strategies that they can use in real life situations on the job. Finding games that require your team members to communicate in order to solve a problem, navigate an obstacle, or otherwise "win" gives you a chance to see how they work together (or don't) and how they communicate (or don't) in real time. Some communications games to try:

- **The Human Knot:** Have 6-8 people stand in a tight knot. Have them take hands. Now tell them to untie the knot and form a circle without letting go of hands. They must communicate how to get untangled.

- **Listen to Me!** Discuss traits of good and bad listeners. Then have team members get into pairs. While one team member talks, the other plays the role of "bad listener." Then have the listener play the role of "good listener." Switch roles. Then reflect.

- **Make a Team With...:** Similar to the Sort and Mingle, in this exercise team members have to build a team quickly depending on a characteristic you call out – shoe type, hair color, etc. This shows different ways to quickly communicate and form teams.

Games for Conflict Resolution

Like games for communication, games for conflict resolution offer a chance to try out skills in a low-risk environment. Finding creative ways to solve a conflict or problem is a valuable skill, and using games is a fun and low-stress way to explore it. Having your team work on conflict resolution skills in a game setting helps them feel comfortable enough with those skills that they are able to apply them in real-life conflicts later. Many games that are used to build communication skills generally can be used to build conflict resolution and negotiation games. Some idea for conflict resolution games include:

- **Advocacy and Inquiry:** Have team members experiment with different ways of acting in conflict situations. Then discuss how they might handle the situation more effectively.

- **Like a Dog With a Bone:** Have each person write down a workplace conflict involving them which is unresolved. Place the papers in a bowl – these are the "bones." Then pick bones from the bowl and discuss as a group how the situation can be resolved.

- **I Statements:** Practice using "I statements" as a way to resolve conflict productively.

Activities

Sharing activities is another way to build teams. Team building activities sometimes get a bad rap as boring, cheesy, or pointless. However, well-constructed team building activities can bring many benefits – better communication, better camaraderie, greater exchange of ideas. Finding activities that engage your team is a great way to build skills, create an atmosphere of collaboration, and create a stronger team overall.

Activities to Build Camaraderie

Sharing in an activity together builds camaraderie among your team members. The sense of having a shared experience can be a powerful way to form bonds and encourage team members to build relationships. Infusing activities with a sense of fun and play also encourages laughter and camaraderie among your people. Whether you choose to use activities that have many of the features of games, or find activities that are more focused on building relationships and skills for your team, the benefits in enhanced relationships, which brings a host of other benefits. When choosing activities that build camaraderie, focus on activities in which people participate as equals, and in which everyone can participate. One strategy is to break your team up into smaller groups, which allows for more one on one interaction. Some activities to consider as you build camaraderie on your team:

- **Building Challenges:** Teams build a product – bikes are a popular option – that will be donated to charity.

- **Charity Drive:** Teams collect for an agreed-upon charity. Food pantries or toy drives are common choices.

- **Office Olympics:** Teams compete in a variety of office-themed events, with fun prizes

Activities for Idea Sharing

The most successful teams share ideas. Hopefully your team shares their ideas in the course of their regular work. Activities that focus on sharing ideas can help team members get more comfortable speaking up about their ideas, and with hearing the ideas of others. Activities that focus on sharing ideas can also do much to build communication skills and camaraderie. When you encourage your people to really listen to each other when they speak, they are learning more than just the specific ideas that are surfaced. They are reinforcing good listening skills, which are invaluable. Some ideas for activities for sharing ideas include:

- **Graffiti:** Place poster boards or flip boards around the room with a concept listed at the top of each one. Have team members circulate and write words the associate with the concept on the board. Then discuss.

- **Brainstorm:** Generate ideas as a group to solve a problem, plan an activity, or otherwise use shared ideas. Have someone write these on a flip board. Use a ball or other item to make sure each person gets to speak.

- **Think, Pair, Share:** Give the team time to think over an idea. Then have them pair up to discuss ideas. Finally, bring the whole group back together to share what they came up with.

Activities to Build Trust

Much like trust-building games, trust-building activities help your team develop confidence in themselves and others. Activities designed to build trust help your team members take calculated risks in a relatively safe, supportive environment. This can help them feel more empowered and confident to take those risks outside the activity session as well. Sharing in an activity where one has to take a risk and succeeds not only builds trust in his or her team mates, but helps to build camaraderie. Having shared in an activity in which they were vulnerable together changes people's relationships, and typically makes them more willing to trust each other and be vulnerable in other instances. In addition to the trust-building games mentioned earlier, some popular trust-building activities include:

- Obstacle courses

- Bungee jumping

- Ropes courses

- Parasailing

- Active listening

- Boundary breaking

Activities to Stimulate Interaction

Most activities you might choose for your team will stimulate some level of interaction. However, you can choose activities which are specifically geared to generate interaction as well. These activities encourage people to get to know each other in a new way, share ideas, and collaborate or cooperate. Techniques such as the Sort and Mingle and Think, Pair, Share are excellent ways to stimulate interaction among your team. You may also choose to engage in activities such as volunteering, participating in a community event, or engaging in an event such as a scavenger hunt. The goal is to get your team interacting in ways that transcend their workday interactions, so that they get to know each other and expand their understanding of one another. When people interact outside a task-oriented context, it helps to round out their relationship and may give people a chance to interact meaningfully with people they have little contact with in a work setting.

More Team Building Activities

Activities go a long way toward building a strong, cohesive team. Activities are chances to build and practice skills, strengthen relationships, and interact on a deeper level. Team activities give members shared experiences, which they draw on in creating a team identity. Activities can also be used to motivate your team, improve team work, strengthen communication and conflict resolution, and generally create a greater sense of unity.

Activities to Motivate

Activities can serve as a great motivation. One way to use activities to motivate is to use them as a reward, though this is not the only way. Engaging in shared activities in which they learn new skills, contribute to the organization or community, and otherwise stretch themselves and their abilities can be a powerful motivating force for a team. You can also use activities to help team members – and the team as a whole – discover their motivators. Getting clear on what motivates your people and your team makes it easier to offer appropriate rewards and motivators. Almost any activity can be used to generate motivation.

Activities to Improve Working Together

Activities are an excellent tool for improving cooperation, collaboration, and other aspects of working together. Activities such as building challenges or cooperative games and sports are ideal for focusing on the way a team works together. When a team has to create a product, navigate an obstacle, or complete a puzzle as a group, they employ skills in communication, collaboration, negotiation, and more. Working together in an activity also adds a level of fun and take some of the pressure off as well. When teams can polish their skills in working together in a fun, supportive, low-stakes environment such as a group activity, they are better able to see what they do well and what needs work. They can then take this and apply it to real work situations.

Activities to Build Communication

Activities also offer a chance for team members to build communications. Games and formal training scenarios can help communication, but may feel artificial. Engaging in group activities, whether it's a team sport or organizing a charity drive, requires that team members communicate. Because activities are generally lower risk than work deliverables, they give the team a chance to experiment with new communication strategies. Team members may also work with colleagues in activities that they don't interact with regularly in their work duties, so activities offer chances to communicate with a variety of different people. Activities may also offer a chance to communicate in different ways than team member's everyday tasks require, which gives them a chance to try out new skills.

Activities for Conflict Resolution

Activities offer a great setting for conflict resolution and negotiation. This is true of activities specifically designed to simulate workplace conflicts and allow team members to work on conflict skills. However, it is also true of activities in which people must work together more generally. Conflicts and the need for negotiation arise when people must communicate and cooperate. Team activities offer an environment where team members can try out conflict resolution and negotiation skills. And because activities take place in an environment which is supportive and collegial, people may feel safer trying out negotiation and conflict resolution skills here than they would in conflicts that arise on the job. Studies show that one of the benefits of team activities, whether sports or theater or any other group activity, for children is improved ability to negotiate and resolve conflict. This holds true for the adults on your team, too! Activities allow people a chance to work things out on their own, try out different ways of negotiating and solving conflict, and experiencing how others do these things as well.

Social Gatherings

Social gatherings are another way to build your team. Always be mindful that social gathering outside of work hours might be difficult for some of your team members, especially those who have family obligations or who have long commutes. However, finding ways for your team to socialize together can help build relationships and create camaraderie that is difficult to achieve in a structured work setting. Use a variety of social gatherings, timed at different times, to encourage your team to socialize together.

Singing/Karaoke

Nearly everyone loves to sing. Singing or karaoke can be a great activity to help your team have fun and grow closer. Whether you go to a karaoke spot in your city, or bring a karaoke machine into the office, this is a fun way for everyone to take a little risk and be creative with their colleagues. Encourage everyone to participate, stressing that the point is to have fun and try something new – and maybe a little scary --- rather than to be the "best" singer. Even those who choose not to sing can be there to cheer and support their team mates. And often, people who are resistant to the idea of singing at the beginning of the event get their courage up by the end, after seeing all their colleagues up on stage.

Dinner/Potlucks

Sharing food as a method of bonding is a human universal. While your team may sometimes share lunch and other meals as part of their work, creating social gatherings where the point is to share and enjoy food and not talk about work is an excellent way to encourage team building. You can plan a dinner out, or you can institute regular potluck dinners. Potlucks give people a chance to showcase their cooking, and are more budget-friendly than always going out. Organize potlucks with a theme, and have a sign-up sheet so that people know what's being brought. Be sure to take into account team members with special dietary needs (vegetarian, gluten-free, kosher).

Physical Activities

Another great way to build a team is to engage in physical activities together. This can include competitive sports, such as golf or volleyball. But you can also schedule gatherings around activities just for the sake of engaging in some physical exercise. Activities such as nature walks, ice or roller skating, dancing (including dance lessons), and biking can be even more fun when shared. You might also investigate activities like mini golf and laser tag which, while competitive, are as much about the fun of playing as they are about winning. Keep in mind team members who might have physical differences or challenges, including those who use wheelchairs or other mobility equipment, when creating gatherings focused around physical activity. You can always find activities in which these members of your team can participate, and many venues have specialized equipment or other assistance. When creating a gathering focused around physical activity, encourage everyone to participate. Put the focus on the shared experience and the fun, not on being the best or more proficient at the activity.

Meetings

Meetings aren't exactly at the top of the list when people think of fun social gatherings. However, you can use your regular meetings to help build your team in several ways. Have time to check in with each other. Include lunch or snacks to make the meeting more enjoyable. Encourage people to interact and share during the meeting. Meetings can also be held in places outside the office, whether over a meal or just in a different location, to add some variety. Meetings need not be a burden. And given that you are likely having regular meetings with your team, they are a built-in opportunity for some team building.

Common Mistakes When Team Building

Even the most carefully created team building plan may fall prey to mistakes. Because people are all different, what works in one group may be less successful in others. There are some common mistakes that occur when team building. Being aware of these mistakes ahead of time can help you avoid them. And if they do occur, you'll be able to quickly spot them and correct course.

Allowing Cliques to Develop

One of the most common errors when team building is allowing cliques to develop. This happens when a group of people become insular and only want to interact with each other. They may exclude others, gossip, or simply keep themselves apart from the rest of the team. Clearly, this is exactly the opposite of what we want to happen when we are engaging in team building. The other side of cliques developing is that certain people may be consistently left out, ostracized, or otherwise excluded. Be attentive if you see cliques developing. Some signs that cliques are developing may include:

- People only wanting to team or pair with each other

- The same groups or teams consistently forming

- The same person being consistently left out or left until last

You can help avoid clique formation by encouraging (or even requiring) people to team or pair with different team members. Encourage interaction with the whole group. Also make conscious effort to include everyone and invite everyone to participate.

Not Delegating Tasks

A failure to delegate can undermine team building. Be sure to delegate tasks when you facilitate team building. Also make clear that, when working in groups, tasks should be delegated. It is not uncommon for team members who are very focused on "winning" or "being the best" to take over group activities and not delegate to their group members. Reinforce how important this is, and that the goal is not winning at all costs. You might include activities which teach and reinforce delegation skills. When tasks are not delegated, the team does not get the experience of working together – they are simply led by the "expert." This can create resentment and lead to negative feelings and interactions among the team.

Rewarding in Private/Criticizing in Public

Feedback is a key component of team building. A common mistake people make when team building is to only give negative or developmental feedback when with the whole team, while reserving rewards and positive feedback for private times. This is especially egregious if there are one or two team members who are consistently criticized in public but only rewarded in private (or worse, not rewarded at all). Developmental feedback is important, but if a team has a sense that they do nothing right, or that they are going to be called out or humiliated in public, they develop resentment and low morale. Be sure to save individual developmental feedback for private meetings with the person. You can give developmental feedback to the whole team when you are together. And make sure to praise as openly as you offer developmental feedback.

Disjointed Plans of Grandeur

As dangerous as it is not to have a team building plan, having a plan that is too complex or grandiose is also something to avoid. A common mistake when creating a team building plan is to pack the schedule with too many activities, trainings, and meetings. This makes your plan unnecessarily complex. Also be wary of expecting miracles – that one session of broomball or one potluck will solve any interpersonal problems in your team. Keep your team building plan interesting, but avoid making it too ornate, multi-faceted, or complex. Plans like this are frustrating to administer and manage, and even more frustrating for the team members who have to engage in the activities. They may result in resentment of you and the program, which does little to build your team!

Formatting a Team Building Plan

Like any other key initiative, team building needs a plan. Take the time to format a solid team building plan so that you know where you're going. This helps you keep your team abreast of what's happening, what they can expect, and what they need to do. Create your team building plan with input from your team, as well as your own research. Create a plan that is manageable and realistic, yet diverse and fun.

Define the Goal

The most important step is to define the goal of your team building plan. Just saying you want to "build a team" isn't enough. What needs to change or improve on your team? This will help you focus your team building efforts. Also take into account the circumstances of your team. Are you spread out over many office locations? How large is your team? What special considerations are there, such as remote employees or heavy travel schedules? Some common goals for team building include:

- Improved interpersonal communication

- Improved collaboration

- Higher morale

- Greater camaraderie

- Integration of new team members into an existing team

- Motivating the team

Based on your goal or goals, choose activities that best support what you are trying to achieve. Be sure to evaluate your plan regularly in case your goals change.

In addition to an overall goal for your team building plan, it is key to define a goal for each team building activity and clearly articulate it.

Consult Team Members

Your team members are your best source of information when you plan team building activities. There is no sense in scheduling social gatherings, for example, that no one comes to! Take the time to ask your team what kind of activities they'd like to engage in and what they would like to do. Also ask them what they think could be improved about your team and how you might go about making those improvements occur. Taking time to consult your team shows that you want to create a team building plan that works for them, and that you are invested in what they care about and have to say. Check in with your team often about different activities. Also encourage your team to come to you when they have new ideas for team building activities.

Research and Create Structure

After you've consulted your team, research their suggestions. Look at what industry leaders and your colleagues are doing in terms of team building. Spend some time surfing the Internet, which is a wealth of team building ideas, as well as looking at books of team building activities and games. Figure out what types of activities are possible and practical for you to do. This may include creating a budget, contacting outside vendors and consultants, and otherwise examining the logistics of various activities. Then create a structure. Decide in what order you will do activities or what goals you will address first. Determine whether you'll have monthly, bimonthly, or more/less frequent team building activities. If possible, start putting these on a calendar. Then communicate with your team what this schedule will be like. Let them know what to expect. Having a structure in place helps make it easier to consistently implement your team building activities and plans.

Keep It Fun

Perhaps the most important thing when creating a team building plan is to keep it fun! If team building is a drudgery, your team is not likely to benefit from it. Find ways to keep even meetings and trainings infused with a sense of fun. Balance more task-oriented sessions with fun activities. Have a sense of play. Make note as you research of ideas for infusing team building with levity and fun. This will help ensure that your team gets the greatest benefit from your plan. And don't be afraid to revise your plan if you start to implement is and realize that no one's having any fun!

Evaluate

Always take time to evaluate your team building efforts. This way you know what works well and what can be changed or gotten rid of. There are some steps you should take after each team building activity, and then at the end of the year or period to evaluate the entire team building plan. Be sure to take these steps so that you can make your team building efforts the best they can be. Never be afraid to switch things up or alter your team building to better suit your team's needs. The goal is always to best serve what the team and the organization need.

Was the Goal Met?

After each team building exercise, ask whether the goal was met. You can ascertain this by handing out evaluation forms or seeking other feedback from participants. You can also watch over the following days to see if any related changes take place. If the goal was met, you know that the team building activity or exercise was a quality one. If you find that the goal was not met, it is important to evaluate why. It may not mean that the activity itself was inherently poor, but that other factors might have interfered with its effectiveness. Take time to honestly evaluate each team building activity. Also take time to evaluate the whole plan at the end of the year, quarter, or other logical time period.

Was the Team Building Cohesive?

Also ask yourself if the team building was cohesive. Did it flow logically? Did the different parts of it make sense? Did the team understand the goal of the team building activity? Again, seeking feedback from your team is one excellent way to help determine this. Also reflect on your own observations or participation in the activity. Was there a piece that seemed out of place? What worked? What didn't? Reflect on any incoherencies and address them in other team development activities. Also be sure to evaluate the entire team building plan to see if it is cohesive, with all the parts supporting each other.

What Did the Team Think of the Team Building?

Ask your team what they thought of the team building. Did they enjoy it? Did they find it helpful? Would they like to the same or similar activities in the future? If they did enjoy the team building, ask them specifically what they enjoyed or appreciated. This will help you choose future activities. By the same token, if your team did not enjoy a team building, ask them what they disliked. This will give you valuable data on what works and does not work for your team. When you find activities that your team enjoys, find ways to offer the same or similar types of team building in the future.

How Can the Team Building Be Improved for Next Time?

Keep a continuous improvement mindset when it comes to team building. What can you do differently to improve the team building next time? Even successful team building activities may have room for improvement. Feedback from the team comes in here. If the team didn't enjoy a team building, ask them what you could do differently next time. If you discover that a team building did not achieve its goal, work to determine why it failed, so that you can improve it the next time. Seek out areas where the team building is not cohesive or seems to break down, and see if you can improve it and future team buildings.

Chapter 33 – Business Acumen

Many people believe you are born with business acumen, which is loosely defined as the ability to assess an external market and make effective decisions. Knowing what is necessary to navigate and create a successful business seems innate for certain people. For example, Steve Jobs showed great business acumen. Fortunately, it is possible for the rest of us to improve business acumen. The right training combined with experience will improve your business savvy.

At the end of this chapter, you should be able to:

- Know how to see the big picture

- Develop a risk management strategy

- Know how to practice financial literacy

- Develop critical thinking

- Practice management acumen

- Find key financial levers

Review the following questions before continuing with the chapter:

1. How would you describe business acumen?

2. Have you ever taken a course to improve your acumen? What was the focus?

3. Where do you feel your business acumen is weak?

4. What do you hope to learn from this course?

Seeing the Big Picture

Business acumen requires an understanding of finance, strategy, and decision making. Most managers and employees, however, are responsible for specific areas, and they have little understanding of the impact their decisions have on other areas. When too much focus is placed on one aspect of the business, it is difficult to make decisions for the good of the company. In order to make effective decisions, it is necessary for you to examine the big picture.

Short and Long Term Interactions

When looking at the big picture, it is necessary to consider long term as well as short term interactions. Short term interactions are immediate, single exchanges, and they are necessary for the company to survive. Without looking at the big picture, however, short term interactions may hinder long term success. For example, you may damage a business relationship by using aggressive sales techniques, costing you sales in the future.

Long term interactions are processes or relationships that are essential to growth. Long term business success requires the long term interactions. The relationships with customers, vendors, and employees need to be carefully cultivated. Failure to cultivate relationships occurs when there is a lack of communication or communication is not respectful. Long term relationships help guide the future of the business.

Improving Long Term Interactions

- **Build relationships:** Relationships must be based on mutual trust, respect, and support.

- **Use feedback:** Request feedback and listen to complaints.

- **Offer value:** Provide value in product, services, and compensation.

Recognize Growth Opportunities

It is essential for every organization to recognize growth opportunities to ensure long term success. An opportunity is any project or investment that will create growth. Opportunities, however, can be overlooked when we do not pay attention to the big picture. Individuals with business acumen are constantly recognizing opportunities for growth. If recognizing opportunities does not come easily for you, there are steps to take that will ensure that you do not overlook growth opportunities.

- **Identify market trends:** Monitor changes in the market such as technological advancements.

- **Actively research customer needs:** Conduct market research and anticipate customer needs, which you will fulfill.

- **Pay attention to competitors:** Take advantage of a competitor's weakness and learn from their strengths.

- **Monitor demographic changes:** Changes in demographics indicate potential shift in customer base or needs.

- **Consult employees:** Do not overlook employee ideas; encourage brainstorming.

- **Monitor abilities of the workforce:** Pay attention to employee skills. Offer training or hire new employees in response to growth opportunities.

Mindfulness of Decisions

Decisions need to be made carefully and mindfully. In stressful situations, it is easy to make decisions based on emotions or external pressure. Recognize these events which increase the risk of making a poor decision that can have long term consequences. Mindful decision making combines reason with intuition to come up with decisions that are based in the present.

Decision making Steps:

Step 1 Be in the moment: Pay attention to how you feel physically and emotionally. This allows you to reach your intuition and understand any feelings of conflict and their source. The source of the conflict may evolve as you become mindful. For example, conflict over the cost of change may shift to conflict that the change goes against company values. Naming the conflict will help you make the decision without fear.

Step 2 Be Clear: Investigate for clarity. Begin by investigating your feelings and identifying the type of decision you are making. A neutral decision, for example, should not create a great deal of stress. Once you identify the decision, make sure you have collected the necessary information to make the decision. Additionally, you should consult the people who will be affected by your decision.

Step 3 Make a choice: Once you have all the information, listen to your intuition, and write down your decision. Take some time to consider this decision. If you are still comfortable with the decision after a few days, act on it.

Everything is Related

In business, it is necessary for each person to perform specific roles and functions. Every business role is related to each other. For example, poor production and poor customer service will affect sales. Too many sales returns cost the company money, damaging the profits. Each aspect of the business relies on the others. Most people only focus on their specific roles, without considering how they affect the other departments. Looking at the big picture allows you to see how everything is related, and it begins with the leadership. The leadership of the company is responsible for the culture and values. These guide the other aspects of business, which are: operations and marketing, finance and governance, and information and people.

How to Relate:

- **Be Comprehensive:** Monitor every area of the business to make sure each one is reaching their goals.

- **Be Balanced:** Make sure that each area of the company is sustainable, and make adjustments as necessary.

- **Be Incorporated:** Integrate every aspect of the business with the others. Show employees how they affect each other and the company as a whole.

KPIs (Key Performance Indicators)

Understanding when goals are reached is a necessary aspect of business acumen. Key performance indicators (KPIs) are metrics that show when goals are met. Each company will have a different set of KPIs, depending on individual business needs. Creating and managing KPIs will improve the success of your business as well as your own business acumen.

Decisiveness

KPIs need to be developed decisively. This requires an understanding of which performances need to be measured and how they should be measured. Creating random metrics will not help gauge the effectiveness of your organization.

Decisive KPIs

- **Define areas to monitor:** Determine which areas are successful and which ones need improvement.

- **Identify criteria:** Brainstorm ideas, and use them to create criteria that need to be monitored. For example, criteria would include customer conversion or units per transaction,

- **Define the measurements:** Create specific SMART goals to monitor. An example would be an average of three units per transaction.

Once you have decided the type of KPIs you want, you need the buy in of the stakeholders. Communicate the information decisively and make sure that everyone understands the purpose.

Flexible

While it is necessary to be decisive with KPIs, they must not be static. Flexibility is necessary in every aspect of business, including KPIs. They must change as the goals change. It is important to remember that KPIs can be improved even when they are successful, which means that they need to be reviewed and altered accordingly.

KPIs are often driven from the top down, and they are less effective when the initiative is inflexible. Allow the different departments to adjust KPIs according to their needs, and give them the authority to time implementing the KPIs so that their employees understand and embrace them. Employee buy in is essential to the KPI success. Additionally, coordinating the KPIs on a large scale can cause confusion. It is better to allow different role out times to avoid mistakes.

Strong Initiative

Showing initiative is having the ability take charge over a new or unknown situation. Having initiative is a way for employees to be more automatous in their day to day tasks. It will lead to and produce better problem solving skills. Mistakes will happen, but do not treat them as mistakes or errors, use them as learning events. Taking the responsibility to look after an issue or event by finding the answer, is what having a strong initiative is about.

Developing initiative:

- Recognize spots for improvement.

- Show some confidence, if you have an idea share it.

- Look for solutions, not problems.

- Offer to fill in when gaps occur.

- Don't focus on or get discouraged by mistakes, learn from them.

Being Intuitive

Key Performance indicators can work from the top down or the bottom up. KPIs are created from the top down when they are used in dashboards because dashboards focus on operational goals rather than strategic goals. The dashboard provides intuitive and useful information to users. They require targets to be established for each KPI ahead of time. In order to use a dashboard, all business users need to be involved thus you should interview users to determine the dashboard metrics.

- Which questions need answers?

- Who is affected by the question?

- Why do you believe the question is important?

- Which data do you use to answer the question?

- Will creating KPIs create more questions?

- What action needs to be taken?

- What metrics will you use?

Once you determine metrics, use them to guide and coach employees. Individuals with business acumen understand that metrics should encourage employees to be successful rather than beat them down when the numbers are not met.

Risk management involves different strategies. The purpose is to identify and assess risks and prioritize them in order to monitor and reduce threats to the company. Implementing risk management requires looking at the big picture in the future and taking the proper steps for the good of the organization. Certain risks may be transformed to opportunities, and risk management is essential to business acumen.

Continuous Assessment

A risk assessment will help identify the different dangers and opportunities you may face. There are different types of risks assessments you can implement, depending on the specific objective and the needs of the business such as strategic risk, internal audit, market risk, and customer risk. A risk assessment needs to be a continuous part of the business cycle to be effective.

Risk Assessment Steps:

1. **Recognize objectives:** The scope of the assessment is based on specific objectives, created using SMART goals.

2. **Identify potential events:** Use prior and possible events to determine risks. Identify external factors such as the economy, politics, technology, and the environment as well as internal data. The information identifies risks and opportunities.

3. **Identify risk tolerance:** Determine the variation from the objective that is acceptable with risks.

4. **Determine the probability and impact of risks:** Assign an impact and probability rating to risks based on data.

5. **Outline responses for risks:** Assign a response for each risk. These may be to accept, avoid, reduce, or share the risk.

6. **Determine the impact and possibility:** Evaluate the controls and response.

You should evaluate the assessment to determine what risks are connected between departments and to each other.

Internal and External Factors

Managing risk requires identifying the external and internal factors that affect the company. In certain cases, internal factors and external factors will overlap. In fact, many internal hazards are external hazards. These factors are essential to the risk assessment. The key risks that every business faces are financial, strategic, operational, and hazard. You must determine which factors affect your business and how to address them.

Internal Factor Examples:

- **Financial Risk**: Internal risks include liquidity and cash flow.

- **Strategic Risk**: Intellectual capital and R&D are examples of strategic risks.

- **Operational Risk**: Accounting and the supply chain are examples of internal operational risks.

- **Hazard Risk**: Employees and products are internal hazards.

External Factor Examples:

- **Financial Risk**: External risks include taxes, interest rates, and credit.

- **Strategic Risk**: Competition and customer demand are examples of strategic risks.

- **Operational Risk**: Regulations, culture, and the supply chain are examples of external operational risks.

- **Hazard Risk**: Suppliers, natural risks, and products are external hazards.

Making Adjustments and Corrections

As we established earlier, risk management requires constant monitoring and assessment. As you gather information using KPIs and other tools designated to monitor progress, you will determine which management strategies are successful and which are unsuccessful. Correct and adjust the strategies to improve performance as necessary. Additionally, risks are subject to change. For example, a competitor who suddenly offers a similar product at a cheaper price changes your threat assessment. This will require adjustments and corrections in your objectives, strategies, and actions.

Knowing When to Pull the Trigger or Plug

There are risks in every aspect of business, and not every program will be successful. Risk management strategies help you determine when to go for a win and when it is necessary to cut your losses. Allocating your resources to an ineffective strategy is wasteful. However, pulling resources from potentially successful opportunities may equal a loss. Individuals with business acumen understand how to allocate resources.

Sometimes knowing where to invest is obvious. A program that hemorrhages money year after year, despite adjustments, needs to be cut. Similarly, rolling out a product that has consumer interest is probably a risk worth taking. Other answers are not so clear-cut, even when you have collected extensive data. In these cases, taking advantage of opportunity costs will help determine which risk is worth taking.

Opportunity Cost:

Opportunity Costs are defined as the value of an alternative decision. It is the actual monetary cost as well as the cost of value. In order to determine opportunity cost, however, it is useful to convert everything to dollar amounts. For example, the complete cost of employee training when sales are slipping could be calculated, and the alternative would be the complete cost of not training employees. When calculating opportunity costs, it is important to remember that it is based on projected costs, but it still provides useful information.

Opportunity cost = selected action – the alternative decision

Recognizing Learning Events

Every day is an opportunity to learn something new. Individuals with business acumen are able to recognize learning events and take advantage of these opportunities. To be successful, you must always be learning. As you gather knowledge, you will find yourself learning from your mistakes and improving your decision making process. The ability to recognize learning events will benefit you as well as the organization.

Develop a Sense of Always Learning

Every encounter offers a learning experience. The key to recognizing learning events is to develop a sense of always learning. Identifying the eight different ways that we learn, will ensure that you do not overlook learning opportunities.

1. **Imitation:** We learn from observing and imitating others such as instructors or respected mentors.

2. **Reception/Transmission:** Reception is the experience that requires you receive a transmitted message. It may be written or verbal, and it can include values as well as academic understanding.

3. **Exercise:** Actions and practice create learning experiences. These can occur in any action that you practice such as writing, meditation, or computer programs.

4. **Exploration:** Searching for answers or discovering information requires individual initiative. This comes from websites, interviews, books, etc.

5. **Experiment:** Experimenting or assessing the success of a project shows different possible outcomes and influences problem solving.

6. **Creation:** The creative process is also a learning process. These can be individual or group projects. The process ranges from painting to developing a new survey.

7. **Reflection:** Analysis before, during, or after an action is a learning opportunity. This can be done on a personal level or with the help of friends and colleagues.

8. **Debate:** Interactions with others cause us to defend or modify our perspectives. These are potential learning experiences.

Evaluate Past Decisions

Our past decisions often guide our current actions. Both successful and unsuccessful decisions need to be evaluated in order to identify errors in judgment as well as effective thought processes. Ask yourself a few questions after each decision, and learn from your mistakes and achievements.

Questions:

- What was the outcome?

- Did the outcome meet expectations?

- Would you repeat the same decision?

- What information or advice can you take away from this decision?

When you take the time to learn from all of your decisions, even your ineffective choices will bring you success.

Problems Are Learning Opportunities

People prefer to avoid problems or mistakes. However, problems are not always avoidable. When problems arise, you have a chance to learn from them and turn them into opportunities. The first step to learning from problems is to correctly identify the problem. For example, a shortage in cash flow may be caused by loss of sales or unexpected expenses.

Once the problem is identified, consider different solutions or opportunities. For example, a change in the market may provide you with an opportunity to introduce a new product you have been considering. If the problem is familiar, what were your past solutions? For example, did a price reduction help increase sales and improve cash flow? Once you consider the different opportunities associated with your problem, you must make a decision. If you make a mistake, embrace it. If you face the same problem again, you will know what to avoid.

Recognize Your Blind Spots

We all have blind spots in our lives, and they can easily transfer to our business success. Blind spots are parts of our personalities that are hidden to us. They may be deep-seated fears, annoying habits, or judgmental attitudes. Allowing blind spots to persist will cost your company in innovative ideas. Blind spots will also permit ineffective activities to continue. Recognizing your blind spots is not difficult, but it does require the courage to make necessary changes.

- **Request Feedback:** Ask trusted friends and colleagues for honest assessments.

- **Reflect:** Take the time to reflect on your decisions, thought processes, and actions. If you are honest with yourself. You will identify blind spots.

- **Study:** Use books, courses, etc. to help you become more in tune with your views and potential blind spots. Figure out what you don't know and strive to learn.

You Need to Know These Answers and More

Running a business is a complex enterprise. In order to look at the big picture in your business, you need to know the answers to some basic financial questions. It is not enough for your accountant to know this information. Business acumen requires you to be aware of these answers so that you will be able to guide your company to success.

What Makes My Company Money?

The purpose of every business is to make a profit. You need to make money in order to survive, but in order to do this; you must identify what makes your company money. You need to examine your products and services to determine which ones are actually making money for the company. For example, a bakery makes croissants, cookies, and cakes. The croissants account for 80% of the sales, and the cakes make up 15% of the sales. Cookies make up 5%, and some days most of them are thrown out. Knowing what makes your company money will provide influence and help steer the future of the company.

What Were Sales Last Year?

Companies need to grow to stay competitive. You are able to identify growth only when you see an increase in sales over time. Knowing last year's sales is essential to understanding the current status of your company. For example, you should use last year's sales to calculate the rate of change.

Rate of change:

Subtract the difference between last year's sales from this year's sales. Last year's sales were $90,000 and this year is $100,000.

$100,000 - $90,000 = $10,000 increase

Divide increase or decrease by the previous year.

10,000/ 90,000 = .111

Multiply the rate by 100.

.111 x 100 = 11% increase

What is Our Profit Margin?

Every business needs to make a profit. The profit margin indicates how well the company is running. A large, successful company typically has a 13% net profit margin. The higher the profit margin, the more efficient the business is run. There are two types of profit margin: gross profit margin and net profit margin.

Both are found when the profit is divided by the total revenue. The difference between the two is that the net profit margin is profit after tax and operating costs.

Example:

Revenue = $150,000

Gross profit = $50,000/150,000 = 33% gross profit margin

Net profit = $10,000/150,000 = 10% net profit margin

What Were Our Costs?

A company's costs affect other financial aspects such as profits. This is why it is so important to control costs. Many companies choose to increase profits by cutting costs. However, this can backfire when the costs you cut directly affect the customers' experience.

Basic Costs:

- **COGS:** Cost of goods sold is also called direct cost. This includes costs associated with production, materials, labor, inventory, distribution, and other expenses. The individual COGS must stay below the sale price to make a profit.

- **Operating expenses:** Overhead expenses are included in operating expenses, which is any expense necessary to keep the company running that is not COGS. Examples include support function salaries, rent, marketing, R&D, utilities, equipment, travel, etc.

- **Interest and other expenses:** Interest on loans or investment losses are not part of running the business from day to day, but they affect the bottom line. Other expenses include lawsuits and selling an asset.

- **Taxes:** Federal, state, and local taxes are unavoidable costs of doing business.

Financial Literacy

Financial literacy is essential to business acumen. In order to see the big picture, you have to understand every aspect of the company's finances. Fortunately, anyone can improve financial literacy with some basic instruction and practice. This module and the next will provide you with information to improve your understanding of financial literacy.

Assets

Assets are anything of value that the company has that will create a profit or improve revenue. Many assets are listed on a balance sheet such as a building or product. Some assets, however, are not listed on the balance sheet. Assets such as customers and employees are not listed, but they are the most valuable assets that companies have.

A company's strength is determined by its assets, especially its liquidity. A liquid asset is cash or is easily converted to cash, making it more stable in times of emergency. However, businesses are not supposed to hoard cash; they are meant to invest in other assets and utilize them to increase the return in productivity. For example, you may purchase a machine that increases production. The key is balancing liquid assets with the assets you utilize.

Financial Ratios

Financial ratios are formulas that provide information about the company's status. The information used to find financial ratios is typically taken from the financial statement. Ratios are used to find a variety of information, including trends, liquidity, profitability, assets, and financial leverage. We have already examined some ratios in the previous module. The following are some more basic ratios you will need to navigate your financials.

Ratio Formulas:

- ROA (Return on Assets) = Net income/Total assets x 100

- Inventory Turnover = Cost of Goods Sold/ Inventories

- Revenue Sales Growth = This year's revenue/ last year's revenue -1 x 100

- Earnings Per Share Growth = This year's EPAs/Last year's EPAs -1 x 100

Liabilities

Liabilities are money that you owe or a debt. Mortgages or credit balances are liabilities. Liabilities are a measure of financial health. Too many liabilities are an indication that the company is in trouble, particularly if the liabilities exceed the assets. Liabilities may be short term or long term. Short term liabilities are considered mature within a year, and they typically have lower interest rates. Long term liabilities last longer than a year. They are a greater risk, and have higher interest rates.

Equity

Both assets and liabilities are used to determine equity. Your equity, in turn, will determine what type of business risk you are. Lending institutions and investors examine your equity carefully. Good equity is associated with being a low risk investment and it makes you a low risk borrower.

Equity Equation:

- Assets – liabilities = Equity

- Essentially, equity is what you have left after paying off all of the debts that you owe.

- Issuing stocks to shareholders can create equity. For stockholders, equity is what they would have after liquidation. A higher equity ratio indicates that they will earn more money.

- Equity Ratio = Shareholder equity/Assets x 100

- Understanding equity and what it influences is necessary to improve your business acumen.

Financial Statements

Financial literacy requires you to read and understand different reports such as the income statement, balance sheet, and cash flow statement. These internal reports along with external information that you gather, will help you lead a financially stable business. Although it is not glamorous, financial literacy is a necessary part of business acumen.

Income Statement

The income statement allows you to see what money the company made. It is also called a profit and loss statement because it shows the profits or losses for a period, typically a quarter or year. An income statement shows information from the two previous reports, allowing you to determine growth. Each income statement is unique, but there are six measures need to be included.

Parts of an income statement:

- Revenue: Sales or gross revenue

- Cost of goods sold: COGS or the cost of sales

- Gross profit: Revenue – COGS

- Operating expenses and income: Itemize each expense to calculate income

- Net income: Net profit

- EPS: Earnings per share is for public companies

Other expenses and income may also be included if necessary.

Balance Sheet

A balance sheet shows you where your company stands at a given time by showing assets, liability, and equity. Balance sheets are prepared the last day of the month, quarter, or year. The balance sheet allows you to determine the financial health of an organization. While balance sheets are created based on the needs of each company, there are specific topics that need to be addressed.

Items on a balance sheet:

- **Current assets**: specifically liquid assets

- **Total assets**: includes long-term assets such as investments

- **Current liabilities**: liabilities paid within a year

- **Total liabilities**: includes liabilities to be paid past 12 months

- **Stockholders' equity**: Stockholders' equity is used in public trading. If the company is private, equity is the difference between total liabilities and assets.

Cash Flow Statement

A cash flow statement is exactly what it sounds like. It provides information about the cash generated and how it was used. It is also called a sources and uses of cash statement. Cash flow statements are usually generated every quarter or year and contain the three most recent reports. You can use the information in the cash flow statement to define the net increase or decrease in cash equivalents.

Equation:

Cash from operations +/- cash from investments +/- cash from financing = Net increase or decrease

Each cash flow statement is unique, but there are specific items that should be included on the report.

Items on a cash flow statement:

- Net cash (used or provided by) operating activities

- Net cash (used or provided by) investing activities

- Net cash (used or provided by) financing expenses

You begin the cash flow statement with the net income from the income statement, and it ends with the cash equivalent, the beginning of the balance sheet.

Read, Read, and Read

Financial literacy requires continuing education. Do not become complacent in your learning. Read everything that you find concerning financial literacy. You need to read relevant trade publications and periodicals to keep up with the current information. Once you find pertinent information, consider different ways to integrate it into your company's financial strategies.

Source of information:

- Books

- Periodicals

- Trade publications

- Government publications

- Blogs/websites

- Databases

Business Acumen in Management

Business acumen requires careful cultivation of resources, specifically one of the most important resources, employees. Managing people is a complex process, but developing your management skills will help you become an effective manager who achieves significant results. Pay careful attention to talent management, change management, asset management, and organizational management.

Talent Management

Talent management differs from employee management in the development process. Rather than abandoning employees to tasks, managers develop employee talent to benefit the organization. Studies have shown that talent management can increase productivity and decrease turnover. There are many different strategies involved in talent management. Below, you will find a few strategies that will improve employee development and increase productivity.

Strategies:

- **Mentor:** Develop mentorship programs, and team up new employees with more experienced ones.

- **Invest:** Invest in effective training programs that develop individuals and make them feel valued.

- **Communicate:** Communicate effectively, which involves active listening and being open and honest.

- **Evaluate:** Choose tools and measures to evaluate the effectiveness of your strategies such as surveys, employee feedback, productivity, etc.

Change Management

Change is inevitable in any organization. Unfortunately, human beings are not wired to accept change easily, so tensions may run high as people resist changes. You can help alleviate the stress associated with change with effective change management. Smoothly implementing change will reduce lost productivity as well as improve workplace culture.

The Process:

Step 1 Prepare:

- **Define the change**: Identify the change, communicate with employees, and assess the needs as well as potential resistance.

- **Choose a team**: Find team members to lead the change.

- **Sponsor**: Determine how leadership will actively sponsor the change.

Step 2 Manage:

- **Develop plans**: Create a change management plan and communicate the details.

- **Act**: Implement the change management plan, and continue to communicate the expectations.

Step 3 Reinforce:

- **Analyze change**: Use surveys and feedback to determine success.

- **Manage resistance**: Understand the causes, look for gaps, and communicate the need for acceptance.

- **Correct or praise**: Praise individuals who implement change effectively, and give corrective actions for resistance.

Asset Management

Asset management is a plan that you implement to define your assets and how they are used. Mismanaged assets will affect your, equity, credit, and reputation. Implementing asset management may be easier with the help of different software programs available.

Steps:

- **Involve the departments:** Determine which departments have assets that need management and coordinate with them. The individual departments are responsible for their assets.

- **Create a list:** Create a list of assets along with the price paid, maintenance, devaluation, and disposal costs. Each department should create its own list.

- **Identify assets to manage:** Choose the different assets that require management. They may be physical, intellectual, etc.

- **Develop a plan:** Use a separate plan for each of the following: facilities management, maintenance plan, capital development.

Organizational Management

Organizational management is unique to each company, depending on structure. It assumes that each singular element is linked to others. The individual unit as a whole must be managed effectively. It requires planning that will lead to company goals.

In organizational management, each employee needs to be part of the plan. You begin with a wide scale plan, and work your way down to the individual employee level. The responsibilities outlined in the plan should fall along the organizational structure of the company. The structure is what links the different positions. For example, there may be regional managers, divisional managers, and departmental managers who oversee different employees. The plan should reflect the distinct divisions. When this is done correctly, all employees will understand the expectations on them and how they contribute to the success of the company.

Critical Thinking in Business

In business, you are constantly bombarded with information. You rely on this information to make important decisions. Business acumen requires that you do more than absorb information. You need to think critically to about information and make your decisions accordingly.

Ask the Right Questions

Critical thinking requires you to ask questions continually. You should question people, information, plans, etc. The key to critical thinking is asking the right questions. The questions should:

- Identify assumptions: Is it verified?

- Explore perspectives: What is another point of view?

- Examine evidence: Why did this occur?

- Attempt to understand: What do you mean?

- Consider different implications: Is this important?

For example, a critical thinking question about statistics would be, *"Is this source credible?"* By asking the right questions, you will weed out useless or harmful information and utilize the information that will help you in your endeavors.

Organize Data

Critical thinking and decision making requires you to analyze different data sets. Organizing your data will make it easier for you to analyze. There are programs that will help you get organized. Data may be grouped together for specific reasons, or they may follow certain patterns. For example, you would want to group financial statements together when organizing data. Once you organize your data, you will see trends emerge as you draw conclusions. For example, market trends will become apparent once you organize your research on external business factors. The trends that you see in the data will help guide and shape your business.

Evaluate the Information

You must always evaluate information and conclusions before making any decisions. You should differentiate between a fact and an opinion by using one of the right questions. You also need to identify information and conclusions for any signs of bias. For example, does a conclusion you are reading consider all of the information available? Even when information is factually based, it may not be relevant to the argument, which indicates possible bias. For example, the fact that it was cold one night does not provide information about the lunar cycle. You need to identify facts that are relevant, substantial, and applicable before you draw your own conclusion from the information presented.

Make the Decision

Critical thinking is useful in the decision making process. You already know how to ask questions and evaluate information. Once you have done both, you have a few more considerations before you make the decision. Once you have evaluated everything, make the decision and act on it. You can feel secure knowing that you based your decision on accurate and relevant information.

- **The effects of your decision:** How will the decision affect you, your business, and others? Is the effect long term or short term?

- **Options:** Do you have more than one option?

- **Your feelings:** Are you comfortable with the decision?

Key Financial Levers

There are key financial levers that drive any business. These financial levers may be overlooked, but you do so to the detriment of the business. Identifying the levers is the first step to addressing them correctly. Once you understand these key levers, you will increase your business acumen.

Investing in People

People are a key financial lever in any business; people are your greatest asset. The people associated with your business are your customers and your employees. If you do not invest in your people, you are making a disastrous mistake.

Employees: Many companies cut back on expenses related to employees to save money. However, this can backfire and cost you qualified people. Consider investing in employees the following ways:

- Training

- Bonus

- Fair salary

- Relationships

- Opportunity for advancement

Customers: Your job is to anticipate customer needs and wants. You invest in your customers when you offer them what they need. Consider the following customer investments:

- Create new products

- Develop a customer experience

- Improve relationships

Effective Communication

Business knowledge and acumen are not useful if you are incapable of communicating effectively. Communicating is a key to the success of any business, and it begins with listening. You must actively listen to people so that you can answer their questions accurately. Before you begin a conversation, you should also become familiar with the topic.

Communication Techniques:

- **Be honest and concise**: Communicate honestly and quickly with people.

- **Be clear**: Use clear, concise language to avoid confusion.

- **Be polite**: Always answer questions and never interrupt.

- **Be friendly**: Use a conversational tone and avoid confrontation.

Process Improvement

Process improvement is used to analyze business processes. It is also used to introduce a new process or changes to existing ones. Benefiting from process improvement requires you to follow some basic steps:

Steps to Improvement:

- **Identify**: Identify processes to change and prioritize the order of the change process.

- **Establish measures**: Determine objectives and measures used to determine the performance.

- **Determine and validate**: Determine if there are obstacles and the exact path necessary to reach objectives

- **Support**: Get buy in from leadership

- **Data**: Collect and analyze data from surveys, metrics, etc.

- **Options**: Provide different change options.

- **Revise**: Revise the project based on the options chosen.

- **Implement**: Use change management strategies to implement to plan.

- **Approval**: Gain acceptance from stakeholders.

- **Evaluate:** Evaluate the success of the process

Goal Alignment

Part of looking at the big picture of business is goal alignment. Goal alignment is aligning the goals of all managers and employees with the goals of the business. Aligning individual goals is done at the team level. For example, a team goal to increase production 10% over the next month will affect the individual goals.

Team goals are based on the information from cascading goals. These start with goals at the top of the company and change as they cascade down to the different employee levels. Once you have team goals, you can identify your individual goals. Remember, they must be based on company goals. It is also wise to create SMART goals that are specific, measurable, attainable, relevant, and timely.

www.ingramcontent.com/pod-product-compliance
Lightning Source LLC
Chambersburg PA
CBHW080408270326
41929CB00018B/2936